MANAGEMENT
Foundations
and Practices

Dalton E. McFarland M.B.A., Ph.D.
University Professor and Professor of Business Administration
University of Alabama in Birmingham

MANAGEMENT
Foundations
and Practices
Fifth Edition

MACMILLAN PUBLISHING CO., INC.
New York

COLLIER MACMILLAN PUBLISHERS
London

Macmillan Publishing Co., Inc.
866 Third Avenue, New York, New York 10022

Collier Macmillan Canada, Ltd.

Library of Congress Cataloging in Publication Data

McFarland, Dalton E.
   Management.

   Includes bibliographies and index.
   Industrial management.   I.   Title.
HD31.M17   1979   658.4   78-4854
ISBN 0-02-378890-9

Printing: 1 2 3 4 5 6 7 8   Year: 9 0 1 2 3 4 5

Preface

This textbook has been written to provide students with a practical, analytical framework for their study of management. It presents a systematic description of management concepts and practices relevant to all types of organizations. The book provides a rational synthesis of research, concepts, and techniques that comprise the field of management.

Although special emphasis is given to business organizations, the analytical treatment and the selection of examples make the contents widely applicable to the management of governmental, religious, social, educational, and voluntary nonprofit organizations as well. The text utilizes a behavioral-science point of view that will help readers occupy an effective place in the organizations they choose to serve.

This fifth edition is the product of many changes from the previous edition. New cases have been added, including an incident case for each chapter, to assist the student in applying the material to practical situations. References and illustrations have been updated wherever possible. New material on organizational staffing, managerial careers, and organizational development has been included. The entire text has been reorganized and rewritten for what I hope is greater clarity and readability.

Many persons have helped me in preparing this edition, and I wish to express my appreciation for their thoughtful efforts. Managers, students, and teachers have provided invaluable insights, criticisms, and suggestions. Clients have generously allowed me to adapt case materials derived from consulting work. Several reviewers made detailed suggestions that enabled me to strengthen the final version of the manuscript. These included Richard A. Cosier, Indiana University, Thomas A. Natiello, University of Miami, and Dr. James Dilworth, of the University of Alabama in Birmingham. For her excellent research assistance, for proofreading the final draft of the manuscript, and for ably performing many other tasks, I thank Mrs. Michael Neilson. For her expert typing and processing of the manuscript I wish to thank Miss Robbie Armstrong. I also acknowledge with gratitude the environment of support and encouragement provided by my colleagues in the School of Business at the University of Alabama in Birmingham. Finally, I express my appreciation to my wife, Jean A. McFarland, for reviewing and proofreading the entire manuscript, for helpful suggestions, and for her encouragement and support as the work progressed.

D. E. McF.

Birmingham, Alabama

Contents

_____ Part **I**

THE FIELD OF MANAGEMENT: BASIC CONCEPTS

1. Management: Theory and Practice   *3*
2. Historical Perspectives in Management   *22*
3. Managers and Their Careers   *41*

Cases

A. Frankfort Milling and Farm Supply, Inc.   *67*
B. Shipley Enterprises, Inc.   *68*
C. Courting Disaster   *70*
D. The Career of Henry Dale   *71*

_____ Part **II**

MANAGERIAL DECISION AND ACTION

4. Decision Making: Fundamentals   *75*
5. Decision Making: Quantitative Tools and Processes   *98*
6. Planning   *121*

7. Objectives   *145*
8. Policies   *167*
9. Coordination and Control   *185*
10. Leadership and Supervision   *213*
11. Staffing   *237*

Cases

A. Hillside Lumber and Supply Company   *257*
B. Helen McGinley   *258*
C. Markham Pharmaceuticals, Inc.   *259*
D. Farrell and Wheelan Corporation   *261*
E. The Allison Power Company   *262*
F. The Ruggles Company, Inc.   *264*
G. Leadership in a Large Bank   *265*
H. The Claremont Milling Company, Inc.   *266*
I. Vanguard Insurance Company   *268*

Part

THE DYNAMICS OF ORGANIZATION

12. Organizations and Their Environments   *273*
13. Organization Design: Bureaucratic Systems   *296*
14. Organization Design: Adaptive Systems   *327*
15. Authority, Responsibility, and Power   *354*
16. Organizational Change   *383*
17. Organizational Conflict   *404*
18. Organizational Effectiveness   *425*

Cases

A. The State Hospital   *443*
B. The Tough Manager   *445*
C. Axtelle Company, Inc.   *446*
D. Designing an Organization Structure   *448*
E. Human Relations in the Office   *449*
F. The Tarfield Company   *449*
G. Norton Candy Company   *450*
H. The Industrial National Bank and Trust Company   *451*
I. The Corporation and Its Environment   *452*
J. Company A, B, and C   *453*

_____ Part **IV**

ORGANIZATION DEVELOPMENT AND MANAGERIAL BEHAVIOR

19. Organization Development *459*
20. Organizational Climate and Morale *487*
21. Managerial Performance: Appraisal and Improvement *515*
22. Motivation *541*
23. Communication *565*
24. Managerial Ethics and Social Responsibility *593*

Cases

A. Lawrence Pharmaceuticals, Inc. *621*
B. The Pembroke Company *622*
C. The LTD Corporation *625*
D. Qwik-Kleen Linen Supply Company **626**
E. U.S. Postal Service *628*
F. Bill Fremont *629*
G. The Program Clerks *631*
H. Wellington Electronics, Inc. *631*
I. Oliver White *632*

_____ **Appendix:**

ANALYZING MANAGEMENT CASES

Purposes of Case Analysis *635*
Approaches to the Exercise *637*
Preparation of Analyses *637*
Alternative Oral Techniques of Presentation *639*
Suggestions for Written Reports *640*
Index *641*

PART I

The Field of Management: Basic Concepts

Chapter 1

Management: Theory and Practice

A manager is best
When people barely know that he exists.
Not so good when people obey and acclaim him.
Worse when they despise him.
Fail to honor people, they fail to honor you.
But of a good manager, who talks little,
When his work is done, his aim fulfilled,
They will all say, "we did this ourselves."

—Lao Tzu, 600 B.C.

CHAPTER GUIDE

"It is becoming more and more apparent that the most successful corporations are those which are translating modern management theory into practical action rather than continuing to depend upon traditional individual managers' experience and trial and error . . . the very best results are achieved only when separate management program elements are consciously and carefully integrated and put to work in a unified, interdependent environment."

—Senior vice president, insurance firm.

Questions to keep in mind as you read this chapter:

1. What are the limitations of "trial and error" as an approach to management?
2. What skills are needed if managers are to improve the integration of theory with practice?
3. What is theory? How does it relate to the practice of management?

Management is the basic, integrating process of the organizational activity that surrounds our daily life. The need for management arises out of the scarcity of resources that satisfy human wants, and out of the diversity and complexity of human activities. Management is also one of humanity's most notable discoveries. According to Drucker, it is a key social institution:

> The emergence of management as an essential, a distinct, and a leading institution is a pivotal event in social history. Rarely, if ever, has a new basic institution, a new leading group, emerged as fast as has management since the turn of this century. Rarely in human history has a new institution proved indispensable so quickly; and even less often has a new institution arrived with so little opposition, so little disturbance, so little controversy.[1]

Management is not confined to factories, stores, or offices. Homes, clubs, and one's personal affairs all need to be managed. However, the management processes explained in this book are fundamental to all complex, purposive organizations, such as businesses, hospitals, schools, or government agencies.

Today's organizations display an enormous variety. There are single-purpose and multipurpose organizations; there are temporary and permanent ones. Organizations also vary as to size, complexity, goals, financial stability, structural patterns, and other characteristics. There are also subtle but important differences in management styles, leadership effectiveness, employee morale, organizational health, and ability to innovate. Although these variations complicate the study of organizations, basic patterns make possible an orderly analysis. This analysis begins with the topics discussed in the remainder of this chapter: (1) definitions of management, (2) the importance of management theory, and (3) management as a profession.

WHAT IS MANAGEMENT?

The word *management* has several meanings, depending on context and purpose. There is no universally accepted, standard definition of management. However, that the word *management* has multiple uses does not remove the need for precision. The loose usage of the word as a synonym for business administration, for example, will be avoided.

The word *manage* seems to have come into English usage directly from the Italian *maneggiare*, meaning "to handle," especially to handle or train horses. It traces back to the Latin word *manus*, "hand." In the early sixteenth century *manage* was quickly extended to the operations of war and used in the general sense of taking control, taking charge, or

---

[1]Peter F. Drucker, *The Practice of Management* (New York: Harper 1954), pp. 3–4.

directing. Later it became confused with the French word *menager,* meaning "to use carefully." In the seventeenth and the eighteenth centuries, the words *manage* and *ménage* overlapped in usage, and today's meaning of the word *manager* is colored by these early variations. *Management* was originally a noun used to indicate the process for managing, training, or directing. It was first applied to sports, then to housekeeping, and only later to government and business.[2]

The following sections explain four important uses of the word *management,* as (1) an organizational or administrative process; (2) a science, discipline, or art; (3) the group of individuals running an organization; and (4) an occupational career.

Management as a Process

The most important and consistent use of the term in this book views management as the fundamental integrating process designed to achieve organized, purposeful results. *Management is therefore defined as the process by which managers create, direct, maintain, and operate purposive organizations through coordinated, cooperative human effort.*

This definition implies four ideas: First, management is dynamic. It does not consist of formulas or fixed patterns. Second, management activities are continuous. Third, change is a way of life in organizations; the process is ongoing and unceasing. Fourth, managerial action directs and controls the nature, extent, and pace of activities in the organization.

Management as a process is reflected in the manager's responsibility to guide, direct, influence, and control the actions of others in working toward objectives. Goal-directed managerial behavior initiates and monitors a myriad of activities. *Management* is the name for the process of ongoing decisions and activities by which an organization's work proceeds.

Figure 1-1 shows a simple diagram of the planning, action, and feedback system that describes the process of management. It begins with the recognition and definition of a need or problem, leading to the development of plans. Actions based on planning generate consequences, which are observed and evaluated by comparing them to the intent of the plans. This comparison leads to further planning and change, and the cycle begins again. Of course actual management processes are much more complex than the diagram shows.

The process of management is largely a social one, involving the interrelationships of people at work. However, organizations are more

---

[2]Raymond Williams, *Keywords: A Vocabulary of Culture and Society* (New York: Oxford U. P., 1976), pp. 156–158.

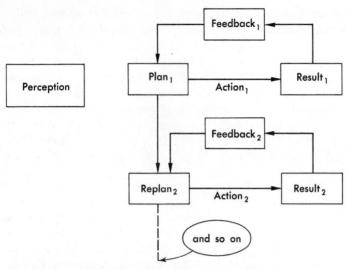

FIGURE 1-1. Fundamental Management Process.

Source: From *Management in the Future* by Richard N. Farmer. © 1967 by Wadsworth Publishing Company, Inc., Belmont, California 94002. Reprinted by permission of the publisher.

accurately described as sociotechnical systems. Technology, machinery, engineering processes, physical properties, financial assets, and other nonhuman elements are utilized through human efforts directed by managers. Management thus integrates the efforts of individuals, groups, and available resources. Management devoid of this social nature is inconceivable, for ultimately all management takes place through people.

Management and Administration

In general, the terms *management* and *administration* are synonymous. Although this book focuses on management, most of what is said is also applicable to administration.

Usage also provides some minor distinctions between these two terms. In government agencies, for example, *administration* is the preferred term, although in recent years *management* has become more widely used. In government units, policies and goals are set primarily by legislators, to be executed by administrators. Another distinction between *management* and *administration* is related to the level of the organization. In business firms, *administration* refers to higher, policy-determining levels. One seldom regards the first-line supervisor as an adminsitrator; he is a manager. In the health care fields and in many service organizations, *problems* (such as an individual's

chronic disease) are managed, but *programs* (such as flu vaccine distribution) are administered.

Management as a Discipline

A second meaning of the term *management* describes a field of learning. Management is an organized, formal discipline researched and
taught in institutions of higher learning. The over-all field of management is integrative in nature, bringing together the relevant aspects of
other disciplines while at the same time developing its own body of
theory.

As a discipline, the boundaries of management are not exact, a
condition true of all disciplines even in the natural and physical sciences. Management, for example, is related to the larger disciplines of
business administration and economics, but parts of these two disciplines are nonmanagerial in character. The organization of the various
branches of learning is constantly changing, and disciplines are often in
conflict. The areas of marketing or financial administration, for example, overlap with management. No discipline, including management,
can be isolated from others or be completely self-contained. However,
because management is complex enough to need the total efforts of
large numbers of scholars and practitioners, so that it becomes the basis
of occupational focuses in society, it is likely to remain a definitive field.
However, there are subfields in management—such as production
management or financial management—which are important disciplines in their own right.

The status of management as a discipline increases as it (1) wins
adherents, (2) discovers and compiles verified knowledge, and (3)
organizes and disseminates that knowledge to mankind. The central
elements in the emerging discipline are its theoretical knowledge
derived from research, and its practical applications. Yet some deny
that management can be taught, insisting that (1) management is
learned by experience, (2) it consists primarily of on-the-spot, common-
sense decisions, (3) managers are men of action, not of thought or
philosophy, and (4) management is an art, not a science. These ideas
reveal an important truth, but one that is easy to exaggerate. Management cannot be learned entirely from books or within the classroom;
experience counts, and management remains a mixture of science and
art.[3] Nevertheless, formal training in management is important, for it
provides the benefits of accumulated knowledge and interpreted experience, and the application of research findings. It is thus a short cut to

[3]Peter B. Baill, "Management as a Performing Art," *Personnel* 53 (July/August 1976),
12–21.

one's education for a career in management, and a source of guidance for new endeavors not previously experienced.

Management as People

A third use of the term *management* covers, in a collective sense, the managerial group within the organization. The word *administration* is similarly used. For example, a newspaper may report that a company is negotiating with a labor union, and that "management has refused demands for a wage increase."

The manager group in a company includes all who exercise supervisory authority over others. In a factory, for example, management includes the first-line supervisors (often called foremen), all department heads, division heads, and all executives up to and including the chief executive. The typical organization separates its managers from its nonmanagers, who include rank-and-file, clerical, technical, and sales employees.

Collective references to management are often ambiguous. For example, when one says that the management of the Standard Oil Company is efficient, it is not clear whether one means the managers as a group, the process by which they manage, or both. Therefore, we will restrict the term *management* to refer to the process of managing and use the term *managers* to refer to the people who run the organization.

Management as a Career

The fourth use of the term *management* is to denote a career or occupation. As we remarked above, certain business careers are non-managerial; and some of these, such as being a stockbroker or an insurance salesmen, may provide lucrative and challenging livelihoods. One begins to follow a management career by accepting the responsibility for achieving results by directing the work of others. A career in management means that an individual is devoting his working lifetime to the practice of management.

As a career or occupation, *management* is a broad concept. Management itself can be regarded as a career, but it also presents a variety of interesting and challenging careers focused on specialized occupations in such fields as marketing, finance, and personnel.

THEORY IN MANAGEMENT

The second objective of this chapter is to analyze the problem of management theory and its relationship to the practice of management.

The purpose of a scientific theory is to provide a framework for the explanation and interpretation of facts, so that phenomena can be explained, understood, predicted, and controlled. Concepts are developed to organize the theory and help managers apply their own ideas, facts, business know-how, and the "conventional wisdom" of the management community. A tested theory of management can lead to improved decision making and action.

At present there is no unified, comprehensive theory *of* management, but there is an accumulating body of theory *in* management. Some researchers focus on organization theory, some on administrative theory, and others on human relations—or group—theory. Others see decision theory as the critical element in explaining managerial behavior and action. Still others prefer to emphasize the manager's tasks and functions. A number of theoretical approaches with varying hypotheses, assumptions, and propositions have, accordingly, evolved. Koontz has aptly described this proliferation of parallel theories as "the management theory jungle."[4] However, several have suggested that variations in theoretical approaches are not as much in conflict as they at first appear, and that integrative forces are at work to bring about a synthesis.[5]

State of Management Theory

The effort to reduce the confusion in management theory by developing a more integrated theory of management still has far to go. Theory emerged slowly prior to the turn of the century, but it has developed more rapidly since then. Three stages can be identified in the evolution of management thought since the early 1900s: (1) scientific management, (2) the human relations movement, and (3) management science and related systems approaches.

The three periods cannot be precisely separated or dated. The era of

[4]Harold Koontz, "The Management Theory Jungle," *Journal of the Academy of Management* 4 (December 1961), 174–188; see also Douglas Austin Woolf, "The Management Theory Jungle Revisited," *Advanced Management Journal* 30 (October 1965), 6–15; Harold Koontz (ed.), *Toward a Unified Theory of Management* (New York: McGraw-Hill, 1964).

[5]Edwin B. Flippo, "Integrative Schemes in Management Theory," *Academy of Management Journal* 11 (March 1968), 91–98. For an optimistic statement of the possibilities for a comprehensive general theory of management, see William C. Frederick, "The Next Development in Management Science: A General Theory," *Academy of Management Journal* 6 (September 1963), 212–219; for the other viewpoint, see Orlando Behling, "Unification of Management Theory: A Pessimistic View," *Business Perspectives* 3 (Summer 1967), 4–8; see also Leonard Sayles, *Managerial Behavior* (New York: McGraw-Hill, 1964), Chapter 1. For a comprehensive review and analysis of management theory, see John B. Miner, *Management Theory* (New York: Macmillan, 1971), and Raymond E. Miles, *Theories of Management: Implications for Organizational Behavior and Development* (New York: McGraw-Hill, 1975).

scientific management began about 1910; it waned in the 1950s as the human relations movement burgeoned, but many of today's management precepts go back to the original ideas of the scientific management movement. Human relations research altered management practices with respect to goup processes and interpersonal relations, and its precepts continue to be useful today. But its contributions to management theory were limited in that large, complex organizations were not studied. The management science stage that is now current emerged from the work of "revisionist" researchers, who saw the limitations of previous research and increased the use of scientific methods of behavioral and quantitative empirical research. Their theorizing has led to improved conceptualization. These three historical periods are analyzed in greater detail in Chapter 2.[6]

Theory building moves slowly because researchers do not concentrate on comprehensive theories and concepts. In 1956, for example, Litchfield advanced a series of fundamental propositions around which he proposed a total theory of administration.[7] Although at first management researchers found these propositions stimulating, their impact faded and researchers have paid relatively little attention to them.

The theoretical work of March and Simon met a fate similar to that of Litchfield.[8] In an attempt to develop a general theory of organization, they stated a large number of propositions for researchers to test. Although their work stimulated researchers at first, its influence faded without much impact on a general theory of management.

Adequate management concepts are needed before principles can be developed. Such concepts permit the description, in terms relevant to theory, of empirically observable situations; without them, the pursuit of adequate empirical research would be inhibited.[9] Forrester has noted, furthermore, that without concepts management theory would lack the unifying structure that is so essential to a system of knowledge.[10] And although there is evidence of an increasing interest in comparative research (that is, studies cutting across cultural or national boundaries), many studies show relatively little concern for the prob-

---

[6]The term *management science* attaches more precision to the term *science* than did early practitioners of scientific management. To say that management is a science is to describe it, not necessarily to praise it. See also Luther Gulick, "Management Is a Science," *Academy of Management Journal* 8 (March 1965), 7–13; Peter P. Gil and Warren G. Bennis, "Science and Management: Two Cultures," *Journal of Applied Behavioral Sciences* 4 (January/February, 1968), 75–108.

[7]Edward H. Litchfield, "Notes on a General Theory of Administration," *Administrative Science Quarterly* 1 (June 1956), 3–29.

[8]James G. March and Herbert A. Simon, *Organizations* (New York: Wiley, 1958).

[9]Herbert A. Simon, *Administrative Behavior*, rev. ed. (New York: Macmillan, 1961), p. 37.

[10]Jay W. Forrester, "The Structure Underlying Management Processes," *1964 Proceedings of the Academy of Management* (Bowling Green, Ohio, 1965), 58–68.

Clearly there are discrepancies between management theory and management practice. Theory is still in a state of development. Some draw peculiar conclusions from this fact, claiming that the discrepancies disprove the theories, or that no adequate theory is possible. There is reason for concern over the state of both management theory and management practice, but there is no need to rely only on the pragmatic.

One reason for the gap between theory and practice is that a time lag occurs between the discovery of a theory and its translation into the decisions and practices of managers. Eventually academicians, writers, and consultants spread new information into wider channels, thereby encouraging the trial of new ideas. But this process takes time. Five or even ten or more years may pass before many managers learn of a major discovery. And even after a manager encounters something of interest, he finds it difficult to apply. Like the farmer who refused the advice of a county agent because "I'm not farming as good as I know how to now," managers do not always manage as well as they know how. They postpone improvements until conditions are more propitious or until the changes can be sold to the more conservative or influential people in the organization.

Good theory is better than poor theory, or no theory. In the absence of appropriate theory, managers will provide their own, which may or may not be right. The test of good theory is whether it explains observed phenomena and is useful in predicting behavior and controlling results.

Comparative Management Theory

In recent years, researchers and teachers of management have paid greater attention to problems of comparative theory. The term *comparative management* describes two sets of phenomena. First, it examines the management process cross-culturally, that is, across the boundaries of nations or of cultural groupings of nations, such as those in Latin America compared to Europe. Pressures for economic and industrial development throughout the world have led to cross-cultural studies comparing the impact of the social, political, economic, and cultural environment on management.

The second use of the term *comparative management* reflects variations within a given culture. For example, one may compare management processes in schools with those in hospitals, or those in hospitals with those in business, and so on. Comparative management in this sense recognizes that all forms of organized, institutionalized effort require the application of management theory and skills.

Two basic questions underlying both approaches to comparative management are the extent to which management theory exists universally, and the extent to which management theory in one sector is transferrable to other sectors. Researchers seek common, universal management principles through comparative analysis, even though they also recognize the need for uniqueness and differentiation among cultural or institutional patterns. These are still open questions, but they are being actively studied.

Systems Theory

Among the trees in the management theory jungle there is one, systems theory, that may potentially integrate the other streams of knowledge with each other and with the ongoing practice of management. General systems theory implies the possibility of the unity of all science, and it is increasingly important in the biological, physical, and behavioral sciences. Management science, in both its behavioral and quantitative aspects, makes extensive applications of general systems theory.[16]

Beer defines a system as "anything that consists of parts connected together."[17] More specifically, a system is composed of parts of a whole related to each other in varying ways under varying conditions. The subsystems are in a state of mutual interdependence, such that a change in one part is related to changes in one or more of the other parts. The system itself relates to, and is affected by, relevant aspects of its environment.

The definition of a particular system is arbitrary, depending on the observer's purpose. Thus, an automobile, or the engine of the automobile, or the engine's carburetor, may be viewed as a system. There are systems within systems. The universe appears to consist of sets of systems. The gasoline in a carburetor is made up of systems of molecules; the automobile operates on a roadway, and together the automobile and the roadway are a larger system. The highway network is a still larger system, and is part of the transportation system, and so on.

There can be little doubt that systems theory is a powerful concept for the analysis of organizations and organization behavior as well as for the design of organization structures and policies. This is true whether we are considering organization from the standpoint of technology or engineering or from a behavioral point of view.

Early scientific management thinkers, many of whom were engineers, saw in the development of machines the possibilities of the

[16]For an exposition of systems thinking from the point of view of the philosophy of science, see Ervin Laszlo, *The Systems View of the World* (New York: Braziller, 1972). See also *Academy of Management Journal* 15 (December 1972), a theme issue on general systems theory; C. West Churchman, *A Challenge to Reason* (New York: McGraw-Hill, 1968); Ludwig von Bertalanffy, *General Systems Theory* (New York: Braziller, 1968); and C. West Churchman, *The Systems Approach* (New York: Dell, 1968).

[17]Stafford Beer, *Cybernetics and Management* (New York: Wiley, 1964), p. 9.

"automatic factory"—in effect, a production system integrating the flow of inputs, processing, and the flow of outputs into a whole. Even now much of the application of systems analysis has an engineering and mathematical basis. The total organization is still an important part of systems analysis, but the production function has been the subsystem most thoroughly explored by means of systems theory and the quantitative tools of operations research. Nevertheless, many other aspects of organizations are proving amenable to systems analysis, including the marketing and distribution systems, engineering and scientific functions, financial activities, and interrelationships of people at work. Almost every type of organization can employ systems thinking. Any organization can be designed or studied as a system, with the aid of the computer and accompanying simulation techniques. The initial design, either existing or desired, can be simulated on a computer that will then generate data and reports concerning such factors as manpower, capital equipment, and market strategies. Different policies and different assumptions can then be used; their effect on the total results of the system can be tested, and the possible effects of changes can be predicted.

Systems may be either relatively open or relatively closed. A system is open to the degree that it can be affected by influences from the environment. It is closed to the degree that there is relatively little or no influence on the system coming across its boundary from outside. Most systems are relatively open systems, but some are more open than others. Although no system, particularly one with living components, can be completely closed, a closed system may be assumed to exist for analytical purposes. Moreover, much traditional organization theory appears to have been based on closed-system assumptions, and the newer approaches to organization theory have advanced by assuming organizations to be open systems.

Contingency Theory

Another recent theoretical approach emerging in the past decade is known as contingency theory. Contingency theory harmonizes with systems views: both approaches consider organizations as managed systems or subsystems interacting in relevant environments.

Contingency theory provides a way of looking at organizations and their managers with emphasis on the situational nature of events and activities. Managers must act under conditions of uncertainty and risk under a variety of needs and conditions. The managers and their organizational system need flexibility and openness to change in order to cope with change, meet society's demands, and exploit the opportunities presented to it. Thus the open-systems concept described in Part 3 of this book find their best rationale in contingency-theory views.

The prescriptive and normative postulates of the scientific management movement have not resulted in any definitive theory that covers the enormous variation in the types, aims, and methods of organization. Therefore we find that traditional or classical theories may be useful for some purposes, whereas systems and contingency theories are necessary for others.[18] This is essentially the theoretical position of this book—that the full range of alternatives for managing organizations must be considered, and ultimately included in a general theory of management.

_____ **MANAGEMENT AS A PROFESSION**

The third main topic of this chapter is the analysis of management as an emerging profession. Although management is not yet fully a profession, it fits some of the necessary conditions. The main benchmarks of a profession include (1) a body of specialized knowledge or techniques; (2) formal training and experience; (3) an organization to espouse professionalization; (4) an ethical code for the guidance of conduct; (5) the licensing of practitioners; and (6) a commitment to service rather than to monetary rewards.

By these standards, management is only in part a profession. Licensing is nonexistent; no large-scale movement for licensing managers is under way. No single organized group professes to speak for all managers, although a number of associations assist particular groups such as personnel managers. There is no universal code of ethics, although many subgroups within management have advanced their own codes. Also, it is doubtful that concepts of service transcend the importance of salary or fees for most managers.

Not everyone agrees that management should be a profession. Drucker, for example, sees difficulties:

> No greater damage could be done to our economy or to our society than to attempt to "professionalize" management by "licensing" managers . . . or by limiting access to management to people with a special academic degree . . . any serious attempt to make management "scientific" or a "profession" is bound to lead to the attempt to eliminate those "disturbing nuisances," the

_____

[18]For further information on contingency approaches, see John M. Newstrom, William E. Reif, and Robert M. Monczka (eds.), *A Contingency Approach to Management: Readings* (New York: McGraw-Hill, 1975); Henry L. Tosi and W. Clay Hamner (eds.), *Organization Behavior and Management: A Contingency Approach* (Chicago: St. Clair Press, 1974); Gary Dessler, *Organization and Management: A Contingency Approach* (Englewood Cliffs, N.J.: Prentice-Hall, 1976); Don Hellriegel and John W. Slocum, Jr. *Organizational Behavior: Contingency Views* (St. Paul, Minn.: West, 1976); Howard M. Carlisle, *Management Concepts: A Contingency Approach* (Palo Alto, Calif.: Science Research Associates, Inc., 1976); Fred Luthans, *Introduction to Management: A Contingency Approach* (New York: McGraw-Hill, Inc., 1976).

unpredictabilities of business life—its risks, its ups and downs, its "wasteful competition," the "irrational choices" of the consumer—and, in the process, the economy's freedom and its ability to grow.[19]

Management Consulting

Professionalization in management is revealed by the rapid growth in the numbers of individuals and firms providing consulting services. In 1940, there were only about 2,000 consulting firms. In 1958, there were nearly 13,000 business and management consulting establishments. By 1963 that number had doubled, and by 1967 it had nearly doubled again. It doubled again by 1972, when approximately 82,000 establishments were listed, but the census category this time included public relations consulting firms.[20]

The number of firms is hard to specify precisely, because the categories do not appear to be consistently defined. The same is true for counting individual consultants. The number of persons doing full-time, bona fide management consulting either with consulting firms or in solo practice was estimated to be between fifty and sixty thousand in 1976.[21] However, it is hard to know exactly how many persons actually work as consultants. In addition to those working as full-time consultants for firms or for themselves, consulting is also part-time work for many. Retired executives and umemployed persons often turn to consulting. Attorneys, engineers, accountants, and other professionals with or without other full-time work also engage in consulting. Because consulting is not subject to government regulation, entry into the field depends mainly on the ability to find clients. Furthermore, some individuals claim to be consultants when they are merely free-lance workers.

A management consultant is an outside specialist retained to help a manager or an organization do things it is unable to do alone, or for which it would not be economical to develop a permanent staff. Consultants apply expertise obtained from a wide experience in many organizations, and from specialized training. There are over a hundred recognized areas of specialization in consulting, such as quality control, plant location, organization behavior or personnel management. Consultants frequently form firms with partners or associates, much as lawyers do, and are thus able to provide consulting groups or teams.

[19]Drucker, *Practice of Management* pp. 9–10. For a study of the characteristics by which certain occupations acquire professional status, see J. A. Jackson, *Professions and Professionalization* (New York: Cambridge U.P., 1971).

[20]U.S. Bureau of the Census, *U.S. Census of Business*, Vol. V., Selected Services, Summary Statistics, pt. 1 (Washington, D.C.: U.S. Government Printing Office, 1967); U.S. Bureau of the Census, *1972 Census of Selected Service Industries*, Final Report, Subject Series (Washington, D.C.: U.S. Government Printing Office, 1975).

[21]The Association of Consulting Management Engineers, correspondence dated July 22, 1976.

Consultants are usually paid on a daily-fee basis, plus expenses, but sometimes charges are based on project or contract arrangements.

Consulting services are generally advisory, investigative, technical, and temporary. Consultants are helpful in developing new projects or programs, especially those requiring knowledge and experience in specific techniques such as wage incentive systems, job evaluation programs, or attitude surveys. Consultants are also valuable in conducting independent management audits, reviews, and research projects, and in planning and problem solving. As advisers to top managers, they may assist in organization design, policy formation, product planning or market strategies. One of the consultant's important roles is that of outsider; as such, he can bring perspectives, objectivity, ideas, and information that have already been tested elsewhere.

The relationships between consultants and clients are complex, requiring special skills and understanding for both. Among the possible difficulties that limit the use and value of consultants is that, as outsiders, they need time to become familiar with each situation. Another is that the likelihood of change arouses resistance among insiders, who may be defensive, jealous, or angry, and thus hostile and ready to interfere with the consultant's work. The consultants may be blamed for the change, or made to look bad when regular organization members do not cooperate.

A good consultant knows how to guard against these difficulties and keep them from affecting the progress of the work. He can minimize the difficulties by (1) developing a trained capacity for observation of details, especially emotional patterns in people; (2) accepting consultations only in his areas of competence; (3) avoiding situations that entail undue risk of failure; (4) resisting tendencies to overdependence by clients; and (5) openly and directly facing the anxieties and hostilities of organization members in the early stages of his work.

Clients can get the most out of their consultants by (1) carefully defining and clearly specifying the problems for which help is desired; (2) carefully selecting consultants; (3) clearly defining the consultant's role, in terms of expected results, to other organization members, with explanations made in advance; and (4) designating a specific person or persons with authority to make decisions as the work proceeds.[22]

[22]The Conference Board, *Consultants: Selection, Use and Appraisal, Managing the Moderate Sized Company,* Report No. 13 (New York: 1970); Philip Shaw, *How to Get the Best Results from Management Consultants* (New York: Association of Consulting Management Engineers, 1965); Theodore M. Becker and Robert N. Stein, "The Human Relations Business: Information and Guidelines for Clients of Consulting Firms," *MSU Business Topics* (Winter 1972), 44–52; John F. Sullivan, "The Several Hats of a Consultant," *Compensation Review* 8 (Fourth Quarter, 1971), 33–38. For an extensive annotated bibliography on consultants, see Stanley C. Hollander and Stephen B. Flaster, *Management Consultants and Clients,* MSU Business Studies (East Lansing, Mich.: Division of Research, Graduate School of Business Administration, 1973); Jean Pierre Frankenhuis, "How to Get a Good Consultant," *Harvard Business Review* 55 (November–December 1977), 133–139.

SUMMARY

The practice of management is pervasive in American life and vitally important to the survival of the organizations on which we rely for goods and services. *Management* is defined as the basic integrating process by which organizations are created, maintained, and developed in the production of goods and services.

Management theory today shows considerable variation in schools of thought, assumptions, and formulations. The prospect for achieving a unified theory of management is not great, nor is the need for such a theory entirely clear. But the work of the revisionists, including both behavioral and management scientists, holds much promise for producing a better understanding of organizations and organizational behavior. Process or functional theories are not inherently incompatible with advancing revisionist theories.

The development of management theory has been enhanced by growing recognition of the widespread applicability of management knowledge to different types of organizations. The application of management theory and practice to these different kinds of organizations will be considered throughout this book.

Several trends reflect the extent of the professionalization of management: (1) the increased body of knowledge and the growth of special skills and techniques; (2) a higher level of formal training and education for practitioners; (3) the expanding use of consultants; and (4) the growth of specialized trade and professional associations that help managers to identify with their specialities. In spite of these trends, however, it is not likely that management will become a full-scale profession by the strictest standards.

As a field of activity in which people earn their livelihoods, management seems destined to undergo considerable growth in the years ahead. Society places much responsibility on the manager, and management is therefore dynamic and sensitive to the undercurrents of inevitable social change. The task of management is to adjust to change, but also to create change—a dynamic quality that is the source of many challenging problems.

INCIDENT CASE

A few years ago, the editor of a trade journal selected the following five companies as the best managed:

- —Xerox, for executive motivation
- —Pfizer, for paramount penetration of global markets
- —Mobil, for corporate flexibility
- —Du Pont, for operational creativity
- —Eastman Kodak, for marketing processes

Questions:

1. Do you think this list would hold true today?
2. What are the possible criteria used for judging the firms?

QUESTIONS FOR STUDY

1. Is "management as people" an oversimplification? Why or why not?

2. Do the definitions of management and administration seem too abstract? How would you compare them?

3. Put in your own words what is meant by "management as process."

4. Look up as many definitions of the word *management* as you can find. Which are the best, and why?

5. Explain the basis for claiming that management may be evolving into a profession. Which of the reasons seem to you the strongest? The weakest? Give reasons for your answers.

6. Outline the arguments pro and con for the statement "Management is a universal process, and its skills and understandings are transferable from one company to another, and from one culture to another."

7. What are the advantages to a company of using a management consultant in working out its problems? What kinds of problems do you think it would be particularly helpful to use consultants for? What relationships should be developed between companies and their consultants?

8. What are the main problems, as you see them, of evolving a general management theory? What kinds of research do you feel are needed to improve management theory?

9. What are the obstacles in the way of establishing a general or a "unified" theory of management? What shall we do in the meantime?

10. Explain your understanding of the role of the revisionists, as compared with the role of earlier theorists. Where do the human relations theorists fit in? Where do management scientists fit in?

SELECTED REFERENCES

ARGYRIS, CHRIS. *Intervention Theory and Method*. Reading, Mass.: Addison-Wesley Publishing Co., 1970.

BELASCO, JAMES A., DAVID R. HAMPTON, and KARL F. PRICE. *Management Today*. New York: John Wiley & Sons, Inc., 1975.

BLAKE, ROBERT R., and JANE S. MOUTON. *Consultation*. Reading, Mass.: Addison-Wesley Publishing Co., 1976.

BUCHELE, ROBERT B. *The Management of Business and Public Administration*. New York: McGraw-Hill Book Company, 1977.

DREYFACK, RAYMOND. *Sure Fail: The Art of Mismanagement*. New York: William Morrow & Co., Inc., 1976.

DRUCKER, PETER F. *Management: Tasks, Responsibilities, Practices*. New York: Harper & Row, Publishers, 1974. Chapters 1–4.

FARMER, RICHARD N. *Management in the Future.* Belmont, California: Wadsworth Publishing Co., Inc., 1967. Chapters 1, 2.

FAYOL, HENRI. *General and Industrial Management.* New York: Pitman Publishing Corporation, 1949.

FUCHS, JEROME H. *Making the Most of Management Consulting Services.* New York: AMACOM, 1975.

GANNON, MARTIN J. *Management: An Organizational Perspective.* Boston: Little, Brown and Co., 1977.

KAHN, MELVIN. *Dynamics in Managing: Principles, Process, and Practice.* Menlo Park, Calif.: Cummings Publishing Company, 1977.

KELLOGG, MARION S. *Putting Management Theories to Work.* Houston, Tex.: Gulf Publishing Company, 1968.

KOONTZ, HAROLD, ed. *Toward a Unified Theory of Management.* New York: McGraw-Hill Book Company, 1964.

KUBR, M., ed. *Management Consulting: A Guide to the Profession.* Geneva: International Labors Office, 1976.

LILIENTHAL, DAVID E. *Management: A Humanist Art.* Pittsburgh: Carnegie Institute of Technology, 1967.

METCALF, HENRY C., and LYNDALL F. URWICK. *Dynamic Administration.* New York: Harper & Row, Publishers, 1940. Chapters 5,.6.

MILES, RAYMOND E. *Theories of Management: Implications for Organizational Behavior and Development.* New York: McGraw-Hill Book Company, 1975.

MINER, JOHN B. *The Management Process.* New York: Macmillan Publishing Co., Inc., 1973.

MINTZBERG, HENRY. *The Nature of Managerial Work.* New York: Harper & Row, Publishers, 1973.

MOORE, WILBERT E. *The Professions: Roles and Rules.* New York: Basic Books, Inc., Publishers, 1970.

NEWMAN, WILLIAM H., and E. KIRBY WARREN. *The Process of Management: Concepts, Behavior, and Practice.* Englewood Cliffs, N.J.: Prentice-Hall, Inc., 1977.

ROBBINS, STEPHEN P. *The Administrative Process: Integrating Theory and Practice.* Englewood Cliffs, N.J.: Prentice-Hall, Inc., 1976.

SHELDON, OLIVER. *Philosophy of Management.* New York: Pitman Publishing Corporation, 1935.

WORTMAN, LILLIAN A. *Successful Small Business Management.* New York: AMACOM, 1976.

VON MAANEN, JOHN, ed. *Organizational Careers: Some New Perspectives.* New York: John Wiley & Sons, Inc., 1977.

Chapter 2

Historical Perspectives in Management

We face few problems today that have not been confronted in other times and other societies.

—Ariel Durant

Every great commanding moment in the annals of the world is the triumph of some enthusiasm.

—Ralph Waldo Emerson

CHAPTER GUIDE

Henry Ford once said that "history is bunk." Msgr. Fulton J. Sheen once observed: "History? The British never remember it. The Irish never forget it. The Russians never make it. And the Americans never learn from it."

Questions to keep in mind as you read this chapter:

1. What are the implications of these statements with respect to the history of management thought?
2. How can an understanding of management history help the practicing manager?

Management history repays careful study, for in history lie the roots of wisdom as well as of knowledge. In the evolution of management thought, ideas have been tested and developed. Yet because they are oriented to action, managers tend to ignore the past, even though to disregard the events and ideas of history is to risk repeating its mistakes.

The pressure of contemporary events can easily overshadow the influence of history. In organizations, managers daily face urgent decisions that make it difficult to reflect on the past or consider the future. Yet to focus one's actions only upon the present is to draw a very narrow view of the manager's responsibilities.

As a formal discipline, the history of management is relatively brief. However, it is enriched by the growth of other disciplines, such as economics, business administration, and public administration, as well as of the behavioral and quantitative sciences. The necessary historical perspectives thus include not only management thought as such, but also the development of ideas from related disciplines.

The evolution of management thought may be divided roughly into four main periods: (1) early influences; (2) the scientific management movement; (3) the human relations movement; and (4) the revisionist movement. This chapter examines these movements and their implications for management.

EARLY INFLUENCES

Systematic management thought in the United States dates from the early 1900s, but the roots of management thinking are found in antiquity. Plato and Aristotle made many observations that are surprisingly relevant to management today. Awareness of management is also apparent in Biblical times. Moses, for example, "chose able men out of all Israel, and made them heads over the people, rulers of thousands, rulers of hundreds, rulers of fifties, and rulers of tens. And they judged the people at all seasons: the hard causes they brought unto Moses, but every small matter they judged themselves."[1] This is the first recorded use of an organizational hierarchy.

Yet management embraces more than random observations by the ancients. Early in the nineteenth century, the British mathematician Charles Babbage perceived that the methods of science and mathematics could be applied to the operation of factories. He recommended the substitution of accurate observations, exact measurements, and precise knowledge for guesswork, hunches, intuition, and opinion in making decisions in factories.[2] To Babbage goes the credit for introducing the fundamental thinking that preceded the formulation of a science of

[1]Exodus 18:25–26, King James Version.
[2]Charles R. Babbage, *On the Economy of Machinery and Manufactures*, 4th ed., enl. (London: C. Knight, 1835).

management.[3] Babbage appears to have greatly influenced the thinking of the pioneers of the scientific management movement in the United States.[4]

Military and Religious Influences

Among the early historical influences are the applications of management and organization practices in military and religious institutions. The rise of large-scale armies, as during the days of ancient Rome, posed problems of communication, logistics, organization structure, and selection and training of manpower. More recently, the concept of the general staff in military organizations is seen in patterns of management in other organizations.[5] The interest of military groups in leadership, decision making, planning, and organization has also led to substantial research on these matters.

Some authorities feel that we have borrowed too heavily from military management, thus failing to devise better management practices. Perhaps management has too readily accepted some of the tenets of military organization. Nevertheless, military organization has contributed concepts which still shape present-day management thought.

The Catholic Church affords a notable example of applied organization and management practices that have endured for centuries. The principles of hierarchical, large-scale organization are readily identifiable, as are the principles of authority and its delegation. The impact of both military history and religious history on managerial thought is analyzed in a classic book by Mooney and Reiley.[6]

Management in Early America

Management problems were much simpler in colonial times than they are today. Focused on an agrarian economy and on handicraft, domestic, and local production systems, management was largely in the hands of the owners of resources, who were often workers as well.

The Industrial Revolution brought the growth of the factory system, enlarged markets, and new, large-scale production technologies. The factory system brought large concentrations of workers and raw materials together, posing the problems of organizing, directing, and control-

[3]Lyndall F. Urwick and E. G. L. Brech, *The Making of Scientific Management,* vol. 2 (London: Sir Isaac Pitman & Sons Ltd., reprinted 1953), p. 8.

[4]John H. Hoagland, "Management Before Frederick Taylor," in Paul M. Dauten, Jr. (ed.), *Current Issues and Emerging Concepts in Management* (Boston: Houghton Mifflin, 1962), pp. 19–30.

[5]See, for example, Ernest Dale and Lyndall F. Urwick, *Staff in Organization* (New York: McGraw-Hill, 1960), chaps. 5, 6.

[6]James D. Mooney and Alan C. Reiley, *The Principles of Organization* (New York: Harper, 1939).

ling work. Businessmen were industrialist entrepreneurs who thought more about problems of machines, materials, money, equipment, and labor than about management activity as such. Workers were given relatively scant attention as individuals, and human problems were tolerated as a necessary condition of the new systems of enterprise.

But the Industrial Revolution was not merely technical; it also had an impact on values, beliefs, social customs, and society at large. The meaning of work began to change; growth and efficiency of production systems emerged as a social and economic goal; people saw hope in the emerging society for prosperity, wealth, and the welfare of all, through the ability of such a system to provide for the wants and needs of people. These changing values were important because they later strengthened the trends that brought about the scientific management movement.

THE SCIENTIFIC MANAGEMENT MOVEMENT

Not until after the Civil War did the basic ideas now labeled *scientific management* slowly begin to take shape in forms useful to practicing managers. Today's concept of management is the product of a long and complicated evolutionary process that is still under way.

Drucker has indicated the importance of scientific management:

> Altogether scientific management may well be the most powerful as well as the most lasting contribution America has made to Western thought since the Federalist Papers. As long as industrial society endures, we shall never lose again the insight that human work can be studied systematically, can be analyzed, can be improved by work on its elementary parts.[7]

The scientific management movement began as the search by practical managers for better ways of running their businesses. They deduced "principles" that they thought to be necessary for improving management practices in industry. The aims were pragmatic, but the methods were only in part those of science: measurement, observation, and analysis. The origins of the scientific management movement were in Europe: the work of Babbage in England, and of Henri Fayol in France. Fayol was one of the first to identify basic principles of administration that are still widely followed in analyzing managerial tasks.[8]

The initiator of the scientific management movement in the United States was Frederick J. Taylor, whose writings are still essential reading for students of management. Taylor experimented with work situations to improve the performance of workmen. He published two

---

[7]Peter F. Drucker, *The Practice of Management* (New York: Harper, 1954), p. 280.

[8]Henri Fayol, *General and Industrial Management* (London: Sir Isaac Pitman and Sons, Ltd., 1949). First published in 1916.

principal works reporting his observations and conclusions. The first, *Shop Management,* was originally a paper presented before the American Society of Mechanical Engineers in 1903. The second, *Principles of Scientific Management,* appeared early in 1911. These writings, together with Taylor's testimony before a congressional committee in 1913, constitute the major primary sources for a study of Taylor's views.[9]

Taylor advocated "scientific management" to cope with certain conditions that he saw as problems of the industry of his time. Among these were (1) unclear concepts of managerial responsibility; (2) lack of measured standards for defining the workers' tasks; and (3) widespread inefficiency of labor and persistent "soldiering on the job."

Management Responsibilities

Taylor believed that managers should accept special responsibilities for planning, directing, and organizing work. He advocated that the planning of work be separated from its execution, so that each individual could work efficiently and could be compensated accordingly. He thought that management should develop a science of doing work and that each kind of work had its own "science":

> Under the old type of management success depends almost entirely on getting the "initiative" of the workmen, and it is indeed a rare case in which this initiative is really attained. Under scientific management the "initiative" of the workmen (that is, their hard work, their goodwill, and their ingenuity) is obtained with absolute uniformity and to a greater extent than is possible under the old system; and in addition . . . the managers assume new burdens, new duties and responsibilities never dreamed of in the past. The managers assume, for instance, the burden of gathering together all of the traditional knowledge which in the past has been possessed by the workmen and then of classifying, tabulating, and reducing this knowledge to rules, laws, and formulae which are immensely helpful to the workmen in doing their daily work. In addition to developing a *science* in this way, the management takes on three other types of duties which involve new and heavy burdens for themselves. . . .
>
> *First.* They develop a science for each element of a man's work, which replaces the old rule-of-thumb method.
>
> *Second.* They scientifically select and then train, teach, and develop the workman, whereas in the past he chose his own work and trained himself as best he could.

[9]Frederick W. Taylor, *Shop Management* (New York: Harper, 1911); *Principles of Scientific Management* (New York: Harper, 1911); *Testimony, Hearings Before Social Committee of the House of Representatives to Investigate the Taylor and Other Systems of Shop Management Under the Authority of House Resolution 90,* vol. 3, pp. 1377–1508. These three sources are reprinted in a single volume, F. W. Taylor, *Scientific Management* (New York: Harper, 1947).

Third. They heartily cooperate with the men so as to insure all of the work being done in accordance with the principles of the science which has been developed.

Fourth. There is an almost equal division of the work and the responsibility between the management and the workmen. The management take over all work for which they are better fitted than the workmen, while in the past almost all the work and the greater part of the responsibility were thrown upon the men.[10]

The tasks that Taylor posed for management were indeed far-reaching, for they initiated changes that are still evident in the industrial system. Taylor's separation of planning and control from the execution of work, for example, is reflected in our modern production control departments in factories; his ideas on the selection, training, compensation, and discipline of workers are embodied in the functions of modern personnel departments.

Work Planning and Measurement

Taylor believed that solutions to problems of efficiency should begin with a study of each job or task. It was to be management's duty, not the worker's, to determine how work should be done. Taylor contended that management did not know what should constitute a day's work for a workman. In conducting his experiments on work peformance, Taylor used a stop watch to get precise measurements of various parts of the work. He made thousands of stop-watch observations in a shoveling experiment alone. This was the beginning of the use of time and motion study to set work standards.

Taylor wrote that "employers derive their knowledge of how much of a given class of work can be done in a day from either their own experience, which has frequently gone hazy with age, from casual and unsystematic observations of their men, or at best from records which are kept."[11] The scientific approach requires that management judgments and decisions be based on accurate, first-hand knowledge procured from systematic, detailed observations, experiments, and studies. Guesswork, hunches, and intuition are rejected.

The tenets of scientific management have greatly influenced work methods and production techniques. Common examples include work simplification, tool and equipment engineering, improved physical facilities, and production control processes.

Work simplification is an industrial engineering technique designed to discover and apply improved ways of doing work. Techniques of work simplification are widely used to conserve time, money, and

---

[10]Taylor, *Principles of Scientific Management,* pp. 36–37.
[11]Taylor, *Shop Management,* p. 33.

energy in all walks of life, from home management to factory operations. The technique may be applied in all parts of an organization. Industrial engineers assist by making independent studies of tasks, jobs, and work methods. The findings are used to set the methods and standards for doing work. The principal tools are process flow charts, job descriptions, and time and motion studies.

Because tools, machines, and equipment are an integral part of the work situation, the study of work methods has been extended to include tool and equipment engineering. The trend is to design tools and machinery that are more compatible with human characteristics. In the shoveling experiments, for example, Taylor found that the workers were using a variety of sizes and shapes of shovels, which they furnished themselves. Taylor had the company furnish a standard-sized shovel for each kind of shoveling task. To determine the standard daily output that workers should attain, he had to standardize the equipment used. Today, such factors as size, shape, weight, and properties of control knobs, handles, levers, and dials are scientifically decided, so that workers can more easily and accurately use them.

Physical facilities have also been carefully studied under the impetus of scientific management. Research on the effects of lighting and air conditioning are prime examples. Every task has optimum conditions; for example, the improved use of color in offices and plants has resulted from psychological experiments. Plant layouts have been improved for greater accessibility to machines, tools, and materials and for greater safety and comfort of workers.

Production control processes in use today had their initial roots in Taylor's plan to divide factory work into several components, each in charge of a specialist. Taylor envisioned such functionalization at the supervisory level; but that never proved practical, primarily because workers disliked taking orders from several bosses (the functional specialists) and because of the difficulty of defining the scope of each function. Nevertheless, the eight main functions Taylor suggested (route clerk, instruction card clerk, cost and time clerk, gang boss, speed boss, inspector, repair boss, and shop disciplinarian) find their counterparts in central staff and service departments. Production control departments, for example, plan the routing, scheduling, and dispatching of materials in process.[12]

Incentive Wage Payments

Taylor advocated strong systems of reward and punishment. He had observed that many "first class workmen" did not put forth their best efforts, and felt that workers should be paid according to their effort, by piece rates. Those who could not produce according to the standards

[12]Ibid., p. 104.

were to be penalized by reductions in pay. Piece-rate systems were in use in Taylor's time, but without accurate determination of work standards by employers. Furthermore, according to Taylor, systematic "soldiering" (in which workers deliberately keep employers ignorant of how much work can be done) arose because employers were focusing on the amounts they thought "right" for each class of employee to earn per day, thus causing workers to fear that the employer would compel them to do increased work without additional pay.

Taylor recommended that the aims of each factory should be to (1) give each worker the highest grade of work for which his ability and physique made him fit; (2) require each worker to turn out the maximum amount of work that a first-class man could do and thrive; and (3) pay each worker who worked at the best pace of a first-class employee from 30 per cent to 100 per cent beyond the average of the class.[13] Such policies involved a basic principle that still holds for today's managements: *high wages* and *low labor cost*. According to this principle, managers should focus on labor cost per unit of product, rather than on the absolute value of wages. Taylor demonstrated in his experiments that high wages and low labor costs per unit go hand in hand, to the extent that high wages induce good workmen to do their best.

Appraisal of Scientific Management

Opinions of Taylor's contribution to the scientific management movement range from exalted worship—he is designated as the "father of scientific management"—to discounting him as an unoriginal recipient of undue credit.[14] Recent studies provide a more balanced perspective on Taylor and on the scientific management movement. Some of his thinking is surprisingly in keeping with recent approaches to administrative science. He was aware of the worker as an individual and of the influences of groups upon individuals. He understood the pressures leading to soldiering on the job and deplored the evils of wage systems that foster it.

Taylor's work has not always been well understood by modern critics.[15] By the time he first outlined his principles, Great Britain had been an industrial country of the first order for nearly a hundred years. Even though scientific management was not a sudden "invention," Taylor served as the catalyst in the codification and statement in coherent and logical form of the practices which had been developing in well-managed factories for some time.[16]

Taylor insisted that the essence of scientific management was the

---

[13]Ibid., pp. 28–29.
[14]Hoagland, "Management Before Frederick Taylor," pp. 19–20.
[15]J. Boddewyn, "Frederick Winslow Taylor Revisited," *Journal of the Academy of Management* 4 (August 1961), 100–107.
[16]Urwick and Brech, *Making of Scientific Management*, p. 7.

"mental revolution" it implied. Although Taylor used the word *science* loosely, he demonstrated that the philosophies, attitudes, and thought processes of the managers of his time were inadequate. Through his advocacy of measurement and experimentation he revolutionized thought patterns that had been tolerating rule-of-thumb methods.

Unfortunately, Taylor's contemporaries frequently misunderstood his methods and applied them unwisely. "Efficiency experts" appeared everywhere to promote increased production. Many companies engaged in rate cutting, that is, imposing rate reductions on workers whose earnings exceeded what managers thought they ought to earn. Rate cutting and the frequently tactless behavior of the efficiency experts gave the scientific management movement a bad reputation, especially among labor unions.

Taylor's writings show that his attitudes toward workers and unions were reasonable, but his work incurred the opposition of organized labor. Taylor's forthright statements that workers had to be taught, that they could not know without instruction how a job should be done, and that they needed strong guidance and stern discipline, were not pleasant words to workers. Moreover, his system of piece-rate wage payments aroused fears of speedup and unhealthy pressure upon workers. These threats were not inherent in Taylor's ideas, but erroneous interpretations and applications that Taylor himself had never intended alarmed the workers. Taylor's protests of respect for the working man did not stem the tide of adverse opinion. Taylor denied that he was antiunion, although he did say that if his principles were widely used there would be no need for unions, and did largely ignore group processes and the informal organization that were discovered by later theorists to be important.

Drucker suggests a perspective in judging Taylor's contribution by urging its relevance for "knowledge work," saying that in the society of the future, knowledge workers—scientists, technicians, engineers, educators, and other professionals and specialists, including managers—will be numerous and powerful. Therefore, scientific management should do for them what it did for manual workers at the turn of the century: increase productivity, earnings, and job satisfactions.[17] However, it is unlikely that scientific management will be as relevant to organizations of the future as Drucker's view implies. Today's organizations, and indeed our entire society, require much more than the useful beginning provided by scientific management thinkers.

Although many ideas from the scientific management movement remain useful, it has declined as a *movement*. It became one because it captured the imagination and enthusiasm of people in all walks of life,

[17]Peter F. Drucker, "The Coming Rediscovery of Scientific Management," *The Record* **XIII** (June 1976), 23–27.

as well as of leaders in business and government. It met many needs. Efficiency became literally a craze that transcended its industrial origins. Now the emotional impact has faded, and emotions and efforts are focused on social needs such as consumerism and environmental protection. Goals of efficiency are subordinate to other needs, although pressures for the efficiency of society itself may be growing, and the efficiency of individual enterprises remains important.[18]

Other Management Pioneers

Taylor's ideas stimulated many contemporaries, and his close associates were deeply committed to advancing the cause. In applying Taylor's principles, however, they developed divergent views. Such pioneers as Henry L. Gantt, Frank Gilbreth, and Harrington Emerson helped to extend scientific management beyond the factory settings in which Taylor did most of his work.[19]

Gantt, who had worked with Taylor in the Midvale Steel Company in 1887, did consulting work in industry and government, enlarging and improving upon many of Taylor's ideas. He developed improvements on Taylor's piece-rate system and widely installed his own incentive pay system. Understanding worker psychology better than Taylor, he saw the importance of morale and of the use of nonfinancial rewards. He believed that management should create environments that had favorable psychological effects on workers. Gantt also developed new planning and control processes in the form of scheduling charts, which related facts to relevant units of time.[20]

Gilbreth, although a contemporary of Taylor, became interested in work methods prior to his writings while he was working as a bricklaying apprentice. Subsequently he developed improvements in bricklaying methods that increased productivity and contributed to the health and safety of bricklayers. He introduced new concepts of work planning and of training workers in correct methods, first in the bricklaying and construction trades and later in other kinds of work. He too showed great regard for the human factors in work, a concern shaped, in part, by his wife and collaborator Lillian. After Gilbreth's death, Mrs. Gilbreth became internationally famous as she carried on his work.

Emerson wrote two important books on the subject of efficiency, emphasizing the importance of effective organization to achieve high

---

[18]Dalton E. McFarland, "Whatever Happened to the Efficiency Movement?" *The Record*, **XIII: 6** (June 1976), 50–55.

[19]For brief biographical sketches of over seventy management pioneers, see Lyndall F. Urwick, *The Golden Book of Management*, edited for the International Committee of Scientific Management (London: N. Neame, 1956). See also Harwood F. Merrill (ed.), *Classics in Management* (New York: American Management Associations, 1960).

[20]George Filipetti, *Management in Transition*, rev. ed. (Homewood, Ill.: Irwin, 1953), chap. 4.

productivity and advocating the line-and-staff type of organization structure that characterizes many organizations today. He cited a number of "principles" of efficiency that still apply, although further studies are needed in this area. He stressed the goal of eliminating waste and asserted the need for strong leadership to reconcile conflicting relationships within management.[21]

Bureaucracy

The evolution of the concept of bureaucracy preceded and later paralleled scientific management. Bureaucracy was elaborated by the German sociologist Max Weber in the 1920s. However, Weber's work was not translated into English until 1947, so that Taylor and other scientific management writers probably were unaware of it. Weber foresaw the development of large-scale, complex organizations and the need for formal management and administrative procedures that would make such organizations possible and efficient.[22]

The compatibility of Weber's ideas with those of the scientific management movement produced a number of important management and organization concepts having to do with levels of authority in the hierarchy of organizations; specialization of work; the command structure; the rules and duties applying to position-holders; coordination; and control.

Researchers later attacked the precepts emerging from this body of work, but the gap between the scientific management–bureaucratic views and modern views was bridged by four important writers: Follett, Barnard, March and Simon. These writers perceived the ideas of bureaucracy and scientific management in such a way as to remain an important force in the evolution of modern theory. March and Simon are currently well within the modern group; their work was inspired by that of Follett and Barnard.[23]

————————————————————————— **THE HUMAN RELATIONS MOVEMENT**

The human relations movement of the 1940s and 1950s filled many gaps in knowledge about work in organizations, but it did little to fill

[21]Harrington Emerson, *Efficiency as a Basis for Operation and Wages* (New York: Engineering Magazine Company, 1911); *The Twelve Principles of Efficiency* (New York: Engineering Magazine Company, 1913).

[22]Max Weber, *The Theory of Social and Economic Organization* (New York: Oxford U.P., 1947).

[23]Henry C. Metcalf and Lyndall C. Urwick (eds.), *Dynamic Administration: The Collected Papers of Mary Parker Follett* (New York: Harper, 1940); Chester I. Barnard, *The Functions of the Executive* (Cambridge: Harvard U.P., 1938); James G. March and Herbert A. Simon, *Organizations* (New York: Wiley, 1958); Herbert A. Simon, *Administrative Behavior*, 3rd ed. (New York: Free Press, 1976).

major gaps in management theory or to advance the theory of organizations. The movement accepted scientific management's goal of efficiency, but it focused on individuals and on small-group processes
rather than on large organizations, stressing communication, leadership, and interpersonal relations, particularly between employees and
their bosses. Like that on scientific management, research on human
relations focused on the lower levels of organization rather than on the
middle and upper groups, so that it lacked the comprehensive scope
that theory demands. Behavioral scientists became interested in companies as research sites, but aimed at building their own separate
disciplines—or at establishing a science of human relations, rther than
a science of management.

The keynote of the human relations approach is found in the rapid
advances made in the sciences dealing with man and his behavior.
Psychology, sociology, social psychology, and social anthropology have
made rewarding contributions to the study of organizational problems
through research on the behavior of people, both as individuals and as
members of groups.

Industrial Psychology

Parallel with the evolving field of scientific management was the
growth of a branch of psychology that applied that science to industrial
problems. In 1913, Hugo Munsterberg first outlined the approximate
boundaries of the new discipline.[24]

In its early stages, industrial psychology, like scientific management,
was concerned with task-oriented work effort and problems of fatigue,
monotony, and efficiency. It was also concerned with the design of
equipment, the arrangement of lighting and other working conditions,
and the influence of these factors on working efficiency.

Later, industrial psychology explored the problems of selecting and
training employees and, spurred by the manpower problems of World
War I, developed techniques of psychological testing and measurement. Managers accepted these techniques, and many companies
incorporated testing, selection, and training into their personnel programs just as they adopted the systems of wage payment and methods
engineering advanced by the scientific management movement. At
later stages, industrial psychologists introduced systems of performance
rating and techniques for measuring and improving employee morale.

A major contribution of industrial psychology is the fact that it was
more rigorously experimental and scientific than the scientific management movement itself. Industrial psychology had the benefit of the
scientific methodologies of general psychologists. A new sector now
developing in the field is called organizational psychology.

---

[24]Hugo Munsterberg, *Psychology and Industrial Efficiency* (Boston: Houghton Mifflin, 1913).

Industrial Sociology

During this same period, the evolving field of sociology emerged. Whereas psychology focused upon the individual, sociology emphasized the study of groups, both large and small, as well as on problems of society itself. Gradually there emerged a branch of sociology concerned with work groups in industry and with the nature of work in society. Researchers in industrial sociology became interested in studying business firms as social systems, as well as with the cultural meaning of work, thus triggering the emergence of a new field, organizational sociology.

Applied Anthropology

The field of anthropology grew out of the work of early sociologists who specialized in the study of cultures, devoting themselves to the study of mankind and to the manifold arrangements, both past and present, by which humans have organized their living patterns. Among the anthropologists were those who came to feel the urgency of studying scientifically the impact of cultural elements on particular groups. Thus emerged a field of applied anthropology, the study of human organizations.[25]

Researchers in applied anthropology have contributed to management practice through studies of business firms, government activities, organizational relationships, and the impact of cultural differences on organization. Applied anthropologists such as William Foote Whyte, George S. Homans, and Melville Dalton were also active in the human-relations-in-industry movement of the period from 1940 to 1960.

Social Psychology

Psychologists soon recognized that the behavior of individuals is greatly affected by their experiences in groups and their presence in society; likewise, sociologists became aware that group behavior is intertwined with individual behavior. Those who sought to study these interrelationships eventually identified a discipline known as social psychology. This development marked a significant step toward the interdisciplinary approach that came to characterize the human relations movement. Social psychologists, too, found business organizations fruitful places for research and investigation. Social psychology is also concerned with problems of mass communications, propaganda analysis, rumor transmission, and similar phenomena.

[25]The American Association of Applied Anthropologists publishes a quarterly journal called *Human Organization*.

Human Relations as a Discipline

As each of the sciences of human behavior advanced, it confronted other sciences that were at work on the same problems, but from differing points of view and with different methodologies. It has been difficult for researchers from the human sciences to maintain a single interdisciplinary movement. Attempts at team research have met with some success, but progress toward genuinely integrated behavioral science is slow. At the level of applications to concrete problems of management, however, the interdisciplinary concept has been more successful. From its inception, the human-relations-in-industry movement was based upon concepts of integrating the work of all disciplines concerned with the human problems of management.

The human relations school of thought had its beginnings in the late 1930s and early 1940s. In 1941, Roethlisberger and Dickson published a landmark study reporting the results of the elaborately conceived psychological experiments of Elton Mayo and his colleagues at the Hawthorne, Illinois, plant of the Western Electric Company.[26] These studies revealed that the performance of workers is conditioned not only by tangible factors in the environment but by more intangible elements, such as the group and the social processes inherent in work situations. This monumental study marked a turning point in the path of research in industrial psychology and industrial sociology; it revolutionized management thinking, focusing attention on the components of job and work satisfaction on the part of the employees. Morale, motivation, and employee attitudes became important subjects of research and practice. One of the key concepts receiving great attention in the Hawthorne studies and thereafter was employee counseling. The researchers also developed new methods of interviewing that are still widely used today.

In 1943, the Committee on Human Relations in Industry was created at the University of Chicago, to conduct interdisciplinary research on human relations and to train competent researchers and teachers in these areas. On this committee were Neil Jacoby, then a vice president of the University of Chicago, and faculty members from the School of Business (George Brown and Burleigh Gardner), the Department of Education (Allison Davis and Robert Havighurst), and the Department of Anthropology and Sociology (W. Lloyd Warner, Everett Hughes, and William Foote Whyte).[27] Books on human relations in industry began to appear, a pioneer text being that of Burleigh Gardner.[28] Research and

[26]Fritz Roethlisberger and William J. Dickson, *Management and the Worker* (Cambridge, Mass.: Harvard U.P., 1941). The Hawthorne studies have in recent years been severely criticized for the lack of vigor of their research methods and the lack of validity of their conclusions. Nevertheless, their impact was substantial.

[27]Delbert C. Miller and William Form, *Industrial Sociology* (New York: Harper, 1951), p. 10.

[28]Burleigh Gardner, *Human Relations in Industry* (Homewood, Ill.: Irwin, 1945).

writing increased rapidly, and soon universities were adding courses and degrees in the subject.

The field of group dynamics emerged during the human relations era. Pioneers in this field were Bales, who developed methods of observing and measuring roles and other group processes;[29] Lewin, who is considered the founder of group dynamics and who developed action research concepts to apply group theory to actual problems;[30] and a number of researchers at the University of Michigan.[31] The research on group dynamics has remained influential in the modern era of revisionist approaches.

The human relations movement made significant advances in both the theory and the practice of management. As with the scientific management movement, practitioners misapplied research findings; fads captured the attention of well-intentioned businessmen; consultants oversold concepts of human relations. As a consequence, human relations could not solve all the problems it promised to, and in the late 1950s serious signs of disillusionment appeared. Some authorities even recommended going back to a philosophy of benevolent authoritarianism.[32]

On balance it is clear that only further research will provide an assessment of the validity of human relations concepts. Meanwhile, as the human relations approach evolves into the better-established field of organization behavior, tempered by a growing degree of realism and by increasing research and experience, the practice of management will benefit.

THE REVISIONIST MOVEMENT

The revisionist movement dates from the mid-1950s, when Litchfield's propositions appeared. In the years following, a number of books emerged directly analyzing the state of management or organization theory.

Revisionists assert that "principles" developed by the deductive reasoning of the scientific management thinkers are inadequate or even wrong. They do not discard all the early theory, but they insist on rejecting what is not verified.

[29]Robert F. Bales, *Interaction Process Analysis* (Reading, Mass.: Addison-Wesley, 1950).

[30]Kurt Lewin, *Field Theory in Social Science* (New York: Harper, 1951).

[31]Dorwin Cartwright and Alvin Zander (eds.), *Group Dynamics*, 3rd ed. (New York: Harper, 1968).

[32]Malcolm McNair, "What Price Human Relations?" *Harvard Business Review* **35** (March–April 1957), 15–18; Robert McMurry, "The Case for Benevolent Autocracy," *Harvard Business Review* **36** (January–February 1958), 82–90.

The Emerging Science of Management

In the earliest stage of revisionist movement, researchers combined streams of effort in the behavioral sciences with those in mathematics, statistics, and the use of computers, at the same time preserving verifiable concepts from scientific management and human relations theory.

In the scientific management movement, quantitative theorists were predominantly oriented to engineering, and behavioral scientists were mainly industrial psychologists. During the era of human relations, behavioral scientists made valuable studies of job satisfaction, morale, productivity, and conflict resolution. In the management science era that is now under way, revisionist researchers include many types—not only behavioral scientists but also systems theorists, operations research specialists, decision theorists, statisticians, computer experts, and others skilled in quantitative research and decision methods. This powerful combination portends a greater rigor in the research that forges a management science. With the strengthening of the contributions of the basic disciplines underlying management science and an increased understanding of the application of behavioral, statistical, and mathematical tools, we can expect better management theory to emerge, for it will then be based on rigorous testing of propositions and more reliable knowledge of management processes and techniques.

Bennis has used the term *revisionist* to describe a current and increasingly large group of researchers in the field of organization and administrative theory.[33] The works of Simon, March, Argyris, Haire, Likert, and others are illustrative. The starting point of the revisionists' writings is dissatisfaction with the concepts espoused by the scientific management and human relations movements. Revisionists believe that neither of these early movements was sufficiently rigorous to provide valid principles and theories. Condemnation of the principles of scientific management is even more severe than for human relations, for many revisionists were themselves the product of human relations training in universities, so that they are more closely bound to their recent experiences.

Revisionists have contributed important perspectives to the practice of management, and their work will be closely followed in this book. Their skepticism about the beliefs and findings of earlier management thought have been largely justified, and they have perceived that management is at the threshold of new and exciting discoveries in the fields of organization and administration. Their work incorporates the most recent advances in the methodology of research and the use of mathematics and computers for many kinds of decisions. The hallmark of the revisionist movement is its emphasis on sophisticated research

[33]Warren Bennis, "Leadership and Administrative Behavior," *Administrative Science Quarterly* 4 (December 1959), 259–301.

methods, empirical investigation, and rigorous testing of propositions. Thus we are moving from "scientific management" to a true science of management.

_____ **SUMMARY**

Scientific management is a social and economic movement that is still evolving from its early American and British roots. The movement has advanced far beyond the day-to-day shop activities in which Taylor presented and tested his ideas. His original concepts of wage payment, worker selection and training, and work measurement for the purpose of setting standards remain in modified forms today. Management as it now exists is a mixture of practices and concepts in all kinds of organizations. Around these practices are developing bodies of scientific theory which, when wisely applied, can do much to improve both practice and theory. Rudimentary scientific efforts to explain, analyze, and predict behavior in the business world were developed by Frederick W. Taylor and his contemporaries. The human relations movement added perspectives overlooked by early scientific management thinkers, particularly in the realm of workers and their attitudes toward work and in the managerial techniques of supervising workers.

Revisionists have noted weaknesses, defects, and gaps in previous streams of thought and have insisted on the use of more rigorous methods of research. They seek to explain behavior in organizations through better theory and greater integration of the many studies of human beings at work.

The scientific management school developed an organization-centered body of theory with a central emphasis on efficiency, leading, in turn, to descriptive research, theories based on deductive evidence, and emphasis on the management functions such as planning, organizing, and controlling. The human relations movement took a small-group, person-centered approach to the study of management. Research became more experimental, but theory remained basically descriptive and highly deductive. Finally the revisionists challenged both earlier movements, using behavioral and quantitative tools of analysis to conduct research that is more inductive, more experimental, more rigorous, and more inclusive than ever.

_____ **INCIDENT CASE**

Two company presidents were arguing at lunch one day. "All I need to do to have a successful company," Smith said, "is to guess right about the future. The present will take care of itself, and the past no longer has any meaning. Henry Ford was correct when he said 'History is bunk.'" Greene, the other president, disagreed: "History is fun; history is instructive. Those who ignore it are doomed to repeat it."

Question

1. Who is right, and why?

QUESTIONS FOR STUDY

1. Just how scientific is management? Explain your answer fully.
2. Should management be more scientific than it already is?
3. Describe the changes in present-day scientific management, as compared with that of Frederick W. Taylor's day.
4. Give some explanations for the unfavorable attitudes toward scientific management expressed in Taylor's time by both management and labor. To what extent do these attitudes prevail today?
5. Explain Taylor's attitude toward the working man and toward labor unions.
6. What aspects of Taylor's work are now found in major departments in business organizations?
7. What elements of human relations activity or philosophy do you think should be retained? What should be discarded. Why?
8. How did the human relations approach seek to modify the scientific management approach?
9. Who are some of the major revisionist researchers, and what implications do you see in their work for management in the future?

SELECTED REFERENCES

AITKEN, HUGH G. J. *Taylorism at Watertown Arsenal: Scientific Management in Action, 1908–1915.* Cambridge, Mass.: Harvard University Press, 1960.

BAUGHMAN, JAMES, ed. *The History of American Management.* Englewood Cliffs, N.J.: Prentice-Hall, Inc., 1968.

DEL MAR, DONALD, and ROGER D. COLLINS. *Classics in Scientific Management.* University: University of Alabama Press, 1976.

FILIPETTI, GEORGE. *Management in Transition.* Homewood, Ill.: Richard D. Irwin, Inc., 1947. Chapters. 1, 2, 4, 6.

HABER, SAMUEL. *Efficiency and Uplift: Scientific Management in the Progressive Era, 1890–1920.* Chicago: University of Chicago Press, 1964.

KAKAR, SUDHIR. *Frederick Taylor: A Study in Personality and Innovation.* Cambridge, Mass.: The M.I.T. Press, 1970.

MEE, JOHN F. *Management Thought in a Dynamic Economy.* New York: New York University Press, 1963.

MERRILL, HARWOOD F., ed. *Classics in Management.* Revised edition. New York: American Management Associations, 1972.

NADWORNY, MILTON J. *Scientific Management and the Unions, 1900–1932: A Historical Analysis.* Cambridge, Mass.: Harvard University Press, 1955. Chapters. 1, 2, 9.

PERSON, H. S., ed. *Scientific Management in American Industry.* New York: Harper & Row, Publishers, 1929. pp. 1–39.

POLLARD, HAROLD R., *Developments in Management Thought.* New York: Crane, Russak and Company, Inc., 1974.

SPRIEGEL, WILLIAM R., and CLARK E. MEYERS, eds. *The Writings of the Gilbreths.* Homewood, Ill.: Richard D. Irwin, Inc., 1953.

TAYLOR, F. W. *Scientific Management.* New York: Harper & Row, Publishers, 1947. Contains *Shop Management* and *Principles of Scientific Management.*

URWICK, LYNDALL F., and E. F. L. BRECH. *The Making of Scientific Management.* London: Sir Isaac Pitman & Sons, Ltd., reprinted 1953. Vols. 1 and 2.

WREN, DANIEL A., *The Evolution of Management Thought.* New York: The Ronald Press, 1972.

WOLF, WILLIAM B. *Conversations with Chester I. Barnard.* Ithaca: New York State School of Industrial and Labor Relations, January, 1973.

WOLF, WILLIAM B. *The Basic Barnard: An Introduction to Chester I. Barnard and His Theories of Organization and Management.* Ithaca, N.Y.: Cornell University Press, 1973.

Chapter 3

Managers and Their Careers

A great society is one in which its men of business think greatly of their function. *—Alfred North Whitehead*

Every man who manages another is a hypocrite. *TRUE!* *—Thackeray*

Administration is not only the faculty upon which social stability rests but it is possibly the highest faculty of the human mind. *—Brooks Adams*

CHAPTER GUIDE

Guard: Your secretary came out to inspect the no-parking signs we put up at the drive-in teller.
Assistant Manager: Hey, that was no secretary. That was my boss.
    The boss was a 31-year-old black woman who earns more than $25,000 per year as manager of the branch bank.

Questions to keep in mind as you read this chapter:

1. What management problems does this incident reflect?
2. What does this incident reveal about role stereotypes?
3. What, if anything, should the assistant manager do next?

Managers are the agents of activity and change in organizations. They require a high capacity for analyzing problems and isolating their

41

causes, marshaling resources, and initiating the actions of colleagues and subordinates. As decision makers, they are responsible for identifying and achieving the purposes of the organization.

Managerial roles are numerous, complex, and diverse. Claims on the manager's time, attention, and energy are severe, and frustrations are inevitable. Nevertheless, reasonably effective and politically sensitive individuals can achieve fulfillment and substantial rewards from managerial careers in organizations.

At the center of action and change in organizations, managers have become the focus of increasing research. This growing interest in studying managers scientifically arises because their ability to manage is vital if organizations are to be effective. In addition, research findings provide managers with valuable knowledge about themselves, their careers, and the leadership of their organizations. This chapter presents an overview of the growing body of knowledge about the manager as a key participant in the organization. First, several terms and concepts are defined; then the critical roles, responsibilities, and characteristics of the manager are examined; finally, the concept of managerial careers will be discussed.

DEFINITIONS

The terms *manager, executive, administrator, businessman* and *entrepreneur* are closely related, and are sometimes used interchangeably despite technical differences. None has a precise, universal definition. The terms are so imprecise that it is impossible to obtain an accurate count of the number of persons in the different categories.

Businessman is the most general term of all. Chapter 1 indicated that not every businessman is an executive or a manager. There are many occupations in business such as that of a stockbroker, that are nonmanagerial; and many managers are not businessmen because they work for the government, trade associations, or other nonprofit and service agencies such as hospitals or schools.

The term *entrepreneur* describes a special type of businessman— one who is generally the owner and initiator of a business, and who may or may not be a manager in it as well. The term should be distinguished from the terms *executive* and *manager*. Entrepreneur is an ambiguous term, and economists differ in their definitions of it. It originally denoted the business risk-taker or owner, or the creator of new enterprise. (The word *entrepreneur* is a French word meaning enterpriser.) More recently it has been used to indicate the aggressive businessman or business leader. Today's organizations are more and more directed by managerial employees, whose behavior is the subject of this book. The terms *executive* and *manager* denote the managerial employees who run our organizations. In this book, the word *entrepreneur* will be used to indicate only the innovators and venturers, including owners, who undertake risks through establishing new organizational units.[1]

That entrepreneurs differ significantly from managers and executives has been argued by Collins and Moore, and corroborated by Giesbrecht on the basis of observations in Taiwan, where there has been much enterprise development. Giesbrecht concludes that entrepreneurs are a special breed: they behave differently and have different motives, backgrounds, and origins than managers. Furthermore, he believes that entrepreneurs do not develop into managers.[2]

The terms *manager, executive,* and *administrator* are often used interchangeably. The term *manager* as used throughout this book is interchangeable with the terms *executive* and *administrator.* When the words *executive* or *administrator* are used, their special meanings will be clear from the context. The main differences among these terms are in the level and type of the organization in which the usage occurs, but even these distinctions are not clear cut. In most organizations, the terms *executive* and *administrator* denote those in or near the top echelons; in others, the term is applied at the middle levels. Some companies differentiate executives from managers by salary classifications. Figure 3-1 shows several of these distinctions by level of organization.

The Top Management Group

The term *top management* includes the corporate officers and the echelons of presidents, executive vice presidents, vice presidents, and assistant vice presidents, who may also be referred to as executives or administrators. Corporate officers are elected from the group at the top, as shown in Figure 3-1. They usually include the chairman of the board of directors, board members, the president, executive or group vice presidents, and frequently, several vice presidents. Corporate officers are concerned primarily with the major direction of the enterprise, over-all policies, large-scale and long-run strategies and commitments, legal matters, the security of the company and its assets, the choice of major goals, and the profitability that ensues from all these elements. The roles and responsibilities of corporate officers are specified in

---

[1]This concept is in fairly general use by economists. See Robert Aaron Gordon, *Business Leadership in the Large Corporation* (Berkeley: U. of California Press, 1961).

[2]Orvis Collins and David G. Moore, with Darab B. Unwalla, *The Enterprising Man* (East Lansing, Michigan: Bureau of Business and Economic Research, Michigan State University, 1964); Martin Gerhard Giesbrecht, "Entrepreneurship vs. Modern Management: A Co-aim for Business," *MSU Business Topics* **16** (Winter 1968), 22–31. See also John Kenneth Galbraith, *The New Industrial State,* 2nd ed. (Boston: Houghton-Mifflin, 1971).

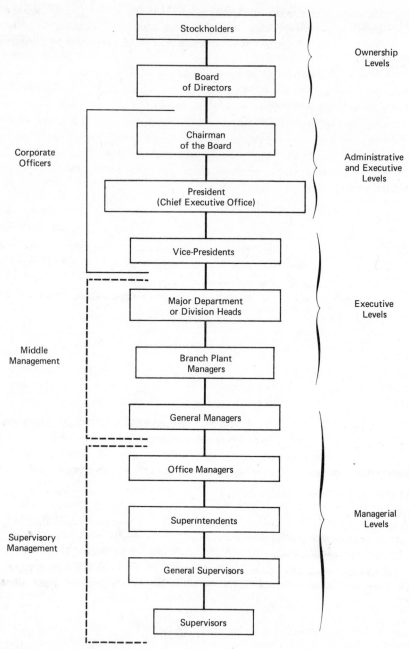

FIGURE 3-1. Executives and Managers by Levels.

44

corporate bylaws, and are governed by the laws of the state in which the
organization is incorporated.[3]

At executive levels, vice presidents, major department or division
heads, or the manager of a plant formulate and carry out policies,
decisions, and plans. They are also concerned with the implementation
and communication of basic administrative decisions pertaining to
goals, strategies, and policies. These managers perform the top-level,
day-to-day management work of the company, with responsibility for
major actions affecting the company's success. The term *executive* aptly
pertains to the members of this group.

Middle Management

Figure 3-1 also identifies, approximately, a group known as *middle
management*. This term, popularized by Niles in the early 1940s,
identifies a group that tends to overlap the executive and lower management groups.[4] The concept of middle management does not refer to
exact boundaries, but it provides a useful focus for examining certain
critical management problems, such as promotions, training, career
aspirations, organization design, human relations, communications, and
leadership.

At intermediate levels of an organization, the term *manager* comes to
supplant *executive*, but the term also applies to those at the lower
levels of the management hierarchy, such as first-line supervisors;
middle management usually includes managers below the vice-presidential level, such as the heads of functional departments, and the
managers of technical and staff units such as purchasing, engineering,
and research and development.

Supervisory Levels

At the supervisory level, typically, are general foremen, group supervisors, and first-line supervisors. Essentially these positions relate closely
to operating units such as maintenance, manufacturing, or office-clerical supervision. General foremen or departmental superintendents

[3]For detailed information on boards of directors, see J. M. Juran and F. Keith Louden,
The Corporate Director (New York: American Management Associations, 1966); Harold
Koontz, *The Board of Directors and Effective Management* (New York: McGraw-Hill,
1967); Stanley Vance, *The Corporate Director: A Critical Evaluation* (Homewood, Ill.:
Dow Jones-Irwin, 1968); Jeremy Bacon, *Corporate Directorship Practices* (New York:
National Industrial Conference Board, 1968); Courtney Brown, *Putting the Corporate
Board to Work* (New York: Macmillan, 1976); The Conference Board, *Corporate Direc-
torship Practices: Compensation* (New York: The Conference Board, 1975).

[4]Mary Cushing Niles, *Middle Management* (New York: Harper, 1941). See also Cyril
Sofer, *Men in Mid-Career: A Study of British Managers and Technical Specialists* (New
York: Cambridge U.P., 1970).

supervise first-line supervisors, who in turn are in direct contact with rank-and-file blue-collar, office-clerical, or technical workers.

The supervisory levels are considered to be managerial in character (although supervision is also a *function* that administrators and executives perform). Managers usually have less discretion in the manner of carrying out their responsibilities and less scope for policy decisions than executives. Their function is to carry out operating plans, policies, and procedures within frameworks developed by higher levels. The term *manager* is most frequently applied to persons who direct relatively small and well-defined units or who operate at close to a day-to-day level of responsibility.

The Hierarchy

The managerial relationships just described pertain to what is technically known as the hierarchy. An organization consists of levels, each having an appropriate status and degree of authority for position holders. This hierarchy is of central importance to organization theory and practice, which will be examined in later chapters. It is also a key factor in understanding managerial behavior. The hierarchy poses difficulties for managers: its very existence has an impact on their judgments, actions, thinking, and decisions. Moreover, the way the hierarchy operates has much to do with career advancement within an organization.

The hierarchy consists not only of levels but also of horizontally differentiated units at each level, thus permitting the scope of the various positions to be defined in terms of tasks and responsibilities so that managers can specialize in a major function within a limited sphere of action. Some organizations put less emphasis on the use of a carefully contrived organizational hierarchy. These subjects will be considered in detail in Part Three of this book.

What Managers Are Like

Managers as a group reflect a great diversity, and there is no typical set of characteristics. A few basic generalizations are possible, however.

Most organizations, obviously, distinguish managers from nonmanagers. The latter group, often called the rank and file, includes such categories as assembly-line or other operations workers, salespersons, or office-clerical employees. That workers are distinguished from managers is a matter of convenience, custom, and usage; it does not imply that managers do not perform "work" in the sense of productive effort. The importance of the distinction lies in the nature of managerial tasks compared to the work of rank-and-file employees. Separated from the performance of operating tasks, the work of managers assumes a less tangible quality. It is predominantly mental and conceptual in nature.

Despite the distinction between executives and "workers," it is important to note that managers themselves are also employees. In many respects they view themselves as job holders, and their basic needs are similar to those of other employees: adequate compensation, opportunities to advance, job satisfaction, and recognition. The differences are in degree rather than in kind. Although managers may own stock in a number of companies, including the ones they work for, their role as owners is similar to that of other stockholders. With some exceptions, managers fulfill the role of employees rather than that of owners: they are the agents or representatives of owners. However, as professional managers they are a special kind of employee.

Certain stereotypes affect our thinking about what managers are like, and thus inhibit clear thinking about the roles and tasks of managers. One such view is that of the "organization man," an unthinking conformist. Others include the image of the manager as an overworked, heroic type, as a rugged individualist, and as a practical person.

Managers are often depicted as aggressive, intense, and busy, making quick decisions, and issuing sharp orders to subordinates. The Hollywood movie version is not much better. Here managers are invariably suave and expensively dressed, either young and handsome or old and distinguished-looking. Subordinates cower before them. They have risen to the top through brute force, with little or no education. They thrive in opulent settings, free from the oil and grime of the factory.

The idea of the practical has a wide appeal. It is part of our frontier heritage, in which the image of the rugged individualist and the "self-made man" looms large. Managers prefer action to words, deeds over thought, decision rather than philosophy. In our early history, the practical view had great value, and it still does. Organizations today need people who are able to take realistic, practical actions. However, the practical is no substitute for theory, and worship of the rugged individualist can cause undue reliance upon intuition, past experience, and hunches. To make a fetish of the practical is to overlook the need for synthesis and integration at the level of management theory and philosophy.

There is evidence that stereotyped views of the manager are changing. Long ago, Follett pointed out that "the image of the masterful man carrying all before him by the sheer force of his personality has largely disappeared."[5] The view of the manager as a ruthless machine, unremittingly energetic, unable to make mistakes, dispensing wisdom on all matters, is no longer appropriate. Management by hunch is fading. In the place of these unrealistic stereotypes is emerging a very different

---

[5]Henry C. Metcalf and Lyndall F. Urwick, *Dynamic Administration: The Collected Papers of Mary Parker Follett* (New York: Harper, 1940), p. 119.

prototype:—the manager whose demeanor is essentially modest and whose guiding light is verified knowledge.[6]

MANAGERIAL ROLES, TASKS, AND RESPONSIBILITIES

A role is a set of related activities or behavior patterns that fulfill the expectations of others in given contexts. Roles result in a general degree of predictability of behavior in recurring, frequently encountered situations. Organizations prescribe official task roles through job titles and descriptions, but roles also have a more informal content consisting of the expectations of superiors, subordinates, peers, or even customers or suppliers. In a given society, people come to learn a number of socially acceptable roles, which are drawn upon almost automatically to meet frequently occurring situations; in the same way, people learn useful roles in organizations.

The complexity of the manager's role arises from the varied sources of the expectations. Some of the demands come from the external environment, some from technical aspects of the work, others from internal associations and conditions, and still others from the manager's own view of his tasks. Moreover, the demands may be in substantial conflict with each other. Therefore, managers face the problem of synthesizing and rationalizing these role demands. They must also select appropriate roles, and shift from one to another to meet ongoing situations. Organizations as well as managers need the stability and predictability that derive from skillful role performance, but the formal and informal pressures of expectations dictate resilience and flexibility on the manager's part.[7]

Changes in Basic Roles

The external and internal conditions affecting managerial roles are continuously changing. Expectations, technology, and managers change; therefore roles also change. Some important roles have undergone substantial change over time. The role of owner was once very important in the business enterprise. The owner was closely involved with the company's day-to-day activities. Now, in corporations at least, the ownership role is diffused among many stockholders who act through elected boards of directors. Direct owner influence is minimal in large organizations and in many small ones.

[6]Tony Ellis and John Child, "Placing Stereotypes of the Manager into Perspective," *Journal of Management Studies* 10 (October 1973), 233–255.
[7]Douglas McGregor, *The Professional Manager* (New York: McGraw-Hill, 1967), chapter 3.

Like the role of the owner, the leader's role too has changed. Great leaders have been replaced by organizationally created leaders. Whereas such men as Ford, Rockefeller, Sloan, Chrysler, and others were few in number but prominent, powerful, wealthy, and influential, leaders today are more numerous, and they appear at every level. They are the product of corporate training programs and professional schools. Leadership is expected of the newest supervisor as well as of the highest executive.

As some roles change or disappear, others come into being. As "great leaders" were superseded by trained leaders, and as organizations grew in size and complexity, the manager's role became more bureaucratic. *Bureaucracy* refers to the highly rational, systematic, hierarchical organization structure, and to the accompanying assumptions that most organizations employ today. Managers occupy assigned positions in the hierarchy, with corresponding duties and rewards. The manager's primary role is to participate in the system according to its well-developed rules. The content of the manager's various roles is based on the logic of task requirements and on the demands of the hierarchical system. Roles typically involve considerable specialization of task or function. Bureaucratic roles tend to be somewhat independent of the role occupant, so that managers may change but the organization's needs continue to be met.[8] Many organizations today are trying to reduce the emphasis on bureaucratic roles, replacing them with roles more oriented to innovation, employee participation, and involvement.

Male and female roles are changing rapidly in the light of society's pressure to achieve equality of status and treatment of men and women, and laws that seek to eliminate discrimination on the basis of sex. Roles that were traditionally male or female are now being redesigned to remove the male-female dimension from them. By law, with few exceptions, jobs may not be limited solely to men or women.

In addition to change, an important characteristic of roles is that they can be both learned and taught. A great deal of educational activity, both formal and informal, is centered upon the cultivation of appropriate roles. Many roles are learned through observation and imitation. The performance of a role is often automatic and subtle rather than consciously contrived. An example is the "bedside manner" of the physician.

Finally, it is important to note that managers play a number of roles all at once, or change roles to fit different situations. The existence of multiple roles is usually not a problem, because people have learned

[8]Bureaucracy and its problems will be analyzed in several later chapters. For a discussion of historical changes in the roles and images of administrators, see Craig C. Lundberg, "Evolving Concepts of the Administrator," *MSU Business Topics* 16 (Winter 1968), 67–72.

the roles that are the most useful in the typical situations they confront. Thus an individual may take roles as a parent, a son or daughter, a teacher, a spouse, or a boss.

Some Key Roles of the Manager

There are an infinite number of possible roles for managers and executives, and an infinite number of styles with which a manager may play particular roles. Let us look at some examples.

Sonthoff describes the manager as *actor, catalyst, guardian, friend, owner,* and *technician.*[9] These roles represent kinds of behavior that are vital to organizations. As *actors,* executives are doers, persons of action; they have goals, and they act to achieve them. As *catalysts,* they harmonize the conflicting interests that they encounter. As *guardians,* they husband resources to facilitate the growth and welfare of the organization. As *friends,* executives display attitudes that strengthen their relationships to others and enhance their ability to guide subordinates. As *owners,* executives work to make the business grow, displaying a commitment to objectives that test their moral and ethical values. As *technicians,* executives find that management can be learned; that there are techniques and processes to master, and that they are in a sense craftsmen. To the roles that Sonthoff enumerates, we may well add the role of *professional.*

The roles described by Sonthoff are relatively metaphysical and philosophical; that is, they express the nature of possible inner attitudes the manager may have toward himself and his organization. We have previously alluded to roles that are essentially managerial in nature, such as planning, organizing, leading, or bringing about change. Clearly the mix and patterning of roles become important. Role behavior can be misdirected or inappropriate when the executive misinterprets the context of other people's expectations; roles can be in conflict and can exist in varying degrees of importance, relevance, and significance. Therefore managers need, from day to day, a sensitivity to the role skills appropriate to their tasks and aims.

A given job role may vary in different organizations, a fact that has an important bearing on personnel management. Katzell and his associates studied the relationships between each of nine executive role dimensions and various features of the organizational setting. The roles of the executives varied with differences in the work setting. Organizational features most prominently associated with variations in role included

---

[9]Herbert Sonthoff, "What Is the Manager?" *Harvard Business Review* 42 (November–December 1964), 24–30. See also David A. Emery, *The Complete Manager: Combining the Humanistic and Scientific Approaches to the Manager's Job* (New York: McGraw-Hill, 1970); F. D. Barrett, "How to be a Subjective Manager," *The Business Quarterly* 41 (Autumn 1976), 82–89.

the mission and level of the organization, the job family of the executive, and his span of control. The role dimensions that were most likely to vary with the situation were staffing, controlling, and time spent with others. Executives whose roles emphasized administrative more than technical features received high average performance ratings from their superiors.[10]

Lopez distinguishes four key managerial roles that may be observed alone or in combinations with each other: *entrepreneur, leader, storekeeper,* and *controller.* Their characteristics are shown in Figure 3-2. These roles are not the only possible managerial ones, but they are worth considering in connection with hiring new managers. When testing and evaluation procedures are used to assess the degree to which the major characteristics are present, individuals can be better matched to the role demands associated with particular functions.[11]

The work of the manager is not only complex but vast in scope. The manager's day is filled with frequent interaction with other people from within and without; with details as well as with grand strategies; with failures as well as successes; with boredom as well as enjoyment. The demands on the manager's physical, mental, and emotional energies are enormous.

Our views of managerial tasks have changed as revisionist research has caused modifications in earlier scientific management thought. Early views depicted managers as positioned in a chain of command with the tasks of planning, organizing, controlling and coordinating. These and other managerial functions, to be analyzed in Part Two of this book, are vital to the organization; but they are not sufficient for a complete understanding of the complexities of mangerial work.

Current approaches see managers as a critical component of the organization viewed as a sociotechnical system. The manager is the creator as well as the creature of this system. The manager's primary task, therefore, is to survive and succeed in this system, of which he is in part a deviser and controller, and in part its victim and agent. The manager that emerges from this view is a person whose capabilities are determined by energy, intelligence, experience, and political and social skills as well as knowledge. And, more deeply, managers need a philosophy and set of values that lend confidence and integrity to their work.[12]

[10]Raymond A. Katzell, Richard S. Barrett, Donald H. Vann, and John M. Hogan, "Organizational Correlates of Executive Roles," *Journal of Applied Psychology* **52** (February 1968), 22–28.

[11]Felix E. Lopez, "The Anatomy of a Manager," *Personnel* **53** (March–April 1976), 47–53.

[12]Rosemary Stewart, "To Understand the Manager's Job: Consider Demands, Constraints, Choices." *Organizational Dynamics* **4** (Spring 1976), 22–32. Peter B. Baill, "Management as a Performing Art," *Personnel* **53** (July/August 1976), 12–21.

FIGURE 3-2. Personality, Ability, and Performance Variables in Four Selected Role Types.

Entrepreneur	Leader	Storekeeper	Controller
Able to make decisions	Power-oriented	Affiliation-oriented	Reliant on past experience
Has positive outlook	Seeks responsibility	Has defensive attitudes	Strong determination
Achievement-oriented	Likes to direct others	Of average intelligence	Status-oriented
Relates to environment	Good supervisor	Has high security needs	Defensive
High self-regard	Bright	Apprehensive about life	Conformist
Accepts responsibility	Has strong verbal skills	Unaggressive	Self-controlled
Dominant	Conceptual thinker	Needs guidance	Follows rules
Sociable	Has high activity level	Practical-minded	Believes in being systematic
Adventurous		Conventional	Avoids ambiguity
Intelligent		Well-controlled	Avoids interpersonal problems
Conceptual thinker		Deferential	Likes structure
		Modern expectations	Of average intelligence
			Serious and thoughtful
			Highly organized
			Neat and orderly

Adapted by permission of the publisher from Felix E. Lopez, "The Anatomy of a Manger," *Personnel* 53 (March–April 1976) pp. 47–53. © 1976 by AMACOM, a division of American Management Associations.

Managerial Work vs. Technical Work

In addition to managerial work, every manager also performs a measure of technical or operational work. However, the job mix changes with the level of organization. The higher one rises in the management hierarchy, technical or operating activities become less important and conceptual and managerial processes are more important. Conceptual work involves thoughts, philosophies, and highly general analytical skills, whereas technical work deals with procedures, technical processes, physical or tangible entities, and so on. Setting a new policy is conceptual and managerial; buying a machine is technical and nonmanagerial. These functions are illustrated in Figure 3-3. When nonmanagerial workers are first promoted to supervisory positions, they quickly learn that a gap separates management from other work activities. They no longer can "do" the work directly—their work is to get others to do it. They are now immersed in human relationships and large complex tasks with uncertain results.

Thus the manager is a rational analyst, a monitor of internal and external environments, and a collector and synthesizer of information. Although managers meet their responsibilities through the performance of managerial functions, such as deciding, planning, controlling, or coordinating, today's successful managers also need sophisticated philosophies and leadership styles.[13]

Two researchers have provided unusual insights about ways in which managers do their work. Sayles has suggested that managerial work can be classified into three main categories. The first views the

[13]See Robert Presthus, *The Organizational Society* rev. ed. (New York: St. Martin's, 1978); William R. Dill, Thomas L. Hilton, and Walter R. Rietman, *The New Managers* (Englewood Cliffs, N.J.: Prentice-Hall, 1962); James L. McKenney and Peter G. W. Keen, "How Managers' Minds Work," *Harvard Business Review* **52** (May–June 1974), 79–90.

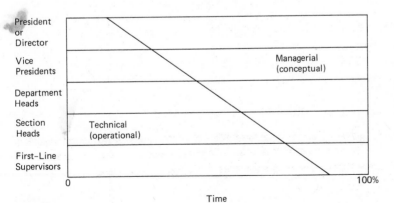

FIGURE 3-3. The Manager's Job Content Mix, by Level of Organization.

manager as a participant in external work flows. The manager interacts with others, primarily peers, colleagues, and subordinates; such interaction provides the connective tissue that holds the subsystems of the organization together. The second category views the manager as a leader: acting as initiator, he attempts to elicit from others, usually subordinates, a group or a team response. The leader directs subordinates so as to get group action, responding to initiations from subordinates, and representing subordinates or interceding for them when necessary. In the third role—that of monitor—the manager observes the system, becoming aware of disturbances, deviations, and problems; inteprets the significance of the latter; decides on corrective actions and predicts their effects; and maintains efforts to cope with change and to produce new strategies, plans, and aims.[14]

The second study, by Mintzberg, is based on detailed observations of managerial job performance. Mintzberg rejects planning, organizing, controlling and similar functions as explanations of what managers really do. He depicts managers as persons who work at a fast pace in contexts of discontinuity, variety, and brevity. They not only deal with problems and the exceptional cases; they also have distinct duties in the form of rituals and ceremonies, negotiations and mediations, and contacts with outsiders. Mintzberg sees three major roles for managers, involving interpersonal relations, informational processes, and decision making.[15]

The ideas of Sayles and Mintzberg are important because they yield perspectives for a more realistic view of traditional managerial functions and add useful insights for understanding those functions. The functions help explain managerial processes, whereas the Sayles and Mintzberg approaches help us picture the realism of the day-to-day behavior of managers. These distinctions are shown in Figure 3-4.

The managerial functions, such as planning or controlling, lie beneath the surface of manifest or overt behavior. By observing the manager at work, one sees overt acts, such as speaking, writing, or attending meetings, as well as the results of these activities. Planning may result in a written plan. Organizing may result in an organization chart. Therefore the act of managing occurs at several levels, ranging from the latent, functional aspects to overt actions and observable consequences.

Managerial Responsibilities

There are two general types of managerial responsibilities. One is *responsibility for* desired outcomes; the other is *responsibility to* a number of groups having a stake in what is happening. In the perfor-

[14]Leonard R. Sayles, *Managerial Behavior* (New York: McGraw-Hill, 1964), pp. 46–57.
[15]Henry Mintzberg, *The Nature of Managerial Work* (New York: Harper, 1973).

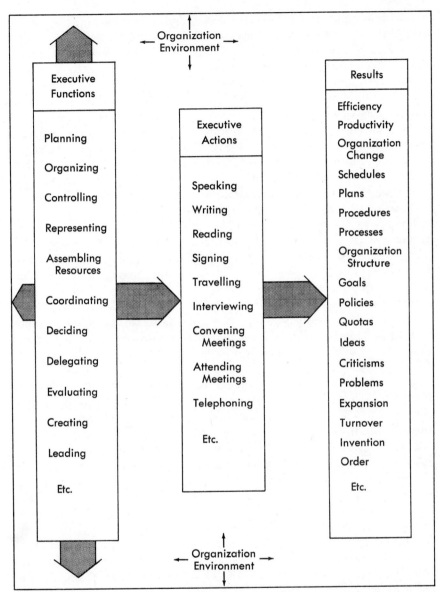

FIGURE 3-4. Relationships Among Executive Functions, Executive Actions, and Results.

mance of their complex tasks, managers are the focus of seemingly diverse streams of effort deriving from the needs of both internal and external individuals and groups. The managers of organizations bear responsibilities with respect to society at large and to related constituents inside and outside the organization.

Leadership is one of the most fundamental of the manager's responsibilities. The leader thinks conceptually, and takes the initiative in planning, policy formation, and reflecting long-range strategies and goals. The leader develops and utilizes group consensus and intiates actions designed to achieve goals.

One of the important factors bearing on managerial action is the way society gets what it wants and needs from organizations, by supporting appropriate roles for managers and by setting up mechanisms to encourage or require managers to work toward desired ends. Managers have both a broad responsibility to society generally and limited responsibilities to specific subgroups within society, such as the consumer, the community, and the management profession itself.

Society allocates to managers the utilization of a large share of our economic and social resources. Government sets up a framework of property rights, legal codes, and regulations, but managers are free within those limits to make decisions that ultimately affect vast numbers of people. In return, managers must accept the responsibilities that such power entails.

Allocating responsibility for the wise use of scarce resources (both material and human) is a broad social problem. Managers who understand the economic and social phenomena with which they deal can contribute to solutions that are needed. Such responsibility requires foresight, planning, and continuing research efforts. For example, limits in available crude oil supplies make it necessary for the oil industry to conduct a continuous search for new sources. In addition, oil companies develop new and improved refining techniques by which greater use can be made of the oil available. Engine manufacturers also contribute through attempting to produce engines that will operate on lower grades of fuel or on nonpetroleum sources of power.

Conflicts in Responsibilities

In a more ideal world, conflict would perhaps be absent, or would be less frequent. Realistically, however, the manager's responsibilities to owners, workers, consumers, the community, and other groups are not strictly compatible, but fraught with strains and tensions that managers must try to resolve in their day-to-day activities. The manager tries to avoid being tossed about like a cork on a stormy sea, but whenever his actions favor one group, others may complain. To a large degree managers must find compromises among the conflicting pressures that are channeled through them.

How managers resolve the conflicts presented by the various groups to which they have responsibilities differs from one to another. There is no rule for determining priorities. However, in practice, managers pursue actions that minimize the tensions and conflicts arising out of the differing demands of the several groups. The effect is to balance the interests of the various groups so that the ends of society are ultimately served. An illustration is the apparent conflict between the pursuit of profit and the fulfillment of community responsibilities—a dilemma that is real only when managers go too far in one direction.

The needs of a community are immediate, but the needs of society are too general for individual managers to relate to directly. Therefore, they chart their course for profits, whose social value and economic contribution are important. Thus social and private objectives are merged, and to an extent the same behavior will help in attaining both.

It should be recognized that, after all, responsibilities to broad social groups are much less compelling than the continuing requirements to meet each situation day by day. The organization—with its customs, traditions, and policies—has much to do with the way managers understand and interpret their social responsibilities. An organization, therefore, is the framework within which at least some of the competing social pressures are resolved. However, the corporate form of organization, whatever its economic and social advantages, makes ownership remote from management. Today's managers are an elite group relatively free from direct ownership supervision; the latitude they have in decision making means that the nature of their task is one of substantial moral as well as economic and managerial complexity.

MANAGERIAL CAREERS

The term *career* refers to the private work history of an individual over a lifetime of job holding or professional practice. Early use of the term was confined to the arts, where painters or singers worked independently to achieve reputations and acceptance. Nowadays most people pursue their careers within and among organizations.

Some persons spend their entire career in one job, often with little sense of its being a career. Others devote their careers to a single occupation, but change jobs and even employers during their working life. Still others develop careers across several different occupations. Some plan their careers carefully; others are indifferent to career planning.

The conscious idea of a career implies focused and deliberate education and training, together with advancement or progress measured by increased rewards, responsibilities, or contributions to society. Career plans guide individuals through their working lifetime toward long-range goals that urge them to develop and use all their capabilities. For the career follower, work becomes a central interest in life.

Managers aspire in varying degrees to higher positions, salaries, status, and other rewards over a lifetime career. Our social system and its values, and the existence of organizational hierarchies, induce individuals to advance their own welfare. Although some individuals, such as lawyers, doctors, and salesmen, are self-employed and are free of the hierarchical constraints of a formal organization, avenues of advancement still exist in the form of such rewards as higher status or money income. This movement of persons in the interests of their own advancement is called *upward mobility*. It may be a social or cultural mobility, seeking mainly status and position, or an organizational mobility, seeking greater financial rewards as well. Occupations themselves have different values and statuses, so that *occupational mobility* occurs when individuals change occupations, usually to one of higher status. Occupational mobility frequently requires individuals to change not only to other positions but also to other organizations. However, considerable upward mobility of persons occurs within the framework of a particular organizational hierarchy through institutionalized promotion and development procedures. A manager should make careful distinctions among his social status, his organizational status, his career, his occupation, and his job.

The degree to which an individual wishes to be upwardly mobile is called his *level of aspiration,* a characteristic in which persons vary widely. It is not an easy one to measure, and may lie hidden within the complexities of human personalities. To a large extent, our perception of someone's level of aspiration is an interpretation of what is communicated, either by word or by action.

Bureaucratic Types

Presthus has described three kinds of persons in organizations: the upward-mobile, the indifferent, and the ambivalent.[16] These are bureaucratic types that have accepted the inevitability of bureaucratic structures and have found an accommodation to life in this environment. The *upward-mobiles* have high morale and high job satisfaction, and can identify strongly with the organization. They usually achieve disproportionately high rewards from the organization, in power, income, and satisfaction. The *indifferents* include those who tend to withdraw from the system, disdaining the frustrations of fighting their way up in the organizational hierarchy; they derive most of their satisfactions in life from off-the-job interests. A typical indifferent rejects values of success and power that are important to the upward-mobile. This type includes vast numbers—the majority of blue- and

[16]Presthus, *The Organizational Society.*

white-collar workers, according to Presthus. The *ambivalents*, finally, find that their values conflict with bureaucratic claims for loyalty and adaptability, but are unable to reject the opportunities of success and power. They do not want to play the roles required to compete in this system. They are sensitive to the need for change, and innovative in their outlook. They have high aspirations, but are introverted and self-effacing. The ambivalent is often a specialist or an independent professional—one who thrives on autonomy and on being independent of the hierarchy or the boss.

These types, it should be recognized, are broad conceptual categories for which there is substantial and persuasive, though not completely definitive, evidence. They are "ideal types," conceptual configurations that explain much about how bureaucracies operate. There is no empirical basis for counting the persons in each type or for explicitly categorizing particular individuals.

Politics in Organizations

One's organizational career inevitably confronts problems of a type that is loosely called "political." The central focus of political behavior is power. Seeking power may be for worthy or unworthy ends, but in either case it leads to competitive, perhaps destructive, conflict.

Political behavior requires skill in interpersonal relationships. The unfavorable connotation often given to political factors arises from implications of unfairness, favoritism, nepotism, or the willingness to gain at the expense of others. The saying "it isn't *what* you know, it's *who* you know" reflects a common view of politics; but, it is a cynical, distorted view, a half-truth. There is a constructive sense in which managers recognize political skills as one facet of their relationship to an organization. Dimock expresses this idea as follows:

> These survival factors are the stuff out of which the executive must fashion his strategy, based upon timing, influence, and the right use of power. The administrator does not operate in a self-contained vacuum. His work is part of the flow of social forces. He is placed in a managerial position for a purpose, but it is not self-perpetuating. It is more than mere housekeeping. It is more than the application of textbook theories, important as these are. The executive is a tactician and a philosopher. He must live by his wits, his competitive instincts, his understanding of social forces, and his ability as a leader. He does not operate in a fixed environment. He must change his environment or adapt to it where necessary, and then try to influence it in any ways which seem indicated in the accomplishment of the ultimate purposes of his program.[17]

[17]Marshall Dimock, *The Executive in Action* (New York: Harper, 1945), pp. 65–66.

Dimock's statement suggests that successful executives have many of the qualifications of successful politicians. Here we must be clear that we are not talking about the stereotype of the politician-manager who is insincere and devious, manipulating people for selfish ends. If we use the term *politician* in the professional sense, where the office holder is serious and turns in an honest performance, the comparison is a fair one.

Many in our society today believe that it is impossible for persons of honesty and integrity to get ahead in business, because they must "play politics." This is a fallacy. Administrators who attempt to substitute chicanery and corruptness for knowledge and skill will nearly always fail. Power and influence may be used without sacrificing integrity, and the political nature of the manager's task is not necessarily evil.

Opportunism vs. Ability

Opportunism is one type of political behavior. The myth of opportunism finds expression in such statements as "The best way to get ahead is to marry the boss's daughter" or "Know someone with a lot of pull." Doubtless many persons advance on some basis other than merit; yet it would be foolish to neglect adequate preparation and to rely on fortuitous events. No one disputes that friends in high places may aid one's career, but ultimately friendships alone cannot sustain a person of mediocre capacities in a position of high responsibility.

Individuals working in organizations often are surprised to learn that honesty, sincerity, energy, enthusiasm, and above-average mentality are not the assets they thought. Our society places a high value on such attributes, and we grow up expecting to capitalize on them in our work. Without questioning the correctness of these social values, one must recognize that sometimes persons indifferent to these values rise higher than those who strictly adhere to them—a disillusioning and frustrating discovery, but not a typical one.

Why should such a situation exist? A contributing factor is the very size of organizations. The individual and his set of values seem lost in a maze of complex interactions among people who may all be strongly motivated to attain financial success. Personalities that correspond closely to group norms attract little attention from higher managers, who deal with exceptions. Exceptionally vivid personalities get attention, and therefore, linger in the consciousness of those higher up. A manager needs insight and finesse to follow a career, balancing the need to move ahead with the need to maintain the respect of others and to conform to what appear to be the important norms of society and of his own conscience. The manager's own attitudes, beliefs, and values are important conditioners of the kind and degree of success that it is possible to attain.

Career Strategies

The alternative to opportunism is career planning. Despite the abundance of advice on career planning,[18] managers tend to be unsystematic and opportunistic in their career decisions.

An aggressive career strategy goes beyond the confines of a single organization. A career inevitably confronts critical turning points where a decision is required as to job, organization, or occupation. The general objective is advancement and mobility in a hierarchical system of jobs and activities that carry prestige as well as salary gradings. A strategy for those uncertain of their own interests and abilities might be to work at several jobs for a year or two each in a small company, getting broad experience in a variety of responsibilities. Once one is committed to a managerial career, broad experience rather than job continuity with a single firm becomes desirable. To get this broad experience managers may change organizations frequently in their early and middle years. During this time, training and educational programs add to one's repertory of skills and knowledge. As the manager approaches the top, strategy changes to a clear-cut striving for positions of power and influence in a particular organization. The manager becomes a generalist, and needs knowledge of the over-all aspects of the work. Dedication to the organization becomes more important at this point, and the achievement of these goals involves complete commitment and arduous effort.

An important aspect of strategy for those aspiring to a career in management lies in the choice of educational preparation. For some, technical and trade schools are sufficient; other seek an undergraduate college degree in the liberal arts, with a general background in humanities, social and political science, or economics. Many find schools of business administration or schools of engineering provide the most direct preparation. There are no rules for this choice; the circumstances of each individual are unique. The aim is to find an entry point in an organization. From that point on, experience and internal training programs will fill in gaps and teach the individual how to apply knowledge to concrete situations.

A major study has found that some degree of undergraduate specialization is helpful in getting a job, but that there is little connection between college preparation and job satisfaction. Of more than four thousand graduates surveyed, 60 per cent said they were "very satis-

[18]For example, see Fred. W. Billmeyer and Richard N. Kelley, *Entering Industry: A Guide for Young Professionals* (New York: Wiley, 1975); Edgar H. Schein, "How Career Anchors Hold Executives to Their Career Paths" *Personnel* **53** (May/June 1975), 11–24; Dalton E. McFarland, *Action Strategies for Managerial Achievment* (New York: AMACOM, 1977); George de Mare, *Corporate Lives: A Journey into the Corporate World* (New York: Van Nostrand Reinhold, 1976); Douglas T. Hall and Francine S. Hall, "What's New in Career Management?" *Organizational Dynamics* **5** (Summer 1976), 17–33.

fied" with their positions, and only 4 per cent indicated dissatisfaction. The history of college preparation, or the lack of it, had no effect on job satisfaction. Also, there was no difference in job satisfaction between those who made early preparations for their careers and those who postponed their choices.[19]

There are two important facts about managers and their jobs: (1) practically every manager—at whatever rank or salary and at whatever degree of job satisfaction—can be lured into accepting a new position; and (2) most managers show little skill in seeking jobs and selling themselves. These two conditions together lead to peculiarities in the behavior of the labor market for managers. On the one hand, openings are numerous and managerial mobility rates are high; on the other, information and communication channels are confused and complex. Although the market is active, managers typically do not follow up its advantages by skillful job-finding techniques.

There are three broad categories of job-seeking managers. The first includes persons of ackowledged ability, stature, and reputation. Whenever someone in this category is available, numerous employers seek to hire him. Such appointments are usually at the officer or the high vice-presidential level, and this hiring is done by other officers or by the board of directors. Informal contacts largely provide the recruitment for this category, although some newspaper advertising is directed toward the presently employed, highly successful, top-level manager. Placement agencies often specialize at this level.

The second category is that of managers whose reputations are mainly within closed company circles or are limited to an industry group. These managers are often looking for jobs, either out of frustration with their present ones or out of unsatisfied ambitions, drives, and aspirations. They are the backbone of executive-search-firm efforts. They are at the higher and middle levels of organizations; they will investigate and respond to advertisements in trade journals and newspapers, as well as follow up contacts from acquaintances. The advertisements tend to follow functional lines—that is, accounting, production, marketing, finance, engineering, or research positions, as well as general management.

A third group of available managers may overlap the other two. It consists of those forced out of their companies, through a reorganization, merger, consolidation, or economy drive, or else have been discharged for inadequacy or incompetence. Whatever the reason, most people who are forced to seek new jobs have great difficulty. They respond to all known vacancies, whether advertised or not, and even explore possibilities in organizations where there are no known vacan-

[19]Lewis C. Solomon and Ann Stoufer Bisconti, *Job Satisfaction After College* (Bethlehem, Pa.: CPC Foundations, 1977).

cies. Many become consultants, at least temporarily while they are seeking a position. The executive who can hang onto a job while seeking another has an obvious advantage.

In following their career strategies, managers are not always aware of critical turning points. They are unsure about when to change jobs, as well as how to change jobs. When an individual has a poor boss, or one he cannot get along with or learn from, or when the work becomes dull and boring, the individual probably should change jobs. Through inertia, fear of the unknown, or the difficulties of the job market, he hesitates to make the change.

The strategies of managers are frequently linked to the strategies and fortunes of other managers, so that one changes with the fortunes of others. One way of advancing is to attach oneself to a successful, upward-moving superior, becoming essential to a team. Certain paths are more fruitful for advancement than others; the fields of finance and marketing, for example, are better routes to the top than manufacturing or staff work like personnel management.

The Gamesman

Although many managers do not systematically plan their careers, Maccoby contends that a newly discovered managerial type is the careerist par excellence: the gamesman. Three other types he calls the company man, the craftsman, and the jungle fighter. The company man resembles the classic "organization man" popularized by Whyte much earlier—the conformist who requires the protectiveness of the organization.[20] The craftsman likes making things and values tangible accomplishment. The jungle fighter is power-hungry, entrepreneurial, action-oriented; he often turns out to be an empire builder. Maccoby views the craftsman and the jungle fighter as virtually obsolete today.[21]

The gamesman is a new kind of leader becoming dominant in corporations. In earlier years, gamesmen did not reach the top of large corporations, but the modern climate of competition and innovativeness, the existence of interdependent teams of managers, and the need for flexibility and a fast pace of change all help produce this new breed. Gamesmen are cool under pressure and tension; they concentrate on their careers; they view things in their own self-interest; they need action, excitement, and challenge; they are good at selling ideas and projects; they enjoy competition and problem solving; their attitudes are flexible and positive.

Gamesmen are unlikely to do something completely new, and they can encounter problems. They may avoid failures by moving out of the

[20]William H. Whyte, *The Organization Man* (New York: Simon & Schuster, 1956).
[21]Michael Maccoby, *The Gamesman* (New York: Simon & Schuster, 1976).

zone of responsibility; they may enjoy the game more than the substance of things; they may come apart, become alcoholics, or show other strains in their personalities; they may drive an organization in the wrong direction; they go by the rules, so will do anything the rules allow. Honesty is, however, a problem to gamesmen. They may make co-workers feel manipulated or confuse an issue to get their way.

From the standpoint of an organization, it is important to be aware of Maccoby's types and their possible combinations. Like other typologies, his set of categories is inexact, and it is risky to classify actual people in this way. But the categories do illustrate common tendencies in the way managers approach their careers.

SUMMARY

This chapter has examined several key aspects of the manager's role and task in an organization. Although there are technical differences, the terms *manager, executive,* and *administrator* are often used interchangeably. Organization structures take the form of hierarchies or levels, and the terminology of titles and positions varies according to the level in the organization to which it is applied.

Executive roles and tasks were described. The executive learns to respond to recurring situations by means of roles. Through roles he meets many of the demands the organization poses. Roles provide a range of acceptable, useful, and relatively predictable behavior, but not necessarily behavior that is rigid or automatic. Roles describe in part what an executive *is* as well as what he *does*.

This chapter also examined the many-faceted problem of the manager's responsibilities for effective results and his responsibilities to the constituent groups of society and the organization. Resolving conflicting needs and pressures from customers, suppliers, owners, employees, and the community looms large in the task performance of the manager.

Finally, career strategies were analyzed. The management of one's career requires self-understanding, recognition of critical turning points, and decisions about changes in job, organization, or occupation. Career planning avoids opportunism and reliance upon chance or upon purely political behavior. These are ethical considerations to be faced, including the nature and uses of power and the way one deals with other people.

INCIDENT CASE

Charles West finished high school in 1977. He investigated several careers, most of which required a college education. He decided that he wanted to study business administration and become a manager. He talked to his boss, the manager of an auto parts firm where he held a part-time job. The manager said, "Don't bother to go to college. You can learn all you need to know by experience on the job. You can stay here and learn from me. Book learning won't do you any good."

Questions

1. Size up the importance of this situation in the light of your understanding of management.
2. What factors are at work in this case?
3. What should Charles say to his boss, and why?

QUESTIONS FOR STUDY

1. Make a list of the things you think amount to important claims on the daily time of the executive.
2. Explain the principal differences among the terms *manager, executive, administrator,* and *enterpreneur.* What are the similarities in usage?
3. Is the board of directors a regular part of management? What are the main functions of board members?
4. State the major arguments for and against the existence of "the organization man." Which set of arguments do you favor, and why?
5. What are executive stereotypes? Give some examples.
6. Define the concept of the executive role. What benefits does this concept yield to the executive? To the organization?
7. How would you refute the assertion that managerial roles are artificial, and that they are illusory?
8. Set up a case in which an interviewer is talking to a prospective managerial employee. Examine and analyze the possible actions of the interviewer and the prospect by means of the concept of role.
9. What responsibilities do managers have? What forces in society regulate or produce the fulfillment of these responsibilities? If his responsibilities are so widely dispersed, why isn't the manager really accountable to no one?
10. How do you think managers resolve the conflicts and counterpressures of their many responsibilities? What problems may arise from this situation?
11. What factors account for rather haphazard approaches to career management on the part of managers?
12. Read Maccoby's *The Gamesman* and evaluate the concept of the gamesman.

SELECTED REFERENCES

AQUARIUS, QASS. *The Corporate Prince.* New York: Van Nostrand Reinhold Company, 1971.

ARAM, JOHN D. *Dilemmas of Administrative Behavior.* Englewood Cliffs, N.J.: Prentice-Hall, Inc., 1976.

CAMPBELL, JOHN P., et al. *Managerial Behavior, Performance, and Effectiveness.* New York: McGraw-Hill Book Company, 1970.

DRUCKER, PETER F. *The Effective Executive.* New York: Harper & Row, Publishers, 1967.

DYER, LEE, ed. *Careers in Organizations: Individual Planning and Organizational Development.* Ithaca, N.Y.: New York State School of Industrial and Labor Relations, 1976.

GRAHAM, GERALD H. *Management: The Individual, the Organization, the Process.* Belmont, California: Wadsworth Publishing Co., 1975.

HEGARTY, EDWARD J. *How to Succeed in Company Politics.* 2nd ed. New York: McGraw-Hill Book Company, 1976.

HODGSON, RICHARD C., DANIEL J. LEVINSON, and ABRAHAM ZALEZNIK. *The Executive Role Constellation: An Analysis of Personality and Role Relations in Management.* Boston, Mass.: Division of Research, Graduate School of Business Administration, Harvard University, 1965.

KOTTER, JOHN P., and VICTOR FAUX. *Self-Assessment and Career Development.* Englewood Cliffs, N.J.: Prentice-Hall, Inc., 1978.

LEVINSON, HARRY. *The Exceptional Executive.* Cambridge, Mass.: Harvard University Press, 1967.

MCGREGOR, DOUGLAS. *The Professional Manager.* New York: McGraw-Hill Book Company, 1967.

MINTZBERG, HENRY. *The Nature of Managerial Work.* New York: Harper & Row, Publishers, 1973.

READY, R. K. *The Administrator's Job.* New York: McGraw-Hill Book Company, 1967.

REDDIN, W. J. *Managerial Effectiveness.* New York: McGraw-Hill Book Company, 1970.

STEPHENS, JAMES C. *Managing Complexity.* Mt. Airy, Md: Lomond Publications, 1977.

VON MAANEN, JOHN, ed. *Organizational Careers: Some New Perspectives.* New York: John Wiley & Sons, Inc., 1977.

Cases for Part I

A. FRANKFORT MILLING AND FARM SUPPLY, INC.

Frankfort Milling and Farm Supply, a firm over eighty years old, was until 1977 a family-owned and -operated company. In late 1977, the owners sold it to Fuller Enterprises, a large holding company based in Lexington, Kentucky. At this time the annual sales volume was nearly $28 million, and there were over 450 employees.

The new owners retained the former owner as president, but appointed new vice presidents of finance, manufacturing and marketing. Because most employees had worked at Frankfort for many years, the company suffered from inbreeding and was slow to react to changes in the industry. The structure was highly bureaucratic, with the president holding virtually all authority. Decision making was centralized in the president's office, with little delegation of that authority to lower managers.

In early 1978, the following events were related by Charles Hasbrook, a marketing research specialist employed three years earlier to work on special projects:

March 19, 1978
I was informed by the president that I would be assigned to the Executive Committee on a half-time basis to work on some marketing-oriented problems. I mentioned that this would mean putting aside some other projects and/or delaying their completion. There was no comment. I told both the president and Chairman of the Executive Committee that the new project would probably take four to six weeks.

April 2, 1978
The chairman of the Executive Committee asked me about the status of the new assignment. I reported limited progress because the president had given me

67

another high-priority project. His remark was, "It must be difficult working for two bosses with both of them expecting their work to be done first." I replied, "Amen."

April 5, 1978
I was given still another project by the president with instructions to start it "immediately."

April 9, 1978
I was asked again by the chairman of the Executive Committee about its project. I reported little progress since April 2 and gave him the reasons why.

April 17–20, 1978
In the field doing work necessary to gather data for the project of the Executive Committee.

April 21, 1978
Upon my return the president voiced displeasure with my absence. I explained the purpose of the travel. He wanted to know how much more time would be needed. When I told him two to three weeks he appeared displeased but said nothing.

April 26, 1978
The president asked me for my resignation. He stated that profits were down and that he was cutting back on marketing research.

QUESTIONS

1. What problems in career management does Charles Hasbrook face?
2. What problems does this case reveal for the company?
3. What is likely to happen next? As chairman of the Executive Committee, what should you do?

B. SHIPLEY ENTERPRISES, INC.

Robert Shipley was a rugged individualist who ran Shipley Enterprises with a firm hand. He had founded the business in 1940 and had the lifelong habit of success. As the business grew, he gave increasing responsibilities to his two sons, and continued to run the business as a family enterprise dominated by his strong personality and abundant energy.

In 1972, Shipley moved the national headquarters to Dallas, Texas, the location of its biggest regional district. By this time the firm had eight marketing and service regions, each with a number of state and local units, and the firm was operating in 32 states at this time. The move and the subsequent restaffing and transfer problems were traumatic at first, but after a few months those problems seemed to stabilize. In the late sixties and early seventies, both volume and profitability increased substantially.

Although Shipley's operating responsibilities grew as his sons increased their experience and competencies over the years, the marks of his philosophy were lasting ones. The business was efficient; its employees were loyal and hard-working. Shipley's imprint on the organization took the form of an emphasis on loyalty and hard work. Many managers and staff people worked overtime without complaint or overtime pay. It was a demanding organization, and continued to be so after Shipley's two sons became the key figures in its operation. The company rewarded loyal high performers well but insisted on complete dedication to the firm and its family.

The following incident illustrates the impact of the Shipley philosophy on the life of one of its managers:

James Shipley, the oldest son, headed the marketing function at the corporate level. In May of 1974, he discharged the marketing manager in the Western Region for not achieving the volume of business he thought could be obtained in that region. He then reviewed his list of probable successors, determining that Bill Martin from the Rochester, New York, office should be given the assignment.

Shortly after reaching this decision, James Shipley telephoned Ralph Sims, manager of the Rochester office, saying that he intended to offer the Western position to Martin. Sims stated that although he hated to lose Martin, "it will be a good move for him and he deserves the opportunity for advancement that it will provide." Shipley then said, "Fine, I'll let you explain the situation to him. When you have the answer, call me. No later than Friday."

The following conversation then occurred between Sims and Martin:

Sims: Bill, come in and sit down. Better fasten your seat belt, though. I've got some good news for you. Jim Shipley just called to let me know he wants you in our Western Region to beef up the marketing function out there. He's really sold on you for that job.

Martin: Oh, no! Don't tell me this is serious.

Sims: It's serious. As you know, the transfer will carry a $3000 salary increase plus the usual allowances and moving expenses. It's a big opportunity, Bill.

Martin: But I—

Sims: Wait, Bill. Think a while before you react. You've been here three years now, and that's a bigger deal out there than you can expect to develop here. Besides, you know Jim when he has his mind made up.

Martin: Didn't you try to keep me here?

Sims: I don't believe in keeping anyone from getting ahead. I endorsed your capabilities and agreed to talk with you about the opportunity.

Martin: This is a big jolt right now. You see, Alice is pregnant and—

Sims: You know that our company policy is very firm. You have 24 hours. We want a yes or no answer by 5:00 P.M. Friday, tomorrow afternoon. I can assure you that if the answer is no, we won't hold it against you. The Shipleys, including Jim's father, have always felt that before an offer is made it should be fixed up so well that it can hardly be turned down.

Martin: I can't decide in 24 hours. That's crazy.

Sims: You never thought it was a bad policy when you went after someone, Bill.

Martin: Whatever put this idea into Shipley's mind, anyway?

Sims: All I ever heard him say was that if you give a man longer than 24 hours, his wife will start thinking of all the reasons why they shouldn't do it.

They'll talk each other into turning it down. But in 24 hours they'll tend to see the best side of it.

Martin: We both know that's too simple.

Sims: Simple or not, that's the way it is in this outfit.

Martin: You've got to give me until next Monday. Surely I'm entitled to the weekend.

Sims: Shipley expects my call Friday afternoon.

Martin: Call him now and tell him I'm not deciding until Monday.

Sims: I doubt if he'll make an exception, but if you insist. I'll call him now and ask.

Martin: Call him.

Martin left Sims's office. Sims made the call and got the extension of time approved. On Monday at 5:00 P.M., Martin told Sims that he would accept the transfer. Sims notified Martin that he was to be on the new job on the following Wednesday, and that he could arrange the details of moving later.

QUESTIONS

1. Analyze the key roles at work in this situation.
2. How would you apply communications principles to this case?
3. Could either Martin or Sims have acted differently?

C. COURTING DISASTER

Homer Walpole, over a five-year period, earned two successive promotions in a very large manufacturing firm. Having a Ph.D. in mathematics, his position as senior mathematician in the firm's research laboratories was very satisfactory. He received several merit pay increases and extensive training at company expense. After two years in this position, however, he concluded that his chances of rising in the managerial ranks would be better in a company with less technical depth in personnel and facilities. Therefore he joined another firm, also a large manufacturing concern, at a substantial increase in salary.

Before long Mr. Walpole headed a forty-person department that was assigned the responsibility for developing computerized production processes. For the next year and a half he ran the department and developed equipment that he claimed saves the company over $1 million annually. During this time he received a favorable performance review, made orally, from his superior. It was the only performance appraisal he had received at the end of seven years' employment with this firm.

With a managerial position that paid over $30,000 per year, Mr. Walpole thought he was doing very well in his career. Suddenly, however, his future looked bleak. His boss was promoted, and a personality clash occurred between him and his new boss. Without warning, his department was abolished. He was demoted to the supervisory level, but retained the same pay as before. The company said the change was necessary to eliminate duplication of effort, but Mr. Walpole thought he was the victim of internal political warfare.

Ready to quit, he cast about for other jobs but saw that to move he would have to take a substantial cut in pay. Therefore he stayed on, hoping to be promoted back to his former level. Instead, he was given routine, "make-work" assignments with no potential for real achievement or advancement.

Two years later Mr. Walpole was laid off as part of a cutback of 25,000 salaried workers, caused by the recession. When he was called back to work, he found that several younger men had been promoted to positions he felt qualified to fill.

On July 1 of this year, Mr. Walpole filed suit against the employer, demanding reinstatement to his former management job and half a million dollars in damages. He said, "My demotion was unjustified, but if they had treated me like a gentleman I would have waited for a promotion back to the manager's level. But there was no internal due process or mediation procedures." In the suit, Mr. Walpole demanded to see the company's list of exceptional or "fast track" employees. The company admitted that it had such lists but denied using them in a discriminatory manner. It argued that the appearance of one's name on such a list was no guarantee of employment. The court ordered the company to disclose certain aspects of the lists in question.

"In this company," Mr. Walpole said, "if you're on the list you can get promoted only if you know someone, like a director or a vice president. It's a sponsor system, and it has nothing to do with proper management." As a result, Mr. Walpole felt that the company wasted millions of dollars by underutilizing people who have high salaries; concerning the suit he said, "I've lost a lot of sleep over all this. I can't take less money and change my life style now."

QUESTIONS

1. What management issues and problems are highlighted by this case?
2. Does Mr. Walpole seem to have a good case on which to base a lawsuit? Why or why not?

D. THE CAREER OF HENRY DALE

Henry Dale, after a year at law school, took a summer job with the Allison Manufacturing Company in 1957. He liked his work so well that he decided to abandon law to remain with Allison. In successive promotions he was assigned alternately to branch plant and headquarters positions. While assigned as office manager for the Detroit sales operation, Mr. Dale decided to specialize in selling. He was made a salesman and then a manager in one of the Canadian plants, following which assignment he went to Atlanta. In 1973, he was transferred to the headquarters office as national sales manager for the chemical processing division.

The chemical division was experiencing falling sales. Mr. Dale was aware of the risks of attempting to turn this part of the business around, but a vice president, his boss, assured him that his job would be protected. By 1976, however, his boss was transferred. Meanwhile the entire company suffered a huge, recessional drop in profits, and it announced a reduction in force of 553 middle managers. Mr. Dale was fired.

With a wife and four children, this event posed a serious turning point in Mr. Dale's career. Allison had long been famous for its extreme paternalism. It was a company of 6500 employees, with headquarters in a city of only 16,000. Many families had worked at Allison for several generations. Allison was regarded as a company with a very high respect for individual employees at all levels.

The firings consequently shocked the community and the remaining employees. Earnings fell by 75 per cent in 1976, and sales were down by 40 per cent. By cutting back immediately on losing operations and letting managers go, the company estimated that it could save $20 to $25 million a year on salaries alone. The board chairman regretted not being able to spread the cuts over a longer period, but thought that business had turned bad too quickly for that. (A year later, however, the business rebounded with a profit increase of 169 per cent).

Most of those fired departed within minutes, but Mr. Dale remained long enough to put things in order for whoever might come in to close up the division. In the next six weeks he returned several times to help out. He received six months' severance pay, and had been saving hard for the past year, anticipating the difficulties. The company provided expert counselors for helping the fired managers relocate, and helped to place a few of them in other companies. Mr. Dale was not among these, so he launched a vigorous job search.

Mr. Dale spent over $1000 for phone calls, stamps, and stationery. He worked ten hours a day for seven days a week in conducting the search, and wrote over eight hundred letters to prospective employers, friends, and search firms. He found that over 30 per cent of the firms contacted did not even reply. He finally obtained nine job interviews in widely scattered locations. Four firms offered Mr. Dale a job. He had eight separate interviews with the firm that hired him, three months after his discharge. He was one of the few of those fired to obtain a position within six months. He liked his new company, and said, "I have no bitterness toward Allison. If I were running it I probably would have made the same decision the board chairman made." However, the frustration, discouragement, and emotional stress were substantial for Mr. Dale and his family.

QUESTIONS

1. What mistakes do you think were made by this firm?
2. Evaluate the decisions, activities, and philosophies of Mr. Dale.
3. Analyze the problems and pitfalls of his job search techniques.

PART II

Managerial Decision and Action

Chapter 4

Decision Making: Fundamentals

I have many decisions to make, and some of them are wrong. But I have learned that there is something worse than a few wrong decisions, and that is indecision.

—Ray Lyman Wilbur

Not to decide is to decide.

—Anonymous

CHAPTER GUIDE

. . ."Most men are poor executives because they fail to understand that decision making does not consist in weighing all the facts as they come in and then making the most reasonable judgment, but rather moving before all the facts are in and anticipating their consequences."

—Sydney Harris

Questions to keep in mind as you read this chapter:

1. Evaluate the above statement in the light of decisions you yourself have made.
2. Why do managers sometimes make the wrong decisions?
3. Why does a manager make some decisions and not others?

Decision making is every manager's primary responsibility. It is also a process affected by the organization's needs and characteristics. The manager's decisions are determined by his personal skills and abilities, and also by the resources and constraints that organizations provide.

Major Influences		Major Techniques	
Internal Factors	External Factors (Stakeholders)	Standard Techniques	Sophisticated Techniques
Experience	Consumer needs and preferences	Schedules	Statistical analysis
Judgment	Market strategies	Plans and forecasts	Operations research methods
Group thinking	State of the environment	Scheduling charts	PERT–CPM
Member participation	Stockholder opinions	Budgets	Systems analysis
State of the art	Creditor influences	Cost control	Computers
Privileged information	Labor unions	Price structures	Linear programming
Observation	Community needs and influences	Historical data	Information systems
Temperament	Industry characteristics	Research studies	Control systems
Emotions	Vendors and suppliers	Policies	Complex problem solving
Organization Politics		Standard operating procedures	Queuing theory
Values		Organization design	Simulation
			Management games

FIGURE 4-1. Major Influences and Techniques in the Decision Process.

Collectively, the decisions of managers give form and direction to the work an organization does.

An organizationwide model of the decision process is needed as a guide for the individual decisions of managers. Each organization should develop its own model, but a general model of the type shown in Figure 4-1 is illustrative. This is a model depicting the major influences and techniques that have a bearing in the decision process. This chapter explains the fundamental problems and processes of decision making from a qualitative, behavioral point of view. Chapter 5 analyzes decision techniques with special emphasis on operations research and complex information systems.

THE NATURE OF DECISION MAKING

Management as both science and art is nowhere better illustrated than in decision making. On the side of art lie the intuitive judgments, personalities, and abilities of deciders. On the side of science are decision concepts and techniques based on computers, operations research, and the findings of behavioral science. Both science and art go together, and management science has not yet eliminated subjectivity and intuitive judgments from the decision-making process.

The simplest view of decision making is that of a manager choosing one of several alternatives. Sometimes the result is intangible, but more often it produces tangible results, such as changes in plans, policies, or procedures. However, a decision not to decide is still a decision, where the status quo is preferable to the uncertainty of change.

The Process of Decision Making

Viewing decision making solely as a choice among alternatives is too simplistic, although some minor decisions may be made in this way. Complex decisions are not unique, isolated events; they reflect prior behavior and anticipated consequences. Focusing only on the moment of choice among alternatives, according to Simon, leads to a false concept of decision, and "ignores the whole lengthy, complex process of exploring and analyzing that precedes the final moment."[1]

The process nature of decision making reveals the influence of time: (1) the past, in which problems develop, information accumulates, and the need for a decision is perceived; (2) the present, in which alternatives are found and the choice is made; and (3) the future, in which decisions are carried out, evaluated, or changed. Moreover, major deci-

---

[1]Herbert A. Simon, *The New Science of Management Decision* (New York: Harper, 1960) p. 1.

sions involve a series of related and increasingly detailed decisions as time unfolds and consequences appear.

The fact that decision making is a process is frequently obscured by the sudden appearance that some decisions seem to make. The forces behind a particular decision are often hidden or unknown. For strategic reasons, managers may reveal decisions only after a great deal of planning. For example, a company president who decides to close a plant in Hoboken and build another in Rochester may not announce the decision until after planners have at least partially dealt with the anticipated consequences, such as employee reactions. Critical decisions require months of planning, fact gathering, and analysis. But even in the "snap" decision, in which the manager responds to an urgent stimulus, background conditions have influenced the mental processes that are involved. The urgency has merely altered the timing.

The Concept of Commitment

Decisions acquire a degree of permanence described as *commitment*— a sticky quality that arises in part because the decider and the organization become committed to the decision's success. The manager's reputation may depend on the decision, so that reversal is difficult. Commitment is also inherent in the manager's need for time to carry out a decision and to observe its consequences. Once made, a decision provides an element of stability for both the organization and its members. Money is often invested, adding to the commitment. Decisions are frequently interrelated, so that a change in one area will affect other areas. For example, a credit decision may affect sales, which could in turn affect production, purchasing, and other facets. Such a decision, once cleared or checked with the affected areas, requires a general acceptance that reinforces commitment, for all but the most routine decisions are hard to change or reverse.

Commitment is not, however, equivalent to support. Support may exist while a decision is tried out, but it may fade while commitment continues. Commitment can develop without support through the general expectations of the authority system. Once a decision is made, a dissenting manager says, "I didn't agree with this decision, but I'll go along with it and see if it will work." The manager's role as leader frequently calls for persuading subordinates to carry out decisions that are unpopular. He may try to gain their support, if not their commitment. Sometimes the commitment is inevitable and irreversible, as in the case of a decision to merge two business firms. Where the finality of the decision is less clear, commitment may gradually fade. Release from commitment may follow from a decline in support, or the recognition of new, face-saving factors that reduce the impact of that commitment.

Ultimately, commitment rests on the judgments of managers and on the impact of forces that reveal the wisdom or error of a given decision so that pressures for change arise. As the need for change increases, the constraint of commitment fades. Commitment permits a decision to endure until it is tested by experience. Where commitment is based largely on saving face for the decider, the pressure to change will grow to a high intensity.

Rationality in Decision Making

A human being who has the ability to learn, to imagine, to remember, and to organize complexity is highly rational. By rational analysis, managers may choose among alternative decisions according to purpose. Purpose provides a rational standard against which to compare results.

Decision theory, however, cannot rely exclusively on assumptions of pure rationality. For example, rationality might dictate that an obsolete organization can be scuttled, yet such organizations often continue long after their purposes have eroded. Inside all organizations are nonrational impulses, complex political and power struggles, and people with emotions as well as brains. The rational and the emotional are intertwined.

Rationality is thus a relative concept. It does not produce perfect decision making. The *principle of bounded rationality*[2]—the notion that rationality is limited in explaining decision making—is based on the premise that a manager at any time is exposed to a bounded area of information that often does not include all the information he needs. According to this principle, managers can seldom find the optimum decision. Instead, they consider reasonable, probable outcomes, and select a strategy calculated to result in a satisfactory, but not necessarily optimum, outcome.[3]

Rationality implies that the decision maker tries to choose the best action for achieving the optimum solution to a problem. If decisions were fully rational, managers would consider all possible choices; practically, however, this degree of knowledge is not possible. Decision makers face not only the limits of time and imperfect knowledge, but the existence of multiple, complex, and often conflicting goals. They also face inner conflicts of emotions, attitudes, and beliefs. The fact that the manager cannot be perfectly or objectively rational does not invalidate the concept of rationality, which remains the model of most decision-making behavior. Short of attaining perfection, the man-

[2]Herbert A. Simon, *Administrative Behavior*, 3rd ed. (New York: Macmillan, 1976), pp. 38–41, 80–81, 240–244.
[3]David W. Miller and Martin K. Starr, *The Structure of Human Decisions* (Englewood Cliffs, N.J.: Prentice-Hall, 1967), pp. 42–50.

ager accepts necessary limitations and attempts to make the best possible decision within given constraints of cost and time. Choices depend on manager's ability to determine the alternatives and the time available to find them. Some factors are beyond control, and others are beyond the decider's knowledge. Hence rationality is limited.

Types of Decisions

It is useful to distinguish between (1) organizational and personal decisions and (2) basic and routine decisions. Although in practice this dichotomy becomes blurred, understanding these two elements will make the decision process clearer.

Organizational and Personal Decisions

Barnard suggests a useful distinction between personal and organizational decisions.[4] In their official or formal roles, managers make organizational decisions, which can be, and frequently are, delegated to others. They usually call for supporting and elaborating decisions by other executives and touch off chains of behavior to carry on the work of the organization.

The right and the responsibility to decide confer substantial power on managers, assuring them of influence and control over the activities and resources of the organization. Although decisions are largely intended to further the interests of the organization, the manager's personal interests and those of the organization are so intertwined that it is difficult to separate them.

Personal decisions pertain to managers as individuals. Throughout their careers, they make many choices in their own interest. Personal decisions cannot be delegated. However, most such decisions also affect the organization, as in the case of a president deciding to resign. Conflicts between personal and organizational goals are discussed elsewhere in this book.

Many managers view their personal and their organizational decisions separately. Some make organizational decisions that contradict their personal beliefs. By identifying decisions as "organizationally required," they are free to make decisions they could not accept on personal grounds. For example, a manager who personally espouses racial equality may tolerate racist hiring as an organizational norm. In the final analysis, the distinctions between personal and organizational decisions are a matter of degree. Managers are to some extent person-

[4]Chester I. Barnard, *The Functions of the Executive* (Cambridge, Mass.: Harvard U. P., 1937), pp. 188–189.

ally involved in any organizational decision they make, and they need to resolve the conflicts that occur between organizational and personal decisions.[5]

Basic and Routine Decisions

Decisions range along a continuum whose polar types are (1) basic and (2) routine.

Basic decisions are unique, one-time decisions involving long-range relatively permanent commitments and large investments—decisions in which a mistake might seriously hurt the organization. They are difficult to decide in view of uncertainties in the environment. An example of a basic decision is one concerning plant location. To select a site involves the investigation and analysis of many complex social and economic factors—markets, population movements, transportation, raw material supplies, power availability, and others. The investment is large and relatively permanent, and an error would be costly.

Most policy decisions at higher levels in the organization are basic decisions, as are the decisions on organization design, capital expenditures, and the selection of key executives. Such decisions provide the context in which routine decisions occur.

Routine decisions, which require relatively little deliberation or are made repetitively, tend to have only minor effects on the welfare of the organization. Standard procedures can be established for making large numbers of such decisions, which require little investigation and analysis and can easily be canceled or reversed. Many, perhaps most decisions—by the estimate of some managers, more than 90 per cent—are repetitive and routine. An important task for the manager, in fact, is to separate routine from nonroutine decision making and develop appropriate policy approaches for each category.

Programmed and Nonprogrammed Decisions

Borrowing from the language of computer technology, Simon presents a classification of decisions as either programmed or nonprogrammed, as shown in Table 4-1. These categories correspond roughly to those of basic and routine types that have been described, and are also polar types describing the two extremes of a continuum. Decisions are programmed to the extent that they are repetitive and routine and to the extent that systematic procedures are devised so that each one does not have to be treated as a unique case. Decisions are nonprogrammed (and

---

[5]John D. Aram, *Dilemmas of Administrative Behavior* (Englewood Cliffs, N.J.: Prentice-Hall, 1976), chap. 4.

TABLE 4-1. Traditional and Modern Techniques of Decision Making

Types of Decisions	Decision-Making Techniques	
	Traditional	Modern
Programmed:		
Routine, repetitive decisions	1. Habit	1. Operations research:
Organization develops specific processes for handling decisions	2. Clerical routine: Standard operating procedures	Mathematical analysis. Models. Computer simulation.
	3. Organization structure: Common expectations A system of subgoals Well-defined informational channels.	2. Electronic data processing.
Nonprogrammed:		
One-shot, ill-structured, novel, policy decisions	1. Judgment, intuition, and creativity.	Heuristic problem-solving techniques applied to:
Handled by general problem-solving processes	2. Rules of thumb. 3. Selection and training of executives	1. Training human decision makers. 2. Constructing heuristic computer programs.

Source: Herbert A. Simon, *The New Science of Management Decision,* rev. ed. Englewood Cliffs, N.J.: Prentice-Hall, Inc., 1977. p. 48.

basic) to the extent that they are novel, unstructured, ill-structured, or consequential. The decision to change to a decentralized form of organization, for example, would be a nonprogrammed decision. The selection of new product markets is another example. An advantage of the categories *programmed* and *nonprogrammed* is that they facilitate the use of the tools of quantitative analysis described in Chapter 6.

Group Decisions

Group decision making refers to the process whereby individuals participate as a group in reaching a decision. This most frequently occurs in task or problem-solving groups, or in management teams or committees. Research on group behavior supports the idea that group decisions are under certain conditions better than those imposed by the leader on a group. Task accomplishment and member satisfaction improve under conditions of group decision.

A major factor in the success of group decision is the significance of the decisions for the members. When people contribute to decisions that are important to themselves, they perform better. Group decision gives individuals a chance to express their views and to persuade others. In such a climate, individuals feel free to make suggestions, air grievances, or otherwise disclose their feelings. They gain a sense of satisfaction from being part of an effort greater than their own. In some group settings, research indicates that a group will take greater risks than would individuals acting alone.[6]

Although group decision concepts can be fruitful, there are also uncertainties and limitations. One is that the ultimate responsibility for the outcome of decisions may be unclear. Groups may be better at discovering and defining alternatives than at making final choices. In some studies, group decision methods were unsuccessful in increasing productivity. Also, problems of personality change, emotional involvement, and other psychological phenomena affect the ability of group members to work with one another. There may be a leveling effect in which the results are reduced to a common level to get the agreement of a majority. Finally, the participation of a group adds to the time required in reaching decisions.

The need for group decision results from the complexities inherent in modern organization. Major decisions require the interaction of many individuals, even though the decisions may be formalized by individual managers. Group or team management is widely used; in large organizations, the scope of activity is simply too vast for an individual manager, no matter how competent. Major decisions, especially those that deal with the future demand collective judgment. For example, a president may decide an issue, but he usually does so on the basis of an interaction of minds, with consequent compromises, and with discussions to find an ultimate consensus. It is the decider, however, who must bear the responsibility of a decision made in this way.

The primary technique of group decision is group discussion, which is designed to find information, clarify problems, and bring forth alternatives for evaluation. Several new techniques have also emerged. *Nominal grouping* methods are used to reduce verbal interaction and to increase the deliberation and contributions of individual members. The nominal group follows a highly structured procedure involving several stages. First each member writes down his ideas. A structured session follows, in which each member shares his best idea, which is written on a blackboard or flip chart for all to see. The next step is another structured session, this time for analysis, clarification or discussion of the ideas listed. The final stage is for each member privately to vote on a ranking or priority. The group decision is the arithmetic outcome of the individual votes.[7]

[6]Daniel Katz and Robert L. Kahn, *The Social Psychology of Organizations* (New York: Wiley, 1966); see also N. F. R. Maier, "Assets and Liabilities in Group Problem Solving: The Need for an Integrative Function," *Psychological Review* 74: 4 (1967), 239–249.

[7]Andrew L. Delbecq, Andrew H. VandeVen, and David H. Gustafson, *Group Techniques for Program Planning* (Glenview, Ill.: Scott, Foresman, 1975).

Another group decision technique is the *Delphi process.* This technique employs a sequence of written questionnaires distributed to a panel of experts or resource persons. At each round of questionnaires, summary results of the previous round are reported to the panel members. In the next round, the participants can reassess and independently evaluate their earlier responses. The result is a consensus estimate that refines the decision through group judgment. The central element is that the panel members are anonymous, unknown to each other. The entire procedure is by mailed questionnaires. Often the process goes through several rounds, although the results are seldom changed after two rounds. The Delphi technique is widely used in estimating various kinds of change, such as predicting the future of "management by objectives" programs in the next hundred years.[8]

Committee Decisions

Committees are of two main types: (1) ad hoc and (2) structural. Ad hoc committees are temporary, appointed for specific tasks or projects. They are usually formed to assist decision makers by conducting studies, pooling information, gathering data, or investigating problems. Their decisions take the form of recommendations, which must usually be adopted or accepted by appropriated decision makers.

Structural committees are permanent features of the top levels of an organization. They are sometimes called standing committees, and are typically elected or appointed under the bylaws of corporation boards of directors, trustees, or other administrative boards. In corporations, the responsibilities of structural committees are broad, and they are relatively permanent. The members are generally senior corporate officers. Examples are the corporate finance committee, or the executive committee of the board of directors.

The advantages of committees in decision making are numerous. One is that the problems of large-scale, complex operations are made more manageable. Basic decisions can be made with inputs from major sectors of the organization, with specialists contributing their knowledge and points of view. Because most committees operate by consensus or majority vote, decisions are more acceptable. Committees can also generate authenticity and support, increasing the confidence of those in lower levels of the organization. A further advantage is that others share the burden and the risks of the top administrator, although ultimate responsibility is retained.

There are also drawbacks to the use of committees. Structural committees may dilute the power and authority of certain managers; a

---

[8]Andrew H. VandeVen, *Group Decision Making and Effectiveness.* Kent Ohio: Kent State University Press, 1975).

strong executive committee, for example, may make the top executive appear to be a mere figurehead. A second problem is that the machinery for decisions may become too slow and ponderous. A third difficulty is that the need for agreement on a decision may result in the discouragement of aggressive individuals who may be creative and daring in their views. This is called the leveling process, in which compromise as a goal may tend to water down the quality of the decision in order to get the agreement of members. A fourth difficulty is possible confusion about the responsibility for results, so that a manager might tend to blame a poor decision on the committee that produced or influenced it.

DECISIONS AND PROBLEM SOLVING

To a large degree, decision making is directed at solving problems. This is particularly true in the use of advanced techniques of operations research, described in Chapter 5. The earlier scientific management approach was centered on John Dewey's directive: (1) state the problem, (2) list the alternatives, and (3) select the best alternative. The newer approaches of the quantitative-decision theorists—labeled "Modern" in Table 4-1—describe the problem solving and decision making in terms of such concepts as model building, statistical probability, and degree of certainty and risk. For additional comparisons, several patterns of problem solving and decision making are illustrated in Figure 4-2.

Problem solving is an important generator of decision-making behavior, but one must not exaggerate its importance. Emphasis on problem solving stresses the need for answers, whereas it may be more important to find the right question, or to prevent problems from occurring. Moreover, the problem-solving decision often tends to be the unimportant, routine, short-range, or tactical decision, rather than the important, strategic, long-range decision. Problem solving, therefore, must be broadly conceived as more than mere answer getting.

If undue rewards go to problem solvers, there is a danger that some will create or find problems solely to win such rewards, so that wasted effort is devoted to false or unnecessary problems. Nevertheless, appropriate problem solving should be recognized in the reward system of the organization.

Perceiving and Defining Problems

The process of correctly identifying and defining the problem is the starting point of successful decision making. Perceiving problems clearly and promptly is not easy. Delays result from uncertainty about the nature of the problem and its causes. Perhaps vital facts are missing

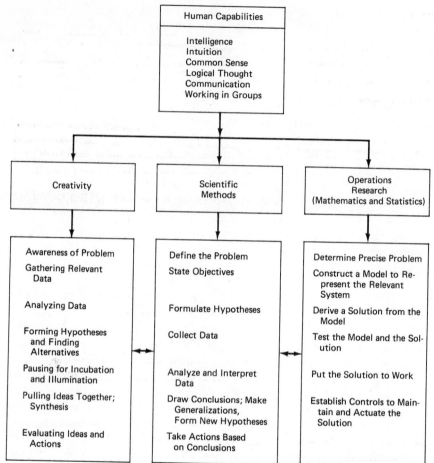

FIGURE 4-2. Fundamental Approaches to Problem Solving and Decision Making.

or are in conflict, requiring skillful interpretation. Reluctance to acknowledge problems is increased where managers, for personal or other reasons, hesitate to grapple with change.

Taking Action on Problems

Perception and definition of a problem are necessary but not sufficient conditions for effective decisions. Action can follow only when there is sufficient consensus that a problem exists and should be dealt with. Managers need an understanding of the norms or standards that govern the selection and definition of problems. In some cases, norms are specific. For example, a given amount of office space becomes overcrowded, and more space must be acquired when space per clerical office worker is less than fifty square feet. In other cases, however, the norms are less precise, as for example when it must be determined whether a company's relations with a labor union have deteriorated to an unsatisfactory level.

It is imperative to define a problem in terms that make action possible. Suppose, for example, that a manufacturer of toys finds that sales are lagging and profits are declining. To say the company is losing money is a *description of a situation* and not an analytical statement of a problem. To correct the situation, the executive must describe and analyze causes. The problem can then be put in the form of a logical hypothesis.

The hypothesis gives direction to the information-gathering activities that lead to testing it. It is true that "selection" has been introduced and that some facts are not sought because they do not accord with the hypothesis. However, if the hypothesis is initially tenable, this selectivity reduces the time and cost of getting the information required for action. Information is gathered by search techniques such as observation, interviewing, questionnaires, special reports, and other sources of information. Information from persons close to the problem is particularly desirable, even though such information may contain biases. Even where a problem is well defined, however, there may be trouble over which facts are relevant and how these facts apply. The admonition to "get all the facts" is not valid: it is usually impossible to get the facts— even all the pertinent ones. It is important to get as much significant data as economical and timely effort permit. However, problems arising from turbulent, uncertain environments may not be amenable to the logic of finding causes and developing hypotheses.

When the facts are weighed and their meaning analyzed, they can be used to test the hypothesis. For example, the hypothesis might be advanced that a drop in sales and profits is caused by a sales manager who does not know how to market the company's products. However, the profit decline may be general throughout the industry. This would not necessarily absolve the sales manager, but would throw doubt on the original hypothesis, making it necessary to modify it and to conduct further research. Thus the testing of hypotheses may proceed until the causes of the problem are pinned down.

Any decision with regard to a problem must consider the influences that the decision itself will generate. For example, when an employee becomes a chronic absentee and does not respond to disciplinary action, his boss is tempted to discharge him. However, the decision to discharge the man is both a problem-solving decision and a problem-creating one. It affects the removal of the obstinate individual but raises the problem of a replacement, and of avoiding the same behavior on the part of a new employee.

_____ **EFFECTIVE DECISION MAKING**

The effectiveness of a decision cannot be known with certainty in advance, nor are there concrete measures of the quality of decisions. Bad or wrong decisions become evident through their undesirable consequences, as brilliant, outstanding decisions are recognized in their desirable consequences. Between these extremes lies a wide range of ordinary decision making that sustains an organization from day to day. Within this range of decisions—from bad to excellent— Mintzberg describes four key decision roles of managers: (1) the entrepreneur; (2) the disturbance handler; (3) the resource allocator; and (4) the negotiator.[9] Performing these roles well is essential for effective decision making.

In the role of *entrepreneur*, the manager is the initiator and designer of the controlled change in an organization. Decisions emerging from this role involve exploiting opportunities, evolving strategies, and solving broad, long-range problems. The entrepreneurial decision leads to the improvement of some aspect of the organization's activities. It is made at the discretion of the manager or his team.

The role of *disturbance handler* is needed to deal with events that demand the attention of managers. A crisis occurs or a problem becomes acute. The manager deals with an involuntary situation which is at least in part beyond his control. Forces beyond the manager initiate the action. For example, a conflict may arise between two subordinates, and that conflict must be solved to prevent the difficulty from getting worse and harming the organization's work.

The role of *resources allocator* involves important choices that reflect the organization's basic strategies. Resources—people, money, time, materials, equipment—are scarce, and are demanded by competing interests. The decisions of the resources allocator include the scheduling of time, the programming of work, and the authorization of actions, projects, or programs.

The fourth decision role, that of *negotiator*, represents a bargaining function. The manager must deal with other managers, with special groups, and with representatives of other organizations. Bargaining with labor union officials is a common example of negotiations, but many other situations—such as settling a customer complaint—involve transactions that are negotiated. The manager must have the authority to resolve the issue under negotiation, committing resources if necessary.

The decision roles just described may be, and often are, performed in conjunction with each other. Thus the role of negotiator may accom-

[9]Henry Mintzberg, *The Nature of Managerial Work* (New York: Harper, 1973), pp. 77–94.

pany that of disturbance handler, or the entrepreneurial role may also involve that of resource allocator.

Evaluating Decisions

Some decisions can be evaluated by objective criteria; others must be judged by qualitative standards. Purchasing a new machine, for example, has the benefit of specific technical and cost data that can greatly reduce uncertainty as to the payoff and the outcomes: the wisdom of such a decision is highly measurable. In contrast, deciding which of three vice presidents to promote to the presidency entails substantial uncertainty, and performance must be judged largely by qualitative assessments.

Evaluation is difficult for managers. They may hesitate to acknowledge failure. The factor of commitment intensifies the fear of evaluation and may lead to defensive or covering behavior by the manager. Decisions are sometimes made for the sake of appearance or for the enhancement of the record, rather than for inherent validity or logic. Moreover, satisfactory or even brilliant decisions may go unnoticed, but one bad decision, even if relatively unimportant, may attract quick criticism.

The need to be right puts pressure on decision makers. The more basic the decision, the greater the penalties for error and the greater the difficulty in reaching and evaluating the decision. However, managers are suprisingly unable to analyze their own decision -making behavior. They tend to maintain a generally optimistic, confident faith in results. Top managers say such things as "I don't think businessmen know how they make decisions. I know I don't"; "There are no rules for it"; "You don't know how you do it, you just do it." Such statements do not necessarily mean that these managers are ineffective, but the attitudes they embody divert attention from the obstacles and failures in decision making, focusing instead on a cultivated image of decisiveness.

Optimism is reinforced by the belief that some percentage of error is only human. Managers can be overconfident about the outcomes of decisions—one said, for example, "It sounds cocky, but I am always sure of the result when I make an important decision." More often, however, managers look at outcomes in terms of probability; unable to attain absolute certainty, they believe in trying for a good batting average. A healthy enterprise, of course, has more leeway for mistakes and reduces the pressure of the need to be right.

Managers are notably conservative in their views about decisions, so that the level of expectations in decision making is reduced. One manager said, "Very few things are black and white; most are gray. . . . I'd say that 300 is a good batting average in our business." A corporation president said that "the difference between a successful executive and an unsuccessful one is the difference between being right 52 per cent of the time and being right 48 per cent of the time." Another president estimated that an error of 15 per cent occurs in the best decisions. Managers try to minimize error and maximize success, keeping mistakes small or undiscovered and arranging that the mistakes that are discovered will be seen by friends or subordinates rather than by bosses or jealous colleagues.

Judging a decision is complicated by the fact that there is often a long time between the making of the decision and its outcome. For example, DuPont spent 12 years and $27 million in research and development to get nylon into production. Before R.C.A. sold its first television set, it put $50 million into research and development. The Minnesota Mining and Manufacturing Company needed five years and "multimillions" to develop a new color copying machine.

A dilemma in the evaluation of decisions is whether to measure a decision by its outcomes, or to assess the process by which it is made. Focusing on outcomes is a common practice; it is an easy method, because one can reduce the problem to a single criterion: "If I like it, it is good." This allows for considerable subjectivity, especially in the absence of objections or criticisms from others. Through habit and custom, the results of a decision are taken as the reality to be faced, and hindsight is deplored as a basis of criticism.

However strong may be the temptation to evaluate outcomes, one must also evaluate the decision process itself. It is impossible to evaluate each and every decision individually. Evaluation processes differ for various types of decisions and decision situations, and by focusing on processes the manager can take steps to improve the quality of whole classes of decisions. The organization can then foster and reward good decision-making processes of managers, and act preventively to avoid all but the most unexpected decision failures.

The spectrum of decisions ranges from routine ones to novel, one-time, ill-structured decisions, as shown earlier in Table 4-1. Routine decisions are made under conditions of either certainty or risk. For these, decision rules or standard operating procedures can be set up according to the evaluator's system of values, preferences, and beliefs (in which case subordinates will then make common-sense decisions); or else subordinates can be made to develop, defend, and carry out their own decision procedures.

A more complex process is required for novel, ill-structured, one-time decisions, which involve considerable uncertainty or even ignorance. In such cases the decision makers must be subjected to controls and to planned guidance, training, and experiential learning procedures. It is important that the decider learn effective decision techniques—how and when to make and communicate decisions and what values, beliefs, and assumptions are present in himself, in the evaluators, and in the organization. To gain experience in making decisions in ill-defined situations, managers should be given opportunities, under guidance, to make actual decisions, to take risks, and to feel the responsibility for them. Another helpful practice is for superior and subordinate to study past decisions, both good and bad, to learn how decision processes may actually work out.[10]

Satisficing

The degree to which specific decisions will be correct depends on a number of factors, including the amount and accuracy of information on which they are based and the abilities of deciders. As noted earlier, it is impossible to make a purely rational decision, nor is it always necessary to find an optimal or perfect solution. For most situations, any of several decisions will be "good enough." Simon calls such solutions "satisficing." *Satisficing* occurs when the decision maker selects an alternative that is reasonably good but not perfect. The alternative chosen is suitable enough to permit halting the costly search for further information or additional alternatives. It is satisfactory enough to minimize criticism, and does not seem to warrant further delays. For example, a sales manager may decide on a bonus system for salesmen after a reasonable effort to compare alternative reward plans, but it is very possible that a better reward system could have been found.[11]

Satisficing decisions are related to the need for *suboptimization*, which occurs because goals typically cannot be pursued independently, one at a time, but are interdependent, related, and often in conflict. If the attainment of one goal in a multiple-goal system results in a lower degree of attainment of one or more of the other goals, suboptimization occurs. For example, increased sales may be obtained by harder selling, but credit losses may increase, or the morale of salesmen may fall. Suboptimization is inevitable where goals are in conflict, as when a company wishes to expand its work force rapidly and at the same time to improve communications among the workers. Furthermore, although a manager may approximate an optimal decision at a given point, optimization may fade as long-run considerations overtake the short run. It is difficult to forecast the future well enough to assure durably optimal decisions. Thus managers tend to suboptimize when the costs in terms of time or effort became greater than they

[10]Douglas R. Emery and Francis D. Tuggle, "On the Evaluation of Decisions." *MSU Business Topics*, Spring 1976, 42–48.

[11]Satisficing phenomena have been supported empirically by the research of psychologists and economists. For further evidence, see Herbert A. Simon, "Theories of Decision-making in Economics and Behavioral Science," *The American Economic Review* 49 (June 1959), 253–283.

wish to pay, or when goals are in conflict. We will return to the subject of goals and suboptimization in Chapter 7.

Factors Influencing the Quality of Decisions

The following factors affect the quality of decision making in an organization: (1) the environment of decision, (2) the personalities of deciders, (3) the timing and communication of decisions, and (4) the participation of those affected by decision making. These factors will be analyzed in the following sections.

Environment

Decision-making behavior has a contagious quality that arises from the way decisions relate to each other and from the tendency of managers to emulate their superiors and one another. Often an atmosphere of indecisiveness engulfs an organization, paralyzing the actions of managers. This situation can be prevented by vigorous leadership. Such a case prevailed in a major corporation, which was forced into reorganization because of years of loss. The new president moved quickly to supplant decision-making lethargy with vitality. By exercising strong personal leadership, he demanded timely and appropriate decisions from the managers. Clearly a key factor in the decision environment is the expectation by top managers that adequate decisions will be made at the right time and place and by the right people. Decisiveness on the part of top managers will help create decisiveness throughout the rest of the organization.

Authority is a pervasive influence in the environment of decision, and this topic will be examined in detail in Chapter 14. Here it is important to note that authority is one of the limitations on decision making. If the nature and amount of authority are unclear, the manager's decision making tends to be uncertain, erratic, or nonexistent. Rather than endure criticism or challenge, the manager becomes too cautious and slow to decide. It takes time to check decisions with those above or to make sure of the favorable reactions of others.

The environment of decision is both internal and external. Internally, managers work in a sociopsychological environment, interacting with other individuals and groups. In this context the manager tests his capabilities as a decision maker. The internal environment includes not only physical elements, but also the intangibles of human interaction among executives and employees, the decision-making behavior that we have noted, the organizational framework, and the network of both formal and informal authority and communications.

In the external environment are the social, political, and economic phenomena of the community, the state, the nation, and the world as well as the actions and decisions of competitors, the evolution of science and technology, the banking and financial system, government regulations and controls, and many other elements.[12]

Psychological Elements in Decision Making

Decision making is intimately associated with the psychological characteristics of deciders. The personal factors that influence a manager's decisions include status, prestige, feelings of security, and personality factors such as temperament, intelligence, energy, attitudes, and emotions. The sociopsychological view of decision making is that the whole person—that is, the total personality of the deciding individual—affects the decision-making process.

Managers vary with respect to temperament. Some are disturbed when they cannot reach a decision immediately, and others debate endlessly with themselves over possible actions they should take. Managers differ, too, in their speed of action and reaction and in their willingness to "go out on a limb." Some are conservative, patient, and slow to decide; others are brash and vigorous in making up their minds. Both impulsive eagerness and unnecessary delay are disastrous to effective decision making. The manager's personal profile of competencies, skills, attitudes, aspirations, and career objectives is a critical factor.

Timing and Communication of Decisions

Managers need to be aware of the elements of strategy involved in decision making, for decisions are the mechanisms by which strategy goes into action. Moreover, a decision reveals a strategy to opposing interests, such as competitors. Hence the timing of decisions is important.

Timing is important not only to deciders, but also to their associates and subordinates. Decisions affect the spirit of an organization through their effects on people. Those affected by a decision like to know of it in a timely manner, the better to carry out their part in relation to it. Moreover, superiors should learn of decisions ahead of their own subordinates and should be the primary link in communicating the decision downward. Thus if the production manager decides to shorten the lunch hour, key people should be alerted before it is announced to the entire organization. One such individual would be the personnel manager, who may have to answer questions and handle complaints resulting from the change; another key group in this case would be the first-line supervisors in charge of the work force.

[12]Chester J. Barnard, *The Functions of the Executive* (Cambridge: Harvard U. P., 1938), chap. 12.

Central to timing is a sensitivity to the degree of urgency involved in a decision and to the appropriateness with which a decision fits into other events. A second factor is an awareness of how the probable consequences can be incorporated into the timing plans.

Decisions must be formulated not only with reference to timing within over-all strategies, but also to the timing of their announcement. If the announcement of a decision is too long delayed, those affected will have difficulty adjusting to it. Moreover, in the meantime, the informal system or grapevine will begin to function, perhaps distorting the information or causing undue concern over what the future may hold. Managers often deplore the grapevine's premature revelations, though they withhold formal announcement. But as people perceive that a decision is near, recognize deadlines, and see data accumulated, they feel the pressure of uncertainty. In such cases, decisions should be communicated promptly and rapidly, and formally disseminated throughout the interested and affected parts of the organization.

Some decisions, however, carry complex political, organizational, or personal connotations for members of the organization, and especially for the decider. Frequently the release of such decisions occurs according to the personal or political strategies at work. For example, if executive A is promoting executive B and bypassing executives C, D, and E, he may delay announcing his decision until he has found a way to deal with executives C, D, and E, who understandably may be disappointed or even angry. The essential dilemma is whether to risk the disadvantages of an information leak and rumors, some true and some not true, or whether to face openly the fact that a decision is imminent.

An important decision about decisions is how to communicate them. Too frequently a decision is couched in language that arouses antagonism. One such communication read as follows: "Beginning immediately, employees are prohibited from parking their cars in the Factory Annex Lot. Until further notice, employees will use the public facilities on Second Street." Such a notice raises many unanswered questions. Those affected may first question its source and authenticity, and will immediately wonder what ulterior reasons prompted the decision. The notice is too abrupt, too impersonal, and too uninformative. Announcements of decisions should be clearly stated and carefully distributed; they should include a rationale, and show sensitivity to the consequences.

Participation

Another element in effective decision making is participation. Participation encourages the members of an organization to influence and contribute to decisions. It can be depicted on a continuum, as in Figure 4-3, which shows that participation exists in degrees ranging from little

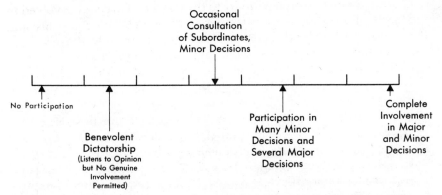

FIGURE 4-3. Continuum Showing Degrees of Participation in Decision Making.

or none to extreme involvement of individuals and groups in decisions. The extent to which participation exists in an organization depends primarily upon the willingness of managers to listen, as well as upon the way they manage the participation process. The roots of participative decision making lie in company philosophy and managerial style, and in the over-all climate of the organization.

Organizations in which participation is at a minimum are said to be authoritarian. Organizations with greater participation are to that extent democratic. In an authoritarian organization, direction and control are lodged at the top. Decisions are made primarily by one or a few top executives, and when the decisions are communicated, unquestioning obedience is expected. In democratically managed organizations, lower echelons have a bigger voice and responsibility in decisions.

The idea of participation does not allow managers to abdicate their authority or to avoid responsibility for decisions. Nor does it mean subjecting all decisions to a voting process or the dilution of supervisory tasks. But participation to encourage individual growth and development, self-expression and innovation, and commitment to decisions has a major place in the management of decisions.

The idea of participation is currently a popular management concept, but its origins are in the movement for industrial democracy dating from the turn of the century, coupled with the influence of the human relations movement of the forties and fifties. In 1916, for example, Henry Gantt wrote:

> The industrial leader of the future must practice methods which are approved by the people, and they must be such as not to take unfair advantage of anybody. . . . The fact . . . that our industries have been handled in general in an autocratic manner is no sign that they will continue to be so handled, and almost every day we see increasing symptoms that people are realizing what true democracy means.[13]

[13]Henry L. Gantt, *Industrial Leadership* (New Haven: Yale U. P., 1916), pp. 22–23.

We shall turn next to elaborating decision-making processes by considering the newer contributions of management research and practice.

———————————————————————————— **SUMMARY**

This chapter has examined the executive's decision-making function, identifying decisions as focal points in a process occurring through time. Decisions are interrelated and have a mutual influence on one another; they produce in turn a need for other decisions. Therefore decisions must be understood in terms of their past and future as well as their present.

Decision making is a highly rational process by which managers choose objectives and methods of attaining them. But decision making is not perfectly rational, because perfect information and forecasting of future events are not possible. Accordingly, the manager satisfices rather than maximizes—takes actions that will be good enough in view of the time and other costs known to him, although these decisions are less than optimal. In complex organizations, group decision making widely occurs.

From the standpoint of effective decisions, the main problems are (1) the degree of correctness desirable and possible, (2) the timing and the communication of decisions, and (3) the extent and nature of subordinate involvement in the process.

———————————————————————————— **INCIDENT CASE**

The Henry Company is a large manufacturer of steel auto parts, operating at full capacity and making abundant profits. Its problems are chiefly those arising from growth and success. Recognizing that production had reached full plant capacity, the president submitted to the board a proposal to build a new plant in another town twenty miles away. This plant was to be devoted to increasing the output of steel parts, and also to enter the growing field of making plastic parts. The president prepared a written proposal asking for the board's decision at its next meeting. None of the other top executives supported the plan, arguing that the factors against it were extensive.

Question:

1. What decision do you think the board should make, and why?

———————————————————————————— **QUESTIONS FOR STUDY**

1. What is meant by a "basic" decision? Why are basic decisions important?
2. Do the facts in a situation automatically determine what the decision should be? Why or why not?

3. What are the principal roles in decision making? What do managers actually do when they decide?

4. What can you suggest to speed up recognition of poor decisions so that improvements and changes can be made?

5. What happens in organizations to prevent the adequate communication of decisions? Cite examples.

6. What causes "buck-passing" in making decisions? How would you prevent it?

7. What is meant by satisficing behavior? Explain this concept as it applies to the firm and to the individual executive.

8. What are the limits on rational decision making? Why cannot decision making be completely rational?

9. Analyze the phenomenon of group decision. Find some examples and make comparisons.

_____ **SELECTED REFERENCES**

BEER, STAFFORD. *Decision and Control.* New York: John Wiley & Sons, Inc., 1966.

DRUCKER, PETER F. *The Effective Executive.* New York: Harper & Row, Publishers, 1967. Chapter 6.

DUNCAN, W. JACK. *Decision Making and Social Issues.* Hinsdale, Ill.: The Dryden Press, 1973.

EASTON, ALLAN. *Decision Making: A Short Course in Problem Solving for Professionals.* New York: John Wiley & Sons, Inc., 1976.

EBERT, RONALD J., and TERENCE R. MITCHELL. *Organizational Decision Processes: Concepts and Analysis.* New York: Crane, Russak & Company, Inc., 1975.

HARRISON, E. FRANK. *The Mangerial Decision-Making Process.* Boston: Houghton Mifflin Company, 1975.

LERNER, ALLAN W. *The Politics of Decision Making: Strategy, Cooperation, and Conflict.* Beverly Hills, Calif.: Sage Publications, Inc., 1976.

Chapter 5

Decision Making: Quantitative Tools and Processes

> One of the troubles of our age is that habits of thought cannot change as quickly as techniques, with the result that as skill increases, wisdom fades.
>
> —*Bertrand Russell*

> Many people will tell you that an expert is someone who knows a great deal about his subject. To this I would object that no one can ever know very much about any subject. I would much prefer the following definition: an expert is someone who knows some of the worst mistakes that can be made in his subject and how to avoid them. —*Niels Bohr*

CHAPTER GUIDE

According to Herbert Simon, "it is traditional to observe, in any discussion of the modern decision making tools, that the knowledge of these tools runs far in advance of application, and that the domain of application has been limited largely to decisions that are well-structured or "programmed" and quantitative in character. . . . Whether this limitation on applications is inherent or temporary is a more controversial question. One of the important tasks now before us is to see how far we can go in extending the applicability of the new decision-making tools to areas that are ill-structured, and qualitative, calling for 'judgment,' 'experience,' and even 'creativity.'" (*Public Administration Review* 25 [March 1965], p. 33).

Questions to keep in mind as you read this chapter:

1. Can computers think? How does the computer compare to the human brain?
2. Why is there a gap between decision theory and its use in organizations?
3. What are the major contributions of operations research specialists to the decision-making process?

Today's new quantitative methods are playing an increasingly important part in decision making. For certain types of decisions, particularly those of a problem-solving or data-based nature, such methods provide faster, more accurate decision making. Although the skillful blending of objective and subjective elements is still required, quantitative techniques greatly increase the rationality and effectiveness of many types of decision problems.

Quantitative techniques draw together several aspects of the decision process: problem definition, the search for alternatives, information storage and processing, estimated probabilities, statistical and mathematical tools, and computers. Detailed descriptions of these techniques are beyond the scope of this book, but an overview of (1) the nature of operations research, (2) operations research concepts, and (3) the main types of decision problems and methods of operations research will be presented in the sections that follow.

OPERATIONS RESEARCH

Operations research is a term denoting the quantitative aspects of management science. The field consists of the work of applied mathematicians, statisticians, management scientists, and other decision theorists. Their common interests are in rigorous analysis, theory building, and the development of scientific methods of problem solving and decision making. Such specialists, along with behavioral scientists, are among the revisionists in management theory. The field of operations research is highly interdisciplinary, including not only management science practitioners in private and public organizations, but also numerous consultants, teachers, and researchers.

Operations research builds upon the work of engineers and the early practitioners of scientific management. It is a logical extension of their concepts. As Simon says, "it is not clear that operations research embodies any philosophy different from that of scientific management. Charles Babbage and Frederick Taylor will have to be made, retroactively, charter members of the operations research societies." [1] This sense of history gives rise to assertions that operations research is "what we've always been doing under another name."

Operations research is defined by Miller and Starr as "applied decision theory," which deals rationally with problems by using any scientific, logical, or mathematical means.[2] The array of operations research methods is large and growing larger, but all these methods embrace the

[1]Simon, Herbert A. *The New Science of Management Decision,* rev. ed. (Englewood Cliffs, N.J.: Prentice-Hall, 1977), p. 15.

[2]David Miller and Martin K. Starr, *Executive Decisions and Operations Research,* 2nd ed. (Englewood Cliffs, N.J.: Prentice-Hall, 1969), pp. 131–133.

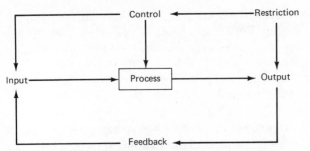

FIGURE 5-1. Simplified Systems Model.
Source: Stanford L. Optner, *Systems Analysis for Business Management,* 2nd ed., © 1968, p. 27. Reprinted by permission of Prentice-Hall, Inc., Englewood Cliffs, N.J.

attitudes and philosophy of science. Operations research can cope with situations involving even astronomical numbers of variables through mathematical, statistical and computer techniques. Computers increase the ability to put decision problems into forms by which mathematical solutions can be obtained through rapid computation. Electronic data-processing equipment makes it possible to store, sort, and manipulate large quantities of data.

Systems Framework for Decisions

Much of the work of operations research comes to a focus in the systems approach, in which the interrelatedness of decisions is a major element. Analysis starts with the system as a whole. Then elements of the system are identified and designed so that decisions are made in the light of their implications for the system as a whole. Economic analysis, engineering, and psychological and sociological concepts are brought together with mathematical and computer techniques for analyzing the dynamic behavior of complex systems.[3]

Optner defines a system as an ongoing process of a set of elements, each of which are functionally united in the achievement of an objective. Such a system is composed of six elements, as shown in Figure 5-1: input, output, process, feedback, control, and a restriction. Input, process, output, and the restriction are *systems parameters* whose limiting values can be specified. The restriction consists of imposed guidelines that bound a problem, and is composed of the objective and the constraint. Feedback, which is required for control, is achieved by comparing output with a standard or criterion. Control is exercised over input, process, and output through the feedback principle. To illustrate, Figure 5-2 applies the general system model to a business firm. The

[3]George A. W. Boehm, "Shaping Decisions With System Analysis," *Harvard Business Review* **54** (September–October, 1976), 91–99.

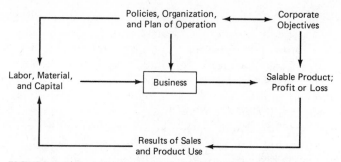

FIGURE 5-2. Systems Framework for the Business Firm.
Source: Adapted from Stanford L. Optner, *Systems Analysis for Business Management,* 2nd ed., © 1968, p. 35. Reprinted by permission of Prentice-Hall, Inc., Englewood Cliffs, N.J.

firm itself is a system, in turn composed of many other systems and subsystems.[4]

Systems may be classified according to their relevant characteristics for decision making. For example, Beer classifies systems according to (1) their complexity, and (2) whether they are deterministic or probabilistic. Systems may be simple and readily described, or complex but describable, or exceedingly complex ones and not precisely describable. Systems thus range along a scale of degrees of complexity. A deterministic system is one in which the parts interact in a predictable way; given the state of the system and the knowledge of its dynamic network, it is possible to predict its next state without risk of error. An example of a deterministic system would be that of a machine adjusted to cut steel bars to a given length. In a probabilistic system, on the other hand, no detailed or precise predictions can be made. There is no predetermination of outcome, and predictions are subject to the limitations of the probabilities in terms of which the system's behavior must be described. An example of a probabilistic system would be that of offering money to an employee to induce a specific behavior; predicting how a human being will react is a matter of probabilistic logic.[5]

Management Information Systems

A key requirement for effective decisions is the ability to obtain and analyze a sufficient quantity of relevant information. By treating information flows as one type of system, and by using computers to obtain necessary information, store it, and make it quickly available, decision processes are greatly improved. The development of sophisticated operations research methods for decision making has proceeded alongside the rapid and extensive evolution of computer technology.

[4]Stanford L. Optner, *Systems Analysis for Business Management.* 2nd ed. (Englewood Cliffs, N.J.: Prentice-Hall, 1968), chaps. 1–2.
[5]Stafford Beer, *Decision and Control* (New York: Wiley, 1966), pp. 12–19.

At first, computers had only minor effects on decision making; they were used mainly to speed up routine clerical tasks. Today's computers, however, can provide support for a complete information flow system of interacting parts. Formerly segmented activities such as planning, market analysis, financial considerations, scheduling, manpower development and many more can come together as part of a total decision system based on information flows. An example is the emergence in supermarkets of electronic cash-register systems, which can provide detailed information on sales, inventories, accounting data, billing procedures, sales forecasts, credit checking, and much more.

Management information systems, when properly designed, usually bring about changes in organization patterns and management responsibilities. Such information systems must be individually designed for each organization, tailor-made to particular purposes and objectives.[6]

_____ **CONCEPTS OF OPERATIONS RESEARCH**

Conceptually, operations research is based on scientific methods: observation, analysis, hypothesis formulation, experimentation, and verification. The general procedure is to compare a problem by analogy to problems in other and different areas. Common elements of decision making, such as fact-finding, exist in widely different problem situations.

The operations researcher (management scientist) translates the methodology of science into a special framework: (1) discovering strategies and states of nature, (2) handling large numbers of decision strategies, (3) determining the outcome of applying various strategies to particular states of nature, and (4) selecting an appropriate strategy with respect to a given problem.

Figure 5-3 shows the general operations research approach to problem solving. The steps are basically the same, whether mathematical or nonmathematical processes are used. However, the development of models and the use of quantitative tools help to generate alternative solutions. A computer calculates the optimum solution, which then must be interpreted and applied.

Simon, summarizing Churchman, gives the general methodology of applying mathematical tools to management decisions:

1. Construct a mathematical model that satisfies the conditions of the tool to be used, and at the same time mirrors the important factors in the management situation to be analyzed.
2. Define the *criterion function,* the measure that is to be used for

_____

[6]Robert G. Murdock and Joel E. Ross, *Introduction to Management Information Systems* (Englewood Cliffs, N.J.: Prentice-Hall, 1977).

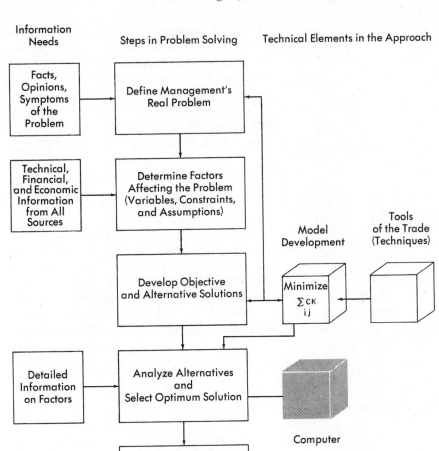

FIGURE 5-3. An Operations Research Approach to Problem Solving.

Source: Robert A. Hammond, "Making OR Effective for Management," *Business Horizons* 5 (Spring 1962), p. 81. © Foundation for Economic and Business Studies, Indiana University, Bloomington, Ind., 1962. Used by permission.

comparing the relative merits of various possible courses of action.

3. Obtain empirical estimates of the numerical parameters in the model that specify the particular, concrete situation to which it is to be applied.

4. Carry through the *mathematical process* of finding the course of action that, for the specified parameter values, maximizes the criterion function.[7]

[7] Simon, *New Science,* pp. 16–17.

Simon cites the key conditions for a problem to be amenable to the application of mathematical tools. It must be possible to define important mathematical variables that describe the situation being analyzed and to quantify the measures used in comparing possible courses of action. There must also be ways of making actual numerical estimates of the parameters of the problem, and the particular tools to be applied must be appropriate for the type of problem at hand. Finally, the problem must be of such a scale that it can be handled with reasonable costs in the time available.[8]

Classes of Decisions

The methods of operations research and decision theory are related to the nature of the decision problems that are faced. For this purpose, the basis of classification is the amount of information available to the decision maker about the likelihood for various states of nature to occur. Four main types of decision-making situations, each involving important procedural differences, most frequently occur: (1) decision making under certainty, (2) decision making under risk, (3) decision making under uncertainty, and (4) decision making under conflict or competition. Such categories are an analytical convenience, however; in reality the amount of information available to a decision maker falls along a continuum ranging from certainty to uncertainty.

These categories can be illustrated by a device known as a payoff matrix, shown in Figure 5-4. States of nature—environmental conditions over which the executive has no control—are represented horizontally at the top, as S_1, S_2, . . . , S_j. Strategies are indicated on the vertical axis, A_1, A_2, . . . , A_i. Payoffs are indicated in the cells, P_{11}, P_{12}, and so on.

In decision making under certainty, there exists only one state of nature, and the decider knows what that state of nature is. However, there are frequently a large number of strategies from which to choose. The rational decider will choose the strategy that is most likely to yield the desired goals; for example, economic theory assumes that a businessman will wish to maximize profit or minimize costs. Among the costs, outputs, and prices in a given environment, it is assumed that only one choice will maximize profits. Multiple solutions are sometimes possible, however, and further analysis must be made. Many of the manager's decisions are made under conditions approaching certainty. But whereas economic theory employs marginal analysis to explain how a firm operates, the form of analysis used by operations researchers is called mathematical programming. Linear programming, for example, is used to find the optimum combination of several limited

[8]Ibid, p. 17.

	S_1	S_2	S_3	S_4	... S_j
A_1	P_{11}	P_{12}	P_{13}	P_{14}	P_{1j}
A_2	P_{21}	P_{22}	P_{23}	P_{24}	P_{2j}
A_3	P_{31}	P_{32}	P_{33}	P_{34}	P_{3j}
...	...	...	...	...	...
A_i	P_{i1}	P_{i2}	P_{i3}	P_{i4}	P_{ij}

← states of nature

FIGURE 5-4. Payoff Matrix.

Where:

Sj = State of Nature

Ai = Alternative Decisions

Pij = Conditional payoff if alternative i is
    selected and state of nature j occurs.

resources to achieve a given objective, such as the maximization of profits.

In decision making under conditions of risk, the decider estimates the mathematical probabilities with which each of two or more states of nature will occur. In many managerial decisions, the decider can determine from past experience the objective probability and relative frequency of the occurrence of various conditions. Past experience becomes available in measurements and in records kept for various purposes. The decision maker's problem is to estimate the various probabilities. For each strategy in the payoff matrix, there will be a number of payoffs—one for each possible state of nature. The decision problem then becomes one of selecting a strategy. The rational decision maker will select that strategy calculated to yield the largest expected utility, or, as it is often called, the expected value. Table 5-1 translates a payoff matrix into probable payoffs in terms of dollars.

TABLE 5-1. Payoff Table for Space Problem

	States of Nature	
Course of Action	Good Financial Conditions (S_1)	Poor Financial Conditions (S_2)
A_1—Build new building	$120,000	$18,000
A_2—Add to present building	80,000	56,000
A_3—Continue present arrangement	32,000	22,000

When the decision maker cannot assign objective mathematical probabilities to the states of nature that affect the payoffs of strategies, conditions of uncertainty exist, and there arises the question of what criterion the decision maker can use for selecting a strategy. Such criteria are subjective and somewhat personal to the decider, who constructs a unique payoff table. Some criteria are optimistic and others are pessimistic. The pessimistic criterion assumes that nature will be malevolent and will attempt to minimize the decider's payoff. The optimistic criterion assumes, on the contrary, that nature will be kind.

The fourth category of decision problems, that of conflict and competition, is found where opponents are in conflict of interest. Contenders for a share of a fixed market would be an example. In making decisions, opponents take into account the actions and probable actions of others. This type of decision is analyzed as game theory, which will be more fully examined later in this chapter. Decisions made in negotiations with labor unions are illustrative.

Models

A model is a way of describing a situation or set of conditions so that behavior within it can be described, explained, predicted, or controlled. An operations research model is a simplified representation of a problem or operation, utilizing only those aspects of elements that are deemed crucial to the problem being studied. For example, three-dimensional scale models may be prepared for studying plant layouts. A model of the exterior surfaces of an airplane may be used in a wind tunnel to test its aerodynamic qualities, instead of using the actual airplane itself.

Models need not be composed of physical or quantitative dimensions; they may also be conceptual. For example, a description of the duties and responsibilities of a particular job is actually a model depicting the company's expectation as to what work shall be done. Such intangibles as time, employee satisfaction, or customer preference may be components of a model. Ideas about "the kind of employee we want in this company" are, in effect, a model representing what the prospective employee should be like.

Models may thus employ words to describe reality in a manageable way; but most models in operations research, and in the sciences generally, are mathematical in form, consisting of equations or sets of equations relating key variables to the desired outcome, say profit maximization, or minimum cost, or time. Some models are precise and are used in situations of relative certainty—that is, under conditions in which change is not a large factor. In decisions under conditions of certainty, quantitative analysis takes the form of maximizing an objective, subject to necessary constraints; for example, a company producing to fill a large backog of unfilled orders may employ an exact model in its production scheduling. Conditions of certainty exist in the form of measurements—known speeds and feeds, machine capacities, spoilage rates are examples.

Other models are probabilistic—that is, they are used in decision making under conditions of uncertainty. Decisions are based on estimates of the relevant factors in the problem, with the decider being willing to base his actions on these estimates. The behavior of consumers in response to particular forms of advertising, for example, is highly uncertain; therefore models used to solve problems in advertising are highly uncertain, and such models—selection of formats, media, and so on—usually employ probabilistic methods. The decider is guided by past experience in estimating the probabilities of consumer responses to different possible actions. Because risk and uncertainty are characteristic of a great deal of business behavior, the mathematics of statistics and probability have been greatly developed and widely employed in model building for business decisions.

Quantitative models are of two kinds: (1) problem-solving models and (2) optimum-value models. Problem-solving methods are used to find relationships among variables, to find pertinent variables, and to discover outcomes of strategies applied to states of nature. A problem can be solved by following one of several alternative strategies, and problem-solving models are used to discover the outcome that will result from the use of the different strategies. For example, a personnel executive observes manufacturing operations and knows from past experience that a given level of output requires certain quantities of various kinds of labor. If production is to be increased, the application of a model of the output-to-labor ratio makes it possible to specify the added labor required—always assuming, however, that the technology and the state of the economy will remain relatively stable, and that the manager has not necessarily established the optimal production system.

Most strategies of action and decision generate sequences of outcomes, rather than only one, so that feedback principle occurs in which an outcome itself becomes an input affecting the state of nature by generating another outcome. A household furnace thermostat is an example of a feedback process; when room temperature falls (input signal), a switch operates to increase the flow of heat, raising room temperature (outcome). The raised temperature in turn signals the source of heat about the new conditions (input) and causes the system to cease supplying heat (new outcome). Thus room temperature fluctuates within the controlled limits, with outcomes in a sequence. Figure 5-5 shows a simple model of a feedback system. The cartoon shows a humorous version of a closed-loop system.

Optimal outcomes, as are problem-solving outcomes, are obtainable by experimental or by mathematical methods. The optimal outcome is

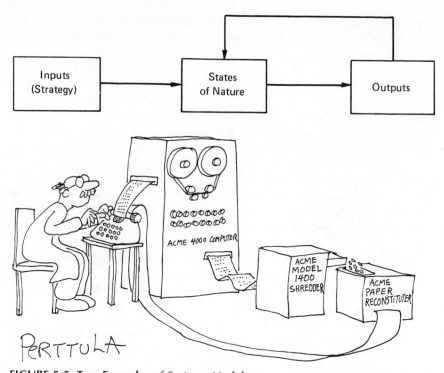

FIGURE 5-5. Two Examples of Systems Models.
Source: Cartoon reproduced from *Saturday Review*, August 23, 1975, p. 8, by permission of Jerry Perttula.

the best that can be produced from available alternative strategies. Through mathematical methods, a large number of outcomes can be examined to find the one that maximizes the attainment of the specified objective. Usually, however, optimal results are not obtainable even with advanced quantitative methods; hence suboptimization occurs. Unexpected events can change what had appeared to be an optimal decision. Decision systems have almost no reversibility. By the time a decision appears to have been wrong, it is impossible to return to the previous condition. Accordingly, decisions should include provision for the best possible predictions of future expectations.[9]

Simulation

Simulation is a way of using models to simplify a problem, or problem system, such as an organization; to identify its basic components; and

[9]Miller and Starr, *Executive Decisions*, chap. 3; George S. Gaines, Charles Lamar, and Leonard S. Simon, "Managers' Uses of Models," *Omega* 4 (1976), 253–263.

through trial and error to find a solution that, although not optimum, is reasonable. Simulation can be used to achieve satisfactory solutions to problems that are not amenable to more precise quantitative techniques. Through simulation models, managers can compare alternative courses of action and see the probable future impact of factors over which they have varying degrees of control. Simulation methods have been used in studying organizational changes, job-shop scheduling, model changeovers on the assembly line, and problems involving waiting lines or time sequences. Management games also employ a type of simulation theory.[10]

The general idea of simulation is to construct a simplified version of the reality being dealt with and to manipulate the model as though dealing with the reality. This technique is useful where it is costly or impossible to work with the reality directly or until simulation teaches the best way to deal with its. It is a way of operating a business, or some segment of it, "on paper" or in a computer, and of testing alternative strategies.

Scale models—such as wind tunnels, pilot plants, or the mock-up of an automobile design—are common simulation techniques. This is a qualitative level of simulation. More abstract are the analog simulation models used by operations research workers. Analog models usually incorporate the use of probability mathematics. War games and business games (described later in this chapter) involve analog simulation. The variables and the relationships are complex, so that computers are usually needed. In this type of simulation, states of nature can be made to appear randomly in relation to assigned probabilities. As in war games, for example, competitive strategies and states of nature, such as weather conditions, can be simulated so as to predict possible outcomes.

There are two basic types of simulation models: those that analyze the risks of single ventures, such as whether a new plant should be built, and those that are used to help decide the continuing policies of day-to-day operations. The latter type is more sophisticated, and involves feeding into the computer the rules by which it makes its decisions. Varying these decision rules produces different results that can be compared. With such a model, a manager can put a new procedure or policy into the console and immediately see the probable results. Figure 5-6 is an illustrative, generalized model of computer simulation.

[10]For details on simulation models, see C. William Emory and Powell Niland, *Making Management Decisions* (Boston: Houghton Mifflin, 1968), chap. 11; Rodney D. Johnson and Bernard R. Siskin, *Quantitative Techniques for Business Decisions* (Englewood Cliffs, N.J.: Prentice-Hall, 1977), chap. 16.

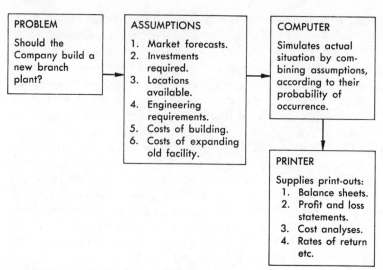

FIGURE 5-6. A Generalized Model of Computer Simulation.

--------------------------------- **DECISION PROBLEMS AND METHODS**

Applications of operations research methods will be described according to four main kinds of decision problems: (1) resource allocation, (2) inventory control, (3) waiting lines, and (4) game models. In addition, two additional techniques, decision trees and heuristic programming, will be described.

Resource Allocation Problems

Allocation problems arise from limited resources. The decision problem is how to make these allocations so as to achieve the best combination of resources for attaining a given objective. The alternate uses of resources are measured in terms of opportunity costs—that is, opportunities that are foregone because limited resources are used in the chosen ways and therefore cannot be used in other income-producing ways. An example is an investment in new machinery: the income foregone by not using the capital in other ways is part of the cost of using it this particular way. Linear programming is frequently used in resource allocation decisions.

Linear Programming

Linear programming is an analytical method of finding the optimum combination of limited resources to achieve a given objective. It describes problems in the form of algebraic equations in which the symbols represent quantities of inputs, such as machine capacities. Solving the algebraic equations yields the optimum combination, as measured by an algebraic statement of the payoff criterion.

Simple allocation decisions can often be made by observation and experience, but in large operations the problems are complex, involving thousands of possible choices. Linear programming is a sophisticated, shortcut technique that makes it possible to achieve, in a few hours, solutions that would otherwise require too much time to obtain. Computers are programmed with standard solutions to many linear programming problems, thus cutting computational time. Linear programming represents a general formulation of a very wide range of allocation problems whose basic characteristics are similar. For example, it has been used to find the optimal blending of gasoline, the minimum-cost diet meeting certain nutritional standards, the smoothing of production patterns, the optimal scheduling of airline flight crews, and the assigning of salesmen to territories.

Linear programming is a method of planning whereby some objective function is minimized or maximized while at the same time it is made to satisfy the various restrictions placed on the potential solutions. A linear function is optimized (minimized or maximized), subject to a set of linear constraints in the form of equalities or inequalities. The conflict in possible allocations is put into the model in the form of equations showing the limitations in various combinations of activities—limitations that may be in terms of time, money, space, or other resources. The linear model requires that these restrictions be linear with respect to each of the activities involved; that is, each additional unit of the activity must add a constant amount to the quantity being restricted. If the linear programming model corresponds closely to an actual problem, it will be useful in solving that problem. Many real problems involve activities that are linear. Moreover, some linear programs can be applied to problems or aspects of problems that are not linear.[11]

An illustration of the uses of linear programming is found in a typical machine-mix problem. One company had a seasonal product that could not be stored in inventory. It had estimates of monthly demand for the next five years under two alternative assumptions about the economic environment. This forecast indicated that the capacity of the machines on which the product was produced would soon be insufficient. The problem was to find out how many machines should be modified, how many new machines should be built, and how many old, unmodified machines should be kept in order to meet the forecasted demand at minimum costs. Operations researchers put this problem into a linear

[11]Richard I. Levin and Rudolph P. Lamone, *Linear Programming for Management Decisions* (Homewood, Ill.: Irwin, 1968).

programming matrix, using a computer program that was set up to handle a large number of variables. Thus the operations researchers could test the effects of varying economic environments and hence varying demand forecasts; they could also test the effect of different operating-costs estimates to find out which were the critical elements in the problem. The decision makers had a way of knowing the cost of varying from the optimum.

Linear programming also permits the modification of problems to take into account changes in any element of the problem. Once the basic model is set up, a change in a variable such as the cost of labor can be substituted in the equations without redoing the entire analysis. Linear programming provides information on the most desirable mix of resources, as well as problems of product mix and the movement of materials from origin to destination.

Linear programming is one of a class of decision methods known as programming. Among the other kinds of programming are heuristic programming, nonlinear (quadratic) programming, and dynamic programming. All programming methods have the common element of relating the decisions to time sequences and multistage problems. Most programming employs algebraic methodologies.[12]

Inventory Control

Inventory control is in reality a special case of the resource allocation problem, but they are so numerous and have been so extensively worked on by operations researchers that they form a special category of their own.

Inventory decision models deal with the storage of tangible or intangible resources to meet future demand. Stocks of machine parts and supplies of consumer goods in a warehouse are examples of tangible items stored for future use; money and available bank credit, examples of storing intangible items. The storage of items for future use involves numerous items of cost, such as warehouse overhead, interest charges, insurance premiums, and spoilage costs. These costs must be weighed against the costs of not storing for future demand—risks of losing customers, holding up assembly lines, handling back orders or special orders, and having to produce items in economical quantities.

Inventory decisions involve determining the costs that pertain to a given situation, measuring those costs, and analyzing the relationship

[12]For further details on linear programming and other programming methods, see Leonard W. Hein, *The Quantitative Approach to Managerial Decisions* (Englewood Cliffs, N.J.: Prentice-Hall, 1967), chaps. 3–6; Max D. Richards and Paul S. Greenlaw, *Management Decision Making*, 2nd ed. (Homewood, Ill.: Irwin, 1972), chap. 16; Billy E. Goetz, *Quantitative Methods: A Survey and Guide for Managers* (New York: McGraw-Hill, 1965), chap. 9; Ronald L. Gue and Michael E. Thomas, *Mathematical Methods in Operations Research* (New York: Macmillan, 1968), chaps. 3–5.

between various levels of storage and costs. The aim is generally to minimize the total operating costs of the firm, although other criteria, such as stable production levels or customer good will, may be important. Two mutually interrelated inventory decisions that affect total costs are (1) the size of each lot to be purchased or manufactured, and (2) the average inventory levels to be maintained. As these two quantities (lot size and average inventory) increase, other costs decrease. Various formulas can be applied under different conditions of decision making. Under conditions of certainty, where demands for an item are known and the lead time for procuring it is also known, optimum solutions can be obtained through the use of economic order quantity (EOQ) models. However, when demand and lead times are uncertain, conditions of risk or uncertainty exist. Here the two main approaches are holding lot size constant and varying the time between placing orders for the scheduling of production runs; and conversely, holding the time between the placing of orders or the starting of production runs constant but varying the lot size. These methods will permit satisficing (acceptable) rather than optimal (ideal) decisions.

Waiting Lines

Waiting-line problems occur whenever a service is required to meet irregular demands. The manager has to decide how much service to keep available to meet such demands. For example, in a battery of machines, breakdowns will occur randomly, and whenever the maintenance service falls below that demanded by the breakdowns, a waiting line of unrepaired machines forms. This idle capacity is a cost that has to be balanced against the cost of keeping maintenance services available.

Mathematical techniques known as *queuing theory* are applied to any situation that produces a need to balance the cost of increasing available service against the cost of letting units wait. Queuing theory has been used to balance the timing of red and green lights at traffic intersections, to plan the arrival of production parts at inspection stations, assembly points, or shipping rooms, and to determine the number of service workers required. It is also used to determine how many forklift trucks or cranes are required to move materials from one point to another and in other situations requiring the company to find the most efficient number of pieces of equipment to provide.

Demands for service are usually unavoidable; they must be met promptly if costs of waiting time are to be avoided or reduced. Probability mathematics is helpful in this kind of problem. Predicting the amount of waiting time in a given situation depends on the probability of receiving a demand for service and the probability that facilities are in use with prior calls. With the knowledge of key facts—such as the relationship between the group demanding the service and the service facility available, the priority rules on assignment of services, the calling-interval distribution, and the service-time distribution—mathematical determinations of the waiting time can be made. Simulation methods are also widely used to solve waiting-line problems.[13]

Game Models

The fourth category of quantitative decision models consists of game models, or competitive strategies. Game theory, which has been developed by mathematicians, economists, and other scientists,[14] has not been widely applied to the solution of actual problems involving competitors, but it has provided useful insights into situations involving elements of competition, bargaining, and negotiation.

Game theory is relevant to decision situations when a rational opponent is involved, so that resulting effects are dependent on the specific strategies selected by the decision maker and the opponent. This assumes that an opponent will carefully consider what the decision maker may do before he selects his own strategy. There exists a definite conflict of interests between the opponents, as in the case of games played for fun.

Games are classified according to the number of opponents and the degree of conflict of interest. Games involving only two opponents have been the most widely studied; those involving more than two opponents have been less thoroughly studied and are exceedingly complex. Classified by degree of conflict of interest, games are termed zero-sum or non–zero-sum. In a zero-sum game, there is complete conflict of interest, and what one opponent gains, the other loses. In non–zero-sum games, the conflict of interest is less than complete. Most business decisions involving rational opponents are of the non–zero-sum type. In a struggle among competitors for sales volume, for instance, one competitor may gain sales not all of which would be at the expense of competitors, for the struggle among competitors may increase the total size of the market in which all are selling. On the other hand, a struggle to increase a company's share of a finite market, as occurs in the automobile industry, is a zero-sum game situation: one firm's increase in the share of the market can be gained only by reduction in the shares of one or more of the competing firms. Thus, non–zero-sum situations involving more than two opponents are more typical or practical busi-

[13]For further information on queuing theory and waiting-line problems, see Hein, *Quantitative Approach*, chaps. 11–12; Richards and Greenlaw, *Decision Making*, chap. 18; Gue and Thomas, *Mathematical Methods*, chap. 7; Goetz, *Quantitative Methods*, chap. 11.

[14]A pioneering work in game theory is that of Oskar Morgenstern and John von Neumann, *Theory of Games and Economic Behavior*, 3rd ed. (Princeton: Princeton U. P., 1953). See also John McDonald, *The Game of Business* (New York: Doubleday, 1975).

ness decision problems. Game theory has contributed few applications to this typical situation, but many useful insights into competitive situations have been provided.[15]

Game theory has been applied experimentally and tentatively to bargaining and negotiating interactions in business, as for example in union-management negotiations or in business-contract negotiations. Applications of game theory are embodied in games used for management training.

Decision Trees

A decision tree is a graphic method by which a decision maker can more readily visualize alternatives, together with the risks, possible outcomes, and information needs involved in each choice. Decision trees are used primarily to visualize over a time span decision making under conditions of uncertainty. Hence the basic data of a decision-tree diagram could be the data from a problem's payoff matrix. It is useful to prepare a decision tree where the decision maker must make a choice or a series of choices from alternative courses of action, and where such choice or choices will ultimately lead to some uncertain consequence dependent upon an unpredictable event or set of conditions.

To illustrate the payoff matrix and decision tree, consider the problem of deciding whether more manufacturing space should be provided now, and if so, how it should be provided. The manager starts by isolating three alternatives shown in the payoff matrix, Table 5-1, shown earlier. Financial conditions over the forthcoming period are uncertain, ranging from good to poor. Using interest rates, building-cost data, and other financial information, the manager determines for each state of nature and each alternative the probable or expected payoffs, expressed in dollars—information that can be diagrammed in a decision tree, as in Figure 5-7. Shown in this decision tree are decision points, branches representing alternative courses of action, chance events, and consequences or resulting states of nature.

The outcomes depicted on the tree or matrix may be based on the experience and judgment of the decision maker, and are thus subjective estimates supported by computational data available within the firm's records. In more complex problems, it is desirable to use probability statistics to derive conditional payoffs and expected values of the various alternatives. The use of probabilities allows the decision maker to

[15]For an excellent critical analysis of game theory applied to decision making, see Miller and Starr, *Executive Decisions*, pp. 552–553. For some applications to industrial organization, see Martin Shubik, "Game Decisions and Industrial Organization," *Management Science* 6 (July 1960), pp. 455–474. For application to the problem of cumulative voting for corporate directors, see Gerald F. Glasser, "Game Theory and Cumulative Voting for Corporate Directors," *Management Science* 5 (January 1959), pp. 151–156.

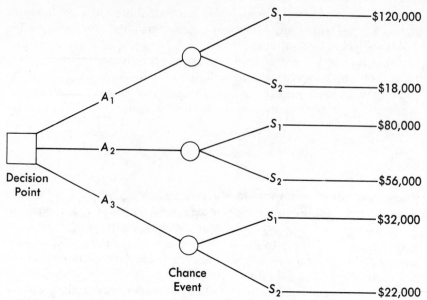

FIGURE 5-7. Decision Tree on Space Problem Described in Table 5-1.

quantify his personal preferences and personal judgments concerning the factors that favor and oppose desired or expected events. A more complex decision tree showing the use of probabilities is presented in Figure 5-8.

The decision tree does not provide an obvious solution or necessarily indicate a single right or correct decision; but it does allow the decision maker to base his choice on the important alternatives and their probable consequences. Normally the decision maker locates himself at the left side of the diagram and thinks ahead in time. But he can also start at the right side of the diagram and think back through future decisions until he arrives at the one he is about to make at a given point in time. His final choice may then be made on the basis of criteria deemed most important.[16]

Heuristic Programming

Heuristic programming, sometimes called heuristic problem solving, is an approach to decision making that has gained increasing use; in fact, it is a branch of simulation model analysis. It is applied to problems in

[16]For further information on decision trees, see Paul E. Green, "Bayesian Statistics and Project Decisions," *Business Horizons*, Fall 1962, 101–109; John F. Magee, "Decision Trees for Decision Making," *Harvard Business Review* **42** (July–August 1964), 126–135; Emory and Niland, *Making Management Decisions*, chap. 5.

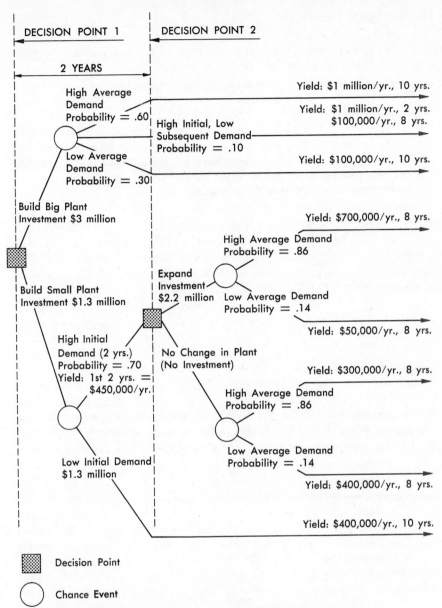

DECISION POINT 1 | DECISION POINT 2

2 YEARS

High Average
Demand
Probability = .60

Yield: $1 million/yr., 10 yrs.

High Initial, Low
Subsequent Demand
Probability = .10

Yield: $1 million/yr., 2 yrs.
$100,000/yr., 8 yrs.

Low Average
Demand
Probability = .30

Yield: $100,000/yr., 10 yrs.

Build Big Plant
Investment $3 million

Yield: $700,000/yr., 8 yrs.

High Average Demand
Probability = .86

Expand
Investment
$2.2 million

Build Small Plant
Investment $1.3 million

Low Average Demand
Probability = .14

Yield: $50,000/yr., 8 yrs.

High Initial
Demand (2 yrs.)
Probability = .70
Yield: 1st 2 yrs. =
$450,000/yr.

No Change in Plant
(No Investment)

Yield: $300,000/yr., 8 yrs.

High Average Demand
Probability = .86

Low Average Demand
Probability = .14

Yield: $400,000/yr., 8 yrs.

Low Initial Demand
$1.3 million

Yield: $400,000/yr., 10 yrs.

▨ Decision Point

◯ Chance Event

FIGURE 5-8. Decision Tree Showing Probabilities and Financial Data.

Source: John F. Magee, "Decision Trees for Decision Making," *Harvard Business Review* 42 (July–August 1964), p. 131. Copyright © 1964 by the President and Fellows of Harvard College; all rights reserved.

such areas as assembly line balancing, plant layout, job shop shceduling, warehouse location, inventory control, and resource allocation.

A heuristic is any device or procedure used to reduce problem-solving effort. A commonly used heuristic is the "rule of thumb"—for example, "when there are only twelve units of part A in bin C, reorder the part," or "don't drink liquor and drive a car." Much business behavior and much of everyday life is guided by this kind of rule. It is important to note, however, that although heuristic systems involve rules, they also involve the recognition of how the rules should be applied at the time the needs are identified.

When heuristics are combined to solve a problem, a heuristic program is formed. Complex programs require computers for their solution. Heuristic programs are used whenever the problem is too large or complex to solve by mathematical or statistical techniques, such as linear programming, and when dealing with ill-structured problems that cannot be stated in mathematical terms, so that quantitative techniques are unsuitable. Operations research and heuristics are thus on opposite ends of the scale as far as rigor of methodology is concerned. But heuristic programming provides shortcuts over computational methods. The chief inputs in heuristic programming are subjective judgments, based on the manager's past experience; the pooling of the knowledge and judgments of colleagues; the use of judgment, intuition, creativity, learning processes; and other qualitative variables. The decision maker immerses himself in the total problem, and searches by trial and error for a satisfactory solution in a reasonable time and at a reasonable cost, rather than striving for an optimal solution at any cost.[17]

SUMMARY

The use of increasingly sophisticated mathematical tools is an important characteristic of decision making. Operations research specialists use a variety of techniques, in which managers have only limited expertise. But managers need to know the uses and limitations of operations research tools, which consist of practical applications of statistics, mathematics, and computers. Problems in a wide variety of managerial functions are amenable to quantitative techniques: marketing, finance, production, and personnel administration have all been fruitful areas for these methods. Moreover, the interrelationships among the functions can be more readily taken into account.

Among the key types of problems that have been primarily amenable

[17]Herbert A. Simon and Allen Newell, "Heuristic Problem Solving: The Next Advance in Operations Research," *Operations Research* 6 January–February 1958), 1–10; Jerome D. Weist, "Heuristic Programs for Decision Making," *Harvard Business Review* 44 (September–October 1966), 129–143.

to the newer quantitative and statistical tools are inventory problems, waiting-line problems, and resource allocation problems. Linear programming has been one of the most widely applied quantitative techniques. Simulation, particularly with the aid of computers, has also been widely used.

That elements of rationality, judgment, subjectivity, and logic are inherent in decision making was considered. The role of the decision maker under conditions of certainty, risk, and uncertainty was analyzed. Payoff matrices and decision trees were described as decision tools of increasing use and importance.

INCIDENT CASE

Charles Smith has been in charge of computers and data processing in the Ball Machinery Company for two years. He is an operations research specialist, and his primary responsibility is to plan the improved use of operations research methods throughout the company. Recently he voiced considerable frustration: "Managers in this company don't want to bother with real data. Hunch and intuition are good enough for them. I've shown them a dozen ways to save money, but they won't accept the new methods of decision making." At the same time, the production manager remarked that "Charlie is an annoyance. He's always sending us data we can't use, much less understand. He doesn't understand our set-up, so how can he tell us how to solve our problems?"

Question:

1. How do you think this situation could be resolved?

QUESTIONS FOR STUDY

1. Explain what you feel are the main components of operations research approaches.

2. What is a model? How does this concept relate to quantitative analysis for decision-making purposes? Give some examples of models that have been applied.

3. What weaknesses or limitations do you see in the quantitative decision-making approaches described in this chapter?

4. Might there be a department of operations research in a large manufacturing company? A bank? An insurance company? Why or why not?

5. Describe the points in problem solving, as presented in this chapter, in which judgment and opinion still play a key role. How does the element of judgment limit the utility of quantitative analysis?

6. What are the main advantages of the use of decision trees? How are they constructed, and where do the data come from that are used in them?

SELECTED REFERENCES

AGEE, MARVIN H., and PAUL E. TORGERSON. *Quantitative Analysis for Management Decisions.* Englewood Cliffs, N.J.: Prentice-Hall, Inc., 1976.

BEER, STAFFORD. *Decision and Control.* New York: John Wiley & Sons, Inc., 1966.

CHURCHMAN, C. WEST. *Prediction and Optimal Decision.* Englewood Cliffs, N.J.: Prentice-Hall, Inc., 1963. Chaps. 2–5.

EMORY, C. WILLIAM, and POWELL NILAND. *Making Management Decisions.* Boston: Houghton Mifflin Company, 1968.

JOHNSON, RODNEY D., and BERNARD R. SISKIN. *Quantitative Techniques for Business Decisions.* Englewood Cliffs, N.J.: Prentice-Hall, Inc., 1976.

LYON, JOHN. *The Data-Based Administrator.* New York: John Wiley & Sons, 1976.

MILLER, DAVID W., and MARTIN K. STARR. *Executive Decisions and Operations Research.* 2nd ed. Englewood Cliffs, N.J.: Prentice–Hall, Inc., 1969. Chaps. 4–9.

MURDOCK, ROBERT G., and JOEL S. ROSS. *Introduction to Management Information Systems.* Englewood Cliffs, N.J.: Prentice-Hall, Inc., 1977.

NORLEN, URBAN. *Simulation Model Building.* New York: Halsted Press, 1975.

RAIFFA, HOWARD. *Decision Analysis: Introductory Lectures on Making Decisions Under Uncertainty.* Reading, Mass.: Addison-Wesley Publishing Company, Inc., 1968.

RAMALINGAM, P. *Systems Analysis for Managerial Decisions.* New York: John Wiley & Sons, 1976.

RICHARDS, MAX D., and PAUL S. GREENLAW. *Management Decisions and Behavior.* Rev. ed. Homewood, Ill.: Richard D. Irwin, Inc., 1972.

ROSS, JOEL E. *Modern Management and Information Systems.* Englewood Cliffs, N.J.: Reston Publishing Company, 1976.

SIMON, HERBERT. *The New Science of Management Decision.* Rev. ed. Englewood Cliffs, N.J.: Prentice-Hall, Inc., 1977.

SHUBIK, MARTIN. *Games for Society, Business, and War: Towards a Theory of Gaming.* New York: American Elsevier Publishing Co., Inc., 1975.

VOICH, DAN, JR., HOMER J. MOTTICE, and WILLIAM A. SCHRODE. *Information Systems for Operations and Management.* Cincinnati: South-Western Publishing Company, 1975.

WAGNER, HARVEY M. *Principles of Management Science.* 2nd ed. Englewood Cliffs, N.J.: Prentice-Hall, Inc., 1975.

WEINBERG, GERALD. *An Introduction to General Systems Thinking.* New York: John Wiley & Sons, Inc., 1975.

WHITE, D. J. *Decision Methodology.* New York: John Wiley & Sons, Inc., 1975.

WOOLSEY, ROBERT E. D., and HUNTINGTON S. SWANSON. *Operations Research for Immediate Applications: A Quick and Dirty Manual.* New York: Harper & Row, Publishers, 1975.

Chapter 6

Planning

All change is not growth, as all movement is not forward.   *—Ellen Glasgow*

The greatest thing in the world is not so much where we stand as in what direction are we going.   *—Oliver Wendell Holmes*

I like the dreams of the future better than the history of the past.
                                                    —Thomas Jefferson

CHAPTER GUIDE

In 1965 a large conglomerate built around defense contracts and various domestic and foreign ventures embarked on a systematically planned growth program through diversified acquisitions. The company was so confident in its planning that it made its long-term goals public. "It's risky, but it keeps our toes to the fire," said the chief executive. The goals of doubling sales and cutting defense work to 50 per cent of the product mix were achieved. In 1970, another five-year plan, again doubling sales and maintaining defense work at 50 per cent, was adopted. The plan was fulfilled one year ahead of schedule. In 1975, new corporate officers launched another five-year plan; this time they scrapped the tradition of publicly announcing the plan's details. Reasons cited were uncertainties caused by the energy shortage, inability to discern the future mood in the federal government, and the need for more caution in the company's acquisitions program.

Questions to consider while reading this chapter:

1. What are the advantages and disadvantages of public announcement of five-year plans in this firm?
2. How do you evaluate the reasons given for abandoning the traditional policy?
3. How does planning for long-range goals differ from other kinds of planning?

Planning is both an organizational necessity and a managerial responsibility. Through planning, organizations choose goals based on estimates or forecasts of the future, giving form and direction to the efforts of managers and workers. Concern for the future is intensified by the fact of relentless, unremitting change. The purpose of planning is therefore twofold: to determine appropriate goals, and to prepare for adaptive and innovative change.

No organization is free of change, so all must plan effectively for survival and growth. Whether dealing with external or internal forces, planning helps an organization avoid being the helpless victim of change; instead it gains a measure of control and influence over its destiny. To make plans is to consider decisions and their probable consequences. Adopted plans become benchmarks against which to judge the ongoing work.

The Impact of Change

Planning needs arise externally from economic, social, political, and technological change. For example, such organizations as the YMCA or the Boy Scouts of America have in recent years had to redesign their objectives and activities to take account of changed social patterns in a society that has undergone a transition from a rural, frontier culture to an urban, industrialized one. Cycles of recession and prosperity, also, intensify the need for planning.

Economic, social, political and technological changes call for internal changes in size, organization structure, staffing, work methods, and products or services. To visualize the scope of change, consider today's automobile, with its 13,000 parts, compared to the automobile of forty years ago, which resembled the horse-drawn carriages of its day. Some have estimated that half our work force is producing and selling things unheard of in 1900, and many are at work on products new since 1930. Half the working population in the year 2000 may be making and selling things that are as yet unknown. Furthermore, there are constant changes in consumer demand for products and services. For example, detergents have virtually replaced soap flakes. Paper and plastic cartons have displaced glass milk bottles. Newsreels, fountain pens, trolley cars, and inner tubes are going out of existence, along with convertible automobiles and wringer washing machines. Emergency rooms in hospitals are used in place of physician's house calls.[1]

Not only have products and services changed; so have the management skills and methods used to produce them. The management skill required to run successfully an eighteenth-century shoe factory fades into insignificance compared with the skill required to manage a mod-

---

[1]For analyses of future change potentials, see Herman Kahn and Anthony J. Wiener, *The Year 2000: A Framework for Speculation on the Next Thirty-three Years* (New York: Macmillan, 1967).

ern shoe factory's highly styled products, its methods of mass marketing and production, its fierce worldwide competition, and the demands of its workers. The tremendous size of many of today's organizations would not be feasible under the management methods of one hundred years ago.

Planning Defined

Planning is defined as the activity by which managers analyze present conditions to determine ways of reaching a desired future state. It embodies the skills of anticipating, influencing, and controlling the nature and direction of change. Planning is a pervasive and continuous function involving complex processes of perception, analysis, conceptual thought, communication, decision, and action.

Planning is a process rather than behavior at a given point in time. Some authorities define planning as all the thinking that takes place prior to actions or decisions. Its central concern is with the future. Thus Ackoff defines planning as "anticipatory decision making." Planning is done to decide what to do and how to do it prior to taking action.[2]

We will now examine the planning process according to: (1) basic elements, (2) obstacles to effective planning, and (3) methods of effective planning.

BASIC ELEMENTS IN PLANNING

There are five important fundamental activities that are basic to the planning process: (1) evaluation of present conditions, (2) the factor of time, (3) the problems of forecasting, (4) the collection and analysis of data, and (5) the coordination of plans.

Evaluation of Present Conditions

A central task in planning is to recognize in present conditions inadequacies that point to the desirability of change. Dissatisfaction with current goals, programs, or activities generates planning as a way to achieve improvement. The dissatisfactions may arise from lack of progress toward goals, from the need for new goals, or from the recognition of critical problems. Planning is needed to prevent or correct problems and to give the organization its forward momentum.

An example of how problems lead to planning is provided by a firm that recognized that its production facilities were becoming inadequate. The managers planned a series of actions to meet the problem.

[2]Russell L. Ackoff, *A Concept of Corporate Planning* (New York: Wiley, 1970), chap. 1.

They studied various locations, and acquired land for a new plant. When the plant was built, they were ready with plans for moving into it from the old location, and for disposing of the old properties. Suppose, however, that the managers had not been alert to the growing pressure on the company's facilities. The result would have been an urgent need for expanded production capacity and too short a time to act. Fortunately, by planning well in advance, the managers accomplished the changes gradually and systematically. This example makes it clear that an important ingredient of successful planning is attention to the needs of the future. Expediency, the usual alternative to planning, is unreliable and often costly.

It is not easy to recognize when conditions require planning. Change is often so gradual that only after a problem has emerged is the cumulative impact recognized. In all but the simplest problems, the number of alternative actions is great, and even a simple problem may have several alternatives.

Planning activities cover a range of types of problems. Some recurring problems can be the subject of *standing plans*, which continue to meet an enduring or continuing need. An example might be a customer service plan detailing policies and procedures for assuring customer satisfaction. It is not known what specific problems will arise, but the plan recognizes that events needing orderly attention will occur.

Many plans, particularly major ones, are *single-use plans*—broad, inclusive plans to accomplish a particular purpose, such as installing a new job evaluation system. They may contain sets of related subsidiary plans.

Another important type is *contingency plans*, which look into varying time spans in the future, and attempt to take account of the possibilities for rapid, major changes such as those described earlier in this chapter. Through contingency planning, executives watch current conditions and map out probable alternatives of varying degrees of risk and benefit. The purpose of contingency planning is to consider alternative futures and to keep plans orderly, coordinated, and current. Such plans require great flexibility; often they are discarded or changed before their actual use.

The Factor of Time

For analytical puspooses, planning may be viewed in both the short run and the long run. However, planning is continuous; in practice, the significant plan is that which people are following at a given time.

Short-run planning is concerned with the relatively near future—the next month or even the next one to two years. A store manager planning a clearance sale is an example. On the other hand, long-range planning attempts to foresee conditions and courses of action for five, ten, or even twenty-five or more years ahead. Planning a new model of an automobile requires three to five years, and even minor changes may require at least eighteen months. Creating a nationwide market for a new product would be a goal requiring intricate long-range plans. Long-range plans center on the organization's basic goals and strategies for growth and development.

As the time span increases, the accuracy of planning tends to decrease. A greater span of time affords more opportunity for unanticipated events to occur. The more remote the future the manager is considering, the more difficult it becomes to foresee what will happen.

Another time factor is that the present plays a stronger role than the manager may realize. Present conditions weigh heavily in planning; by overshadowing future needs, they may sometimes result in errors of judgment. One company, for example, recognizing the trend for expansion, planned a new building one-third larger than the one they occupied. Within a year after occupying the building, it became clear that the company's growth had been grossly underestimated. In the first year, the company had to make an addition to the new building. This example shows how present conditions produce conservative plans. The present is seldom so bad that it is not somewhat preferable to the unknown future.

The long-range future is far more difficult for an executive to consider in his planning than is the short-range span of time. The factors that a manager desires to take into account into planning, such as new technology, consumer tastes and desires, business conditions, change rapidly and often unpredictably. It is easier to estimate the significance of elements like these in the short run, but over long periods of time only approximate trends can be forecast—and with increasing loss of accuracy. The relative difficulty of long-range planning has led to the tendency to concentrate heavily on short-range planning, where managers feel more confident in their ability to be right. It is tempting to concentrate on plans for improving the company's grievance procedure rather than on ways of working out relationships between workers and supervisors so that fewer grievances would arise.

Long-range planning is generally strategic planning. That is, it concerns the appropriateness and nature of goals and of ways of attaining them. Strategic planning requires the utmost skill in anticipation of the future and in relating to the external environment.[3] Contingency planning is a form of strategic planning.

The importance of short-range planning should not be underestimated, however. Short-range plans tend to be more accurate than

[3]Peter Lorange and Richard F. Vancil, "How to Design a Strategic Planning System," *Harvard Business Review* **54** (September–October, 1976), 57–81; T. H. Naylor and M. J. Mansfield, Jr., "Corporate Planning Models: A Survey," *Planning Review* **4** (May 1976), 8–12; Peter Baiardi, "The High Visibility of the Long-Range Planner," *MBA*, November 1975, 29–39; Charles W. Hofer, "Research on Strategic Planning: A Survey of Past Studies and Suggestions for Future Efforts," *Journal of Economics and Business* **28** (Spring/Summer, 1976), 261–286.

longer-range plans. More managers in the organization will be involved in making and carrying out short-range plans. The day-to-day work of members of an organization consists of completing plans currently in process and developing plans designed to deal with situations antici- pated in the relatively near future.

Forecasting

Forecasting embodies procedures and techniques for predicting condi- tions or events that are expected to prevail in the future. Forecasting may apply to any relevant aspect of the future, but the most important focus is on the general level of conditions in the economic, governmen- tal, and social sectors in which the organization operates. For a business firm, economic conditions, financial conditions, the level of consump- tion, and population changes are critical. For a government agency, constituent needs for service, population trends, and legislative actions are important. For a hospital, changing trends in health care, govern- ment policy, and medical technology are important.

Forecasting is not an exact science, for uncertainties abound. A matter of judgment will always remain something of an art. We have no economic Geiger counter to identify the right policies or decisions, but executives are making forecasting more and more a science and less an art. Many firms employ professional economists and other experts to make careful and detailed forecasts for use in planning. Large firms such as Standard Oil Company of New Jersey may employ as many as one hundred economists with planning and forecasting responsibili- ties. The Bell Telephone Laboratories has a systems engineering department, with approximately 250 to 300 full-time planners, whose sole concern is to anticipate future needs and to speculate about how these needs may best be met. Clearly this magnitude of planning accompanies large-scale organization in which factors of technological innovation, population growth, and expanding physical facilities are interrelated. However, small organizations also have access to a great deal of economic and business data, and are aided in their forecasting by consultants, industry, and trade association analyses, university bureaus of business and economic research, data from federal and state governments, and sometimes by small staffs of economic analysts.[4]

Forecasting Strategies

Three basic strategies in forecasting have been summarized by *Busi- ness Week:* the loaded deck, oaks from acorns, and the test tube.[5]

The loaded-deck strategy consists of finding out what has happened

---

[4]For perspectives on planning problems see Peter F. Drucker, *The Age of Discontinu- ity* (New York: Harper, 1969). See also *Economic Forecasting and Corporate Planning* (New York: The Conference Board, 1973).

[5]"Business Forecasting," *Business Week,* Sept. 24, 1955, p. 90.

or is happening before anyone else finds out, and using information available before someone else thinks of using it. The strategy requires inside information, reported quickly and accurately. The methods most useful are being an insider, knowing an insider who will tell you what you want to know, spotting the initial steps of process that require considerable time to carry out, or observing factors that cannot change much during the forecast period. For example, the initial step in an expansion move might be the purchase of a tract of land—the tip-off for a possible building program.

The oaks-from-acorns strategy hypothesizes that the future grows out of the present. Another useful idea is that changes are often rhythmic or cyclic in nature, going through alternating phases of expansion and contraction. Hence the principal technique of this strategy is trend extrapolation of data, as shown in Figure 6-1. Projecting these trends assumes that they will tend to continue unless interrupted by some event. The difficulty is that a turning point may occur to render the extrapolation invalid.

The third strategy, test-tube forecasting, is the development of theoretical economic models that can be used to establish relatively permanent principles which can then be applied to past, present, or future situations. These theoretical abstractions can then be experimentally manipulated by the professional economist. The science of ecometrics (economics, mathematics, and statistics) is studying these aspects of forecasting.

The executive need not rely on any one of these strategies and techniques, but can employ them in many combinations, to produce forecasts of general economic conditions. They serve to indicate the complexity of economic forecasting and to suggest how managers can take practical steps to facilitate their planning.

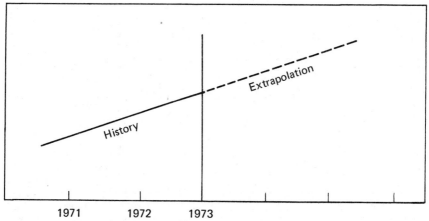

FIGURE 6-1. The Concept of Extrapolation.

General and Specific Forecasts

In addition to forecasts of general business conditions, a great deal of specific and short-run forecasting is done in many organizations. In a firm, for example, the nucleus for this is the sales forecast. After studies of market demand the sales department forecasts the volume of sales it expects to make, usually in a year. Two kinds of data emerge: seasonal variation and secular trends. Seasonal peaks tend to occur annually; secular trends show general economic changes over longer periods. From the sales forecasts, other managers can draw up forecasts of labor requirements, materials required, production schedules, budgets, and direct and indirect costs. These specific forecasts are of course closely geared to the estimates of general economic trends. They are the cornerstones of the activities of the major operating units of the business.

As Figure 6-2 shows, the range of forecasting techniques is large. Some techniques are judgmental and subjective, but for many purposes they are adequate. Model-based forecasting methods may be explanatory or statistical; the latter requires extensive sophistication in the use of computers and advanced quantitative approaches.

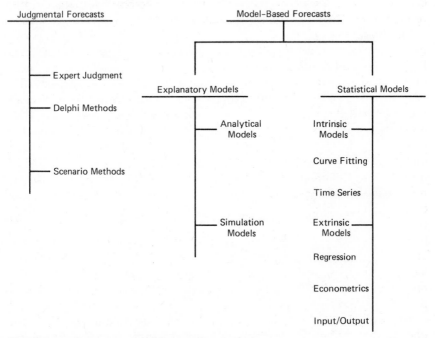

FIGURE 6-2. A Taxonomy of Forecasting Techniques.

Source: William K. Hall, "Forecasting Techniques for Use in the Corporate Planning Process," *Managerial Planning*, November–December 1972, p. 6. Used by permission.

Four conclusions about forecasting can be stated. First, it is clear that equally astute executives, who have the same facts available, reach different conclusions about future conditions, showing that the factors they consider are complex, particularly when chief significance of those factors lies in their combinations and interrelationships. Second, it takes courage and confidence to make a decision involving large sums of money, based on a forecast of general conditions that at best can be only approximately right. Always there is the danger of unforeseeable and unforeseen events that might upset the general forecast. Third, forecasts and expectations have a psychological characteristic: they are contagious. One optimistic forecast tends to breed others. Fourth, the accuracy of general forecasts of trends, like any planning activity, lessens the farther ahead one tries to project the future. A six-month estimate will be more reliable than a five-year one.

Collection and Analysis of Data

A fourth important element in planning is information. Effective planning depends on the quality and quantity of data available to the planner. Planners need to establish reliable sources of information and get the information in a timely manner. The information must be organized, evaluated, and distributed to those who need it. Storage and retrieval systems must be established.

Information is perceived and evaluated differently by the groups or individuals involved in a program, even if accurate information is found. For example, firms in energy industries—coal, oil, gas, and electric power, as well as nuclear power producers—compete with each other; they face long-run, total increases in demand for energy as population increases; they face shortages of supply. They are also enmeshed in complex relationships with the government. The election of a new president, for example, causes change and uncertainty for the energy industry because the government influences it through import quotas, pollution-control policies, mine supervision, public land leases, reserve allowances, price controls, and so on. Moreover, a new administration brings changes in key government posts that make energy policies and decisions. Therefore, the energy supply firms must judge the impact of these extensive changes. Skill is therefore required not only in collecting and organizing information, but also in interpreting facts and drawing conclusions. Knowing what information is relevant, the planner has guidelines for reducing his monitoring efforts to a reasonable level.

Among the economic phenomena watched by managers and other planners are changes in money in circulation, installment credit, department-store sales, freight-car loadings, mortgage loans, business failures, production of steel or other basic commodities, employment levels, stock-market averages, and many other indicators. Many different schemes exist for analyzing these economic indicators, no single one of which is demonstrably superior to any other for specific predictions.

Information used in planning is both internal and external. Internal data consists of records of costs, production, sales, labor requirements, and other strategic matters describing the ongoing situation. Vital internal information also includes knowledge of targets, quotas, objectives, expectations, and the entire network of plans and operational activities. Internal data are provided systematically by periodic or regular reports, special memoranda, and statistics compiled from records. External sources supply information on industry, community, and governmental trends and on general economic conditions. These sources include newspapers, periodicals, trade publications (such as reports from associations to which the company belongs), and the bulletins, newsletters, charts, and documents published by commercial research organizations and the federal government.

A significant factor in the use of information, both for planning and for decision making, is the cost of obtaining and storing it. It is not possible to gauge the need for information accurately, but most organizations tend to overestimate the amounts required. A penalty for over-estimation is the cost of getting and presenting the information, plus the cost of the time required to read, digest, and analyze it. The manner of organizing and presenting data at the point of use also poses problems, for complete data on almost any question may be cumbersome; yet digests or abstracts often leave gaps. Some compromise usually attends the collection, compilation, and use of data, chiefly because of the time and money costs involved. In this area the use of computers has brought many changes.

The Coordination of Plans

The fifth major element in planning is the fact that plans relate to each other vertically and horizontally, leading to problems of coordination. Plans form a hierarchy corresponding approximately to the levels of the organization. That is, plans range from those of a broad, long-run scope, which are primarily the responsibility of those executives at or near the top of an organization, to short-run plans oriented toward day-to-day operating problems being faced by managers at the lower levels in the organization. Figure 6-3 shows a hierarchy of long-range planning, beginning with over-all strategy developed by top management and extending into project plans by operating management.

As one goes from the lower levels of the organization to the higher levels, the scope and coverage of planning tend to become broader and

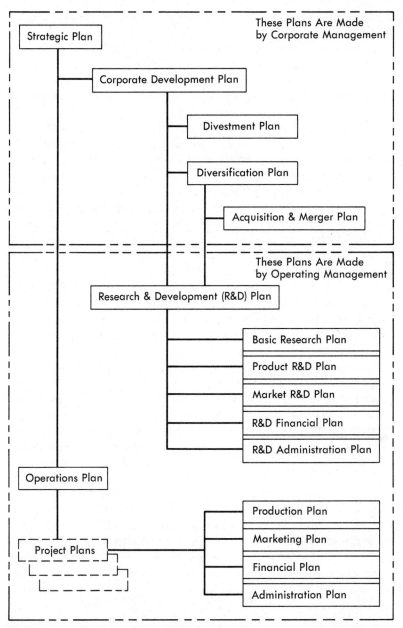

FIGURE 6-3. Elements of a Long-Range Plan, Showing Planning at the Corporate and Operating Levels.

Source: Business Week, June 1, 1963. Copyright 1963. Used by permission.

longer-range. The advantage of visualizing plans arranged in a hierarchy is that they present a better picture of the entire range of planning in an organization, so that the planner can see how a given plan must fit into other existing or contemplated plans. This does not necessarily mean that plans are actually developed in the sequence depicted by the hierarchy, but it does indicate that the end result should be a coordinated whole.

Budgeting procedures provide a useful illustration of the hierarchy of plans. A budget is a device for both planning and controlling the activities within an organization for a given period of time. The planning phase results in the preparation of the budget, based on expected or desired activities. Each unit builds its budget on the budgetary plans of its own subdivisions. Thus each level plans its budget, and the successively higher levels incorporate the budgetary plans of those below. Finally, the over-all budgetary plan can be completed.

Looking at an organization as a whole, we can see that the hierarchy of plans corresponds approximately to the variations of authority and responsibility assigned to the kinds of job within it. Table 6-1 illustrates the different types of planning activity that tend to be concentrated at each of the main levels in an organization.

Another form of coordination relates to time and timing. Long-range planning and short-range planning are two aspects of the same ongoing process. Success depends on integrating the two types. Short-range planning can be successful only if it is carried out in the context of adequate long-range planning, so that shifts in the long-range view may be taken into account in the short-range plans. For example, a telephone company might plan year after year how many miles of telephone wire it will need, but to do so without reference to the long-range possibility that messages in the year 2000 may be transmitted by radio signals rather than by wire might be reckless indeed. Time spans are especially important in governmental organizations, for actions and programs are often tied to annual budgeting, program completion dates, or tenure of elected or appointed administrators

Plans may also succeed or fail depending on timing. The difficulty

TABLE 6-1. Planning Activity by Levels

Level of Organization	Types of Planning
Top management	Goals, policies, long-range plans, companywide sphere
Middle management	Quotas, programs, supplementary goals, policies
Supervisory management	Projects, schedules, short-range goals, supplementary policies, operational planning
Nonmanagerial workers	Work routines and minor procedures only

arises in timing various steps in a particular plan and in fitting a particular plan into the time dimensions of the other plans that are also going forward. The starting and completion of plans must also be related to other complex strategies. For example, the marketing department may be planning an expensive but experimental advertising campaign, only to discover that the finance executives have been planning a cost-cutting drive. Such wasted effort can be prevented if communication and coordination are adequate, but the timing of forward planning is always an intricate problem.

The factors of timing may often be decided by knowledge of necessary lead times for various objectives, based on prior experience. Thus an automobile firm knows the time required to produce a major change in its product, and the associated market factors of seasonality, customer preferences, financial conditions, and similar matters have an important bearing on timing.

It is important to note that plans may originate at any point in the vertical or lateral structure of the organization. Plans initiated by the middle levels become increasingly specific as they move downward but they should unfold in relation to broader plans from higher up. Plans from higher levels are subject to reactions and responses from lower levels. Therefore higher-level plans should be developed with the aid of those below who are affected by or who must execute the plans.

OBSTACLES TO EFFECTIVE PLANNING

The lack of effective planning in many organizations is surprising. Special efforts are needed to assure that planning is rewarded and recognized, and that managers have opportunities to learn and practice the necessary skills. Planning at its best is a habit, a mode of thought that gives attention to future outcomes. Planners cannot be effective as single individuals; the total organization must nurture and emphasize continuous, integrated planning throughout.

The chief obstacles to effective planning can be grouped in two broad categories: (1) administrative problems and (2) human factors.

Administrative Problems

The central administrative problem in planning is to create an organizational climate in which planning thrives. Planning for planning is essential, for it makes clear that planning is expected and facilitated.

In view of the importance of planning, it is strange that not everyone in an organization approves of it. Even those who approve it in principle may inhibit planning without realizing it. Planning is somewhat discredited by a negative reaction to social planning that exists in the United States. Planning failures—which are inevitable—tend to discourage further planning. Plans imposed arbitrarily arouse resistance, as do plans that have involved hard work but then are filed and forgotten. Some administrators feel that planning is useless because it *looks* useless: it often displays little overt physical activity, so that a planner appears to be doing nothing, which runs counter to the old-fashioned concept of keeping all employees busy.

The principal administrative problems lie in the flow of information, the allocation of planning responsibilities, and the matter of the costs of planning.

Information Flows

Planning may be inhibited by lack of sufficient information or by deficiencies in accuracy or quality. As we have seen, managers have access to immense amounts of general information, and such information poses a problem because it must be sifted, organized, interpreted, and related to specific needs. This process entails complex judgments.

The quantity of information, as well as its quality, is partly a function of the time period involved in the planning. The time available for search is limited. A balance has to be struck between acting on inadequate information or not acting at all while waiting for complete information. Experience teaches executives how to judge when they have enough information for a reasonably useful plan and how to know when a plan is shaky by reason of missing knowledge that may still be obtained.

An oversupply of information (information overload) occurs when large amounts of information, relatively unanalyzed or unorganized, are distributed. This often happens when a large corporation centralizes its computers and other information handling systems in the headquarters office to achieve economies of scale. Although there may be advantages to this centralization, subsidiary units may receive much unwanted data and be forced to sift and reprocess data to find and organize what they need. Moreover, with information specialists in the central office, there is a tendency not to employ them in the subsidiary units or at lower levels where the need for them may be as great. This problem can be resolved if the using units make their needs known to the central group, and inform them of the problems they have with data provided.

Once key planning processes and the principal planners are identified, information flow problems can be worked out as part of a total management information system. Distinctions can be made as to what planners need to know and what they would like to know; but what is irrelevant is often difficult to determine.

Authority and Responsibility for Planning

Another obstacle to effective planning is failure to relate the responsibility for individual manager's planning to various types of specialist planning groups. The work of formal planning units necessarily overlaps that of individual planners, who may also be responsible for accomplishing the plans. For example, the personnel department may perform manpower planning work as a staff unit servicing the entire organization. But the production manager is directly concerned with specific operating manpower problems in his unit. If the production manager abdicates his planning responsibility on the grounds that the personnel department is doing it, a valuable effort will be lost. Therefore, the utilization of formal planning groups should integrate their work smoothly into the work of the entire organization.

Planning Costs

A further administrative difficulty is that planning is costly. It requires money, time, and information. Planning costs include not only the salaries of executives who plan, but the costs of false starts that result when planning, as it often will be, is incomplete or incorrect. Costs are incurred in acquiring, storing, and retrieving planning data, and in training planners.

Although planning may be regarded in general as having many payoffs, it often is severely curtailed when economic conditions deteriorate. Those disillusioned with the results of planning are quick to attack it as a waste of money. Planning specialists may be released or reassigned to other work. Plans under way or about to start may be canceled or delayed.

Planning costs are part of overhead, or fixed costs. They must be paid regardless of the organization's productivity levels. The salaries of personnel workers, for example, continue even when workers are not being hired or trained. Organizations can save money by careful control of planning costs.

Opposition to Plans

Even after plans are fully developed and officially approved, resentful organization members may block them or fail to carry them out. Plans may also be blocked or attacked by external dissidents, such as clients, constituents, or the public.

Government organizations often face this kind of problem. Public clamor may interfere with or change the plans after they are announced. For example, the U.S. Postal Service encountered enormous political difficulty with plans to reduce the number of its small uneconomic offices. Military branches experience similar outcries over plans to disestablish major bases. Highway departments encounter difficulty locating highways. Companies can also experience such problems, as when they move their offices from the city to the suburbs, or when the federal government attempts to block a merger plan. These problems can be partly offset by considering external impacts during the early planning stages and prior to the announcement of decisions.

It is important to realize that an individual executive's planning occurs within a limited area of discretion. Forces inside and outside the organization influence the progress of planning as it moves toward the decision-making stage. External forces such as laws, government regulation, trade associations, and the actions of competitors may impede or influence the character of the planning. Internal forces include chiefly the latitude allowed an executive for planning and the amount of resources available for that purpose.

The Human Element

Many inhibitions to planning are psychological, relating to the individual planner. The principal psychological barrier to planning is that managers, like most people, have more regard for the present than for the future. Not only is the present more certain, but it may also be preferable to the unknown.

Resistance to change is common. Planning often depends on the recognition of needed changes that many would prefer to ignore. For example, a manager who is merely told to coach and groom a subordinate for advancement may understandably feel insecure. In planning a merger of two companies, the planners know that their jobs may be in jeopardy. Involvement of those affected and full communication with them helps to reduce this problem.

Planning that lacks consideration for humans and for relations among them runs into difficulties. Planning connotes changes, and change for many produces anxiety. Planners should realize that they cannot make changes solely in tangible arrangements, and that every change affects the relationships among workers, between workers and management, and among managers. For example, the introduction of a new technology for long-wall coal mining in British coal mines caused the realignment of work groups. It broke up long-standing, close-knit work teams and informal groups, leading to dissatisfaction and decreased productivity rather than the increased productivity expected from the new technology.[6] Better planning might have prevented some of these difficulties.

[6]Eric L. Trist et al., *Organizational Choice* (London: Tavistock Publications, 1963).

Another human difficulty in planning is that it is essentially intellectual. A plan is the tangible evidence of the thought process—the ability to manipulate a complex array of variables in their various combinations. Thought requires effort and, furthermore, often involves the painful contemplation of unfortunate and undesirable events, such as past errors. The mental process required by planning is by necessity passive. The manager habituated to action is not favorably inclined to sit at his desk and think.

Planning and strategy formulation require conceptual skill—the ability to recognize how various functions are related to one another and how changes in one affect the others. For example, when a change in financial policy is made, those who see the probable effects on production and personnel management as well as on financial matters can make better decisions.

Creative abilities are always in short supply. They are best drawn forth by relaxed but moderately stimulating atmospheres, although strains, pressures, and tensions may also provoke thought. Mental activity is frequently ridiculed by those who lack respect for it, and some individuals are so sensitive to ridicule that they go to great lengths to avoid being caught thinking.[7]

A final obstacle to planning occurs when plans, once made, are not acted upon. The investment of time and effort seem wasted, and top management appears to have been "crying wolf." Plans should be kept flexible and up to date to prevent them from being unnecessarily filed or scrapped. Where a plan cannot be implemented for unexpected reasons, these reasons should be clearly explained.

METHODS OF EFFECTIVE PLANNING

The third and final main subject of this chapter is that of developing effective planning methods. The following aspects of this problem will be analyzed: (1) criteria for judging the effectiveness of plans, (2) organization for planning, (3) simulation and planning, and (4) participative approaches to planning.

Criteria for Evaluation

Effective planning requires top management direction and support. It also needs an appropriate organizational climate in which planning is made meaningful at all levels. The supreme test of effective planning is

[7]For further information see David W. Ewing, *The Managerial Mind* (New York: Free Press, 1964); see also Ben Heirs and Gordon Pehrson, *The Mind of the Organization* (New York: Harper, 1977). For an excellent analysis of the human aspects of planning see David W. Ewing, *The Human Side of Planning* (New York: Macmillan, 1969).

pragmatic: does it lead to actions that move the organization forward toward choosing and achieving objectives? Within this framework, the following criteria are important:

1. *Objectives* must be clearly defined and properly selected.
2. *Simplicity* is preferable to complexity.
3. *Reward* and *recognition* for planners motivates better planning effort.
4. *Flexibility* should be built in so that plans can be adjusted while they are under way.
5. *Feasibility* standards show the wisdom and reality of plans compared to realistic conditions.
6. *Acceptance* by those affected or who must execute plans is vital.
7. *Completeness* indicates that nothing important will be taken for granted.
8. *Writing* the plans sharpens thought, enhances preparation, provides valuable learning experiences, and aids in the dissemination and follow-up processes.

Because not all elements of a situation are important, and some are more important than others, getting to the heart of problems requiring planning requires raising crucial questions and searching for strategic factors. Typical questions are the following:

1. How long do we have before definite action must be taken?
2. Have we tried anything like this before?
3. What makes this problem so urgent?
4. Why do some departments withhold cooperation in this matter?
5. Who is available to help us work on this?
6. Have we succeeded in defining the real problem?
7. Where can we get more information?
8. How much money do we have available to spend?
9. Who gains and who loses by what is going on?

Organization for Planning

The problems of planning can be handled within the planning process itself. Planning itself must be planned and organized. Although planning is a managerial function and hence the task of every manager, certain types of coordinated, long-range planning in complex organizations require structural and administrative devices to pool and coordinate planning. Among them are the use of (1) central corporate planning groups, and (2) planning specialists.

Central Planning Units

While formal, comprehensive planning groups are relatively new as structural devices in today's organizations, more and more organizations are establishing central planning staffs in their headquarters, with smaller corollary units in branches, divisions, or departments. Schools, hospitals, government units, and trade associations, as well as business firms, increasingly use planning groups of various types.

Planning staff groups often report directly to top management, and frequently to the chief executive. They are headed by persons bearing such titles as "Director of Long-range Planning." The corporate structures of large firms have their counterparts in the various divisions. Central planning groups help to integrate companywide planning efforts, providing guidance and eliminating duplication and overlapping. They initiate broad, strategic, long-range plans, review plans prepared by others, and assist in developmental objectives. Sometimes, particularly in nonbusiness organizations, such planning is done by committees or governing boards.[8]

Central planning staffs, working closely with top management, can greatly increase the scope and intensity of the planning effort. The placement of planning responsibility at this level, and the identification of a specific department, give visibility and prominence to planning activities. Another function of planning groups is to provide leadership, creativity, and innovation. A group removed from operating problems is free to do creative planning, to exploit the processes of inevitable change, and to capitalize on emerging opportunities.

The use of central and corporate planning staffs has certain drawbacks. Confusion and conflict may arise over differences between responsibility for central planning and the planning by divisions and functional specialists. Central market strategies, for example, could conflict with marketing plans in several subsidiary units. To offset this problem, management must carefully coordinate the total planning effort. One facet of such coordination from the top is the specification of objectives. It is also necessary to provide a clear philosophy and motivation from the top. In the Potlach Company, for example, a new president brought in to turn the company's performance around stressed planning and changed the firm's objective of growth by acquisition to growth by getting better at what it already did. He put planning itself on a May-to-October cycle that ended as annual planning began, and set up processes directed at training managers to plan.[9]

Another difficulty of highly centralized planning is that planners below will be tempted to abdicate their responsibility for planning—the "let George do it" philosophy. Again, the remedy is involvement, together with rewards for good planning and the training of managers in planning skills.[10]

[8]George A. Steiner (ed.), *Managerial Long-range Planning* (New York: McGraw-Hill, 1963), pp. 311–326; Frank F. Gilmore and Richard G. Brandenburg, "Anatomy of Corporate Planning," *Harvard Business Review* **40** (November–December 1962), 61–69; *Planning and the Chief Executive* (New York: The Conference Board, 1972).

[9]*Business Week*, November 10, 1975, pp. 129–133.

[10]*Planning and the Corporate Planning Director* (New York: The Conference Board, 1974).

The risks of centralized, long-run strategic planning can be high, and there has been a trend toward caution in corporate planning. For example, the General Electric Company reduces the dangers by taking risks in bite sizes. Rather than single ventures of major dimensions, the company's entrepreneurship consists of smaller projects in larger numbers.[11]

Planning by Specialists

Much of the planning in organizations is assigned to units set up as staff groups in specific functional areas, such as personnel management or research and development. Frederick W. Taylor's early concept of functional foremanship included the idea of separating out all the planning activities from the work of foremen and assigning those activities to persons who would specialize in the type of planning called for. Although functional foremanship did not prove practicable, the principle of separating the planning work and assigning it to specialized units appears in modern organizations in the form of departments organized on a staff basis.

The creation of staff units to aid in planning provides the advantages of specialization and the allocation of specific resources to planning, but not without a price. Separating planning from doing has in many cases gone too far, creating confusion as to the responsibility for ultimate results. Moreover, removing the planning from the actual work activity tends to rob the work of interest and meaning to the individuals involved. It is impossible to separate *all* planning from the job of doing something, and planning is done most effectively by involving those who are to carry out the plans. Removing planning from the persons who do the work decreases motivation and leads to abdication. In matters that are broader than any single responsibility—those involving companywide problems—specialized planning is desirable despite its drawbacks. In narrow areas of responsibility, however, executives can do a large share of their own planning. For example, it is wise to organize the personnel department as a separate, specialized planning unit because of the need for uniform personnel practices throughout the company. On the other hand, it may be better to organize market planning in the marketing department, for not to do so would constitute an unnatural division of the responsibility.

Simulation and Planning

The simulation techniques discussed in Chapter 5 are useful in planning and development. *Game simulation* is a suggested technique for

[11]*Business Week*, April 28, 1975, pp. 46–54.

helping planners determine which action will improve a system's performance. Game simulation represents a combination of business games, which are relatively unstructured, and traditional computer simulation, which is rigidly controlled. The technique was developed by the Rand Corporation to help the U.S. Air Force with management planning; it has the advantage of incorporating the human element (managerial actions) into the model of a future organization, project, or other management system, thus yielding better predictions. When various decisions and actions are put into the simulation model, managerial systems can be experimentally changed. The managers can undergo training and development before actual changes are made. Much can then be predicted about the behavior of executives and about whether executives will function better or worse than someone thinks, or how to divide responsibilities of managerial decision between headquarters and field groups. Game simulation, however, has certain limitations. One is that it tends to involve the participation of large numbers of executives over long periods of time, and hence it can be more costly than all-computer simulation techniques.

The output of simulation models is used chiefly by senior managers. Researchers found that in at least half of the 346 firms they surveyed, the outputs were utilized by top managers. Other users were model builders or the sponsors of simulation projects. The models were used mainly for financial planning, control, and review, and most were based on a deterministic, "what-if" model.[12]

Participative Approaches to Planning

Some organizations foster a kind of participative management, emphasizing the importance of ideas, suggestions, feelings, and opinions from the appropriate members of the organization. This process facilitates planning by keynoting problem areas and by bringing more resources to bear on them. Committees, group discussions, suggestion systems, and opinion surveys help provide a system of pooled thinking that can stimulate improved planning. In addition, such participation increases the understanding and acceptance of plans and improves the search for information. Those who are affected can contribute points of view that are not known to the planner, and can prevent disaster or the lack of success of a plan by suggesting something overlooked by the fact-gathering process. Just as valuable is the feeling of dignity and importance that people get from being consulted.

Top executives cannot possibly be familiar enough with operating

[12]Naylor and Mansfield, "Corporate Planning Models," pp. 8–12. For further analysis of applications to planning, see James L. McKenney, "An Approach to Simulation Model Development for Improved Planning," Fall Joint Computer Conference, Vol. 38, Part I, 1968, American Federation of Information Processing Societies Press.

conditions and problems to be able to make a final and complete determination of plans. Managers who are close to actual operations are sensitive to problems and bottlenecks that hinder their work. They see the need for plans that will help them work their way out of the unsatisfactory conditions. In this way, a connection is made in management between the broad, high-level planning of top executives and the planning behavior of the managers at the lower levels of the business.

Plans imposed on managers by higher echelons often incur resentment and resistance among those forced to accept a plan made elsewhere. Budgeting supplies a good example. A common reaction to the annual budget preparation is that it is a waste of time. When the final version is submitted, people sigh with relief and hope not to be bothered until next year. Using persuasive and educational tactics rather than pressure or force helps minimize this problem. The budget becomes a tool for better planning and for the improvement of operations, generating fuller cooperation in the planning, and creating working documents that are useful throughout the planning period.

SUMMARY

Planning is a managerial function that helps provide purpose and direction for the members of an organization. It is also a problem, for planning must be coordinated throughout the enterprise, and certain types of plans require the efforts of planning groups rather than of individuals.

The central element in planning is the constant fact of change. Change brings about the need for planning and affects the nature of the planning. Administrators can stimulate planning by providing conditions and motivations that are conducive to it. These conditions include (1) the budgeting of time, money, and other resources; (2) free and open channels of information and communication; (3) attention to developing skills and procedures involved in planning; and (4) rewards for effective planning.

In this chapter we have considered four major themes in planning: (1) what it is, (2) who does it, (3) obstacles to effective planning, and (4) examples of planning methods, including those of staff specialists and central planning departments. The following chapters will elaborate on the concept of planning by considering objectives and policies.

INCIDENT CASE

"Planning should be very important in government agencies," said the city manager of a large suburb near a metropolitan city. Therefore he issued the following memorandum to all city officials:

Beginning on January 1, 1979, all managers and supervisors will set aside the hour between 4:00 to 5:00 P.M. for the purpose of planning. Each one is to clear his desk of all work at 4:00, in order to concentrate on the development of ideas, plans, and suggestions for improvement. All but the most urgent matters should be held until the next morning. I will be in touch with each of you concerning the planning effort.

Question:

1. What is wrong with the city manager's thinking?

QUESTIONS FOR STUDY

1. What is planning? What is executive or managerial planning? Are there any differences?

2. What considerations give rise to the need for planning in an organization?

3. Does the size of the business make any difference as to whether planning is important or not? What are the reasons for your position? Is planning done differently in large firms and in small ones?

4. Specify some of the administrative costs involved in planning.

5. What controls would you advocate to keep excessive time and money from being devoted to planning?

6. Suppose you were running an engineering or scientific laboratory and you wanted conditions there to encourage planning. What conditions would you establish?

7. What kinds of executives in a business organization do the planning? Cite some examples, giving as much detail as you can about their work.

8. How does planning differ at the supervisory level, as compared to planning done by the vice-president in charge of divisions or departments? What are the relationships?

9. What are the tools most useful to executives in planning?

10. Outline the main hindrances to the planning process. How can these be minimized or guarded against?

SELECTED REFERENCES

ACKOFF, RUSSELL L. *A Concept of Corporate Planning.* New York: John Wiley & Sons, Inc., 1970.

ACKOFF, RUSSELL L. *Redesigning the Future: A Systems Approach to Societal Problems.* New York: John Wiley & Sons, Inc., 1974.

ANSOFF H. I., R. P. DECLERCK, and R. L. HAYES, eds. *From Strategic Planning to Strategic Management.* New York: John Wiley & Sons, Inc., 1976.

ANTHONY, ROBERT N. *Planning and Control Systems: A Framework for Analysis.* Boston: Division of Research, Graduate School of Business Administration, Harvard University, 1965.

ARGENTI, J. *Systematic Corporate Planning.* New York: John Wiley & Sons, Inc., 1974.

BOULDEN, JAMES. *Computer Assisted Planning Systems: Management Concept, Application, and Implementation.* New York: McGraw-Hill Publishing Company, 1975.

BUTLER, WILLIAM F., ROBERT A. KAVESH, and ROBERT B. PLATT, eds. *Methods and Techniques of Business Forecasting.* Englewood Cliffs, N.J.: Prentice-Hall, Inc., 1974.

CHAMBER, JOHN C., ATINDEREZ K. MOLLICK, and DONALD D. SMITH. *An Executive Guide to Forecasting.* New York: John Wiley & Sons, Inc., 1974.

COTTON, DONALD B. *Company-Wide Planning: Concept and Process.* New York: Macmillan Publishing Co., Inc., 1970.

EMERY, JAMES C. *Organizational Planning and Control Systems: Theory and Technology.* New York: Macmillan Publishing Co., Inc., 1969.

HEIRS, DON, and GORDON PEHRSON. *The Mind of the Organization.* New York: Harper & Row, Publishers, 1977.

HUSSEY, DAVID. *Corporate Planning: Theory and Practice.* Oxford: Pergamon Press, Inc., 1974.

ISHIKAWA, AKIRA. *Corporate Planning and Control Model Systems.* New York: New York University Press, 1975.

JONES, HARRY. *Preparing Company Plans: A Workbook for Effective Corporate Planning.* New York: John Wiley & Sons, Inc., 1974.

KASTENS, MERRITT L. *Long-Range Planning for Your Business.* New York: AMACOM, 1976.

KING, WILLIAM R., and DAVID I. CLELAND. *Strategic Planning and Policy.* New York: Petrocelli/Charter, 1977.

LORANGE, PETER, and RICHARD F. VANCIL. *Strategic Planning Systems.* Englewood Cliffs, N.J.: Prentice-Hall, Inc., 1977.

MARGERISON, CHARLES J. *Managerial Problem Solving.* New York: McGraw-Hill Book Company, 1974.

NEWMAN, WILLIAM H. *Administrative Action.* 2nd ed. Englewood Cliffs, N.J.: Prentice-Hall, Inc., 1963. Chapters 2–6.

O'CONNOR, ROCHELLE. *Corporated Guides to Long-Range Planning.* New York: The Conference Board, 1976.

RANDOLPH, ROBERT M. *Plan Management: Moving Concept Into Reality.* New York: AMACOM, 1975.

SCHEER, WILBERT E. *How to Develop an Effective Company Growth Plan: The Fundamentals of Corporate Long- and Short-Range Planning.* Chicago: Dartnell Corporation, 1975.

STEINER, GEORGE A. *Top Management Planning.* New York: Macmillan Publishing Co., Inc., 1969.

WARREN, E. KIRBY. *Long-Range Planning.* Englewood Cliffs, N.J.: Prentice-Hall, Inc., 1966.

WHEELWRIGHT, STEVEN C. *Forecasting Methods for Management.* New York: Wiley-Interscience, 1973.

———, ed. *Managerial Long-Range Planning.* New York: McGraw-Hill Book Company, 1963.

———, and WARREN M. CANNON. *Multinational Corporate Planning.* New York: Macmillan Publishing Co., Inc., 1966.

Chapter 7

Objectives

A fanatic is one who redoubles his energy as he loses sight of his aim.
—*Santayana*

Perfection of means and confusion of goals seem—in my opinion—to characterize our age. . . .
—*Albert Einstein*

It is a paradoxical but profoundly true and important principle of life that the most likely way to reach a goal is to be aiming not at that goal itself but at some more ambitious goal behind it. . . .
—*Arnold Toynbee*

CHAPTER GUIDE

A large manufacturing firm listed seven goals it wished to achieve. One of them was "to maximize the value of the shareholders' investment in the company over the long term." Another was "to have fun."

Questions to keep in mind while reading this chapter:

1. How would you evaluate these two objectives from the point of view of (a) merit, (b) clarity, and (c) legitimacy?

The selection, definition, identification, interpretation, and pursuit of objectives are basic for effective management. Carefully planned objectives serve to integrate and coordinate the complex activities of the organization, and reflect the caliber of that organization's leadership. Knowledge of objectives transforms otherwise random behavior into logical, effective action.

This chapter details the problems and methods of developing and attaining objectives in organizations of all types, including business, educational, governmental, and voluntary organizations.

OBJECTIVES DEFINED

Objectives are the results that organizations expect to achieve. They are related to the future in the sense that their attainment is distant in time and hence must be the subject of careful planning. Some objectives are broad and long-range, such as those specified in a corporate charter. Others are immediate and specific. Still others are in the intermediate range. Like plans, objectives are related vertically in a hierarchy, according to the level at which they are being implemented. As objectives are elaborated, they become more complex, with a tendency to be in conflict or to overlap. The pursuit of multiple objectives with differing degrees of importance at different times poses problems for managers.

The need for planning of objectives is continuous, but it is intensified at times of organizational crisis. For example, in a severe economic cutback, a firm may have to cancel building plans or postpone research efforts. A fund-raising agency may have to limit its efforts. A school may have to delay the expansion of its faculty.

The words *aim, goal, mission, objective,* and *purpose* are often used interchangeably, with little attempt to differentiate their meanings. Some distinctions, however, will give a clearer picture of the processes of management with respect to the results sought by organizations.

The word *mission* is a general term describing an organization's fundamental reason for existence. It implies considerable idealism with respect to objectives. Missions are based on the need for strong commitments by organization members, and typically call for impossible or very difficult results. For example, labor unions have the mission of "organizing the unorganized and representing the organized workers." thus emphasizing the solidarity of members and the mobilization of forces toward ultimate purposes. A mission reflects the nature of an organization's basic long-run commitment, helping to establish its identity and direction. The concept of mission is more widely used in nonbusiness organizations than in business firms. Government programs for fighting poverty, unemployment, or pollution problems are examples. Regulatory bodies have a mission of control. The school's mission is to educate succeeding generations of people to live in a complex society.

Many organizations state their missions in writing; others use informal methods, such as statements by the president. Most declarations of the organizational mission are very broad, reflecting values, beliefs, and a philosophy of management. Some are stated as company creeds. The following statement by a company president is representative:

> We want to render values, usually new ones that men have not enjoyed before. . . . We want to be part of an industry that gives men something worth getting . . . to add new dimensions to the ways they communicate . . . to make increasing knowledge more broadly useful.[1]

Gross provides some useful definitions. He does not mention missions, but he ranks purposes, objectives, goals, and norms, in order of increasing specificity. He regards *purpose* as an all-inclusive term referring to any commitments to desired future situations. An *objective* is a specific category of purpose that includes the attainment by an organization of certain states or conditions, such as the satisfaction of the interests of organization members, the production of goods and services, efficiency, the mobilization of resources, rationality, and the observance of codes or disciplines behavior. A *goal* is even more specific than an objective or purpose—an objective expressed in terms of one or more specific dimensions, such as the quantity or quality of production, or costs per unit of output. Finally, he uses the term *norm* to indicate a goal having a cardinal or an ordinal value or a rough order of magnitude, such as increasing production by 20 units per man hour per week. When used to evaluate individual performance, a norm becomes a standard.[2]

Figure 7-1 provides a visual description of how the key concepts of planning and objectives are related to each other and to charters, policies, philosophies, and creeds. The hierarchy of objectives is shown, along with the relationship between long-range and short-range objectives, and between general and operating objectives.

The Advantages of Objectives

Clearly objectives provide a basis for planning and for the coordinating of the many persons who work together in organizations.

Careful planning helps managers give organization members the sense of direction and purpose that is essential to effective results. One of the primary responsibilities of managers is to point out what accomplishments they expect from their subordinates. Energy, time, and

---

[1] Reprinted by permission of the publisher from AMA Research Study No. 74, *Objectives and Standards: An Approach to Planning and Control,* by Ernest C. Miller. © 1966 by the American Management Association.

[2] Bertram M. Gross, *Organizations and Their Managing* (New York: Free Press, 1968), p. 292.

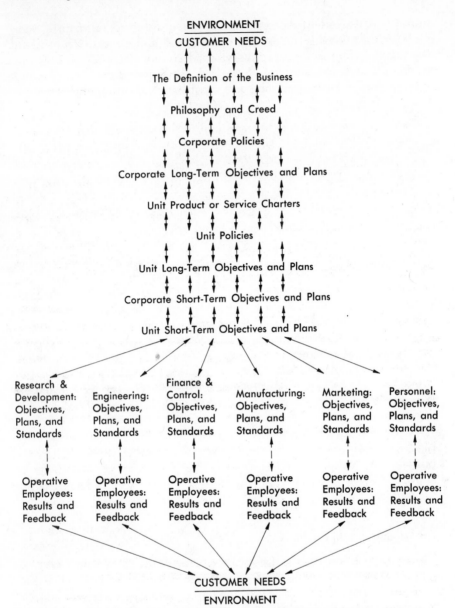

FIGURE 7-1. Relationship Among Planning, Objectives, Policies, and Standards in a Business Enterprise.

Source: Reprinted by permission of the publisher from AMA Research Study No. 74, *Objectives and Standards: An Approach to Planning and Control,* by Ernest C. Miller. © 1966 by the American Management Association.

money are wasted when individuals pursue objectives of their own choosing. It is costly to let the parts of an organization veer off in different directions, uncoordinated and uncontrolled. Objectives are the focal points around which managers mold the efforts of their team.

Among the specific benefits of sound, carefully chosen objectives are the following:

1. *They embody the basic ideas and fundamental theories as to what the organization is trying to accomplish.* The work of the people associated with the business must have meaning and direction. It is dangerous to assume that the organization's objectives will be understood automatically. If they are expressly formulated they provide evidence that top management has performed its planning responsibility.
2. *They serve to identify the organization and to link it to the groups upon which its existence depends.* An organization does not exist apart from groups that have an interest in it, such as customers or workers. It needs to emphasize its individuality and to clearly exhibit its *raison d'être.* One business, for example, describes itself as "The World's Best Motel," and by so doing invites the customer to draw comparisons. An objective forthrightly expressed reflects the uniqueness of a firm within its industry.
3. *They provide a basis for guiding, leading, and directing an organization.* The objectives serve as targets for which people strive. Progress toward the objectives can be observed and used to influence further efforts.
4. *They provide standards that aid in the control of human effort in an organization.* The evaluation of current efforts requires observations of the degree to which selected objectives are being attained.
5. *They help motivate people.* Objectives stimulate productive responses from subordinates, who are better able to release their energies toward constructive ends. Individuals have a framework into which to fit their personal aims. Objectives help provide the sense of unity, harmony, and accomplishment that are essential for cooperative effort.

GENERAL OBJECTIVES

Top executives determine the over-all objectives that the members of an organization try to achieve. Governing boards, trustees, boards of directors, and executive committees approve, authenticate, and disseminate the objectives. In this function they are guided by the chairman of the board or the president in the performance of their leadership roles. Any of these persons or groups may initiate a change in objectives or propose new objectives. They also monitor, and approve or disapprove, subordinate objectives developed at lower levels in support of the major ones.

General objectives are the broad aims that the total organization pursues. They are long-run in nature. For example, Drucker has indicated basic objectives for eight key areas that affect performance and results: market standing, innovation, productivity, physical and financial resources, profitability, manager performance and development, worker performance and attitudes, and public responsibility. Developing key objectives enables managers to (1) organize and explain the whole range of business phenomena in a small number of general statements, (2) test those statements in actual experience, (3) predict behavior, (4) appraise the soundness of decisions when they are still being made, and (5) analyze their own experiences and, as a result, improve their performance.[3]

Certain long-range objectives are common to all organizations, although from time to time the emphasis may shift. The following sections will analyze survival, growth, social obligations, and profit making.

Survival

Although some organizations are temporary, and are terminated when their aims are accomplished, survival is a basic objective of most organizations. It is not always explicitly stated, because it is the minimum possible objective. An example of the survival objective of one large company is "To conduct throughout the world, under all economic and political conditions consistent with the corporate nature of the company, a profitable, continuous, independent business in the manufacture and sale of. . . ."

For a company, the ability to survive is the ability to earn profits sufficient to attract outside capital, which in our economy depends in turn upon the company's selling its products and services at a competitive price for a given standard of quality. Survival depends upon the ability to cover the costs of staying in business. Survival thus represents the minimum conditions under which owners of resources will continue to employ them in that particular way. Survival is a function of (1) general business conditions in the economy as a whole, (2) the financial strength developed by the company, (3) factors applying to the health of its industry, and (4) the management skills applied by the firm's executives. An upswing in the general level of business activity, a cushion of

---

[3]Peter F. Drucker, *The Practice of Management* (New York: Harper, 1954), p. 63.

strong financial resources, and the development of management teams contribute to the chances of survival. In addition, the industry of which the firm is a part must be a surviving one: no amount of management skill could prevent a buggy-whip manufacturer from going out of business along with the whole industry, without a change in objectives.

Survival is particularly urgent during adverse economic conditions. When survival is relatively assured, managers choose objectives that far exceed mere survival. Organizations whose survival is threatened often find it possible to continue in some other form by reorganizing or selecting new objectives. Marginal firms may be the targets of merger or acquisition plans of other companies, or they may fail.

In nonbusiness organizations, survival is also important, but the criteria are more elusive. In companies, the organization ends when assets are liquidated to satisfy creditors, or when legal steps dissolve the firm. In nonbusiness organizations, survival does not depend on profits but rather on the accomplishment of a mission, the disappearance of purpose, or the absence of funding. However, such organizations often survive by changing their purposes, acquiring new missions, and finding new funding. Tenacity and endurance are strong qualities in both business and nonbusiness organizations. They fight hard to survive.[4]

A new development in public organizations is that the federal government and many state legislatures are considering the enactment of "sunset" laws that periodically require bureaus, agencies, and departments to expire unless they can justify their continuation.

Growth

Growth is a key objective in most organizations. Some managers say that an organization cannot stand still—it must either move forward or die. Some firms, however, deliberately limit their output and growth; for example, Steuben Glass limits the quantity of its products to maintain their prestige and value as art objects. A school or college department limiting its enrollment to maintain quality education is another example. The Hewlett-Packard Company has pursued a slow-growth policy rather than a price policy aimed at increasing its share of the market for electronic instruments; according to the board chairman, the firm should concentrate on developing products so advanced that customers will pay a premium for them.[5]

Goals of size are measured by number of employees, amount of capital invested, net value of assets, dollar volume of sales, quantities of

[4]For an excellent analysis of the phenomenon of organizational mortality, see Herbert Kaufman, *The Limits of Organizational Change* (University: University of Alabama Press, 1971).

[5]*Business Week,* June 1975, pp. 50–58.

raw materials processed, gross or net value of assets, dollar volume of sales, quantities of raw materials processed, gross or net profits, production and marketing capacities, or combinations of these elements. Galbraith asserts that firms try to achieve the greatest possible rate of corporate growth, as measured by sales. He argues that such a goal is a buffer against contraction, which is painful to the corporate enterprise, and that it also provides for expansion of the jobs, opportunities, and pecuniary rewards of the managers themselves. Hence the goal of growth takes precedence over that of profit maximization.[6] However, it is more realistic to view the firm as pursuing a number of related goals simultaneously.

Growth is affected by external conditions as well as by internal management practice. For example, growth may be influenced by strategic factors affecting the market position of a company and the nature of its product. In planning its future, therefore, a company must take into account changes in economic, political, and social factors in the environment, translating these changes into market opportunities.

Growth can be considered along five dimensions: (1) local operation, (2) small territory operation, (3) large territory operation, (4) national operation, and (5) international operation. Each organization faces such limiting factors as the nature of its product or service and of current or possible markets. For example, stores, warehouses, or repair shops operate best in local or territory patterns. Companies providing unique, differentiated, quality products for mass consumption, such as autos, watches, tires, or books, operate typically on a national or international scale. For some kinds of technology, such as steel manufacturing, autos, or chemicals, minimum size is determined by the economics of scale that are inherent in the technologies.

Nonbusiness organizations, too, seek growth, for typically they provide much-needed services in which economic considerations are secondary to the imperatives of the services themselves. Thus hospitals may provide services for which they receive little or no payment. The Salvation Army gives food and comfort to the indigent, covering the costs by obtaining donations from the more affluent in society. Schools receive fixed appropriations for which they try to provide as much educational service as possible. Growth in such organizations depends on their ability to raise funds from such sources as donors, appropriating agencies, and membership dues. Growth may be limited also by technological factors or by public coordinating agencies. Hospitals, for example, may have to secure the permission of local health planning agencies before adding beds, space, or equipment.

Growth can bring problems as well as benefits. Rapid growth may

[6]John Kenneth Galbraith, *The New Industrial State* (Boston: Houghton Mifflin, 1967), pp. 171–178.

enlarge the scope of activities and interests so extensively that the abilities of managers are no longer adequate for control, effectiveness, and profitability. The growth of business organizations raises the problem of monopolies and the domination of markets by giant corporations. Large corporations bent on expansion may face action under the antitrust laws. In addition to legal matters, there is the further question of whether there are any practical criteria for establishing how big a company should get. The criteria for judging whether a company has achieved a size harmful to the public interest or has become too unwieldy to be efficient are not clear.

Even though we grant that there may be limits to efficiency and to the public welfare in unrestrained growth, the phenomenon of growth itself is a powerful motivating influence on organization members. An environment of growth stimulates creativity, ingenuity, morale, and opportunities for progress in the careers of individuals. Growth is a matter of pride to managers. Figure 7-2 shows four dimensions of growth in the Clark Equipment Company—size, net income, cash dividends, and net worth. Note also that growth has been very steady over a twenty-year period.

Social Obligations

The long-range goals of an organization inevitably focus upon its contributions to the needs of society, tangible and intangible. Its contribution may be in terms of goods or of services, or both. The nature and extent of these contributions may change from time to time, as society or the organization perceive shifting demands and needs.

In recent years, organizations have given increasing attention to broad social obligations, at local, national, or international levels. This trend is attributable in part to the natural affinity of organizations for

		Average Annual Performance Amounts in Thousands		
Period	Sales	Net Income	Cash Dividends	Period-End Net Worth
1956–58	$ 143,689	$ 8,026	$ 4,962	$ 57,953
1959–61	192,758	8,930	5,628	70,620
1962–64	280,426	16,678	7,042	101,464
1965–67	479,987	25,712	11,012	154,667
1968–70	615,465	33,938	15,668	210,884
1971–73	923,710	41,551	18,987	321,142
1974–76	1,352,049	54,935	22,247	415,870

FIGURE 7-2. Growth Data for the Clark Equipment Company, 1956–1976.
Courtesy of Clark Equipment Company, *Annual Report,* 1976.

relationships in the community or in society which help to meet their needs. Organizations need an environment that is safe from crime, is clean, and is well governed by responsible officials. They need good transportation, and communications systems, churches, schools, and social agencies, so that they can attract and hold good employees. But the needs are reciprocal: public agencies also need the help and cooperation of all types of organizations.

The importance of social obligations in organizational goals has been spurred by an increasingly demanding public clamor for various reforms. These pressures have arisen to meet several social problems such as crime, inequality, urban decay, or environmental pollution. The public acts through governmental means to regulate organizational activities and to achieve prevention and improvement. Thus special organizations, such as the Equal Employment Opportunity Commission, have social goals as their primary reason for existence.

Organizations meet social obligations in several ways. One is philanthropy, but philanthropy depends on some degree of affluence plus the desire to assist others. Another way is being "a good citizen." Many organizations encourage members to be active in civic affairs, often at company expense. But the severity and complexity of social problems will require in the future a much more active involvement in finding solutions. This matter and related ones will be discussed more fully in Chapter 24.

Profit Making

The acceptance of social responsibilities does not require the substitution of philanthropy for profit. To conduct a business in the light of social purpose and the full range of human needs is not only compatible with profits, but indeed may even be essential to them.

Profit lies at the core of business activity, but as an objective it is too general and diffuse. It is also misconstrued as an objective that managers seek to maximize. On the contrary: managers do not try to maximize profit as a sole objective. They must consider profit along with other objectives and with the long-run interests of the business. The vital functions of profits include assuring the amount needed for safety and survival and for attracting future supplies of capital, or of providing it through earnings.

Profits provide only a rough measure of the effectiveness of organizational effort and the competence of managers. Many forms of organizational behavior are unrelated to profit making. There are no objective standards by which to judge various degrees of profitability, or the nature of the efforts that produce it. Profit may be greatly affected by conditions not directly within the control of managers.

The *profit objective* is often confused with the *profit motive*. We have little trouble visualizing the economic functions of profit and its role in the survival of a business. The profit *motive* is much less well understood. In a general way, opportunities for profit may stimulate the efforts of individuals, but the nature and degree of these efforts vary, and the complex conditions underlying motivation through financial gain are not clear. Indeed, the chance to make additional profit may stimulate less prodigious efforts than will the imminence of catastrophic failure.

_____ **SPECIFIC OBJECTIVES**

Within the framework of over-all objectives stated in general terms, managers must determine the specific objectives that they and their units of organization seek to attain. Specific objectives tend to be—but are not necessarily—short-range in character; and they also tend to have definite time limits within which executives expect to attain them. For example, a specific objective might be to open a branch store in a new suburb by a certain deadline. The following are examples of other specific objectives for various types of organizations:

A. Companies
   1. To diversify the line of products.
   2. To reorganize the firm.
   3. To liquidate an unprofitable division.
   4. To establish market contacts abroad.
B. Trade Associations
   1. To increase the number of member companies.
   2. To lobby for or against a bill in Congress.
   3. To launch a management development program for member firms.
C. Government
   1. To adopt a new city ordinance.
   2. To launch a consumer assistance program.
   3. To establish a new bureau.
D. Schools
   1. To establish an in-service teacher training program.
   2. To secure increased research funds.

The more clearly and succinctly specific objectives can be stated, the more readily they can be worked into the fabric of the organizational effort. Stating specific objectives in writing and disseminating them properly permit plans to be built for their achievement.

Specific objectives arise out of, and are related to, broad general objectives and the basic strategies of the organization. For example, in pursuing the objective of diversifying its line of products, a company needs to keep carefully focused on the definition of its business to make sure it stays within the realm of its capabilities. For example, a supermarket that defines its goal as "selling food and household items" might be cautious about adding lines of clothing or furniture.

In addition to organizational objectives both general and specific, managers have personal objectives—for to be human is to have objectives. Personal objectives are both general and specific. "Living a good life" is a general one; "getting promoted next year" is specific. It is important that insofar as possible the personal goals of organization members be in harmony with organizational goals, so that the same actions bring about both sets of goals. This is an ideal situation, a goal to strive for but never completely attainable. Personal goals are often largely hidden or kept subservient to organizational goals. They are often implicit in the manager's behavior, rather than being overtly expressed.

EFFECTIVE MANAGEMENT OF OBJECTIVES

One of the primary functions of managers is to specify clearly the goals for their group and its members. Broad organizational goals must be translated into specific aims to guide their efforts. As leaders, their task is to blend the specific and several objectives into an integrated pattern.

The over-all pattern of goals consists of a hierarchy that corresponds roughly to the levels of an organization. The approach to goal management needs to vary at the different levels. At the top levels, goals are broader, more strategic, and of longer range. At the middle and supervisory levels, goals are less strategic and increasingly related to operations. At the level of the individual organization member, goals are almost entirely operational. The following sections will explore the management of goals according to problems of (1) strategy, (2) evaluation, (3) multiple goals, (4) acceptance, (5) changes, and (6) individual goals and MBO programs.

Strategies

Strategy is defined as behavior whose purpose is to achieve success for organizational or personal goals in a competitive environment, based on the actual or probable actions of others—chiefly rivals, market competitors, suppliers, customers, employees, and governmental units—and on probable events occurring in the organization's environment. Strategy includes the choosing of goals, the unpredictability and uncertainty of events, and the need to adjust tactics to the probable or actual behavior of others, principally opponents or competitors.

Strategies should be distinguished from tactics. Tactics are actions based on the executive's judgment and experience in a strategic situation calling for a decision. By contrast, strategy involves planning for possible alternatives; setting policies, standards, and objectives; and making decisions that indicate what tactical decisions should be made. Strategy helps remove uncertainty from the choice of tactics. Strategic plans provide constraints over the tactical behavior of managers. As strategies develop over time, they become institutionalized and known to outsiders, calling for further work on both strategy and tactics.[7]

Moore indicates that elements of unpredictability, chance, risk, incomplete knowledge, extraneous influences, and the sheer complexity of operations constitute both a source of opportunity and a source of insecurity for the manager. The purposeful manager can pick strategies that help establish advantageous relationships with the internal and external environment, with a consequent reduction in risk and insecurity.[8]

Types of Strategies

The patterns of goal-directed activities reflect a strategic posture for the organization with respect to the actions and strategies of other organizations or groups. Managers choose or modify strategies in response to forces both inside and outside the organization. Strategies may be explicit or implicit. Implied strategies exist in all courses of action or inaction. The knowledge of deliberate strategies is often kept restricted to limited numbers of persons, for their revelation to or perception by opponents would limit or destroy their value. Restricted strategies become known, and hence become explicit strategies, after observers take note of managerial or company behavior and deduce the strategy from it. Both the implied and the explicit strategies require continuous adjustments dictated by changes in the internal and external environments. Hence the selection of strategies involves predictions about future events and the probably behavior of the organization.

Moore presents a useful classification of company strategies, consisting of three types: (1) external economic strategies, (2) external social strategies, and (3) internal organizational strategies.[9] External economic strategies relate the company to economic and technological elements of its environment—particularly those having to do with sources of capital, raw materials, tools, and equipment—and also to its customers. These strategies center upon inputs and outputs and define the company's economic activities and contributions.

Relationships with the community at large, including government units, public welfare associations, and the general public, generate the

[7]Sherrill Cleland, "Toward a Managerial Theory of the Firm," in Kenneth E. Boulding and W. Allen Spivey (eds.), *Linear Programming and the Theory of the Firm* (New York: Macmillan, 1960), pp. 208–215.

[8]David G. Moore, "Managerial Strategies," in W. Lloyd Warner and Norman H. Martin, *Industrial Man* (New York: Harper, 1959), p. 219.

[9]Ibid., p. 224.

company's external social strategies. The company desires to fulfill its obligations to stakeholders and also to maintain the economic, social, and political rights and privileges to which it is entitled.

Finally, those strategies that define or describe how a company allocates and uses its resources to accomplish its objectives are the internal organizational strategies. Examples of such strategies are the development of organization structures; personnel assignments; plans for the use of labor, tools, and equipment; and the distribution of authority.

Strategies and Organization Structure

The organization's structural design is, among other things, an instrument of corporate strategy. Thompson and Tuden have presented a significant typology based on the interrelationships of objectives, strategy, decision, and organization structure. They assert that decisions made in an organization depend on (1) the extent of agreement on objectives, and (2) whether cause-and-effect relationships are known, so that agreement is possible on how to attain the objectives. Combinations of these two factors yield four types of decision strategies and organization patterns:

1. *Computational strategies.* If there is agreement on both the objectives and the methods of attaining them, decisions can be based on rational calculations. This is the foundation for a rational, formal, bureaucratic organization structure, following the Weber model.
2. *Judgmental strategies.* If there is agreement on objectives but cause-and-effect relationships are not well known, judgmental strategies employing the use of insight will be used. The preferred organizational type is that of a colleague group or self-governing board, such as the board of directors of a company.
3. *Compromise strategies.* If there is agreement on how to achieve objectives, but the priorities among objectives are in dispute, compromise strategies make action possible. This situation is typical in representative bodies, such as legislatures.
4. *Inspirational strategies.* If there is little or no agreement on either objectives or how to achieve them, inspirational strategies may produce action and decision. This situation occurs where there is little or no formal organization to foster the decision process.[10]

[10]James D. Thompson and Arthur Tuden, "Strategies, Structures, and Processes of Organizational Decision," in James D. Thompson, et al. (eds.), *Comparative Studies in Administration* (Pittsburgh: University of Pittsburgh Press, 1959), pp. 195–216. See also Alfred D. Chandler, Jr., *Strategy and Structure* (Cambridge, Mass.: The MIT Press, 1962).

Evaluating and Choosing Objectives

In their role as leaders, managers must help subordinates see the differences in emphasis desired for objectives of varying importance. The leader has the responsibility for pointing out which objectives are primary and which are secondary and of keeping subordinates aware of changes. For example, a department manager in a large store would not wish to have a clerk refuse a reasonable refund to a customer to keep his sales record intact. The manager could explain that a higher goal— long-range profitability based on favorable customer attitudes—is preferable to protecting the record. The choice among alternative objectives to be emphasized cannot be left to subordinates alone, although they may provide valuable inputs.

Standards for measuring goal achievement can be more readily specified for operational goals than for strategic goals. Making a 10 per cent gain in sales is more measurable than the goal of "improving customer relations." Measurement also depends on how the goal is stated. If the goal of improving customer relations is stated as "getting a 5 per cent reduction in formal customer complaints," it is not only clearer but also more readily measured.

Goals are sometimes kept purposely vague and ambiguous to avoid objective measurement. Managers may prefer ambiguous or unstated goals to give them added flexibility, or to hide their own limitations. They may be unwilling to pin down specific goals because they may be evaluated by how well they are achieved.

Good achievement alone is not an adequate measure of organizational performance or effectiveness; there remains the larger question of whether the right goals are chosen. Also, goals may fade or conditions change as the achievement of those goals nears, so that measurement is less significant.

In a study of the goal-determination behavior and attitudes of 1,072 managers, England found that goals could be classified into four levels according to their importance with respect to content and to managerial behavior. "Organizational efficiency," "high productivity," and "profit maximization" form a set of goals that are behaviorally very important and can be viewed as maximization criteria and alternative generators. This is the most important set of goals. The second set includes "organizational growth," "industry leadership," and "organizational stability." This set is moderately important behaviorally; it serves what is largely an alternative-testing function in the decision process. The goal of "employee welfare" constitutes the third set; it has low behavioral relevance and most often serves an alternative-testing function. Finally, the fourth set, goals pertaining to "social welfare," was found to have still lower behavioral relevance. England's study found a high degree of similarity of goal patterns in different types and sizes of organizations and among different groups of managers, regardless of organizational affiliations and personal values. Another finding was that actual goals may be related more closely to the personal characteristics of managers than to the broad characteristics of business.[11]

Multiple Goals

Managers face multiple objectives and have to make decisions that are most often directed toward courses of action that deal with a number of constraints at once.

Often some of the objectives an organization chooses are in conflict with one another. The objective of profits, for example, might seem to rule out the expenditure of funds for improving worker morale or for improving community relations. The goal of quality in a product is not entirely compatible with the requirements of mass production. Economy drives throughout a company may necessitate the canceling of otherwise desirable objectives. It is hard to compare long-range objectives in monetary terms. In practice, managers use their best judgment to determine how such conflicts can be adjusted. Expenditures for building worker morale may not contribute to a measureable, immediate profit, yet many companies undertake such a goal in the belief that the long-run interests of the company will flourish.

There are several ways of coping with the problem of multiple goals. One is to make satisficing decisions rather than optimal ones. That is, choose a set of goals that will satisfy the need for goals even though they are not ideal or cannot be fully achieved. Another way is to keep stated goals intangible, idealistic, or even ambiguous. However, this may result in *goal displacement,* and the real goals evidenced in the organization's behavior will come to differ from stated goals.

The frequent displacement of intangible organizational goals by tangible goals has been ascribed by Merton, Selznick, and others. Goal displacement is behavior in which the organization neglects its stated major goals in favor of goals associated with building or maintaining the organization.[12] Thus goal displacement represents an inversion of means and ends, with the means becoming ends and displacing major goals. The intangibility of the major goals expressed by some organizations appears to be a primary generator of goal displacement. This intangibility of goals has advantages and disadvantages. Because goals are multiple, intangibility promotes the ability to accommodate diverse and even inconsistent subgoals. More people may feel satisfied with what the organization does. Intangible goals provide a measure of

---

[11] George W. England, "Organizational Goals and Expected Behavior of American Managers," *Academy of Management Journal* 10 (June 1967), 107–117; see also Gary P. Latham and Gary A. Yukl, "A Review of Research on the Application of Goal Setting in Organizations," *Academy of Management Journal* 18 (December 1975), 824–245.

[12] Robert K. Merton, *Social Theory and Social Structure,* rev. ed. (New York: Free Press, 1957); Philip Selznick, *Leadership in Administration* (New York: Harper, 1957).

flexibility and adaptation, and the ability to change short-term, immediate working goals. Intangible goals help leaders dramatize needs and secure the commitment of followers: they give the organization the appearance of being effective. Offsetting these possible advantages, however, is the likelihood of (1) generating expectations that cannot be accomplished, leading to frustration and disappointment; (2) creating anxiety and role conflict through ambiguous or contradictory directives; and (3) letting intangible goals fade, as disillusionment over failure to accomplish them increases.[13]

Goal displacement in a business organization occurs when decision makers substitute tangible goals for broader, riskier, more uncertain, longer-range goals. For example, procedures and forms may be emphasized over the substance of what they are intended to accomplish. Risky but creative activity may be avoided in favor of following rules and sticking to past experience. Managers may "play for the record" and be numbers-oriented, rather than focus on the actual goals.

Goal displacement is even more prevalent in development organizations, voluntary associations, and government and public-service organizations such as prisons or hospitals. The lines of attack on goal displacement lie within the spheres of an organization's structure and design, executive role behavior, the structure of the organization's reward and penalty system, and the use of leadership skills.

Goal Congruence

Another problem of multiple goals is that of achieving a reasonable degree of congruence among the different goals, and between individual goals and organizational goals.

Goals need to be examined for possible conflicts across the departmental or functional structure of the organization, as well as among the vertical levels. Otherwise possible conflicts in subgoals will emerge. For example, the primary goals of a marketing unit and those of a production unit differ, but they can be made congruent by coordination or goal planning. Thus the marketing department's desire to sell as much of the product as possible must be fitted to the constraints of production technology. Similarly, lower-level operating objectives should be fitted to the structure of broader goals higher up.

Congruence between personal and organizational goals requires getting goals accepted by organization members by means of clarifying a degree of identity between the two sets of goals. Coordination is also frequently achieved by setting up coordinating units in the structure of the organization.

Some managers tend to assume the acceptance of organizational aims

[13]W. Keith Warner and A. Eugene Havens, "Goal Displacement and the Intangibility of Organizational Goals," *Administrative Science Quarterly* **12** (March 1968), 539–555.

by subordinates or to impose aims without regard for the effects that lack of acceptance might bring. Successful managers try to clarify objectives, both general and specific, so that their subordinates understand them. Such understanding will be more conducive to acceptance and cooperation than force, threats, coercion, or the stern application of authority. The aims favored by management may not necessarily be shared by workers. The aims of top management are not automatically adopted by middle managers, supervisors, or workers. Acceptance may at times be reluctant and partial, often because the organizational aims appear to be incongruent with the aims of individuals. For example, many managers feel that workers do not understand the role of profits in our economic system; but in addition, workers may perceive the desire for profits as a threat to wage increases and therefore incompatible with their own aims. Moreover, workers may feel that they produce the profits for the company, but cannot share directly in them.

According to Barnard, the inculcation of belief in the existence of a common purpose is an essential executive function.[14] However, an important question is how far to go to gain acceptance. Does it mean relinquishing part of one's managerial authority? Does it mean that aims must be leveled down to a least common denominator? How much say should subordinates have in determining objectives? Does acceptance imply that the objectives are sound? Will concern over acceptance prevent the company from keeping pace with needed but unpopular change?

A practical approach to the problem of acceptance of objectives involves recognizing that the manager's responsibility as a leader is to state objectives in terms that invite confidence and produce positive attitudes in subordinates. Managers can also consider the advice, feelings, and opinions of associates and subordinates, as well as of superiors, in formulating objectives. The manager need not fear the objections of others, but should boldly face the task of persuading them that the chosen objectives are sound and logical, showing them how their personal aims coincide with over-all objectives.[15]

Changes in Objectives

An organization is not static, and a set of objectives cannot be static if it is to succeed. Executives must be constantly alert to the need for change in the broad as well as the specific aims the organization has established.

In keeping abreast of change, executives seek information indicating

[14]Chester I. Barnard, *The Functions of the Executive* (Cambridge, Mass.: Harvard U. P., 1938), p. 87.

[15]Greg R. Oldham, "The Impact of Supervisory Characteristics on Goal Acceptance," *Academy of Management Journal* 18 (September 1975), 461–475.

the need for change in objectives. They observe the results of research both within and outside the organization, and set up channels of communication and contact that will provide a flow of information affecting current and planned objectives.

Often the changes in objectives are drastic, although close study will usually reveal a logical progression of events coupled with the perception of changing events. An example is provided by the John Bean Division of the Food Machinery and Chemical Corporation. Its original purpose was to produce a fruit tree sprayer. When the gasoline-powered automobile appeared, owners discovered that their power sprayers could remove the mud from their cars; the company capitalized on this discovery by creating a new manufacturing division for automobile-washing equipment. Next the owners found that the sprayers were effecting in putting out fires; the company researched the effect of water pressure in putting out fires, leading to the development of special fire-fighting equipment and a third main division of the company.

Changes in objectives often become necessary because of changes in the habits and life styles of customers. The goals of an electric fan manufacturer, for example, cannot be confined to selling more and more fans without considering that people may increasingly prefer air conditioning. Food merchandising provides another example of the way management focuses on long-range objectives relating to consumers. Food merchandising since World War II has concentrated on the goal of providing convenience items for housewives. Foods are prepared in advance and packed for ease of preparation. In the 1970s, however, this trend slowed down because of pressure from health-conscious consumers and their reactions to inflationary food costs.

Management By Objectives

The term *management by objectives* (MBO) has been widely used to describe organizationwide programs providing for the meshing of personal and organizational objectives. It stresses the involvement of all managers in planning their own objectives in collaboration with their bosses. At supervisory and middle-management levels, the objectives are related primarily to operations activities. At higher levels, the objectives focus on broad, integrative problems such as budgeting, fiscal planning, or organizational development. Although MBO is best viewed as a companywide program, individual segments of an organization can profit from its use.

An MBO program consists of mutual goal planning by superiors and subordinates, periodic performance appraisal by superiors, and feedback interviews in which both superiors and subordinates analyze progress and restate the objectives for the next period. The idea is to specify performance goals, in both the personal and the organizational sectors. The goals are used as standards for the performance review, and for guiding the further development of managers. Management by objectives stresses results rather than personal traits, and focuses on mutual agreement on performance targets by bosses and subordinates. Problem solving rather than personality reform is its central focus.

The standards and reviews are based on results rather than opinions and generalities. The periodic discussions of goals and performance generally lead to improved superior-subordinate relations because they result in a mutual agreement as to the targets to be met, and because the reviews can then be based on objective criteria rather than values and biases of the superior alone.[16]

In MBO programs, managers learn how to work with subordinates by cultivating a continuous helping and teaching relationship. Such programs establish systematic checkpoints for reviewing and evaluating performance. They provide a philosophy of management and a way of life for the manager at work. Each situation requires tailor-made MBO programs, which entail the learning of new skills, such as interviewing and counseling, not widely utilized by managers in conventional settings. Traditional rating scales are often used in MBO systems, but they are subordinate to the larger developmental concepts that make up an MBO program.

SUMMARY

Objectives and strategies serve to identify the organization and its mission, and to provide a central focus around which human effort and organizational resources can be put to work.

The clear, vigorous determination of objectives is a requisite of effective management. Objectives are statements of aims or purposes for which the organization strives. Objectives, like plans, are imbued with considerations of the future and with the aspirations and values of managers.

Objectives assist managers in their leadership roles by providing a basis for uniting the efforts of organization members. Objectives help to establish the organization's relationships with society and with its environment. They help give the organization recognition and status. In addition, objectives motivate individuals and provide a basis for evaluating the total performance of the organization.

[16]Steven Kerr, "Overcoming the Dysfunctions of MBO," *Management by Objectives* **5** (January 1976), 13–20; Frank P. Sherwood and William J. Page, Jr., "MBO and Public Management," *Public Administration Review* **16** (January/February 1976), 5–11; Fred E. Schuster and Alva F. Kindall, "Management by Objectives: Where We Stand: A Survey of the Fortune 500," *Human Resource Management* **13** (Spring 1974), 8–11; John C. Alpin, Jr., and Peter P. Schoderbek, "MBO: Requisites for Success in the Public Sector," *Human Resource Management* **15** (Summer 1976), 30–36.

Objectives are set forth in broad general terms by top management. Successively lower levels of the organization base their more specific objectives on the general ones. Thus there is a hierarchy of objectives corresponding to missions at each level.

Organizational strategy develops an over-all plan or set of objectives. Tactics are actions or decisions that apply to the immediate situation. Both strategies and tactics focus on competitive elements—the awareness of an opponent and his strategies, and his estimates of the organization's strategies. Objectives should be made clear, precise, and accurate, reflecting the real purposes of the organization.

_____ INCIDENT CASE

In the middle of the year, the department heads in a large manufacturing firm were instructed to call their supervisors into a conference meeting to plan their objectives for the next fiscal year beginning January 1.

Questions:

1. On what conditions and factors will the success of these meetings depend?
2. As a department head, how would you plan for this meeting? How would you conduct the meeting?

_____ QUESTIONS FOR STUDY

1. As a chief executive, what procedures would you follow to explain the company objectives to interested groups, such as supervisors, workers, owners, or customers?

2. What is the purpose of general objectives? Are workers interested in them? Why or why not?

3. Does a labor union local have objectives? Are they general or specific, or both?

4. How can a manager know when a particular objective should be changed?

5. Are there any disadvantages to setting up definite objectives? If so, what are they?

6. Relate the concept of strategy to the concepts of planning, policies, decision making, and objectives.

7. What are the practical values of strategies? Can organizations train people in strategic behavior so as to get more of these advantages?

8. Under what conditions would you recommend a change in strategy? What would be your checkpoints or signs of needed change?

9. How can companies provide for the systematic development and application of strategy?

10. Look up the details of a typical MBO program, and explain the conditions that are needed to make such a program effective.

11. How do strategy problems in educational or governmental organizations differ from those in business firms?

12. Explain what is meant by goal displacement, and give several examples.

13. How can the leader gain subordinates' acceptance of goals?

SELECTED READINGS

ANSOFF, H. IGOR. *Business Strategy*. London: Penguin Books Ltd., 1969.

BUSKIRK, RICHARD H. *Handbook of Managerial Tactics*. Boston: Cahners Books, Inc., 1976.

CARROLL, STEPHEN J., and HENRY L. TOSI, JR. *Management by Objectives: Applications and Research*. New York: Macmillan Publishing Co., Inc., 1973.

CHANDLER, A. D. *Strategy and Structure*. Cambridge, Mass.: The M.I.T. Press, 1962.

COPEMON, GEORGE. *The Chief Executive and Business Growth*. New York: Leviathan House, 1971.

DRUCKER, PETER F. *Management: Tasks, Responsibilities, Practices*. New York: Harper & Row, Publishers, 1974. Chapters 5–10.

GROSS, BERTRAM. *Organizations and Their Managing*. New York: The Free Press, 1968. Chapter 11.

MIGLIORE, R. HENRY. *MBO: Blue Collar to Top Executive*. Washington, D.C.: BNA Books, Inc., 1977.

ODIORNE, GEORGE. *Management by Objectives*. New York: Pitman Publishing Corporation, 1965.

RAIA, ANTHONY P. *Managing by Objectives*. Glenview, Ill.: Scott, Foresman and Company, 1974.

WARR, PETER, ed. *Personal Goals and Work Designs*. New York: John Wiley & Sons, Inc., 1976.

———. *Management Decision by Objectives*. Englewood Cliffs, N.J.: Prentice-Hall, Inc., 1969.

SMITH, THEODORE A. *Dynamic Business Strategy*. New York: McGraw-Hill Book Company, 1977.

Chapter 8

Policies

Before we embark on the noble, we must first embark on the useful.
—Aristotle

The most involved act in the world could have been faced when it was simple. The biggest problem in the world could have been solved when it was small. *—Lao Tzu*

"We did the wrong thing, but we were only carrying out company policy."
"There's the right way, and then there's the company way."
"There's no reason for it. It's just company policy."

Questions to keep in mind while you read this chapter:

1. What is the significance of these three statements?
2. How can managers avoid the problems implied by these statements?

The work of planning and of determining objectives becomes effective when it is supported by a network of appropriate policies. Decisions at all levels are aided by policy, and one of the fundamental skills of the manager is to create policy and to use it.

Policies spell out the organization's intentions with respect to the appropriate actions of people. Policies are vital to decision making:

167

they provide a basis for relating actions to objectives and help to assure that decisions result in coordinated and successful endeavors.

POLICY DEFINED

Policies are guides to the actions or decisions of organization members. They are the planned expressions of the organization's formally approved decision guidelines. Official policies are statements that tell the members of an organization how to meet specific situations that occur frequently and affect a substantial number of people. Potential decisions are appraised in the light of policy.

Specific policies anticipate that many problems requiring decisions occur repeatedly and need to be treated consistently. For example, managers know that many workers who have already had their vacations will ask for more time off at deer hunting season. Their supervisors want satisfied employees, but at the same time production must not suffer. Clearly a policy is needed that will treat all employees fairly and preserve the company's goals. Without a policy, there is the risk of excessive unauthorized absences, and the likelihood of unfair treatment of employees by considering each case as unique.

General policies are also needed to guide decision making in situations that are nonrecurring but that need to be made consistent with broad, long-range goals and strategies. For example, companies marketing a product abroad face a difficult problem: how much should they decentralize to permit custom tailoring of market policies to fit individual countries? Most multinational firms start out highly decentralized, but many are beginning to centralize. The General Foods Corporation has followed a policy of decentralized distribution, pricing, and advertising, with centralization of product and market research.[1]

Further Examples

In the example cited before—that of time off during hunting season—the policy needed might be stated as follows:

> Requests by employees for time off beyond regular holidays and vacations can be granted only if the supervisor approves and if it is clear that there will be no interference with production. Such time off, if granted, will take the form of an unpaid leave of absence.

The above policy spells out how such a request will be handled, placing responsibility on the supervisor for deciding each case, and indicating the cost to the employee. Another policy would be needed to govern unauthorized absences from work.

[1]*Business Week*, March 16, 1974, p. 99.

Policies are also useful as instruments of planning and control. To meet inflationary turbulence, many firms must carefully control product problems with respect to cash flow and return on assets. An example of such a policy in a large manufacturing concern is: "Focus cash flows on the aggressive funding of growth opportunities, and withdraw from businesses that provide neither cash nor growth."

Policies are also related to the organization's objectives. One company expressed the relationship between objectives and policies as shown in Figure 8-1, which shows the central over-all objective, operational objectives, product objectives, financial objectives, planning objectives, and organizational objectives, each with relevant sets of policies. Also shown are the operating policies for the key functions, such as sales, manufacturing, and accounting.

Differences Among Policies, Rules, and Procedures

There are significant distinctions between policies and rules, both of which are statements designed to influence the behavior of people in

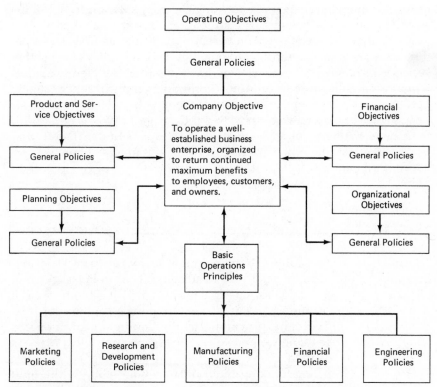

FIGURE 8-1. Relationships Among General Objectives, Policies, and Operations in a Typical Firm.

an organization. The differences, though important, are largely in degree. Policies are usually broader than rules and are stated in more general language; they imply a measure of discretionary action allowable to managers, whereas rules specifically state what must or must not be done. Rules are usually reinforced by specific, stated penalties, but policies allow a wider, more general scope for disciplinary action if needed. An example is provided in the field of safety. The list of safety rules a company follows is often long: smoking is prohibited in paint rooms, for example, and safety glasses must be worn while at work on grinding machines. Policy on safety, however, is much different. A typical safety policy might say that the company will pay for safety clothing and equipment, and will conduct periodic educational campaigns on safety. The example of safety also shows the interdependence of rules and policy. The policy establishes a guiding framework for the safety rules, which otherwise may be overlapping, full of conflicts and ambiguities. Once the policies are adopted, management can devise rules that support and augment the policies.

There are also fundamental differences between policies and procedures. Procedures reflect explicit policies, and often unstated policies as well. Moreover, procedures may deviate from policy at least briefly, as in the case of a company that instructed its supervisors not to answer any employee grievances without clearing with the central personnel director's office. The company did not alter its basic policy of expecting supervisors to settle grievances whenever possible, but merely made a temporary change in procedures to permit the training of supervisors in decision making under the new labor agreement.

Rules and procedures are always subordinate to policy, and policy making is a higher order of managerial responsibility. Those who establish rules and procedures must work within the framework of appropriate policy. To think of rules and procedures in isolation from policy invites poor coordination.

POLICY MAKING

As guides to action, policies anticipate that many recurring decision-making situations can be dealt with in advance. Thus policies covering classes of decisions are labor-saving devices, curtailing the burden of handling problems one at a time. Moreover, policies endure for relatively long periods of time, providing stability for the organization and an orientation base for new employees. The organization's way of life is expressed in its body of policies.

To influence policy thinking in an organization is one of the most important personal goals of managers. The greater their influence on policy, the greater their contribution and the greater their status. This in part accounts for the deference and respect accorded to top-level managers.

Policies are formed or changed when managers become aware of a need to guide the decisions of organization members, when recurring problems demand attention, or when strategies or operations are being implemented.

The Structure of Policies

Policy formation may begin at the top, middle, or lowest levels of management, but the weight of policy making is from the top. It is important to note the process character of policy formation as it links the levels of an organization together. Policies beginning at the top arise out of broad, basic needs perceived and defined by top management. Thus the General Motors Corporation, for example, follows a strategic policy of organizational decentralization, in which each division is highly autonomous. This policy requires centrally coordinated planning and control by means of clear policy guidelines.

Once a policy is established at the top, it becomes the guide for supporting policies at successively lower levels. A policy of growth through increased sales, for example, causes production managers to devise appropriate policies covering equipment, inventory, and production processes. The personnel director needs to fit manpower policies to new potential manpower demands. Marketing policies may require change. Further down, the pressure for increased output may force the shop supervisors to alter their policies on time off or on dividing up overtime work.

Policy may also originate at or near the bottom of an organization, through pressures that are strongly influential there. If the higher-level managers are receptive to the ideas, feelings, and attitudes of those below, they will derive valuable policy inputs from them. The openness of upward communication and the use of participative management methods can do much to generate upward influences on the processes of policy formation.

The existing policies of an organization generally conform to its hierarchical structure. Thus a number of policies exist simultaneously and are interrelated in a complex structural pattern, and each policy varies in its importance and scope of coverage; policies, therefore, like plans and objectives, exist in a hierarchy. The policies with maximum scope and importance are administered from the top, and those with narrower, more operational and specific applications are administered lower down in the organization. Other policies range between these extremes in a pattern of ascending importance as we look upward in an organization.

It is important to understand the hierarchical structure, which shows how policies relate to one another. Policies at lower levels make sense when they are consistent with and supportive of higher policies. For example, if top management declares a policy of good corporate citizenship in its community, the maintenance supervisor might follow a policy demanding scrupulous attention to the cleanliness and appearance of the plant's properties. This in turn might induce a policy among first-line supervisors not to permit workers to eat their lunches outside.

POLICY MAKERS

The right to select or approve policies confers substantial power upon executives. Certain constituencies of an organization, however, may influence policy even though they cannot control it.

Many groups and individuals have an interest in policies because their welfare and degree of success may depend heavily upon them. Stockholders, employees, customers, investors, suppliers, and even the general public all have a vital stake in organizational policy. Because policies reflect the thinking of managers and the basic strategies of management, those with a stake in the organization are often critical and cautious observers of its policies. In companies, stockholders know that policies may affect the profitability and safety of their investment. Workers know that policies determine how satisfied and secure they can be in their jobs. Customers like policies designed to assure satisfaction in their transactions. All stakeholder groups can to some extent influence an organization's policies by making known their points of view. Specifically declared policies serve to inform all those who are interested in or affected by the organization's activities.

Owners and Policies

Whereas outside groups such as suppliers or customers may *influence* policy, the *control* of policy decisions is in the hands of managers. But in corporations, managers are legally the representatives of owners— that is, stockholders—and the mechanisms by which owners influence or control managers are complex.

Legally, the property and other rights that owners have in a business permit them to say how its assets may be used. The interest of owners is in the success of the business and the security of their investment. Thus the adequacy of the policies is important to them. Owners are represented by a board of directors that guides the actions of the executives who actually operate the business. Through these directors, stockholders may express their views and vote on issues concerning the management of the company. Managers are hired to run the business and are responsible to the stockholders through the board of directors.

In actual practice, the influence and control of top management are much greater in relation to that of owners than is suggested by formal corporate mechanisms. Stockholders are widely scattered, and only a relative few hold substantial amounts of stock. Moreover, most stockholders are not financial wizards, but ordinary people intent on a good return on their investment. Stockholders tend either to be indifferent to policy questions and major decisions, or else to be ineffective in mobilizing major efforts for change. Furthermore, the board of directors is to a considerable extent composed of the managers themselves and thus serves as an adjunct to management, so that policies adopted by the board frequently originate with and represent the thinking of the managers. It is physically impossible for thousands of individual stockholders to manage a company directly. Many of them own shares in a number of companies and hence cannot devote undivided attention to any one of them. Accordingly, managers have a great deal of scope for action within the broad legal requirements of corporate organization.[2]

In nonbusiness organizations, procedures similar to those of the corporation's ownership exist in the form of boards of trustees, as in hospitals, or constituencies, as in the case of governmental units. Boards of trustees carry out policy requirements in ways that are similar to those of the boards of directors. Constituencies, however, are seldom formally organized, and seldom act without an issue or event that causes their members to coalesce and make their wishes known to administrators.

Top Management and Policies

Corporate executives in top management have the over-all responsibility for operating the business. Therefore they exercise a major influence over company policy. We have seen that such managers are hired and empowered to act by the owners of the business, through the board of directors. We have also seen that there is an element of indirectness in this procedure that gives managers considerable latitude in how they operate the business. However, certain policies cannot possibly be determined by any group other than top management. For example, whether to secure additional capital through the sale of stock or of bonds depends on the company's general financial policies. Or again, a policy of resisting the organization of a new labor union must be made by top management. A policy of making component parts rather than purchasing them from suppliers cannot be made by production departments.

Corporate policies are a reflection of the skills and abilities of top managers, who earn the right to determine significant policy issues

[2]A classic study of the influence of stockholders is Adolph A. Berle, Jr., and Gardiner C. Means, *The Modern Corporation and Private Property* (New York: Macmillan, 1933); for a critique of corporate forms of organization, see George C. Lodge, *The New American Ideology* (New York: Knopf, 1975).

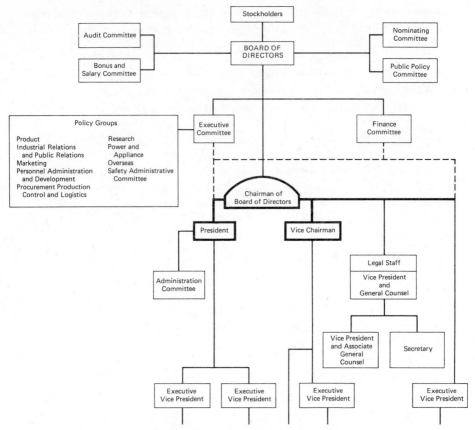

FIGURE 8-2. Top Levels of Organization in the General Motors Corporation.
Source: Courtesy of General Motors Corporation, 1977.

through years of experience and opportunities to test their judgment. Figure 8-2 illustrates the policy-making group at the top management level in the General Motors Corporation.

Nonbusiness organizations find that policies are often embodied in legislation (as in government) or in statements from boards of trustees. The public interest in such policies is high. Nevertheless, although top administrators are constrained by their boards or by legislation, they have considerable latitude in designing policies appropriate to their mission.

An illustration of how a formally adopted top management policy provides an expression of company action and intent in a given area is provided by the following policy statement of a large corporation:

> Recognizing that effective performance in community relations is vital to the long-range success of any company, it is the policy of the Company to

conduct itself at all times as a good corporate citizen of every community in which it operates.

To ensure that the Company consistently acts upon its responsibilities for good corporate citizenship, it is a further policy to conduct continuing community relations programs in plant communities and other localities where the size of the Company's operation warrants formal programs.

The necessity for community relations programs arises not alone from the desire to have the community *think* well of us and our actions, but also from the need to have the community *act* well toward us.

Community relations is the sum total of what our neighbors in our plant and community think and do about us.

Middle-Management and Supervisory-Level Policies

At operating levels, policy making is restricted to a narrower focus according to the nature of the work. Department heads or supervisors determine policies as needed to accomplish the tasks assigned. Building relationships with subordinates entails forming policies for dealing with them and their problems. However, the managers must not only stay within prescribed limits of authority, but also must keep policies free from conflict with those at higher levels and with the top management. Deviations and conflicts risk the possibility of corrective action by managers higher in the hierarchy.

First-line supervisors are in direct contact with workers and can control policies within the scope of their jurisdiction. They are vital connecting links in the channels of communication through which policies are disseminated from above and through which important information affecting policies is transmitted upward. To the extent that higher managers foster upward communication, first-line supervisors can influence broader and more general company policies. Through daily contacts with workers, they are able to discover the feelings, opinions, and information that are needed for setting policies at higher levels. Also, as spokesmen for management, first-line supervisors tell workers what policies are in effect as directives from higher management. To individual workmen, whose day-to-day activities depend upon either the policies the first-line supervisor actually sets or the manner in which he interprets and carries out policies from above, he appears as the main determiner of policy. Similarly, first-line supervisors in nonbusiness organizations are policy makers with respect to the scope of authority delegated to them. They are also policy executors and interpreters in the day-to-day operations of their organization.

POLICY ADMINISTRATION

The best of policies can fail unless they are properly administered. Managers learn to use policies by thinking and acting in policy frameworks. Nothing is more futile than a dormant, unused, or irrelevant policy. But even a good policy cannot be effective without the capable, observant judgment of the managers who carry them out.

No organization can exist without policies. In poorly managed organizations, policies are erratic, haphazard, undisciplined, unsystematic, and usually unwritten. Nevertheless, they exist. Effective policies are not only soundly conceived; they are carefully administered.

Policy Dissemination

Policies may be either stated or implied. The problem of dissemination exists for both, but in different ways. Implied policies are generally less effective than formally stated policies, and they are harder to use in a meaningful way.

Implied Policy

In most organizations the problem of implied policy gets far too little attention. Implied policies are those that have little or no official statement or expression of approval, but that fulfill the function of guiding managerial decisions. Not all executives believe that policies can or should be expressly stated; some believe that some policies can be stated, but that others cannot. Policies that exist but are not stated officially are implied policies—consistent forms of managerial behavior that have not been formalized or expressed as statements of organizational intent.

The occasional claim that an organization has no policy is an inaccurate notion founded on circumstances that are more apparent than real. What is usually absent is a body of *stated* policies. Implied policies can be observed only indirectly, by noting the actual behavior of members of the organization in specific instances. For example, a company may seem to have no policy with respect to the upper age limits for hiring employees, yet examination of the ages of newly hired persons might indicate that no one over fifty years of age was hired. The implied policy, then, is not to hire persons over fifty years of age. Implied policies are difficult to perceive and must be dealt with carefully because they represent an interpretation of observed behavior.

The effects of implied policies may be either favorable or unfavorable. Companies that try to give each customer fair treatment, for example, may not actually state this intention as a policy; yet to state it would strengthen it and increase its utility, both inside and outside the organization.

The reluctance of some managers to operate under expressed policies is generated by the constraints that formal policy imposes. Some policies are difficult to state in such a way that the organization's interests are protected while the needs of those affected are met.

Managers sometimes believe that their success depends upon having complete freedom to act. Personal discretion and judgment in particular situations are adequate, they feel. Such a rationale includes the idea that situations are unique and so cannot be grouped under the umbrella of policy. Also implied policy is protected from public view: only trained or alert observers can notice it. The dissemination of implied policy is very informal; usually it is left to chance. Implied policy is often used when the organization's true policy is not likely to merit the approval of one or more groups. For example, a company may want to engage in cutthroat competition, or to discriminate against minorities. A hospital may not want to take charity cases. But to express these policies explicitly would be to risk severe criticism or other penalties.

Managers have no choice of whether to have policies, but rather must choose those policies to which they wish to give attention. It is dangerous to leave too much to the realm of implied policy, for the organization's worthy intentions may lose respect through faulty inter-pretations. Rationalizations in support of undue reliance on implied policy are weak: they are defensive in character and timid in their approach. They often are used to shield inept administrators and to protect them from facing pressure, criticisms, failure, or complaints. On the other hand, however, the policy structure of an organization proba-bly cannot be complete, and it is therefore the case that some policies, particularly at operating levels, are influenced more by the informal organization than by the formal authority system.

Stated Policy

Stated policy not only disseminates the policy guidelines in writing; it also includes, either explicitly or by implication, the backing and authentication of top management. Even though it is difficult to write policies clearly, misunderstandings of stated policy are fewer than if policies were left to chance or shrouded in mystery. Moreover, the process of putting policies in writing aids in sharpening the policies and in improving the policy skills of managers.

Formal, official policy statements in writing offer the following advantages: (1) they become available to all in the same form; (2) they can be referred to so that anyone who wishes can check the policy; (3) misunderstandings can be referred to a particular set of words; (4) they indicate a basic honesty and integrity in the organization's intentions; (5) they can more readily be disseminated to all who are affected; (6) they can be more easily taught to new employees; (7) the process of writing forces managers to think more sharply about the policy, thus helping achieve further clarity; and (8) they generate confidence among people in the organization that the top leadership is good and that everyone will be treated substantially the same under given conditions.

The above advantages accrue primarily to organizations operating in relatively stable environments. Indeed, securing these advantages helps to produce stability of the organization itself. In more turbulent environments, policy administration is difficult because of the time required for amending and adjusting policies.

The degree of detail involved in the policies of a particular unit of organization is important. Where the time factor in carrying out a policy is urgent, it is more desirable to be explicit and detailed as to the policy's applications, as for example in the policies to be followed during and after an emergency, such as an explosion in the plant. On the other hand, if time is not short and if the abilities and experience of the persons concerned have invited the confidence and trust of a superior, he may be less detailed in policy without serious consequences.

Media for Disseminating Policy

When a policy is put into effect for the first time, or when an existing policy is modified, it is important to pave the way for understanding the new policy. Prior to announcing it, those who are affected or those who can contribute ideas concerning it should be consulted as early as practicable. The unexpected announcement of new policies or policy changes generates fears and antagonisms. Behavior with respect to policy is long-range, in the sense that people grow accustomed to existing policies and can best adapt to changes if they have time to think about the effects of the change. They feel less hostile if they have a voice in such matters before the policies are adopted.

Media for disseminating policy include written statements that appear as bulletins, letters, handbooks, manuals, pamphlets, or news releases. Policy is also disseminated by word of mouth, through key people in the organization. Each executive, manager, or supervisor may take part in the procedure of dissemination. Written statements may be issued in support or confirmation of the spoken policies.

Whether or not writing is used to disseminate policy, the question of timing is important; it should be worked out so that each manager is the first to tell subordinates about the policy change, thus protecting the manager's status as a leader and avoiding the pitfalls of fear and distrust that occur when people learn what they need to know too late or learn it from unofficial sources. Moreover, people usually cannot ask questions of these unofficial sources to achieve a quicker, more accurate understanding of the situation.

Policy Criteria

The ultimate objective of any policy is to influence effectively the performance of organization members in the collective achievement of goals. A critical factor in the success of policy is the degree to which it is accepted by those who are affected and those who administer it. Without cooperation and acceptance, any policy stands in danger of destruction through subtle forms of resistance. The following administrative considerations can enhance the possibilities for the acceptance of policies: flexibility, consistency, fairness, and judgment.

Flexibility

Flexibility is not necessarily built into the actual statement of policy, although some statements of policy indicate the tolerance to be allowed by such phrases as "whenever possible" or "under usual conditions." Flexibility is primarily the result of the way managers apply policy. As noted earlier, excessive flexibility may destroy or weaken a policy. Flexibility serves the useful function of permitting a policy to be applied intelligently to conditions that are sufficiently different that the usual application is sometimes undesirable, yet not so different as to call for an official change of policy. Tolerance represents the extent to which ignoring or substantially altering the application of the policy will be permitted before corrective action is instituted. The basic idea of flexibility in policy administration can be illustrated by the policy of putting no limits on the expense accounts of salesmen, on the theory that salesmen will react by being reasonable about the matter. This policy would not, however, preclude placing such limits on a particular salesman who was thought to be abusing the system, and to do so would not eradicate the policy itself. The idea of tolerance is represented in this example by the fact that a sales manager would be subject to criticism if he allowed a salesman to abuse this privilege.

Consistency

The criterion of consistency pertains to the way policy administration appears to those affected by it. People who see a policy applied in one way on one occasion feel disturbed when they see it applied differently at another time. The feeling arises from a sense of unfairness, from fear of biases, or from the dislike of preferential treatment. Inconsistency introduces uncertainty, which makes planning of future behavior exceedingly difficult. Seemingly rapid and surprising policy changes in an organization are often found on close analysis to be the product of the eccentricity, or the mercurial or vacillating temperament, of a manager. Inconsistency is most apparent in incidents that involve short periods of time. Over longer periods the reasons for differing applications have time to become more apparent. Inconsistency also appears between various units of an organization, presenting managers with a problem of coordination. An example of inconsistency occurred in one company with respect to its policy of requiring executives to participate actively in the life of the community. One department head had subordinates spending nearly half their time in outisde organizations; another required only a token recognition of the policy.

Fairness

Fairness is a quality that people attribute to the application of policy. It represents a value judgment on their part, one that is not necessarily based on rational and logical analysis. Most managers try to be fair, but they realize that in some cases an honest decision on their part may not be judged as fair by those affected. If a particular application adversely affects an individual, he may consider it unfair unless he can be convinced that the manager applying the policy considered the relevant facts and issues. This can be illustrated by the policy of systematic wage administration through job evaluation. The object of such a policy is to ensure relative fairness in wage rates, that is, to pay rates that correspond to the relative importance of the work to be done. Yet the system itself cannot deliver all the fairness desired by the over-all policy, and fairness to individuals includes still another policy of adjusting employees' wages according to the quality of their work.

Judgment

Managers often regard judgment as one of the most necessary traits for competence. Judgment is hard to define, but it is not difficult to see in particular situations. Judgment in applying policy is demonstrated by the ultimate wisdom of the behavior it generates. We say a manager has judgment when his decisions exhibit insight, perspective, and a substantially correct analysis of relevant matters. In policy administration, judgment is required for the flexible application of policies; it is also required in determining the need for new policy or for changes in current policies. An example of the factor of judgment in applying policy is provided by the company that has a policy of not permitting its executives to speak for fees. However, outsiders occasionally disregard such a policy, bestowing an honorarium upon a manager for some unusual service. A department head in this case may choose to ignore this payment, even though that choice is contrary to policy; in doing so, he may make a judgment that the executive concerned earned the reward, that he is not spending an excessive amount of time outside, and that others will not be unduly upset if an exception is made in that case.[3]

[3]See Ray Brown, *Judgment in Administration* (New York: McGraw-Hill, 1966), and Geoffrey Vickers, *The Art of Judgment* (New York: Basic, 1965).

Conflicting Policies

In the over-all administration of policy matters, it is important to develop a body of policy whose constituent parts fit together with as little conflict and confusion as possible. For example, the policies of one firm to diversify and also to decentralize were combined in an integrated way, but they required one further policy: near-total disclosure of operating information to those carrying decentralized responsibilities. The company believed that highly confidential data must be communicated to a large number of people to allow them to make the right decisions. The extent of this policy is revealed by the fact that the type of data on which the company depends to improve management efficiency is information that in many firms would be restricted to the executive or board-of-directors level.

On the other hand, policies that are in conflict cause confusion by pointing in opposite directions. For example, a company might have a policy of recruiting and training as many engineering personnel as can be obtained, in the anticipation that future needs might increase. However, if another policy dictated the cutting of labor costs, the two policies would not be consistent. Neither the personnel department nor the departments needing engineers could know from these policies how best to carry on.

Changes in Policies

Policies are characterized by considerable inertia. Once established, they persist. Written policies tend to become relatively permanent, particularly when published in a handbook or manual. As situations calling for policies change, the need for altering policies gradually increases. However, mechanical difficulties, such as the expense and work involved in publishing the manual, often cause companies to wait until the need for change justifies the cost of a general revision. One way to avoid this difficulty is to maintain stated policy in loose-leaf binder systems so that changes can be made without a large-scale revision.

The tendency of policies to persist beyond the point of maximum need or usefulness seems to arise from the fact of their success. Executives become reluctant to change or discard any policy that has worked well for a long period of time. Executives need to acquire skill in sensing the obsolescence of a policy and recognizing when a policy is out of date. For example, the Richman Brothers clothing stores, which formerly sold only for cash, eventually came to recognize the consumer demand for credit selling.

Changes in policies often seem abrupt, and often reverse the former policy. A change in a major policy like decentralization, for example, must be in the direction of more centralization, and even a slight move in this direction will seem of great magnitude and significance to the people in the organization. Changes are further impeded when they are made without informing those affected or without inviting their help and participation.

Policies that have existed for a long time introduce rigidities that are difficult to overcome. For example, policies may continue to be very desirable for a division or a department, yet become undesirable for the company as a whole. In such cases, it is hard for top management to effect changes, particularly where a unit's executives have acquired great power and influence. This power may derive from long-standing independence and the freedom of a department to determine its own policies, or else from lack of leadership on the part of top management. Top management may adopt a technique of breaking the entrenched rigidity by destroying the power bloc through reorganization, rather than attempting to force through a change in policy directly. Clearly this technique should be necessary only when conditions have become so rigidly severe that less drastic methods seem fruitless. Constant attention to the entire hierarchy of policies, as they relate to each other, is at least a partial safeguard against the evolution of such problems.

SUMMARY

Policies are guides to action, rather than rules. They are broader than rules or procedures, which tell exactly what must be done or not done. The effectiveness of policy making depends on sound content, as well as on the extent of authentication from the top. The administration of policies is as important as their creation and dissemination. Stated policies are preferable to implied policies.

In the management of policies, consistency and fairness of application are important. Acceptance is necessary to obtain the compliance and cooperation of organization members. Acceptance is enhanced by the participative involvement of those affected, and by the clear assignment of responsibility for policies throughout the organization.

Policies, like plans and objectives, exist at all levels in an organization's hierarchy. It is important to develop the proper relationships among the policies at the different levels. Policies must be kept up to date.

Policies have roots that extend to all parts of an organization. To activate conditions so that policies are lived, not merely practiced, is a challenge to all managers.

INCIDENT CASE

For many years, Company X had a firm policy of preventing the unionization of its workers by all possible legal maneuvers, and by a quality of management such that workers would not want to be unionized. Over the years, considerable paternalism had crept into the company's management philosophy and practices. Suddenly the firm became organized as the workers voted in favor of establishing a UAW local.

Question:

1. What are the implications of this situation for the effective management of company policy?

QUESTIONS FOR STUDY

1. Talk with an executive and find out what he thinks a good policy should be like. Can he give you some examples of policies?

2. What standards would you apply in order to judge the policies of a particular company?

3. Why do some executives dislike too much formal determination of policies?

4. What are the advantages and disadvantages of putting policies in writing?

5. Can workers do anything about the policies of their supervisors? What can they do, and why?

6. Suppose a department head disagrees with a company policy he is asked to carry out. What should he do, and why?

7. Can policies be enforced, or is persuasion the only way to keep them in effect? What penalties would you suggest for deviations from policy?

8. What are the most serious or difficult problems in policy management, as you see them?

9. Write a policy of your own, considering matters of good policy formation and application.

SELECTED REFERENCES

BAUER, RAYMOND A., and KENNETH J. GERGEN, eds. *The Study of Policy Formation.* New York: The Free Press, 1968.

BONGE, JOHN, and BRUCE R. COLEMAN. *Concepts for Corporate Strategy.* New York: Macmillan Publishing., Inc., 1972.

BROWN, RAY E. *Judgment in Administration.* New York: McGraw-Hill Book Company, 1966. Chap. 3.

HANER, F. T. *Business Policy, Planning, and Strategy.* Cambridge, Mass.: Winthrop Publishers, Inc., 1976.

KATZ, ROBERT. *Management of the Total Enterprise: Cases and Concepts on Strategy.* Englewood Cliffs, N.J.: Prentice-Hall, Inc., 1970.

KING, WILLIAM R., and DAVID I. CLELAND. *Strategic Planning and Policy.* New York: Petrocelli/Charter, Inc., 1977.

KLEIN, WALTER H., and DAVID C. MURPHY. *Policy: Concepts in Organizational Guidance.* Boston: Little, Brown and Company, 1973.

KOONTZ, HAROLD. *The Board of Directors and Effective Management.* New York: McGraw-Hill Book Company, 1967.

LEWIN, ARIE Y. *Policy Sciences: Methodologies and Cases.* New York: Pergamon Press, 1977.

McNICHOLS, THOMAS J. *Executive Policy and Strategic Planning.* New York: McGraw-Hill Book Company, 1977.

PAINE, FRANK T., and WILLIAM NAUMES. *Strategy and Policy Formation: An Integrative Approach.* Philadelphia: W. B. Saunders Company, 1974.

ROGERS, DAVID C. *Business Policy: Text and Cases.* Englewood Cliffs, N.J.: Prentice-Hall, Inc., 1976.

VICKERS, GEOFFREY. *Towards a Sociology of Management.* New York: Basic Books, Inc., 1967.

———. *The Art of Judgment.* New York: Basic Books, Inc., 1965.

Chapter 9

Coordination and Control

"The most fertile new ideas are those that transcend established specialized methods and treat some new problem as a single task."

—*Lancelot Law Whyte*

Peter F. Drucker writes in his book *Management* (Harper & Row, 1974) that huge international auditing firms such as Arthur Anderson & Company simply are not manageable. More and more of the top people spend more and more of their time trying to coordinate, administer, and hold together a vast mass of professionals, each of whom has to do his work in his own way and yet to professional standards. In a professional practice, standards must be set by example, not by rules. Yet in a huge firm, the senior people are too remote from junior staff to function as mentors. Partners can't discipline their people, and it's harder to dislodge a partner than to fire a corporate executive.

Arthur Anderson & Company has a "Marine-like tradition" of instilling discipline and providing the example of professionalism. The firm "cultivates strong, outspoken and audacious leadership in a profession never noted for elan." (*Wall Street Journal*, October 2, 1975, p. 1).

Questions to keep in mind while you read this chapter:

1. With its 944 partners, 14,000 employees, and 55,000 clients (1975), what kinds of coordination and control problems are likely to exist in the Anderson firm?
2. Are there reasonable alternatives to the firm's hard-charging, aggressive style, hard training programs, and heavy use of discipline and doctrine?

Coordination and control are not only two important functions of management, but also desirable states of being for the organization. To achieve coordination and control, managers need to make continuous efforts to adjust discrepancies between actual and intended efforts.

Coordination and control are closely linked, and both are interrelated with the planning function. The degree of coordination and control achieved is derived from elements that are built into the system by planning processes.

_____ **COORDINATION DEFINED**

Coordination is *the process by which managers achieve integrated patterns of group and individual effort. To coordinate is to develop unity of action in common purposes.*

This definition is concise, so further elaboration is in order. First, note that coordination is one of the manager's leadership responsibilities. Coordination is often wrongly confused with cooperation. Individuals or organizational units will not automatically be coordinated, no matter how much they cooperate. Any degree of coordination so achieved is coincidental, and managers cannot risk relying upon coincidence to get results. Although cooperation is always helpful and the lack of it can destroy the possibility of coordination, its mere presence is not enough to produce coordination.

A second important feature of the definition is that of process. The idea that coordination is a fixed entity that either exists or does not exist is unrealistic. Coordination is present in varying degrees.

A third aspect of the definition is the need for orderly arrangements of group effort. Coordination applies to group, not individual, effort. When a number of individuals must work together, integration and orderliness become significant. The extent to which coordination produces a united effort is an important element of efficiency in running an organization. Undue confusion is a symptom of poor coordination.

A fourth factor is the concept of unity of effort. This is the heart of the coordination problem. Unity of effort means primarily that managers have so arranged the nature and timing of activities that individual efforts blend into a harmonious stream of productive action. Unity of effort demands effective leadership. A successful leader achieves coordination by providing a focus around which tasks are divided among group members and brought together again in a meaningful whole.

Finally, the definition states that the object of coordination is a common purpose. The degree to which the organization achieves its intended purposes is at least a partial index of the extent to which the chief executive has been able to coordinate it. Unity of effort requires that participating individuals understand the goals toward which they are working as a group, and that there be no excessive and costly overlap of their methods and activities.

Self-Coordination

Self-coordination applies primarily to simple situations in relatively simple organizations. Simon suggests an interesting concept of adjustment. In doing work, it is expedient for employees to adjust their efforts to the work of others. As an example, Simon refers to a group of painters working together. For the most part they work silently, each taking a part of the work, fitting in as he thinks best, being careful not to get in the way of others. These adjustments are in the nature of self-coordination. A more elaborate example is provided in the case of a group attempting to move a heavy load. If all members of the group accept one individual as leader, they can adjust their movements to his and thus achieve a measure of coordination.[1]

Self-coordination, like cooperation, is no substitute for the coordinative effort of the leader. Clearly, some self-coordination is required for an organization to run smoothly. Yet there remain the deeper conflicts of interest that only a leader can resolve. It is unrealistic to expect the heads of subunits automatically to put the good of the total organization over their own interests. As an organization increases in complexity, coordination becomes a necessary constraint upon the autonomous impulses of managers. Such coordination is not accidental. It must be brought about deliberately through direct decisions.

_____ **CONTROL DEFINED**

The idea of control sometimes arouses opposition in societies that value freedom, individualism, and democracy; yet every organization requires a measure of control to provide for stability and predictability in the system. Many social controls, such as traffic laws, are generally accepted even though deviations occur. Control is thus blended into our daily experience so that we seldom recognize how the need for order restricts the autonomy of the individual. An organization is also a type of society, made up of people who have chosen to work together. The members of an organization, by joining it, implicitly subject themselves to control in order to make their collective efforts feasible. The word *control* is often preceded by a modifier to designate a specific control problem. For example, we speak of inventory control, quality control, production control, manpower control, and even adminstrative

[1]Herbert Simon, *Administrative Behavior*, rev. ed. (New York: Macmillan, 1957), p. 104.

control. Administrative or managerial control is the most comprehensive control concept. All other types may be subsumed under it. Administrative control implies a managerial function, accomplished through policies, plans, decisions, and the design of systems and procedures.

Control may be viewed as a system state, as a managerial function, and as a process. Therefore a good working definition of control holds that it is *the process by which managers make sure that intended, desirable results are consistently and continuously achieved.* A definition of control as the state of a system is "that function of a system which provides direction in conformance to the plan" or "the maintenance of variations from system objectives within allowable limits." System control is established by causing outputs or end results to be fed back as signals to the input and processing parts of the system. Although not all control problems are subject to this built-in feedback process, it is an efficient method for many types of situations. Turbulent environments, or conditions involving for continuous human judgmental inputs, require corrective actions that are difficult to embody in automatic feedback systems.

Planning and Control

Control and planning are closely related. In fact, the terms *planning* and *control* are used interchangeably in the designation of departments that carry out production planning, scheduling, and routing. Thus some companies have a production planning department; others a production control department.

Like other managerial functions, control is important because of the scarcity of resources and the need for order and system in the activities of organization members. Control is thus a measure of the effectiveness of planning, organizing, and coordinating. It is an axiom that the manager must first make sure that all other managerial functions are performed in the light of control problems. Control is not something that is applied after all else is done. If control is an integral part of managerial effort, the number and extent of corrective decisions can be minimized.

The highly integrated nature of planning and control is reflected in a research report by Robert N. Anthony, who postulates three related conceptual areas: (1) strategic planning, (2) management control, and (3) operational control. Strategic planning is the process of deciding on objectives, on changes in objectives, on the resources used to attain objectives, and on policies that govern the acquisition, use, and disposition of resources. Management control is the process by which managers assure that resources are used efficiently to accomplish the organization's objectives. Operational control relates to specific controls over procedures, tasks, or processes of work. Because money is a common denominator, Anthony sees the financial system as central to management control. His framework requires distinguishing between the types of planning and control, but he concludes that management control is so subjective a problem that it is unrealistic to view it as a total system based only on computers and mathematical models.[2]

Following Anthony's framework, Deming made a detailed study of one company's management control system. He concluded that the Anthony framework provides distinctions critical to the effective design of management control systems. Deming subjected his data to review by a committee of experts on management control systems. Their conclusions were then evaluated by the company's top management, and Deming analyzed all the information thus obtained. His findings stressed the importance of stating objectives in specific, measurable terms wherever possible, and of long-range planning and the allocation of funds among competing demands, including capital budgeting. Considerable attention was devoted by the company to the fundamental economics underlying its business. Thus profit planning, cost-price-volume relationships, allocation of fixed variable costs, and other economic considerations occupied a prominent place in the control process. Finally, analysis of the information system indicated the importance of proper facts to produce profit-oriented actions. Other elements of the information system included the need for relating reports to each other and for concentrating information at the proper points. Deming's study shows the relevance of an integrated approach to planning and control.[3]

Planning and organizing logically precede the control phase of executive action. But seeing the elements in a circular relationship is actually more descriptive, because control is the result of particular

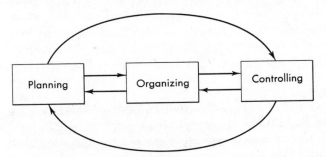

FIGURE 9-1. Reciprocal Relations Among Planning, Organizing, and Controlling Functions.

[2]Robert N. Anthony, *Planning and Control Systems: A Framework for Analysis* (Boston: Division of Research, Graduate School of Business Administration, Harvard University, 1965).

[3]Robert H. Deming, *Characteristics of an Effective Management Control System in an Industrial Organization* (Boston: Divison of Research, Graduate School of Business Administration, Harvard University, 1968).

plans, objectives, or policies, and because it occurs within the context of a particular organization. Planning and organizing not only affect control but also are affected by it. These reciprocal relationships are illustrated in the form of a feedback cycle shown in Figure 9-1.

———————— SOURCES OF COORDINATION AND CONTROL PROBLEMS

Problems of coordination and control in organizations arise from the presence of constant change, weak or passive leadership, and the complexities inherent in large-scale organizations. The sources of coordination and control problems will here be analyzed according to three aspects: (1) human attributes, (2) functional differentiation, and (3) specialization.

Human Attributes

The greater the number of persons involved in an organization, the more complicated the problems of coordination and control. Individuals are unique, acting to serve their own needs as well as those of the organization. They have their own habits of work, approaches to situations, and relationships with others. Moreover, individuals act emotionally as well as rationally; their behavior is not always well understood or completely predictable.

Problems of coordination sometimes arise out of the perverseness of human beings in organizational settings. Silly or routine questions may be pushed up to higher levels than necessary, in the name of coordination, by individuals seeking contacts, reassurance, or notice from their superiors. The manager plagued by needless coordinating decisions may feel contemptuous of those below, resenting their intrusions and interferences. People also develop self-interests that make them reluctant to have their work coordinated. These difficulties can be partly offset by actions designed to clarify authority, to delegate properly, and to control effectively.

The need for control is reflected in the psychological makeup of individuals. In the absence of control, people tend to allow results to stray from plans or orders. They gradually slide off standard. Suppose, for example, that in an office the workers are to arrive at 8 A.M.. Also suppose that there are no time clocks and that the supervisor arrives at 8:30. Under these conditions, some workers would begin to arrive late. To be sure, they would have "reasons," but the problem could be greatly reduced by control procedures or by a better example provided by the supervisor.

Control is vital to the strength and morale of an organization. Members do not like things to be out of control, for they cannot predict what will happen to them. They become the victims of caprice rather than the beneficiaries of control. The manager is likely to be considered unfair, for in the absence of control they cannot be sure that everyone is treated equally. Thus, in the above example, the office workers with plausible excuses might fare better than those too scrupulous to make up good stories. Morale falls when the manager has no way of discriminating between the honest and the not-so-honest excuses.

In all organizations, workers are exposed to serious temptation. Many must be trusted with large quantities of money, trade secrets, and valuable raw materials, tools, and machinery. In the absence of effective control, employees tend to yield to these temptations. Although control cannot cure habitual dishonesty, managers are irresponsible if they do not establish order and discipline among employees.

Human attitudes toward control greatly affect its success. Some executives are hesitant to exert control; they ignore deviations, hoping that self-correcting influences will save the day. In part, this reluctance to control results from an awareness that subordinates resent control, particularly if it is heavy-handed. Even where there is respect for order and control there is also, in society generally, a sentiment against control that supports opposition to it. Some persons are disorderly in their work habits and thought processes; some use disorder and confusion as a strategy for manipulating and controlling a situation for private benefit. The manager who creates confusions that only he can understand thereby becomes indispensable.

Functional Differentiation

The need for coordination and control arises out of the complex functional interdependencies within organizations. The operation of one unit, such as the manufacturing department, depends heavily on the other units, such as purchasing, labor relations, and marketing. Yet the manufacturing unit has no direct authority over these other departments. Coordination and control must, therefore, be accomplished by a manager who has a larger scope of authority than the manager of the individual units. Coordination and control are therefore necessary to link the interdependent functions together and assure their contribution to the total result.

Problems arise not only from interdependence of technology and work flow, but also from conflicts over authority and jurisdictions among differentiated units. Coordination and control are difficult when managers create unusual groupings of duties that overlap with those of other units. For example, when one firm established a department of automation to apply new techniques for improving production, other departments resisted the effort.

Problems of coordination and control may arise because domains become solidified; rigid barriers grow between them, with each unit trying to perform its mission in isolation from the others. Sometimes functions are grouped illogically, or managers take the expedient route rather than the logical one. For example, in one firm the function of hiring accountants was assigned to the accounting department rather than to the personnel department, primarily because large numbers of accountants were needed. However, this arrangement entailed the use of untrained recruiters and led to the objections of the personnel director.

Nonbusiness organizations also have problems of functional coordination and control. A prime example is the hospital, which must coordinate the services of physicians with the tasks of patient care, laboratory management, and housekeeping, under strict conditions of control. A hospital may also engage in teaching, with medical and nursing training programs that have to be coordinated with patient care services.

As a further example, consider the operations of sales and production departments in business firms. The sales department tries to sell all it can. Left to its own devices, the sales staff might sell more than the production department can make. Sales departments often demand a product that is designed for customer preference but that is inconsistent with cost and technical constraints important to the production unit.

Specialization

Specialization presents unusual problems of coordination and control. Specialization arises out of the complexities of modern technology, as well as from the diversity of tasks and persons needed to carry them out.

Specialists believe that they are the best judges of the scope, nature, and kind of work they perform, and that they alone are qualified to judge each other by professional criteria. However, if specialists are allowed to work without constraints or confinement to restricted missions, the results can be costly. Because specialists in staff units generally perform work that could be done by other units were it not for the desire for specialization, conflicts between the specialized and the regular units readily arise. Control and coordination efforts are needed to minimize such conflicts.

An interesting example of technical specialization leading to problems of coordination is found in government agencies, where the locus of coordination is external to a specific organization but internal to a social unit such as a city, county, or state. In 1975 in New York City, for example, there were over forty public agencies specializing in manpower problems. To achieve coordination, not to mention control and efficiency, among such an array of governmental units is difficult. Internal, independent specialization can have a similar effect. In one large city, for example, several hospitals were found to have duplicated expensive equipment, such as highly specialized heart machines that were often idle.

ACHIEVING COORDINATION

Administration is sometimes defined as the art of continuously resolving differences. It is virtually impossible to achieve a mechanically perfect system of clear-cut jurisdictions. Conflicts of jurisdiction may serve useful purposes. They provide tests of managerial thought and action, ensuring that no one function or specialist ignores the interests of others. The possibility of reckoning with others helps shape the manager's thinking. Conflicts inevitably arise in the interrelated actions of position holders, as well as from matters of timing, communications, and the degree of mutual understanding among individuals.

To minimize undesirable conflict, overlapping, and disorganization, managers can focus on the following ways of achieving coordination: (1) clear delegations of authority, (2) making decisions that establish or restore coordinated efforts, and (3) setting up coordinating units in the organization structure.

Delegating Authority and Responsibility

Coordination is required in both the horizontal and the vertical dimensions of an organization. Clarity of delegated authority and responsibility is important in achieving both types.

Vertical coordination harmonizes the work delegated to the various levels of an organization. It is important to assure that units at each level act in accord with those at other levels and with policies and objectives. This is done through careful delegation of authority. For example, the need for coordinating sales and production efforts is not restricted to the work of the heads of the two departments, but extends downward to the shop foreman and the outside salesmen.

Horizontal coordination pertains to relating the efforts of functional, divisional, or territorial units to each other. If the horizontal units, each created for special functions, are to work together in harmony, each needs to know the expected limits of its domain. Clarity of authority is not easy to achieve, however; authority needs constant interpretation in the contest of daily actions. Also, some overlapping of authority may be desirable even though it produces difficulties of coordination. For example, both the market research department and the public relations department might have the authority to conduct opinion surveys among customers. Such an overlap might be permissible, but a problem of coordination is to avoid having the same customer groups bombarded by questionnaires at the same time. For some problems, the two departments could use joint surveys. However, for different specific objectives, the overlapping and duplication would be justifiable.

Coordination Decisions

Good delegation alone cannot prevent all failures of coordination. Managers must observe ongoing activities and deal with coordination problems that do arise. The manager looks particularly for actions or decisions that are out of harmony with one another, for results that point to a lack of coordinated effort, for sources of misunderstanding or conflict, and for unnecessary duplication of effort.

All key decisions can be reviewed to consider their impact on coordination. Established systems and procedures help to develop coordinated effort. For example, Companywide or interdepartmental information can be provided by periodic reports and records, which managers can scan to detect soft spots in the interrelations of the units or people being coordinated. Coordination also involves continuous, judicious, personal contact with subordinates. During such contacts, many forms of communication may take place, includiing checking and observation.

Managers must inevitably make some decisions for the purpose of coordination. Such cases involve dealing with conflicts and finding the reasons why the lack of coordination has developed. These are hard many forms of communication may take place, including checking and observation.

Organizational Mechanisms

Some organizations establish units or positions that are primarily for the purposes of coordination. For example, state university systems in which each unit has a president may be coordinated by a chancellor. Some large companies coordinate all staff units, such as personnel management, legal affairs, and public relations, under an "administrator of staff services."

Committee structures included in the organization's design are useful in the over-all analysis and problem solving that lead to better coordination. The central task of such committees is to administer policy matters at the top echelons of the organization. Ad hoc committees, which may be appointed from time to time for coordination purposes, usually have narrower, specific jurisdictions and missions; they are also temporary, and are dissolved after their mission is completed.

Among the benefits of committees as coordination devices are (1) the application of participative or consultative supervision, contributing to greater uniformity of direction in the organization; (2) coordination of long- and short-term programs; (3) flexibility in emergency situations; (4) broader experience for managers and greater interchangeability of management personnel; (5) pooling of resources for problem solving in situations having no clear-cut answers; (6) coordination of related functions where each unit has its part in a predetermined or inevitable decision; and (7) greater acceptance and better execution of decisions because those affected have been consulted in advance and allowed to participate.

Staff meetings or other group conferences can provide further opportunities for coordination if leaders encourage free and open discussion and the interchange of ideas, proposals, and solutions. Improved understanding of organizationwide matters leads to better coordination. The group meeting provides for the focusing of face-to-face communication. Moreover, the atmosphere that is conducive to group decision is more likely to produce coordinated effort. As people work together in groups, lack of coordination tends to become apparent, and group processes tend to restore it. Group norms emphasizing the need for coordination can be developed.

ACHIEVING EFFECTIVE CONTROL

Effective control is achieved through two interrelated approaches: (1) overcoming human limitations through education, training, and supervision, and (2) appropriate administrative effort in the form of attention to the control cycle.

The fact that these two approaches go hand in hand is illustrated by the problem of safety in a manufacturing plant, where accidents cannot be minimized by mechanical means alone. Although safety devices are important, employees who think that they interfere with their earnings often disconnect them, hoping not to be detected. Moreover, some workers like to live dangerously and out of sheer bravado will flout safety rules. Clearly an additional approach is needed. To improve the attitudes and behavior of workers, supervisors are trained to be "safety-minded," so that they, in turn, can train workers to value accident prevention. In addition, continuous safety education campaigns use films, posters, meetings, contests, and the like to increase safety awareness.

Improving the Human Factor

Education and training are valuable ways of improving the degree of control that is present in an organization. They provide a positive approach that recognizes the dignity and importance of individuals.

People often like to behave as though control efforts do not apply to them, believing that controls are good for others but not for themselves. Managerial control procedures must take account of the desire for autonomy, at the same time rejecting the notion that "rules are made to be broken." Coercion or power is not effective in meeting the human problems of control. The best alternative is an approach that (1) recognizes the dignity and worth of human beings, and (2) allows their self-expression and participation in matters affecting them, and (3) enlists their cooperation by persuasive and educational means.

Control is most effective where it is least obvious. Managers should therefore plan their control efforts at the minimum needed for desired results. Control methods should be chosen with a view to minimizing objectionable features and maximizing the positive aspects. Control becomes more acceptable if it is part of a general atmosphere of competent, successful work and if managers make clear the reasons for control. One manager, for example, ordered a subordinate to submit a weekly report of his work. The subordinate grumbled about the additional effort, but when the manager explained that the reports would help to justify a larger budget, and that they could be brief, the subordinate accepted the control device.

The involvement of those who are affected by necessary controls helps win their acceptance. For example, in one company, workers were demanding their vacations in too limited a time, so that operations suffered. When confronted with the problem, they helped to work out an orderly priority system that eliminated the difficulty.

Control is best aimed at results, not at people as such. The purpose of control is to assure that intended results occur, not that employees be dominated, regimented, or reformed. The purpose of time clocks, for example, is to establish the habit of punctuality and to set up controlled measures of time worked, rather than to trap workers who are assumed to be cheating the company. Avoiding worker abuse of the time-clock system may require additional controls, but here again these controls should be focused, not on workers, but rather on the need for accurate measurement.

The Control Cycle

The control process, whether administrative or operational, is best viewed as a feedback cycle (Figure 9-2), which shows the basic elements upon which the manager focuses in maintaining any system in a state of control.

The control cycle functions at its most objective level for mechanical, operational, or routine controls, and where concrete measurement of the standards and results is possible. Administrative controls use the

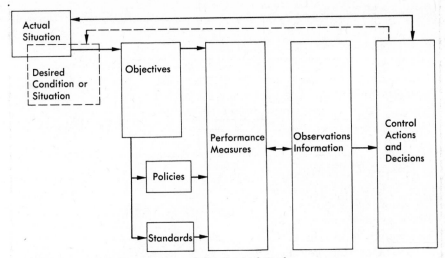

FIGURE 9-2. Schematic Diagram of the Control Cycle.

same elements, but because measurement is less precise, the functioning of the cycle is more subjective. Wherever possible, the factors entering into a problem of control should be mechanized or computerized in order to reduce the impact of subjectivity.

Let us now consider the key elements in the control cycle: (1) standards, (2) information about existing conditions, and (2) corrective actions.

Standards

The first step in control is to select a standard against which to compare results. Precision in stating such standards is important. In many areas of management, great precision is possible. Product specifications, for example, are determined by engineering techniques within ranges that make the product desirable and useful to users at a reasonable cost. In some areas, however, standards are less precise. An example is the set of performance standards a manager uses in directing subordinates. Even in such situations, however, systematic procedures can do much to make the control function concrete and effective.

Standards are usually stated in terms of a range—minimum to maximum—outside of which results are not acceptable. Within that range, there may be fluctuation and variation in results. The extent of the tolerance depends largely on the nature of the activity, the costs of compressing the range, and the uses of the end product. See Figure 9-3.

Standards also include (1) the setting of examples; (2) standing limitations; (3) standing rules, orders, and procedures; and (4) budgets.

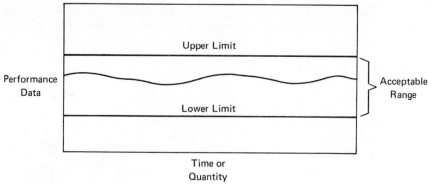

FIGURE 9-3. Control Range.

The Setting of Examples

Managers often find that setting an example helps control results. The example of the leader becomes the norm of the group. A supervisor who can operate a machine at a hundred units an hour (even though most union-management contracts do not permit him to) is in sounder position to demand a hundred units an hour from subordinates than one who cannot. A manager who can conceive broad plans himself is more likely to get subordinates to plan than one who works from day to day.

Setting an example works better where managers do not defy group norms but instead choose norms that strengthen their standing in the group. Managers who work late if they ask subordinates to work late usually strengthen their influence. A manager who is eager to show off by making others look inferior will lose people's support. It is seldom necessary—and indeed usually impossible—for managers to possess capabilities precisely equal to those of subordinates. But by providing good examples in their own behavior, managers help subordinates see expected standards in action.

Standing Limitations

Where subordinates are empowered to exercise considerable latitude in decision making, it is frequently desirable to place definite limits beyond which they may not go without permission. For example, a secretary may be authorized to use a fund for petty cash, but required to clear any items in excess of five dollars with a superior. A purchasing agent may be permitted to spend up to $10,000 but required to secure approval for contracts exceeding that amount. In this way, the higher manager prevents possible misuses by reserving an ultimate responsibility for exceptions beyond the limit. It is important, when in setting control limitations, to adapt them to the level of the manager, to the scope of his authority, and to the capabilities of the individual.

Standing Orders

By establishing rules, orders, and procedures, managers control routine behavior and can develop the performance habits of subordinates. *Rules* generally specify prohibited forms of behavior which, if allowed, would disrupt orderly effort or endanger people or the organization. *Standing orders* tell individuals what to do under given conditions that are repetitive or that may occur at any particular time. For example, standing orders may allow the members of a volunteer first-aid team to leave their jobs and to go to the scene of a disaster without waiting for specific orders. *Standing procedures* spell out correct sequences of events, or the series of activities through which work is accomplished. For example, to help control absenteeism, a standing procedure may require an employee to report the reason for his absence by a given time. When the report comes in, the procedure continues by the official recording of the absence, the compilation of statistics, the notification of the proper people, and so on.

As with other control devices—like records and reports—rules, orders, and procedures can be misused. Abuse and failure can be avoided if they are carefully planned and periodically audited. After an audit they can be modified or eliminated, if necessary.

Budgets

A budget is a planning instrument while managers are creating it, and a standard for comparing progress and evaluating results after it is established. Therefore, budgets are both planning and control devices.

Control through budgets comes from the fact that a budget provides limits to the activities it covers. It is true that the budget need not be, and indeed usually is not, rigid and inflexible. Even though the limits imposed by a budget are not fixed, however, the budget controls decisions and programs, for it is a continuous guide. Managers who exceed their budget need good reasons for requesting additional funds, and they can be criticized for poor planning if the need could reasonably have been anticipated. Managers who do not expend available funds may be censured for poor planning, for padding their original requests, or for not using the resources allocated to do the job assigned.

Usually managers participate in budgetary planning and control by submitting budget plans for their units. Higher management may modify this budget, but the process of initial planning has a controlling influence over the managers, providing pressure to make accurate estimates of needs. If managers are too far above realistic needs, the budget may be severely cut back. If the budget is too far below potential needs, top management may try to raise the manager's sights.

Information and Observation

The second major element in the control cycle is information. The presence of standards implies a corresponding ability to observe and comprehend existing conditions and to ascertain the degree of control achieved. Thus the whole pattern of information and communication is a key element in control.

The information system relating to the process of control provides two kinds of data: the results of measurement and appraisals of nonmeasurable factors. These are standards with which to test results. The process of measurement enters into both the determination of standards and the evaluation of results, but intended results expressed in terms other than those of mathematics or of engineering standards are more difficult to utilize. When intentions are expressed as objectives, plans, or policies, the planning process itself is substituted for measurement. Planning lends credence, authenticity, and precision to the manager's intentions. In the case of standards, the element of measurement is more significant. F. W. Taylor, for example, introduced the idea of determining output standards by stop-watch observations of work methods.

The process of measurement is fundamental in comparing results against intended performance. The success of such comparisons depends upon the quality of the measures used, so that managers must be sure that their intentions are as clear as possible, that performance is evaluated as fairly and accurately as possible, and that precise standards are used wherever applicable.

The fact that measurement of results against intentions cannot always be in quantitative terms, and that there must be an element of estimation and appraisal, need not deter one from attempting to achieve adequate control. In Drucker's words:

> It should indeed be an invariable practice to supply managers with clear and common measurements in all key areas of business. These measurements need not be rigidly quantitative; nor need they be exact. But they have to be clear, simple, and rational. They have to be relevant and direct attention and efforts where they should go. They have to be reliable ... and ... self-announcing, understandable without complicated interpretation or philosophical discussion.[4]

All managers must work with some nonmeasurable factors, judging what relative weight to give to measurable and nonmeasurable ele-

---

[4]Peter F. Drucker, *The Practice of Management* (New York: Harper, 1954), p. 131.

ments. Nonmeasurable items include human elements such as attitudes, beliefs, moral views, human abilities, thought processes, and personalities. Tools such as attitude surveys have been developed for appraising these factors and drawing appropriate conclusions, but they are far from exact, and statistical pitfalls exist to trap the untrained executive. It is possible to make a fetish of precision and measurement. Some managers cannot stand uncertainty, but the top-flight ones know where it is impractical or uneconomic to insist on certainty, and learn to operate within the range that is practical and feasible. It is highly important, moreover, that managers know what is actually important to measure. One utility executive reported that more than half of the monthly statistical data he automatically received was useless.

Records and reports have considerable control value, but they can also clog the organizational machinery by becoming too numerous, too burdensome, and too time-consuming. Many reports are not read; many records are not consulted. There is no justification for records and reports that are unused or unusable. Most organizations can save money by studying their records systems and report procedures, eliminating those that have become archaic.

Observation of Subordinates

The fact that managers systematically observe the work methods and results of their subordinates exerts a controlling influence, as does their mere presence, even without overt observation. The possibility of being observed, often unpredictably, has an inevitable effect on workers. There is some truth in the adage that "when the cat's away, the mice will play." Much depends, of course, on the skill with which a manager creates the illusion of being present even during his absence.

Workers know that observation leads to evaluation (of themselves as well as of their work). Sometimes this causes them to perform "for the record," trying to impress the boss. In spite of these and other defects, observation remains a strong ally of control, and should be planned and systematic. There is no substitute for frequent personal contacts with subordinates, not to exchange pleasantries but to make needed observations.

Auditing

Personal contacts cannot do the entire job, however, primarily because of the difficulty of piecing together a number of fragmentary observations so as to see the enterprise or a segment of it as a whole. To do that, a system of audit or review may be used. Auditing involves preparing a plan to assure that key facts will be observed. Critical measures are then applied. A good example is the financial audit: when a company has drawn up its annual financial report, it is customary to retain an outside accounting firm to audit the company's books.

Many companies have instituted continuous systems of internal auditing that are not restricted to financial matters. The internal auditor is an employee whose job may include, in addition to finance, auditing the performance of company policies, practices, and plans. The auditor points out defects, neglected situations, or problems, and makes suggestions based on careful analysis.

Review is similar to auditing except that qualitative rather than quantitative factors may be emphasized. For example, policies may be reviewed periodically to make sure they are sound and up to date. Personnel requirements may be reviewed to bring recruiting into perspective with production changes. Managerial performance may be reviewed by superiors who wish to develop their subordinates.

Control Actions and Decisions

The third major element in control is that of taking actions or making decisions that maintain the desired degree of control. In simple systems, control may be established or restored by altering one or more of a few variables. In complex systems, the processes of detecting disequilibrium, disharmony, or lack of control are often slow and difficult; consequently remedial decision and action may also be slow. In such complexity, the conditions for achieving control are always changing.

Actions and decisions required by the problem of control vary. Managers may make different interpretations of similar situations and use different methods of control. Where control can be built into a system through planning, or incorporated into computer systems, control becomes automatic, as in the case of information-feedback processes.

Haberstroh found, in studying a steel company, that the characteristics postulated by cybernetic theory for self-regulating systems have their correlates in human organizations. Feedback performance and objectives were found to have a major influence on two types of decisions: the programming of routine work, and innovation in the organization of executive functions. A self-regulating system such as a thermostat operates in a state of equilibrium put there by engineering design. In a complex organization, however, such an exact control cannot be established because existing conditions are the result of so many factors. One of the most significant factors is the conscious intent of those who designed the system and operate it. Because these intentions are part of the communications network, they can be observed and even measured. Managers can form a common picture of their collective and individual intentions, and can then act and react so as to maintain or control the system at a desired level of performance.[5]

Disciplinary Action

Disciplinary action functions as a control to the extent to which it can be made preventive and corrective in nature. This is difficult to do, but deviations from orderly and effective behavior cannot be allowed to go unheeded. If they are, they will grow worse and more numerous. Even after positive controls—such as motivation, example, and records— have been utilized, some deviate behavior will occur.

The theory of disciplinary action is not well understood. The general idea is that control results from the desire of employees to avoid the penalties for undesirable behavior. The deterring nature of specific penalties cannot be doubted, but it is often exaggerated. Control is the net result of many factors, one of which may be the threat that disciplinary action will occur. In spite of limitations in the theory, however, practical actions often require recognition that orderly behavior cannot be obtained from every individual and that in severe cases an employee may have to be discharged

Censure or reprimand are mild forms of disciplinary action that may help in some cases; in others, more drastic measures, such as wage penalties, layoffs, or discharges, are needed.

Although most executives favor positive forms of control, negative sanctions may be required. For example, a worker who is often absent from work may be restrained somewhat by a report-and-record procedure and the superior's known dislike of such behavior. Some workers who are not so restrained, however, become chronic absentees. At this point, the supervisor may use censure in the form of an oral or written reprimand.

Censure is unpopular among employees: unions try to protect members against unfair punishment, and subordinates usually dread censure, reprimand, ridicule, or any form of criticism or disapproval. Hence, it is imperative for managers to use censure with wisdom and understanding. Used recklessly, with cruelty or unfairness or in a thoughtless manner, it can become a dangerous weapon. On the other hand, it is also unwise to avoid using censure where it can help someone. Some managers too readily avoid censuring subordinates because it is an unpleasant duty, requiring considerable skill if it is to be effective. Discharge, the most severe form of disciplinary action, is usually a last-resort procedure.

[5]Chadwick J. Haberstroh, "Control as an Organizational Process," *Management Science* 6 (January 1960), 165–171.

Social Controls

Among the more interesting and least-studied types of controls in organizations are those classified as social in character. The term *social* means determined by the system as a whole—institutionalized requirements enforced by social pressures from associates acting not as individuals, but as members of a small group.

Among the social controls in organizations are norms, customs, conventions, unwritten laws, habits, practices, status and prestige systems, organizationally determined and disseminated values, myths, and folklore. Some social controls are, of course, manifested in formal rules, regulations, and other control devices. But the sanctions that are brought to bear in order to control the behavior of individuals are more diffuse and subtle for infractions of social requirements than for deviations from formal organizational requirements.

Peer-group pressure is often at work. Social pressures brought to bear upon "rate busters" or "eager beavers" are familiar to anyone who has worked in a plant or office. Few persons can withstand the contempt of fellow workers aroused by departure from standards determined by and accepted in the immediate work group.

The Statistical Aspects of Control

Wherever possible, control based on objective, measurable standards is preferable to the use of subjective judgment. The same is true for controls that can be built into cybernetic, computerized, or automated systems. Between the extremes of judgmental and automatic control lies a kind of control that can be established by statistical means.

To illustrate the statistical element in control, let us consider the problem of maintaining the quality of the firm's product. Most manufacturing companies have departments of quality control; other firms simply call them inspection departments. The basic idea, in any case, is to make sure that customers get a product without defects, and that each item conforms to the standards which the company wishes it to meet.

Because it is uneconomical or impossible to inspect every unit of a product, inspection is often a statistical process. Statistical quality-control procedures consist of measuring probabilities that tell the number or percentage of items to check in order to predict with a given degree of accuracy that the remainder of the items are like those actually checked. The items are checked by sampling procedures. Manufactured items may seem to be identical,but they have variations from piece to piece. These variations, if measured, will fall into a frequency distribution. The patterns of variation repeat themselves indefinitely within predictable limits, unless some cause intervenes to throw the expected pattern off.

Control is at the desired level if the variations fall within the tolerance limits established for the items being produced. The production supervisor does not become alarmed unless the control charts indicate that the variation is exceeding the tolerances. Thus we see that quality control involves the human element—a manager concerned with the limits of quality to which the product is being made and one or more workers. It also involves technical elements such as control charts and statistical analysis. In addition, a number of devices, such as scales, gauges, and the like, aid inspectors in measuring variations from standard.

Some products, like fine furniture, may require complete and individual visual inspection. Products such as piston rings for automobile engines, however, are turned out by machines in huge quantities and to such finely drawn specifications that mechanical means of inspection and concepts of statistical quality control must be employed.

Automation and Control

In recent years a concept known as *automation* has taken root in the management of organizations. The term has been identified with the "push-button factory," with the concept of feedback mechanisms, with automatic machines with improved materials handling, and with assembly lines. However, automation is not a mere extension of concepts of mechanization and mass production, as such identifications might imply. Automation applies not only to factories, but to any repetitive and large-volume process, such as billing or payrolls. It includes, but goes beyond, automatic, mechanized, or assembly-line production. It is a totally new way of looking at the problem of organizing and performing work. It extends to the design of the product and to the planning of work processes.

Automation views production processes as an integrated system and not as a series of individual steps divided according to the most economic distribution of human skills—or even of individual machines. Automation is a philosophy rather than a particular technology or set of devices; it is a conceptual innovation as revolutionary as Ford's concept of the assembly line. According to Drucker, automation "is not technical in character. Like every technology it is primarily a system of concepts, and its technical aspects are results rather than causes." Rather than organizing work according to the product, as in assembly-line production or mass production, automation focuses on the processes, "which it sees as an integrated and harmonious whole."[6]

Automation is an application of the systems idea. It exists at levels of abstraction ranging from the technical to the philosophical. By linking

[6]Peter F. Drucker, *The Practice of Management* (New York: Harper, 1954), p. 19.

processes or machines to other processes or machines and utilizing computers and feedback mechanisms, automatic controls, and sensing devices, continuous automatic production can be envisioned, with a consequent reduction in the use of labor. Man appears outside the process as planner, innovator, or controller, rather than within the process as laborer.

Although automation is often considered as a factory or manufacturing concept, its nontechnical character and its philosophical and conceptual nature make it applicable to management problems in all kinds of organizations. Retail stores, banks, insurance offices, hotels, and other service organizations find automation useful. Automation concepts are also widely used in such nonbusiness organizations as schools, government units, and hospitals. However, research and practice in these areas has lagged behind that in business firms.

Within the broad concept of automation there are four main areas: (1) automatic machinery, (2) integrated materials handling and processing equipment, (3) control mechanisms, and (4) computers. The first three are generally directed and controlled by some form of computerization.

Through greater speed and accuracy of data processing, and the systems analysis that precedes the installation of computer centers, better prediction and control result. The feasibility studies used in planning computer facilities often discover duplications and wasted effort, but some of this overlap is necessary for the service and control that are being provided by the new system. New data-processing equipment is not an improvement if it lowers costs by reducing services and controls.

The computer's major contribution to the concept of control lies in its role as a component of information-feedback control mechanisms. An information-feedback system consists of decisions leading to changes which in turn affect future decisions. The character of decisions or conditions over time can be determined by the nature of preceding decisions or conditions.

The use of computers to control complex production processes provides an interesting example. Many factories are now being constructed around computers that control their production and product-mix processes. Computers are used to produce steel, chemicals, paint, petroleum products, power, and paper at a level of efficiency beyond the reach of human operators managed by direct supervision. At first computers were developed for continuous-flow production processes, such as those just cited; but many believe that computers may be similarly applied to "discrete-parts" production systems. General Motors has installed the automobile industry's first computer-managed transfer line; it uses this complex of automated tools to help assemble rear axles. IBM, Inc., has installed computers to guide the flow of city traffic; Digital Equipment Corporation sells small computers to control laboratory equipment; and the Mobil Oil Corporation has a process computer to oversee a 351-well oil field.

The influence of computers is spreading into office and clerical processes; there they are used in ways similar to electronic data processing. Furthermore, process computers are being linked to each other and to electronic data-processing computers to form an electronic chain of command. Thus there is a hierarchy of the concept of control in the utilization of computers.

PERT

Production control has been greatly improved by the use of PERT techniques through computerized scheduling techniques.

PERT is an acronym for Program Evaluation and Review Technique, sometimes called Critical Path Method (CPM). It is a network system model for planning and scheduling work projects, and hence it is a control technique as well. It was developed jointly by the Navy Special-Projects Office and Booz, Allen & Hamilton management consultants, in conjunction with the Fleet Ballistic Missile Program. It was successfully used in producing the Polaris Missile, and has since been increasingly used in industry.

PERT involves (1) identifying all key activities in a project, (2) devising the sequence of activities and arranging a flow diagram, and (3) assigning duration times for the performance of each phase of the work. The sum of the estimated durations along the most lengthy sequence of activities gives the estimated total time span for the entire project. PERT uses time as a common denominator to reflect three basic factors in work projects: time, use of resources, and performance specifications. By adding mathematical concepts and the use of computers, PERT represents an advance over former systems of planning and scheduling such as Gantt charts. Its basic principle, however, is similar to Gantt chart scheduling.

The critical path of a program is the longest possible time span along the system flow. The critical path is obtained by organizing the events in sequence, beginning with the final event in the total network and working backwards. Simple sequences can be worked out manually, but more complex ones are programmed on computers. Observation of the network plan and the critical path makes possible the comparison of progress in each part of the project with the target dates of completion. Frequent review and reporting procedures are established. Inputs into the network are assembled and programmed into the computer, which then prints out a report on the status of the time interval estimates compared to the actual reported progress. Figure 9-4 shows one type of PERT flow diagram based on the Critical Path Method (CPM). The circles show the key events, such as "redesign" or "build prototype."

CPM network for Antismog Device Redesign Project

CPM Activity Designations and Time Estimates

Activity	Designation	Immediate Predecessors	Time in Weeks
Redesign	A	--	21
Build Prototype	B	A	5
Evaluate Tooling	C	A	7
Test Prototype	D	B	2
Write Tooling Report	E	C,D	5
Write Methods Report	F	C,D	8
Write Final Report	G	E,F	2

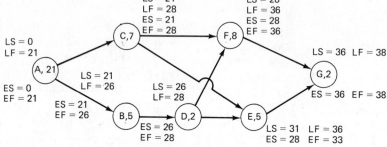

Slack Calculations and Critical Path Determinations

Activity	LS–ES	Slack	On Critical Path
A	0-0	0	✓
B	21-21	0	✓
C	21-21	0	✓
D	26-26	0	✓
E	31-28	3	
F	28-28	0	✓
G	36-36	0	✓

ES = Earliest time to start an activity.

LS = Latest time to start an activity and keep project on schedule.

EF = Earliest time to finish an activity.

LF = Latest time to finish an activity and keep the project on schedule.

FIGURE 9-4. A CPM Diagram Showing Activities, Times, Work Flows, and Critical Path.

Source: Richard B. Chase and Nicholas J. Aquilano, *Production and Operations Management,* rev. ed. (Homewood, Ill.: Richard D. Irwin, Inc., 1977 ©), p. 558. Reproduced by permission of the publisher.

Arrows indicate the sequences of events, and the codes along the arrows show the number of days available for starting and finishing an activity. Activities A, B, C, D, F, and G are on the critical path, with slack shown for Activity E. This procedure provides a basis for comparing actual production schedules at each stage to the main plan and its over-all target of 38 days.[7]

[7]Perhaps the best piece of writing on PERT is the pamphlet with which the Navy introduced it, *PERT Summary Report Phase 1* (Washington, D.C.: U.S. Government Printing Office, 1958). A procedural approach is given in IBM's General Information Manual, *PERT . . . A Dynamic Project Planning and Control Method,* E20-8067, published by IBM, 112 East Post Road, White Plains, New York, 10601.

The fact that PERT is a total systems approach results in desirable program perspectives. Each program, moreover, is planned in detail by the participants, making possible better teamwork and communication. Applications of PERT indicate promise for (1) handling resource allocation and interproject scheduling relationships, (2) providing increasingly accurate estimates of the probability of timely completion of projects, and (3) making meaningful evaluations of the quality of the past activity time and cost estimates and work performance. Although PERT was originally designed for very large network systems, smaller projects are more typical in business, and PERT has been successfully applied to them as well.

The original emphasis in PERT plans was on the factor of time in complex projects. An extention of PERT/Time is known as PERT/Cost, a system that monitors plans and controls progress as well as the time progress of a project. Cost breakdowns are obtained and associated with the relevant steps in the time process. Alternative costs can also be compared. Although this variation of PERT has numerous values, such as improvement of financial planning, it has not been widely adopted as PERT/Time has been.[8]

_____ **SUMMARY**

Coordination is defined as the leadership activity designed to establish unity of effort toward a common purpose. It is the blended, integrated, total performance that is primary. Coordination is a leadership responsibility and a managerial duty of utmost importance. Top administrators, in particular, find coordination a pressing matter.

The need for coordination arises from the size, complexity, and functional differentiation of an organization, as well as from geographical or physical dispersion. It is also made necessary by the vagaries and unpredictability of human behavior, and from ever-present problems of communication and change.

The development and maintenance of effective coordination involves (1) keeping authority and responsibilities clearly defined; (2) checking, observing, and appraising the nature and extent of conflicting elements; and (3) facilitating effective communication.

Control is a situation in which results are occurring as planned or intended according to standards. Methods of control are designed to keep actual results in line with intended results. Measurement processes are valuable in setting standards and in comparing results, but some results are not capable of being reduced to measurable terms, so

_____

[8]For further information on PERT, see Jerome D. Wiest and Ferdinand K. Levy, *A Management Guide to PERT/CPM* (Englewood Cliffs, N. J.: Prentice-Hall, 1977); Peter P. Schoderbek, *Management Systems*, 2nd ed. (New York: Wiley, 1971).

that executives must learn to balance consideration of what can only be estimated with what can be measured.

Coordination and control have similar roots in an organization and pose similar problems. If coordination and control are deficient, the accomplishments of the organization will suffer. Although a certain degree of coordination and control can be designed into the managerial and organizational system, or engineered into the technological system, the executive's personal activity and attitudes are critical for successful coordination and control.

Positive control and coordination decisions are preferable, although many situations require the use of censure, reprimand, discharge, and other disciplinary actions.

INCIDENT CASE

The output of Department A is an input for Department B. The output of Department B is an input for Department C. The output of Department C is an input for both Departments D and E. Department B consists largely of professional engineers who tend to behave in a highly independent manner. The output of Department B has recently become very inadequate, containing errors, and it is not being transmitted to Department C according to the schedule.

Question:

1. As the general supervisor over all these departments, what steps can you take to achieve better coordination and control?

QUESTIONS FOR STUDY

1. What factors do you believe strongly inhibit the coordination of two or more functions or activities? How can executives eliminate or minimize these factors?

2. Analyze the statement "What's good for my department is of necessity what is best for the company."

3. Can coordination occur spontaneously? If executives are capable, intelligent, and experienced, and are men of good will, can coordination be expected to follow automatically?

4. What interconnections can you describe between "management by the exceptions principle" and coordination? Can you relate decision-making concepts to your answer?

5. Explain the concept of self-coordination. Can you find examples from an actual organization in which you have had experience?

6. What are the specific symptoms or manifestations of poor coordination?

7. How will computers and automatic data-processing techniques affect problems of coordination?

8. Do problems of coordination vary from one kind of company to another, from one industry to another, or in companies of varying sizes?

9. Describe the principal elements that constitute the process of executive control.

10. What is the relationship between planning and control? What are the main similarities and differences?

11. What is happening in a situation where there is lack of control?

12. What does an executive do when he is controlling? What steps does an executive take to maintain control?

13. How can a situation be controlled without causing problems in human relations? Are such problems inevitable?

14. Discuss the merits and disadvantages of close supervision as a means of control over the work of subordinates.

15. How does one control the activities of professionals such as engineers, lawyers, or psychologists in the organization?

SELECTED REFERENCES

ANTHONY, ROBERT N. *Planning and Control Systems.* Boston: Division of Research, Graduate School of Business Administration, Harvard University, 1965.

BEER, STAFFORD. *Decision and Control.* New York: John Wiley & Sons, Inc., 1966.

DALTON, MELVILLE. *Men Who Manage.* New York: John Wiley & Sons, Inc., 1959. Chapters 7, 8, 9.

DAVIS, RALPH C. *The Fundamentals of Top Management.* New York: Harper & Row, Publishers, 1951. Chapters 17, 19.

DEMING, ROBERT H. *Characteristics of an Effective Management Control System in an Industrial Organization.* Boston: Division of Research, Graduate School of Business Administration, Harvard University, 1968.

JOHNSON, RICHARD A., FREMOND E. KAST, and JAMES E. ROSENZWEIG. *The Theory and Management of Systems.* Rev. ed. New York: McGraw-Hill Book Company, 1968. Chapters 1–6.

LAWLER, EDWARD E., III, and JOHN GRANT RHODES. *Information and Control in Organization.* Pacific Palisades, Calif.: Goodyear Publishing Company, 1976.

LIKERT, RENSIS. *New Patterns of Management.* New York: McGraw-Hill Book Company, 1961. Chapters 5, 13.

McGREGOR, DOUGLAS. *The Professional Manager.* New York: McGraw-Hill Book Company, 1967. Part IV.

MOCKLER, ROBERT J. *The Management Control Process.* New York: Appleton-Century-Crofts, 1971.

MODLER, JOSEPH J., and CECIL R. PHILLIPS. *Project Management with CPM and PERT.* New York: Van Nostrand Reinhold Company, 1971.

NEWMAN, WILLIAM H. *Constructive Control.* Englewood Cliffs, Jersey: Prentice-Hall, Inc., 1975.

PETIT, THOMAS A. *Fundamentals of Management Coordination: Supervisors, Middle-Managers, and Executives.* New York: John Wiley & Sons, Inc., 1975.

SAYLES, LEONARD. *Managerial Behavior.* New York: McGraw-Hill Book Company, 1964. Chapter 10.

TANNENBAUM, ARNOLD S., ed. *Control in Organizations.* McGraw-Hill Book Company, 1968.

THOMPSON, VICTOR A. *Modern Organization.* New York: Alfred A. Knopf, Inc., 1961. Chapter 9.

WIEST, JEROME D., and FERDINAND K. LEVY. *A Management Guide to PERT/CPM.* 2nd ed. Englewood Cliffs, N.J.: Prentice-Hall, Inc., 1977.

WILLIAMSON, OLIVER E. *Corporate Control and Business Behavior.* Englewood Cliffs, N.J.: Prentice-Hall, Inc., 1970.

Chapter 10

Leadership and Supervision

A tale is told of a man in Paris during the upheaval in 1848, who saw a friend marching after a crowd toward the barricades. Warning him that these could not be held against the troops, that he had better keep away, and asking why he followed these people, he received the reply, "I must follow them. I am their leader."   —*Attributed to A. Lawrence Lowell*

—in short, in integrity lies the answer to that ever returning question, *Quis custodes ipsos custodiet?* Who is to supervise the supervisors? —*Alan Gregg*

CHAPTER GUIDE

Why aren't leaders bolder and more imaginative? It's because people do not like them that way, say many psychologists. Unlike animals, which are led by the strongest and toughest member of the group, humans prefer as their leader the most effective talker, the one who can articulate most clearly the group aims.

People expect a leader to be active and assertive, to espouse new ideas and to lead them into new areas. But they also expect him to be safe and careful. New ideas must not be too different or too sudden. And the decisions that the leader makes must be those that most group members would make.

Questions to keep in mind while you read this chapter:

1. How do leaders know how far ahead of their followers they can get without losing them?
2. In what respects should leaders be like members of their group, and in what respects should they be different?

Leadership is an area of managerial responsibility that follows from the needs, discued in previous chapters, to develop plans and set objectives that help the organization cope with the future and meet the demands of the environment. It also stems from the needs of organization members for guidance and direction in doing their work.

Leadership is vital to the survival and effectiveness of organizations, which consequently spend substantial sums to find and train leaders. As organizations have grown and the expectations about their performance have increased, demands for leadership have multiplied. The technical, economic, social, and political characteristics of organizations bring about continuing needs for the innovation, creativity, and imagination of leaders.

People capable of exercising effective leadership in organizations are scarce relative to the need for them. Leadership ability, therefore, is a valuable skill, and those who possess it reap high rewards. The almost universal scarcity of effective leaders causes organizations to search constantly for them and fosters development and better utilization of existing leadership potentials in people.[1]

The shortage of leaders is a problem because there are no good substitutes for effective leadership. Weak managers are sometimes tolerated in the false belief that a strong organization structure can support them. According to Dimock,

> A serious and common mistake . . . is to assume that a weak man in a pivotal position can be bolstered by surrounding him with one or more persons of capacity, making it necessary for several to do what the top man should be able to accomplish alone. Almost without exception, the makeshift fails.[2]

A major cause of the shortage of leaders is that organizations too often fail to provide conditions under which leadership can flourish. Organizations should create a climate in which leadership thrives—one that encourages managers to practice leadership skills under the guidance of competent superiors, and rewards them for success as leaders.

This chapter discusses both the theoretical and the practical aspects of leadership according to three main topics: (1) leadership theory and research, (2) modes by which organizations develop effective leaders, and (3) the concept of supervision as an application of leadership theory.

LEADERSHIP: THEORY AND RESEARCH

A basic definition of leadership is *the ability of an individual to influence others to work beyond ordinary levels to achieve goals.* Such

---

[1]James A. Reichley, "Our Critical Shortage of Leadership," *Fortune* **84** (September 1971), 88–93.

[2]Marshall Dimock, *The Executive in Action* (New York: Harper, 1945), p. 150.

a definition applies particularly to leadership within organizations, although it could also apply to the leadership of great men of influence in the community and in society.

Leadership is more fully defined as a complex phenomenon combining the personal traits of individuals as well as significant variables in group or organizational contexts. The earliest theories of leadership focused almost exclusively on personality traits, whereas current theory emphasizes the context or situational elements.

Research on leadership has often been highly normative. It has tried to find the best way of leading, or of developing leaders in organizations. This complicates the research, because the dimensions of leadership that are used as variables may come to have evaluative rather than descriptive or analytical meanings. It is difficult to specify the variables, because the popular image of leadership views it as one-dimensional—the "tough" leader or the "authoritarian" leader, for example. Values are apparent in such labels. Much of the research has considered leadership behavior as an independent variable, comparing differences in leadership behavior with dependent variables such as group productivity and employee satisfaction. Properties and activities of the group thus become intervening variables. Research treating leadership as a dependent variable may be needed.[3]

Research on leadership can be divided into three interrelated categories: (1) the early period, which focused largely on traits and which viewed leadership as one-dimensional, (2) the discovery that leadership is multidimensional, and (3) the discovery of the importance of the situational and contextual factors that produced a contingency approach to leadership.

The Early Period

Gordon has summarized the early research on leadership,[4] including studies of the authoritarian leader, the emergent or natural leader, and formal leaders in bureaucratic organizations; he also covers the problems of training leaders. Applewhite has summarized much of the research on leadership roles and functions, the question of why people attempt to lead, leadership under stress conditions, the relationship of communication to leadership, the problem of leader assessment, and the concept of leadership styles.[5]

Studies of authoritarian leaders have focused on dictatorial political leadership and have explored the meaning of power and authority in

---

[3]For further discussion of the problems of leadership research, see Abraham Zaleznik and David Moment, *The Dynamics of Interpersonal Behavior* (New York: Wiley, 1964), pp. 418–427.

[4]Thomas Gordon, *Group-Centered Leadership* (Boston: Houghton Mifflin Company, 1955), pp. 46–51.

[5]Philip B. Applewhite, *Organizational Behavior* (Englewood Cliffs, N.J.: Prentice-Hall, 1965), chap. 6.

society.[6] Research on the emergent or natural leader involves, primarily, the study of small, informal groups, with emphasis on leadership as a group role. These studies, in the field of "group dynamics," have many applications where small groups within large organizations can be identified.[7] Studies of formal leaders within organizations include observations of actual leaders to see what factors apparently led to their positions of leadership.[8] Finally, the problem of training leaders has encouraged the investigation of methods by which effective leaders can be discovered, developed, and helped to lead their groups more satisfactorily.[9]

Trait Theory

The earliest theories sought to establish the personal traits necessary for effective leaders. Until the middle 1940s, leadership research centered on identifying the traits or personal characteristics of individual leaders. Such traits as *honesty, loyalty, ambition, aggressiveness, initiative,* and *drive* were deemed important. The earliest theories held that traits are inherited, and that certain people are born to be leaders. Traits are carried in the genes, and persons endowed with appropriate traits were "natural" leaders. Later, these theories held that traits could also be developed through learning and experience.

Trait theory gained wide credence, but convincing evidence failed to emerge. It was a highly plausible theory, corresponding closely with commonly observed experiences. Studies of successful leaders nearly always indicated that there were similarities in personality and character traits; but many good leaders did not possess the expected traits, and the presence of the traits did not reliably predict leadership behavior. Moreover, trait theory failed to consider the influence of situational factors. Leadership cannot be understood apart from its relationship to contexts as well as to individuals. It has not been possible to identify universal, specific traits common to all leaders; and the degree to which managers possess given traits does not vary directly with measures of effective leadership.

[6]T. W. Adorno et al., *The Authoritarian Personality* (New York: Harper, 1950). Studies in military leadership also bear upon authoritarian and democratic leaders. See, for example, Fillmore H. Sanford, *Authoritarianism and Leadership* (Philadelphia: Institute for Research in Human Relations, 1950).

[7]The vast literature of group dynamics and social psychology contains much work on leadership in small groups. See Warren Bennis, Kenneth D. Benne, and Robert Chin, *The Planning of Change* (New York: Holt, 1961), chaps. 9–12; John W. Thibaut and Harold H. Kelley, *The Social Psychology of Groups* (New York: Wiley, Inc., 1959).

[8]See, for example, Chris Argyris, *Executive Leadership* (New York: Harper, 1953); Eugene E. Jennings, *An Anatomy of Leadership* (New York: Harper, 1960).

[9]The work of the National Training Laboratory in group development is illustrative. See Edgar H. Schein and Warren G. Bennis, *Personal and Organizational Change Through Group Methods: The Laboratory Approach* (New York: Wiley, 1965); Warren G. Bennis et al., *Interpersonal Dynamics* (Homewood, Ill.: Dorsey, 1964).

Gouldner cites the following additional weaknesses in trait theory: (1) lists of traits usually do not indicate which ones are most important and which are least important; (2) traits are often not mutually exclusive—as, for example, in the case of judgment and common sense; (3) trait studies do not distinguish between traits that are needed for *acquiring* leadership and those that are necessary for *maintaining* it; (4) trait studies describe, but do not analyze, behavior patterns; and (5) the trait theory is based on debatable assumptions regarding personality, which for example, ignore the fact that a personality is not the mere summation of a collection of traits, but is a function of the total organization of the individual.[10]

Leadership as Influence

During the early period of leadership research, leadership was also defined as a process of influence.

McGregor specifies the main variables of the leadership relationship as (1) the characteristics of the leader; (2) the attitudes, needs, and personal characteristics of followers; (3) the characteristics of the organization, such as its basic purpose, habits, customs, traditions, structure, and the nature of the tasks performed; and (4) the social, economic, and political milieu.[11] However, specifying the variables in this way says nothing about how the variables affect one another. Tannenbaum has used variables similar to McGregor's, connecting them by the idea of influence. He defines leadership as "interpersonal influence, exercised in situations and directed, through the communication process, toward the attainment of goals.[12] This definition implies that leadership is a process of purposive behavior, continuous through time.

The process of influence has been intensively studied in behavioral science, although much of the research has concerned propaganda analysis and influence in large groups such as societies.[13] But our knowledge of leadership in organizations has been greatly advanced by viewing the executive as being a leader to the extent that he is able to influence others by initiating activity for them. Whyte's theoretical work in human relations has defined leadership, in the sense of influencing others, as initiating actions for others.[14] Whyte's definition helps

[10]Alvin W. Gouldner (ed.), *Studies in Leadership* (New York: Harper, 1950), pp. 23–24, 31–35. For a study more favorable to the theory of managerial traits, see Lyman W. Porter, "Perceived Trait Requirements in Bottom and Middle Management," *Journal of Applied Psychology* 45 (August 1961).

[11]Douglas McGregor, *The Human Side of Enterprise* (New York: McGraw-Hill, 1960), pp. 182–185.

[12]Robert Tannenbaum, Irving R. Weschler, and Fred Massarik, *Leadership and Organizations: A Behavioral Science Approach* (New York: McGraw-Hill, 1961).

[13]See, for example, Elihu Katz and Paul F. Lazarsfeld, *Personal Influence* (New York: Free Press, 1955).

[14]William Foote Whyte, *Organizational Behavior: Theory and Application* (Homewood, Ill.: Irwin, 1969).

to distinguish leadership based on formal positional authority from a more fundamental concept of leadership based on persuasion, example, and social skills rather than on the use of force, power, threats, or command. The concept of influence connotes the ability to accomplish much more in association with others than the strictly formal components of organizational action would predict.

Zaleznik and Moment express the idea of influence in their definition of leadership as follows:

> An interaction in which the conscious intentions of one person are communicated in his behavior, verbal and otherwise, with the consequence that the other person wants to and does behave in accordance with the first person's intentions.[15]

Power and Influence

Influence is the result of a variety of forces that work in differing combinations for each position holder in an organization. The concept of power as the capacity to influence is central to the understanding of organizational leadership. According to French and Raven, there are five major sources of power that result in the leader's ability to influence others: (1) legitimate power, (2) reward power, (3) coercive power, (4) referent power, and (5) expert power.[16]

Legitimate power comes from delegated authority and is recognized by others as necessary in the performance of assigned responsibilities. *Reward power* consists of the ability to bestow money, praise, promotions, or other benefits upon subordinates. *Coercive power* derives from the ability to apply punishment or to withhold rewards. *Referent power* is based on the leader's personality and the ability to inspire and attract the support of others, as well as on the leader's alliances with other influential persons. Finally, *expert power* comes from the leader's special skills, abilities, and knowledge.

Thus we see that leaders draw on many sources for their ability to influence others, and that power embraces a number of these sources. For influence to become leadership, there must be a significant increment of influence over and above compliance with routine duties. Leadership is present when a person goes beyond ordinary performance, and in so doing realizes more fully the potentials of his influence. This quality accounts for the differences among persons who show better performance than others in positions whose formal requirements are technically the same.

[15]Zaleznek and Moment, *Dynamics,* p. 414.

[16]J. R. French and B. Raven, "The Bases of Social Power," in Dorwin Cartwright and Alvin F. Zander (eds.), *Group Dynamics,* 2nd ed. (Evanston, Ill.: Row, Peterson, 1960), pp. 607–623.

Leader-Follower Relations

Employees at all levels tend to evaluate their jobs and their organizations according to the kind of leadership behavior their bosses exhibit. Democratic values are predominant in Western societies, and such institutions as schools, labor unions, and churches help foster these values in political, economic, and social affairs. At the same time, authoritarian leaders are numerous and are often effective.

An authoritarian leader gets others to follow orders through actual or implied threats, the authority and prestige of an organizational position, or a hard-boiled demeanor. Authoritarians strongly insist on getting their own way, feeling little or no need for the ideas of others. Authoritarian leadership exalts the leader at the expense of others in the group. Often the authoritarian leader takes credit for accomplishments but blames failure on followers. Yet authoritarian leadership is not necessarily uncomfortable to followers: many people feel more secure under strong leaders.

Democratic leaders lead mainly by persuasion and example rather than by force, fear, status, or power. They consider the opinions and feelings of followers, make them feel important, and attempt to put group and individual goals above their own personal objectives. They encourage participation in decision making.

Of course, autocracy or democracy is a matter of degree. Few leaders are at either extreme, and most are in between. Research indicates that in most situations the democratically led group is likely to be superior in accomplishment to a group led by an authoritarian. The classic study reporting such findings was conducted by Lewin, Lippitt, and White, who studied autocratic, laissez-faire, and democratic leadership in boys' groups. They concluded that democratic leadership produced less aggressive behavior, less dependence on the leader, more group initiative, and more productive behavior than the other two types of leadership.[17]

The case for the superiority of democratic leadership over authoritarian leadership is not yet conclusive, however. Leavitt asserts that even though people cooperate better and indicate higher job satisfaction when they participate in decision making, the decisions themselves are not necessarily better.[18] It is well to note Leavitt's caution, but also to recognize that participation can take many forms, some more helpful than others. The extent to which group members value participation varies. If they want it and do not have it, they usually resist imposed decisions. If they are expected to participate when they do not strongly

[17]R. Lippitt and R. K. White, "An Experimental Study of Leadership and Group Life," in T. M. Newcomb and E. L. Hartley (eds.), *Readings in Social Psychology* (New York: Holt, 1947), pp. 315–330.
[18]Harold Leavitt, "Unhuman Organizations," *Harvard Business Review* **40** (July-August 1962), 90–98.

feel the need, they may give only lip service rather than inspired compliance. Difficulties arise when managers use participation of subordinates as a shield, delaying a difficult decision by keeping it before the group. They can also abdicate responsibility for decisions on the grounds that "the group decided."

Democratic leadership, however, is not an absence of leadership. It is a mistake to define participation as the equivalent of anarchy or majority votes. Laissez-faire leadership may create more anxiety and tensions than either democratic or autocratic leadership, because the people and the organization flounder from lack of direction and control.

There are several reasons for the apparent superiority of the democratically led group. In a critical moment followers may desert the authoritarian leader, who can influence only those who have uncritical minds and dependent personalities. Good people will seek other employment that is more likely to demand their best. A second factor is that subordinates can sabotage an activity or a project simply by doing as they are told, withholding their views and information, or letting their bosses hang themselves by their own mistakes. Such action takes courage, for the subordinate also suffers when the boss fails. The authoritarian leader can only expect to encounter mounting resistance in its more subtle and troublesome forms. A third factor is the inherent weakness of organizations built around the authoritarian behavior of one individual. When that one person goes, the entire organization may collapse, for such a leader has not allowed others to develop.

An interesting problem in leader-follower relations is the potential conflict between formal and informal leaders. Formal leaders are those appointed to positions of authority. Informal leaders emerge through group processes, in which group members identify their natural leader. The informal leader is more responsive to group norms, values, and beliefs than to the requirements of a formal structure.

In some cases the formal and the informal leader may be the same person. If so, the formal leader has earned the respect, loyalty and emotional commitments of group members. However, where the formal and the informal leadership become lodged in two different persons—a common situation—potential conflict becomes real when the interests, objectives, and needs of the individuals are no longer perceived as compatible or parallel. Thus informal leaders may influence followers in directions contrary to those of the formal leader. Even when group members are consulted in the appointment of their formal leader, and even if their informal leader is chosen for the appointment, rifts may develop between the formal leader and the group, which often rallies around a new informal leader who can express and solidify their opposition to the formal leadership.

An interesting example of the influence of informal leaders is found in the phenomenon of "soldiering on the job." Appointed leaders of work groups, such as supervisors, try to get workers to produce at the highest rates; but workers in groups develop a conception of how much work should be done, which is less than the boss desires, primarily out of fear of "using up all the work." This is called a group norm—that is, a standard evolving out of a substantial consensus in the group. The informal leader of such a group is sensitive to such norms and appears to the group as one who can play a strong part in setting norms as well as maintaining them.

The typical leader-follower relationship in an organization is the superior-subordinate dyad, a relationship that exists at all levels but has presented particularly acute problems at the level of the first-line supervisor.

In a laboratory experiment, Herold demonstrated that leaders' behaviors and attitudes varied as a function of subordinate performance, and that subordinate behaviors and attitudes varied as a function of leaders' behavior. This reciprocal relationship was found also in studies by Greene, and by Kochan and his co-workers.[19]

Multidimensional Theories

Early theories viewed leadership behavior as scalable in a single continuum, such as the range between authoritarian versus democratic. With the decline of trait theories, researchers turned to studies of the relation of leaders' behavior to desired outcomes such as job performance or employee satisfaction. These studies introduced the concept of the situation; because they also considered personality effects, at least two dimensions were needed to explain leadership.

Two sets of investigations are illustrative of this period: The Ohio State Leadership Studies, and the Michigan Studies. Investigators in both sets of studies carried out many projects over a period of years beginning shortly after World War II.

The Ohio State Studies used a Leader Behavior Description Questionnaire, which underwent modification as the research progressed. Two composite dimensions of leader behavior emerged: (1) consideration, defined as friendship, mutual trust, respect, and warmth, and (2) initiating structure, defined as the extent to which leaders organize and define the relationship between themselves and their followers. Although these two dimensions were the ones that held up over the range of studies, two others—production emphasis and social awareness—showed some relevance but were subsequently dropped.

[19]David M. Herold, "Two-Way Influences Processes in Leader-Follower Dyads," *Academy of Management Journal* **20** (June 1977), 224–237; Charles N. Greene, "The Reciprocal Nature of Influence Between Leader and Subordinate," *Journal of Applied Psychology* **60** (April 1975), 187–193; Thomas A. Kochan, Stuart M. Schmidt, and Thomas A. DeCotis, "Superior-Subordinate Relations: Leadership and Headship," *Human Relations* **28** (April 1975), 279–294.

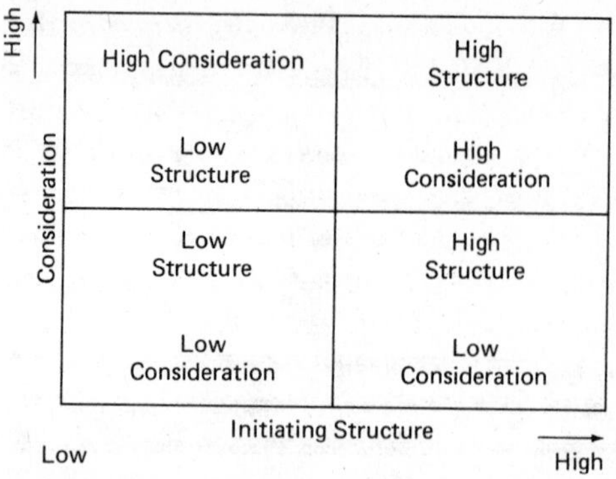

	High Consideration Low Structure	High Structure High Consideration
	Low Structure Low Consideration	High Structure Low Consideration

Consideration (vertical axis: Low to High)

Initiating Structure (horizontal axis: Low → High)

FIGURE 10-1. The Ohio State Leadership Studies, Dimensions of Leadership Style.

Source: Adapted from Ohio State Leadership Studies, Dimensions of Leadership Style, from *Current Developments in the Study of Leadership,* edited by Edwin A. Fleishman and James G. Hunt, Copyright © 1973 by Southern Illinois University Press. Reprinted by permission of Southern Illinois University Press.

Initiating structure and consideration were found to be prime dimensions of leadership in many different situations. These dimensions were analyzed in terms of the high or low degree of their presence, resulting in the four leadership styles depicted in Figure 10-1. Research was then directed at comparing these styles with job performance and worker satisfaction. No single style, however, emerged as best for all situations. Although high consideration–high initiating structure (Quadrant 2) led most frequently to high satisfaction and performance, it was also found that negative consequences often appeared. Therefore, it appears that consideration and initiating structure are specific to some situations but not to others.[20] The style quadrant appropriate at a given time tends to vary with the level of maturity of the subordinates.

The influence of the Ohio State studies has been extensive. Many researchers have used their measuring instruments, although a great many other scales developed to measure leadership came to be labeled *consideration* and *initiating structure* without using the concepts in precisely the same way. The concepts of consideration and initiating structure have had a high intuitive appeal to practicing managers, so that many training programs have made use of them.

In the Michigan studies, the direct aim was to study the factors influencing employee performance and satisfaction. Some investiga-

[20]The research reports on the Ohio State Studies are voluminous. See, for example, E. A. Fleishman, E. F. Harris, and H. E. Burtt, *Leadership and Supervision in Industry* (Columbus: The Ohio State University, Bureau of Educational Research, 1955); R. M. Stogdill and A. E. Coons, *Leader Behavior: Its Description and Measurement* (Columbus: The Ohio State University Bureau of Business Research, 1957); also Ralph M. Stogdill, *Handbook of Leadership* (New York: Free Press, 1974), which contains summaries of over three thousand leadership studies.

tions were made of concern for employees related to concern for production, with findings similar to those at Ohio State for consideration and initiating structure. The two dimensions were independent of each other, and it was concluded that effective leaders use both dimensions to varying degrees, depending on the situation. The researchers also found that another dimension, closeness versus looseness of supervision, were dependent upon the situation.[21]

Situational and Contingency Theories

In the third period of theoretical development, the situational dimension became a central focus, although leadership traits have not been completely discarded. Situational approaches view leadership as a group or organizational process in which the context greatly influences leadership behavior. The situational view emphasizes interpersonal relationships and defines leadership as a process of influence.

The origins of situational analysis go back to the studies of the preceding period. Pigors was among the first to point out that leadership cannot be properly studied apart from the group or the organization.[22] Hemphill,[23] Stogdill,[24] and others in a long series of studies at Ohio State University also took the situational approach, as did Gibb,[25] Homans,[26] and McGregor.[27]

A purely situational view of leadership has one shortcoming: it fails to take into account that leadership is a complex process in which the individual's traits may well play a part. Like trait theories, the situational theories by themselves represent a limited and incomplete explanation. The situationists may be overlooking the possibility that at least some traits influence people to attain leadership responsibilities and that in some cases traits may increase the chances of their becoming leaders. Gouldner has advanced the view that a theory of leadership can and should involve both traits and situations. Some traits could be specific and unique to groups; others might be common to all leaders.[28]

[21]See, for example, Daniel Katz and Robert L. Kahn, *The Social Psychology of Organizations* (New York: Wiley, 1966).

[22]Paul Pigors, *Leadership or Domination* (Boston: Houghton Mifflin, 1935).

[23]J. K. Hemphill, *Situational Factors in Leadership,* Ohio State University Studies, Bureau of Educational Research Monograph No. 32 (Columbus: Ohio State University, 1949).

[24]In 1948, Stogdill concluded after surveying a large number of leadership studies that the traits and skills required in a leader are determined to a large extent by the situation in which he is to exercise leadership. See Ralph M. Stogdill, "Personal Factors Associated with Leadership: A Survey of the Literature," *Journal of Psychology* **25** (January 1948): 63.

[25]Cecil A. Gibb, "Leadership," in *Handbook of Social Psychology,* vol. 2, Special Fields and Applications (Reading, Mass.: Addison-Wesley, 1954).

[26]George C. Homans, *The Human Group* (New York: Harcourt, 1950), pp. 415–440.

[27]Douglas McGregor, *The Human Side of Enterprise* (New York: McGraw-Hill, 1960).

[28]Gouldner, *Studies.*

It seems clear that both the trait and the situational theories have added to our understanding of leadership in management, and that the situational explanations hold a predominant place in current theory.

Contingency Theory

Fiedler has developed a situational model of leadership known as contingency theory, an approach based on measuring the leader's need structure and comparing it to how favorable the situation is for him. The need structure is measured by a questionnaire that assesses the esteem in which the leader holds his Least Preferred Co-worker (LPC). Both the LPC scales and the interpretations thereof have changed as the research progressed, throwing some doubt on exactly what is being measured.

Situational favorableness is measured by three factors: (1) *affective leader-member relations* (quality of personal relations between leader and followers), (2) *task structure* (degree to which the group's task is structured), and (3) *position power* (legitimate power and reward power). Fiedler plotted leadership style and performance against the degree of favorableness, as shown in Figure 10-2. From data such as this Fiedler concluded that under both favorable and unfavorable situations low-LPC or task-oriented leaders are most effective. In situations of moderate favorableness, high-LPC (relationship-oriented) leaders are more effective. A leader who describes a least preferred co-worker in a relatively favorable manner tends to be permissive, human-relations–oriented, and considerate of others. But a person who describes a least preferred co-worker in an unfavorable manner tends to be highly directive, task-controlling, and less concerned with human relations.[29]

Although Fiedler's contingency model has been widely criticized on technical, conceptual, and methodological grounds,[30] his view that a group's performance will be contingent upon the appropriate matching of a leadership style and the degree of favorableness of the situation for the leader represents a substantial advance in leadership theory. However, the implications for management pose difficulties. For example, the model suggests that group performance can be improved either by modifying the leader's style, or by modifying the group's task and situation. But Fiedler concluded that organizations cannot afford expensive selection techniques to find able leaders that fit job specifica-

---

[29]Fred E. Fiedler, *A Theory of Leadership Effectiveness* (New York: McGraw-Hill, 1967).

[30]George Graen, Kenneth Alvares, James B. Orris, and Joseph A. Martella. "Contingency Model of Leadership Effectiveness: Antecedent and Evidential Results," *Psychological Bulletin* **74** (December 1970), 285–296.

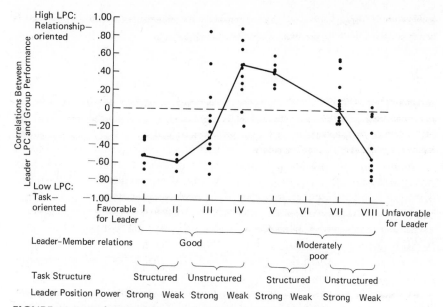

FIGURE 10-2. Task-Oriented vs. Relationship-Oriented Leaders.

Source: Fred E. Fiedler, *A Theory of Leadership Effectiveness,* p. 146. Copyright 1967 by Fred E. Fiedler. Used with permission of McGraw-Hill Book Company.

tions;[31] nor does he believe that training provides adequate answers to the problem of leadership.[32] The most feasible alternative, in his view, is to engineer the job to fit the manager. Because the type of leadership called for depends highly on the favorableness of the situation, the organization would find it easier to change the situation than to transfer people from one job to another or to train them in different styles of interaction with group members. The organization can affect the leadership style by altering such factors as the power associated with the leader's position, the task structure of the group, or the composition of the group's membership.[33]

An important benefit of Fiedler's contingency model is that it provides measurement scales for the major dimensions of leadership

[31]Fred E. Fiedler, "The Leadership Game: Matching the Man to the Situation," *Organizational Dynamics* 4 (Winter 1976), 6–16.

[32]Fred E. Fiedler, "The Trouble with Leadership Training Is That It Doesn't Train Leaders," *Psychology Today,* February 1973, 23–30 and 92.

[33] Fred E. Fiedler, "Engineer the Job to Fit the Manager," *Harvard Business Review* 43 (September-October 1965), 115–122. See also Irwin M. Rubin and Max Goldman, "An Open System Model of Leadership Performance," *Organizational Behavior and Human Performance* 3 (May 1968), 143–156; and Orlando Behling and Chester Schriesheim, *Organizational Behavior: Theory, Research, and Application* (Boston: Allyn and Bacon, 1976), chap. 12.

behavior. These scales and their uses have been modified and improved as Fiedler's research has progressed.

Path-Goal Theory

Path-goal theory is based on recent theories of motivation. It is a situational theory built around two propositions: that (1) the leader's function is supplemental, and (2) the motivational impact of a leader is determined by the situation. The situational elements include the characteristics of followers, as well as the environmental demands and pressures that affect the work and needs of subordinates. House, the originator of path-goal theory, believes that leader behavior is accepta- ble to subordinates to the degree that they perceive it as an immediate or future source of satisfaction. If subordinates have needs they can fulfill independently, they will tend to perceive a considerate leader as a source of satisfaction. If they are highly task-oriented, they may desire a more directive leader.

Path-goal theory focuses on the perceptions and expectations of subordinates, regarding the relation of effort to performance, the rela- tion of performance to the expectations of reward, and the strength of the subordinate's desire for the rewards expected. The leader is viewed as a motivator whose task is to increase personal payoffs to subordinates who attain work goals, and to make the path to these rewards easier by clarifying it, eliminating pitfalls or blocks to progress, and providing sources of satisfaction along the way.[34]

Summary of Contingency Approaches

Contingency approaches, which have virtually replaced trait theories and other earlier approaches, represent a deeper development of ideas and concepts originating earlier; in addition, they are in accord with emerging psychological and sociological theories dealing with motiva- tion, teams, groups, and other aspects of human behavior. The Ohio State and Michigan studies brought leadership theory to a significant turning point. Fiedler's contingency model and House's path-goal the- ory have extended the manager's capabilities for applying our knowl- edge of leadership to practical situations.

[34]Robert J. House, "A Path-Goal Theory of Leader Effectiveness," *Administrative Science Quarterly* 16 (1971), 321–338; Robert J. House and Gary Dessler, "The Path-Goal Theory of Leadership: Some Post Hoc and A Priori Tests," in J. G. Hunt and L. L. Larson (eds.), *Contingency Approaches to Leadership* (Carbondale: Southern Illinois University Press, 1974); Gary Dessler and Enzo R. Valenzi, "Initiation of Structure and Subordinate Satisfaction: A Path Analysis Test of Path-Goal Theory," *Journal of the Academy of Management* 20 (June 1977), 251–259.

EFFECTIVE ORGANIZATIONAL LEADERSHIP

The structure of an organization provides the technical apparatus through which leadership is made effective and operable in human activities. Often an informal structure will suffice, and indeed for certain objectives it might be preferable; formal organization structures, on the other hand, provide orderly and systematic frameworks within which both appointed and informal leaders operate.

Every organization needs strong and able leaders at all levels—not just a strong president, but strong supervisors and middle managers as well. The members of an organization cannot respond effectively to dull, lifeless, and unimaginative leadership: their full powers will remain untapped, their abilities will lie idle, their ideas will go untried. The organization will drift.

Leadership is not necessarily the same as administrative ability. A manager may be a capable administrator in the sense of doing the job at reasonable costs, yet he may offer little or no leadership. Perhaps the manager does not have the ability to try new ideas or the skill of eliciting the last ounce of effort from subordinates. Perhaps the elements of imagination and creativity, and the willingness to innovate, are absent. Such factors, important in leadership, can be absent, yet current activities may continue.

When we talk about leadership, we are talking about something more than administrative behavior. Although leadership and administration are not synonymous, leadership exists in different forms and degrees at each level. Administrative leadership is important in an organization, for it initiates the formulation of ends, secures their acceptance, and guides the total effort toward the attainment of those ends.

Administrative Problems

It is important for organizations to maintain an appropriate structure and climate conducive to the development of leadership. Selection and promotion policies, as well as training and development opportunities, need to be managed with leadership requirements in mind.

Leadership has an intangible quality that makes its potentials hard to predict,[35] a factor that increases the difficulties of training and development. One helpful approach is to maintain manpower inventory systems that ensure that persons with leadership capabilities are identified and available for new opportunities. Long-range career planning is also needed. Many managers do not carefully plan their careers. Appropri-

[35]Jeffrey Pfeffer, "The Ambiguity of Leadership," *Academy of Management Review* **2** (January 1977), 104–112.

ate opportunities for actual "firing-line" experience are also needed by those with leadership potential. These activities need to be incorporated into definite plans and policies for guiding leadership experience.

It is often asserted that managers should not be "drivers" and that putting pressure on subordinates is bad. The fact is, however, that many "drivers" are effective when judged by their accomplishments. For example, one organization had lenient administration and high morale, yet operated at a loss. A new leader used pressure to motivate subordinates to peak performance. Eventually the business became profitable. What is needed, of course, is to use judgment in applying pressures.

Being an aggressive and energetic leader does not necessarily eliminate democratic leadership. The desire to operate an organization democratically cannot absolve a leader of ultimate responsibilities for decisions. There are times when split-second decision making becomes necessary, and occasions when the leader must issue unequivocal orders. In so doing, the leader may act ruthlessly—that is, place results ahead of other values. Through a democratic approach to his followers, the leader frees the energies and abilities of subordinates, but they may have to be restrained and controlled when conditions warrant.

What cannot be done individually can be accomplished by groups, but to be effective the group needs wise and able leadership. No one knows what really creates the powerful leader, or why some persons can take charge of a situation and others cannot. Nor do we know why so many unwise and inept persons retain their positions of leadership. Almost every person is a leader in some situations and a follower in others. In addition to training and developing leaders, therefore, it would be plausible for organizations to train people to be followers.

By its very nature, leadership implies change. The leader's task is to identify the need for change, to set up plans for accomplishing change, and to persuade followers that new things need to be done and new ways devised to do them.[36]

There is a relationship between the kind of organization and the degree of dynamic leadership required. In a research organization, or a control board such as the Interstate Commerce Commission, the pace required of the organization and hence of the leader is more deliberate than it would be when the organization is a dynamic action agency, which needs aggressive, energetic, and action-oriented leadership. The leaders in such an organization set the pace for the others in it, and because it is unrealistic to expect dynamic leadership from a lethargic or slow-paced individual, a "driver" might be needed under such conditions.

The size of the organization has an important effect on leadership.

[36]Chris Argyris, "Leadership, Learning, and the Status Quo," *Organizational Dynamics* 4 (Winter 1976), 29–43.

For example, Miles and Petty found in a study of small social service agencies that the initiating structure of the leader is more effective in smaller agencies than in large ones, and that the effectiveness of a leader's consideration does not appear to vary with agency size.[37]

Leadership Styles

In practice it has been hard to translate research findings into pragmatic actions for leaders in actual organizations. One reason for this gap is that the behavior of managers is influenced by a complexity that goes beyond leadership itself. For example, Figure 10-3 shows the relationships among theories of motivation, leadership styles, and organizational climate. The horizontal dimension shows a continuum ranging from the bureaucratic system of the scientific managers to the organic, adaptive models of the revisionists. The vertical dimension indicates key researchers and their ideas as they range along the continuum.

A review of leadership styles in the light of evolving theory will shed light on how managers lead in practical settings. We shall consider (1) charismatic leadership, (2) the great organizers, and (3) leader-follower relationships.

Charismatic Leadership

In his studies of bureaucracy, Max Weber described prebureaucratic leadership as charismatic. The leader with charisma is one whose authority has a legitimacy based on charismatic grounds—that is, on "devotion to the specific and exceptional sanctity, heroism or exemplary character of an individual person and of the normative patterns or order revealed or ordained by him."[38] Charisma is a mystical, inspirational quality that some persons reflect in their social relations. The charismatic leader leads by inspiring—by winning the emotional commitments of followers and by arousing their loyalty and enthusiasm. However, Zaleznik and Moment conclude that this kind of emotional interaction is a mass phenomenon, rather than a group event in which problem-solving goals and methodologies evoke rational action. Furthermore, although the charismatic leader is highly influential, he strives for general goals rather than detailed ones. He does not consciously try to engineer measurable outcomes, and his leadership has a ritualistic, symbolic element. Therefore charisma is less appropriate for conceptualizing leadership in organizations than are the situation-

[37]Robert E. Miles and M. M. Petty, "Leader Effectiveness in Small Bureaucracies," *The Academy of Management Journal* **20** (June 1977), 238–250.
[38]Max Weber, *The Theory of Social and Economic Organization* (New York: Free Press, 1947), p. 328 and passim.

	Hierarchically-Directed		Participative, Self-Directed, Team Interactive	
Theories about Motivation — Abraham Maslow	Physiological, safety, and security needs	Belonging and esteem needs	Self-actualization and growth needs	
Frederick Herzberg	Dissatisfiers and hygiene factors		Satisfiers and motivating factors	
Chris Argyris	Dependence, submissiveness, frustration		Aspirations toward psychological success	
Theories about Style of Leadership — Douglas McGregor	Theory X cosmology		Theory Y cosmology	
Rensis Likert	*System 1* Exploitive authoritative	*System 2* Benevolent authoritative	*System 3* Consultative	*System 4* Participative group
			Principle of supportive relations	
Blake and Mouton	*Style 9, 1* Maximal concern for production, minimal concern for people	*Style 5, 5* "Middle-of-the-road" concern for both production and people	*Style 9, 9* Maximal concern for both production and people	
Theories about Organizational Climate — Warren Bennis	Bureaucratic organization		Organic-adaptive organization	
Burns and Stalker	Mechanistic systems		Organic systems	
Systems Theory	Closed system		Open system	

FIGURE 10-3 (opposite). Parallel Theories About Motivation, Style of Leadership, and Organizational Climate.

Source: Reprinted from Wendell French, *The Personnel Management Process: Human Resources Administration,* 3rd edition by Wendell French. Copyright © 1974 by Houghton Mifflin Company. Used by permission.

based theories we have described.[39] Charismatic individuals are more often found leading social movements in the pursuit of larger missions or goals.

The Great Organizers

There are organizational leaders who exhibit a degree of charisma. An example is found in the "great organizers"—men of vast ambition, talent, and energy that they devoted to the building of huge industrial empires. Henry Ford, John D. Rockefeller, and Walter P. Chrysler are examples. Such men were not entirely charismatic, yet they had style and commanded a following partly because of what they were as well as because of what they knew. Most were hard-working, astute individuals who could successfully exploit financial and industrial opportunities. They were men of action, able to command the allegiance of able followers. In their relationships with others, however, they remained dominant.[40]

Leadership of the "great-organizer" type is far less possible today, although we are perhaps seeing a resurgency of it in the empire builders who put together huge conglomerate firms. Some see the conglomerate—the firm built by mergers and acquisitions and having widely diversified product lines—as one element in the important transformation from bureaucratic administration to vigorous, get-up-and-go organizations that create and take advantage of change. However, although many managers have charismatic traits, and many have the qualities of creativity needed by conglomerates, the vast majority do their work within the bureaucratic mold. Organizations manufacture their own leaders to their specifications and expectations. Leadership is thus more of a bureaucratic construct than a charismatic force. All leaders employ their personalities in the leadership process, but most play their roles as members of teams rather than as dominant personalities. To let an organization rely too strongly on a single leader is to jeopardize the security of the organization if the "great leader" is lost.[41]

[39]Zaleznik and Moment, *Dynamics,* p. 415.

[40]Ernest Dale, *The Great Organizers* (New York: McGraw-Hill, 1960).

[41]For a treatment of the broad social, political, and psychological implications of leadership and its developments in a business society, see Eugene E. Jennings, *An Anatomy of Leadership,* (New York: Harper, 1960); *The Executive: Autocrat, Bureaucrat, Democrat* (New York: Harper, 1962). See also Philip Selznick, *Leadership in Administration* (New York: Harper, 1957).

SUPERVISORY LEADERSHIP

All managers, at whatever level, perform a supervisory function. At the top levels of an organization, however, the proportion of direct supervision in each position is smaller than at lower levels. Hence we generally use the term *supervision* to describe the responsibilities of first-line supervisors (sometimes called "foremen") and general supervisors at the next higher level or two. At these levels leadership focuses on operational rather than strategic matters. It is more closely focused on interpersonal relationships and on the day-to-day work of the group. Persons at supervisory levels constitute in most cases the largest proportion of the managerial group.

Supervision does not automatically connote leadership, but the most effective supervisors have substantial leadership skills. Therefore they can move their group beyond routine, average performance. Supervisors are so vital to operations that organizations plan carefully their selection, training, development, and progress. Supervisory levels provide a pool of managerial talent from which to build middle and upper-middle management groups.

Much of the work crowded into the supervisor's day has little to do with leadership. Supervisors process records, hold meetings, scan reports, monitor production, and deal with special problems. To fulfill their leadership functions, they need top management's understanding and support. Instead supervisors often experience conflicts with higher management, and attitudes that prevent them from feeling confident in their work.

In one sense supervisors are employees governed by the same motivating forces and influences as those they supervise. They regard their relationships with their own bosses as important. They want a good job, adequate pay, fair treatment, and good working conditions. They want recognition and status, and like to be an important member of the management team. Whereas workers have unions to make sure their complaints are heard, supervisors have only their own resources in communicating with top management. It is unrealistic to expect supervisors to develop adequate relationships with their subordinates unless good relationships also prevail between themselves and their superiors.

The first-line supervisor occupies a strategic place in the hierarchy of an organization. As management's representative at the point of contact with rank-and-file workers, and as the workers' first point of contact with management, first-line supervisors are a vital link in the upward and downward flow of communications, and key individuals in the lives of those who work for them. To the extent that they earn workers' confidence as leaders, supervisors are looked up to for ideas, information, suggestions, approval, guidance, and even criticism. Workers look to them for decisions, for timely information, for friendly counsel, and for answers to questions that arise. They expect them to be fair and to use common sense in working with them. In short, they want their leaders to lead.

In many organizations, there is considerable antagonism between workers and supervisors. Sometimes workers develop fears, hatreds, and frustrations that produce conflict and stress in their jobs; they express their resentment and anger toward the supervisor. The attitudes of subordinates toward the supervisor are conditioned by general organizational conditions, policies, and values and by their own experiences with particular supervisors. The supervisor is the distributor of rewards and punishments and hence may evoke positive or negative feelings on the part of subordinates.

The over-all problem of first-line supervisors in management today centers on a conflict in role expectations. They face pressure from subordinates and from higher managers. These pressures produce conflict, confronting supervisors with two sets of expectations that are often at odds. Higher managers value higher output, lower costs, and the fulfillment of exacting production schedules. Management also defines a "good" supervisor not merely as one who gets a high level of performance from subordinates but also one who is completely loyal to top management. On the other hand, workers expect their supervisors to put a high priority on sympathetic understanding of their problems and on considerate treatment of their personal needs. Roethlisberger sums up this basic conflict: "Nowhere in the industrial structure more than at foreman level is there so great a discrepancy between what a position ought to be and what a position is."[42]

Most supervisors find themselves caught in the middle at one time or another, but they need not experience role conflict continuously. It is possible for a supervisor to belong to his management group and to his own work team without excessive conflict and dissatisfaction, provided that management recognizes the existence of the bid for dual loyalties and does not attempt to capture the exclusive loyalty of the supervisor. It is important for the supervisor to be an accepted member of both groups, and for the goals and expectations of the two groups to be generally clear and compatible.[43]

The expectations of higher managers with respect to communica-

[42]F. J. Roethlisberger, "The Foreman: Master and Victim of Double Talk," in Schuyler D. Hoslett (ed.), *Human Factors in Management,* rev. ed. (New York: Harper, 1951), p. 39. See also Roberta G. Simmons, "The Role Conflict of the First-Line Supervisor: An Experimental Study," *American Journal of Sociology* **73** (January 1968), 482–495; Thomas H. Patten, Jr., "The Authority and Responsibilities of Supervisors in a Multi-plant Firm," *Journal of Management Studies* **5** (February 1968), 61–82; L. W. Wager, "Leadership Style, Influence, and Supervisory Role Obligations," *Administrative Science Quarterly* **9** (March 1965), 319–420.

[43]For further treatments of the supervisor's role and task see M. Gene Newport (ed.), *Supervisory Management: Tools and Techniques* (St. Paul, Minn.: West, 1976); Robert M. Fulmer, *Supervision: Principles of Professional Management* (Beverly Hills, Calif.: Glencoe, 1976).

tions are exacting. By designating first-line supervisors as a vital link in the channels of communication, their superiors make them responsible for communicating orders, policies, information, and ideas to workers. Frequently, they also expect them to report on worker opinions, attitudes, and other problems. The first-line supervisors' role in communications is vital because they inevitably must interpret and translate the communications, and because the possibility of filtering and distortion is high.

Some researchers have suggested that the "man-in-the-middle" supervisor holds priorities more like those of managers than like those of nonmanagerial employees. For example, one study found that supervisors assign lower values to human relations than their supervisors, and view the variables of human relations as instrumental for achieving productivity goals rather than as ends in themselves.[44] This is not surprising in view of the pressure for productivity that most firms exert on supervisors, and of the large amounts of money spent on trying to make supervisors feel psychologically an integral part of the management team.

SUMMARY

Leadership is one of the central problems of managers and executives at all levels. This chapter has defined and described the process of leadership and presented an analysis of trait and situational approaches to understanding leadership in organizations.

Leadership is the capacity to guide, direct, and influence the behavior of others, imaginatively, toward given ends. The trait theory holds that leadership is inherent in the psychological makeup of individuals. The situational pattern views leadership as contingent on the needs and resources of a given situation. In a synthesis of these two patterns, we concluded that both have contributed ideas of value, that neither approach alone is satisfactory, and that the dominant approach now current is based on theories of the contingency type.

This chapter also examined the role of first-line supervisors and the general process of supervision as a management function. The supervisor is traditionally viewed as "the man in the middle"; but although this is often a fair portrayal of his role, in reality his beliefs are closer to those of other managers than to those of nonmanagerial employees. Organizations vary widely in the efforts they make to integrate their supervisory staffs fully into the management network. Because supervi-

[44]William Weitzell, Thomas A. Mahoney, and Norman M. Crandall, "A Supervisory View of Unit Effectiveness," *California Management Review* 13 (October 1971), 37–42.

sors are highly influential in relation to rank-and-file employees, their managerial skill is highly important to operating results.

INCIDENT CASE

Joe Miller worked for several years as a machinist in an automotive parts firm. His performance ratings and work record were excellent. He served for two years' as secretary of the union local, and was elected as president in 1978. He was popular among his fellow workers, and was an aggressive, intelligent union president. After a year as president, he was offered the position of first-line supervisor, with all the machinists in his department reporting directly to him.

Question:

1. What problems of leadership are associated with this situation?

QUESTIONS FOR STUDY

1. Should a leader be a "driver"? Under what circumstances will such behavior succeed? Under what conditions will it fail?

2. What physical, mental, and emotional traits do you feel are essential to managerial success? Why?

3. Do you agree that there are important distinctions between leadership and administrative ability? What are these differences?

4. In what ways can you apply the concept of situational leadership to your knowledge of business and industry? Of other organizations?

5. Think of someone you have known whose leadership you disliked. Why did you dislike it?

6. What connections, if any, do you see between the concept of coordination and the concept of leadership?

7. List the factors that make the quality of leadership important to a subordinate.

8. What have the social sciences contributed to our knowledge of leadership in a field of management?

9. What are the main variables in Fiedler's contingency model of leadership?

10. Why do organizations have extensive problems in the areas of supervisory leadership? What steps can companies take to minimize these problems?

11. Find some examples of how a given situation helped or hindered a leader, apart from the question of that leader's ability.

12. Outline your ideas about the kinds of training concepts, activities, and policies you think appropriate to improve leadership processes in a given organization.

13. Explain the nature of role conflicts among first-line supervisors and show how these problems can be minimized.

14. Argue for or against the concept that the first-line supervisor is a "man in the middle."

SELECTED REFERENCES

Administrative Science Quarterly, Special Issue on Organizational Leadership 16. March 1971.

ARGYRIS, CHRIS. *Increasing Leadership Effectiveness.* New York: John Wiley & Sons, Inc., 1976.

BERNSTEIN, PAUL. *Workplace Democratization: Its Internal Dynamics.* Kent, Ohio: Kent State University Press, 1976.

BLAKE, ROBERT, and JANE S. MOUTON. *The Managerial Grid.* Austin, Texas: Gulf Publishing Company, 1964.

FIEDLER, FRED A., and MARTIN M. CHEMERS. *Leadership and Effective Management.* Chicago: Scott, Foresman and Company, 1974.

FIEDLER, FRED E., MARTIN M. CHEMERS, and LINDA MAHAR. *Improving Leadership Effectiveness.* New York: John Wiley & Sons, Inc., 1976.

FLEISHMAN, EDWIN A., and JAMES G. HUNT, eds. *Current Developments in the Study of Leadership.* Carbondale: Southern Illinois University Press, 1973.

GEORGE, CLAUDE S., JR. *Supervision in Action.* Reston, Va.: Reston Publishing Company, 1976.

HUNT, JAMES G., and LARS L. LARSON, eds. *Contingency Approaches to Leadership.* Carbondale: Southern Illinois University Press, 1974.

HUNT, JAMES G. and LARS L. LARSON, eds. *Leadership Frontiers.* Kent, Ohio: Kent State University Press, 1976.

KATZ, DANIEL, and ROBERT L. KAHN. *The Social Psychology of Organizations.* New York: John Wiley & Sons, Inc., 1966. Chapter 11.

KNOWLES, HENRY P., and BORJE O. SAXBERG. *Personality and Leadership Behavior.* Reading, Mass.: Addison-Wesley Publishing Company, 1971.

MACCOBY, MICHAEL. *The Gamesman: The New Corporate Leader.* New York: Simon & Schuster, Inc., 1977.

McCALL, M., and M. LOMBARD, eds. *Leadership: Where Else Can We go?* Durham, N.C.: Duke University Press, 1977.

METCALF, HENRY C., and LYNDALL F. URWICK. *Dynamic Administration: The Collected Papers of May Parker Follett.* New York: Harper & Row, Publishers, 1950. Chapters 7, 12, 13.

NEWPORT, M. GENE, ed. *Supervisory Management: Tools and Techniques.* St. Paul, Minn.: West Publishing Company, 1976.

"Philosophers and Kings: Studies in Leadership." *Daedalus* **97** (summer 1968).

SELZNIK, PHILIP. *Leadership in Administration.* New York: Harper & Row, Publishers, 1957.

STOGDILL, RALPH M. *A Handbook of Leadership: A Survey of Theory and Research.* New York: The Free Press, 1974.

STEINMETZ, LAWRENCE, and H. RALPH TODD. *First-Line Management: Approaching Supervision Effectively.* Dallas: Business Publications, Inc., 1975.

Chapter 11

Staffing

"System to all things is the soul of business."

—*George Washington*

No man in a business suit ever reads employment ads in public.

—*John R. Coleman*

In 1977 Ralph Beasley had worked eleven years for a large building supply firm as vice president of sales for the western region. He began in that region as a salesman and advanced rapidly to district sales manager, then to his vice presidency. Two years after achieving the vice presidency, he was transferred to a similar post in Dallas. Two years later he was transferred to Atlanta. He was successful in all his work, and the advances brought him increased salaries and a reputation for effective management. In July of 1977 he was notified of a transfer to Detroit, with higher pay but without a promotion. He put his home in Atlanta up for sale and prepared to move to Detroit. Two months later, he was notified that his assignment in Detroit would last for only eighteen months, and that he should be prepared for another move at that time.

Questions to keep in mind while you read this chapter:

1. What does this case reveal about the company's staffing policies?
2. How typical do you think this example is?
3. How would you feel personally about this kind of staffing decision, and what would you do about it?

People and organizations come together by means of the managerial function called staffing, a mutually selective process with choices made by both. Managers decide who will be offered employment. Applicants decide which available offer to accept.

The fact that staffing consists of separate decisions by the organization and the individual does not mean that the two are on an equal footing. Except in rare cases, the individual needs a job more than the organization needs any one person. Organizations are usually careful in selecting new employees. Individuals, who generally do not have the time and money for an extensive job search, are less exacting and more opportunistic in choosing jobs.

_____ **DEFINITION OF STAFFING**

Staffing is *the function by which managers build an organizations through the recruitment, selection, and development of individuals as capable employees.* This concept is broad enough to cover rank-and-file employees as well as managerial ones; this chapter, however, will focus on the staffing of managerial positions.

Staffing gives managers the opportunity to surround themselves with subordinates of their own choosing. This fact is most evident when an outsider is hired, because the selection activities and the applicants are visible. Yet the retention of subordinates also reflects staffing decisions, tacit though they may be. Thus, staffing is more than merely hiring new employees. Managers cannot build an excellent organization solely by hiring; the concept of staffing, therefore, is broadened to include many activities frequently assigned to personnel departments, such as transfers, discharges, resignations, retirements, training, development, and orientation.[1] This concept widens the decision horizon of managers, but it entails a sharing of the staffing function with the personnel department.

The Role of Personnel Departments

Personnel departments vary in their capabilities for assisting managers in their staffing function. The extent to which managers draw upon the services of the personnel department depends largely on their confidence in the capabilities of the personnel staff, usually based on its record of past performance. It also depends on the aggressiveness by which the department asserts claims to a role in the staffing function.

---

[1]Gulick and Urwick define staffing as "the whole personnel function of bringing in and training the staff and maintaining favorable conditions of work." Luther Gulick and Lyndall Urwick (eds.), *Papers on the Science of Administration* (New York: Columbia University Press, 1937), p. 13.

Historically, personnel departments have focused on dealing with rank-and-file employees, because of the large numbers of such employees and also because of the complexities first of preventing unionization and later of dealing with unions. Personnel and labor-relations specialists were placed in staff departments to help the line manger develop and carry out the procedures of employee relations. However, the techniques, policies, and expertise needed for dealing with rank-and-file employees were not adequate for dealing with managerial and higher-level executive employees. Until recent years, therefore, personnel administration was routine and nominal for managerial employees. Now many organizations, especially large ones, have sophisticated, well-developed programs explicitly designed for managerial as well as rank-and-file personnel administration. Such departments give managers vital assistance in staffing.

It is important for managers to maintain ultimate control over staffing decisions in their own units, subject only to broad guidelines, policies, and technical assistance from the personnel department. Although it is sometimes necessary for managers to accept or retain subordinates who are not of their own choosing (as happens when managers are promoted to supervise an existing group) the manager's right to hire and fire is the primary assurance of effectiveness in staffing. For this reason, personnel departments provide facilitating services, but the final decisions to hire, retain, or discharge an individual are the responsibilities of line managers.

Manpower Planning

Many organizations have developed manpower planning units. Manpower planning is a more inclusive concept than staffing; the term describes formal procedures designed at any of four levels of analysis: (1) programs for replacement of individuals who vacate positions, (2) forward personnel planning by staff personnel departments, (3) manpower and employment policies in the economy as a whole, and (4) the planning, development, and implementation of comprehensive programs of selection, training, and education to meet the needs of manpower forecasts.[2] The traditional view of staffing has been related to the filling of jobs, with an emphasis on replacement. Now, however, the concept of staffing focuses mainly on the human-resources approach, which we have listed as procedure (4). Therefore manpower planning provides the over-all rationale within which staffing activities occur.

---

[2] Thomas H. Patten, Jr., *Manpower Planning and the Development of Human Resources* (New York: Wiley, 1971), pp. 31–33; Peter Mears, "A Manpower Evaluation Program and Reporting System," *Managerial Planning* 23 (May–June 1975), 29–31; Lane Tracy, "The Control Process in Personnel Management," *Personnel Journal* 55 (September 1976), 446–449.

Staffing must be carried out in relation to existing manpower programs and policies, and to forecasts of needs over future periods.

_____ **STAFFING PROCEDURES**

Prior to any staffing action the existing organization structure should be examined and if necessary improved. A personnel vacancy provides an opportunity to review the work assigned to that and related positions. Perhaps the position should be changed, or even abolished. The organizational system should be thoroughly reviewed for possible redesign before all but the most routine vacancies are filled. Manpower planning data are also considered.

Following the assessment of the state of the organization and its needs, procedures of recruiting, selection, placement, orientation, and development are carried out.

Recruiting

The recruiting phase of staffing includes (1) finding candidates for employment, (2) considering outside applicants who initiate contacts with the organization, and (3) finding candidates from among the existing employees. The search for candidates with desired qualifications is normally the most reliable way to proceed, although persons who themselves initiate employment inquiries should not be overlooked as potential candidates.

External recruiting is through advertising, word of mouth, public and private employment agencies, or the visits of recruiters to schools and colleges. Internal recruiting involves searching among current employees for those who may be promoted or transferred.

Recruitment itself is selective by nature: it can be directed toward the sources that are shown by experience to provide good managerial talent. Recruiting college graduates, for example, results in a certain selectivity as to educational qualifications.

Recruiting must be fitted to the goals of equal opportunity for disadvantaged persons. It must conform to the requirements of civil rights legislation banning discrimination as to race, creed, age, nationality, or sex. Special sources and extra efforts are required to meet these goals. The term *affirmative action programs* denotes this aspect of staffing. Many firms try to live up to the spirit as well as the letter of these laws. The requirements also pose procedural problems not only in recruiting but in the content of interviews, application forms, and testing.

To perform successfully in the light of genuine affirmative action programs, recruiters should have a commitment to the program's goals. Some recruiters are unwilling to make the additional effort to locate

good sources and to find places for the disadvantaged in the organization. The recruiter's commitment is largely a reflection of attitudes and
commitment on the part of others in the organization, particularly those
with whom the disadvantaged persons are to be placed.

Because recruiters are often the first contact of the organization with
its potential members, it is essential for them to work skillfully, with
tact and sensitivity. First impressions are important influences on those
who are eventually hired; it is also desirable to leave a good impression
with those who are not hired.

The recruiting of managerial personnel should be approached from a
long-range point of view. That is, the recruiters should over time build
ongoing relationships with sources of supply, such as college placement directors, and with candidates who, if not immediately hired, may
become candidates later. This is an argument in favor of professional
personnel recruiters in the central personnel department—people who
are responsible for recruiting throughout the organization. Line managers need not refrain from recruiting efforts; indeed, they would be
abdicating their responsibilities if recruiting and other selection procedures were left entirely to personnel workers. In some highly specialized areas, line managers feel they can recruit more effectively than
full-time recruiting specialists. Purchasing agents, for instance, may
prefer to recruit other purchasing agents. Often this issue is resolved by
the use of recruiting teams, made up of the full-time recruiter accompanied by a representative of the area being recruited for.

The recruiter needs either a job description or a set of specifications
indicating the managerial capabilities sought. Many organizations do
not use formal job descriptions for management positions, but the
recruiter searching for applicants needs definitive guidelines, which
are best provided by the managers doing the staffing.

External Sources

Public and private employment agencies are one important external
source of candidates. Such agencies provide many services: they not
only handle recruiting, but also do a preliminary screening of candidates by collecting biographical data, conducting initial interviews, and
making tentative evaluations of applicants.

Public agencies—state units participating in a federal system built
around unemployment compensation legislation—are best for locating
supervisory or middle-management persons. For higher-level executives and managers, private agencies are particularly useful. Public
agencies charge no fees to employers or applicants; private agencies
charge substantial fees, which are generally paid by the employer.

Private employment agencies often specialize by salary range (under
$20,000 per year, over $25,000 per year, or over $100,000 per year, for

example), or else by functional fields such as accounting, marketing, and the like. Some go by fancy names emphasizing their particualr specialities. There are private agencies that sell testing, career guidance, counseling, or resume preparation services to applicants, but the fees for such services are high, and some firms are less than scrupulous about the needs of applicants for these services. Although most agencies operate within accepted ethical guidelines, some are overly aggressive in selling services to applicants, or too careless and hasty in gathering information and making referrals to clients.

Employment agencies are in effect go-betweens in the markets for managerial services. Applicants come to them for referrals to job openings, and organizations retain them to locate applicants. Some aggressive private agencies, however, are dubbed "headhunters." Headhunters are aggressive in finding candidates to recommend to clients, and in finding clients. They even contact people who have not planned to change jobs and attempt to persuade them to try for a better one. Headhunters do not always make blind contacts, but instead utilize an informal and perpetual information network carefully built up over time to provide the names of able people; they also follow up on discontent in companies that have low morale or are undergoing merger or reorganization. They advertise regularly to keep their name before those who may become applicants or clients.[3]

Other external sources should be considered, including applicants' initiation of contacts with the organization, word-of-mouth referrals, and advertising. Applicants from these sources may require more and better screening than do candidates from other sources.

Many critical staffing decisions are made concerning candidates who apply on their own. Their success in getting considered depends on their skills of searching for openings. Getting an initial interview is very difficult. Such candidates need effective resumes that will get the immediate interest of potential employers. It is bothersome for managers to handle the often voluminous intake of inquiries from would-be candidates. Even so, each person should be given fair and considerate treatment, and inquiries should receive prompt and clear replies, whether affirmative or negative. Often an outstanding person can be obtained by means of candidate initiative.

Word of mouth is helpful in disseminating information about a vacancy and in bringing able people to the organization's attention. Relatives and friends of current employees are numerous, but assuming that screening is careful, there are no serious drawbacks to word of mouth as a source.

Advertising, carefully done, helps bring potential applicants to the attention of employers, but many replies often do not meet the sought-

[3]Allan J. Cox, *Confessions of a Corporate Headhunter* (New York: Trident, 1973).

for qualifications. The device of requesting replies to box numbers controls contacts with unqualified applicants.

Internal Sources

Manpower planning, equal opportunity legislation, the desire to distribute job opportunities fairly among existing employees, and the difficulties of using external sources all point to the value of considering current employees as a talent pool from which to carry out staffing processes.

The use of internal sources reduces recruiting and training costs, and contributes to the morale of employees. It is essential that recruiting from within be systematic and carefully planned. Manpower inventories, performance appraisal records, and the recommendations of supervisors are helpful. Another advantage of turning to current employees in staffing is that their performance and achievement histories are better known, and known more objectively, than is the case with outsiders who may apply.

In most cases the selection of an existing employee to fill a position will involve a promotion decision, although it can sometimes be done through a transfer. Later in this chapter the policy of promotion from within will be discussed.

Selection Processes

Selection procedures are usually handled by the central personnel department; but the manager engaged in staffing should stay aware of what is done, know how applicants are treated, and have opportunities to cooperate in the procedures. The personnel department is well equipped to apply organizationwide policy, to develop and maintain records, to conduct interviews and tests, to make preliminary assessments of candidates, and to do other technical work, but the manager himself should make the final decision. Hunch and intuition are inadequate; systematic analysis is imperative. The decision should be made on the basis of as much factual information as can be feasibly obtained. These standards do not automatically eliminate subjectivity, whim, or personal opinion, but at least the subjective elements should come into play only after systematic screening produces satisfactory candidates from which to choose.

Selection procedures are, in effect, a screening of candidates according to a progressive series of steps designed to eliminate those who in some ways are unsuitable. Their elimination should be based on well-informed judgments; thus, for each kind of measurement or data gathering, standards for rejection or acceptance are necessary. Such standards are not precise, nor are their results fool-proof. Decisions are made on the basis of information collected and analyzed by statistical methods, chiefly sampling. By means of probability statistics, the validity and reliability of the results of each step in the process can be evaluated. But there will always be a margin of error in all selection procedures, because it is impossible to collect all possible relevant data.

It is essential to get the information best calculated to predict each applicant's successful job performance. This requires skillful use of information gathering and analysis techniques, which in turn depend on knowing the performance characteristics of jobs against which the data obtained are to be compared.

The personnel specialists carry out the technical procedures, and the screening steps they follow generally include application blanks, preliminary interviews, testing, physical examinations, and interviews with potential colleagues or superiors. Where applicants are not eliminated by one of the steps in the procedure, it is important that the final decision be based on an analysis of the total information obtained, so as to avoid undue reliance on any single step, such as tests.

The Applicants

Job seekers are often not highly skilled in the activities necessary to land a good job. Individuals do not even become applicants until they find organizations willing to consider them. Many applicants are opportunistic in their approach—they take the first reasonable job they encounter, relying on tips or advertisements rather than systematically searching for opportunities.

Job seekers should prepare a concise, informative resume giving their work history, skills, education, interests, and personal data. Resumes need not be elaborate, but they should be attractively prepared. The main object of the resume is to secure job interviews with prospective employers. The next stage is to prepare for the interview by studying the organization in reference books and in other ways, so that the interview can be conducted intelligently.

During the interview the applicant should listen carefully to learn what the interviewers or recruiters are seeking. It is important to ask questions of the interviewer. The interview situation is not without tension for the applicant, but in most cases the interviews can be safely regarded as straightforward opportunities for mutual exchange of information.

Skills of the Manager

To fulfill the staffing function properly, managers themselves need personnel skills. Relying solely on the personnel department is an unnecessary risk and amounts to abdication of responsibility.

The candidate will already have been interviewed several times by recruiters, employment personnel, psychologists, or even physicians. The candidate will have presented a resume, filled out an application blank, and taken tests. The hiring manager's interview is one of the last and most critical screening events in a long series of information exchanges. At this point the interviewing manager has a large amount of information to use as a guide.

The personnel department will, if possible, have made referrals of several applicants, all of whom have met the basic requirements. The objective of the final interview is to facilitate a match between the alternative candidates and the opening available. The manager will want to recheck any doubtful points, obtain missing information, and clarify the applicant's intentions and objectives. The applicant will have questions that should be heard. This is the most critical step in the screening process, and is best regarded as a two-way exchange of information.

The manager needs well-developed interviewing skills. These can be learned, but practice is needed.[4] The manager also needs to know how to interpret test scores and other information; otherwise he is forced to rely on the personnel department's interpretations. A balanced view is ultimately needed to properly review and assess the potential benefits and risks of the decision about to be made.[5]

The final decision, whether favorable or otherwise, should be communicated promptly to the applicant, without equivocation or subterfuge.

Employment Contracts

Formal, written contracts are occasionally used in connection with employment of top-level, professional managers or executives, and are often sought by candidates of high ability considering a position involving considerable personal uncertainty or risk, such as launching a new firm, introducing extensive change, or salvaging a foundering company.

The effect of an employment contract is to protect the new manager in the high-risk first years of his employment by committing the organization to certain agreements about employment, including length, pay, benefits, and conditions of termination. For example, Charles E. Selecman, chief executive officer of E. T. Borwick Industries, Inc., was brought in "to save the company from financial ruin." In a few months,

---

[4]Fredric Jablen, "The Selection Interview: Contingency Theory and Beyond," *Human Resource Management* 14 (Spring 1975), 2–9; Felix M. Lopez, *Personnel Interviewing* (2nd ed.), (New York: McGraw-Hill, 1975); Walter R. Mahler, *How Effective Executives Interview* (Homewood, Ill.: Dow Jones–Irwin, 1976).

[5]Marvin D. Dunnette, *Personnel Selection and Placement* (Belmont, Calif.: Wadsworth, 1966).

during which financial progress was made, he was given an employment contract with the following provisions:

1. Four years' duration.
2. Annual salary of $125,000 until March 1977 and $150,000
   thereafter.
3. Eligibility for bonuses.
4. Options to buy 100,000 shares of common stock for $1.50 each
   (the current price, although it had traded for as high as $29.00 per
   share).
5. Two years' salary ($300,000) if the contract is terminated against
   his will.[6]

Employment contracts are decreasing in popularity.[7] They are essentially one-sided: the company is obligated but the executive is not
bound because the company generally benefits little from forcing an
executive to remain if he wants to leave. Such contracts are hard to
enforce in the courts, and the company may be stuck for a large sum if
the executive turns out to be a poor choice. The primary benefit to a
company is that such a contract may attract a capable person who would
not otherwise be interested. For a time it was a fad among managers to
boast of a contract that guaranteed their employment even if the company no longer provided work.

In essence, the relationship between a manager and an organization
is a moral obligation rather than a legal one, whereas an employment
contract attempts to set up a legal relationship. Informal "termination
agreements"—which make no pretense of being legal documents and
are less inclusive in their guarantees—are sometimes used instead.
Whereas an employment contract may run to 15 or more pages, specifying what happens under an enormous range of eventualities, termination agreements merely give the executive a few months' salary after
dismissal for specified causes.

PROBLEMS IN STAFFING

A number of important issues complicate the staffing processes just
described. Among them are (1) problems of matching individuals and
jobs, (2) mobility, and (3) promotion from within policies.

[6]*Business Week*, November 29, 1976, pp. 81–82.
[7]*Business Week*, July 7, 1973, pp. 42–43. See also Frank F. Beaudine, "The Termination Agreement as a Recessionary Tool," *Personnel Journal*, June 1975, 345–356.

Matching Individuals and Jobs

"Square pegs in square holes, round pegs in round holes" is a cliché that has long clouded the staffing function. Such a statement makes a number of assumptions that are less true than many suppose. It assumes that the "holes" are clearly definable positions, and that individuals must be sought who "fit in." It assumes that positions do not affect their occupants. These views, however plausible, are oversimplifications. The fact that some organizations seem to operate by these assumptions does not thereby make them valid.

Most managerial positions are not routine in nature. The roles associated with each job may be played in many different ways by position holders. Where an organization is run as a "tight ship," concrete, well-defined positions ease the burdens of staffing, but preclude flexibility and innovation. On the other hand, positions too loosely structured may be unappealing to prospective employees and hence more difficult to staff.

One way out of this dilemma is to view the basic organization structure as consisting of relatively permanent, key positions, but also to be open to creating special opportunities in the structure to accommodate unusual persons who become available. In this view, staffing is not only a matter of "matching" people to jobs, but of matching jobs to talented, innovative, or highly specialized people. Many organizations hire individuals, such as college graduates, mainly for their interesting or unusual capabilities even when there are no specific vacancies. Often such employees are assigned to temporary positions or to rotational plans for acquiring practical training and experience. Thus many interesting positions are those that the organization did not know it needed; they are invented by persuasive persons who know how to create their own jobs.

The need for exact matching of people and jobs is often exaggerated, and under certain conditions it may be better for an organization to put a square peg in a round hole and let the two adapt to each other. Still, it is wise to recognize that serious cases of mismatching can and do occur. Selection processes can go awry. Individuals may make wrong choices. Substantial over- or under-qualification for positions may bring about the risks of low morale and job dissatisfaction.[8]

Manager Mobility

Those who yearn for the absolutely stable and predictable organization are in most cases doomed to disappointment. Change is the more

[8]Robert A. Luke, Jr., "Matching the Individual and the Organization," *Harvard Business Review* **53** (May–June 1975) 17–23.

constant reality. The better the manger, the more likely that others will want that manager too. Also, the better managers are interested in advancement and are more likely to plan their working careers carefully and to make strategic changes.

From the individual's point of view, advancement in a career is more important than mere advancement within an organization. Career-oriented professional managers meet critical turning points in their careers that often make it desirable to move to a new organization. It is true, however, that in very large organizations there is a great deal of opportunity for managers to develop and advance without leaving.

Mobility thus dictates that the staffing function be continuous. It often turns out that one's least able subordinates stick to their jobs like mustard plaster, whereas the best are drawn away by other parts of the organization or by outsiders. Managers face the inroads of attrition: deaths, resignations, transfers, and promotions create staffing problems. In many organizations, managers are specifically rewarded for their ability to develop subordinates who can replace them or move ahead. Yet the pain of separation from a friend or colleagues is nonetheless real, and the prospect of going through it all again can be frustrating.

It is all to easy for a manager to become overdependent on subordinates (as well as for subordinates to be too dependent on their bosses). But the manager who tries too hard to retain a subordinate to avoid the problems of replacement does a disservice to the individual. The strategy may have short-run success at the expense of long-run problems. The manager who holds someone back for selfish or even logical reasons will earn an undesirable reputation.

When a good subordinate decides to move to a new organization, the staffing problem is how much effort to make to retain the individual. The usual practice, if the person is an effective employee whose loss would be a setback to the management team, is to make a strong attempt to meet the conditions of the subordinate's offer. However, some persons collect offers with no real intentions of leaving, using them as leverage to gain improvements in their present organization; this tactic can be blunted by not being gullible about the genuineness of the offer or the individual's strategies.

It is possible to manifest too great a dependence by trying too hard to retain even a very capable person. The costs of retention have to be measured against a realistic appraisal of the person's capabilities and weaknesses. Trying too hard overcommits the organization and paves the way for continuous pressure to extend those commitments. If the ploy is successful, others will repeat it.

An unusual staffing problem occurs when an executive takes to a new organization a team of associates he has developed in a previous organization. To get the key manager, the new organization must accept the others. In any case, new managers coming in at or near the top usually insist on the freedom to replace existing staff members with individuals of their own choice. The advantage of the team is that its members have developed a way of working together that was successful in a previous assignment. Later the team may again move on. A disadvantage is the unusual cost of moving whole teams from one firm to another.

The "key manager plus a team" idea is built around the concept of sponsorship, but sponsorship is an aspect of many other relationships of the boss to subordinates. Sponsorship is the technique whereby a manager informally selects a subordinate for special coaching and development. The advancement of the subordinate is tied to the advancement or influence of the superior. In effect, this technique identifies persons whose advancement potential becomes widely noted and legitimated by the attitudes and actions of their sponsors. Although it is no guarantee of promotion, ambitious managers often benefit from establishing a favorable relationship with a sponsor. On the other hand, the individual so sponsored wins the risk of being labeled a "fair-haired boy" by his peers.

Promotion from Within

In most organizations, staffing begins with consideration of changes that can be made by advancing or transferring individuals already employed—a policy that is often called "promotion from within." Such a policy benefits employee morale by giving an opportunity to be considered for advancement. Having a strong internal candidate for a vacancy removes uncertainties that accompany the hiring of an outsider candidate. The internal candidate has a visible record, continuous performance appraisal, and a shorter learning time in new responsibilities. Outsiders are needed, however, to permit expansion, to germinate new ideas, and often to change old ways for new.

Several procedures facilitate staffing changes from within. First, a manpower inventory system keeps on record the performance and development histories of at least the key managers. Such records are usually kept by the personnel department, thereby fostering an organizationwide talent pool that can cut across departmental or other domains.

A second component of the promotion-from-within concept is systematic training and development, both in the form of formal programs and in more informal methods such as coaching and sponsoring.

A third set of techniques involves performance appraisal. Appraisal systems give specific attention to fair, objective evaluations based primarily on effective results, but also with some consideration of potential for handling greater responsibilities. Finally , career counseling can be utilized to assist individuals in carrer planning and decisions.

The policy of promotion from within entails a corollary responsibility of providing an organizational climate in which executives may develop their abilities and talents in directions that are useful to the organization and satisfying to themselves. It is neither necessary nor desirable to guarantee that all who work for the organization will be promoted at regular intervals, but it is important to give assurance to those who are associated with the organization of a reasonable opportunity to learn, to experiment, to study and observe, and to be associated intimately with others of greater ability and achievements. Employees tend to favor an organization in which opportunities to advance are wisely managed.

Critiques of Promotion From Within

The policy of promotion from within has the merit of appearing fair to existing employees. Companies that are actively recruiting use the inducements of this policy. In times of scarce labor supplies, companies cannot afford to overlook any source whatsoever. Promotion from within encourages internal mobility and adds flexibility to the work of organization planners. Changes that occur gradually and according to systematic planning are healthy in an organization and help create a climate of success.

However, there are limits to such a policy. First, employees may question particular promotions from within, and may not agree with the choice. They may also disagree with respect to outsiders, but morale is often not so greatly endangered as when internal promotional policies do not seem to be working well. A second problem is the fact that overstressing the policy results in "inbreeding" in organizations—the lack of new, fresh ideas that are likely to originate with outside talent coming from other organizations. Inbred organizations have operated too long on their own narrow set of ideas, experiences, and policies. The problem is particularly acute in organizations which depend heavily on ideas, such as an advertising agency or a business requiring skillful engineering of its products and the development of new products.

A third difficulty is caused by the fact that organization structures generally adhere to the pyramidal shape, so that the number of available openings declines as one approaches the top. Competition for promotion becomes keener, and the need to set standards for promotion is greater. Other factors partly offset the difficulty of winning promotions. Compensation levels, for example, can rise without requiring an increase in responsibilities, whether the cause is inflation, added fringe benefits, reduced hours, longer vacations, easier manual labor, better equipment and working conditions, or improved leadership and communication. Finally, there are individuals who do not want promotions. They may have reached a point where further progress does not seem worth the struggle. Or they may be performing to the top of their capacity. Such employees may continue to do their present jobs capably, but they are poor risks for promotion.

A fourth weakness is often found in the practice of "using what we have." Recognizing that it is impossible to get a perfect fit in the position, people abandon efforts toward systematic selectivity, and take the easy way out—namely, to utilize any person who happens to be available and shows no marked drawbacks. This is a risky way to develop a staff. The difficulty is perpetuated by a general reluctance to remove the less capable individual when a better person is available. Operating by expediency may solve a current problem, but it may also create serious long-run problems.

A fifth and very important difficulty with policies of promotion from within is that persons with upward aspirations tend to identify with the group to which they aspire to belong, rather than the one to which they actually belong. Thus subordinates act like and take on the values of persons above them. If they are promoted, such roles and values would stand them in good stead. If they are not promoted, however, their roles and value behaviors have separated them from the group in which they are destined to remain. In other ways, aspiring candidates for promotion may alienate their current group. They may make less of an investment in the group they seek to leave; they appear to have less involvement and commitment than the group would like; they appear to reject the present group in favor of another one. The disruptive effect of anticipated promotion can be particularly serious in situations characterized by high task interdependence—situations in which ineffective performance would have critical effects on the total process.

Internal promotions also have effects on those who are not promoted. The passed-over individual has to explain what happened, be driven to find satisfactions outside the organization, and, in extreme cases, may leave. The bypassed manager who remains could become a problem of morale and motivation. Problems can be prevented by explaining the reasons for the decision to the passed-over individual.

Striving for promotion may lead to biases and blind spots in the training and development of individual managers, who may overlook areas within their field, as long as they are not important to the particular organization. Thus long careers with one organization increasingly preclude changing organizations or types of organizations.

Strong emphasis on promotion-from-within policies may intensify the normal resentment that often meets the acquisition of an outsider. Some may feel that the job could have been filled from within when it was not. Moreover, the outsider often is brought in with a strong "mandate," either expressed or implied, to solve problems or correct conditions that existed previously. New ideas or an organizational shake-up appear to be necessary. Furthermore, the new manager has probably had a good job in a previous company, and the new company has to offer a relatively more attractive position in terms of salary, job level, title, and degree of cooperation. A new manager sometimes enters an organization to do the same job that competent individuals already in the organization have been trying to do for years. Being new confers the advantage that the manager can ignore established procedures with the excuse of unfamiliarity. The new manager can override traditions and habits. These factors may be advantages, but they may have the disadvantage of lowering the morale of older employees, disrupting the salary scales, and eliciting resistance to change.

Assessment Centers

Staffing is greatly facilitated by establishing assessment centers. Such centers represent a new technique usually found in large organizations: a systematic approach to promotion policies. They bring together in one program all the procedures for recognizing and evaluating the capabilities of individuals available for selection, development, and promotion. Center approaches are applicable to both managerial and nonmanagerial employees, but are used mainly for assessing managers. Most employees look favorable on centers because they substitute systematic decisions for the whims of supervisors, and assure that talented persons will not be overlooked.

A typical assessment center conducts periodic programs consisting of group exercises that simulate actual management situations. The exercises include in-basket tests, leaderless group discussion, and other situational devices to appraise the individual's ability to think in action. Psychological tests, peer evaluations, depth interviews and other familiar techniques are also brought together. An enormous quantity of subjective and objective information is developed.

Assessment sessions can take from one day to two weeks, depending on the scope and difficulty of the effort. Each group consists of six to eight employees. An observer is appointed for each two group members. Observers are both psychologists and line managers, but for middle- and top-level candidates more psychologists are used.

Assessment centers are costly to establish and operate. The time required for observers is extensive, usually twice that of candidates, so that they can make analyses and evaluations. However, if the numbers to be assessed are sufficiently large, the per capita cost may be feasible. The chief benefits lie in the systematic and rigorous gathering and interpretation of information, the fair treatment of internal candidates for advancement, and the use of highly trained psychologists and other specialists in planning and conducting the assessments.

For most persons, going through assessment center procedures does not result in immediate advancement. The individuals may be retained in a talent pool or manpower inventory system, while being designated as having potential for advancement.[9]

Over a twenty-year span, AT&T made a Management Progress Study to appraise the effectiveness of its assessment center. The goal of the study was to uncover basic information about managers' ability and performance; 442 managers were studied, some of whom were college graduates and some of whom had simply been promoted to managerial positions. In an analysis of the college graduates' first eight years on the job, AT&T found that the assessment center had an excellent batting average. Of those expected by the center to reach middle management, 64 per cent had already achieved it, and of those predicted not to reach it, only 32 per cent had made it.[10]

Discharge

Too little attention is paid in most organizations to discharge as part of the staffing function. Organizations that pride themselves on a humane spirit may do so at the cost of retaining obsolete, incompetent, or inadequate persons who not only remain on their jobs but also compete in the promotion system. The accumulation of dead wood in many organizations is astounding and can make an organization moribund and difficult to change.

Discharge is properly a last-resort form of disciplinary action. It is drastic and painful to carry out, yet it is often the best action for the individual released, although he may not believe it at the time. There are humane ways of effecting a discharge: giving the person plenty of time to relocate, assisting in the job search, supplying office and clerical services during the relocation period, and offering separation pay.

It is often overlooked that retaining a person who ought to be discharged affects the work of many others whose tasks and quality of

---

[9]Harold S. Alexander, John A. Buck, and Robert J. McCarthy, "Usefulness of the Assessment Center Process for Selection to Upward Mobility Programs," *Human Resources Management* **14** (Spring 1975), 10–31; Kristen Amundsen, "An Assessment Center at Work," *Personnel* **52** (March–April 1975), 29–36; John P. Bucalo, Jr., "The Assessment Center: A More Specified Approach," *Human Resource Management* **13** (Fall 1974), 2–13; Ann Howard, "An Assessment of Assessment Centers," *Academy of Management Journal* **17** (March 1974), 115–134; James R. Huck, "Assessment Centers: A Review of External and Internal Validities," *Personnel Psychology* **26** (Summer 1973), 191–212; James O. Mitchell, "Assessment Center Validity: A Longitudinal Study," *Journal of Applied Psychology* **60** (October 1975), 573–579; Allen I. Kraut, "New Frontiers for Assessment Centers," *Personnel* **53** (July–August 1976), 30–38.

[10]Douglas W. Bray, "Management Development Without Frills," *The Record* **12** (September 1975), 47–50.

performance are closely related. Discharge will make sense to this group; retention results in continuous annoyance and frustration. One library, for example, retained a catalog specialist who was unable to keep up with the flow of materials arriving each day. The resulting backlog was evident in the large room full of unattended material, in user complaints, in the disorderly environment, and in the low morale of other professional librarians.

SUMMARY

The mobility of managers is a fact of life; therefore staffing must be a continuous concern. *Staffing,* defined broadly, includes not only the replacement of persons who leave but also the development of people in their careers. Merely matching people to positions precludes fitting positions to the special abilities of people. Therefore a two-way relationship prevails between persons and positions.

This chapter has discussed several aspects of managerial staffing. In performing these responsibilities, the manager must have a close working relationship with the personnel department, which maintains overall perspectives vital to the interests of all and to the total organization. It recommends and carries out policies bearing on staffing, and maintains records and carries out screening activities that are too technical for nonspecialists to perform.

Managers should take a long-range view of their staffing problems. They need to be aware of external and internal sources of supply, factors in the managerial labor market, growth patterns, and the demands of changing technology.

Staffing skills include planning analysis, interviewing, and information interpretation. The manager needs to consider each vacancy as an opportunity to review the organization's structure, and the tasks and duties of the vacant position as well as those related to it.

INCIDENT CASE

Company X is famous for its "fast-track" program. Top-notch persons are hired from leading colleges around the country and given an intensive training program emphasizing rotation on a variety of job assignments. The work is real, not mere training exercises. Some department heads, however, resent the trainees. Edward Norton, a trainee, remained in the program for one year. He then resigned to "take a real job in another company."

Question

1. What went wrong?

--- **QUESTIONS FOR DISCUSSION**

1. In what ways can staffing be considered more than merely matching people to jobs?

2. What are the characteristics of a successful job interview from the organization's point of view? From the applicant's point of view?

3. What steps can be taken to reduce or prevent fraud and exaggeration on the part of applicants for managerial positions?

4. Explain how the recruiting and selection of managers may differ from recruiting and selecting rank-and-file employees.

5. What are the advantages and disadvantages of employing managers as groups or teams?

6. What are the pros and cons of a policy of promotion from within?

--- **SELECTED REFERENCES**

BURACK, ELMER H. *Strategies for Manpower Planning and Programming.* Morristown, N.J.: General Learning Corporation, 1972. Part 6.

COX, ALLAN J. *Confessions of a Corporate Headhunter.* New York: Trident Press, 1973.

DALE, ERNEST. *Management Theory and Practice.* 3rd ed. New York: McGraw-Hill Book Company, 1973.

GLUECK, WILLIAM. *Personnel: A Diagnostic Approach.* 2nd ed. Dallas: Business Publications, Inc., 1978.

GRINOLD, RICHARD C., and KNEAL T. MARSHALL. *Manpower Planning Models: Modeling of Long-range Manpower in Large Organizations.* New York: Elsevier North Holland, 1976.

GRUENFELD, ELAINE F. *Promotion: Practices, Policies, and Affirmative Action.* Ithaca, N.Y.: New York State School of Industrial and Labor Relations, Cornell University, 1975.

HALL, DOUGLAS T. *Careers in Organizations.* Pacific Palisades, Calif.: Goodyear Publishing Company, 1976.

LOPEZ, FELIX M. *Personnel Interviewing.* 2nd ed. New York: McGraw-Hill Book Company, 1975.

MILES, RAYMOND E. *Theories of Management: Implications for Organizational Behavior and Development.* New York: McGraw-Hill Book Company, 1975. Chapter 10.

MILLER, KENNETH M., ed. *Psychological Testing in Personnel Assessment.* New York: John Wiley & Sons, Inc., 1975.

PETROFESA, JOHN. *Career Development: Theory and Research.* New York: Grune and Stratton, 1975.

PORTER, LYMAN W., EDWARD E. LAWLER, JR., and J. RICHARD HACKMAN. *Behavior in Organizations.* New York: McGraw-Hill Book Company, 1975. Part 2.

RICHARDS, MAX D., and WILLIAM NIELANDER, eds. *Readings in Management.* Cincinnati: South-Western Publishing Company, 1974. Section F.

SCHNEIDER, BENJAMIN. *Staffing Organizations.* Pacific Palisades, Calif.: Goodyear Publishing Company. 1976.

SHAEFFER, RUTH G. *Staffing Systems: Managerial and Professional Jobs.* New York: The Conference Board, 1972.

WHITE, HARRISON C. *Chains of Opportunity: Systems Models of Mobility in Organizations.* Cambridge, Mass.: Howard University Press, 1970.

YODER, DALE, and HERBERT G. HENEMAN, JR., eds. *Staffing Policies and Strategies.* ASPA Handbook of Personnel and Industrial Relations, vol. 1. Washington, D.C.: BNA Books, Inc., 1974.

Cases for Part II

Hillside is a national conglomerate firm selling and manufacturing lumber and building supplies; it also operates a chain of over four hundred retail establishments covering hardware, furniture, farm machinery, and household products. Its growth by acquisitions resulted in a tripling of sales in the past ten years, but profits failed to keep up the same pace. In 1967 its return on equity was 15 per cent, but by 1971 the figure fell below 2 per cent. In 1978, it suffered a net loss of over $22 million.

To turn the firm around, the board put a moratorium on growth, limited its capital expenditures, and pruned its debt. The most drastic move, however, was reshuffling the executive suite. Whereas many firms in such circumstances fire the existing managers and hire new ones, Hillside fired no one, but instead reassigned 17 senior executives, changing their titles, duties, and responsibilities. Several managers had less responsibility under the new structure; others received more.

The president explained that the firm would thus be in a position to deploy its best managers into the businesses in which it wanted to grow, and to cut back on others. By assigning the best talent to areas of greatest potential, the firm lessened its emphasis on troublesome, weak, or relatively unimportant areas of activity.

This new organization design was one suggested by a major consulting firm after a four months' study. The board chairman denied that this reshuffling resulted in demotions. The president and the executive vice president shouldered increased responsibilities, but several executives ended up with narrower roles, including in some cases reassignment to lower units they had previously commanded. The chairman stated that he expected a few people to be upset, but they were not.

The managers with more responsibilities faced tough challenges. Hillside's recycled managers talked about their aim to stimulate growth, but company officials

257

generally seemed to favor a go-slow policy derived from bad experiences with unprofitable acquisitions. Their firm's business for the most part is highly cyclical, and there is little room for improvement through greater operating efficiency.

QUESTIONS FOR STUDY

1. Discuss the wisdom of the turn-around strategy described in this case.
2. What conditions are significant relating to a decision of this type?

B. HELEN MCGINLEY

Helen McGinley is a 32-year-old black female executive who manages a large branch bank located not far from the main bank of which it is affiliated. The branch is in the financial district of a large metropolitan area. Mrs. McGinley has a salary of $30,000 per year, and 26 bankers, tellers and clerks report to her as branch manager.

Thus Mrs. McGinley occupies a middle-management position within the estimated 6 per cent of female workers in the nation at this level. She aspires to achieve the vice presidential level or higher, which would include only about 1 per cent of all female workers. Mrs. McGinley is aware of these difficult odds—the pressure to compete and the threat she poses in a male-dominated hierarchy. Physicians and teachers foster guilt feelings by implying that the woman executive, being unavailable in the daytime, can't adequately care for her children. Inside the company, the woman executive cannot socialize with male colleageues the way men do. She cannot participate in lunches, golfing, or drinking sessions, and is thus barred from the inner networks of the informal organization. Even more difficult is the fact that the woman executive cannot be a protégé of a senior executive who can serve as a sponsor in a system of upward mobility. Mrs. McGinley feels that despite these obstacles, females are expected to perform their work better than men in similar positions. All these factors tend to produce emotional stress.

Mrs. McGinley's personality is not that of the typical hard-driving, ambitious executive. She is quiet, shy, soft-voiced. She entered upon a full-time business career against the wishes of her husband, searching not for power but for fulfillment and peace of mind through getting out of the house every day. Her progress to branch bank manager was slow and difficult, achieved through persistence and concretely demonstrating her capabilities for management. She was the bank's first female officer, and is now one of one hundred executives, only three of whom are black. The total work force of the bank is twelve hundred employees.

In her previous job, as sales manager in charge of the family banking division, Mrs. McGinley was in charge of 35 bankers, mostly men. A few of these men were uncomfortable with Mrs. McGinley's supervision, and complained to her boss. Customers were sometimes dubious about her authority. Nevertheless, she was promoted to branch manager before the new branch opened, and directed the construction, design, equipping, and staffing of the new facility. In this job she had for the first time to work with men in other bank departments. She had trouble keeping them interested in her priorities: "They tended to put my programs on the back burner, and I had to prove myself with them."

In meetings with other managers at the main office, Mrs. McGinley found herself often fighting to protect her domain. However, the competitive elements were in general friendly and low-key. Mrs. McGinley followed a policy of thorough preparation, including efforts to become part of the informal social system. She adapted quickly to office politics. In the new branch, things moved ahead of schedule and were running smoothly, with high morale in the group. However, she worked 19-hour days, taking a full brief case home at night. She also enrolled in evening courses two nights a week at a local college offering an MBA program.

In February, 1977, Mrs. McGinley's boss called her in to say that he had noticed signs of stress and tension caused by overwork and the feelings associated with her role as a female executive, her neglected family, and her heavy responsibilities. He asked whether she would consider a transfer to a staff position in the main office. She replied, "I am doing what I like to do, I am successful, and don't have any problems I can't overcome. I haven't really completed what I set out to do in the branch."

QUESTIONS

1. Analyze the situation from the point of view of Mrs. McGinley.
2. Does Mrs. McGinley's boss have any real cause for concern? Why or why not?

C. MARKHAM PHARMACEUTICALS, INC.

Markham Pharmaceuticals, Inc., is a well-established firm with a reputation as one of the leaders in the ethical drug industry. Its aggressive marketing policies are credited with achieving substantial growth and profit results over the past decade.

The company's field marketing system consists of "detail men," each with an assigned territory. They are organized into districts in charge of a district sales manager, who directs the efforts of 15 to 20 detail men, and is responsible for their sales volumes as well as for recruiting, training, and supervising them.

Fred Malcolm was a district sales manager in one of the eastern regional divsions of the company. In 1975, he employed Mrs. Wanda Harper as a "detail man." Mrs. Harper, an attractive divorcee, applied for the position advertised in a local newspaper. Her previous experience in selling cosmetics was only indirectly related to drug sales, but her resume indicated that she had a successful record in selling, and that she had favorable recommendations from a number of people including past employers. Fred Malcolm sized her up as an ambitious, hard-working young woman with the ability to learn, and consequently with great potential for his organization.

Mrs. Harper, one of the few women in this kind of work, was paid a starting salary of $14,500 per year, and was eligible for bonuses based on sales. During her first year, she earned $2000 in bonuses, and Mr. Malcolm seemed to regard her work as satisfactory. An attractive, well-groomed blonde, always elegantly dressed, Mrs. Harper gained the confidence of the physicians on whom she called and was able to greatly increase the sales of company products in her territory, which consisted of eight counties, two of which were sites of urban medical centers.

With strong ambitions to make good and become established in her field of work,

Mrs. Harper applied for admission to and was accepted in an MBA evening program in a local college. By taking one or two evening courses she could acquire course credits leading eventually to a graduate degree in business.

Mrs. Harper described her experiences in Markham Pharmaceuticals as follows: "I'll admit I was pretty lost at first calling on all those doctors. But it got easier as I went along, and I got so I was increasing the sales in my territory about 40 per cent over what they had been before. It was hard, too, to be competing with a bunch of men, but I felt that I was doing as well as any one else in this kind of job.

"Mr. Malcolm taught me a lot about selling and about the drug industry. He seemed to take pride in my success, and he has been good to work for all these months. He does get on my nerves at times, though. He is always after me to make more calls. He checks up on me all the time, and even calls me at odd hours as though he doesn't believe I'm following the schedule I gave him. You see, we fill out a weekly sales call plan, so he can know what I'm going to do. So he should know from that where I am. But he'll call on Saturday or Sunday and ask why I'm not out making sales calls. I don't understand how I could be calling on anyone then. Besides, I regard my weekends as my own and it's none of his business what I do on my own time. We have so many company forms to fill in that I could spend all weekend just on them. In fact Mr. Malcolm gets mad at me, as I am often late in sending in the reports. He expects them to be followed exactly and in the field you know you have to adapt and adjust.

"At first, Mr. Malcolm went with me on my calls to doctor's offices. This was good training for me. He'd help me, or make observations and go over everything that happened. But I thought he would only do this at the start. He keeps on, though, and I never know when I'll get a call from him saying he'll meet me and make calls with me for a couple of days. There's no pattern to it—it's so unpredictable, and he's a problem to me anyhow. It just puts pressure on me to have him interfering. And he's so critical I can't stand it.

"Mr. Malcolm has changed a lot since I first met him. His wife divorced him three months ago and he has become a heavy drinker. I think he is an alcoholic. I can't see why the company isn't on to him. I suppose he is good at covering things up.

"You know, I don't know how much more of this I can take. I like the work, and I feel I am doing very well and getting better. I make pretty good money—but this Malcolm is putting on too much pressure. It must be that the company is pressuring him. He has a lot or worries, maybe that's why he drinks and is so hard to get along with."

Six months later not much had changed, according to Mrs. Harper. "I am still getting along all right but my boss is getting worse. He is more demanding and more unreasonable than ever. He gets upset at little things, and yells at me when I do something wrong. The other day he caught me filling in sales visit forms with information that wasn't strictly true. I got so tired of all the red tape that I just filled in the forms and sent them in so he'd think I was working. I had to take a day course at school last term, but I didn't dare tell him about school. I suppose it wasn't too honest of me and he had a right to be angry. I think I ought to quit this job and try something else. The reason I don't is that I like the work. It is a good job except for the way my boss acts.

"A counselor I talked to suggested that I try confronting him and telling him how I felt about his behavior. I decided to do it. After all, it was worth a try. He couldn't do anything more than fire me, and I couldn't go on the way it was. When I pointed out how he was too strict, too inflexible and unreasonably demanding, he seemed startled at first, then he asked some questions. Finally he said that he realized my point and that he thought it could all be worked out to our mutual satisfaction. He mentioned some of his problems to me and he really has some. Now that I've told him my reactions to his supervision, maybe I can hold on and see if this job will develop."

Four months later Mrs. Harper recounted another major event: "I was fortunate, I felt, to be selected for a two-week special company school in New York, all expenses paid. I just got back, and I'm so mad and hurt by what happened. You see, the training man said that he wanted our opinions and ideas as the program went along. Most of the participants didn't say much, but I thought of it as an opportunity to contribute the benefit of some of my field experiences so others could learn. So I guess I was pretty outspoken. But no one said anything then. At the end we were to give our evaluation, which I did, and it was a very favorable one. Imagine my surprise when I got back to get this call late at night from Mr. Malcolm. He demanded to see me right away the next morning, and I could tell he was angry. When I met with him he screamed at me for disgracing him at the training program. The training director had reported me to be the worst of the thirty participants, arrogant, smart-alecky, and a know-it-all. Mr Malcolm said he thought he would have to fire me, as he couldn't stand to have anyone that bad work for him, and he didn't want the company to think he was too soft to take the necessary action. However, he hasn't actually fired me yet. He talked quite a while about the program, and he decided to let things go another two or three weeks and see if I improved my attitudes . I'm really hurt. That's why I'm crying. And I'm afraid I'll get fired. Do you think I should quit and try to get another job? Besides all this, my daughter has been hospitalized and I can't find out what's wrong or how she is. She is in my ex-husband's custody."

Six more months passed. Mrs. Harper reported as follows: "Yes, I'm still with Markham and working for Mr. Malcolm. His drinking is worse and his demands more unreasonable. He hasn't forgotten that black mark I got in the training program. But I think he knows I can sell and his record looks good with me doing so well. Now I've got another job opportunity. It's still in selling, similar to what I've been doing. It's selling supplies and equipment to hospitals. I'll have to move to another city, but that's okay with me. I'm trying to decide whether to take this job or not. It would be with a smaller company, but it seems very successful. Markham is so damned bureaucratic—all those forms to fill out every day. It takes me at least four hours a day just to keep records and fill out reports. I think I could make more money, and I don't think Pelman Industries is nearly as bad as Markham."

QUESTIONS

1. As a career counselor, how would you analyze this case?
2. What would you advise Wanda Harper to do next, and why?

D. FARRELL AND WHEELAN CORPORATION

Farrell and Wheelan Corporation is a relatively new, highly diversified corporation, formed in 1958 by merging Farrell, Inc., founded in 1882, and the Wheelan

Company, founded in 1908. Wheelan manufactured high-quality bicycles, wagons, and other nonmotorized wheelgoods in the toy industry, and Farrell, Inc., operated a chain of about ninety hardware stores in the southern and eastern portions of the United States. The merger helped integrate the Wheelan Company by providing its own retail outlets, and assured Farrell, Inc., of a planned supply of merchandise and other benefits. The merged corporation succeeded almost from the start.

Success brought the means to continue expanding the firm. Several more retail chains were purchased and melded into the group. The company moved boldly into the manufacturing of hardware items, auto supplies, and in recent years, into the insurance, apparel, electronics, and recreation industries. The firm thus joined the ranks of the giant conglomerates—with the corporate headquarters operating through central financial controls, central policies, and central evaluations of the autonomous units.

Speaking to a huge throng of executives at a trade association meeting in one of the industries in which the company holds several firms, the president of Farrell and Wheelan outlined his company's philosophy toward growth: "Our industry has entered the jet age of corporate management on full power. The major business of management is management, and an important part of every Farrell and Wheelan acquisition is getting new managerial talent." However, he was addressing the leaders of an industry in which his firm's own units were lagging behind the industry averages on profits.

In 1978 Farrell and Wheelan aggressively attempted to acquire a major firm in an industry they had heretofore been unable to penetrate. It was reported in the local newspapers that "in view of the company's policy that they acquire firms to obtain managerial talent, it is inconceivable how they could have wanted to acquire this firm, whose management could be described as the worst in its industry."

According to the president, "Through our company headquarters staff . . . we run one of the busiest management-consultant services in the world." He said Farrell and Wheelan's headquarters staff assists in handling problems that "temporarily" block satellite progress. In return the company received valuable management contributions from the satellites.

QUESTIONS

1. What inconsistencies exist in this company's policies? Why do you think they occur?
2. Evaluate the acquisition philosophy and practice described in this case.
3. Evaluate the growth philosophy expressed in this case.

E. THE ALLISON POWER COMPANY

The Allison Power Company, a large public utility serving the eastern part of the United States, is a corporation organized into districts, territories, and divisions according to major functions. Divisions are further subdivided into departments and departments into sections.

Of its 12,000 employees, about 4,000 are in clerical, professional, and managerial categories. The company is widely known for its progressive personnel policies and the low turnover of its employees. The company hires large numbers of mechanical and electrical engineers, many of whom become managers.

By 1977, John Knowles had been the head of the Test Equipment Department for three years. In this department are located all activities connected with designing, building, procuring, and maintaining test equipment used throughout the company. Trained as an electrical engineer, Knowles had been with the company for 13 years. Early in 1977, his immediate supervisor, Ralph Lerner, manager of the company's service division, asked Knowles if he would accept a newly created position in the Industrial Development Division. Because the position was new, the Industrial Development Division wanted someone experienced in company policies and procedures to fill the position temporarily for one year. After that time, the position was to be made permanent or else to be eliminated. Knowles was invited to fill the position because of his reputation as a highly skilled engineer. Lerner told Knowles that he was reluctant to lose him even temporarily, but, acting in accordance with the long-standing company policy of filling vacancies from within, he wanted Knowles to make the decision. The new position would represent an advancement for Knowles to the next higher supervisory level, with a commensurate increase in salary. Knowles asked for and received a week's time to think the offer over. He concluded that the position offered a new challenge and that he would accept the position.

On the following Monday, Lerner called Knowles into his office to discuss the matter of his replacement. It was recognized that at the end of the year Knowles might want to return. In considering his three subordinates, Knowles did not feel certain in his own mind which of the three, if any, would be the best successor. Larson, head of Section A, had the broadest experience and longest tenure in the company, but was considered by Knowles to be rather hasty in his judgments and prone to make mistakes that were not easy to rectify. Dexter, the head of Section B, was a competent workman, but never showed any indication of the imagination and creative ability that Knowles thought to be important in the department. The head of Section C, George Keyes, had an aggressive and ambitious temperament, but often found it hard to maintain smooth working relationships with colleagues. Because Knowles could not see a clear-cut choice, he proposed to Lerner that Larson, Dexter, and Keyes take turns as acting head of the Test Equipment Department for a four-month period each. Then, if Knowles did not return, a choice could be made among the three on the basis of their actual performance. Lerner agreed to this proposal and put the plan into operation.

Nine months later, while Keyes was acting head of the Test Equipment Department, Lerner was unexpectedly transferred to another division. Fred Winston was immediately appointed to Lerner's post as manager of the division. Prior to his departure, Lerner briefed Winston on the situation in the Test Equipment Department. When Winston asked Lerner what tentative evaluations he had come to, Lerner replied that although Keyes had not yet served out his four months, he appeared to be the best of the three men for the job. In fact, Lerner said, "I have indicated to him more or less indirectly that he has a strong chance to get the job." Winston decided to let Keyes finish out the quarter as acting head before making a choice.

Toward the end of the year, Knowles was notified that his new position was permanent and that he would not be returning. When Winston received this information, he decided to interview each of the three eligible subordinates. He prepared for the interviews by a close scrutiny of their personnel records, past appraisal records by their former supervisor, Knowles, and systematic notes he had been making on the performance of the three men. During the interviews, he discovered that considerable animosity and jealousy had developed among the three men. It had been a year in which they had competed with one another for the vacant position. Larson had taken a positive approach and had attempted to do a conscientious and efficient job of running the department. Dexter was more flamboyant, and had attempted to introduce some innovations that met with opposition from his two colleagues. Keyes had tried to do everything himself so as not to give the others much opportunity to show what they could do. Each of the three believed the assignment should be given to him. After careful analysis of the interviews and the records, and an assessment of the objectives of the department and its future, Winston decided that neither Larson, Dexter, nor Keyes was capable of developing this department at the high level he expected.

On June 1, 1978, it was announced that Gordon Miles, a section head from the Experimental Research Division, had been named head of the Test Equipment Department.

QUESTIONS

1. How would you evaluate the decisions of the key persons in this case?
2. What factors appear to be at work in the managerial environment that are influential in problems of this kind?
3. What do you think will happen in the next few months in this company?

F. THE RUGGLES COMPANY, INC.

The Ruggles Company is a moderate-sized but rapidly growing manufacturer of machine tools. For several years it has had a small planning section whose assignment is to assist top management in special projects, long-range planning, and problem solving where complex analysis is required.

James Randall was recently appointed general manager of the company, and the planning section, which he headed prior to his promotion, reports directly to him. That section is now headed by Larry Paxton, whom Randall appointed right after his own promotion. Randall has been with the firm over fifteen years, is forty years of age, and is generally acknowledged to be an effective supervisor and leader of men. Paxton is relatively new with the company, having been employed three years earlier; he is thirty-six years old, with a reputation from prior assignments as a dynamic, aggressive leader.

Shortly after these changes were made, a troublesome incident occurred. Randall, having recently been the supervisor of the planning section, was familiar with the work being done. On several occasions since becoming general manager he requested special projects, and after Paxton assigned the work to one of his analysts, Randall worked directly with that analyst to expedite the project.

Recently Paxton assigned such a special project to Albert Harrison. While working in close contact with Randall, Harrison asked permission to discuss something of a personal nature. Randall encouraged Harrison to talk with him, whereupon Harrison stated that he was highly dissatisfied with the way Paxton was allocating project assignments. He believed that Paxton did not appreciate his unusual qualifications for the work, and that Paxton was not giving him assignments in keeping with his technical background and previous experience covering over fifteen years with the Ruggles Company. In detailing his dissatisfaction, Harrison specified three types of project assignments that he had formerly completed when working as an analyst under Randall, and that were now being done by the other analysts. During the discussion, Randall recalled that Harrison was a widely known expert in his field, and had even written articles for technical journals. He also recalled that he had indicated to Paxton when he first came into the planning section that he thought it would be a good idea to draw up plans for the development of the men in the planning section.

The group of analysts working for Paxton included, in addition to Harrison, Ralph Broker and David North. Broker, 25 years old, had been with the Ruggles Company three years, and was a recent college graduate from a well-known school of business administration—in fact the same school from which Paxton had graduated some years earlier. Shortly after Paxton came into the section as its head, Broker began tentative job explorations with another company. North, 30 years old, had been with the Ruggles Company for six years, and was also a college graduate. He transferred to the Section approximately eighteen months before Harrison's expression of dissatisfaction to Randall. North and Harrison were quite friendly, and shared the feeling that Broker was Paxton's fair-haired boy.

Randall recalled, by reason of Harrison's comments to him, that when he was heading the section, all three analysts—Harrison, Broker, and North—were satisfied with their work assignments and relationships and had worked well as a team.

QUESTIONS

1. What brought about the problems in this case? Is there a central issue involved?

2. What happens next, and why?

G. LEADERSHIP IN A LARGE BANK

The Big Dollar Bank, a corporation operating a chain of banks on the east coast, is the twelfth largest bank in the United States. Before the arrival of its new chairman and chief executive officer, Arthur Lott, it was generally regarded by the rest of the industry as stodgy, halting, and unremarkable. The corporation was barely in the black when Lott arrived in 1977.

Lott was known for his reputation as a dynamo. In his previous position in a financial services company he was aggressive, energetic, and demanding. He saw in his new post an opportunity to infuse the Big Dollar with a new, lively management style that could reverse the near-paralysis into which it had drifted.

Focusing on four dimensions—people, capital structure, marketing, and organization—Lott began hiring executives who were above all else managers, and often not experienced in banking at all. He got rid of two thirds of the bank's senior and middle-level managers, cut the payroll by ten per cent, and began building a management team with an attitude of fast rather than slow growth. The termination of 1500 of the bank's 7,200 employees caused widespread bitterness, uncertainty, and low morale.

Lott drew up a plan to position the bank for rapid growth; the plan included improving the bank's capital base. Instead of slowing the growth rate because growth was outstripping the capital base, he proposed a major restructuring of captial: 1.5 million shares of common stock were to be issued and sold, and there was to be an offer to exchange convertible preferred stock for $70 million worth of convertible subordinated debentures. This plan was expected to result in improving the debt-equity ratio from 0.8 : 1 to 0.5 : 1, allowing it scope to return to the debt market for further expansion of growth.

The bank then moved to penetrate markets it had heretofore ignored, such as investment banking. Lott hired marketing specialists, operations research managers, and special talents from other banks, consulting firms, and corporations. His philosophy was that "old-style management is as obsolete in banking as in any other business." He worked a 14-hour day and expected his subordinates to do the same.

In his first 18 months, Lott created new budgeting, planning, personnel, and research groups, dismantled the bank's awkward regional structure, restructured the key international, corporate, and retail banking divisions, and sharply curtailed the power of the board of directors.

Critics attacked these and other moves. Fellow managers thought him too flamboyant when he put the stamp of his personality on the bank by appearing in TV and newpaper ads. Competitiors attacked the risks he took in unleashing a war by raising savings account interest, creating free checking for senior citizens, calling for longer hours, and instituting other marketing efforts. Lott's image of drive and ambition was thought by many to border on ruthlessness, but he was very effective in helping clients and in curbing the aloofness and snobbery with which the bank had previously dealt with potential customers. Others praised him for leading by example and not by fear, and for his ability to earn the loyalty of those around him. One said, "He is a man of charisma, a motivator, a sparkplug." To those who deemed him overly aggressive, he replied "The world is changing more than most people recognize, and we must make our services more responsive to new and different needs."

--- **QUESTIONS**

1. What components of the concept of leadership are at work in this case?
2. What managerial philosophies are being espoused?
3. Evaluate the strategies being followed, and analyze the risks involved.

------------------------ **H. THE CLAREMONT MILLING COMPANY, INC.**

In 1949, John Blake had purchased a bankrupt flour-milling company. Two years later he had built the firm's business substantially. He acquired a partner named

Albert Cotter, an inventor who held several patents on milling equipment. The business was incorporated in 1958, and in 1962 Blake sold his interest to Cotter, who was then president.

Reporting directly to Cotter was Jim Brown, the plant manager. By 1974 Brown had been with the firm for seven years and was well liked by Cotter. Cotter and Brown played golf together several times a week, and some of Brown's associates felt that he deliberatley cultivated Cotter as a means of holding his job. Although they believed his abilities were somewhat better than average, they also felt that he played politics to be sure of holding his job.

In 1976 Brown hired Sam Green as the new office manager. Cotter and Brown together had been able to keep things rolling, but by 1973, the volume of office activity had increased to the point where they both felt that an office manager was needed to coordinate all the office procedures. Sam Green had had about ten years' experience in office work in banking and insurance companies, and at the time he was hired was working for a large factory as office manager. He told Brown that his main reason for wanting a change of jobs was to get with a smaller company with opportunities for growth.

Before hiring Green—and with his permission—Brown made a routine check with Green's former employer. Green had reported in his factory job to the executive vice president, Edward Clay. Clay told Brown over the telephone that Green was a good, conscientious, worker, with an analytical mind and a pleasant personality. The only negative characteristic Clay cited was that Green's temperament was somewhat slow-moving, rather than being energetic and aggressive. Before making his decision, Brown discussed Green's qualifications with Cotter, and Cotter gave Brown clearance to hire Green.

For about a year, Green did his work efficiently, and both Brown and Cotter felt that they had made a good decision. However, at the annual review held on Green's anniversary date, Green made it clear that he aspired to the job of chief accountant, which would soon become vacant. Brown had not particularly regarded Green as a possibility for that position and had been planning to go outside to fill the job. He did not explain this to Green, but did not act very encouraging about Green's plan.

The next day, Brown told Cotter about Green's aspirations and said that he did not feel that Green had the background for the chief accountant's job. He told Cotter that Green had studied accounting in college, but had never had any work experience in a highly responsible accounting position.

Cotter told Brown not to do anything right then, and that he would think the problem over. Meanwhile, in a foursome at the country club, Cotter was introduced to Clay, from the factory where Green had previously worked. While playing golf with Clay, Cotter mentioned that Green had been on their staff for about a year and had worked out fairly well. Clay replied to Cotter, "Oh yes, I remember him. He used to be our office manager. We thought he was a pretty ordinary fellow. As a matter of fact, it did our organization a lot of good for him to leave, because he was always wanting a promotion that we didn't think he deserved. And you ought to see the guy we got to replace him—he's one of the topnotch office managers in the country." Cotter did not say much, but was disturbed that a man like Clay regarded Green as too ordinary to be worth having.

The next day, Cotter called Brown into his office and said, "I've been thinking about Green, and what you'd better do is discourage him all you can. I don't think we can fire him, but he seems to be only average, so when it's time for raises, just give him a token increase, if any. And I think you ought to tell him that the promotion he wants is out as far as I'm concerned." Brown immediately called Green in and told him, "I know you have been looking forward to the chief accountant's job. Cotter and I have given the matter very careful thought. Our feeling is that you will make a better office manager than a chief accountant, and we want to get a man in that job who has been at least ten years as an accountant." Green replied, "I took this job because I thought there was a lot of opportunity here because you have a growing company. What do you think the chances of advancement here really are?" Brown replied, "That's a hard one to answer. I'd rather not talk any more about it right now, but we'll get together on it just as soon as I get some of these details out of my way here." On three subsequent attempts, Green tried to get Brown to indicate his feelings about the future possibilities for advancement. Each time Brown gave vague and evasive answers. Green quietly proceeded to activate certain contacts he had in the business community, and on a Friday afternoon he entered Cotter's office and told him he was leaving. Cotter showed no surprise and told Green he hoped that he would find the kind of opportunity he wanted. Green's interview with Cotter was short and not very cordial, and during the following week, Cotter and Brown did not speak with Green. One of the other men in the office who had liked Green as a supervisor remarked openly to others in the office that he thought Cotter and Brown had been grossly unfair to Green and he couldn't understand why.

QUESTIONS

1. What is the heart of the problem described in this case?
2. Who is responsible for letting this problem develop? Why?
3. If you were Green, would you have proceeded as he did? Why or why not?
4. What management problems are exemplified in this case?

I. VANGUARD INSURANCE COMPANY

John Evans, 39 years old, had been personnel director at Vanguard for six years. He had joined the firm as office manager two years prior to his promotion to the top personnel position in the company.

Although he reported directly to the president, most of his work involved contacts with two officials: Fred James, vice president for underwriting, and Ted Stuart, vice president and controller. James and Stuart were widely known throughout the state and throughout the insurance industry as experts in human relations. Both made frequent speeches to civic clubs and industry groups on the importance of human relations skills. They were also respected inside the company for their ability to practice what they advocated for others.

Nevertheless, Evans had come to feel that the results of a long-range human relations training program, undertaken with the aid of a consulting firm, were not what they should be. The consultants, however, had apparently performed their services according to their agreement. In his own thinking, Evans concluded that the problem was at the department head level:

The problem arises because our top executives, Mr. James and Mr. Stuart, have succeeded in establishing a changed policy from an autocratically run company to a democratically run company. This change worked fine for them, for it was in accord with their views on human relations. They felt that the ideas were all very sound. This change was also acceptable to most of the other people in the company. The employees liked it because it seemed to give them a better chance to express themselves, to talk about their problems, and to say what they had on their minds. But I think the real trouble is in the department heads. These departments heads are old-timers. They were brought up in the school of hard knocks, and they are used to the autocratically run system. It's hard for them to adjust to this change. They say they agree to it, and they may even try to live up to the ideas of good human relations, and of a democratic organization, but when it comes to actually doing anything, they either let it go or do it the old way. That's why I say they are blocking our human relations.

QUESTIONS

1. What factors do you think may have brought this problem about?
2. Assuming that Evans is right in his diagnosis, what should be done next and who should do it?

PART III

The Dynamics
of Organization

Chapter 12

Organizations and Their Environments

The public must and will be served.

—William Penn

The most beautiful thing is the mysterious. It is the source of all true art and science.

—Albert Einstein

The world has a way of giving what is demanded of it.

—Anonymous

CHAPTER GUIDE

"In the days before oil became so mixed with politics, a happy oil company was an integrated company, with its functions neatly bundled according to their geographical location. But now the demands of more exciting times have the industry reworking its organizational charts. . . .

"Several oil companies have reorganized to develop deintegrated, functional structures. The Sun Oil Company in 1975 formed two separate companies, two of which own its basic oil assets. Four others were formed for exploration, production, refining and petrochemicals, and retail marketing. Its chairman stated that the company hopes 'to improve the effectiveness of the way we cope with the changing world around us.'"

—Business Week, August 18, 1975, p. 24.

Questions to keep in mind while you read this chapter:

1. What is meant by "more exciting times"?
2. What is meant by "integrated company"?
3. What are the functional structures that can be substituted for integrated ones?
4. Why do you think the Sun Oil Company is reorganizing in this way?
5. Are there other industries where you would expect to find a similar trend?

The organization constitutes the manager's immediate task and social environment. Conditions inside the organization, as well as its structure, influence the managers' work; but managers may also influence internal conditions and change the structure. Therefore there is a two-way interaction between managerial actions and the nature and behavior of the organization.

Every organization is a complex sociotechnical system. But it is also part of a larger system. The organization exists in a political, economic, social, and technological ennvironment that greatly affects its success. To explain the relations between organizations and their environments, this chapter will discuss (1) the nature of organizations, (2) the systems view of organizations, and (3) management ecology—the study of the impact of environment on the organization.

THE NATURE OF ORGANIZATIONS

Organization is a basic concept that underlies all cooperative activity. Society's needs are complex and numerous, and organizations reflect this complexity and diversity. An organization is a collectivity devoted to getting work done efficiently and at feasible costs. Organizations provide a concentration of human and other resources focused upon common endeavors; the work that results could not otherwise be done. In some cases, the organization is unobtrusive, fulfilling its purposes with little visibility. In others the organization is more apparent, demanding substantial time and energy. But in every organization managers must adapt the organization to problems of growth, change, development, and effectiveness.

Organization Defined

Prefaced by the article *an*, the word *organization* refers to a particular entity, such as a company. We call the Dow Chemical Company, for example, an organization. However, *the idea of organization itself* is an important analytical concept, and greater precision is necessary in the use of the word *organization* in management thought.

Organization is best defined as *the structure or network of relationships among indiviudals and positions in a work setting, and the processes by which the structure is created, maintained, and used.*

This definition has two interrelated aspects: structure and process. *Structure* consists of a network of specified relationships among individuals, positions, and tasks. This is a static view. *Process*—a dynamic view—denotes a managerial function by which organizations are created and continuously adapted to changing needs. Both aspects are

Source: © 1966 United Feature Syndicate, Inc. Used by permission.

important. Structure helps us observe and classify the main features of organizational anatomy and and to compare one organization with another. The process of organization focuses on the managerial actions that create and change the structure.

The definition just presented describes formal organization, that is, the intended structures that managers create. Structure and process apply also to informal organization, which arises out of the needs, feelings, and interactions of people. This chapter analyzes formal organization. Informal organization will be discussed in Part Four.

Organization Structure

Structure is a key concept in all sciences. The biologist wants to know the structure of cells; the astronomer wants to learn the structure of the universe; the physicist, the structure of the atom. The economist studies the structure of a labor market or of money flows. The reader of a book needs to discover its structure for better understanding. In management, we need to understand how organization structures work, and how they are created.

Formal structure is, in general, the result of deliberate decisions. Managers organize by devising the structural arrangements that they believe to be best for themselves, their work, or their objectives. Structures tend to be relatively permanent, with continuous, gradual change, with major changes occurring at strategic times. Although determining the basic structure is a responsibility of top management, all managers may influence the structure within their sphere of authority. Structure, once established, becomes a framework that can either constrain or facilitate the manager's actions.

The *Peanuts* cartoon illustrates the intrinsic nature of formal organizational structure. A detailed analysis of structural characteristics has been presented in Chapters 3 and 4.

Organization Process

The structural relationships in an organization can only be approximated on charts. Such a view is static because the chart depicts the intended formal relationships at a given time. Organizations must also be viewed dynamically, however: the structure changes over time as managers do their work. Changes may be gradual and slow, or extensive and rapid. In either case we need to see organizations as dynamic systems adapting to change.

The process view looks at organizations as always becoming something else, constantly being created or re-created. Improving the structure, a fundamental task of managers, is always possible. Organization decisions are among the most important that managers make. Therefore it is imperative for managers to develop skills of organizational analysis and change. Managers at lower levels, however, have less opportunity for change than do those at the top. Often they must await opportunities for change that occur as a result of major reorganization or expansion. The production supervisor, for example, finds organizational structure tied closely to operating processes and technology that usually change gradually. On the other hand, stability can be an advantage, and considerable change may go on higher up without great effect on operating levels.

The Functions of Organization

The quality of an organization's achievements depends on designing an appropriate structural system of tasks, technology, and people, and on the skills with which managers create, change, or utilize that structure.

Let us consider five important functions that organization structures may provide: (1) an efficient work system, (2) a system of communications, (3) satisfactions to organization members, (4) organizational and individual identities, and (5) innovation and change.

Efficiency

A major function of any structure is to facilitate appropriate decisions and actions. Resources tend to be scarce, challenging the organization to maximize its output of goods or services with given inputs of resources. Chaos or disorganization work against efficiency, so there is pressure to develop and control the work system through the systematic, orderly, rational, and coordinated efforts we call organization.

Concern for efficiency in organization was a central element of Weber's theory of bureaucracy. The hierarchy of levels, the division of work into logical groupings, and an overlay of rules and procedures are, in Weber's view, the ideal type of organization if efficiency is the primary goal. Later, in the early 1900s, practitioners of scientific management developed management theory around the bureaucratic model. Bureaucracy facilitates not only the practice of efficient management, but also the growth of today's large-scale organizations.[1]

Despite its values and achievements, the bureaucratic concept no longer dominates management theory. Its chief limitations lie in its inability to meet important needs and demands other than efficiency, such as job satisfaction or innovation. These problems have led to new demands on managers for improved leadership and interpersonal skills.

Communication

The designer of an organization is also establishing the pathways and requirements for formal communications. In hierarchial organizations, downward communications predominate. They take the form of commands, delegations of authority, instructions, and information needed by echelons below. Upward information consists largely of reports, responses to communications from above, queries, and the referral of problems that need attention at higher levels. Lateral communication is allowed but not emphasized.

Hierarchical organizations, with their formal positions and prescriptive management styles, are not well designed for purposes of effective communication. Instead, they rigidly prescribe the nature, form, content, timing, and direction of communications. Where effective communications are recognized as an important aspect of the organization's design, progress in both structural improvement and relationships among people have occurred.

Organizations and Job Satisfaction

Because *organization* specifies the desired relations among tasks, responsibilities, and people, organization members evaluate these relationships as well as their own jobs and their relationship to the organization. Individuals like interesting jobs and meaningful work, and most organizations try to meet these expectations.

Organization structure provides members with a "place" to be and to work, and a status that reflects their relative standing. Most people spend a large part of their lives at work associated with organizations; they expect their jobs and their work to provide a reasonable degree of satisfaction, and the framework for this expectation is in the structure of the organization itself.

An organization may be viewed as a transactional system whose

---

[1]Max Weber, *The Theory of Social and Economic Organization* (New York: Oxford, 1947). Details of the bureaucratic model are presented in Chapter 13. For a current view, see Selwyn Becker and Duncan Neuhauser, *The Efficient Organization* (New York: American Elsevier, 1975).

members both give to the organization and receive from it. Members of organizations are aware of what they give and what they get. Thus the organization is a means of achieving both individual and organizational goals. Satisfaction derives from the extent to which these goals are achieved.

Organizational Identity

Organizational identity is affected by organizational characteristics, since positions and their titles provide visible manifestations of the organization's presence. Other factors, such as physical facilities, also help to establish and maintain its identity.

Organizations deliberately shape their identities so that insiders and outsiders may recognize them. Most attributes of organization images are not left to chance, but are carefully planned and maintained through symbols and devices such as organizational names, logos, product brand names, location and appearance of physical facilities, product styling, advertising, and public-relations techniques.

By establishing an identity, the organization becomes known to customers or clients, investors or donors, and employees or members. Organizations thus develop a continuity of existence independent of particular members. If the organization's identity needs are well managed, its external features remain relatively stable even though internal change may be extensive.[2]

Innovation and Change

Organizations need continuity, which can be achieved only through some degree of adaptiability and self-renewal. Hierarchies have orderly procedures for maintenance and development of their structure and organizational processes. Nonhierarchical organizations also face this need, but they accomplish it by different means. They are more open to change, to opportunities in the environment, and to free and abundant communication. Thus they are designed specifically to find, accept, and use new ideas.

Multiple Expectations

Clearly an organization and its structure serve many functions simultaneously; but these functions are often in conflict. The organization cannot serve all the functions equally over unlimited time. Designing an organization to maximize efficiency is not the same as designing one

[2]Thomas Rotondi, Jr., "Organizational Identification: Issues and Implications," *Organizational Behavior and Human Performance* 13 (February 1975), 95–109.

for job satisfaction, and if both characteristics are wanted to some degree in the same organization, organization design becomes a matter of reaching appropriate compromises. Moreover, an organization's needs at one time are not the same as those at another, hence change is inevitable. To make the necessary compromises requires continuous assessment of priorities.

There is no universal, ideal organizational pattern. There is no optimum organization design, merely better or worse ones for given purposes. Moreover, the criteria for evaluating organization structures are uncertain and eclectic. Structural and other deficiencies are found in all organizations, although logical or historical reasons may be advanced to explain them.

Some assert that poorly designed organizations are nevertheless highly successful; this is sometimes true, because of inertia or of willingness to accept a few minor or even major defects rather than risking change. An existing relationship or structural form is a known quantity; changes can be unsettling. However, it does not follow, as some infer, that structures with defects are desirable or that the defects cause the organization's success.

The whole question of ends and means is a complex one in organization theory. One may, for example, view an organizational structure as a means to a given end—a tool by which selected ends are attained. The value of any tool is partly in its own quality and partly in the skill of its user. This view of structure, however, is an oversimplification that has limited value, because managers of bureaucratic bent may behave as though the organization were an end in itself rather than a means. In addition, the concept of organization as a means toward "given ends" belies the organization's ability to change, reject, or create ends as it goes along. Finally, managers may not sufficiently appreciate the intricate interdependencies inherent in organizational variables.[3]

THE ORGANIZATION AS A SYSTEM

Any organization may be viewed from a systems point of view. The concept of systems is widely applied as a way of understanding a variety of processes that occur *within* organizations, such as information processing, problem solving, or decision making. The computer has made it both possible and desirable to treat these internal processes as systems or subsystems. It is also useful to view whole organizations as systems in an environment, as we are doing in this chapter and throughout this book.

[3]M. C. Knowles, "Interdependence Among Organizational Variables," *Human Relations* **28** (July 1975), 431–449.

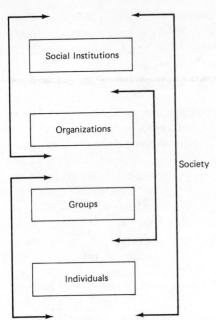

FIGURE 12-1. Interlocking Components of the Social System.

An advantage of the systems concept is that it enables us to analyze behavior at several levels of increasing complexity. One may define a system at whatever level is best for a given purpose. For example, we may consider the individual as a biological system, or we may define a team, task force, or other group as the system we choose to examine. We may also study the relationships of groups to a total organization, and of organizations to each other. The various clusters of organizations in a network make up a social institution, such as *business*, and the relationships of social institutions are the components of society as a system. These interlocking levels of analysis are illustrated in Figure 12-1.

An organization is best viewed as a sociotechnical system.[4] The anslysis of such systems is a central focus of behavioral sciences research. For example, Likert concludes on the basis of his own research findings that traditional atomistic research design is not appropriate for experiments involving organizational theory, and that management systems must utilize a systems approach.[5]

Carzo and Yanouzas utilize a behavioral system in developing their theory of organization. They describe the technical system, the social system, and the power system as interrelated subsystems constituting

[4]Kenyon B. DeGreene, *Sociotechnical Systems* (Englewood Cliffs, N.J.: Prentice-Hall, 1973).

[5]Rensis Likert, *The Human Organization: Its Management and Value* (New York: McGraw-Hill, 1967), p. 123.

the mutually dependent parts of the larger system. These subsystems interact; through that interaction they create new patterns of behavior that are separate from but related to the patterns specified by the original systems. Thus systems behavior is "emergent."[6]

Seiler elaborates an analysis of organizations based on behavioral systems. He describes a system composed of four elements: human inputs, technological inputs, organizational inputs, and social structure and norms. From these inputs he derives the concept of the sociotechnical system, which can be applied to the analysis of specific organizations.[7]

Ackoff and Emery, for example, have presented a philosophical design for the study of human behavior as systems of purposeful events, as have Churchman and others.[8] At the core of systems analysis is the burgeoning development and use of computers.

Elements of Systems

The numerous characteristics of systems include boundaries, interacting and mutually interdependent parts, equilibrium, feedback, and the environment.

Boundaries

The boundaries of a system may be associated with physical facilities, but they are frequently intangible, as in the case of a system of roles assigned to a small work group. The boundary distinguishes the inside of the system from its outside, and is arbitrarily determined by defining the system.

Boundaries encompass the subsystems of which the primary system is a part. If, for example, an organization is taken as a system, the divisions and departments within are subsystems. At the same time one then distinguishes phenomena, such as other organizations, that lie outside and are part of the environment.

The notion that the environment is everything that lies outside the organization is too simple: precisely where an organization ends and its environment begins is not easy to determine. Moreover, as already noted, it is the perceived environment that is important. Parts of the environment act upon the internal elements of the organization, including the managers. Not everything outside the organization is relevant to explaining what goes on within.

[6]Rocco Carzo and John N. Yanouzas, *Formal Organizations: A Systems Approach* (Homewood, Ill.: Irwin and the Dorsey Press, 1967), pp. 237–247.

[7]John A. Seiler, *Systems Analysis in Organizational Behavior* (Homewood, Ill.: Irwin and the Dorsey Press, 1967), pp. 1–72.

[8]Russell L. Ackoff and Fred E. Emery, *On Purposeful Systems* (Chicago: Aldine-Atherton, 1972); C. West Churchman, *The Systems Approach* (New York: Dell, 1968).

At many points an organization becomes intertwined with elements that are technically outside it—clients, customers, or suppliers, for example. Thus organizations are not only part of the external environment for other organizations, but they also interpenetrate the internal environment. For example, a unit of the state police, the county sheriff, and municipal policemen may in a given case be jointly involved. Or the personnel of a vending machine service unit may visit a plant's premises to service the coffee machines.

Managers whose responsibilities include dealing with outside organizations or monitoring environmental influences are called boundary spanners. Any manager can be a boundary spanner, but some positions formally carry boundary spanning responsibilities. For example, a public relations manager deals with the various communications media; personnel managers have contacts with the labor market; corporation presidents deal with the heads of other organizations; and lobbyists deal with legislators.

Successful boundary spanning has much to do with the organization's ability to cope with relevant elements of the environment. Organizations must collaborate, cooperate, compete, and transact exchanges with other organizations. Factors of power, coordination, control, and conflict are inherent in boundary spanning.[9]

Subsystems

The idea of system also implies the interrelationship of its component parts, or subsystems. The concept of mutual interdependence holds that a change in one part of a system leads to changes in other parts. For example, in a company's marketing department, starting a cost-cutting program in sales training might affect the selection of salesmen, the division of territories, or the morale of salesmen. The systems concept emphasizes the totality of the set of interrelated parts, conditions, or activities that are known as subsystems.

One of the most important subsystems is that of the flow of work. Work flows are based on particular technologies, consisting of the processing of raw materials, human inputs, and associated paperwork. The design of the product or service, the tools and equipment, and the

[9]Neil H. Jacoby (ed.), *The Business-Government Relationship: A Reassessment* (Pacific Palisades, Calif.: Goodyear, 1976); Sergio F. Mindlin and Howard Aldrich, "Interorganizational Dependence: A Review of the Concept and a Reexamination of the Findings of the Aston Group," *Administrative Science Quarterly* 20 (September 1975), 382–392; Harold Guetzkow, "Relations Among Organizations," in Raymond V. Bowers (ed.), *Studies of Behavior in Organizations* (Athens: University of Georgia Press, 1966); John R. Schermerhorn, Jr., "Openness to Interorganizational Cooperation: A Study of Hospital Administration," *Academy of Management Journal* 19 (June 1976), 225–236; Richard P. Leifer and George P. Huber, "Relations Among Perceived Environmental Uncertainty, Organization Structure and Boundary-Spanning Behavior," *Administrative Science Quarterly* 22 (June 1977), 235–247.

necessary engineering and management controls are part of the technological subsystem.

Equilibrium

A dynamic system has a tendency to achieve a balance among the various forces operating within and upon it. This balance is called *equilibrium*, or a steady state. Chapple and Coon define equilibrium as a "state in which, if a small force is impressed on a system, the force will produce modifications . . . within the system, and when the force is removed, the system will tend to return to its previous state."[10] Equilibrium takes several forms. A stationary equilibrium exists when there is a fixed point or balance to which the system returns after a disturbance. Dynamic equilibrium exists when the equilibrium shifts to a new position of balance after a disturbance. A stable situation exists where the forces that produced the initial equilibrium are so powerful that any new force has to be very strong before any movement to a new position can occur. An unstable situation is tense and precarious, so that a small disturbance produces large and rapid movements to a new position.[11]

Feedback

Feedback is a central concept in the theory of control as well as the theory of systems. It has also been utilized in communication theory and in the study of organizational behavior. It is a diagnostic concept for the manager, for the breakdown or absence of feedback may be evidence of difficulty in the operation of a system. Feedback is a process by which systems gather and evaluate information about how they are doing, and use it to guide, direct, and control the performance of the system. It is like a self-regulating device, like the ordinary home-heating thermostat that regulates room temperature. A diagram of a feedback mechanism was presented in Chapter 1 as the basic management model, and in Chapter 9 as a mechanism of control.

Feedback may be positive or negative. Positive feedback reports the proper functioning of a system; negative feedback reports errors or malfunctioning that call for corrections in the input or processing part of the cycle. For example, praise from a supervisor operates as positive feedback. Complaints from a customer provide negative feedback. Clearly there are many feedback systems at work simultaneously in every organization.

[10]Eliot D. Chapple and Carleton S. Coon, *Principles of Anthropology* (New York: Holt, 1942), p. 14.

[11]Robert Chin, "The Utility of System Models and Development Models for Practitioners," in Warren Bennis et al., eds., *The Planning of Change* (New York: Holt, 1962), 201–208.

Feedback has become a major tool of the behavioral sciences, and it is the foundation of the science of cybernetics, which emerged in 1947 as the science of communication and control in the animal and the machine. It studies the flow of information within a system and the way the system uses information to control itself. Management scientists as well as physical, biological, and social scientists have found cybernetics extremely helpful. Cybernetics deals extensively with the phenomena of information feedback systems by which living organisms exist. It studies systems in which complexity and uncertainty are high, and for which new ways of measurement must be found. Cybernetics supplies a stream of models for the management scientist, and points the way toward quantification of decisions related to organization design and other problems.[12]

The environment in which an organization exists is also an important component of the system. The balance of this chapter will be devoted to an analysis of management ecology, the impact of environment on organization and the managers within them.

_____ **MANAGEMENT ECOLOGY**

The concept of ecology is borrowed from the field of biology, in which it refers to the study of the organism in relation to its environment. The analogy between biological and management ecology is, however, imperfect; in contrast to biological organisms, human organizations show a greater propensity to change and modify their environments rather than adapting to them or being subject to them. Individuals are in a state of interaction with each other and with the organization as a whole. The organization itself is also in a state of interaction with its environment. The ecology approach fits best those theories of organization that take the organization to be, by analogy, a living, dynamic "organism." Therefore those who reject an organic view of organizations tend also to reject the ecological analogy.

Despite its limitations, however, the concept of environment has a vital place in the systems view of organizations. Eells explicitly identifies "corporate ecology" as a discipline that deals with the relations between the corporation and its environment. Ecology contributes to a philosophy of the enterprise, and is essential for studying it as a dynamic rather than a static system. He points to the obvious economic environment of the enterprise, but suggests also that the political and

[12]For an analysis and description of cybernetics in detail, see Norbert Wiener, _Cybernetics_ (New York: Wiley, 1948), and _The Human Use of Human Beings_ (Garden City, N.Y.: Doubleday, 1954).

social environment confronts the firm with important and often over-looked dangers and opportunities.[13]

A study of the environment is not only theoretically interesting; it has practical implications as well. Among the practical influences of the environment is the fact that it provides challenges and problems—indeed, Toynbee held that civilizations require challenges to survive. But the environment also contains hostilities and dangers that may overcome individuals, organizations, or even civilizations unable to cope with their environments.[14]

Managerial responses depend on the ability to perceive the relevant forces in the environment and to apply the resources of the enterprise to them in a constructive accommodation. Jeuck sees the qualities of imagination, foresight, or vision as centrally important for achieving the necessary creativity and innovation. But it is diffiuclt for managers to really see the environment of which they are a part. Jeuck suggests that Marshall McLuhan's concept of the "extra-territorial man" applies. Whereas many are relatively unaware of their environment, extra-territorial persons sense appropriate configurations and meanings in the environment. Because they are not slaves to their cultural milieu, they can achieve fresh insights and create patterns of action. Their range of behavior is not limited by the irrevelant rules or pointless information that almost always clogs daily experience;[15] an example we considered earlier is the consultant who comes into a company from the outside and hence can take a fresh view of both the internal and the external environments.

Perception of relevant environmental forces is thus an important element of managerial action. Indeed, many managerial actions take the form of influencing, or even creating, aspects of the environment. We have learned to accept artificial physical environments such as air conditioning; in the realm of social and cultural environments, how-ever, we are less knowledgeable but are achieving greater understand-ing through research.

The Impact of the Environment

An organization exists by successfully meeting demands originating in the larger systems of which it is a part. Interactions occur between the organization and the various components of its environment. Thus an

[13]Richard Eells, *The Meaning of Modern Business* (New York: Columbia U. P., 1960), pp. 99–103.

[14]Arnold J. Toynbee, *A Study of History,* abridged by D. C. Somervell (New York: Oxford U. P. 1947).

[15]John E. Jeuck, *School of Business Newsletter,* University of Chicago (Spring 1968), pp. 24–26.

organization is an input-output system where inputs from the environment are processed by the internal system, and returned as products or services to the external environment. The organization as a system is a locus for countless exchanges of people, values, ideas, resources, energy, products, and services.[16]

We shall now examine some pertinent organizational theories that utilize ecological concepts. Such theories envision the organization and its environment as an interacting system of exchanges. We will discuss three types of such exchanges: (1) the flow of people into and out of the organization and the environment; (2) exchanges of information, ideas, and values; and (3) the task environment.

Exchange of People

Among the most conspicuous processes that connect organizations and their environments is that of the interchange of personnel. The mobility of people is both an input and an output of organizations. Organizations thus search for able, creative persons, and compete for the best available. The shortage of such people causes organizations to alter their internal environments to be attractive to outsiders. Because individuals often leave one organization to join another, they may be attracted to the better ones, creating the phenomenon of the leading firm, the outstanding employer. This competitiveness in the environment is a challenge to organizations, which find that recruitment of able people and the rate of innovation tend to be mutually reinforcing. The innovative organization recruits individuals of creative potential, who in turn convert that potential into productive innovation—an attractive internal environment that becomes visible to outsiders and attracts them to the firm.[17]

Information Flows

Wilensky has analyzed the use of knowledge and policy in government and industry. He notes that the external environment may have sub-

[16]D. S. Mileti and D. F. Gillespie, "An Integrated Formalization of Organization-Environment Interdependencies," *Human Organization* 29 (January 1976), 85–100; Richard N. Osborne and James G. Hunt, "Environment and Organizational Effectiveness," *Administrative Science Quarterly* 19 (June 1974), 231–246; M. Douglass, "Organization Environment Interaction and Firm Performance," *Management International Review* 16 (January 1976), 79–88; Stuart M. Schmidt and Thomas A. Kochan, "Interorganizational Relationships: Patterns and Motivations," *Administrative Science Quarterly* 22 (June 1977), 220–234.

[17]Robert K. Merton, "The Environment of the Innovating Organization: Some Conjectures and Proposals," in Gary A. Steiner (ed.), *The Creative Organization* (Chicago: U. of Chicago Press, 1965), pp. 50–65. See also G. Baty, William Evan, and T. Rothermel, "Personnel Flows as Interorganizational Relationships," *Administrative Science Quarterly* 16 (1971), 440–443.

stantial influence on the evolution of the use of "facts and figures men," and hypothesizes that the more an organization sees its external environment and internal operations as rationalized—that is, as subject to predictable uniformities in relationships among significant objects— the more resources it will devote to its intelligence function and the more of those resources will be spent on experts.[18]

Dill has argued cogently that by conceptualizing the environment as a flow of information to participants in an organization (and as a body of accessible information), it is possible to make systematic and meaningful comparisons of the environments of different organizations. Dill has developed the concept of task environment, which has proved useful to other theorists.[19] Let us explore this concept more fully.

The Task Environment

Dill views the manager as a planner seeking to base his actions on information received about environmental events. He designates that part of the total environment that is potentially relevant to goal setting and goal attainment as the task environment. This raises an important problem: that of determining what elements in an organization's environment are relevant to behavior within it. The task environment consists of inputs of information from external sources. The inputs themselves are not the tasks. The task is defined as a goal and a set of behavior patterns appropriate for attaining that goal. The task environment consists of the stimuli to which an organizaion is exposed; the task is the organization's interpretation of what the environmental inputs mean for behavior.[20]

Thorelli has advanced an ecological model of organization in which he recognizes both the internal and the external environments. His model consists of a matrix in which the environment is divided vertically (from factory shop to the administrative environment of the chief executive's office), and horizontally by functions (that is, production, marketing, personnel, and so on). He uses the term "ecosystem" to denote the system comprising the organization and its relevant environment. Thorelli's definition of task environment is not inconsistent with Dill's but is more operational: environment is that part of the total setting with which the organization is interacting and in which it is competing. Thus even beyond the task environment are environmental factors that may affect the organization and be affected by it. Therefore

[18]Harold L. Wilensky, *Organizational Intelligence* (New York: Basic, 1967), p. 14. Wilensky defines "facts and figures men" as organizational experts involved in processing intelligence data. The hypothesis could probably be broadened to include all staff service units, such as personnel, public relations, or research departments.

[19]William R. Dill, "Environment as an Influence on Managerial Autonomy," *Administrative Science Quarterly* 2 (March 1958), 409–443.

[20]Ibid., pp. 410–411.

Thorelli regards the environment as a continuum in which relevance is a matter of degree.[21]

Interpreting Relevant Environmental Factors

Most environmental inputs do not directly indicate appropriate organizational actions. The manager has to attach meanings to the information and bring it into the organization. Therefore a major organizational function is to evaluate, interpret, and combine inputs to devise appropriate tasks for organization members to perform. Tasks thus are the organization's own statements of the goals that it wants to achieve and of the means by which it expects to achieve them. Task statements are then communicated with the authentication and sanction of the insiders who endorse and disseminate them, and who persuade or influence others to act.

Dill notes two main directions of study in the developing theory of environmental influences: (1) isolating environmental variables and using them as behavioral dimensions, as has been done with traits like personality and intelligence, and (2) conceptualizing individuals or organizations as information processing systems, simulating, with the aid of computers, the environment to which they are exposed.[22]

Thorelli's model identifies four sets of variables within any given transacting ecosystem. One set is composed of structural variables within the organization. Another consists of the environmental variables, such as market demands, economic conditions, or government regulations. Between the organizational and the environmental variables are variables that provide a strategy of interaction connecting them, such as a product price. The fourth set of variables consists of results, such as survival or growth. With such classes of variables tentatively posed, one can develop testable hypotheses. Thus Thorelli's model permits the study of a wide range of variables in the external environment.[23]

Dill reasons that with greater environmental complexity, it is harder to know what is relevant. The best strategy for analyzing the environment is not to regard it as a collection of systems and organizations external to what is being studied, but to focus on the environment as it affects the organization. One then treats the environment as information about goals, plans, or strategies that managers make accessible to

[21]Hans B. Thorelli, "Organizational Theory: An Ecological View," *Academy of Management Proceedings*, 27th Annual Meeting, 1976 (Bowling Green, Ohio: 1968), pp. 68–84.
[22]William R. Dill, "The Impact of Environment on Organizational Development," in Sidney Mailick and Edward H. Van Ness (eds.), *Concepts and Issues in Administrative Behavior* (Englewood Cliffs, N.J.: Prentice-Hall, 1962), p. 107.
[23]Thorelli, "Organizational Theory."

the organization. Not all the information that an organization receives or has access to is relevant to its goals and programs. Therefore the manager should seek inputs that bear on goal setting and goal attainment. These elements form, as indicated earlier, the task environment, which has constantly changing dimensions as people within the organization do things that affect intended goals. The dimensions also change as sources of action outside the organization persuade managers to change its goals.[24]

Thompson has utilized the work of Dill, Simon, and others in building a theory of organization that accepts and uses the idea of task environment but also does not reject the notion that potential influences in the rest of the environment may have effects on organizational behavior. Thus he recognizes that no two task environments are identical. For a given organization, the task environment is determined by the requirements of technology, the boundaries of the organization, and the composition of the larger environment. In building a total theory of organization, Thompson relates a number of key types of variables in addition to environmental ones, such as technology, organization structure, human relationships, power relationships, stress variables, and the concepts of organizational rationality.[25]

Terreberry argues that evolutionary processes occur in the environments of organizations. She notes the increasing interdependence of organizations, which indicates the need for a perspective by which any organization, its transactions, and the environment itself can be viewed in a common conceptual framework. She believes that the research to date on environment makes it possible to hypothesize that organizational adaptability is a function of ability to learn and to perform according to changes in the environment.[26]

That the external environment has a great deal to do with the shaping of the internal organizational behavior—goals, structures, and performance—has been confirmed by Lawrence and Lorsch. In a comparative study of six organizations in the same industrial environment, they found that a relationship existed between the extent to which internal states of differentiation and integration in each organization met the demands of the environment and the relative economic performance of the organizations. Thus many characteristics of organizations can be explained as efforts to deal with different kinds and rates of environmental change, and to attain effectiveness in dealing with environmental demands.[27]

[24]Dill, "Impact of Environment."

[25]James D. Thompson, *Organizations in Action* (New York: McGraw-Hill, 1967).

[26]Shirley Terreberry, "The Evolution of Organizational Environments," *Administrative Science Quarterly* 12 (March 1968), 590–613.

[27]Paul R. Lawrence and Jay W. Lorsch, *Organization and Environment: Managing Differentiation and Integration* (Boston: Division of Research, Graduate School of Business, Harvard University, 1967).

Coping with the Environment

The environment of an organization contains both supportaive and antagonistic forces. An organizational system derives support from clients or customers who need its products and services, and from society's protection of property and other rights. But the organization is also subject to the constraints of public regulation, to demands for social responsibility, and to the need to meet a multiplicity of demands that are often conflicting.

It is part of every manager's responsibility to be alert to forces in the external evironment that affect the organization and its goals. Organizations develop adaptive mechanisms and structural devices for coping with these factors, relating them to the internal processes of management. Figure 12-2 shows the way in which environmental factors penetrate the organization and influence decision making within it.

In Chapter 1 it was pointed out that organizations vary in accordance with the degree of openness of the system, and that structural characteristics vary on a continuum ranging from closed to open. This is a matter of managing at the boundaries of an organization to determine the ease with which people and information may interchange from among sets of interrelated organizations. Therefore boundary roles must be explicit, and appropriate boundary-spanning individuals must be recognized.

Boundary spanners have considerable power and undergo substantial stress because they deal with much uncertainty. The creation of multiple boundary-spanning roles distributed over a number of individuals helps to distribute stress among them, and diffuses role conflict. Relationships between boundary roles and internal roles require proce-

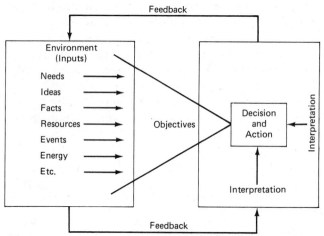

FIGURE 12-2. Relationship of Environment to Decision Making.

dures for maintaining agreement and understanding. Openness to negotiations, adjustment, and coordination is imperative.

The principal way of coping with environmental influences is to design the organization structure with the problem of boundary spanning in mind. One of the fundamental effects of the environment is to produce change; coping mechanisms, therefore, become important.

Qualities of the Environment

Emery and Trist speak of the causal texture of the environment: the increasing interdependencies that cause it to behave as a system. An organization's ability to cope effectively depends on the causal texture of its relevant environment. Emery and Trist describe four types of causal texture, ranged along a scale that goes from placidity to turbulence:[28]

1. *The placid-randomized environment.* Opportunities and dangers are randomly distributed and relatively unchanging. Trial-and-error knowledge is adequate for the situations met. The environment of a "mom-and-pop" corner grocery is an example.
2. *The placid-clustered environment.* Opportunities and threats are clustered, and the environment is more complex, consisting of clusters of influences rather than random ones. For example, if the grocer tries to adapt to competition by supermarkets, there will be clusters of factors in the use of advertising, and the need for new store layouts.
3. *The disturbed-reactive environment.* The presence of organizations is introduced into the elements of the placid-clustered environment. Organizations become competitive, and in need of strategies and tactics to meet objectives.
4. *The turbulent environment.* Turbulence is the chief characteristic of the present-day environment for organizations in a complex society. Turbulent environments cause changes that affect organizations but are independent of any one organization. For example, a corporation today faces complex product safety regulations that were not heretofore present in its environment. Negotiation or compromise may help, but the company cannot eliminate the causes of pressure.

Goodman has shown how the Emery and Trist categories have practical significance for managerial planning. He suggests combining the four types of environment with the concepts of the present and the future. When the environmental textures are similar for the present and

[28]F. E. Emery and E. L. Trist, "The Causal Texture of the Environment," *Human Relations* **18** (February 1965), 21–31.

the future, planning needs to encompass only relatively minor adjustments. However, if there is a mismatch between the present and the expected environmental textures, planning must take account of substantial environmental change; otherwise it would be tied to mistaken short-run strategies. A rich knowledge of the immediate environment shortens the planning horizon, leading to long-term ineffectiveness where there is a mismatch between present and future environments.[29]

Three Examples

The following examples are helpful in illustrating how elements of the environment affect internal decisions:

1. The Federal Trade Commission was created in 1914 for antitrust regulation, and broadened in 1938 to permit attacking "unfair or deceptive acts or practices in commerce." In 1976 it had a staff of 570 attorneys, was conducting 749 investigations, and had an additional 88 cases pending trial or other disposition. In the 1970s the Commission became increasingly activist, with broad powers permitting probes throughout almost every industry. Under complex procedures for investigation and rule making, the FTC has enormous power. It launches massive investigations demanding time, energy, and information from business firms. It administers controls affecting innumerable production, marketing, and financial decisions.[30]

2. The nation's retailers are becoming aware that today's operating environment is vastly different from that of the 1960s. Population growth is slowing, a growing singles market is emerging, and family formations are coming at later ages. More women are entering the labor market. Of the 11 million households in the U.S. today, the dominant consumer segment is headed by persons over 45. By the 1980s this dominant group will be headed by 25- to 40-year-old persons. Therefore merchants must aim to attract these newer and more youthful customers.[31]

3. Simon E. Knudsen, chairman of the board of the White Motor Corporation, "has learned that one's banker can quickly become one's enemy." Several of White's outside directors, under pressure from the banking syndicates to whom the firm owed millions, twice attempted to oust Knudsen from his position. Both attempts were unsuccessful, but the bankers had a dominant influence on

[29]Richard A. Goodman, "Environmental Knowledge and Organizational Time Horizon: Some Functions and Dysfunctions," *Human Relations* 26 (1973), 215–226.
[30]"The Escalating Struggle Between the FTC and Business," *Business Week*, December 13, 1976, pp. 52–59.
[31]Ibid.

many merger, divestiture, and other decisions necessitated by the firm's financial difficulties.[32]

The above examples reflect the diversity and scope of possible signals from the environment and show how the decision maker needs to take such signals into account.

SUMMARY

This chapter has taken a broad overview of purposive organizations, with emphasis on the significance of the external and internal environments. Problems of survival, failure, and adaptation exist, as reflected in the continuous entry and exit of organizations into the world of action and enterprise. The quality of managerial thought and action greatly affects problems of survival and effectiveness.

The concept of management ecology, borrowed from the field of biology, was presented. Both the manager and the firm have environments and must be studied in relation to them. Environments, we saw, affect firms and managers in many ways. Evidence suggests the strong influence of environment in behavior, but the evidence is less conclusive that environment directly affects the level of performance of the organization or the people in it. However, some evidence for the latter proposition appears to indicate a possibility in that direction.

The external environment contains influences that shape the behavior of those inside the organization, mainly through information coming into the organization from outside and helping it to shape its goals. According to his perception of these signals and his interpretation of their meaning, the manager's task environments emerge. Wilenski and Dill, among others, have supplied valuable theoretical insights as to the role of environment through the mechanisms of information transfer. Dill and Thorelli, followed by Thompson and others, have presented models of organization that give an important place to the concept of environment.

Coping with turbulent environments is one of today's major challenges for the managers of organizations.

INCIDENT CASE

The Ko-Mar Chemical Corporation is a well-known producer and distributor of fertilizers, nutrients, and farm chemicals. For several years the firm was managed by its owner, who held all the stock. In 1976, the business went public, selling an issue

[32]Ibid. p. 72.

of stock on the American Stock Exchange. Shortly thereafter, the board of directors elected a new president, a chemist who had risen to the position of vice president for research and development. The board directed the new president to improve the company's ability to cope with relevant factors in the environment.

Question:

1. What should the new president do, and why?

QUESTIONS FOR STUDY

1. What is ecology? What is the source of this concept and how does it apply to our study of management?

2. Can you see how the problem of forecasting is related to problems of the environment? Explain.

3. What is meant by *task environment?* How does this relate to the internal and external environments?

4. Contrast the environmental aspects of the theories of Dill, Thorelli, and Thompson.

5. Give examples of some of the practical questions faced by managers in relation to the external and the internal environments.

6. Explain how the environment operates as a constraint against managers, as well as a resource.

7. Describe the various types of environmental conditions that an organization faces today.

SELECTED REFERENCES

ABARBANEL, JEROME. *Redefining the Environment.* Ithaca, N.Y.: New York State School of Industrial and Labor Relations, Cornell University, 1972.

ABELL, PETER. *Organizations as Bargaining and Influence Systems.* New York: Halsted Press, 1975.

AGUILAR, FRANCIS J. *Scanning the Business Environment.* New York: The Free Press, 1967.

ANSHEN, MELVIN, and GEORGE L. BACH, eds. *Management and Corporations 1985.* New York: McGraw-Hill Book Company, 1960.

BATES, F. L. *The Structure of Social Systems.* New York: Halsted Press, 1975.

CHAMBERLAIN, NEIL W. *Enterprise and Environment.* New York: McGraw-Hill Book Company, 1968.

CHURCHMAN, C. WEST. *The Systems Approach.* New York: Dell Publishing Company, 1968.

CLELAND, DAVID I., and WILLIAM R. KING. *Systems Analysis and Project Management.* New York: McGraw-Hill Book Company, 1975.

EMERY, F. E., ed. *Systems Thinking: Selected Readings.* London: Penguin Books, Ltd., 1969.

EVAN, WILLIAM M. *Organization Theory: Structure, Systems, and Environments.* New York: John Wiley & Sons, Inc., 1976.

FABUN, DON. *The Corporation as a Creative Environment.* Beverly Hills, Calif.: Glencoe Press, 1972.

GOLD, BELA; *Technological Change: Economics, Management, and Environment.* New York: Pergamon Press, 1975.

LAWRENCE, PAUL, and JAY LORSCH. *Organization and Environment: Managing Differentiation and Integration.* Boston: Division of Research, Graduate School of Business, Harvard University, 1967.

LEAVITT, HAROLD J., WILLIAM R. DILL, and HENRY B. EYRING. *The Organizational World.* New York: Harcourt Brace Jovanovich, Inc., 1973.

MATHIES, LESLIE H. *The Management System: Systems are for People.* New York: John Wiley & Sons, Inc., 1976.

MAURER, JOHN G., ed. *Readings in Organization: Open Systems Approaches .* New York: Random House, Inc., 1971.

ROEBER, RICHARD J. C. *The Organization in a Changing Environment.* Reading, Mass.: Addison-Wesley Publishing Co., 1973.

SCHODERBEK, PETER P., ASTERIOS G. KEFALOS, and CHARLES G. SCHODERBEK. *Management Systems: Conceptual Considerations.* Dallas: Business Publications, Inc., 1975.

Chapter 13

Organization Design: Bureaucratic Systems

When you climb the corporate ladder you're afraid of the man above and the one below.
—*Morris West,* Harlequin

As the day is divided into ten periods, so men are apportioned into ten classes, in such a way that the inferiors serve the superiors, while the latter serve the gods. In that manner, the king gives orders to dukes, the dukes to high officers, high officers to gentlemen, gentlemen to lictors, lictors to intendants, intendants to majordomos, majordomos to servants, servants to footmen, footmen to grooms. There are also stableboys to look after the horses, and herdsmen to care for the cattle, so that all functions are filled.
—*Tso Chuan*

An ancient commentary, composed somewhere around the third century B.C., on the Confucian classic *The Spring and Autumn Annals,* a chronology of events in the state of Lu, from 7222 to 481 B.C.

CHAPTER GUIDE

Elliott Jaques suggests in *A General Theory of Bureaucracy* (Halsted Press, 1976) that the organization and control of bureaucracies can be designed to ensure that their effects on behavior are in accord with the needs of an open, democratic society. He also suggests that bureaucratic organization is relevant and workable for the production of all materials and services (educational, diagnostic, therapeutic) where the content of the service is objectively measureable. He asserts also that it is essential to develop humanitarian bureaucratic systems.

Questions to keep in mind while reading this chapter:

1. How do you assess the validity of Jaques' comments?

2. Do service organizations need a different organizational framework from that of business firms?
3. How can bureaucracy become more humanitarian?

The decisions by which managers create, change, or maintain an organization are among the most important they make. The aim is to provide effective structural relationships. Although good structure does not guarantee good performance, poor structure can adversely affect the work even of good managers. Therefore it is important to develop organization structures that enhance rather than inhibit performance.

This chapter will describe and analyze one major type of organization design: that which is designated as bureaucratic. After we have examined key concepts and definitions, the nature of bureaucratic structures and modes of operation will be discussed.

DEFINITIONS AND CONCEPTS

Two key concepts must be explained in detail before we proceed to examine specific structural alternatives: (1) organization design, and (2) bureaucracy and its key assumptions.

The term *organization design* denotes the pattern of relationships that make up the structure of an organization. Design characteristics greatly influence the performance of other managerial functions, such as planning, setting objectives, or controlling. They also influence interpersonal relationships, job satisfaction, leadership styles, communications, and work processes. Thus design patterns are basic to understanding the behavior of organizations and the people who work in them.

The process of establishing or developing an organization design is known as the organization function of the manager. The concept of design implies that managers may choose among a number of alternative patterns. Some designs are unique, because they evolve from unique needs and conditions. Others, perhaps most, are imitative, copied from structures that managers have come to know elsewhere. The range of alternatives is virtually limitless.

Leavitt has suggested that organizations consist of four sectors: tasks, technology, structure, and people.[1] Each covers a broad category of

[1]Harold J. Leavitt, "Applied Organizational Change in Industry," in James G. March (ed.), *Handbook of Organizations* (Chicago: Rand McNally, 1965), p. 1145.

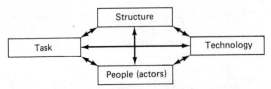

FIGURE 13-1. Key Sectors in Organization Design.

Source: Harold J. Leavitt, "Applied Organizational Change in Industry: Structural, Technological, and Humanistic Approaches," in *Handbook of Organizations*, James G. March (ed.). © 1975 by Rand McNally College Publishing Company, Chicago, p. 1145.

elements with which managers work in designing and utilizing organization structures. Leavitt's model provides a systems view in which the four sectors are interacting subsystems of a total system, as shown in Figure 13-1. Many difficulties that occur in organizations can be traced to the failure of managers to understand the interrelationships among the four components, so that a change in one sector is treated in isolation as though it had no effects on the others. For example, to change structure without considering its impact on people might result in lower morale and the resignation of good managers.

Design decisions require the prior analysis and determination of goals and plans. Then tasks, technology, and staffing capabilities may be analyzed. Finally, structural relationships are established. This structural base may be centered on relatively open or closed systems, as previously described, with tight or loose structures. We turn now to an analysis of bureaucratic structures, which tend to be highly structured and relatively closed systems. Chapter 14 will discuss modifications in bureaucratic design known as adaptive or relatively open designs.

_____ **BUREAUCRACY**

The term *bureaucracy* is commonly used to express anger and frustration over inefficiency and "red tape." This usage does not reveal its technical meaning. *Bureaucracy is best defined as a system of organization and management in which roles, tasks, and the relationships among people and positions are clearly defined, carefully prescribed, and controlled in accordance with formal authority.*

It was Max Weber, a German sociologist, who first elaborated the characteristics of bureaucracy:

1. A hierarchy of authority and levels of organization.
2. Specialization of tasks, duties, and responsibilities.
3. Positions designed as "offices."
4. Planned succession to office.
5. Impersonality of officials.

6. A system of rules and standards for discipline and control.
7. Specified qualifications for individuals holding office.
8. Protection of individuals against arbitrary dismissal.[2]

Weber's concept of bureaucracy was derived from the study of governments. He viewed it as a rational system, an "ideal type" for achieving efficiency. Although the ideal of efficiency cannot be perfectly attained, the concept provides a prototype that is useful in explaining how most organizations function. Emerging at approximately the same time, bureaucracy and scientific management energized each other. Their fundamental tenets were in harmony, and in an era of rapid industrialization they pointed the way both to efficiency and to the growth of large-scale organization.

The methods of both bureaucracy and scientific management highly rational; both permit and aim for measurement, control, and prescriptive procedures. Rationality implies control and decision making through knowledge, order, system rules, discipline, and impersonality. The use of a stop watch to set an output standard, for example, is efficient and rational because it systematizes decisions and can be applied to work methods irrespective of particular job holders.

It is clear that bureaucracy is a normal, logical development of large-scale enterprise. Nor is it surprising that, as they grow, smaller organizations imitate large ones. Some characteristics of bureaucracy are present in all organizations; bureaucracy is a legitimate form of organization that emphasizes orderly, efficient management, although it cannot attain the degree of efficiency represented by Weber's ideal type. Every organization falls somewhere between these extremes.

Managers need to understand how bureaucratic systems work, and how to work in bureaucratic systems. They must also reckon with the weaknesses and limitations of bureaucracy, which, although it is designed primarily for efficiency, institutionalizes and formalizes both the inefficient and the efficient. By overstressing rules and other formalities, an organization sometimes justifies the use of the term *bureaucracy* as an epithet. Yet when the efficient elements are formalized, the welfare of the organization is enhanced.

Another important drawback is that bureaucracy, by stressing efficiency, develops rigidities. It also makes faulty assumptions about human beings, and tends to be somewhat unresponsive to its environment. It finds coping with change difficult. It tends to ignore the informal organization, much as the scientific management movement did. Fortunately, managers can minimize the defects of bureaucracy by

[2]Summarized from Max Weber, *Essays in Sociology,* trans. and ed. by H. H. Gerth and C. Wright Mills (New York: Oxford U. P., 1958), pp. 196–204. See also Max Weber, *The Theory of Social and Economic Organization,* trans. by A. M. Henderson and Talcott Parsons (New York: Free Press, 1947).

effective leadership, by modifying bureaucratic assumptions about people, and by developing management styles open to factors in the environment. It is difficult to establish the necessary stability of purpose and procedure, without suffering the danger of excessive rigidity.

_____ STRUCTURING THE BUREAUCRATIC ORGANIZATION

A manager rarely has the opportunity to structure an entire organization from its inception. In most instances the need is to change an existing structure to meet new demands, such as retrenchment or growth. In all cases, the basic components of technology, goals, and resources are known and can be analyzed. Managers can change the organization structure rapidly or slowly, as conditions warrant, so that the pace of change is adapted to the organization's aims. Decisions regarding the structure itself and the methods of changing it take account of communication and decision patterns, work processes, growth potentials, and many other elements. A relatively stable and continuous pattern that still permits change can usually be established.[3]

We shall now describe the special characteristics and problems of bureaucratic organization structure: (1) the hierarchy, the vertical dimension, (2) departmentalization, the horizontal dimension, and (3) other basic structural patterns.

The Hierarchy

Figure 13-2 depicts the vertical and horizontal dimensions of organizational structure. Bureaucracies tend to take the pyramid form shown because at successively higher levels, there are fewer positions and managers have increasingly broad responsibilities.

The hierarchy is thus composed of vertical levels of responsibility. It consists of three key elements graded into degrees of importance from top to bottom: (1) positions consisting of tasks, duties, or responsibilities, and authority commensurate with them; (2) policies, plans, objectives, practices, and procedures at each level; and (3) roles, statuses, and authorities of position holders. Varying degrees of authority and responsibility are allocated by delegation from the top to successively lower levels. Policies, plans, and objectives, together with operating procedures and practices, are developed hierarchically around assigned responsibilities. Roles and statuses develop formally and informally as work and interpersonal relations blend together.

The existence of scalar levels characterizes all forms of organized,

[3]Lawrence R. James and Allan P. Jones, "Organization Structure: A Review of Structural Dimensions and Their Attitudes and Behavior," *Organizational Behavior and Human Performance* **12** (June 1976), 74–113.

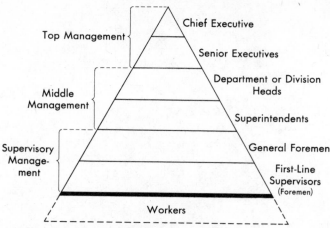

FIGURE 13-2. The Organizational Pyramid.

cooperative effort. In simple, informal groups, two levels exist as soon as a leader emerges. In more complex organizations, the number of levels becomes large and tends to increase with growth. Each successively lower level represents a decreasing scope and amount of authority, and, frequently, a variation in the kind of authority allocated to managers.

The levels depicted in Figure 13-2 are only approximations. In actual organizations the number of levels between supervisors and the chief executive may range from three in a very small enterprise to twenty or more in a giant company.

Figure 13-3 shows how the scalar levels relate to managerial functions and to the distribution of authority. The levels function as transmission stages in the flow of communications and authority. The scalar concept is important in that it throws light on decision making and on how the parts of an organization are created and held together. It is a universal phenomenon that reflects the authority relationships in organizations.

Departmentalization

The term *departmentalization* refers to the horizontal differentiations in an organization—divisions, branches, regional units, subsidiaries, and the like, as well as departments divided according to major functions such as marketing, production, or personnel management.

Departmentalization involves establishing units to which groups of related functions, activities, or tasks are assigned. As an organization expands, it enlarges its horizontal dimension by new units containing logical segmentation of the work to be done. Segmentation by level will occur simultaneously.

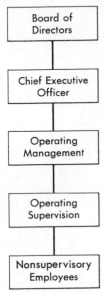

FIGURE 13-3. Scalar Levels by Which Authority Is Distributed Throughout the Line Organization.

Departmentalization subdivides the organization structure so that the several units may specialize within defined ranges of activity. Thus individuals whose abilities and interests vary can focus their work on specific, logical goals and tasks. Departmentalization also guides the managers who direct and control the work, and provides a meaningful unit around which the loyalties of organization members may be formed. The department also provides outsiders with an image of its mission and capabilities, and provides a means of structuring the development that is continuous in a healthy organization.

Departments in organization structures take four main forms: that of function, of process, of product, and of geographical area or location. Most structures are complex enough to possess more than one type of departmentalization at the same time; most large firms use them all simultaneously. Thus *departmentalization* is a generic term that includes any kind of segmentation, such as divisions, branches, sections, or other units. Terminology varies widely on the specific labels used for horizontal segmentation.

Departmentalization by Function

The way an organization segments its major functions depends upon its objectives, its work practices, and its technology. In a manufacturing firm, for example, departments of finance, production, and sales are logical units based on functions related to the company's primary purpose of making and selling its products. Functions of additional

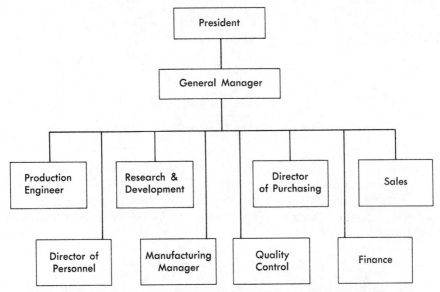

FIGURE 13-4. Functional Departmentalization in a Manufacturing Company.

support are gradually included as a company grows. Such a basis for organization is illustrated in Figure 13-4, which shows eight functional operating departments, each headed by an executive reporting to a manager of operations. Top management creates these departments by defining their most important tasks or missions.

As an organization grows in size and complexity, additional departments may be established. Some may be changed or deleted. New functions that were not previously necessary become desirable. Managers also split off activities into new departments to reduce the burdens on themselves. An increasing number of modern management techniques require specialists who work best when grouped together under specific departmental units. For example, referring to Figure 13-4, the production engineer could logically be included in the manufacturing department. However, with growth, it becomes desirable to make production engineering a separate department, in effect increasing the visibility and status of production engineering, and providing a cohesive team of several production engineers.

Departmentalization by Process

A second way of grouping duties and responsibilities is to organize them according to the processes performed. For example, a foundry might establish units for shipping and receiving, molding, maintenance, shakeout, machining, and inspecting. An organization set up for job shop production in machining small parts might departmentalize

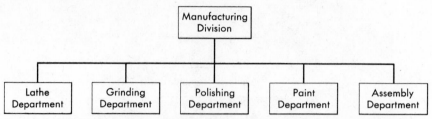

FIGURE 13-5. Departmentalization by Processes in a Job Shop Operation.

processes as follows: boring, milling, drilling, lathe operations, screw machines, painting, and heat treating. A large retail store might have departments for delivery, receiving, pricing, servicing, and so on. A chart of process departmentalization for a factory organization is shown in Figure 13-5.

Departmentalization by Product

Departmentalization by product may or may not be geographical as well, and it may be based on goods or services or both. Sometimes this type is called "commodity departmentalization." Under this form, a manager is in charge of all activities relating to a particular product. The several divisions of the General Motors Corporation are illustrative. The automotive group is subdivided into divisional units for each of its brands of automobiles. It also has a body group, an accessory group, an engine group, a household appliance group, an export group, and many others. Figure 13-6 shows the operating divisions of the American Machine & Foundry Company, which are departmentalized by product. Figure 13-7 shows how product departmentalization duplicates the structures for the functions under each unit. Many firms departmentalize their operations into military contract work and nonmilitary work. Some departmentalize according to the quality of the product or the kinds of markets in which they sell, as when retail stores operate bargain basements that carry lines of merchandise similar to the lines in other parts of the store.

Geographical or Territorial Departmentalization

In addition to departmentalization by functions or processes, departmentalization may be geographical or territorial. As companies grow, they divide their activities among branch plants, branch offices, warehouses, or other facilities away from the main center of operations. To develop an adequate sales program, or a good customer service program, organizations set up groupings by territories, districts, regions, or specific city locations. Some industries *must* departmentalize by geographical area or location because of the nature of their products or

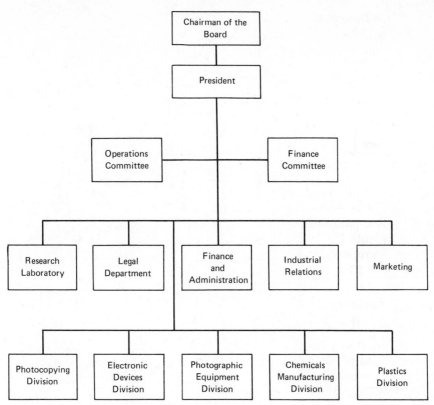

FIGURE 13-6. Product Departmentalization.

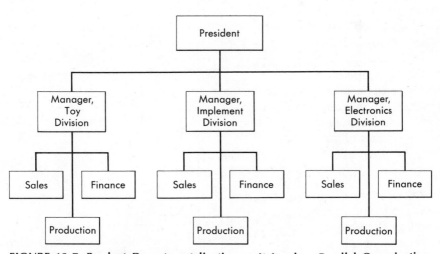

FIGURE 13-7. Product Departmentalization as It Involves Parallel Organization Structures in a Manufacturing Company.

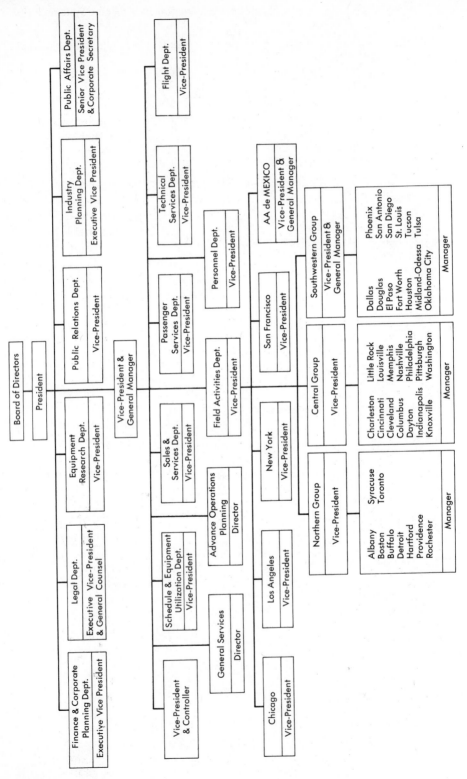

FIGURE 13-8 (opposite). Organization Chart Showing Geographical Departmentalization.

services. For example, railroads, airlines, chain stores, gas and oil distributors, and public utilities, by the nature of their operations, must establish geographical departmentalization similar to that shown in Figure 13-8.

Geographical or locational decentralization has been a noticeable trend in recent years. The decentralization of facilities often arises from the desire to avoid the congestion of large urban centers, as well as from problems of recruiting and utilizing labor. Transportation burdens have posed increasing difficulties. Furthermore, enterprises have moved outward toward receding supplies of raw materials, or closer to shifting markets. They also gravitate to improved tax situations. Geographical departmentalization involves not only social and economic factors but also managerial and economic ones. Planning, controlling, and other functions become more complex.

Positions and Jobs

Positions are the smallest structural unit of an organization. They are dispersed both horizontally and vertically. A position consists of a formally assigned place in the structure. A job consists of tasks, duties, and responsibilities that are logically related or sufficiently homogeneous to be assigned to a position holder. Thus for a given job there may be several positions. The job designated as *machinist*, for example, entails specific tasks, but there may be many machinists holding similar positions.

Positions are supported and made tangible by such devices as titles, job descriptions, organization charts, organization manuals, or wage and salary structures. The relationships among positions, depicted on organization charts and described in manuals, represent the formally intended relationships rather than the working relationships that become superimposed over the formal ones through the interactions of people at work.

Position relationships in formal structures include (1) superior-subordinate relations; (2) peer relations, or relations among members of groups at each given level; and (3) relations that extend beyond and apart from man-boss and peer relations.

Basic Structural Patterns

Four basic structural types can be identified within bureaucratic organizations: line, staff, functional, and committee. These types exist in combined forms in hierarchical organizations. Line organization is the central starting point and also the controlling and directing element of the other three types, which must be considered as modifications of line organization.

A detailed analysis of these patterns must await our study of authority in Chapter 15, for the differences among the types, and the problems in their administration, center on the scope and application of authority. In the following sections, a brief description of each pattern is provided.

Line Organization

Line structure consists of the direct relationships that connect the positions and tasks of each level with each other and with those above and below. It results in a network of superior-subordinate relationships that is sometimes called the chain of command. These line relationships are the designated channels through which authority flows from its source to levels of action below.

Any organization that has differentiated a leader and followers possesses line structure. Every individual in a bureaucracy reports to a "superior"—a supervisory person who gives orders, instructions, help, approval, and criticism.

The line structure is the basic framework for the entire organization. It has a major and pervasive influence over the behavior of all persons in an organization. Historically it is the oldest type of structure: all other kinds of organizational structure are modifications of it and must rely upon it for legitimate action. Line structure is indispensable to all organized effort; any other form must relate to it in such a way that its integrity and effectiveness of action are not impaired. The line structure provides channels of upward and downward communication, linking the various parts together in a system of authority. Charts typically denote the line structure by means of solid lines connecting the positions and groups of positions.

Staff Structure

Staff structure is used to expand and supplement line activities by providing positions for various types of specialists. The staff mechanism is separate from the line, but subordinate to its authority. Staff units perform functions that line managers would otherwise carry out, but they do so with the greater expertise of specialists. As organizations grow in size and complexity, line activities come under pressures which strain the capabilities of line managers. The staff concept separates certain functions and transfers them to the specialists in staff departments.

The special advantages of staff units are that they can (1) achieve organizationwide consistencies in activities that affect the entire organization, such as personnel policies, (2) devote more attention and skill to problem areas, (3) increase the services available to other units, and (4) relieve line managers of work they least prefer or are least capable of doing. Thus staff specialists may carry out delegated activities directly, but they also develop new services such as research, planning, and development. Staff specialists serve in advisory roles to relevant line officials. Line managers have the final approval or veto powers over the actions of staff groups.

Staff structure occurs in two principal forms: the staff assistant and the staff specialist. The staff assistant usually appears on an organization chart, as shown in Figure 13-9; it is a difficult relationship, presenting possibilities of ambiguity as to the sharing of decision-making authority between the manager and his assistant. The staff assistant is usually not a specialist, although the appointing manager usually seeks a person with particular interests, abilities, and experience. Such an assistant performs in the name of the superior, without formal authority to command. This structure often leads to imputing greater authority to the assistant than the superior intends.

The second type, that which incorporates the staff specialist, is the more common structure. It is a modification of line structure and exists always in combination with it. Managers create line-and-staff structure by tying staff departments by specific areas or functions, and delegating a type of limited authority that will be explained in Chapter 15. In general, staff departments do not exercise command authority except in limited cases. Figure 13-10 illustrates a typical line-and-staff combined structure.

An example of a unit organized on a staff basis is the personnel department, a department that does not directly supervise any employees except those within it. Personnel policies and decisions are line

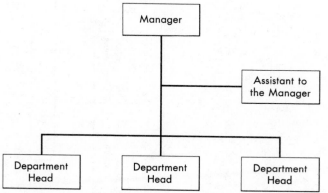

FIGURE 13-9. Organization Structure Showing a Staff Assistant.

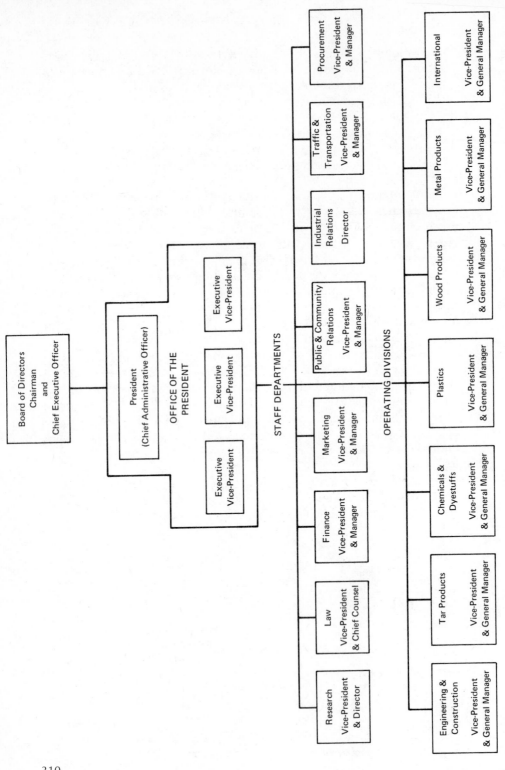

Board of Directors
Chairman
and
Chief Executive Officer

President
(Chief Administrative Officer)

OFFICE OF THE PRESIDENT

Executive Vice-President

Executive Vice-President

Executive Vice-President

STAFF DEPARTMENTS

Research Vice-President & Director

Law Vice-President & Chief Counsel

Finance Vice-President & Manager

Marketing Vice-President & Manager

Public & Community Relations Vice-President & Manager

Industrial Relations Director

Traffic & Transportation Vice-President & Manager

Procurement Vice-President & Manager

OPERATING DIVISIONS

Engineering & Construction Vice-President & General Manager

Tar Products Vice-President & General Manager

Chemicals & Dyestuffs Vice-President & General Manager

Plastics Vice-President & General Manager

Wood Products Vice-President & General Manager

Metal Products Vice-President & General Manager

International Vice-President & General Manager

FIGURE 13-10 (opposite). Organization Chart Showing Designation of Line and Staff Departments by Position and by Notation.

responsibilities, yet personnel techniques are too complex to be handled well by line managers alone. Therefore technical specialists in the various personnel fields assist the line by advice, policy guidance, program planning, and various services and procedures.[4]

Functional Structure

As with staff structure, functional structure is a way of relating specialists to the line organization. Functional structure should not be confused with the elaboration of "functional" operating departments in the line organization. Departments of production, marketing, or finance, for example, are usually line departments, but their identity is according to function. They represent a vertical split in the allocation of line authority and can command within their allocated function.

Large corporations, however, need a much more complicated kind of functional structure. When a company has a central corporate headquarters and a decentralized structure of branches, divisions, or plants, it must give direction to the activities of the subsidiary units.

Two types of functional structures have been used to fill such needs. In the first and most common type, a headquarters manager with given functional responsibilities, such as personnel administration, has responsibilities for the same function in the decentralized units, where there is a counterpart who reports to the general manager of each unit. The general manager has total direction and control, subject to corporate policy and other forms of guidance from the central offices. For example, the top personnel manager in the headquarters of a large multiplant company is a staff executive in the central offices. In each of the subunits, a personnel manager reports to the unit manager on a line basis (although organized on a staff basis within the unit). With staff structure only, the central personnel executive could work only through branch plant managers to influence the branch personnel managers. With functional structure, however, the central personnel executive directly supervises the work of the branch personnel managers through policies, directives, and required consultation and approval. How this arrangement actually works out in practice depends on the temperament, personality, and experience of the managers. Figure 13-11 shows a functional organization of this type.

Clearly a functional relationship subjects managers to multiple supervision. In the example cited, the personnel manager in the branch

---

[4]Charles Coleman and Joseph Rich, "Line, Staff, and the Systems Perspective," *Human Resource Management* **12** (Fall 1973), 20–27.

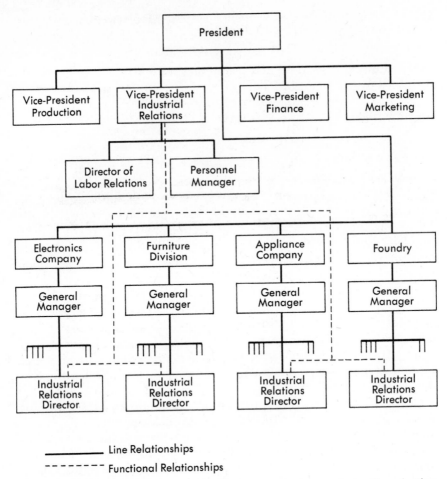

FIGURE 13-11. Organization Chart Showing Central Corporate Organization Structure with Functional Relationships to Counterpart Officials in Subsidiary Units.

unit reports directly to the plant manager, but in personnel activities he also reports to the central corporate personnel officer. Such a duplication presumes that managers can make distinctions in their multiple roles. Those who are subject to higher dual authority may have divided loyalties, and in cases of conflict or doubt they must choose which of the two authorities to obey. Coordination is thus a difficult problem.

The second type of functional structuring arises out of the need to preserve the integrity and coherence of specialized units through several levels of organization, without subjecting them to the command influence of the line manager at each and every level. This situation, less common than the first type, has generally emerged in organizations having numerous relatively small units that have wide geographical dispersion but require that all the functions be carefully performed in the interests of effective customer service. Figure 13-12 shows a partial chart of a public utility company in which the structures of the traffic, commercial, and plant departments extend two levels below their point of coordination and control. The U.S. Internal Revenue Service has a similar pattern of organizational structure, and for similar reasons.

This type of functional structure presents the major problem of coordinating the units that have no central line command but are physically located together. Coordination is generally achieved by designating the key manager from each function as a member of a district or divisional committee, which meets periodically to discuss, coordinate, and act on matters of interest to all. Many problems go all the way up to the level of the general manager for decision, because no one person on the local scene has the power to command or direct all the representatives on duty there.

Committee Structure

Committee structure differs from ad hoc committees, which are temporary and are created for specific and often operational rather than administrative missions. Committee structures assign managers to a permanent committee with authority for action and decisions in assigned areas.

Committee structures can exist at any level, but they are found most often at the top of large organizations. The best examples are executive committees or finance committees. Executive committees, which make decisions regarding major aims and policies and operational problems, consist of the top officers and are headed by the chief executive. These committees are subject to the authority and guidance of the board of directors. Finance committees do long-range financial planning and make decisions as to such matters as resource allocation and capital outlays. An example of committee structure is shown in Figure 13-13.

The strengths and weaknesses of structural committees are similar to those of ad hoc committees. They are one means, but not the only one, of putting talented and experienced executives to work on major problems too complex for a single leader to handle alone. On the other hand, such committees can make mistakes, and it is hard to pin down who is at fault when a group has made the decision. Clearly the success of such committees depends on the leadership abilities of the executive in charge, as well as on the appointment of able members.[5]

---

[5]For an analysis of committee organization see Alan C. Filley, "Committee Management: Guidelines from Social Science Research," *California Management Review* **12** (Fall 1970), 13–21.

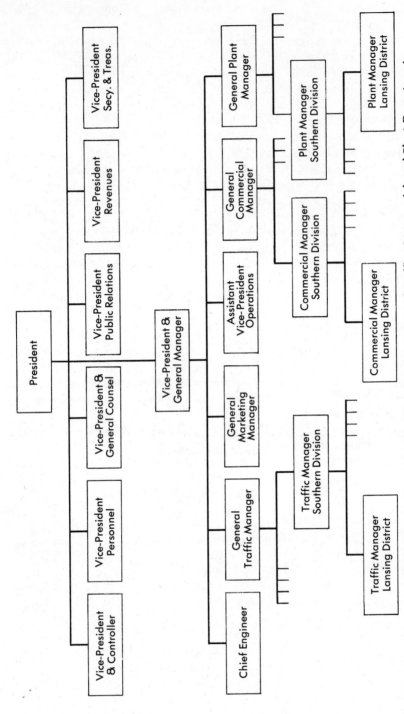

FIGURE 13-12. Partial Organization Chart Showing Functional Structure of Traffic, Commercial, and Plant Departments.

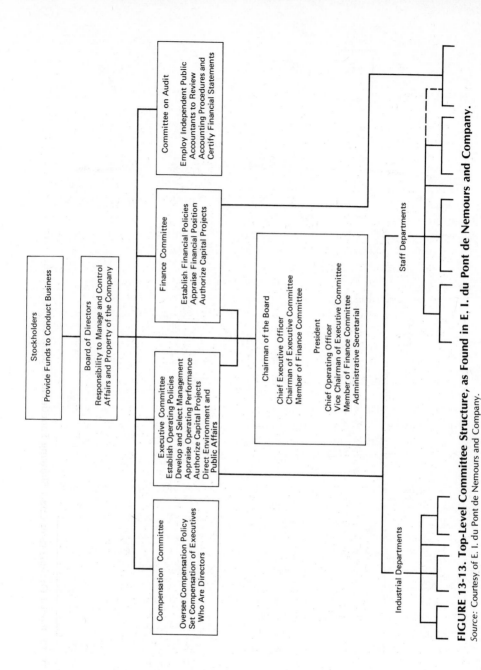

FIGURE 13-13. Top-Level Committee Structure, as Found in E. I. du Pont de Nemours and Company.

Source: Courtesy of E. I. du Pont de Nemours and Company.

315

The Shape of the Bureaucratic Structure

The relationship between the horizontal and the vertical dimensions of organizational structure pose problems of balance and form. Some organizations have tall structures, with many levels; other reduce the number of levels but then must flatten the structure by increasing the number of managers at each level.

Flatness is thus achieved by broadening the span of control (or supervision)—that is, the number of subordinates that a manager supervises. The concept holds that the larger the number of subordinates, the more difficult it is for a manager to supervise and coordinate them effectively. In addition to number, two other variables are critical. The first is the capability of the superior, and the second is the capabilities of those supervised. Many have incorrectly described the span of control as a fixed number of managers whom it is feasible for another to control. The usual number specified is from four to eight. This rigid concept of the span of control is unrealistic: spans of control numbering ten, fifteen, or even forty or more executives are frequently observed. Large spans are feasible where (1) the ability of the supervising executive is high, and (2) subordinates do not need close supervision, enjoy working independently, and flourish under autonomy. However, the capabilities of both superiors and subordinates are limited. They vary in energy, intelligence, training, experience, and other factors that they bring to the job. Communication is more difficult. There is a finite amount of time and energy for supervision, so all spans reach an upper limit. To these human limits must be added the fact that as more individuals are added to a manager's span of supervision, the number of possible relationships among the individuals increases at a geometric, not an arithmetic ratio, as shown in Table 13-1. This situation argues against large spans of control.[6]

A well-known example of the use of large span of control is Sears, Roebuck and Company. At the top level, over forty executives may report to the president; the actual number changes with changes in task assignments. The organization structure is "flat," meaning that for a company of its size it has very few levels. The large span of control is feasible largely because managers are held strictly accountable for results. They must work with other appropriate managers because they are cut off from close and frequent contact with a superior. They are judged more by results than by how they get results.

The flat structure obtained by large spans of high-caliber managers offers numerous advantages. It shortens the lines of communication

[6]See Robert J. House and John B. Miner, "Merging Management and Behavioral Theory: The Interaction Between Span of Control and Group Size," *Administrative Science Quarterly* 14 (September 1969), 451–464.

**TABLE 13-1. Geometric Increase in Number of
Relationships as Span of Control Broadens**

Number in Group	Number of Relationships	Increase in Relationships with Each Addition to Group
2	1	–
3	3	2
4	6	3
5	10	4
6	15	5
7	21	6
8	28	7
9	36	8
10	45	9
15	105	–
20	190	–
50	1225	–

Source: Chester I. Barnard, *The Functions of the Executive*
(Cambridge, Mass.: Harvard University Press, 1968), p. 108.
Used by permission.

between the bottom and the top levels. Communication in both directions is more likely to be fast and timely. The route that communications follow is simple, direct, and clear. Also, the distortions that inevitably occur in long channels of communication in tall organizations are
minimized. Some believe, therefore, that the flat structures result in
higher employee morale than tall structures.

There is an important distinction between the actual process of
supervision and the concept of "access to" a superior. The number
having access may be much larger than the number under direct
supervision. There has been a trend toward freer access to the president of a company combined with intensive supervision of a few. It is
clear that extremely tall and extremely flat structures are exceptional
cases that require special justification for their existence. The usual
practice is to direct the growth of an organization structure in such a
way as to keep its dimensions in reasonable balance.

Critics point out that flat structures have not been widely applied.
Found mainly in retailing, some assert that they are impractical in large
manufacturing concerns. Flat structures put pressure on managers and
exact heavy penalties for failure. Claims for higher morale have not
been proved. Nevertheless, organization design must consider the
balance between the horizontal and the vertical dimensions. Flat and
tall organization structures are illustrated in Figure 13-14.

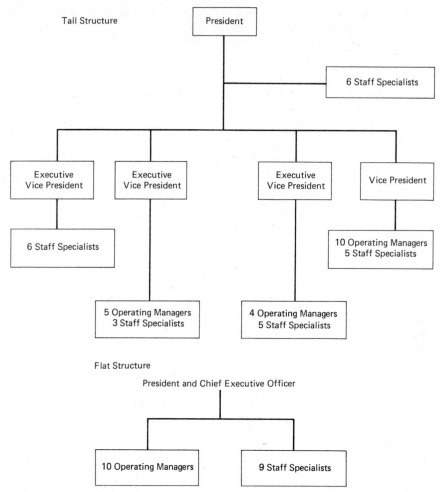

FIGURE 13-14. Tall and Flat Organizational Structures. The tall structure shown for a manufacturing firm was changed to the flat structure shown below.

Organization Charts

An organization chart is a diagram showing the formal organization structure—the relationships of positions and managers. Charts show the hierarchy of levels, the departmentalization, and interrelationships of the main units. They show the over-all pattern from which one may deduce some of their general strengths and weaknesses. They indicate the main lines of communication, and the network of authority, responsibility, and accountability. Charts may be constructed to depict the entire organization or any part of it. Usually, an organization prepares a general chart showing key positions in the hierarchy, and in addition constructs several auxiliary charts giving more detail.

Organization charts have many advantages. The process of drawing a chart causes managers to think more carefully about the organizational relationships that underlie it. Vague relationships not previously articulated may be clarified. Once constructed, organization charts provide information for outsiders or for new employees. They provide starting points for planning organizational changes and for evaluating the strengths and weaknesses of the present organization. A chart provides a ready means of visualizing the general characteristics of an organization.

Because charts are two-dimensional, and because the staff and functional relationships are superimposed over the line relationships, it is difficult to depict such structures on them. Some companies do not try to depict such differences on their charts, leaving to the organizational manual the task of presenting the differentiations of authority. Where distinctions are made on the chart, broken lines may be used, or heavy connecting lines can be used for the line organization and light lines to designate the staff units. Some companies show by positional arrangements that the staff units are regarded as different; a few insert wording along the lines at various levels to indicate the staff and operating groups. Figure 13-10 showed how a chemical company has separated the staff groupings (level 3 counting from the top) and also designated them by inserting wording along the line of the level. This method results in simpler, clearer, and less confusing charts.

Typical organizational charts show horizontal and vertical dimensions. Efforts to depict bureaucratic structures in nonbureaucratic ways have not proved popular. For example, concentric charts show top managers at the center with "lower" levels ranging in circles toward the perimeter. Figure 13-15 is illustrative. A few firms tried reversing the chart by placing "top" management at the bottom and "lower" levels of managers at the top. The purpose was to reflect an emphasis on participative management. These pictorial efforts did little to correct the alleged difficulties of straightforward bureaucratic relationships.

Charts also have many drawbacks, not all of which are inherent in charting; sometimes the problem lies in misuse or poor techniques. Among the disadvantages are the following: (1) charts record organizational relationships at one particular time and quickly become obsolete; (2) human relationships are not susceptible to exact representation on paper, even when they are carefully defined; (3) charts cause hard feelings among people who are sensitive about status and position; (4) charts foster the rigidities of bureaucracy by stressing domains and private jurisdictions; (5) charts foster "buck-passing" and too much formality in communication; (6) charts tell little about actual activities or interpersonal relations; and (7) the costs of preparing, disseminating, storing, updating, and studying charts are high.

On balance there are strong grounds for dispensing with charts. Some managers are reluctant to use them, and many believe that an

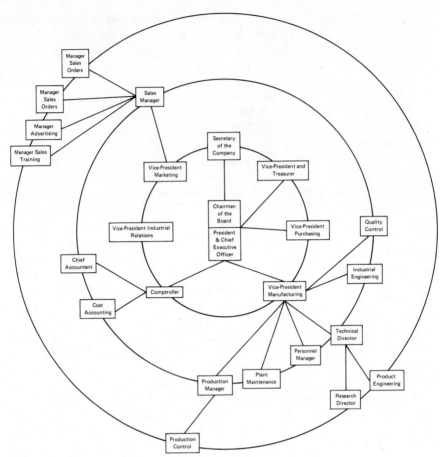

FIGURE 13-15. A Concentric Organization Chart.

organization can be managed better without them. Occasionally, distrust of charts arises from an autocratic or overbearing manager's fear that his power will be weakened if subordinates have a clear understanding of the organization's working structure. The manager who wishes to dominate and control, to maneuver freely, and to manipulate subordinates must control such information. If charts are used, they should be periodically and systematically revised, and should be drawn with the utmost care based on thorough analysis.

Organization Manuals

Organization charts, as has been indicated, cannot possibly include the wealth of detail that is often desirable and necessary for understanding an organization. Someone inevitably has to explain the chart, giving its rationale and justifying its individual peculiarities and departures from custom. This can be done in an organization manual, which supplements charts by including additional details such as more elaborate auxiliary charts, more complete titles, job descriptions (indicating responsibilities and duties), salary, wages, and the like.

The disadvantages of manuals are similar to those of organization charts, except that there is more work involved in writing, compiling, and editing. They are also difficult to keep up to date. Some organizations have found that the manual is not used much. As with charts, the autocratic executive who needs to control information will regard a manual as unnecessary or undesirable, in order to accentuate his hold over subordinates. Their principal value is to establish common practices among the various units of an organization. The process of preparation may be more instructive than the final result.

Position Titles

Practice concerning the use of such terms as *superintendent, vice president,* and other titles varies considerably from one organization to another. Figure 13-2 shows that the management group includes all levels above rank-and-file workers. Occasionally there are "group leaders"—workers who are assigned some leadership responsibility under a supervisor, but are not technically considered part of the management group.

Organizations are generally headed by a chief executive, president, or chairman of the board. These three titles may be used in various combinations. If the chairman is the chief executive officer, the president reports to him. If the president is the chief executive officer, the chairman is usually relatively inactive or is assigned special responsibilities on the board of directors.

Another frequent title, that of group vice president, is used in large corporations with substantial diversity of operations or product lines. When companies reach a sales volume of $500 million and operate three or four distinct kinds of business, they devise a structure that groups logical operating units together to permit the central office to control the diversity. This structure interposes another level between operating units and central corporate managers, reducing their span of control. Such positions also provide training grounds for executives advancing to corporate-level general management positions. In effect, each group becomes a profit center, combining divisions that have natural affinities and relationships.

Group structure also permits economic gains. For example, the group can maintain a larger sales force, which no individual unit could afford to maintain for itself. Group executives are the counterpart of chief executive officers in simpler structures: they have full responsibility and accountability for the group's objectives. The drawbacks of group structure include resistance on the part of the group's units to supervision by the group executive, who is often tempted to reduce the autonomy of operating divisions. Because group executives usually supervise divisions headed by a president, these executives may have less visibility, and hence less prestige and status, than their subordinates, whose positions make them prominent.

More and more companies have used the title *vice chairman*. This title is applied in two ways. First, it may be an honorific title in which the position holder does little; for example, the individual may mark time in it while awaiting retirement. Such a position makes it possible to "elevate" a president to it so that a new president may be moved in. It is also used to place obsolete higher managers without loss of pride and status. A second usage is to assign the title to an active, capable executive who can accomplish special missions, assist the chairman of the board, and even be ready to replace the chairman. Often the vice chairman is a financial analyst, an acquisitions expert, or a good general administrator. Whether assigned as a holding action or as a genuine mission, it is a difficult position because its occupant will appear as "number two."

The drawbacks to the position of vice chairman are even more marked in the case of "assistants to," who are often errand runners. If they gain power or influence it is through the abdication of their superior or through illegitimate means. The position often attracts younger executives because it provides an opportunity to learn through valuable first-hand experience. Others in the organization, however, may be suspicious, unwilling to trust whoever fills the position.

The level below the top group consists of vice presidents or other senior executives who head up the major activities within the enterprise. These first two levels are considered together as the top management group. Examples are the corporation secretary, the treasurer, the vice president of marketing, the vice president of finance, or the vice president of operations. In corporations, some persons from this level are elected under the bylaws as officers by the board of directors. Officers have legal responsibilities and obligations that depend upon the laws of the state of incorporation.

The next two levels in Figure 13-2 represent middle management, positions that are held by intermediate or junior executives. They bear major responsibilities and are in line for advancement to top management positions. These persons are department heads or supervisors of important segments of the company's activities. Examples of middle-management titles are the purchasing agent, the head of traffic and transportation, the production control manager, the works manager, the department store buyer, or the office manager.

In manufacturing organizations, the first-line supervisors represent the connecting level between the middle and top levels and the rank-and-file workers. The wide black line in Figure 13-2 shows that rank-and-file workers are differentiated from the managerial levels.

There are no standard, universal titles for managerial positions; many variations are found, especially in nonbusiness organizations. In hospitals, the top executive is usually called a *director*. In schools, the terms *superintendent* or *principal* are often used. Church, military, and government organizations also use characteristic titles.

Some managers attach great importance to titles; others treat them casually. Some titles imply high status and hence appeal to status-seekers. Often one finds that exaggerated or inflated titles are used, apparently to reward organization members. Although it would seem important to make titles accurately descriptive of the work they cover, many organizations are content to treat position titles with considerable informality.

SUMMARY

Building the structure of an organization is a continuous process that requires the constant attention of executives. Many changes that occur in an organization have implications for organization structure. Hence planning is required to keep structure commensurate with the demands imposed upon it.

Organization structure consists of the interrelationships of the working parts of the organization. It is the web or network of positions and task assignments formally designated by executives doing the organizational planning. Structure is not merely positions on a chart; it is a constant, dynamic interaction between individuals whose positions determine in part, and whose personal abilities determine in part, the behavior of persons and the work that is done in the organization.

This chapter has described the bureaucratic model of formal organization structure. This structure is two-dimensional in nature—having a horizontal and vertical direction. In the horizontal direction—an organization differentiated into major departmental units—and in the vertical direction, the structure is differentiated into scalar levels that represent a hierarchy of authority. Finally, line, staff, and functional types of structures were described. Committee and task force structures were examined, together with an analysis of their major strengths and weaknesses.

The concepts of span of control and unity of command were examined in the context of bureaucratic structure. Finally, the advantages and drawbacks of organization charts were analyzed.

_____

The governor of a large midwestern state decided to press the legislature for approval of a reorganization plan prepared by a major consulting firm he had retained to improve efficiency in the state government. The firm came up with a plan to establish nine major departments with directors at the cabinet level. Directors would each devise their own organization structure, deciding whether to consolidate, leave intact, or abolish the agencies assigned to them. The plan distributed the state's 226 agencies among the nine departments. Approval of each departmental organization rested with the governor, but the legislature would have veto power over the plans. The governor's Committee on State Government Reorganization did not like the plans, feeling that under them the state legislature could not have a significant enough role. The governor himself was unsure of the plan, and tended to agree with the committee.

Question:

1. What factors bear on the possibilities for the success or failure of the plan to reorganize?

_____

1. What do you think are the most difficult problems of building a sound organization structure, and why?

2. Why is there no ideal or perfect structure possible for a given kind of organization?

3. How do formal, bureaucratic structures differ in hospitals, schools, or government organizations, in contrast to business firms?

4. List the advantages and disadvantages of the use of organization charts.

5. Examine the organization manual of a large firm or government agency, and make a critical analysis of it.

6. Why is it that charts do not appear to indicate the actual relationships and activities of an organization?

7. What is meant by the idea of an organization structure? What are the principal characteristics of structures in organizations?

8. Why do organizations have a pyramid-shaped structure? Is this structure necessary? Can you find organizations with some other kind of structure?

9. Why is the "multiple presidency" of a large corporation not an exception to the concept of unity of command?

10. Comment on the advantages and disadvantages of committee structure in organizing a business.

11. What differences in structure are there between large and small business organizations?

12. Explain the chief characteristics of line, staff, and functional organization structures.

13. In what situations would you expect to find product departmentalization a useful and economical way to organize a business?

14. What are the principal variables that determine the appropriate span of control for a particular executive?

15. Under what conditions is organization by process preferable to organization by product?

16. Outline the main precepts of the bureaucratic model of organization.

SELECTED REFERENCES

ALBROW, MARTIN. *Bureaucracy*. New York: Praeger Publishers, Inc., 1970.

BLAU, PETER M. *On the Nature of Organizations*. New York: John Wiley & Sons, Inc., 1974.

BROWN, COURTNEY. *Putting the Corporate Board to Work*. New York: Macmillan Publishing Co., Inc., 1976.

CROZIER, MICHEL. *The Bureaucratic Phenomenon*. Chicago: University of Chicago Press, 1964.

DALE, ERNEST. *The Great Organizers*. New York: McGraw-Hill Book Company, 1960.

DALTON, GENE W., PAUL R. LAWRENCE, and JAY W. LORSCH. *Organization Structure and Design*. Homewood, Ill.: Richard D. Irwin, Inc., 1970.

FAMULARO, JOSEPH J. *Organization Planning Manual*. New York: American Management Association, 1971.

GIBSON, JAMES L., JOHN M. IVANCEVICH, and JAMES W. DONNELLY, JR. *Organizations: Behavior, Structure, Processes*. Revised edition. Dallas: Business Publications, Inc., 1976.

GRUBER, W., and J. NILES. *The New Management: Line Executive and Staff Professional in the Future Firm*. New York: McGraw-Hill Book Company, 1976.

HICKSON, DAVID J., with DEREK S. PUGH. *Organization Structure in its Context*. Aston Studies, vol. I. Lexington, Mass.: Lexington Books, Inc., 1976.

HUMMEL, RALPH P. *The Bureaucratic Experience*. New York: St. Martin's Press, 1977.

JAQUES, ELLIOTT. *A General Theory of Bureaucracy*. New York: The Halsted Press, 1976.

KILMAN, RALPH H., LOUIS R. PONDY, and DENNIS P. SLEVIN, eds. *The Management of Organization Design*. Vols. I and II. New York: Elsevier–North Holland, 1976.

LORSCH, JAY, ed. *Studies in Organization Design*. Homewood, Ill.: Richard D. Irwin, Inc., 1970.

MARCH, JAMES G., and HERBERT A. SIMON. *Organizations*. New York: John Wiley & Sons, Inc., 1958. Chapters 6 and 7.

MEYER, MARSHALL. *Bureaucratic Structure and Authority*. New York: Harper & Row, Publishers, 1972.

NYSTROM, PAUL C., and WILLIAM H. STARBUCK. *Prescriptive Models of Organization*. New York: Elsevier–North Holland, 1976.

O'SHAUGHNESSY, JOHN. *Patterns of Business Organization*. New York: John Wiley & Sons, Inc., 1976.

RICE, GEORGE H., JR., and DEAN W. BISHOPRICK. *Conceptual Models of Organization.* New York: Appleton-Century-Crofts, 1971. Part I.

SEXTON, WILLIAM P., ed. *Organization Theories.* Columbus, Ohio: Charles E. Merrill Publishing Company, 1970. Part I.

SWINTH, ROBERT. *Organizational Systems for Management: Design, Planning and Implementation.* Columbus, Ohio: Grid, Inc., 1974.

THOMPSON, JAMES D., ed. *Approaches to Organizational Design.* Pittsburgh: University of Pittsburgh Press, 1966.

THOMPSON, JAMES D. *Organizations in Action.* New York: McGraw-Hill Book Company, 1967. Part I.

THOMPSON, VICTOR A. *Modern Organization.* New York: Alfred A. Knopf, Inc., 1961. Chapters 5–9.

TOREN, NINA. "Bureaucracy and Professionalism: A Reconsideration of Weber's Thesis." *The Academy of Management Review* 1:3 (July 1976), 36–46.

Chapter 14

Organization Design: Adaptive Systems

Once upon a time there was a traveler drawing for the King of Ch'i. "What is the hardest thing to draw?" asked the king. "Dogs and horses are the hardest." "Then what is the easiest?" "Devils and demons are the easiest. Indeed dogs and horses are what people know and see at dawn and dusk in front of them. To draw them no distortion is permissible. . . . Devils and demons have no shapes and are not seen in front of anybody.

—*Han Fei Tzu*

CHAPTER GUIDE

People who work for an organization often feel constrained by its formalities. Job descriptions, position titles, salary structures, authority figures, and the defined jurisdictions of typical organizational anatomy provide some people with feelings of security and self-confidence, but others regard them as unnecessary restrictions that hamper their performance.

Therein lies the dilemma: how can an organization provide enough structure to stay organized, yet allow its members to move freely enough to give their best efforts to their work?

Many organizations today are letting their employees work at home. Weyerhauser, for example, informally maintains such a policy. The rationale includes greater efficiency, reduction of commuting time, and the opportunity for individuals to work away from telephones, interruptions, and the stress that often prevails at the office.

Working at home or at other locations has been traditional among college professors. It is one of many manifestations of the adaptive organization design.

Questions to keep in mind while you read this chapter:

1. Can you think of other occupations or jobs where the practice of working at home could be used?

2. What do you think are the main drawbacks?
3. Would you like the privilege of deciding where you would prefer to work if you were employed in an organization? Why or why not?

The effectiveness and efficiency of a given organization design depend not only on its structure but also upon the leadership and management styles it fosters. The bureaucratic structures described in the previous chapter are based on rational analysis of goals and tasks. But as managers sought to incorporate more humanistic and social attitudes into management practices, it was inevitable that fundamental changes in both bureaucratic structure and management style would emerge.

The adaptive structures described in this chapter represent an extensive evolution in the theory of complex organizations. Adaptive structures are not merely variations or improvements in the bureaucratic model; they represent extensive departures from its underlying assumptions, theories, structures, and aims. Both the bureaucratic and the adaptive models represent "ideal types" of organization design, with choices between these extremes depending on the balance of benefits desired and their attendant costs.

Probably no organization will exactly fit either of the two models. However, many strongly bureaucratic organizations are moving gradually into the modes of adaptive organization design. Not all bureaucratic characteristics are bad, nor are they all likely to disappear. But organizations of the future will look and work substantially less like the bureaucracies we know today. Organization designers now have a wider array of alternatives to choose from in designing organizations to meet changing and increasingly complex demands.

This chapter will first define the concept of adaptive organizations and then turn to an analysis of the difficulties of bureaucratic structure; finally it will describe a number of the newer adaptive structures.

DEFINITIONS

The term *adaptive* is used here to describe the newer organizational designs. Other closely similar terms include *organic model, open-system model, fluid or flexible model, "natural" model,* and *free-form model.* All these terms convey similar meanings: that model of organization which maintains a high degree of openness to inputs from the internal and external environments, and develops mechanisms by which it remains flexible and amenable to change, innovation, and

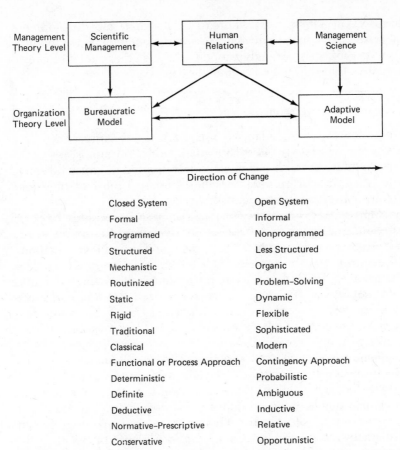

FIGURE 14-1. Comparative Attributes of Bureaucratic and Adaptive Models of Organization.

development. These terms all convey the sense of organizational receptivity to inputs for change and development that come from organization members as well as from the environment of the organization.

Particular organizations range along a continuum of the type depicted in Figure 14-1, which shows how management theory and organization theory parallel one another. The human relations movement is shown bridging the two extremes of the continuum. The columns under the bureaucratic and adaptive model show, respectively, the terms currently in use to describe each model.

In some organizations, both bureaucratic and adaptive structures exist. Perrow calls this a "mixed model."[1] Those functions in which routinization is characteristic, such as a production department, may

[1]Charles Perrow, *Organizational Analysis: A Sociological View* (Belmont, Calif.: Wadsworth, 1970), pp. 68–75.

find bureaucracy satisfactory, whereas the research and development unit may prefer an adaptive design. However, the rationale for adaptive models of organization strongly supports the idea that a total organizational approach has the best likelihood of success.

Origins of the Adaptive Model

The trend toward fluid, adaptive organization structures has been under way since the early 1960s. Spearheaded by revisionist research, the open-systems approach has been widely applied in large and small business firms, in government agencies, and in a host of new and experimental social service organizations.

The adaptive model represents extensive applications of behavioral research, a kind of maturation of the earlier human relations movement. Two significant works started the conversion of human relations thought into what has become the field of organization behavior. The first was a British research report by Burns and Stalker which detailed their views of the organic model. They recognized that some organizations work better as mechanistic, bureaucratic systems, but found that organic systems occurred where aims of creativity, innovation, change, and employee satisfaction prevailed.[2]

The second pivotal influence was that of Warren Bennis, who wrote extensively on the breakdown of bureaucracy and the emergence of change-oriented organizations that were open to their environments.[3] Bennis's prediction of the total demise of bureaucracy, however, was too sweeping, and he later modified his views by recognizing that some degree of bureaucracy is inevitable in large-scale enterprise.[4]

———————— **DYSFUNCTIONAL CONSEQUENCES OF BUREAUCRACY**

The newer developments in adaptive organization designs are founded on difficulties and problems experienced in managing according to the bureaucratic model. These difficulties are called *dysfunctional consequences* because they pose problems that the bureaucratic organization finds hard to cope with. A dysfunctional characteristic is a counterproductive one, producing more drawbacks than advantages.

[2]Tom Burns and G. M. Stalker, *The Management of Innovation* (Chicago: Quadrangle, 1962).

[3]Warren Bennis, *Changing Organizations* (New York: McGraw-Hill, 1966). See also "Beyond Bureaucracy," *Trans-Action* 6 (July-August, 1969), 44–51; "The Coming Death of Bureaucracy," *Think*, November–December 1966, 30–35; and "Organizational Developments and the Fate of Bureaucracy," *Industrial Mangement Review*, Spring 1966, 41–55.

[4]"Conversation with Warren Bennis," *Organizational Dynamics* 2 (winter 1974), 50–66.

One of the earliest signals about the drawbacks of bureaucracy consisted of the recognition of informal organization as a corollary of formal organization. Discrepancies between intended and actual behavior of organization members raise doubts about the ability of bureaucracies to rule out the human equation. Adaptive organizations indicate that there has been a ready accommodation to forms of behavior that bureaucracies call informal but regard as abnormal.

This point can be illustrated by the example of worker-established output norms. The bureaucratic scheme gives managers the authority to set norms or quotas for appropriate output. The open-system model recognizes that where worker-desired norms are strongly held and widely shared in a group, the imposition of other norms by someone "in authority" is unlikely to be successful. Peer pressure can be greater than boss pressure, and the open-system model instructs the manager to find ways of getting the group to improve its own norms. The manager in a bureaucracy worries about the enforcement of its imposed policies; the manager in an open system is more likely to acknowledge the reality of group norms and to attempt to redesign the system to take account of them.

In the main, the dysfunctions of bureaucracy center upon changed expectations as to the benefits and payoffs desired from organizational effort. Bureaucracy primarily emphasizes a single payoff—efficiency. Although efforts are made to achieve "good" human relations, results have the first priority. Now we have come to expect more innovation, more change, more social responsibility, and more involvement of people in their own destinies—results that appear to be more difficult for a bureaucracy than for open systems.

Another source of difficulty in bureaucratic organizations is that the effects of inherent or potential defects are made worse by exaggeration. Bureaucrats can hide behind rules and regulations; they may attach undue importance to trivial procedures; they often carry impersonality to an extreme; they delay decisions under the protection of red tape; they are often more sensitive to the needs of the system than to the people the organization is designed to serve. Another drawback of bureaucracies has been their monocratic posture; that is, they claim that a single line of authority exists so that decision and control are lodged entirely in single positions, with managers acting alone. At least in large bureaucracies, this is not really the case. As was shown in Chapter 4, the most significant decisions are those made by teams, committees, or groups of collaborating managers.

Thompson traces many of the dysfunctions of bureaucracy to their source in specialization. Specialization imparts such qualities as routinization, strong attachment to subgoals, impersonality, categorization, and resistance to change. Managerial behavior exaggerates the characteristic qualities of bureaucratic organization, and this exaggeration leads to excessive aloofness, ritualistic attachment to procedures and routines, resistance to change, and petty insistence on rights of authority and status. Moreover, bureaucratic organizations encourage self-serving behavior and extreme competitiveness in advancing selfish interests.[5] As an example, it is clear that bureaucracies find it difficult to manage and provide job satisfactions for professionals. Lawyers, physicians, scientists, or engineers espouse professional values such as autonomy, independence, open discourse, and freedom from close supervision. They shun having their work appraised by a superior, and being dominated by a boss. Finally, professionals are often in conflict with each other, and bureaucratic management finds it hard to resolve such conflicts.[6]

Argyris has found that hierarchical models predispose to authoritarian managerial styles and are therefore injurious to healthy personality patterns. Like Thompson, he sees the bureaucracy fostering a pathological need to control in managers, whose fear of their subordinates and insecurity may produce autocratic behavior in bosses and a corresponding subservience among subordinates. Emphasis on success and the stress entailed in attaining it produces a high level of anxiety on the part of members of the organization. The boss has strong control over subordinates' needs and personal goals, and an ability to exact subservient behavior through the use of power and fear.[7]

Etzioni reinforces the findings of Thompson and Argyris by pointing out that organizations set norms and enforce them through elaborate rules and regulations and by the power of reward and punishment systems. This use of power alienates organization members, even though it may temporarily enforce compliance. The conformity of subordinates is likely to be limited to matters explicitly backed by power, and they become reluctant to show initiative, to cooperate, or to volunteer information. In a crisis, when the power structure is weakened, organization members are likely to revert to the norms they really prefer.[8]

Bennis has also indicated discontents with bureaucracy: bosses who have no technical competence when their subordinates do; arbitrary and rigid rules; subversive informal organizational apparatus; role conflict; and proliferating unanticipated consequences. He sees an over-emphasis on conformity, control, and subservience, and a lack of inno-

[5]Victor A. Thompson, *Modern Organization* (New York: Knopf, 1961), chap. 8.

[6]James E. Sorenson and Thomas L. Sorenson, "The Conflict of Professionals in Bureaucratic Organizations," *Administrative Science Quarterly* 19 (March 1974), 98–106; Nina Toren, "Bureaucracy and Professionalism: A Reconsideration of Weber's Thesis," *The Academy of Management Review* 1 (July 1976), 36–46.

[7]Chris Argyris, *Personality and Organization* (New York: Harper, 1957).

[8]Amitai Etzioni, *Modern Organizations* (Englewood Cliffs, N.J.: Prentice-Hall, 1964).

vation and communication.[9] Simon and March have also catalogued similar defects in bureaucratic organizations.[10]

Communication Nets

Studies of communication nets by Bavelas,[11] Leavitt,[12] and others show that for certain purposes patterns other than the pyramid-shaped, hierarchical organization structure may be better. What effect, they asked, do communication patterns have upon the operation of task-oriented groups? They studied this problem by means of laboratory experimentation based on different organization patterns.

Three such communication nets are shown in Figure 14-2. The wheel and circle patterns were utilized by Leavitt in exploring Bavelas's earlier theory. The all-channel pattern was tested by Guetzkow and Simon on replication experiments testing Leavitt's findings. The arrows indicate permissible channels of communication. The wheel and circle groups represent restricted communication channels. The all-channel net represents open or unrestricted communication. Experimental groups of five were assigned tasks; group members were seated around a table but were separated. The members could pass messages through slots to each other, according to which pattern was being tested. The groups had first to organize themselves, then to perform the

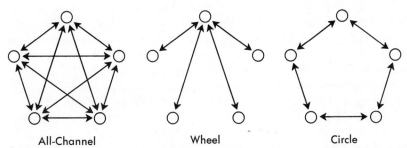

All-Channel   Wheel   Circle

FIGURE 14-2. Open Communication Channels in Three Nets of Task-Oriented Groups.

Source: Harold Guetzkow and Herbert A. Simon, "The Impact of Certain Communication Nets upon Organization and Performance in Task-Oriented Groups," *Management Science* 1 (April–July 1955), p. 237. Used by permission.

[9]Bennis, *Changing Organizations.*
[10]James G. March and Herbert A. Simon, *Organizations* (New York: Wiley, 1958), pp. 36–46.
[11]A. Bavelas, "Communication Patterns in Task-Oriented Groups," *Journal of the Acoustical Society of America* **22** (May 1950), 725–730; "A Mathematical Model for Group Structures," *Applied Anthropology* **7** (Summer 1948), 16–30.
[12]Harold J. Leavitt, "Some Effects of Certain Communication Patterns on Group Performance," *Journal of Abnormal and Social Psychology* **46** (January 1951), 38–50.

task. Factors such as speed, accuracy, or efficiency of task performance could then be observed in the various organizational arrangements that the groups developed.[13]

Leavitt and others testing the Bavelas design found that the group was more effective when the group structure permitted the members to channel communications through a member who occupies a central position than when the structure required communications to be filtered back and forth through each member; therefore a differentiated structure that serves a coordinative function would be more effective than an undifferentiated structure. But the time required for problem solving is greater under those circumstances. Other researchers found that a member having information essential for problem solving tended to become the central member; that a differentiated structure lowered the satisfaction of group members but increased their efficiency; and that productivity decreased in a centrally organized structure.[14]

The Guetzkow and Simon experiments used time-and-motion study to separate organizing efforts from the operational, task-performing elements. The different nets in Figure 14-2 yielded different degrees of organizing difficulty for the groups. The more difficult it was to organize, the longer it took to attain efficient task performance. Once the optimal organization was attained, however, time differences among the groups disappeared. The more restrictions that were placed upon the groups, the more stable the groups became. Open communication on the all-channel pattern exerted a more limiting effect on task performance than communication restricted to specific channels. Either a two- or a three-level hierarchy developed in three or more groups within each of the three nets; groups thus organized performed their tasks efficiently. However, only wheel groups were able to achieve a hierarchical structure with ease; most of the all-channel nets did so, but only three of 21 circle groups developed hierarchies. Therefore, it was established that difficulty of organizing is greatest in circle groups, next in all-channel groups, and least in wheel groups.[15]

In performing group tasks, members tend to adjust their communication patterns to task complexity. They also improve with experience in performing the task. Thus, for example, a group may begin on an all-channel pattern, but if the task is simple or routine, they may find the

[13]The methodology and findings of this research are reported in Harold Guetzkow and Herbert A. Simon, "The Impact of Certain Communication Nets upon Organization and Task Performance in Task-oriented Groups," *Management Science* 1 (April–July 1955), 233–250. Reprinted in Albert H. Rubenstein and Chadwick J. Haberstroh (eds.), *Some Theories of Organization* (Homewood, Ill.: The Dorsey Press and Richard D. Irwin, Inc., 1960), pp. 259–277.

[14]As summarized in Ralph M. Stogdill, *Individual Behavior and Group Achievement* (New York: Oxford U.P. 1959), pp. 228–229.

[15]Guetzkow and Simon, "Impact," pp. 241–243.

all-channel structure inefficient, and transform themselves into a wheel pattern.

The Guetzkow and Simon findings indicate that there is not necessarily a direct connection between complete freedom to communicate and effective functioning. Some restrictions on communication may improve effectiveness. The findings also show how communication is related to the evolution of hierarchy and other patterns of organizational structure. Communication patterns have an important effect on the difficulty a group will have in organizing itself, but restricted patterns do not necessarily increase the difficulty over that of unrestricted patterns.

_____ **ADAPTIVE ORGANIZATION DESIGNS**

Whereas bureaucratic organization designs are frequently described by means of organization charts, it is more difficult to chart open or adaptive systems. The typical organization chart is essentially a bureaucratic device that implies a permanency, clarity, and simplicity that are far from reality. In this section we will present charts or diagrams wherever feasible, but it should be noted that the more open the system the more difficult it is to picture the relationships involved.

Gardner says that a nonhierarchical organization can only be viewed as a scenario rather than a two-dimensional diagram. A key concept, however, is that most work can best be done in small groups, which should be temporary, semiautonomous, self-managing, focused, modular, participative, democratic, changing, and learning.[16]

The general characteristics of an adaptive system are the opposite of the bureaucratic ones postulated by Weber. They include:

1. A reduction of emphasis upon the hierarchy.
2. Greater ambiguity in the system of authority that ties the organization together.
3. Greater autonomy, participation, and involvement of organization members in meaningful decision making.
4. The absence of restrictions on communication patterns.
5. De-emphasis on rules and rule enforcement, and greater reliance on trust, autonomy, and self discipline.

[16]Neely Gardner, "The Non-Hierarchical Organization of the Future: Theory vs. Reality," *Public Administration Review* 36 (September/October 1976, 591–598. See also William H. Starbuck and John M. Dutton, "Designing Adaptive Organizations," *Journal of Business Policy* 3 (1973), 21–28; Martin Landau, "On the Concept of a Self-Correcting Organization," *Public Administration Review* 33 (1973), 533–542; and L. T. Hedberg, Paul Nystrom, and William H. Starbuck, "Camping on See-Saws: Prescriptions for a Self-Designing Organization," *Administrative Science Quarterly* 21 (March 1976), 41–65.

6. Greater recognition of group methods, norms, and sanctions.
7. The use of intrinsic motivation instead of close or punitive supervision.
8. Rewards based on achievement and results.

We will now consider five of the newer structural concepts which, when added to traditional concepts of the bureaucratic model, greatly enrich the repertory of available organization-design strategies: (1) systems designs, (2) matrix and project designs, (3) task forces and teams, (4) free-form structures, and (5) multiple leadership at the top.

Systems Designs

Systems concepts have been applied to four major sectors of management. First, they have been used to analyze and explain existing organizations and their management. The closed-system nature of bureaucracies thus became a prominent part of organization theory. Second, systems concepts have been useful in understanding human behavior in organizations. These aspects will be reviewed in Part Four of this book. Third, systems concepts have contributed to a better understanding of decision making, planning, controlling, and information processing as organizational and managerial functions, as we saw in Part Two. Finally, systems concepts are becoming more and more significant in the design of organization structures, as illustrated by the designs that will be explained in this and following sections.

By viewing organizations as sociotechnical systems, it is possible to include all the other ways in which systems concepts have been utilized.[17] It is one thing to try to understand what exists, and quite another deliberately to design organizations based on available knowledge about systems. If systems theory were to be applied at the time that an organization design is first created, it is likely that the resulting organization would look much different from the organizations we commonly observe. A systems approach to design would begin with the flow of work and information processes; it would consider linkages and relationships, networks, controls, decision points, and time. It would not begin by considering positions into which are collected logically related duties.

Total systems approaches are in their infancy, but the use of computers and related techniques have reinforced the importance of thinking in terms of systems. In particular, the science of cybernetics has advanced our concepts of adaptive, organic structures. Cybernetics is the science of control, or of self-regulating systems. Because organization is the medium through which control is achieved, cybernetics is

---

[17]Kenyon B. DeGreene, *Sociotechnical Systems: Factors in Analysis, Design, and Management* (Englewood Cliffs, N.J.: Prentice-Hall, 1973).

closely related to organization; indeed, according to Beer, one may define cybernetics as the science of effective organization.[18]

According to Katz and Kahn, an open system consists of recurrent cycles of input, transformation, and output. To locate a system, specify its functions, and understand its functioning requires the examination of this cycling process. An open system has (1) *boundaries* for the selective reception of inputs and transmission of outputs; (2) an *internal processing* system; (3) *negentropy* to counteract the tendency of the system to run down; (4) *feedback,* or responsiveness to information provided by the system's own functioning; (5) *homeostasis,* or the tendency to maintain a steady state; (6) *equifinality,* or the use of different patterns to produce the same effect; and (7) *differentiation,* the tendency toward elaboration of the system's structure.[19]

The general process of systems design includes the following steps:

1. *Establish criteria for management information needs,* including the objectives of the system, the current information available, and the decision and report practices that are currently used.
2. *Develop the preliminary design,* statement of system requirements, reporting frequencies, types and routings of reports, and equipment needed. Determine what can be automated, using computer programming, and what to leave as is. Balance current requirements with growth plans.
3. *Evaluate the preliminary design:* establish cost of hardware and other elements, assess training requirements, and establish the nature of expected improvements.
4. *Develop a revised model of the proposed system,* using an analytical or experimental approach, simulation, or gaming to test the design. Involve the ultimate users in developing the revised model.
5. *Determine system specifications:* evaluate alternative means of achieving the proposed design; consider relationship to other system requirements.
6. *Install, debug, modify, and extend the system* by providing for maintenance and updating. Allow for flexibility in operating and modifying the system.[20]

Although open systems de-emphasize traditional structure and hier-

---

[18]Stafford Beer, *Decision and Control* (New York: Wiley, 1966), p. 425. One should read this book for an understanding of the relationships among operations research, decision theory, cybernetics, and organization concepts.

[19]Daniel Katz and Robert Kahn, *The Social Psychology of Organizations* (New York: Wiley, 1966), pp. 452–453.

[20]For further information on designing systems, see John A. Beckett, *Management Dynamics* (New York: McGraw-Hill, 1971); Thomas B. Glans et al., *Management Systems* (New York: Holt, 1968); Anant R. Negandhi, *Organization Theory in an Open System* (New York: Dunellen, 1974).

archy, they do have structural patterns. There is no standard practice with respect to depicting these structures in charts or diagrams. The types of diagrams that have been used display an enormous variation; the meaning of any structural diagram is peculiar to each situation. Many open systems organizations forego charting entirely. Where charts are used, they emphasize groups, rather than positions or individuals. Such illustrations generally depict the main elements of the environment, boundaries of the system and subsystems, boundary-spanning units, and general work levels. To those who are used to standard charts, open-systems diagrams seem vague and mysterious. The reality of any organization, open or closed, is extremely hard to show in any two-dimensional representation.

Most open-system diagrams take circular or irregular shapes that are nonhierarchical. Figure 14-3 shows a circular design. In effect, such

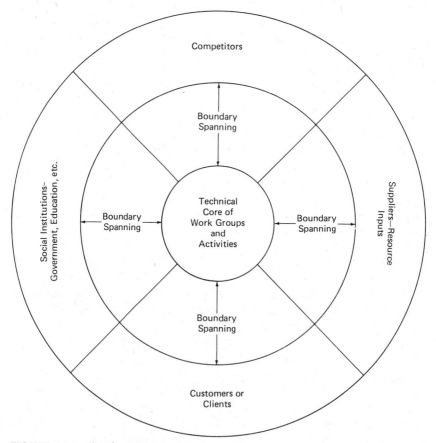

FIGURE 14-3. Circular Pattern of an Open System.
Source: Adapted from Orlando Behling and Chester Schriesheim, *Organization Behavior: Theory, Research, and Application* (Boston: Allyn and Bacon, Inc., 1976), p. 199. Used by permission.

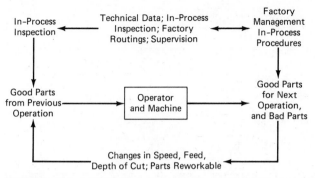

FIGURE 14-4. A Work Flow Diagram for an Organizational Subsystem: the process responsible for the production of scrap.

Source: Stanford L. Optner, *Systems Analysis for Business Management,* 2nd ed., © 1968, p. 38. Reprinted by permission of Prentice-Hall, Inc., Englewood Cliffs, N.J.

diagrams are conceptual schemes rather than organization charts. A traditional chart may be used to depict the technical core of activities represented in the center of Figure 14-3. Another useful technique is to depict various subsystems separately. This is often done in the form of work flow diagrams such as that shown in Figure 14-4.

Matrix and Project Designs

Matrix and project designs are employed in large organizations whose work is diverse, complex, and often highly technical. The designs are found widely in the aerospace industries, for example, as well as in manufacturing firms where major project units can logically be formed.

Matrix structures, the broader category, may be used without project organization, but project structures typically take the matrix form. Figure 14-5 illustrates the structure of an organization set up in a matrix form.

Although matrix organization is not limited to the purpose of combining project and functional structures, it does provide a good way to do so, and to overcome the disadvantages of using either type alone. If project organization is used, technologies are likely to be less developed. If functional structure is employed, important projects may suffer for lack of focused, coordinated attention. Matrix design attempts to secure the benefits of both.[21]

Matrix and project structures are designed less around positional

---

[21]Jay R. Galbraith, "Matrix Organization Designs," *Business Horizons* 14 (February 1971), 29–40. See also John F. Mee, "Matrix Organization," *Business Horizons* 7 (Summer 1964), 70–72. Kenneth Knight, "Matrix Organization: A Review," *The Journal of Management Studies* 13 (May 1976), 111–130; William C. Coggin, "How the Multidimensional Structure Works at Dow Corning," *Harvard Business Review* (January–February 1974), 54–65.

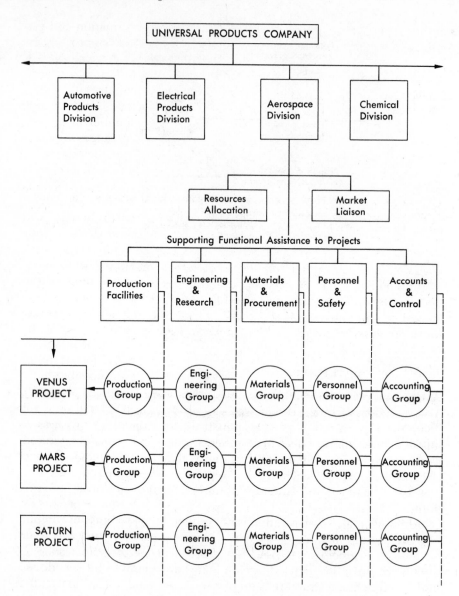

LINE OPERATIONS FLOW OF WORK PERFORMANCE

FIGURE 14-5. Matrix Organization Structure in a Multidivisional Firm.

Source: Fremont A. Shull, *Matrix Structure and Project Authority for Optimizing Organizational Capacity* (Carbondale, Ill.: Business Research Bureau, Southern Illinois University, 1965), p. 81. Used by permission.

authority and more around who has the relevant information and the special skills required for particular, nonroutine missions or projects. In large firms undertaking large and long-range projects, such as the building of a prototype for a supersonic aircraft, project managers are designated to see a project to its completion. When the mission is completed, members of the project team are reassigned. Organization in such a firm, therefore, consists of setting up a number of project groups and administering them through the various stages of their existence. The project manager and his group have specific objectives with a clear terminal point. Such a group does not fit readily into traditional models of organization, although many of the management precepts it adopts are similar.

Project management was introduced in aerospace industries and complex government-industry projects during World War II. Since then it has flourished in a variety of organizations, including universities and military settings. Project organizations work best where large-scale, complex efforts must be coordinated, and where major projects are identifiable as such. Projects and the groups responsible for them are usually temporary, although they may last as long as three or four years. Project structures are useful also to accelerate a program or other result by concentrating efforts and large numbers of specialists for intensive concentration. The Manhattan Project of World War II, for example, accelerated work on the atom bomb, although it would possibly have developed eventually anyway.

The central idea of project organization and associated management techniques is to design the structure around a purpose or a mission, rather than by functions. Where the structure places the functions, such as engineering, production, or research across several projects at the same time, a matrix structure results.

Project structures require temporary allocation of authority and temporary assignments of functional personnel to the project units. For example, if the project requires marketing, financial, production, or research knowledge, these departments assign persons to the project for varying periods of time. When the project assignments are completed, the individuals are redeployed or returned to their functional unit.

Figure 14-6 shows a type of project management in which a central headquarters organization simply sets up project groups or divisions under a manager as needed. The central group provides a permanent source of staff assistance, control, and over-all coordination. Project managers have full authority over projects, but functional activities such as design, testing, and so on are duplicated within each project.

Figure 14-7 illustrates a matrix design in which the functional activities are departmentalized, but managerial authority is shared between functional heads and project managers. Functional managers retain line

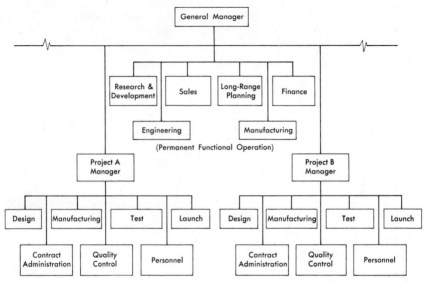

FIGURE 14-6. Pure Project Management, Showing Full Authority of Project Manager.

Source: Reprinted with permission of the Trustees of Columbia University in the City of New York, 1968, from *Industrial Project Management* by George A. Steiner and William G. Ryan.

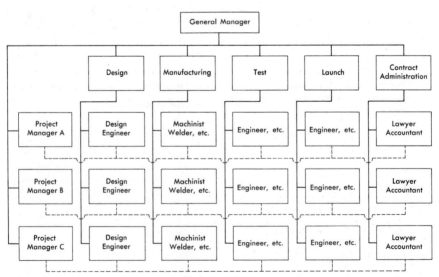

FIGURE 14-7. Matrix Organization in Project Management, Showing Shared Authority.

Source: Reprinted with permission of the Trustees of Columbia University in the City of New York, 1968, from *Industrial Project Management* by George A. Steiner and William G. Ryan.

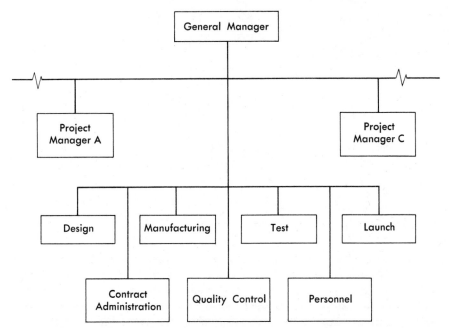

FIGURE 14-8. Influence Organization in Project Management, Showing Monitoring Authority.

Source: Reprinted with permission of the Trustees of Columbia University in the City of New York, 1968, from *Industrial Project Management* by George A. Steiner and William G. Ryan.

authority over their own people, who are assigned to projects temporarily. The project manager builds his team from the people assigned.

Figure 14-8 shows an "influence" type of project organization design, in which the project managers in effect act as staff personnel to the general manager, who supervises the functional groups. The project managers monitor the activities, exerting control through persuasion and influence, with line authority over the functions retained by the general managers.

Project management is used widely in industries with government contracts, such as aerospace industries, in industries in which a considerable amount of planning and coordination must be done, where long lead times intervene between planning and putting a product into production, and where substantial amounts of high-risk research and development work are characteristic.[22] Project management is also useful where management wishes to deal with a one-time project, such as installing a computer system, or where the mission is unfamiliar or

[22]For further information see John Stanley Baumgartner, *Project Management* (Homewood, Ill.: Irwin, 1963); George A. Steiner and William G. Ryan, *Industrial Project Management* (New York: Macmillan, 1968); C. J. Middleton, "How to Set Up a Project Organization," *Harvard Business Review*, 45 (Mar.–Apr. 1967), 73–82.

beyond the managers' previous experience and capabilities, or where the task is complex, involving interdependencies among traditional, functional departments.

Project organization has several advantages and disadvantages. Among the advantages are the accomplishment of major, unusual tasks with a minimum of disruption to the regular organization; improved chances of meeting time, cost, and performance requirements; and the likelihood of innovative approaches. Project methods are most likely to fail when (1) the basis for the project is not sound, (2) the wrong person is appointed project director, (3) top management fails to provide support, (4) task definitions are inadequate, (5) inappropriate techniques are used, or (6) project termination is not planned.[23]

Task Forces and Teams

An evolving structural form, related to committee structure but distinct from it, is that of task forces or teams, consisting of managers drawn temporarily from their regular posts. A task force is similar to an ad hoc committee in that it is usually temporary, but differs in that it has broader powers of action and decision, as well as greater responsibilities for investigation, planning, research, and analysis. Task forces are also usually of longer duration than committees: some, owing to the magnitude of their assignment, have lasted one or even two years. Project designs make use of teams and task forces with members drawn from functional units. They differ from project structures in that they are likely to be of shorter duration, designed for a one-time purpose, and assigned more to planning and study than to execution or operations.

By the task-force device, managers with special qualifications may pool their talents and focus on a major problem with an intensity that would not be possible on their regular jobs. They are freed from the limitations of department-oriented thinking, and from the routine uses of their specialities; the members of the task force can think about the organization as a whole. The advantages of task forces therefore include: (1) unusual training opportunities for the managers so assigned, (2) the effective and economical solving of unusually difficult or unique problems, (3) the release of creative energies not possible under the regular system of authority and communication, and (4) the possibility of introducing innovations in the permanent organization structure by prior trial on a task-force basis.

[23]Ivar Avots, "Why Does Project Management Fail?" *California Management Review* **12** (Fall 1969), 77–82; David I. Cleland and William R. King, *Systems Analysis and Project Management* (New York: McGraw-Hill, 1975); Melvin Silverman, *Project Management: A Short Course for Professionals* (New York: Wiley, 1976); Charles C. Martin, *Project Management: How to Make It Work* (New York: AMACOM, 1976).

Task forces are potentially disturbing to a bureaucratic organization. Department heads must give up the services of key people for an unknown length of time. Moreover, after task-force experience, the members are often promoted or transferred from their original departments; or else, if they return, they are restless. Assignment to a task force marks a manager as unusual in comparison to colleagues and others who have to remain on ordinary jobs. Finally, it tends to create feelings of independence and of being only loosely attached to the formal organization, thus making the managers harder to supervise and complicating the problems of department heads who have been told to build a close-knit group of loyal subordinates. Because these possible difficulties are far-reaching in their significance, the task force should be used with great care.

Free-Form Structures

A type of structure that is compatible with open-systems theory and is also useful in designing large-scale, complex organizations is called the free-form organization structure.

A free-form organization design is constructed so that its major units operate flexibly and independently. It de-emphasizes charts and chains of command; it utilizes independent-profit-center concepts and systems and teams approaches. A small relatively stable central group at the top consists mainly of planners and acts as the center of control and evaluation. The operating units consist of changing combinations of the various functions as different mixes of resources are applied across or within industry lines. Operating divisions are regarded as either temporary or permanent, depending on their potential for generating profit; their additions or deletions are governed by policies on rate of return and on assessments of alternative uses of the resources. Hence a free-form organization is opportunistic, seeking change and development, growth and expansion. It picks and chooses the areas of financial, executive, market and technical capabilities that have high value to the firm's objectives.

Free-form structures have appeared more frequently in some industries than in others, principally in firms whose operations gain or lose by the results. Such a system can be managed as a team or a cohesive group, but its organization structure would be fluid and dynamic.

Free-form structures reduce the emphasis on positions, departments, and other formal units, and on the organizational hierarchy. Forrester even suggests that the traditional superior-subordinate relationship is disappearing; he recommends profit centers rather than functionally divided budgetary units as the major entities. Budgetary units, such as departments of sales or production, are spending units; hence other units must be set up to control them. Thus tensions and conflict arise;

only higher management levels can resolve them, so that a hierarchy is produced. By contrast, profit centers place all contributors to an objective in an integrated, single unit with unified goals, so that all are highly adaptive to products or services on the frontier of public use, such as air-pollution devices, and products meeting an essential and high-demand industrial, consumer, or military need, such as electronic devices. However, the applications vary; there is no universal pattern. The main ingredients are centralized control and decentralized operations, profit-center emphasis, the use of computerized evaluations of performance, and stress on young, dynamic managers willing to undertake personal and corporate risk.[24]

Examples of firms in this group include Litton Industries, Xerox Corporation, and Textron, Inc. The Polaroid Corporation uses a sun-and-satellite concept of free-form chart superimposed on its formal organization. International Minerals & Chemical Corporation uses the idea of "cross-hatching" by employing teams of managers without regard to formal titles or offices, and without the requirement of "only one boss for every manager." Many companies are dispensing with organization charts and manuals, job descriptions, and even position titles to melt the rigidities associated with the lines of formal structures.[25]

Conglomerates

Another example of free-form organization is found in some of the large conglomerate firms. A conglomerate is a company that grows by acquisition and merger rather than by internal means alone, and diversifies into a variety of unrelated industries. The free-form concept is particularly valuable in managing conglomerates because it controls divisions or subsidiaries but allows them autonomy. Not all conglomerates are free form, of course, but many are. In 1967 *Fortune* listed 46 true conglomerates, of which 12 were considered free form.[26] Figure 14-9 shows the 21 divisions of UOP, Inc., formerly known as the Universal Oil Products Company. The change provides a general name for the firm that "encompasses all we do and anything we might do."[27]

Multiple Leadership

The four forms of adaptive organizations just described have one feature in common: they depart from the essentially monocratic nature of

[24]Jay W. Forrester, "A New Corporate Design," *Industrial Management Review* **7** (Fall 1965), 5–17.

[25]John J. Pascucci, "The Emergence of Free-form Management," *Personal Administration* **31** (September–October 1968), 33–41.

[26]Thomas O'Hanlon, "The Odd News About Conglomerates," *Fortune* **75** (June 1967), 175–177.

[27]*Wall Street Journal*, August 7, 1975, p. 9.

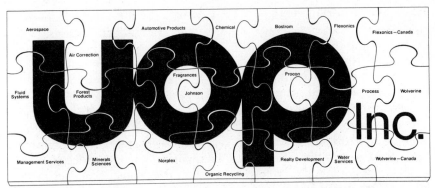

FIGURE 14-9. The 21 Operating Divisions of UOP, Inc. This advertisement appeared in both domestic and international business publications in 1975.
Source: Courtesy of UOP, Inc.

bureaucracy. The advocates of bureaucracy specify *unity of command* as a key principle, but this concept does not hold in adaptive organizations.

Responsibilities and tasks are assigned to units whose superiors are the only ones to possess a legitimate source of authority over subordinates. Communications are vertical, passing upward only through superiors. Jobs must fit completely into supervisory units, and tasks combining activities in two or more parts of the company cannot be assigned to one person. Furthermore, unity of command strengthens centralization and increases the difficulties of integrating staff specialists into the organization. The supervisor's rights to be the only locus of communication and command, and to claim the loyalty of subordinates, restrict subordinates' freedom of interaction with each other across units. The demand of one's colleagues and peers also reinforce this restriction for subordinates; they can hold only one set of legitimate norms and values and enjoy only one set of rights and privileges.[28]

The concept of unity of command has undoubtedly been overemphasized and overidealized by early management writers. There has been little analysis of its assets and liabilities. It has been greatly oversimplified, and advanced as an inviolable tenet. Yet as a principle the concept is belied by the frequency with which multiple-command situations are a fact of life. We are all used to receiving orders of instructions from different authorities present in a situation; a child, for example, typically has two parents to obey.

Revisionists therefore have attacked the idea of unity of command as unrealistic, as unsupportable by evidence, and as thwarting innovativeness and common sense. March and Simon, for example, do not even discuss this concept in their effort to state testable research

[28]Victor A. Thompson, *Modern Organization* (New York: Knopf, 1961), pp. 38, 104, and 107.

hypotheses.[29] Although many situations still call for unity of command (for example lower echelons, military units, small organizations, labor-intensive groups, and organizations that are highly routinized and standardized), students of adaptive organization designs would take account of those situations calling for or benefiting from multiple leadership.

Departures from unity of command should be made only after careful assessment of their consequences for those affected. The risks include the difficulties of putting managers in ambiguous situations, and of increasing the potential for confusion, lack of coordination, and conflict. Uncertainty may lead to error in decisions and other performance characteristics of subordinates. Quick to sense even subtle differences of power or influence among superiors, subordinates are forced to please everyone, ignore orders, or attempt to circumvent the situation.

The President's Office

J. J. Shubert, who with his brother Lee controlled a theater empire, liked to assert his authority. A show that was to open in Boston had run into trouble, and J. J. went to see what was wrong. He found only chaos, with people milling about, but no one taking action. J. J. jumped onto the stage and shouted, "Silence. I want absolute silence . . . From now on there is only one captain on this ship—my brother and me."[30]

Several large firms have adopted the concept of *the president's office*, in recognition of the complexity of decisions and actions at the top. Instead of a single head, the office of the president includes from three to seven executives with equal or nearly equal authority. Among these firms are General Electric, Inc., Mead Corporation, Levi Strauss, Sears Roebuck, and Trans World Airlines.

Multiple presidency systems have the advantage of pooling high-level talent at the top. They also provide a way of adjusting to upper-echelon turnover. By staggering the appointments around retirement ages, for example, continuous leadership can be assured. The office becomes a training ground for executives who otherwise might never get experience in top-level management. One firm, for example, established a president's office in which the holder of the title of president was scheduled for retirement one year later. The vice chairman of the board and an executive vice president made up the president's office. Because the board chairman was scheduled to retire in 1980, this change gave two of the team members ample time to develop the capabilities needed to fill the chairman's slot.

For several years, Levi Strauss & Company has employed an office of the president consisting of the board chairman and the president. Each

[29]James G. March and Herbert A. Simon, *Organizations* (New York: Wiley, 1958).
[30]Jerry Stagg, *The Brothers Shubert* (New York: Random House, 1968).

has specified responsibilities, but each can make decisions in the other's absence. In 1971 they extended the concept one level lower, by establishing a troika to monitor and coordinate operations in all the divisions. One executive was a vice president with responsibility for day-to-day operations; a senior vice president was charged with planning for diversification and new products; another senior vice president was assigned to handle production, distribution, and research.[31]

The Union Carbide Corporation in 1973 established a form of multiple leadership called a Management Committee of the Board. It consisted of four executives: the chairman and the chief executive officer, the president, and two vice-chairman. This committee was formalized to restore top management control, which had been diluted earlier by diversification and decentralization. The committee replaced two devices used by a previous chairman: (1) a general committee consisting of the president and the heads of the eleven operating units, coupled with (2) an informal "president's office" consisting of the president and three senior executives. These changes were made to launch a new, highly structured system of planning to increase central control of budgeting, resource allocation, cost cutting, and development of new markets. The top management system was also changed to emphasize performance objectives rather than human relations, through better planning by individual executives.[32]

Some firms establishing multiple presidencies have reverted to one-person leadership—an indication that the system is not easy to maintain. However, in some of these firms a group system of management remains in some form. The General Electric Company, for example, pioneered the concept of the multiple president's office concept in the early 1960s. The president's office consisted of three vice chairmen who served as a corporate staff for policy making, but who had no direct financial accountability for the operations they monitored. In 1973 a new chairman quietly revamped the entire echelon of the president's office, but without revamping the whole system. The three vice chairmen were given line responsibilities and made financially accountable for the groups reporting to them.[33]

A similar reversal occurred in the Aetna Life and Casualty Company. In 1973 it established a four-person "corporate office," which it described as "not a committee" and "not a decision-making body," but rather a planning and problem-solving group. In 1976, however, this structure was scrapped and "one-man rule" restored. It was believed that the effort to separate planning and decision making did not work, and problems of indecision resulted.[34]

[31]*Business Week*, September 4, 1971, p. 50.
[32]*Business Week*, July 14, 1973, pp. 88–94.
[33]*Business Week*, June 30, 1973, pp. 38–39.
[34]"Making Aetna's Corporate Office Work," *Business Week*, July 14, 1973, pp. 84–85, and "Aetna: Where Group Management Didn't Work," *Business Week*, February 16, 1976, p. 77.

Group Management: An Assessment

Clearly such devices as the president's office and other forms of group or multiple top management have met with mixed success. When established as interim devices to facilitate retirement or turnover problems, they fade when their purpose is accomplished. When they are established by one top executive, they tend to be dissolved when a new chairman or president enters. When established as devices to improve planning and other staff functions, they founder on the shoals of indecision. Still, such techniques have worked successfully for long periods of time, and they appear to be on the increase among large firms.

Unity of command is logical, to an extent, in bureaucracies. Multiple leadership can be expected to function at best in the highest or second highest echelon of a bureaucracy, where executives are more confident, self-assured and successful, and have close personal ties that mold their leadership styles. But further down, there is a greater risk of confusion, doubt, and conflict. Subordinates are insecure or ambitious for advancement and may prefer a single leader. And even at the top, as has been shown, there lingers the thought that one authority at the top is enough. The president of Northwest Industries once said, "In this company if the president doesn't have an opinion, no one else does either"; and "I am the antithesis of free-form management. People do much better when they know what is expected of them and to whom they report. They get nervous and anxious when these things aren't clear."[35]

Multiple leadership plans are well within the concept of adaptive organizations. They are difficult to establish and maintain in the face of bureaucratic structures and assumptions. Indeed, they are a device that, if carefully followed, can cause a system to become more open. Because the concept is usually confined to only one small part of the bureaucracy, it can be utilized without drastically restructuring the entire organization. It can then serve as a role model for other units, if not eventually for the whole system.[36]

SUMMARY

Adaptive organization designs are essentially open systems in which domains or spheres of influence are flexible rather than rigid. Boundaries separating internal relationships from external ones are more permeable. Recognition is given to the fact of high manager mobility

---

[35]*Business Week*, May 26, 1973, pp. 60–61.

[36]John Senger, "The Co-Manager Concept," *Business Horizons* 13 (Spring 1971), 77–83. See also the staff of AMACOM, *The Chief Executive Officer and His Responsibilities* (New York: AMACOM, 1975).

rates and to various devices such as consultantships, whereby temporary affiliations are frequent.

Adaptive models are less compatible with the use of organization charts, because relationships of organization members are flexible and changing. Similarly, job descriptions become less meaningful. Adaptive models favor participative management philosophies, and reward structures are focused on group or individual results rather than on salary grade systems. Motivation derives from system needs and task-related factors, as well as from peer-group pressures, rather from than coercive supervision. Because adaptive models are more ambiguous, they call for staffing with persons high in tolerance for ambiguity, and for self-reliant, independent individuals who do not need close supervision.[37]

We reviewed the significance of systems for organization design, and described five basic types of adaptive structures that go beyond traditional bureaucratic structures: (1) systems designs, (2) matrix and project structures, (3) task forces, (4) free-form organization, and (5) multiple presidencies. These kinds of structures represent open-system applications. With this array of alternatives, managers can build organization designs to fit many purposes, can remain adaptive to the forces of change, and can provide for the growth and development of complex firms such as conglomerates and multinational companies. Each type of structure has major impacts on managerial styles and philosophies.

The price of such adaptive structures appears to be the difficulty of learning to work under conditions of ambiguous authority and unfamiliar reward systems. But the advantages include a higher ability to solve the complex problems faced by modern organizations—problems that are ill-structured and unprogrammable. Creativity and innovation should increase, and job satisfaction should be higher.

_____ **INCIDENT CASE**

At an advanced management seminar, the president of the Mayfair Department Stores, Inc., learned that many organizations are changing to matrix structures. Upon his return to the office, he conferred with Donald Jones, the director of organizational planning, suggesting that Jones look into the matter and assess the possibilities for such a structure at Mayfair. Jones reluctantly agreed to set up a task force to explore the benefits and dangers of the possible change. Jones told the president, however, that he was "not sold on matrix structures" and that the present highly bureaucratized organization design was operating at a very high level of efficiency.

[37]See, for example, Richard Alan Goodman, "Ambiguous Authority Definitions in Project Management," *Academy of Management Journal* 10 (December 1967), 395–407; and John R. Rizzo, Robert J. House, and Sidney I. Lertzman, "Role Conflict and Ambiguity in Complex Organizations," *Administrative Science Quarterly* 15 (June 1970), 150–163.

Questions:

1. As the leader of the task force, what would you do and why?
2. What factors would favor or discourage the proposed idea?

QUESTIONS FOR STUDY

1. Are there any differences in the essentially similar meanings of the concepts of adaptive, organic, natural, free-form, and fluid models?

2. Outline a plan for establishing a task force on new plant location for a company. What instructions would you give?

3. How does the systems concept differ in application between bureaucratic and adaptive models?

4. Depict on paper some of the structural possibilities inherent in the concept of adaptive structures.

5. Why is is said that the manager's role and responsibilities are different in adaptive structures, as compared to bureaucratic structures?

6. What is a conglomerate? Trace the thinking that underlies the design of organization structures for the conglomerate company.

7. Make a list of advantages and disadvantages, as you see them, of the three main types of organization design for project management.

8. To what kinds of industries or situations is matrix organization most readily adaptable? Why?

9. Could you argue that a fixed, rigid structure would be more stable and predictable, and hence a better one for the typical company to use? What support would you use for so arguing?

10. Why do most organizations appear to be of a hybrid type?

SELECTED REFERENCES

BASS, LAWRENCE W. *Management by Task Forces.* Mt. Airy, Md.: Lomond Systems, Inc., 1976.

BATES, F. L., and C. C. HARVEY. *The Structure of Social Systems.* New York: Halsted Press, 1975.

BECKETT, JOHN A. *Managerial Dynamics: The New Synthesis.* New York: McGraw-Hill Book Company, 1971.

BENNIS, WARREN G. *Changing Organizations.* New York: McGraw-Hill Book Company, 1966.

BURNS, TOM, and G. M. STALKER. *The Management of Innovation.* Chicago: Quadrangle Books, Inc., 1962. Chapters 5 and 6.

CARZO, ROCCO, JR., and JOHN N. YANOUZAS. *Formal Organization: A Systems Approach.* Homewood, Ill.: Richard D. Irwin, Inc., 1967. Part III.

CHAPMAN, RICHARD L. *Project Management in NASA: The System and the Men.* Washington, D.C.: National Aeronautics and Space Administration, 1973.

CLELAND, DAVID I., and WILLIAM R. KING. *Management: A Systems Approach.* New York: McGraw-Hill Book Company, 1972.

DAVID, STANLEY M., and PAUL R. LAWRENCE. *Matrix*. Reading, Mass.: Addison-Wesley Publishing Co., Inc., 1977.

DYER, LEE. *Project Management: An Annotated Bibliography*. Ithaca, New York: School of Industrial and Labor Relations, Cornell University, 1976.

EMSHOFF, JAMES F. *Analysis of Behavioral Systems*. New York: Macmillan Publishing Co., Inc., 1971.

GALBRAITH, J., ed. *Matrix Organizations: Organization Design for High Technology*. Cambridge, Mass.: The M.I.T. Press, 1971.

KLEIN, LISL. *New Forms of Work Organization*. (New York: Cambridge University Press, 1976.

MARTIN, CHARLES C. *Project Management: How to Make It Work*. New York: AMACOM, 1976.

MAURER, JOHN G., ed. *Readings in Organization Theory: Open System Approaches*. New York: Random House, Inc., 1971.

MELCHER, ARLYN. *Structure and Process of Organizations: A Systems Approach*. Englewood Cliffs, N.J.: Prentice-Hall, Inc., 1976.

NEGANDHI, ANANT R. *Organization Theory in an Open System*. New York: Dunellen Press, 1974.

PERROW, CHARLES. *Complex Organizations: A Critical Essay*. Glenview, Ill.: Scott, Foresman and Company, 1976. Chapters 1 and 4.

SEXTON, WILLIAM P., ed. *Organization Theories*. Columbus, Ohio: Charles E. Merrill Publishing Company, 1970. Part IV.

STEINER, GEORGE A., and WILLIAM G. RYAN. *Industrial Project Management*. New York: Macmillan Publishing Co., Inc., 1968.

SWINTH, ROBERT L. *Organizational Systems for Management: Designing, Planning, and Implementation*. Columbus, Ohio: Grid, Inc., 1974.

WIELAND, GEORGE F., and ROBERT A. ULLRICH. *Organizations: Behavior, Design, and Change*. Homewood, Ill.: Richard D. Irwin Company, 1976.

Chapter 15

Authority, Responsibility, and Power

Man's greatest challenge is to find someone able to make him do what he is capable of doing.   —*Emerson*

In the setting of today's corporate life . . . the gravest danger comes from those at all executive levels who are adroit enough to wield great power in ways that are pathological, however plausible and effective their bossing methods may momentarily appear.   —*Ordway Tead*

CHAPTER GUIDE

Power is intriguing to those who hold it, as well as to those who labor in its grip. But power relationships are constantly changing, so that organization members must review and perhaps recast their roles in changing power structures. For example, one corporation president, who has seen a decline in the uncontrolled power of chief executives, asserts that board directors must plan an enlarged and more informed role in the management of corporations.

Questions to keep in mind while you read this chapter:

1. What factors have caused this shift?
2. Why do some members of an organization aggressively seek to acquire power, whereas others ignore it or try to avoid it?
3. Is power the same thing as authority?
4. Do leaders need power, or is authority sufficient?
5. How does an organization guard against undesirable uses of power? Of authority?

All organizations must deal with problems of authority, influence, and power. However, bureaucratic and adaptive organizational designs differ in their approaches to these concepts. The purpose of this chapter is to analyze these differences.

The management of the authority and power systems in an organization is more an art than a science. Each organization has a unique pattern of authority; organization members display unique capabilities for influence, power, and responsibility. The structural design of an organization reflects decisions about the formal distributions of authority, but the actual functioning of authority and related concepts is reflected primarily in the ever-changing behavior of people at work.

This chapter describes (1) the concepts of authority and power, (2) the chief types of authority used in designing organizations, and (3) the processes of delegation, responsibility, and accountability.

THE NATURE OF AUTHORITY AND POWER

Numerous concepts of authority exist in everyday life. For example, a person with superior knowledge in a particular field is called an *authority,* meaning an expert. Officials such as the police are referred to as *the authorities.* The expression *authorized dealer* denotes an appointed representative with special rights or permissions. A corporation exists by the sanction of *legal authority.* These meanings of *authority* are useful, but we need a more adequate definition that conveys the meaning in an organizational setting.

We shall define *authority* as *the right of managers to direct the activities of others and to exact from them responses that are appropriate in the attainment of organizational purpose.* The rights of authority are thus not absolute. Rather, they are accompanied by practical limitations, such as responsibilities for decisions and their consequences, and the demands of goal attainment. They are also limited by the contexts in which they are exercised and by the willingness of subordinates to accept the rights as legitimate forms of direction and control.

Authority takes different forms, depending on its source. The most common form is *positional authority,* in which duties, tasks, and responsibilities are associated with defined positions and delegated to the position holder. This process is a bureaucratic one, by which formal expectations as to the nature and scope of authority become explicit.

Positions and titles are approximately indicative of the authority of position holders compared to that of others in the organization, but they are not specific measures of the degree of authority. The mere holding of a position or title does not automatically confer all the authority the manager needs. The true extent of the position holder's authority is measured by the scope delegated by a superior. Moreover, the ability to use this conferred authority depends greatly upon the personal attributes by which managers can win the acceptance of subordinates.

A second form of authority is that derived from knowledge. The *authority of knowledge* belongs not only to professionals or technical specialists, but also, in a sense, to every member of the organization.

Knowledge gives one a degree of authority because those who do not have it risk making wrong decisions. The authority of knowledge is independent of levels or positions. It may not always be prevalent or applied directly, but it can come into play at strategic times. It is a type of authority that points to the use of organic rather than bureaucratic models, for in the former it would assume greater importance. In large organizations, and in those where technology is complex, people with the authority of knowledge are often not managers, or at least not higher managers, thus posing the problem for managers of learning to work with those who know, and to find ways of judging and evaluating the knowledge of others.

The authority of knowledge can sometimes supersede positional or "higher" authority. For example, a company president ordered a product design change without knowledge of its effect on costs. He was forced to rescind the order when a production foreman pointed out his mistake.

A third form of authority is that which depends on a particular situation. In a broad sense, all authority depends on the context, but the term *situational authority* is used most frequently to indicate temporary changes in the distribution of authority. An employee who encounters a fire breaking out does not seek or need a boss's permission to sound the alarm and to order the premises vacated. The situation itself is sufficient to vindicate an action that had no positional or other formal authority to support it. Situational authority is often found evolving in small groups, where leadership roles may shift from one person to another depending on the tasks or problems being faced.

Power and Authority

Authority and power are separate but closely related concepts. Fayol defined authority as "the right to give orders and the power to exact obedience." He distinguished between a manager's official authority of position and his personal authority, which derives from knowledge, intelligence, and experience.[1] Power is the possession of authority, control, or influence, by which a manager directs the actions of others.

[1]Henri Fayol, *General and Industrial Management.* (London: Sir Isaac Pitman & Sons, Ltd., 1949), p. 34.

Power, in effect, reinforces authority, and authority is one of the major sources of power.

Mary Parker Follett introduced the idea of distinguishing *power-over* others from *power-with* others. She considered *power-over* others to be insidious and dehumanizing, and believed that the only legitimate power or authority comes from the mutual influence of superiors and subordinates. If the law of the situation prevails, she wrote, respect for fact and scientific method will assure that "no person has power over another."[2]

Follett's suggestion that power relationships can be eliminated in an organization is unrealistic. In the management of an organization, authority is the central cohesive force. Power reflects political realities within the organization and relates to the subtler, more informal patterns of action and interaction that occur. Power relationships exist with, but also extend beyond, authority patterns within the organization.

Shifts of power occur when key managers leave and are replaced, or when power centers are disrupted by serious events such as financial losses, dramatic changes in technology, or failure to adapt to change. Such events often trigger a power shift in the form of major shakeups at the top. For example, to check a drop in return on assets and a rise in loan losses, and to enlarge the bank's capital base, David Rockefeller, chairman and chief executive officer of the Chase Manhattan Bank, restructured the top management group. He reduced his own power by appointing a new president responsible for all operations, and replaced a four-man executive office with a seven-man committee to back up the new president's activities. Four young and promising executive vice presidents, appointed to the new management committee, were promoted over their peers and in some cases over their bosses. These executives were also given explicit control over staff functions formerly reserved for Rockefeller himself. The underlying aim was to get the entire organization moving in unison and to reduce the power of the separate empires that had become entrenched in the power structure.[3]

Managers acquire power in many ways. Power may be usurped by taking action without appropriate authorization or legitimation; power also accompanies the use of authority in the control, direction, or utilization of wealth and resources. Persons may derive power from greater knowledge, from access to vital information that they can dispense or withhold strategically, or from psychological forms of dominance and aggression directed toward others. Some forms of power

---

[2]Henry C. Metcalf and Lyndall F. Urwick, *Dynamic Administration: The Collected Papers of Mary Parker Follett* (New York: Harper, 1940), chap. 4.
[3]*Business Week*, February 17, 1975.

reside in groups. In every organization there are "power centers," groupings in which managers support one another in efforts to dominate, or to win a struggle for power. Groups in power can apply sanctions or withhold approval or authentication.[4]

Power Strategies

Power strategies reinforce or improve the manager's position in the organization in competition with colleagues or rivals. The hierarchical structure exists, and because it is there to be climbed, it is a challenge. Social and organizational forces press managers to go as far up as they can (although managers differ as to levels of aspiration). Managers who accept the challenge of the hierarchy need strategies focused on this goal. Some are more opportunistic than others, awaiting rather than creating goal-reinforcing events in the environment. Yet many are energetic and determined in their efforts to advance.

Like other types of strategy, power strategies may be positive or negative. Positive strategies favor managers' goals directly by strengthening their position relative to others. Negative strategies reduce or dilute the powers or positions of others in relation to the manager. Both positive and negative strategies may or may not be ethical. The ethical implications of managerial behavior are considered in Chapter 24.[5]

Communications, management styles, and interaction patterns are all instruments of power strategies. By a strategy of selectivity in communicating upward, downward, or laterally, for example, managers keep adverse information under surveillance or tip the balance in their own favor on key decisions. Management styles can be developed to abet strategies reinforcing power and influence. If the strategy is one of rapid, aggressive advance in the system, a hard-driving, hard-nosed management style can help, especially if opponents' styles are quiet, patient, and careful. Interaction patterns are also important. Each day managers make decisions about whom to contact, whom not to contact, and how much time to spend with each person with whom they interact. The strategy of advancement in power, influence, and position requires constant interaction with those who can contribute the most to the manager's goals. This strategy of course can be overdone, and the content of the interaction time is also crucial. But spending time with

[4]Alfred Chandler, Jr., "Structural Conditions of Intra-Organizational Power," *Administrative Science Quarterly* **19** (1974), 22–44; Rami Hofshi and James F. Korsch, "A Measure of the Individual's Power in a Group," *Management Science* **19** (January 1972), 52–61; Virginia E. Schein, "Individual Power and Political Behavior in Organizations: An Inadequately Explored Reality," *Academy of Management Review* **2** (January 1977), 64–72; Rosabeth Moss Canter, *Men and Women of the Corporation* (New York: Basic, 1977).

[5]Many power strategies and tactics, some less ethical than others, are described in Michael Korda, *Power: How to Get It, How to Use It.* (New York: Random House, 1975.

important persons in important places is a key factor in strategies of advancement.

Acceptance by Subordinates

Major contributions to the understanding of authority have been provided by Weber, Barnard, and Simon, who stress the central importance of acceptance of authority by those who are subject to it. Weber was among the first to develop a systematic concept of authority in bureaucratic organizations. He describes a condition of "imperative coordination," defined as the probability that certain commands, or even all commands, from a given source will be obeyed by a given group of persons. This implies a range of conditions under which obedience will occur. Motives dictating obedience will vary from individual to individual and situation to situation. Weber also pointed out that not every case of imperative coordination involves the use of economic means or the presence of economic motives; psychological and sociological elements are always present in the behavior of people in organizations.[6]

Barnard extended the concept of authority, emphasizing the importance of acceptance on the part of individuals subordinate to it:

> Authority is the character of a communication (order) in a formal organization by virtue of which it is accepted by a contributor to or "member" of the organization as governing . . . or determining what he does or is not to do so far as the organization is concerned.[7]

The Barnard concept has widely influenced all current theories of management, including those of Herbert A. Simon, whose pioneering work on decision making accepts and extends this concept.[8]

An essential element of Barnard's definition is that those who are subject to authority voluntarily accept it. Without such acceptance, managers lose whatever power was involved in their authority, and find that their "rights" have become meaningless.

The failure of authority without acceptance can easily be illustrated. Even a casual observer cannot fail to note the many cases in which authority is disregarded by people supposedly subject to it. The United States Constitution, for example, is our ultimate authority in government, yet millions of otherwise patriotic Americans refused to abide by the Eighteenth Amendment prohibiting the sale and consumption of alcoholic beverages. Tremendous legal power could not reverse the

[6]Max Weber, *The Theory of Social and Economic Organization* (New York: Free Press, 1947), p. 324.

[7]Chester I. Barnard, *The Functions of the Executive* (Cambridge: Harvard U. P., 1938), p. 163.

[8]Herbert A. Simon, *Administrative Behavior*, 3rd ed. (New York: Macmillan, 1976).

tide of public unwillingness to accept it. Traffic laws, no-smoking regulations, and many other expressions of high and powerful authority are evaded or disobeyed each day by millions, without lowering, and in some cases even raising, the social standing of the individuals who do so.

Many influences affect the nature of individual responses to the efforts of others to employ authority over them. Among these influences are family life, level of intellectual ability and educational attainment, factors in the environment, personal attitudes, emotions, physical and mental health, and economic circumstances. An individual's response to the exercise of authority may vary considerably from one situation to another. People evaluate each situation at the time they experience it, and respond to it according to complex psychological and sociological variables.

Zones of Indifference

Barnard used the term *zone of indifference* to describe the probability ranges within which organization members accept the authority of others. The idea of a zone of indifference denotes that individuals tend to set specific limits within which they will respond willingly to the exercise of authority over them. Each person defines for himself three categories of possible actions: (1) actions that are clearly unacceptable and will not be carried out; (2) actions that are borderline cases, either barely acceptable or barely unacceptable; and (3) actions that are unquestionably acceptable. This third group constitutes a "zone of indifference." These actions will be performed without question as to the authority that is seeking to put them into effect. An individual accepts these applications of authority because they accord approximately with his understanding of the relationship between himself and his employer at the time he entered into it.[9]

The size of an individual's zone of indifference is related to the values of the inducements to cooperate compared to the burdens and sacrifices involved. According to Barnard, the range of orders accepted will be very limited among those who are barely induced to contribute to the system. From this it follows that the higher the position held in the hierarchy, the wider is the zone of indifference, as shown in Figure 15-1. High-level executives seldom rule out any action or order from higher up. On the other hand, workers at lower levels tend to draw narrow limits in their responses to authority. Their zone of indifference is relatively small. A typist can more readily refuse to do filing than can an executive refuse to join a civic group.

Why is the zone of indifference wider for higher managers than for

[9]Barnard, *Functions*, pp. 168–169.

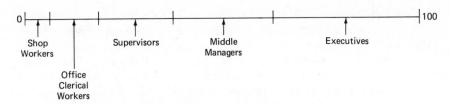

FIGURE 15-1. Zones of Indifference for Various Levels of Employees.

individuals at lower levels? One reason is that organizations give more explicit definitions of lower-level positions for purposes of job evaluation and wage classification. The exacting standards of job definition apply mainly to rank-and-file positions. A more important reason, however, is that managers are trained to accept responsibility and to keep looking upward in the organization for advancement. Managers learn not to count the hours, and to look at their jobs as a 24-hour-a-day proposition. They are expected to think of the total welfare of the institution rather than the narrow confines of their jobs.

_____ **TYPES OF AUTHORITY**

Management practice today makes considerable use of line, staff, functional, and committee authority, and various combinations thereof. All four types can be found in almost every large organization. These types are essentially bureaucratic in nature, and revisionist theories of open systems view them as declining in importance. The organization patterns that accompany these four types of authority were presented in Chapter 12.

Line Authority

Line authority, the basic authority in an organization, is the ultimate authority to command, act, decide, approve, or disapprove—directly or indirectly—all the activities of the organization. It is the authority to direct the work of others and to require them to conform to decisions, plans, policies, systems, procedures, and goals. Line authority is the heart of the relationship between superiors and subordinates.

It is desirable to draw a distinction between the right to decide and the right to direct. Line authority is not *merely* the right to decide but also, more inclusively, the right to direct.

Line authority, although described as a right to direct, is not absolute. Managers are responsible for how they exercise authority and for its consequences. They must use judgment and discretion and stay within the limits of their delegated authority. They must apply authority reasonably to the performance of tasks and the proper execution of policies and procedures. Line authority requires the acceptance of the individuals subject to it.

The primary purpose of line authority is to make the organization work. It does so in numerous ways. First, it provides the basic decisions required for operating an enterprise. It provides the initiating force for actions of all kinds. Second, it makes the leadership process effective by establishing authentic channels of communication. Third, it serves as a means of control by setting limits to the scope of managerial actions. Fourth, it provides points of reference for the approval or rejection of proposals or actions. Without the existence of this ultimate authority, organization members cannot be sure that their activities are appropriate. Securing the approval of higher line authority supports the actions and decisions of subordinates.

Staff Authority

Staff authority is best defined as *authority whose scope is limited, by the absence of the right to direct or command, to such auxiliary and facilitating activities as planning, recommending, advising, or assisting.* In addition, staff units may also have authority to perform certain regular services to the line, such as processing or maintaining records. The need for staff authority arises as the result of problems that managers face as an organization grows larger. Line authority alone becomes inadequate for large-scale organizations, whose managers face an increasing number of details that can best be handled by staff specialists.

Two kinds of staff structures were explained in Chapter 13—the staff assistant, analogous to the general staff in military organizations, which takes the form of "an extension of the leader's personality," and the staff specialist. It is with the staff specialist that we are especially concerned, for this function is the most complicated and difficult staff relationship, and it is in common use in all but the smallest organizations.

A major criterion for distinguishing between line and staff functions is the degree of closeness of the function to the primary objectives of the enterprise. Basic activities, such as production, finance, or marketing, are usually line departments. Activities that consist mainly of assistance, advice, or services cutting across several units are generally set up as staff departments. This does not mean that staff authority is inferior to line authority. It is merely different. The indirect relationship of staff to primary objectives does not necessarily imply any lack of merit or importance.

Pure staff authority has no right to command, except within the staff department itself. In practice, however, this distinction gets blurred. Staff advice or service may be accepted by others much the same as line authority is; staff managers may make command decisions when line managers fail to act or decide; line managers may abdicate their responsibilities; staff managers may be delegated to command authority in certain limited matters.

Staff authority is often misleadingly described as *merely* the authority to advise or to make recommendations to the line. Giving advice does not adequately distinguish between line and staff authority, because line managers may also advise and recommend. The primary distinguishing feature of staff authority is, therefore, that it is devoid of the right to command.

The advisory responsibilities of staff managers are nevertheless tangible and important. They cannot issue orders, so they work by planning, thinking, studying, informing, recommending, persuading, and suggesting. They must be in touch with the problems of top management and of other parts of the enterprise. They must be sensitive to the needs of others and win their confidence by building a record of capable assistance to them. In this manner, they relieve line executives of a burden of details, often technical, which would otherwise be handled less ably or not at all.

The unique contribution made by staff managers consists of specialized skills and complex techniques. Such skills can only be acquired through long training and experience. Managers who staff such units appoint specialists who can direct activities that the managers themselves cannot perform as well. The staff relationship is ideal for this purpose because it permits the specialist to focus managerial attention on major problems that require planning, or that cut across several line functions. An example is the market research specialist who studies consumer preferences so that the design, production, and sales departments may do their work better.

Certain activities and functions are particularly well adapted to staff authority. Among the departments typically classified as staff are the organization's legal, public relations, labor relations, research, and personnel departments. The heads of these departments are staff executives with staff authority. Although results might be affected, such departments could be eliminated, with the functions that were assigned to the staff performed in the line where they originally existed.

A summary of the principal distinctions between line and staff authority is presented in Figure 15-2.

Line-Staff Conflict

A combined line-and-staff structure contains inherent problems of coordination and conflict, which cannot be entirely eliminated but can be managed so as to minimize the problems and gain the benefits of additional staff expertise.

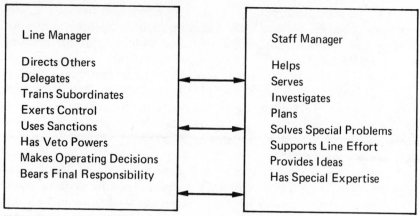

FIGURE 15-2. Comparison of Line and Staff Characteristics.

One approach is to clarify, insofar as possible, the delegations of authority by which each line and staff unit operates. This is a logical step, and written delegations are particularly helpful if one wishes to determine the exact nature of a unit's authority.

Yet even assuming that an effort is made to clarify all delegations, the potential for conflict remains high, for some ambiguity will always remain. Some situations call for line and staff managers to act at the same time without regard to line-staff differences. Often a given department performs line, staff, and functional responsibilities simultaneously, again blurring the distinctions. Finally, the success of line-staff distinctions depends heavily on the attitudes of particular managers. If they do not believe in or approve of the staff concept, it will function with great difficulty.

Confusion between line authority and staff authority is often increased because some staff executives try to exercise line authority. The staff executive exceeds his authority, reaching out for greater power. Frequently the delegating executive abets this process by giving the staff executive a deliberate or implied authority to act in his name. Thus it appears on the surface that a staff executive is exercising line authority, whereas in reality he performs line activities in the name of his superior. These are exceptional cases that must not be allowed to mask the true nature of staff authority.

Line-staff conflict has further sources in the following situations:

1. Specialists may be resented by line executives because of their advanced training or their college educations, and because they differ from managers who came up "the hard way." Some specialists intensify these feelings by their overbearing attitudes.
2. Staff managers are often impatient to put their ideas to work,

losing their sensitivity to tactful and diplomatic persuasion. It is frustrating to see one's ideas held back or delayed.

3. Staff managers may become empire builders by doing unnecessary work or by pushing ideas too hard. Line men often resist change, especially if they do not readily understand what the staff is advocating.
4. Line managers resent the loss of functions that are transferred to staff groups.
5. Line executives with responsibility for high productivity and low costs often see staff managers as impractical. Staff managers spend money fast, and often are highly paid relative to line personnel in the same organization. The staff represents overhead (fixed) costs.
6. Staff managers frequently are closer to top management. Staff gets attention, where line activities are taken for granted.

The above statements represent *possible* differences between the attitudes of line and staff executives toward each other, rather than *necessary* differences. Line and staff executives learn to accommodate many of their differences and to find mutually satisfactory ways of fulfilling their responsibilities by working together.

Functional Authority

The process of departmentalization, which occurs as a differentiation of functions, can take place with all three types of delegated authority—line, staff, and functional. The idea of functional authority must not be confused with the process of functionalizing the organization. Some departments created by this process may be assigned functional authority, but others may receive line or staff authority.

Functional authority, like staff authority, is subordinate to line authority and is a way of putting specialists to work in the organization. The principal difference between staff authority and functional authority is that the latter confers upon its holder the right to command in matters pertaining to that function. Functional authority differs from line authority in that its right to command is limited to a particular, specialized area. Suppose, for example, that a product research department were given functional rather than staff authority; it could then require other parts of the company to follow its orders with respect to meeting consumer product preferences.

The chief weakness of functional authority is that it may subject subordinates to the conflict of multiple supervision. This multiplicity may not always be undesirable, but if it is undertaken the drawbacks should be evaluated. The disadvantage of multiple supervision is mainly that the subordinate dislikes having to choose between an immediate superior and the functional specialist if their orders are in conflict. To some extent, however, the problem is minimized by the fact that line authority—that of the immediate supervisor—tends to prevail in such conflicts. In practice, subordinates often regard the functional managers as important sources of help and guidance as they become aware of their potential contributions.

Functional authority is of limited use. Its main advantage is to provide specialists with a limited scope of command authority. For example, suppose that a production control department found that supervisors were changing the routing and scheduling of materials at will. With functional authority, the production control department could issue final orders on routing and scheduling. Thus functional authority might be delegated temporarily to the production control unit until the supervisors could be trained in correct methods.

Functional authority is most widely used in connection with determining relationships between special groups in a central corporate office and their counterpart groups in a branch or division. For example, the personnel manager in a central corporate office performs staff functions for the corporation as a whole, but in his relationships with the branch plant personnel director he may exercise functional authority in personnel matters. This authority assures that personnel policies are uniform in their main aspects from one branch to another and that the policy influence of the central corporate staff is strong in the affairs of the branch plant.

───────────────── **DELEGATING AUTHORITY AND RESPONSIBILITY**

Every manager has the responsibility of delegating authority. The central idea of delegation is to provide subordinates with a scope of authority appropriate to the responsibilities they undertake. The actual scope of a manager's authority is that received by delegation, as modified by his zone of indifference and the degree to which he aggressively assumes authority not delegated to him.

The manager decides the nature and scope of formal, legitimate authority of subordinates. Authority is not a fixed quantity; it changes as the superior changes the responsibilities of the subordinate. Moreover, a manager may have line, staff, and functional authority at the same time. For example, a personnel director in the corporate office may have functional authority over the plant personnel managers in the branches, staff authority in relation to the rest of the entire organization, and line authority within the personnel office.

The Nature of Delegation

The very core of the organizing process is the establishment of authority relationships among managers and among the positions of those managers within the structure. Delegation is the process by which managers specify the authority of subordinates, so that subordinates share the delegator's work and responsibility. In effect, delegation extends the delegating executive's personal effectiveness and capacities.

In general, authority flows downward from its source at the top. However, this downward flow is not smooth and continuous, for the events that determine this flow are discrete. Moreover, there are upward forces influencing the allocations of authority and instances in which a lateral delegation of authority may occur.

The distribution of authority throughout an organization does not occur automatically. Rather, it is a way for leaders to make authority effective and influential. Without this planned distribution of authority to subordinates, the manager's own tasks become unmanageable.

The subdivision and allocation of work, together with the delegation of authority, account for the establishment of the structural characteristics of an organization. The responsibilities delegated are managerial in character—a subdivision of processes of decision making, planning, organizing, controlling, coordinating, and leading. A vice president in charge of sales, for example, has full responsibility for selling the company's products, but may never contact a customer directly. The need is for the authority to hire sales persons, clerical staff, and advertising specialists and to study market potentials and consumer preferences. It is managerial responsibility rather than a collection of tasks that requires the sales executive's attention.

Accountability refers to the fact that those who are given authority and responsibility will be judged by the manager who delegates. Accountability directs the subordinate's attention to his obligations with respect to a superior, who judges the effectiveness of performance. Accountability grows out of responsibility and goes hand in hand with it. By accepting authority, a person accepts responsibility. To require subordinates to submit their performance for review and evaluation is to hold them accountable for results. This procedure not only requires a form of managerial control but broadens out to include all the techniques and attributes of effective leadership.

Decisions in Delegation

The act of delegating is a deliberate sharing of the delegator's responsibilities with those whose efforts are needed to fulfill them. To delegate wisely, a manager must decide the following questions:

1. What is to be delegated?
2. Why are the selected responsibilities being delegated?
3. To whom are the responsibilities being delegated?
4. What limits should be placed on the authority delegated?

What to Delegate

Deciding what to delegate requires first of all that the manager develop adequate self-understanding. The delegator needs a realistic view of his personal strengths, weaknesses, preferences, and attitudes. Deciding what to delegate results at the same time in decisions about what is retained. The aim is to delegate what can best be done by others and retain the balance for oneself.

Managers who appear to be good delegators often turn out to be delegating work they themselves do not want to do, retaining responsibility for matters in which they are interested or which they have been in the habit of doing. Acitivities they dislike or consider troublesome are delegated without precise thought about the abilities of the subordinates to whom they are assigned. Thus, in many organizations, some people are doing what they should be delegating, and others are delegating what they should be doing.

One may usefully consider what to delegate from three points of view: (1) things that cannot be delegated at all because the delegator can do them best or, for strategic reasons, must keep them; (2) things that can be delegated to others in accordance with their availability and with judgments about their skills and talents; and (3) things that should be delegated because they are so routine that it is sheer stupidity for the delegator to do them. It is not suggested that these categories neatly cover all responsibilities, but they do provide basic guidelines.

In planning the patterns of subdivided responsibility, the delegator may first consider breaking the work into reasonable and logical units that can be performed by others, particularly by people already available. However, certain responsibilities are logically related to more than one group of functions and are therefore difficult to classify. For example, managing customer credit could logically be assigned either to the marketing or to the finance department. The criterion of logical relatedness can be misleading. Strict adherance to the logic of relatedness has often resulted in undue fractionalization of the various parts of integrated processes, with resulting lack of coordination and control. A second important variable for the delegating executive to consider, therefore, is the consolidation of responsibilities and their assignment on the basis of work flows, even though strict logic might suggest some other grouping. Only careful study in each organization will reveal how the criterion of completed work flow should be used to temper the criterion of logic.

Delegations of authority generally consist of broad responsibilities and tasks rather than procedural details.

Why Delegate

The main reason for delegating is to reduce the burden of work the delegator would otherwise have to do. When the quantity of work is too large to perform well, the manager can delegate functions to others who may perform them even better. This device helps to build an organization of people who can do the tasks at which the delegator is less competent or experienced, or else, on the other hand, work that has lost its challenge.

Delegation also occurs as an instrument of developing or changing the organization structure. Although it is often possible to delegate within an existing structure, delegators should also consider the possibilities for structural change. Such factors as the number of levels, effective spans of supervision, and balance in the horizontal and vertical dimensions are relevant to this planning. Moreover, the basic structure is developed by top management, and it is under their continuous scrutiny and control in order to prevent managers from throwing the basic plan out of balance by poor delegating.

A further reason for delegating is the deliberate adjustment and rotation of responsibilities for the purpose of developing subordinates through experience. This takes confidence in the abilities of subordinates. If inadequacies exist, delegating is one means of correcting them. Therefore, effective managers do not hesitate to delegate to weaker subordinates so as to challenge and develop their abilities. Because a group is never wholly perfect, managers must learn to delegate to less-than-perfect subordinates.

Good delegation results in extending the manager's total effort. In effect, managers multiply their personal influence by adroit delegation. They then have adequate time for performing at their best the higher-level duties that come to them by delegation from their own bosses.

To Whom Should Authority Be Delegated?

Among the unfortunate things that can happen with poor subordinates is that work does not get done. When results do not appear, the delegator is accountable. The inability of a subordinate to perform well is a reflection on the delegator, so that the person to whom work is delegated should be selected carefully. The delegator must be sure that the subordinate can carry the responsibility and effort contemplated in the assignment.

This does not mean that the delegator must tailor the work delegated to the precise level of the subordinate's ability. To develop subordinates, or to measure the upper limits of their ability, managers can delegate authority and responsibility designed to stretch their subordinates, who will learn by being pushed beyond their more obvious capabilities. If a goal is set a little beyond the subordinates' reach with average effort, they may show latent abilities that would otherwise never surface. On the other hand, it is not desirable to overdo this. If the goal is too high, the responsibility too great, and the whole effort beyond the attainments of the person even after a hard effort, the subordinate's selfconfidence will be destroyed. Discouragement and frustration will ensue, along with resentment of the boss and organization. Instead of getting work out, the subordinate will tend to resist and to dramatize inner protests.

Clearly delegation should be directed toward those who have the capacity for accomplishment, the talents and abilities needed, and the practical experience of meeting responsibilities. Also, managers delegate best to those they trust and respect, and whose performance they have observed.

Limitations on Authority Delegated

In the process of delegation, the manager confers upon a subordinate the right to act in specified ways and to decide within limited boundaries. The subordinate who accepts the authority exercises it in conformity with the intentions of the superior, within the framework of such controls as that superior sets up.

Delegation outlines the boundaries of what is permissible. Some actions can be classified as planning; others involve the performance of work operations; still others provide for the right of organizing, controlling, deciding, coordinating, or further delegating. The central problem for managers, therefore, is to determine the scope of authority for subordinates, and so frame their communications with them as to map the range of their expected and permitted behavior.

The scope of authority delegated to subordinates is inseparably linked with the nature and number of tasks and duties. We have seen that the range of possible authority available to a delegator is described by the concepts of line, staff, and functional authority. With these variant forms of authority, it is possible to tailor the delegation to the specific needs of each situation. The scope of authority so delegated should be adequate for, but not more than adequate for, the successful performance of the responsibilities assigned, and the kind of authority should be matched to the nature of those responsibilities.

PROBLEMS OF DELEGATION

Five problems must be considered with respect to delegation: (1) responsibility and accountability, (2) delegation without abdication, (3) blocks to delegation and how to overcome them, (4) the exceptions principle, and (5) clarity of authority.

Responsibility and Accountability

Delegations result in the creation of an obligation on the part of subordinates for the satisfactory performance of their assignments.

Some refer to these obligations as *responsibility;* the term *accountability,* however, is better for this purpose, because *responsibility* is more accurately defined as the work or set of tasks assigned to each position holder. The sense of obligation required arises from the way in which the delegator monitors the work to see that it meets certain expectations.

Delegating has the peculiar feature of leaving delegators with as much authority as they had before, even though they have seemingly given it to others. The same is true of responsibility: no matter how much authority is delegated, and no matter what degree of obligation is placed on subordinates, the delegator retains ultimate responsibility and authority for what subordinates do. The delegation of duties does not free managers from personal obligations (responsibilities) concerning them, for he must continue to guide, direct, and hold accountable subordinates to whom he has delegated authority. For example, line executives may delegate hiring to a staff personnel department. The personnel department conducts selection procedures, but the line management, because it retains ultimate authority to accept or reject the personnel department's recommendations, also retains primary responsibility for the success of the hiring program.

Early management theorists declared that delegated authority should "equal" responsibility. This formulation has been attacked because of its spurious mathematical implications. Those who espouse it, however, see mainly a general tendency rather than a mathematical idea. Let us see what kind of case can be stated in favor of an approximately balanced relationship between responsibility and authority.

A state of inequality between responsibility and delegated authority produces undesirable effects in an organization. To see why this is so, we need only question the effects an unequal state. If authority exceeds responsibility, the subordinate is tempted to misuse the authority. An example is provided by the disease "chief-clerkitis," in which a secretary acquires power by acting in the superior's stead, becoming peremptory, condescending, and ruthless in the use of undelegated powers. Unrestrained exercise of authority without responsibility becomes unacceptable to those who are subject to it, producing resistance and subtle forms of nonconformity. Fear, suspicion, and other tensions blight the effectiveness of work under such circumstances.

On the other hand, one who accepts responsibility without authority is in the unfortunate position of being without an adequate means for task performance. Without authority that matches responsibility, managers cannot take appropriate actions; they have no way of compelling others to help them in attaining prescribed goals. In such a position managers become frustrated, losing energy and the desire to be loyal to the organization.

The pressures involved in cases where authority and responsibility are out of balance set up a chain reaction of forces that direct them toward equality. Thus a temporary state of inequality between authority and responsibility is possible. For example, consider the case where a manager is appointed to a new position that will be effective in thirty days. During those thirty days, there is much that he could do if he could act as though he were actually on the new job. In such cases, it is common for the manager to accept certain responsibilities inherent in the new position, on the assumption that when the official change takes place the necessary authority will be his. Others react to him in this interim period as though he actually had the authority that will eventually be delegated to him.

Delegation Without Abdication

A source of concern to managers is the extent to which they lose authority when they delegate it to others. Theoretically, it is retained even though it is delegated to another. Actually, it is quite difficult for a delegator to bestow upon another complete authority and responsibility. It is unusual to find a person in whom the delegator has so much confidence that supervision is unnecessary. It is important in each case of delegation to steer a course midway between two extremes; on the one hand the extreme of laissez-faire attitudes, in which the delegator follows a hands-off policy, and on the other hand the extreme of oversupervision, that is, of annoying the subordinate by constant inquiry and checking.

A reasonable approach to delegation is that the subordinate's results be the objective desired. Authority, in the amount and kind sufficient to get those results, is then delegated to the subordinate. The delegator remains the final arbiter of results. But considerable latitude can be allowed where the subordinate is competent in the selection of methods. Left to determine how to do the work and trusted to work cooperatively and efficiently with others, most subordinates will have performed well under such autonomy.

The subordinate, however, may need or desire the help of the delegator. To avoid the risk of the subordinate blindly accepting the boss's way as best, or becoming too dependent on the boss, the manager should take time to talk at length with him and to raise questions that will lead the subordinate to think constructively about the work delegated. As the work progresses, the subordinate may occasionally check to reaffirm a sense of direction, or the superior may make judicious inquiries to see how the subordinate is doing.

Blocks to Effective Delegation

Some executives do not delegate because they feel compelled to maintain tight control over everything. They have a passion for details, power, influence, and the enjoyment of constant interaction with subordinates. They like the busyness and security of work piled high on their desks. Doing tangible work is pleasurable, whereas thinking, planning, and other less tangible activities are difficult. They become habituated to the constant flattery of subordinates bringing matters to them for approval.

The failure to delegate has four serious weaknesses. First, it prevents the preparation of the subordinate as a replacement. Second, the self-development of subordinates is stifled. They are not properly motivated to make their best contributions to the organization. Third, the dominant manager is so overburdened with details that it is impossible to work efficiently. Fourth, the manager may not be as omniscient and infallible as his failure to delegate implies. The boss can make mistakes and foregoes help that subordinates could otherwise give.

Attitudes Toward Subordinates

Because the delegation of authority is a particular kind of relationship between bosses and subordinates, the manager's attitudes toward subordinates are important for good delegation. Two particular attitudes are blocks to effective delegation: fear or distrust of the subordinate, and lack of confidence in him.

The fear that others cannot do the work as well as the delegator is real. It is often true that performance may suffer when tasks are delegated. But because quality will also suffer when the manager is overburdened, it is better to delegate (provided the delegation is wisely carried out). Part of the manager's job is to teach subordinates and to help them develop their capabilities. Such teaching pays dividends, for when the subordinate acquires experience the delegator is relieved of burdensome detail. Deficiencies in the subordinate's performance are then temporary, and are ultimately the price of better performance by both superior and subordinate.

The fear of a subordinate's potential growth is also real. It takes two forms: first, the subordinate becomes a contender for the boss's job; second, the subordinate may win a promotion to some other part of the organization, and the delegator would thus lose a good employee.

These fears lead to defensiveness on the part of the delegating manager, who simply fails to delegate the scope and kind of authority that would have such results. Unless the delegator has self-confidence and some assurance of moving up, subordinates are widely restrained. Delegation improves when the manager is training a replacement. On the other hand, as delegators level off and get older, they tend to guard their positions more cautiously and in subtle ways will block the growth of subordinates by not delegating more and more complex assignments.

Overcoming Blocks to Delegation

Delegation, like other management processes, can be learned. The behavior of managers who know how to delegate authority properly can be studied and lessons drawn from their experience.

Because the principal blocks to delegation are psychological, it follows that one important requirement in overcoming them is to remove the elements of fear and frustration. It is important to create an atmosphere in which managers feel confident that good delegation will be rewarded and will not penalize them. In one company, once a month, the general manager picks the name of a first-line supervisor or member of middle management at random. The one selected gets an additional two weeks' vacation with pay, provided that he can leave immediately without affecting the organization's work. Although this is a "gimmick," it illustrates how important the company considers delegation and provides tangible rewards for it.

Top management can set good examples to teach those below them that delegation is a prime characteristic of promotable managers. Many companies include the techniques of delegation in training courses by making delegation a definite standard of evaluation.

The Exceptions Concept

Delegated authority, in effect, sets limits within which the subordinate may act. When a situation calls for a decision or an action beyond these limits, the subordinate is usually instructed to refer the matter to the next higher level for an authoritative decision. This is called "the exceptions principle." An example of the way this principle works can be found in the case where a sales representative requests the sales manager to provide a company car. If past policy has been for salesmen to drive their own cars, an exceptional case is now before the sales manager. The decision would then be referred to the next higher level, the vice president in charge of marketing. Thus the exception to the sales manager's right to decide becomes part of the routine decision making that the vice president retains. Decision making at a given level thus may include the handling of problems referred from the level below. Therefore it is important that the delegating manager has allocated decision making to appropriate levels.

Clarity of Delegated Authority

A special problem related to deciding the scope of authority is that of achieving clarity. The manager who has carefully subdivided tasks and distributed authority may feel comfortable about the results without recognizing that subordinates may not agree. It is important that the manager's views of authority are understood and accepted by others.

The need for clear authority has been overemphasized, but the problem is serious. Leaving doubts as to the scope of authority leads to confusion and conflict. If managers are not sure of their authority, their capacity to act is impaired, slowing up the work of the organization, causing conflicts, and paving the way for the illegitimate usurpation of authority.

The best safeguard is to realize the need for constant clarification and interpretation of delegated authority. The manager cannot set down once and for all the scope of authority for subordinates. A manager who delegates authority to another creates a new relationship—one that is continuous and will be subject to many changes throughout its existence.

The delegating executive can use a number of techniques to achieve the goal of sufficient clarity of authority. Organization charts and manuals may provide specific points of reference. Also, all delegations should be in writing. Whenever a delegation of authority remains in oral form, it is subject to distortion, misunderstanding, and forgetting. When the authority is in writing, it is more likely that both parties will understand the exact nature of their working relationship.

A further procedure is for the manager to monitor the performance of subordinates. Through frequent and strategically timed observations of the subordinates' performance, the manager can spot the erosion by which subordinates have either enlarged the scope of their authority or omitted important tasks. An array of communication techniques, such as staff meetings, planned discussions, or open-door policies, can also help to clear up ambiguities. All of these techniques depend, however, on consistent effort to observe what is going on and to keep in close touch with subordinates.

Clarity of authority, important as it is, should not be considered the cure for all problems of organization and management. Unclear authority usually leads to problems, but clarity of authority alone does not eliminate the need for the intelligent application of other managerial skills.

The manager should not be misled by his desire for clear lines of authority. If overly idealized, the need for clear authority can introduce counterbalancing strains that may prove undesirable. To a substantial extent the manager is not really in complete control of the nature or amount of authority delegated. Subordinates manifestly can influence the process of delegation. They do so in three chief ways: (1) by exercising authority beyond the scope allotted to them, or by otherwise becoming instruments through which situational authority is actualized; (2) by a conscious, deliberately planned reaching for opportunities to seize greater authority and to widen their scope of authority either permanently or temporarily; and (3) by deliberately warping, ignoring, or misunderstanding instructions, policies, and so on. If the scope of authority is too rigidly defined, the initiative and individuality of particular managers may be curtailed. Complete abolition of decisions outside the manager's allotted scope of authority probably is not possible, but to the extent that it is achieved it may circumscribe the development of leadership among energetic and aggressive managers.

A certain dread of the empire builder often distorts the thinking of managers. It is true that the empire builder poses a threat to the security and well-being of others. The aggrandizing manager whose empire is built at the expense of the welfare of the organization as a whole is a type we can least well countenance. The danger of empire building lies in the way it can fragment the total effort into a collection of competing rather than cooperating units. This must not be allowed to happen, but it is also well to recognize that often the best contributions of some individuals cannot be elicited under rigidly restricted authority. The striving for results, for better accomplishment, and for recognition from superiors causes managers to strain against narrow ties of authority. Thus managers often wish for employees who are "more willing to assume responsibility." In so doing they may be inviting them to bid for authority that is not granted to them.

It is clear that the delegator's principal problem in determining the scope of authority for subordinates is twofold: first, to encourage self-satisfied managers to give more of themselves to the organization by removing the shackles of rigidly applied authority, and second, to restrain aggrandizing managers who have only their own power and influence in mind.

Authority in Adaptive Organizations

In flexible, adaptive organization structures, authority is much more ambiguous and changing. The demands for clarity, formal delegation, and close supervision are mandates of the bureaucratic model. In adaptive organization designs, authority relationships are more subtle.

The ways in which authority is applied differ substantially in adaptive models as compared to bureaucratic ones. Moreover, the management problems surrounding authority are different. In general, authority in adaptive models is less obvious. It is not considered important for its own sake; it is more flexible, ambiguous, and changing, more closely related to short-run needs. In adaptive organizations, there is a greater emphasis on situational authority and the authority of knowledge, and a lesser emphasis on the authority of positions or other formal delegations. Tasks and work flows form the basis of work teams or groups. Informal relationships, democratic values, and the techniques of persuasion predominate over command. There is a design of information flow so that the proper information reaches the right place at the right time, and no one has access to unneeded or illegitimate information that would enhance individual political power.

Under such organization designs, the manager's role is one of managing change. As structure is fluid, so also is the underlying system of authority. As professionals, managers must work under conditions of more ambiguous authority than heretofore has been thought desirable.[10]

_____ **DECENTRALIZATION OF AUTHORITY**

Large organizations have found it necessary to organize systems of decentralized authority. *Decentralization of authority is* defined as *the degree to which an organization places authority and responsibility for decisions as far down in the organization as efficient management permits.* This is done by creating, under a central organization, a number of relatively autonomous units, and delegating appropriate authority to them. In the General Motors Corporation, for example, each automobile division has full responsibility for results and authority commensurate with that responsibility. The automobile divisions are regarded as competitors with each other with respect to costs, prices, efficiency, profits, and penetration of the automobile market. These units are sometimes called "profit centers."[11]

A program of decentralization was inaugurated in 1940 in the General Electric Company. This program involved extensive decentralization in which each "department" was set up as a business small enough for one manager to take full responsibility. There are now over 80 independent operating units, called departments, organized into 22 divisions, which in turn constitute four major operating groups and one distribution group. The "departments," however, are the basic units of the structure, and in other firms these would be called divisions or subsidiaries.

Decentralization is a necessary policy for the diversification of large corporations, such as holding companies, conglomerates, or free-form organizations. Diversified companies produce a variety of products or services, not necessarily for the same markets or with similar production processes. Esmark, Inc., a holding company made up of the former Swift & Company and several firms it acquired, established one thou-

---

[10]Richard Alan Goodman, "Ambiguous Authority Definition in Project Management," *Academy of Management Journal* 19 (December 1967), 395–407; Richard M. Hodgetts, "The 'Authority-Gap' in the Project Organization," *Business Perspectives* 4 (Summer 1968), 25–29.

[11]Decentralization in General Motors is thoroughly analyzed in Peter F. Drucker, *The Concept of the Corporation* (New York: Day, 1946). See also Alfred P. Sloan, Jr., *My Years With General Motors* (Garden City, N.Y.: Doubleday, 1963).

sand "profit centers," each a "bite-sized bit." Each center has consider-able operating authority, and each reports to one of four major subsidi-ary "holding companies." Decentralization is everywhere except for corporate financial controls. The establishment of the four subsidiaries allowed the chairman to be freed from operating decisions, and to deal only with his immediate staff and the heads of the four major units. It reduced his span of control to four line managers and a few staff executives.[12]

Other principal advantages of decentralization of authority relate to decision making. The larger the company, the more urgent is the need for decentralization, because greater size increases the number and difficulty of decisions for top management. In addition to size, further complexity in decision making is introduced if there are wide variations in the number and nature of products, services, and markets. In such organizations, it is imperative to get decisions made promptly, in a timely manner, and without the undue delay that decentralization involves.[13]

Extreme autonomy of operating units could conceivably have the undesirable result of too much fragmentation, posing problems of coor-dination and control. If the subsidiary units become too independent, will the parent organization lose its identity, its importance, or even its control? And what about the units themselves losing a mutuality of interests in one another? These are real dangers. Both General Motors and General Electric have met these problems imaginatively, however. In both companies, the central organization controls through broad policies; through its right to evaluate performance and set standards; through central programming, financial, and accounting mechanisms; and through the provision of technical staff services. However, decen-tralization of authority as practiced in large corporations is no simple answer to complex problems of organization. Some decentralized com-panies have experienced control and cost problems. The large, decen-tralized conglomerates have faced heavy losses as well as great profits.

Not all parts of an organization can be decentralized. For example, UAL, Inc., the holding company for United Airlines and Western International Hotels Company, decentralized the marketing functions of United Airlines but not its flight operations. Three regional divisions were set up, with 1700 profit centers; marketing was the first function to go under the new divisional structure. The eleven new regional vice presidents found themselves with the authority to establish special promotion packages or to veto the use of corporate advertisements in their regions. Department heads reporting to the vice presidents

[12]*Business Week*, August 3, 1974, pp. 48–49.
[13]Andrew F. Sikula, "Administrative Authority: Its Genesis and Locus," *Business and Society* **15** (Spring 1975), 22–30.

received full authority for all marketing decisions in their units. The result was quicker decision making on the scenes of action, under policy guidance from the central headquarters. Managers of the profit centers were given full responsibility for productivity and cost control.[14]

SUMMARY

This chapter has traced the meaning of the concepts of power, authority, and responsibility in organizations. Authority is a form of power or influence over others; it is made legitimate by the acceptance of those subject to it. We defined three types of authority: line, staff, and functional. Line authority bears the ultimate rights of decision and command. Staff and functional authority are modifications of line authority, each representing a special kind of limitation on the scope of authority. Staff authority is limited to planning, recommending, or advisory rights, stopping short of the right to command. Functional authority has the right to command only in matters directly related to a specifically designated area of activity. Functional authority and staff authority are used chiefly to provide the line organization with the benefit of specialists in particular areas.

The organizational processes that result in the creation and maintenance of organizations are closely centered upon the use of authority. Skill in building, developing, and strengthening an organization structure must be based on a knowledge of the sources from which authority rises and an awareness of the conditions under which authority can make an organization effective in achieving its purposes.

Delegation of authority is the process by which managers legitimize and empower the work of subordinates. Delegation involves three main steps: assigning duties, granting permission to act, and creating obligations for satisfactory performance.

In assigning duties, the delegator considers the scope of the work to be done and how it may best be subdivided among subordinates. In granting permission to act, he allocates specific authority to the particular individuals. The scope of authority depends upon the abilities of the persons, or upon the delegators' estimate of their abilities compared with the needs of the organization. In determining the scope of authority managers must consider the amount and the type (line, staff, or functional) of authority to be delegated. Finally, they must control the whole process of delegating by holding subordinates accountable for

[14]*Business Week*, June 29, 1974, pp. 66–69. See also Ronald G. Greenwood, *Managerial Decentralization* (Boston: Lexington, 1974).

the quality of their performance. Authority must be commensurate with responsibility if tensions and conflicts within the organization are to be avoided. Social and psychological blocks to effective delegation are inevitable, but they can be minimized.

Whereas delegation distributes authority to individuals, the process of decentralization denotes the extent to which authority is distributed downward in the organization.

INCIDENT CASE

Winston Smith, the corporate vice president of personnel relations of a large, multiplant manufacturing firm, decided that changes were needed in the company's program of job evaluation. Because he thought the changes were rather extensive, he devised a new plan and persuaded one of the branch plants to try it out. A committee evaluated the new plan as highly successful in that plant, and Smith ordered the personnel managers in nine other plants to install the new system. Shortly thereafter, he received a telephone call from the personnel manager in Plant X in a distant city, to the effect that "the plant manager here likes the system the way it is, and he doesn't want anyone from the ivory tower telling him how to run his factory. Therefore I don't feel that I can go ahead with the new plan."

Questions:

1. What has led to this problem, and why?
2. What is likely to happen next?

QUESTIONS FOR STUDY

1. Explain in your own words Barnard's concept of authority in an organization.

2. On what basis do employees decide whether the authority of a supervisor may be exercised over them?

3. Define staff authority. Why is it incorrect to define staff authority as the right of the specialist to advise?

4. What is meant by line authority? Could an organization operate without it? Why or why not?

5. How does a manager know how much authority he has?

6. What keeps managers from exercising too much authority or from becoming too domineering through the use of authority?

7. How can an organization be run democratically without sacrificing the "authority" of those in charge?

8. What is the chief difference between line authority and functional authority?

9. List the qualities you think a manager should have in order to be a good delegator. Give reasons for each of the qualities you list.

10. Answer the assertion that a manager who is a good delegator will have nothing to do, because everyone in the organization will be doing the work.

11. Suppose you are the supervisor of a manager who is not good at delegating. What would you do, and why?

12. What would you recommend doing, if anything, about the fact that in many cases a manager can do better the tasks to be delegated to others?

13. How can you prevent overlapping authority in an organization? Is overlapping authority really bad? If so, why and in what way?

14. Should authority and responsibility be equal? Can they be equal?

15. Describe the steps you would take to make sure that the authority you are delegating to others is clear.

16. List some advantages to the manager of *not* keeping lines of authority clear.

17. What are some of the main sources of authority other than delegation?

SELECTED REFERENCES

BARNARD, CHESTER I. *The Functions of the Executive.* Cambridge, Mass.: Harvard University Press, 1938. Chapter 12.

DAHL, ROBERT A. *After the Revolution: Authority in a Good Society.* New Haven, Conn.: Yale University Press, 1970.

DALTON, GENE W., LOUIS B. BARNES, and ABRAHAM ZALEZNIK. *The Distribution of Authority in Formal Organizations.* Boston: Division of Research, Graduate School of Business, Harvard University, 1968.

ETZIONI, AMITAI. *A Comparative Analysis of Complex Organizations: Power, Involvement and Their Correlates.* Rev. ed. New York: The Free Press, 1974.

FILLEY, ALAN, ROBERT J. HOUSE, and STEVEN KERR. *Managerial Process and Organizational Behavior.* 2nd ed. Glenview, Ill.: Scott, Foresman and Company, 1976. Chapters 6 and 17.

GAMSON, W. A. *Power and Discontent.* Homewood, Ill.: The Dorsey Press, 1968.

JAY, ANTONY. *Management and Machiavelli.* New York: Holt, Rinehart and Winston, 1968.

MAHLER, WALTER. *Structure, Power, and Results.* Homewood, Ill.: Dow-Jones–Irwin, Inc., 1975.

MCCLELLAND, DAVID G. *Power: The Inner Experience.* New York: Irvington Publishers, Inc., 1975.

MCGREGOR, DOUGLAS. *The Human Side of Enterprise.* New York: McGraw-Hill Book Company, 1960. Chapters 11 and 12.

———. *The Professional Manager.* New York: McGraw-Hill Book Company, 1967. Chapters 8 and 9.

METCALF, HENRY C., and LYNDALL F. URWICK. *Dynamic Administration: The Collected Papers of Mary Parker Follett.* New York: Harper & Row, Publishers, 1940. Chapter 4.

NISBET, ROBERT. *Twilight of Authority.* New York: Oxford University Press, 1975.

SPRIEGEL, HANS B. *Decentralization*. Fairfax, Va.: Learning Resources Corporation, 1976.

SWINGLE, PAUL G. *The Management of Power*. New York: Halsted Press, Inc., 1976.

THOMPSON, VICTOR A. *Modern Organization*. New York: Alfred A. Knopf, Inc., 1961. Chapters 4 and 8.

ZALEZNIK, ABRAHAM, and MANFRED F. KETS DE VRIES. *Power and the Corporate Mind*. Boston: Houghton Mifflin Company, 1975.

Chapter 16

Organization Change

It must be considered that there is nothing more difficult to carry out, nor more doubtful of success, nor more dangerous to handle, than to initiate a new order of things.   —*Machiavelli,* The Prince

It is not now as it hath been of yore; Turn where so e'er I may, By night or day, The things which I have seen I now can see no more.   —*Wordsworth*

CHAPTER GUIDE

While running for the presidency in 1976, Mr. Jimmy Carter described our government in Washington as a "horrible bureaucratic mess." He promised to give top priority to a drastic and thorough revision and reorganization of the federal bureaucracy, and the procedures for analyzing the effectiveness of its service. Every president from Mr. Hoover to Mr. Nixon has expressed a similar intention to simplify and change the structure of the federal government.

Questions to keep in mind while you read this chapter:

1. Why have our presidents failed to achieve significant improvements?
2. Is more than "politics" involved?
3. Since taking office, to what extent has Mr. Carter succeeded or failed in his reorganization objectives?
4. Are business firms as difficult to improve as government bureaucracies? Why or why not?

The earlier chapters of this book presented a view of the organization process as an evolving one. Organization dynamics depicts the organization as it changes over time. Such changes lead to changing modes and preferences in organization design and leadership style. This chapter presents an analysis of organizational change and the problems it poses for managers.

Change is one of the most pervasive and complex forces with which organizations and their managers must reckon. Changes occur in people themselves, in organizations, and in the social, political, and economic environments. Apart from catastrophic events, changes occur within patterns of stability for both societies and organizations.

The first thing to note about change is the range of attitudes and reactions to it. For some, organizational change is beneficial; for others it is a threat, a danger, and a source of fear. For some, change is a challenging game, a vital life force; for others, it is a disturbance to be avoided or borne with stolidity and patience. The attitudes evoked by change are largely dependent on the context of the situation, the nature and the extent of change, and the manner in which changes are initiated and executed. This is why managerial skills are highly attuned to problems of change.

THE NATURE OF ORGANIZATION CHANGE

It is important to note the difference between organizational change and individual change, although the two are closely related. Organizational change alters prescribed, structured relationships and roles assigned to members. Individual change is behavioral—determined by the characteristics of members, such as their personality, needs, skills, values, and beliefs. Thus a focus of change can be either through the redesign of organizational structure or through attempts to change people by means of training and discipline; or it can be both.

Attempts to make organizational changes by modifying either structure or individual behavior alone run the risk of ignoring the interdependence of the two kinds of change. Hence the complexity of managing change makes it necessary for managers to understand both the structural and the psychological approaches to change.

It often appears that organization structures are fixed, a view that is reinforced by what happens when a vacancy occurs. The procedure is often to keep the position, title, and salary constant, and to "fill it" with a person possessing "the qualifications of the position." Positions are relatively stable, although organization members may change. This phenomenon is one of the main attributes of the bureaucratic model. Slow or infrequent changes are also seen to indicate rigidity.

Actually, however, the static nature of organization structures is illusory. It is the result, in part, of the fact that managers are often conservative about changes, so that gradual changes in existing structure can be mistaken for the absence of any change at all. A further contributing factor is the strong "instinct for survival" that attends an organization structure and its component parts. The very perpetuity of an organization may tend to overshadow the changes going on within its structure.

Some organizational changes are nonstructural in character, though they may arise from, or affect, structural change. Policies, procedures, techniques, and personnel changes may be essentially nonstructural, but they are nevertheless important. Some changes are more visible than others, and hence appear more dramatic. For instance, a shakeup in the top echelon where a president is ousted is readily apparent; changes in the paint department of a manufacturing firm may be noted by a very few.

Changes in organizations may be subject to distortions arising from managerial attitudes. There is a tendency to play down the seriousness of drastic change, and to magnify the importance of small changes to enhance a manager's reputation as a person of action. Changes must be made acceptable, and distortions help to smooth them over. For example, to gain acceptance a change may be described by its proponents as "inevitable," where in reality there are other alternatives.

Change as an Issue

Researchers are not in close agreement about the extent to which organization change occurs. Greiner, for example, describes change as revolutionary rather than evolutionary,[1] whereas Perrow describes change as "glacial."[2] The argument for vigorous change is based on descriptions of the environment as turbulent, with drastic forces, technological and social, forcing change upon the organization. Opposing views, such as those of Perrow, hold that dominant perceptions of change are exaggerated, and that more skepticism is needed.

On balance, it seems right to suggest, as does Perrow, that we have uncritically accepted the idea of rapid, revolutionary change, thereby ignoring the existence of stability in the world of organizations. On the other hand, we cannot ignore the very real changes going on in technology, political systems, values, and beliefs, together with their implications for management practice and organization theory. The position taken in this book is that change is real, and that organizations must cope with it or fail to survive. At the same time it should be noted that

[1]Larry E. Greiner, "Patterns of Organization Change," *Harvard Business Review,* May–June, 1967, pp. 119–130.

[2]Charles Perrow, "Is Business Really Changing?" *Organization Dynamics* 3 (Summer 1974), 30–44.

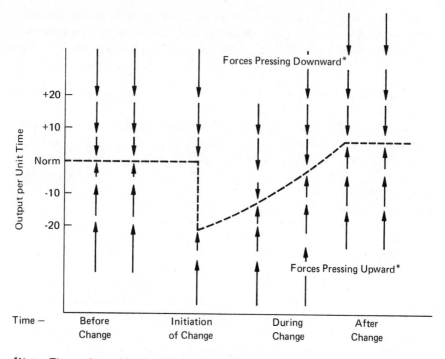

*Note: The number and length of the arrows is roughly a reflection of the number and strength of forces at that point.

FIGURE 16-1. Major Change as a Social Process.

Source: Floyd C. Mann and Franklin W. Neff, *Managing Major Change in Organizations* (Ann Arbor, Mich.: The Foundation for Research on Human Behavior, 1961), p. 63. Used by permission.

all organizations are not affected in the same way by change, and that generalizations about change should be framed with regard for the forces of continuity and stability.

The dynamic nature of organizational structure derives from the fact that it stands in a position of mutual interdependence with almost every major problem or activity. This means that the problems affect the structure and the structure affects the problems. A change in one sector has an impact on the other. Change problems must therefore be viewed within the context of a sociotechnical system, as illustrated in Figure 16-1, which shows how upward and downward forces maintain a system in equilibrium. But when the forces in one direction change in relation to the others, a new constellation of forces will arise, and the level of the ongoing process will change accordingly. This type of change model focuses attention on the idea of a total field of forces at work under given conditions; the element of time before, during, and after the change; and the effects of given strategies of change on the level of activity within an organization.

SOURCES OF CHANGE

There are many sources of organizational change, but their impact depends on whether or not managers notice the forces of change and evaluate them as significant. Some changes, such as new legal restrictions, must be made; others are voluntary and are matters of managerial judgment.

Among the chief sources of change are the following: (1) growth and decay, (2) the internal and external environments, (3) new personnel, (4) change agents, and (5) the domino effect. Although these categories of sources are not mutually exclusive, they provide a useful framework for the sections that follow.

Growth and Decay

Growth presents many problems and opportunities for change. Such change is gradual when growth occurs through internal vigor of product lines, services, or market penetration. Change is more extensive when growth occurs from mergers, acquisitions, or exceptionally rapid success in organizational activities. Growth leads to the need for more employees at all levels, more functions to be established, and old functions to be changed or eliminated. Patterns of work flow must usually change. A greater total effort must be provided for by new organizational arrangements.

Decay, too, poses change problems. The decline of organizational vitality can result from failures to change in appropriate ways. It leads to defensive, restorative changes aimed at survival and the eventual resumption of growth.

Although organizational change is associated with cycles of growth and decay, it may also occur within conditions of static equilibrium. Growth and decay theories take a biological or an organic view: that by analogy the organization is like an organism, with various stages of growth and states of health. Although this view is subject to the limitations of reasoning by analogy, organizations do appear to have alternating periods of growth, stability, and decline, and much light has been thrown on the problems of organizational change by research based on organismic approaches.[3]

Growth-oriented change inspired by potential decay is illustrated by the case of a firm that found its profit greatly eroded by problems of the economy, depressed prices, and overcapacity. Moreover, competition

[3]Mason Haire, "Biological Models and Empirical Histories of the Growth of Organizations," in Mason Haire (ed.), *Modern Organization Theory* (New York: Wiley, 1959); Warren G. Bennis, *Changing Organizations* (New York: McGraw-Hill, 1966), chap. 3; Chris Argyris, "The Organization: What Makes It Healthy?" *Harvard Business Review* **36** (November-December 1958), 107–116.

had grown increasingly fierce. The firm developed a streamlined program that included entering new fields—such as ethical drugs, electronics, consumer educational services, water treatment, and building products—and starting cost-cutting programs. The organization structure was also subjected to drastic change. "People are getting shuffled around so fast I'm not even sure where my office will be tomorrow," said one manager. Organization changes include the acceleration of the move toward establishing each of its twelve major divisions as a "profit center," with complete profit and loss responsibilities. The executive committee, consisting of the president and eight vice presidents, each assigned to act as a primary liaison with one or more of the operating or staff units, was restructured.

Mergers and Acquisitions

Mergers and acquisitions represent a particular problem in reorganization, for structural changes and role assignments are needed to obtain efficient , coordinated operations. Mergers and acquisitions are undertaken for many reasons, such as consolidating or increasing capital, pooling managerial talent, using facilities more efficiently, increasing production and marketing capacity, and achieving vertical integration. In short, mergers and acquisitions are actions that foster growth of at least one party to the change, and are often a tactic against decay on the part of the others.

Mergers may be of the product-extension type or of the market-extension type. Product-extension mergers are the less important. In such mergers, the firm adds to its product line but remains generally within its main industry of field of expertise. The majority of mergers in recent years have been of the market-extension type, such as those of the conglomerates in which the acquiring and acquired firms have few if any common domains. An important goal of organization in this kind of merger is to cope with the problems that arise from managing unrelated acquisitions that are foreign to the existing expertise of the original firm. This process is called product diversification.

When two or more firms combine through merger, or when one or more firms are acquired by a company, organizational problems, including problems of structure, arise. In such cases, companies usually need to consolidate and eliminate positions. Premerger planning can to some extent take account of probable changes, but no one can completely foresee all the impacts of change. A merger or acquisition usually entails major structural changes because of the need to establish an integrated, unified, total organization. The process of consolidating, streamlining, and improving the organization of the newly formed company may take several years, although key changes may be made rather soon.

Brown has analyzed a number of organizational changes that are to be expected in mergers and acquisitions. First, such changes are usually accompanied by an increase in the administrative component relative to the total growth of the organization. The larger organization created by the merger faces greater difficulties and costs of communication and coordination that override the projected economies of scale. Research in school systems found that the larger the size of the containing organization, the greater the proportion of its administrative component. However, later research in hospitals discovered that for them the reverse was true. Second, synergy effects are usually sought in a merger. *Synergy* is defined as the fact that the total effect of two organizations coming together is greater than the sum of the effects taken independently. For example, firm A may be strong in finance and firm B in marketing. Both would gain from the synergistic effects of a merger. Third, the task environment of a new organization is different, especially for growing conglomerates. If the task environment is heterogeneous and dynamic, as it is for most conglomerates, emphasis is placed on flexibility for meeting contingencies and the need for increased decentralization. Fourth, and finally, mergers often involve foreign concerns, which introduce cultural and legal constraints that complicate desirable integration.[4]

Changes caused by mergers or acquisitions lead to substantial impacts on people. There is a high potential for generating feelings of anxiety, fear, or insecurity among managers, from top echelons to foremen, and also among rank-and-file workers. Sometimes these anxieties, if not properly recognized and handled, turn into hostility toward the organization. For example, one demoted executive stole $100,000 within the next year; in another case a controller formed a ring of department heads who rigged a computer and stole $2 million. Personal failings are intensified by extreme change. Some managers are so afraid of losing their jobs that they spend all their time apple polishing, writing memos, building defenses, seeking reassurances, or looking for other jobs.

Reorganization

Any change in assigned roles or in the structure of an organization is in a sense a kind or reorganization. This term, however, is usually applied to major changes in both roles and structure. Profit-oriented organizations such as corporations are reorganized when there are major

---

[4]Warren B. Brown, "Mergers, Managers, and Organizations in the '70's," *Business Topics* 18 (Summer 1970), 49–55. See also T. L. Whistler, "Organizational Aspects of Corporate Growth," in W. W. Albert and J. E. Segall (eds.), *The Corporate Merger* (Chicago: U. of Chicago Press, 1966); J. D. Thompson, *Organizations in Action* (New York: McGraw-Hill, 1967), chap. 6.

changes in goals, technology, or financial requirements. Companies losing money or facing economic cutbacks frequently reorganize. Nonprofit organizations typically reorganize when goals or missions change, or when budgetary requirements indicate the need. Reorganization is one defense against decay.

The term *reorganization* may also refer to the making of basic structural changes on a unitwide basis, that is, throughout a department, plant, or company. However, reorganization usually involves changes at the top echelons of the business. Although in many cases it is possible to arrive at rather sweeping changes through gradual alterations in structure, reorganization implies that significant changes are made simultaneously.

When a new company is just starting out, its executives have an unusual opportunity to plan a pattern that will result in as close to the ideal organization as they can get. It is harder to alter an already existing organization in the direction of the ideal. Commitments and people's expectations impose limitations on the practicability of making rapid, extensive organizational changes. When the changes to be made in an established organization are so extensive as to fall within the concept of the reorganization, there is an implication that serious deficiencies existed in the company. Executives are not always eager to admit the existence of such defects, and hence may hold back the sweeping changes involved in reorganization until conditions force them into it.

Even successful companies may reach a point where they experience serious losses. As losses increase and one losing quarter follows another, pressures increase for radical change to reverse the direction of the firm's affairs. Reorganization occurs, with new managers coming in to set a new course. Although survival is the immediate objective, drastic action is required to restore long-run profitability. One company, for example, reported a loss of $25 million after taxes in one year. A new president was appointed, who reduced the central corporate staff from 1,500 persons to 150 and restructured the firm into 26 divisions and departments. He closed three production facilities. The new president indicated that he thought the company could be turned around in two years, and that in five years it should be producing net profits of 5.5 per cent on sales after taxes and a sales volume roughly double its current rate.

Internal and External Environments

Organization patterns and structures change as a result of forces from internal origins, as well as from external pressures arising in the environment. Change is inevitable and abundant. Many successful managers believe that learning to manage change is the prime requirement for success.

Internal origins of change are in part self-generated, and in part represent responses to external pressures perceived by members of the organization. For example, a number of companies have set up departments designed to cope in new ways with problems of consumer complaints. This strategy is effected by appropriate managers acting in response to mounting outside stress in the public sector.

A certain amount of organizational change may occur almost entirely from internal origins. For example, someone may decide that a particular department is so big and unwieldy that it should be split into two separate units. No doubt, too, some organization changes occur for change's sake, because change can be adventurous and exciting. Change usually follows the appointment of a new manager, even though he inherits a successful unit.

Internal change may also occur in furtherance of individual or group strategies for self-enhancement or the aggrandizement of power. For example, a new unit may be established to provide a job for a favored relative, or to shelve an incompetent, obsolescent, but undischargeable manager. It should be noted that changes originating from political strategies are implicit rather than explicit, and their overt characteristics are couched in the more acceptable rhetoric of "development" or "growth."

The relative openness of an internal environment has important effects on change. Adaptive organizations are designed to be open to the external environment, and flexible in adapting to it. Bureaucratic models are less open to structural or other internal change, and change tends to be more selective and defensive. The range of possible individual changes is greater in adaptive models. Thus the choice of patterns of organization design is influenced by the extent of the organization's need to adapt and change to survive and pursue its goals. The wide variety of existing kinds of organization attests to this point.

Forces for external change arise out of an organization's interaction with elements in its environment. The actions of competitors, suppliers, government units, or public groups may have substantial impacts for change. Social and cultural factors, such as life styles, values, or beliefs, also lead to important changes. Organizations face the need both to *adapt* internally to external forces and to *initiate* changes in the external environment. These needs explain, for example, why companies engage in lobbying for legislation they favor (external influence) but comply when laws not favored are passed (internal adaptation).

Technology and Organizational Change

Technology is a major external source of change. From the standpoint of organization design, there may be a number of alternative patterns for a given technology. However, as organizations keep pace with technological changes, changes in organization structure are frequently required.

Computerization, with its new technology for decision making, provides an excellent example. An entire company, or any of its units or processes, may be simulated on the computer and trial changes made in the model itself to see their effects before actually instituting them. Appropriate organization structures can be developed by similar methods to match changes in operations. Structures can be tailor-made to fit new management styles and changing environmental demands. Major reorganizations could occur very often if desired. By increasing the accuracy and timeliness of information flows, facilitating decision making and planning, and reducing problem-solving time, managerial styles, technologies, and philosophies have been undergoing rapid changes, which in turn appear to be revolutionizing organization theory and practice.

Technology and its relation to organization structure have been extensively studied by Perrow. Bureaucratic organization is appropriate for some types of work but not for others. It is appropriate where the organization tries to control outside influences by the use of staff units and sets of rules and regulations, and by routinizing its processes. Such an organization is oriented toward internal efficiency, as new technologies appear, with corresponding impacts on organization size, objectives, and operating processes. To an extent such changes may be incorporated into bureaucratic models, possibly even increasing the degree of bureaucratization. In some cases, however, the bureaucracy is modified; the advantages of control, specialization, and high-volume production may then be sacrificed to improve flexibility, innovation, and responsiveness to the forces of change. Less bureaucratic and more adaptive structures may be created by transferring routine tasks to machines, leaving people free to deal with nonroutine matters. Line and staff distinctions may be given up and specialists placed closer to the line units they serve. More organizational diversity is created, thus accommodating the organization to rapid and extensive change, and the need to deal with great ambiguity and uncertainty.[5]

One major dimension of organizational change thus clearly consists of shifting from bureaucratic concepts to adaptive, open modes. Adaptive structures evolve to meet needs for which the bureaucratic model is relatively less suitable, but technology plays a significant role in determining the nature of the structures required.

Technological change has become increasingly diverse and complex. Its pace is stepping up, making executives more and more concerned with the adequacy of organization structure and the develop-

---

[5]Charles Perrow, *Organizational Analysis: A Sociological View* (Belmont, Calif.: Wadsworth, 1970), chap. 3. See also Joan Woodward, *Industrial Organization: Theory and Practice* (New York: Oxford U. P., 1965).

ment of new forms of organization to meet new needs. A further reason for managerial concern with technological change in designing organizations is that technological alternatives exist. It is often assumed that the technology in organizations is automatically determined by economic or technical requirements. Yet organizations do convert constraints to choices, and a given technical capability can be used in different ways. Automobiles, for example, may be moved along a line with workers at fixed stations adding parts and components, or work teams can move along with each vehicle as it is assembled, putting together the entire product. Each technological alternative results in different organizational requirements.[6]

New Personnel

The effects of proposed or actual organization changes are difficult to evaluate objectively. Some change is inevitable, because such internal factors as position holders change through death, retirement, transfer, promotion, discharge, or resignation, and elements in the external environment are constantly changing. No two managers have the same styles, skills, or managerial philosophies, or the same personal needs. Managerial behavior is always selective, so that a newly appointed manager may favor different organization designs, objectives, tasks, procedures, and policies than a predecessor. The new executive will not be exactly like the previous one, nor even like those already present. In matters of intelligence, personality, and temperament the new manager may be quite different and still possess the "qualifications for the position." Such differences cannot be overlooked, for inevitably they will influence job performance, making it desirable, if not necessary, for top management to evaluate the effects of these influences to see whether or not results could be increased or improved by making changes in the organization structure. Such an evaluation is not easy to make, and the changes in organization structure that changes in executive personnel make necessary are not always clear.

One of the most frequent reasons for major changes in company structure is a change of executives at the top. They usually begin by examining the structure below them to see if it corresponds to their ideas of what will be needed to do their job effectively. Upon taking over a position at the top, a new manager may make sweeping changes. Moreover, some who opposed the appointment are likely to resign. The filling of these top vacancies, particularly where the new person comes in from outside, presents a strategic opportunity for a reexamination of the entire structure and explanation of the changes to the people

[6]Paul R. Lawrence and Jay W. Lorsch, *Organization and Environment* (Boston: Division of Research, Graduate School of Business Administration, Harvard University, 1967), pp. 233–235.

affected. Often the new top executive appointed from outside brings in an entire top management team of associates from a former position, thus providing himself with colleagues having known capabilities and proven ability to work with him.[7]

Change Agents

Change agent is the technical term for an organization member whose role involves the strategies and procedures for bringing about change. Any individual may be a change agent at one time or another, but many people have positions, tasks, or formal roles in which their main assignments involve dealing with change. A change agent's formal role is primarily to plan and initiate changes rather than to implement them. Change agents serve as catalysts, interpreters, and synthesists. They often work quietly behind the scenes to promote change.

Examples of formal change agent roles can be found in any part of an organization, but they are particularly important in departments or groups assigned to planning, analysis, and other staff functions. Personnel managers, for example, are change agents when they focus on such things as the development of programs for improving human relations or new applications of research findings. Outside consultants are basically change agents. They are retained to solve problems, a procedure that usually results in change. In Part Four we will analyze programs of organization development that widely utilize consultants as change agents.[8]

Many change agents occupy boundary-spanning positions in which they interact with various components of the environment. They acquire information, ideas, and an awareness of demands on the organization, enabling them to participate in the planning of change within their organizations. For example, the top marketing manager might learn at a convention a new approach to market research that would require a restructuring of his department if it were to be instituted.

An interesting kind of change agent is often referred to as "the young Turk." Young Turks are new, usually young employees, eager and ambitious, full of ideas for improvement, and willing to be a bit pushy and obnoxious, or at least persistent, in trying their ideas. Organizations sensing the need for change often deliberately hire young Turks to challenge the status quo. They are not always popular with peers, colleagues, or even their bosses. The best of the young Turks are those

---

[7]Warren B. Brown and Donald L. Helmich, "Successor Type and Organizational Change in the Corporate Enterprise," *Administrative Science Quarterly* 17 (September 1972), 378–381.

[8]Lee Grossman, *The Change Agent* (New York: AMACOM, 1974); James A. Lee, "Leader Power for Managing Change," *Academy of Management Review* 2 (January 1977), 73–80.

who have real talent combined with a measure of tact and patience. But young Turks hired explicitly to foment change often appear to be egocentrc, rebellious, and impatient.

The Domino Effect

A fifth main source of change is change itself. There is often a domino effect in which one change touches off a sequence of related and supporting changes. For example, creating a new department may cause the creation of new managerial or nonmanagerial positions, or changes in assignments within other departments, budgetary reallocations, and office space. Other departments may need to realign their missions, structure, tasks, and staffing.

It is quite common for people to fail to consider the domino effect; such an oversight leads to problems of coordination and control, and necessitates effective planning processes that limit the tendency of individual units to change only in accordance with their own needs. Before any significant change is made, the possible consequences of that change must be examined to see whether undesirable chain reactions will occur.

The decision maker should not necessarily let the possibility of the domino effect prevent necessary action. Opponents of decisions may use the domino effect as a threat to prevent a decision they dislike. For example, a first-line supervisor may say, "I can't fire Jim though he deserves it, because the union will file a grievance, his buddies will resign, my boss will be irritated." He is using potential domino effects as a way of avoiding a hard decision.

_____ **MANAGING ORGANIZATION CHANGE**

Organizations that learn to manage change are more likely to be successful than those that resist or ignore the forces of change. Similarly, managers who can initiate and absorb change are likely to be more successful than those who resist needed change.

Change itself is neither good nor bad. It is the substantive nature of the change that reveals its importance to the organization. The problem, then, is to identify the kinds of change that are beneficial to the organization. Timing is important, but so is having an awareness of the degree of change, the direction of change, and the pace of change.

Among the important problems of managers is the implementation of plans for change. The impacts of such plans on people need consideration, and authentication and legitimacy for the change proposals should be provided. The changes may be instituted by appropriate, accepted authority, such as the board of directors or a top executive. Evidence of

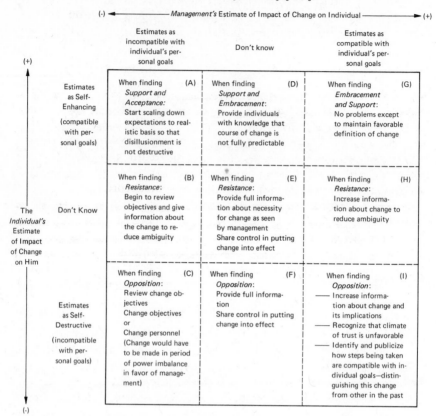

FIGURE 16-2. Strategies for Managing Change.

Source: Floyd C. Mann and Franklin W. Neff, *Managing Major Change in Organizations* (Ann Arbor, Mich.: The Foundation for Research on Human Behavior, 1961), p. 75. Used by permission.

careful planning and staff work improves acceptance. Finally, grass-roots involvement and participation in the planning and problem-solving effort are valuable.[9]

Some possible strategies for dealing with change are shown in Figure 16-2. These strategies are based on management's estimate of the meaning of the change for the individual in relation to the individual's estimate of the impact of change on himself. The figure shows the circumstances under which additional information about changes is required, when participation is essential, and when neither further information nor participation would be useful in introducing a change.

[9]Robert C. Shirley, "An Interactive Approach to the Problem of Organizational Change," *Human Resources Management* **14** (Summer 1975), 11–19.

The Adaptive-Coping Cycle

Schein has described an adaptive-coping cycle that is helpful in organizational diagnosis. This cycle is the sequence of activities or processes that begins with some change in the internal or external environment and ends with a more adaptive dynamic equilibrium for dealing with the change. If one can identify the stages or processes of this cycle, one can also identify the points where organizations typically may fail to cope adequately. There are six stages of the cycle:

1. Sensing a change in the internal or external environment.
2. Importing the relevant information about the change into those parts of the organization that can act on it.
3. Changing activities inside the organization according to the information obtained.
4. Stabilizing internal changes while reducing or managing undesired by-products.
5. Exploring new products, services, or methods that are more in line with the originally perceived changes in the environment.
6. Obtaining feedback on the success of the change through further sensing of the state of the external environment and the degree of integration of the internal environment.

From these stages of the cycle, Schein indicates four conditions for successful coping, conditions that are very similar to the ultimate criteria of organizational health cited by Bennis: (1) ability to take in and communicate information reliably and validly; (2) internal flexibility and creativity to make the changes that are demanded by the information obtained; (3) integration and commitment to the goals of the organization, from which comes the willingness to change; and (4) an internal climate of support and freedom from threat.[10]

Resistance to Change

The influence of the many forces that produce change in organizational structure is cumulative, so that one cannot readily determine, except in urgent cases, exactly when such change becomes necessary or desirable. Caution in making organizational changes is desirable: changes are always disturbing to those who are affected, and considerable resistance to change often arises. Therefore, it is not wise to engage in organizational tinkering—making change for change's sake. Too many managers are persistently restless, unable to leave their organizations

[10]Edgar H. Schein, *Organizational Psychology* (Englewood Cliffs, N.J.: Prentice-Hall, 1965), pp. 98–104. See also George V. Coelho, David A. Hamburg, and John E. Adams, *Coping and Adaptation* (New York: Basic, 1974).

alone. Giving their structure a chance to work out would often be superior to change.

Many managers are entranced by the ease with which organization structures can be changed "on paper," and thus make changes without regard for their impact on those affected. To the manager manipulating the structure, the changes proposed may seem trivial, or else so obviously necessary that no one would question them. But to the people occupying positions, the proposals may be very disturbing. They see all kinds of implications apparently being disregarded by higher management—changes in their status, challenges to their prestige, signals of growing unfavorable attitude toward them, or even the loss of their jobs.

Whether change in organizational relationships arises from positive forces such as growth, or negative forces such as poor management, resistance is frequent. Human relations research has shown that people develop vested interests, rigidities, habits, and preferences that tie them to existing arrangements. They tend to interpret changes in relation to their effects on their personal lives, status, or future, rather than in relation to the welfare of the organization. Change introduces the risks of error, and innovations are troublesome, particularly in situations where people have feelings of insecurity. Accordingly, both the formal and the informal organizations may resist changes. Change produces resistance because it has major impacts on the people.

Although they are relatively closed systems, bureaucratic organizations have considerable ability to change if the *desire* for change is present. Bureaucracies do have built-in, institutionalized modes of change. Yet even logical, institutionalized, and legitimate changes produce tensions and resistances that complicate decision making and call for greater attention to the human factors underlying problems of change.

Nevertheless, it is often true that organizations administer changes carelessly. When managers decide that a certain change is beneficial, they are eager to "get the show on the road." To minimize resistance to change, however, the manager needs careful planning, proper timing of communications, adequate feedback from parts of the organization affected, and the confidence of organization members in the reasons for change. Gradual changes, or changes made by clearly progressive stages, are generally less disturbing than radical, sweeping, scattered, and unpredicted changes made by surprise decree from higher echelons in the organization.

Changes in structure brought about by changes in size, scope, or objectives are easier to perceive and deal with than are changes induced by shifts of personnel occupying specific positions. As has been indicated, the former are precipitated by sharply defined events that presumably already have been planned. The latter are masked in human relationships of infinite complexity, evident only through careful observation over considerable periods of time. To illustrate, take the example of a company deciding to expand by exporting its product on a large scale. The decision to enter the export market entails research and planning. Once the decisiōn is made, however, the next step is to set up an export department and put it in charge of a capable person. The decision compels the managers concerned to consider matters of organizational structure and plan the relationships between the new department head and his associates. The new executive, in facing his responsibilities, will in turn face problems of structure in his evolving unit.

Planning for Change

Most changes can be subjected to the effort of planning, and they should be. In particular, changes affecting organization design require careful planning. Such planning is a function that should be located at top-management levels.

Plans for organizational changes of major dimensions are often detailed and elaborate. For example, when the Bell Telephone Company of Pennsylvania revised its highly functional structure to meet accelerated growth patterns, it developed a detailed plan directed by an officially designated "change agent." Studies were made of other Bell System changes, and an independent consultant was retained to assist in the planning. Two task forces were appointed, one for planning and another as a control group. Many meetings had to be held, investigations made, and reports compiled. Representative parts of the organization were involved. A strategy was devised for gaining acceptance of the ultimate plans, and a plan of implementation and support, including timetables, was developed. Planning for the organizational changes in this situation required 18 months, but it resulted in major alterations in management philosophy and a high degree of interest in and support for the structural changes made.

Organization Planning Departments

Many organizations have set up departments of organization planning, a design strategy that has the effect of identifying organization planning as a staff function. Some of such departments are subdivisions of the personnel or industrial relations departments. Others are separate units.

Two approaches seem predominant: (1) focus on the organization structure, but with emphasis on the human approach (attitudes, opinions, and ways of working with people) and the technical approach (decision-making ability and information flow), and (2) the structural approach only. In the latter approach, departmental directors do not attempt to change people or their abilities in making organization changes.

Glueck found that the purposes of such departments include the following:

1. Effective use of human resources.
2. Adaptation of the organization structure to a changing environment.
3. Control of organization change.
4. The management of conflict.[11]

As managers at the top of an organization exercise their planning functions, long-range targets are set. Plans are started which are calculated to keep the organization healthy, often through expansion and growth. If organizational planning departments are to be utilized, it is important for them to be part of the total planning process; they should be kept informed of major changes in the organization's goals and activities that may give rise to the need for structural change and other forms of organization development.

Formal departments of organization planning have numerous advantages. They can think in terms of organizationwide problems, so that an organization design can evolve as a totality rather than piecemeal. Systematic attention can be given to problems of design before changing conditions force hurried and unplanned changes. Organization planning departments need not wait for difficulties to arise, but can keep in touch with changes likely to lead to structural problems. However, such departments entail the usual risks of staff work: overhead costs, conflicts with line authority, and the possibility of unnecessary tinkering with the organization in the absence of a genuine need for change.

The designation of formal organization planning responsibilities, when assigned to a staff department, is generally at a high level in the organization. For example, in a reorganization of top echelons of the firm, American Can Company placed a vice president of organization planning under the direction of the chairman of the board. At another corporation, there is a vice president for organization who reports to senior vice president, as shown in Figure 16-3. In some companies, however, the function of organization planning is located nearer the middle-management group and frequently within the finance department or controller's office. At a still lower level, systems analysts and office managers often find themselves developing structural changes in the organization. One study indicated that personnel or industrial rela-

[11]William F. Glueck, *Organization Planning and Development* (New York: American Management Association, 1971).

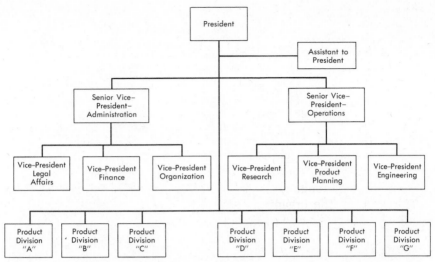

FIGURE 16-3. Organization Structure Showing Vice President for Organization Reporting to a Senior Vice President—Administration.

tions directors by and large have little direct influence over or responsibility for organizational planning. In general, the importance of the organization planning function warrants the status and authority of a position in or near the top echelons.

_____ **SUMMARY**

This chapter has analyzed the processes by which organizations change their structures and designs. Some change is inevitable; some is at the discretion of the manager. Successful organizations and successful managers have developed the capacity to understand change and to utilize it in strengthening and improving their activities.

Organization change differs from individual change, but often the route to successful organization change is through successfully incorporating behavioral changes in people with the structural programs desired. Organization planning departments are increasing in number. They are staff units that plan structural change and development. Some do so with respect to structural goals alone; others take a broad view of their mission and deal with human-relations goals as well.

Organization change was examined in relation to the bureaucratization-debureaucratization process, in which the importance of technology is a fundamental characteristic. The major sources of change were noted as (1) growth, (2) the internal and external environments, (3) changes in personnel (4) change agents, and (5) the domino effect.

_____ **INCIDENT CASE**

Paul Sims had been the president of a large four-hospital system for eight years. The chief administrators of the four hospitals all reported to him. Each hospital had vice presidents in charge of major functions in the hospitals. In one of the hospitals, the chief administrator had worked as an associate of Sims in a hospital in another state. Sims brought him to Linwood Hospital shortly after becoming president of the group, along with four staff specialists for the central office. In 1977, Sims suddenly resigned, and shock waves ran through the organization. The board appointed a temporary president, and began an outside search for a permanent replacement. Three months later, the chief administrator at Linwood also resigned. One month later, Linwood's vice president of operations resigned. A few weeks later, the vice president of business affairs at Linwood resigned. Nine months after Sims had left, a permanent replacement for the chief administrator at Linwood was found, but the presidency of the group was still vacant. This post was ultimately filled. A final problem was the resignation of the vice president for nursing at Linwood, three months after the new chief administrator came on duty. During this period following Sims's resignation, three of the four staff specialists in the central office resigned, two of them to join Sims at his new post.

Question:

1. What problems are involved in this case?

_____ **QUESTIONS FOR STUDY**

1. Explain the main difference between organizational change and individual change.
2. What causes organizational change to occur?
3. How can organizations best meet problems of resistance to change?
4. Explain how mergers cause structural problems in an organization. What can be done about this problem?
5. Elaborate on the proposition that technological change is involved in the shift of organizations from a bureaucratic design to an adaptive (nonbureaucratic) design.
6. What is meant by the domino effect?
7. Argue for or against the establishment of organization planning departments.

_____ **SELECTED REFERENCES**

BASIL, DOUGLAS, and CURTIS W. COOK. *The Management of Change.* New York: McGraw-Hill Book Company, 1974.

BEER, STAFFORD. *Platform for Change.* New York: John Wiley & Sons, Inc., 1975.

BENNIS, WARREN G. *Changing Organizations.* New York: McGraw-Hill Book Company, 1966.

DALTON, GENE, and PAUL R. LAWRENCE, with LARRY GREINER. *Organizational Change and Development.* Homewood, Ill.: Richard D. Irwin, Inc., 1970.

EWING, DAVID W., ed. *Technological Change in Management.* Cambridge, Mass.: Harvard University Press, 1970.

GROSSMAN, LEE. *The Change Agent.* New York: AMACOM, 1974.

GUEST, ROBERT H., PAUL HERSEY, and KENNETH H. BLANCHARD. *Organizational Change Through Effective Leadership.* Englewood Cliffs, N. J.: Prentice-Hall, Inc., 1977.

HAGE, GERALD, and MICHAEL AIKEN. *Social Change in Complex Organizations.* New York: Random House, Inc., 1970.

HUSE, EDGAR F. *Organization Development and Change.* St. Paul, Minn.: West Publishing Company, 1975.

JONES, GARTH N. *Planned Organization Change: A Study in Change Dynamics.* London: Routledge and Kegan Paul, Ltd., 1968.

KATZ, DANIEL, and ROBERT L. KAHN. *The Social Psychology of Organizations.* New York: John Wiley & Sons, Inc., 1966. Chapter 13.

KAUFMAN, HERBERT. *The Limits of Organizational Change.* University: University of Alabama Press, 1971.

LIPPITT, GORDON L. *Organizational Renewal.* New York: Appleton-Century-Crofts, 1969.

MARGULIES, NEWTON, and JOHN WALLACE. *Organizational Change.* Chicago: Scott, Foresman and Company, 1976.

MATHES, SORREL M. *Handling Company Growth.* New York: The Conference Board, 1967.

MCFEELY, WILBER F. *Organization Change: Perceptions and Realities.* New York: The Conference Board, 1972.

QUICK, THOMAS L. *Your Role in Task Force Management: The Dynamics of Corporate Change.* Garden City, N.Y.: Doubleday & Company, Inc., 1972.

SCOTT, WILLIAM G., and TERENCE R. MITCHELL. *Organization Theory: A Structural and Behavioral Analysis.* 3rd ed. Homewood, Ill.: Richard D. Irwin, Inc., 1976. Part IV.

SEASHORE, STANLEY E., and DAVID G. BOWERS. *Changing the Structure and Functioning of an Organization.* Ann Arbor, Mich.: Institute for Social Research, 1971.

THOMPSON, VICTOR A. *Bureaucracy and Innovation.* University: University of Alabama Press, 1969. Page 167.

TUSHMAN, MICHAEL. *Organizational Change: An Exploratory Study and Case History.* Ithaca, N.Y.: New York State School of Industrial and Labor Relations, 1974.

WARNER, AARON W., DEAN MORSE, and THOMAS E. COONEY, eds. *The Environment of Change.* New York: Columbia University Press, 1969.

WIELAND, GEORGE F., and ROBERT A. ULLRICH. *Organizations: Behavior, Design and Change.* Homewood, Ill.: Richard D. Irwin, Inc., 1976. Section V.

Chapter 17

Organizational Conflict

Competition comes in place of monopoly, and intelligence and industry ask only for fair play and an open field.   —*Daniel Webster*

Managers in American corporations are aware of the fact that competitiveness among them can reach unhealthy and damaging levels, according to an American Management Associations survey ("The Manager and Self-Respect: Follow-up Survey," New York: AMACOM, 1977). Survey respondents cited lack of consideration for others, need for recognition and approval, and greed for power as the three human characteristics most often responsible.

Managers in the under-30 and 30-39 age ranges were especially prone to the feeling that "a great deal" of damaging competitiveness exists, on the job, between men and women.

Competition is a major cultural value; competitive skills are refined at home and in school, and are brought to work, but Americans have not been taught to differentiate between healthy and unhealthy competitiveness.

Questions to keep in mind as you read this chapter:

1. What can organizations do to foster healthy competitiveness and minimize unhealthy competitiveness?
2. What other forms of conflict may be present in organizations?

Conflict is widespread in human societies. It occurs among major social institutions—between the church and state, for example, or the state and business. It occurs among organizations, as when firms compete in the same markets. It occurs within organizations, as when departments compete for a jurisdictional domain. Finally, conflict arises among the members of an organization, and within the personality of each individual. The presence of conflict is an everyday reality for all managers.

This chapter will take up the subject of managing internal conflict within an organization, analyzing (1) the nature of organizational conflict, (2) major types of conflict, and (3) how managers and organizations cope with conflict.

THE NATURE OF CONFLICT

Conflict is universal in human affairs, but so are forces that mediate and resolve conflict. Organizations often face a turbulent, ambiguous, and even hostile environment containing forces that generate conflict. Internally, the forces of change and the close collaborations that are needed in doing work produce abundant opportunities for conflict. Conflict goes with change. It is the price of change, and an instigator of change. Conflict is generated in the reordering of interests affected by change.

The absence of conflict, if it occurs, often indicates the success of status quo interests. Yet, paradoxically, conflict highlights the fact that a large degree of cooperation is generally present in well-managed organizations.

Organizational conflict represents the struggle of two or more centers of power for dominance over the others. Conflict may be purely interpersonal in nature, but it is more often associated with formal or informal organizational roles. Organizational conflict centers upon the struggle of departments, divisions, or other groupings to achieve and maintain their identities, missions, and roles compared to others.

Conflict Defined

Conflict describes a situation in which persons or groups disagree over means or ends, and try to establish their views in preference to others. Conflict among groups or organizational units has its base in the presence of competing objectives, methods, philosophies, or missions, and in the desire of managers to protect jurisdictions, control resources, or acquire power. Conflict arises when domains are established and expanded, or when they are defended against erosion or attack. It may also emerge when people experience dissatisfaction or frustration, and it frequently produces anxiety and tension.[1]

March and Simon describe conflict as a breakdown in the standard mechanisms of decision making so that an individual or a group experiences difficulty in selecting an alternative.[2] It seems more appropriate, however, to view conflict as more than a crisis in decision making. Smith defines conflict as "a situation in which the conditions, practices, or goals for the different participants are inherently incompatible."[3] The dimension of goals appears to provide a deeper explanation of conflict.

The latent base of organizational conflict is the self-interest of managers. Tannenbaum describes this base as comprising the processes of adjustment that individuals undertake to resolve differences in their skills, statuses, rewards, authority, organizational position, and tasks. Here hierarchy is of deep significance, for it reflects such differences among organization members. Conflict arises between managers as a result of disparities in advantages relative to efforts to achieve more closely their ideal position or situation.[4]

Conflict As Strategy

Conflict has been studied extensively by game theorists and others, using mathematical or quantitative approaches. Game theory has evolved from studying laboratory groups by experimental methods, and has thrown much light on union-management negotiations and on interpersonal conflict situations where individuals follow strategies of competition and self-interest with respect to opponents.

One way to describe conflict in organizations is to view it as a non–zero-sum game. In such games, competition and cooperation have acceptable and nonacceptable forms. Each side plays by the rules of the game, and each gets some of what it wants; neither loses or wins all. But some conflict situations, such as between organization departments, unions and management, or line and staff units, are zero-sum games, in which one side wins and the other loses; or, in some cases, such as employee strikes, they are non–zero-sum games in which both sides lose.[5] In labor arbitration cases, for instance, there are usually clear-cut

[1]Joseph A. Litterer, "Conflict in Organization: A Re-examination," *Academy of Management Journal* 9 (September 1966).

[2]James G. March and Herbert A. Simon, *Organizations* (New York: Wiley, 1958), p. 112.

[3]Clagett G. Smith, "A Comprehensive Analysis of Some Conditions and Consequences of Intra-Organizational Conflict," *Administrative Science Quarterly* 10 (March 1966), p. 511.

[4]Arnold S. Tannenbaum, *Social Psychology of the Work Organization* (Belmont, Calif.: Wadsworth, 1966), chap. 4.

[5]See, for example, Bernard M. Bass and Samuel D. Deep (eds.), *Current Perspectives for Managing Organizations* (Englewood Cliffs, N.J.: Prentice-Hall, 1970), pp. 441–446; T. C. Schelling, *The Strategy of Conflict* (Cambridge, Mass.: Harvard U. P., 1960).

"winners" and "losers," but sometimes arbitrators give something to both sides, with both feeling that they have "lost."

Emshoff has reported a research method of model building that begins by focusing on small segments of behavior, which can then be integrated sequentially as they become more clearly understood. He applies this method to a project designed to provide a quantitative explanation of human behavior in conflict situations. In developing a systems approach to solving behavior problems, Emshoff makes extensive use of game theory as well as other bodies of theory. By explaining the dynamics of human behavior in conflict situations, an understanding of how such conflicts may be resolved can better emerge.[6]

The Strong and the Weak

The aspects of strategy that emerge in conflict raise questions about the relative strengths and weaknesses of adversaries. By their very nature, organizations are peculiarly fitted to generate conflict; but they are also suited to produce contervailing forces that tend to resolve it. A balance is struck between the strong and powerful and the weak and powerless. In the words of Paul Tournier,

> In any family, firm, association, international organization—there are periods of instability during which the interplay of forces takes a violent form: angry scenes, attempts at intimidation, resort to force, war, flight, panic, bewilderment. But the interrelationship of forces tends to become crystallized in an apparent state of peace which is made up of a pattern of strong and weak reactions. There is then a sort of mutual acquiescence; each individual plays his role, giving way to those he accepts as stronger, and taking advantage of those who are weaker. There are coalitions, alliances, intrigues, a battle going on beneath the surface at every stage, in which it is always the same ones who suffer.[7]

Functions and Dysfunctions of Conflict

Conflict is not always bad for an organization or for an individual. The human relations movement implied that conflict is inherently undesirable and should be replaced by harmony, cooperation, and stability. Conflict was thus seen as a deviation, a malfunctioning of the organization or the individual. A more realistic view is that some degree of conflict, like change, is inevitable. Therefore managers should learn not only to live with it, but to contain it within reasonable bounds and use it to good purpose.

Although some conflict may be generated by troublemakers, it is

---

[6]James R. Emshoff, *Analysis of Behavioral Systems* (New York: Macmillan, 1971).
[7]Paul Tournier, *The Strong and the Weak* (Philadelphia: The Westminster Press, 1963), p. 152.

clear that work situations are often the real cause. Kelly contrasts the human relations view with the newer one. The earlier approach held that conflict was avoidable and was caused by agitators and troublemakers. Managers were expected to "stick to the book" on rules and regulations, and to blame someone for the conflict. The newer approach accepts conflict not only as inevitable, but as functional, and related to such factors as physical surroundings, career patterns, class systems, or organizational designs, as well as human attributes. Conflict is seen as being integral to change, and optimal at a minimum level.[8]

Another value of conflict is that it initiates a search for ways to eliminate or resolve it, leading to innovation and change, and to the polishing and refining of objectives, methods, or activities. An important effect is to make change more acceptable and desirable. Conflict provides some persons with challenges, bringing out their abilities and talents and giving them activities with interest and zest. Conflict may thus lead to shifts in resources and important changes of benefit to the organization and its people. Conflicting views on a given issue enlarge the number of alternatives being considered and enrich the pool of ideas for problem solvers.

Conflict also has strategic implications for bosses and their subordinates. It occupies the time or attention of those who might otherwise be doing greater or unrestrained damage elsewhere. It gives some persons less time to attack their superiors or others, and it can also keep superiors too busy to supervise subordinates closely. A boss may keep subordinates in conflict with each other so they are less likely to conflict with him.

The fact that conflict may be beneficial or constructive does not preclude the possibility of destructive conflict. Some conflicts are so severe, so long lasting, that they drain off energy and resources that could be devoted to better use. For example, trade union history recounts many struggles between warring factions within unions that often weakened the union's position in another conflict, the struggle with management.

Conflict also exacts its toll on the physical and emotional well-being of the individuals involved; intense conflict carries strong emotional forces of involvement, self-esteem, beliefs, and values. Visceral and muscular effects are present. Moreover, conflicts may spread and endure, generating not only additional conflict but also feelings of anxiety, guilt, frustration, and hostility. Often these feelings endure beyond the apparent cessation of the actual conflict. Dread and apprehension also spread throughout the organization, affecting not only those directly involved but all members of the organization.

[8]Joe Kelley, "Make Conflict Work for You," *Harvard Business Review* **48** (July-August 1970), 103–113.

Those who initiate conflict situations for strategic purposes should be aware of the potential dangers, balancing the benefits against the costs.

Conflict and Leadership

Conflict often surrounds the leadership process itself, with consequent effects on the leader's success. Even members of substantial power and ability may find their leadership blunted by conflict arising from an incongruence between status and esteem. If high-status and high-esteem organizational members differ in their respective goals or ideas, conflict is likely. Status without esteem, or vice versa, may generate conflict.

The conflict generated by status-esteem incongruence is predominantly interpersonal conflict. Because status is partly associated with a leader's position in the organization structure, however, there may be an organizational factor in interpersonal conflict. Two or more persons may be in conflict apart from their organizational roles, as in the case of so-called personality clashes. More often, however, the conflict has a task or mission base, or originates in differing philosophies and concepts of management or organization. Accordingly, a problem of organizational design is to review potentials for conflict and to take steps to minimize them.

Managers need to know how and when to create constructive conflict. Conflict need not be feared, but they should understand the origins and nature of conflict and be able to absorb and mediate conflicts. They should also prevent or minimize degenerative, vicious, or otherwise undesirable conflict.

TYPES OF CONFLICT

Conflict appears everywhere, in a variety of forms. Three types will be discussed here to illustrate conflict in organizations: (1) structurally based conflict, (2) role conflict, and (3) institutionalized conflict. These categories are not mutually exclusive. They may overlap, occur simultaneously, or show similarities and differences.

Structurally Based Conflict

As an organization grows, or a simple organization becomes more complex, it becomes increasingly differentiated along horizontal and vertical dimensions. Levels, departments, divisions, and other units increase; built-in conflict, both horizontal and vertical, is inevitable.

In dictating material for a training manual, Colonel Lyndall C. Urwick, the noted British management consultant, referred to the organization chart as a "wiring diagram." Instead, the transcriber typed the phrase "warring diagram." Perhaps this typist had noted that the domains on an organization chart set up ideal jousting grounds for war among builders of empires.

Organizations vary in their tolerance for conflict, according to the nature of their organizational orientation. The traditional bureaucracy can tolerate very little conflict; the human relations–oriented organization can stand somewhat more. The adaptive, fluid organization designs permit a great deal of conflict, but it is less likely to occur as a result of structural rigidities. Rather, it takes the form of conflict between experts, teams, or peers.

Vertical Conflict

Transactions along the vertical dimensions are within the framework of hierarchical authority, between levels. Conflict arises among different kinds and intensities of roles, missions, objectives, and activities at the various levels. It occurs in superior-subordinate relations and in forms that bypass some echelons.

Smith found partial support for three hypotheses regarding vertical conflict: (1) that conflict arises from inadequate communication between echelons, (2) that conflict stems essentially from differences of interests between position holders occupying different stations in the organizational hierarchy, and (3) that intraorganizational conflict arises from a lack of shared perceptions and attitudes among members at different echelons.[9]

Vertical conflict in bureaucratic organizations frequently has a process character. That is, a cycle occurs in the conflict between a superior and a subordinate. When a superior tries to control the behavior of a subordinate, the subordinate tends to resist, causing the superior to increase the use of bureaucratic rule enforcement to gain control. But the subordinate's reaction to rule enforcement is further resistance, resulting in the perpetuation and intensification of the conflict. When subordinates cannot count on their superiors to identify with their goals, autonomy becomes an important value to them, leading them to resist attempts at control. This in turn generates pressure for the superior to further routinize activities and to institute impersonal rules.[10]

[9]Smith, *Comprehensive Analysis*, 504–529. See also, Litterer, *Conflict in Organization*. See also Samuel A. Culbert, "Organizational Renewal: Using Internal Conflicts to Solve External Problems," *1969 Annual Proceedings* (Madison, Wisc.: Industrial Relations Research Association, 1970), pp. 109–119; Louis R. Pondy, "Organization Conflict: Concepts and Models," *Administrative Science Quarterly* 12 (September 1967), 295–320.

[10]Pondy, *Concepts and Models*, pp. 314–316. See also Patricia A. Renwick, "Perception and Management of Superior-Subordinate Conflict," *Organizational Behavior and Human Performance* 13 (June 1975), 444–456.

Structural conflict in the vertical dimension of adaptive organizations is less likely, for the hierarchy is less important.

Horizontal Conflict

Transactions along horizontal dimensions are very important and have been little studied. This form of conflict occurs between departments or other units, such as divisions, sections, and branches. The term *interdepartmental conflict* is used to describe lateral conflict among all types of units or subsystems.

A central element in interdepartmental conflict is the degree of interdependence of tasks among the conflicting units. This interdependence is important in both bureaucratic and adaptive organizations. Pondy has presented a model of interdepartmental conflict from the systems (adaptive) point of view, in which the subsystems are in conflict. The manager's problem is to achieve coordination and articulation of interests, objectives, and activities. The source of conflict between lateral units consists of pressures toward suboptimization. The subunits in the goal-oriented system will have different sets of goals or different preferences for the same goals. If the two subunits having differentiated goals are functionally interdependent, conditions exist for conflict.

Thompson classifies interdependencies into three types: pooled, sequential, and reciprocal. Under pooled interdependence, each unit makes a contribution to the total organization, and each unit receives support from the whole. Branches A, B, and C may or may not have direct interaction with each other, but the failure of any one to perform properly can jeopardize the success of the others or of the whole. In sequential interdependence, unit A must perform adequately before unit B can act, unit B must act before unit C can act, and so on. Each is directly dependent on the preceding performance. In reciprocal interdependence, the outputs of each unit become inputs for other units, with each unit being penetrated by the other. Unit A provides a service for unit B; unit B provides input in the form of a need for that service. All organizations have pooled interdependence; complicated organizations have both pooled and sequential types; highly complex organizations have pooled, sequential, and reciprocal independence. Breakdowns in the performance of interdependent work can lead to serious conflict.[11]

Mutual task dependence is a key variable in interdepartmental conflict, as studied by Walton and Dutton. They define task dependence as

[11]James D. Thompson, *Organizations in Action* (New York: McGraw-Hill, 1967), pp. 54–55. See also R. L. Simpson, "Vertical and Horizontal Communication in Formal Organizations," *Administrative Science Quarterly* **4** (December 1959), 188–196; H. A. Landsberger, "The Horizontal Dimension in a Bureaucracy," *Administrative Science Quarterly* **6** (December 1961), 298–333.

the extent to which two units depend on each other for assistance, information, compliance, or other coordinative acts in the performance of their respective tasks. Such interdependence produces the need for collaboration, but also presents occasions for conflict and the need for bargaining behavior between units over the issues in conflict. Pressures on work loads in one unit or the other intensify the conflict. Walton and Dutton constructed a model of interdepartmental conflict that links contextual factors, such as organizational elements and personalities of managers, with conflict situations. Linkages occur in the form of responses of higher managers, and in the ways the conflicting units manage the interface between them. These linkages are affected by the extent of their desire to collaborate or engage in conflict. Interunit conflict occurs when each of the interdependent units has responsibility for only one side of a dilemma embedded in organizational tasks. The linkage of higher management occurs through coordinating decisions and through the power of manipulating the reward system. This theory suggests that the total lateral relationship is determined by contextual factors operating first upon the way the two parties exchange information, with effects on interaction structure and interunit trust as subsequent reactions. However, personality and status may sometimes be a prior influence on attitudes such as trust, with information exchange and interactions structure being secondary reactions.[12]

Line-Staff Conflict

Line-staff conflict, discussed earlier in this book, is a form of structural conflict, primarily horizontal, between staff and line managers at or near the same level. It also illustrates both interdepartmental and role conflict, for the staff department has its own identity and mission, and pits the specialist's role against the roles of line managers. Line-staff conflict is essentially a clash of domains caused by dividing expertise, authority, and roles.

Thompson has extensively analyzed the interactions between specialist and hierarchical roles, throwing light on staff-line relationships. Staff specialties have flourished in organizations, bringing about conflict through differential role expectations. New specialties also threaten older ones and attempt to crowd them out—for example, "organization development" attempts to replace "personnel management." The problem is intensified when new specialties are formed into separate, competing departments. Furthermore, advancing special-

[12]Richard E. Walton and John M. Dutton, "The Management of Interdepartmental Conflict: A Model and Review," *Administrative Science Quarterly* 14 (March 1969), 73–84; Richard E. Walton, John M. Dutton, and Thomas P. Cafferty, "Organizational Context and Interdepartmental Conflict," *Administrative Science Quarterly* 14 (December 1969), 522–542.

ization upsets status expectations and vested interests. By splitting various functions, low- and high-status persons are forced into interdependent relationships, thereby reducing the status of the latter. As specialties eventually become entrenched, they acquire nonhierarchical authority, which conflicts with hierarchical authority, creating a discrepancy between expected and actual authority.[13]

Belasco and Alutto found in a study of personnel managers that line-staff conflict is less severe than many believe. Perceived conflict was found to be low in that both line and staff managers agreed on the current role definitions of the personnel administrators. The researchers found also that both line managers and personnel administrators idealized similar expectations for more participation by the personnel administrators in decisions. But the personnel administrators expressed a stronger desire for more participation in traditional personnel matters, causing their role expectations to exceed those of the line management role definers. This resulted in more felt role conflict on the part of personnel administrators and more potential conflict between them and the line managers. Line-staff conflict, however, is reduced by outside pressures that affect both types of managers.[14]

Line-staff conflict is further reduced by an accommodation process in which line and staff managers adjust their roles to contain conflict. They learn to go by rules of the game that they themselves work out.[15]

Role Conflict

Organizational roles consist of sets of behaviors expected of each organization member. Some roles are formally prescribed by job descriptions, delegations, assignments, organization manuals, and the like, and are derived from tasks, missions, procedures, or instructions. Others are created by the informal activities of organization members. The individual is allowed considerable discretion in performing both formal and informal roles.

In bureaucratic organizations the most important roles are those of superiors and subordinates, which are usually specified as tasks in job descriptions. In adaptive organizations, important role expectations may also be held by one's peers and others who are not directly in the lines of authority but are bound together by technology, expertise, or shared goals.

Role conflict occurs when an individual must assume roles for different situations that are inconsistent with one or more other roles. For

[13]Victor A. Thompson, *Modern Organization* (New York: Knopf, 1961), pp. 100–101.

[14]James A. Belasco and Joseph A. Alutto, "Line-Staff Conflicts: Some Empirical Insights," *Academy of Management Journal* **12** (December 1969), 469–477.

[15]Dalton E. McFarland, *Cooperation and Conflict in Personnel Administration* (New York: American Foundation for Management Research, 1962).

example, a supervisor is both a boss and a subordinate. The roles are strikingly different, and in certain circumstances they are in conflict. Fortunately, people readily learn the skills of handling multiple roles and develop the ability to shift from one role to another. However, when the roles are so conflicting that the individual is uncertain, anxiety and frustration result. It is hard for anyone to please those above and those below at the same time.

But role conflict is not only within the individual. It is also spread structurally across organizational units. Line-staff conflict thus may be viewed as a type of role conflict in which divergent roles dictate different behaviors on the part of line and staff people in particular situations. Much structural conflict is role conflict, and an understanding of role conflict throws light on both vertical and horizontal structural conflict.

If a system of multiple authority is in use, as is the case in hospitals (separate structures for physicians and for administrative personnel), role conflict readily appears, with consequent hostility and passive resistance on the part of those in conflict. Job dissatisfaction and loss of effectiveness on the part of organization members occurs, but this is the price of providing physicians with control over the professional and technical work.

Ambiguity of job or role prescriptions is a major source of conflict. Ambiguity affords substantial scope for variations in work or role performance by individuals, thereby increasing opportunities for conflict.[16]

Well-intentioned interest groups function unwittingly as provokers of role conflict. For example, John R. Coleman has depicted the college president's job as the center of a web of conflicting interest groups, none of which can be fully satisfied:

> He is, by definition, almost always wrong. If he spends much time meeting with students, he is neglecting the faculty. If he spends much time with the faculty, he is being dictated to by them. If he is off campus, he should be back minding the store. If he is on campus, he should be out raising money. . . . If he changes his mind on an issue, he is wishy-washy. If he doesn't, he is pig-headed. . . . [17]

Power Struggles

Role conflict and interpersonal conflict are intermixed. In the complex web of organizational affairs, leaders and persons of authority fulfill

[16]John R. Rizzo, Robert J. House, and Sidney I. Lirtzman, "Role Conflict and Ambiguity in Complex Organizations," *Administrative Science Quarterly* 15 (June 1970), 159–163; Robert J. House and John R. Rizzo, "Role Conflict and Ambiguity as Critical Variables in a Model of Organizational Behavior," *Organization Behavior and Human Performance* 7 (September 1972), 476–505; Robert H. Miles, "A Comparison of the Relative Impacts of Role Perceptions of Ambiguity and Conflict by Role," *Academy of Management Journal* 19 (March 1976), 25–35.

[17]John R. Coleman, *Blue-Collar Journal* (New York: Lippincott, 1976), p. 24.

such diverse and often conflicting roles as authority figure, judge, object of affection, target of hostility, confidant, catalyst, and symbol of strength. But the performance of such roles is often caught up in power struggles among competing executives. The outcome of power struggles hinges on how the roles are selected and played, as well as the personalities of individuals. Dominant managers take aggressive roles; weak ones play submissive roles. Delegations of authority are contracted and expanded according to personal loyalties. The proposals and actions of one manager may be blocked or diverted by others, not only for logical, technical reasons but for self-protection, advancement, and emotional reasons. Cliques and coalitions are formed to advance and protect entrenched interests or to oust old ones. Thus conflict and competition develop among managers as personal interests merge with organizational needs.

Power struggles are particularly serious at the top of an organization, among the positions of president, chief executive officer, and board chairman. When these positions are filled by separate individuals, role conflict arises from possible ambiguities over who really runs the organization.

How a power struggle can restructure a key top role in an organization is illustrated by events in E. T. Barwick Industries, Inc. Charles E. Selecman was brought in by creditors as chief executive officer in 1975, to save the firm from failure. His predecessor, the founder and principal stockholder, resisted Selecman's efforts. Lender banks then pushed the founder aside by threatening to call their loans. The founder was forced to surrender all authority over operations for the next three years, and not to visit his own office without Selecman's permission. Furthermore, he had to give Selecman the power to vote the 5.4 million common shares he controlled, in electing the ten members of the board of directors. Selecman was required to vote for two directors named by the founder, but the founder was not eligible for nomination as a board member, and Selecman chose the other eight. Two board vacancies were created, to be filled only by Selecman if he felt he needed additional power. "winner" and "loser" are roles that executives must often play in power struggles of this type.[18]

Role conflict often leads to dilemmas of evaluation for the individual organization members. For example, Cressey found that relaxed supervision created pleasant working conditions for prison guards but also complicated the criteria used for judging guard competence. Each guard had to decide between relaxed control approaches (therapeutic) or custodial rigidity with respect to prisoners. For reasons of treatment, guards were to go easy on inmate deviations, but on custodial grounds

[18]*Business Week*, November 29, 1976, pp. 81–82. See also "The No. 2 Man's in the Hot Seat," *Business Week*, January 26, 1976, pp. 25–27; and Alanzo McDonald, "Conflict at the Summit: A Deadly Game," *Harvard Business Review* **50** (March/April 1972), 59–68.

IDEALS

	IDEALS	PURPOSE	SOCIAL	PSYCHOLOGICAL	LEARNING
IDEALS	Be kind and loving vs. Be truthful				
PURPOSE	Be honest vs. Fix prices Be just vs. Pay minimum wages	Produce a lot (quantity) vs. Produce it well (quality)			
SOCIAL	Be truthful vs. Don't squeal	Work as hard as you can vs. Don't be a ratebuster	Meet production norm vs. Help fellow workers		
PSYCHOLOGICAL	Be brave vs. Need to express felt fear	Work hard vs. Conserve my energy Do it the organization's way vs. Do it my own way	Belong vs. Be independent Don't deviate from production norms vs. I want to excel	Need to belong vs. Need to be free	
LEARNING	Adhere to ideals vs. Deviate to get new experience	Do it the standard way vs. Experiment	Conform to our norms vs. Try something new	Fear of taking a chance vs. Try something new to learn	Analytical vs. Clinical

FIGURE 17-1. Examples of Conflict Within and Across Dimensions of Behavior.

Source: Anthony G. Athos and Robert E. Coffey, *Behavior in Organizations: A Multidimensional View,* ©1968, p. 295. By permission of Prentice-Hall, Inc., Englewood Cliffs, N.J.

they needed to enforce inmate compliance with rules. If they insisted on enforcement they risked negative evaluation as rigid, punitive, or neurotic; if they relaxed too much they risked evaluation as lazy or unmotivated. Thus the guards were uncertain of the linkages between expected behavior and organizational rewards.[19]

Figure 17-1 shows a number of examples of conflict within five dimensions of employee behavior: ideals, purpose, social, psychological, and learning. The examples indicate that conflict is not one-dimensional, but rather is a complex web of interrelated pressures.

[19]Donald R. Cressey, "Contradictory Directives in Complex Organizations: The Case of the Prison," *Administrative Science Quarterly* 4 (June 1959) , 1–19.

Institutionalized Conflict

Institutionalized conflict occurs where the social system substantially structures the conditions under which conflict may occur, regulates the conduct and severity of the conflict, and legitimizes the methods by which the conflict is resolved, prescribing appropriate roles, rituals, and ceremonies. Labor-management relations is an example. Line-staff conflict, too, has its institutionalized aspects as the parties to it accommodate their strategies to those of their counterparts.

When the conditions, methods, and reasons for conflict are highly organized, ritualized, and regulated by broad social policy through law, precedent, or practice, conflict becomes institutionalized. To that extent it is accepted as long as the parties abide by the ground rules. Dubin has advanced a theory of conflict and power in union-management relations which considers the strategies of power between the two parties, because power affects conflict. The model considers both conflict and the substitution of nonconflict interactions between the parties. A strike, for example, delineates a clear, specific conflict. On the other hand, the process of negotiating a labor-management agreement may or may not involve significant conflict, or else conflict remains latent until events and strategies turn the negotiations into conflict. The proposed model suggests that the direct relationship between power and conflict, on the one hand, and the points at which substitution of nonconflict methods enters into the bargaining, on the other, supplement each other.[20]

Clark Kerr has also analyzed institutionalized labor-management conflict. He sees such conflict as more than an expression of irrationality or ill will, and asserts that even with mutual good will, conflict is inherent. The desires of the parties are more or less unlimited, but the means of satisfaction are limited. Also, the conflict is between the managers and the managed. If management and labor are to retain their institutional identities, they *must* disagree and *must* adopt appropriate roles. Conflict is essential to survival for the union; lack of conflict would weaken it. Independence is asserted by acts of criticism, contradictions, conflict, and competition.[21]

There are many varieties of institutionalized conflict in labor-management relations. The strike is the most prominent, but there are many kinds of strikes. Also, conflict includes many other forms, such as peaceful bargaining, grievances, debates, boycotts, political action, restriction of output, sabotage, absenteeism, and the like. The presence of hostile acts and aggressive behavior attests to the value for society of

[20]Robert Dubin, "A Theory of Conflict and Power in Union-Management Relations," *Industrial and Labor Relations Review* 13 (July 1960), 501–518.

[21]Clark Kerr, "Management of Industrial Conflict in Society," *The Pacific Spectator* 8 (Autumn 1954), 298–299.

institutionalizing collective bargaining so that the conflicts are restricted. Contained conflict is better than the more violent alternatives available.

Collective bargaining conflicts take place in the open and are usually orderly and backed by practice, precedent, and jurisprudence. Such conflicts are subject to compromise and to definitive solutions. Problem-solving approaches can be used, instead of win-lose power struggles aimed at the total capitulation of the opponent.

CONFLICT RESOLUTION

The ways of minimizing excessive organizational conflict are as varied as its causes, sources, and contexts. Conflict cannot be entirely eliminated, but episodes of conflict that threaten the welfare of the organization or its members can be minimized. Much can be prevented. Continuous undercurrents of conflict that cannot be avoided must be accepted, but with an awareness of their costs as well as benefits.

The parties in a conflict have several alternatives. One is withdrawal, a kind of strategic retreat, which can be either real or simulated. Some conflicts, of course, do not permit withdrawal, as in the case of labor-management conflict, in which bargaining is required and dispute settlement methods are often imposed. Withdrawal is not a satisfactory alternative, usually, and it tends to be a last-resort maneuver. It may also drive the conflict underground.

Another alternative is the pursuit of a win-lose strategy through the use of power, authority, or persuasiveness. Each adversary tries to win and make the others lose. Long-enduring conflicts may be created in which the powers are nearly equal and the balance of power shifts back and forth. This kind of conflict can be costly, for the fighting may be harder and last longer. It is painful for the loser, who loses the argument and "loses face" as well.

Third-party intervention presents a more positive approach to conflict. In this case an outside, neutral party, such as an arbitrator, mediator, or consultant, can intervene, find facts, and provide a decision. In arbitration, the parties agree to abide by the decision. In mediation, the mediator uses persuasion to try to bring the parties into a voluntary agreement. The consultant brings outside expertise in similar problems, and also contributes the objectivity of the outsider.

Organizational conflict is often settled by a coordinating manager who exercises a leadership or coordinating function. The need for containing or reducing such conflict is met by various integrating and coordinating devices, such as committees, councils, boards, or, as in the case of many firms, a central corporate office. A further source of conflict reduction is the assignment of managers to integrating, decision-making roles.

Lawrence and Lorsch found that three factors promote effective resolution of interdepartmental conflict and high organizational performance. First, where there is a separate coordinating person or unit, the unit will be most effective if its degree of structuring and the goal, time, and interpersonal orientations of its personnel are intermediate among the units linked. Second, where there is a coordinating unit, conflict resolution will be more effective if its personnel have relatively high influence based on expertise and if they are evaluated and rewarded on over-all performance measures covering the activities of the several departments. Third, interunit cooperation will be more effectively achieved and organizational performance will be higher to the extent that the managers openly confront differences instead of ignoring them or smoothing them over.[22]

Conflict is minimized in bureaucratic organizations by emphasis on a single chain of command, a dominant line organization that clarifies authority and responsibilities and adjudicates conflicts among them. Role ambiguity is also minimized by the concept of unity of command, so that each employee has only one superior. In more adaptive, less hierarchical organizations, such conflict is dealt with through its managers' result-oriented, problem-solving approach, and through the influence of professional expertise.

Blake, Shepard, and Mouton suggest three approaches to conflict resolution, based on the possibilities for agreement.[23] First, where the parties see the possibilities for eventual agreement, and where they are both skilled at gamesmanship and the use of straightforward strategies well understood by both sides, peaceful coexistence can occur. In peaceful coexistence, each party is alert to the actions of the other and to the possibilities for erupting conflict; but in the meantime they benefit from the healing of time and from their growing strength. The contending parties are approximately equal in their power and strength.

A second approach cited by Blake and his colleagues is through compromise, bargaining, and splitting the difference. It is often found in conjunction with other approaches, such as intervention, arbitration, or mediation. The conflict becomes quiescent or resolved when the contending parties decide that they have obtained as much advantage as they can, given the costs they are willing to bear.

[22]Paul R. Lawrence and Jay W. Lorsch, *Organization and Environment* (Boston: Division of Research, Graduate School of Business Administration, Harvard University, 1967), pp. 54–83.

[23]Robert F. Blake, Herbert A. Shepard, and Jane S. Mouton, *Managing Intergroup Conflict in Industry* (Houston, Tex.: Gulf Publishing Company, 1964), chaps. 7–9, 12. See also March and Simon, *Organizations*, pp. 129–131.

The third approach, that of problem solving, appears to be useful in all realms of conflict, particularly in labor-management relations. In this approach, problem solving is mutual between the parties, who work together to identify the problem and find alternatives. They determine goal priorities and areas of common agreement. They are then in a position to determine intergroup courses of action.

For the most part the approach of Blake, Shepard, and Mouton is supported by research in behavioral science that bears out the value of problem-solving, participative, confrontational approaches. Interpersonal relations receive attention, even though the conflict is between groups or other units. This outlook provides the advantage of being preventive, for participative techniques set up communication patterns that help to avoid conflict or prevent it from developing through resentment and resistance to change. Conferences, meetings, confrontations, committees, staff groups, seminars, problem-solving sessions, teams and task forces, and sensitivity training are all helpful. Administrative practice can do much to resolve or minimize conflict. Policies can be used to maintain a balance of power among contending groups or individuals, as happens in labor-management relations.[24]

Approaches to Role Conflict Resolution

Another means for facilitating conflict resolution is to set up role expectations so as to minimize or reduce conflict. Pondy, for example, has suggested that whereas the bureaucratic model minimizes conflict by altering supervision (the use of such devices as rules and disciplines), organizations using participative management tend to minimize role conflict. Instead of reducing dependence and increasing the autonomy of managers, leadership theories suggest reducing conflict by using persuasion and group pressures to bring subordinates' goals closer to organizational goals. The role conflict approach opens up the possibility of reducing the conflict that is faced by the manager as "the man in the middle."[25]

Thompson suggests that conflict between specialist and hierarchical roles generates role defense mechanisms, which are required to secure and maintain the legitimacy of the role. For example, specialists may abandon their profession and compete for line jobs, and thus escape the hierarchical conflict experienced by specialists. The specialist who remains a specialist may adopt a strategy of separate roles, one for personal values and another for technical values, thus rejecting respon-

---

[24]See Kenneth W. Thomas, "Conflict and Conflict Management," in Marvin D. Dunnette (ed.), *Handbook of Industrial and Organizational Psychology* (Chicago: Rand McNally, 1976).

[25]Pondy, *Concepts and Models*, pp. 315–316.

sibility for the nonspecialist use or consequences of their advice and perpetuating their lower status. They take refuge in being "only staff," and can "only advise." Also, specialists engaged in problem solving consistently evade official prescriptions in order to get the job done. Another device for specialist protection is to join local, state, and national associations, which strengthen professional career groups, providing pressures for due process and procedures for protection of members in their work roles.[26]

Ideologies are another form of role defense. Power holders seek legitimacy as a basis for their power. They find and develop ideas that justify their power, and these ideas become a firm set of beliefs known as an ideology. Generally ideologies show that those who hold power are the most qualified to do so, or that the present authority system is best for all, or that it is right in some sense. Attention is diverted from structure, and any apparent evils are alleged to arise from the nature of things or from the defects of individuals, never from the structure itself.[27]

Miller and Shull found that the decisions of a position incumbent, when confronted with role conflicts, can be predicted with a high degree of accuracy under given perceptions of legitimacy and sanctions. The manager makes judgments about the legitimacy of opposing expectations, and of negative sanctions and contesting claimants. Finally, the manager's personal orientation toward alternative choices is made from a range of morally expedient behaviors, along a hierarchy of personal values that serve as a decision criterion.[28]

Diagnosing conflict situations is both desirable and difficult. Seiler has suggested that a plan for action in conflict situations include stopping to see if action is really required and, if it is, whether it is feasible. Some conflict may run its course or become dissipated. As with a biological organism, it has some capacity to heal itself. In those cases that arise in response to conflicts of authority, as where work flows violate notions of organization members' authority or of their right to assign duties, (1) take whatever steps are available to reduce prestige, ambiguity, and threat; (2) reduce nonproductivity in illegitimate authority relations by reorganizing subunits so that authority and prestige become consistent; and (3) use structural reorganization not only to resolve the authority problem but also to bring clashing points of view into sufficient harmony to destroy communication.[29]

[26]Thompson, *Modern Organization*, pp. 110–112.

[27]Ibid., pp. 114–118.

[28]Delbert C. Miller and Fremont A. Shull, Jr., "The Prediction of Administrative Role Conflict Resolutions," *Administrative Science Quarterly* 7 (September 1962), 143–160.

[29]John A. Seiler, "Diagnosing Interdepartmental Conflict," in Bass and Deep, *Current Perspectives*, pp. 459–475.

Another major strategy for diverting departmental energies to constructive action is intergroup counseling, therapy, or training. Only conflicts in points of view are susceptible to this strategy.

_____ **SUMMARY**

This chapter has analyzed the presence of conflict within organizations. Not all conflict is bad, nor can it always be stamped out. However, conflict should be measured against the possibility of its debilitating, costly effects if too severe or too protracted.

Because a certain amount of conflict is inevitable, managers need a knowledge of the elements of conflicts and experience in dealing with conflict situations. Conflict may be generated as interpersonal conflict among human beings as individuals or as role occupants. Conflict is also generated by the establishment of domains of functional operations and staff specialties whose interests may overlap or whose jurisdictions are unclear. Organization design needs to include the consideration of potential, built-in conflict situations.

Many managers prefer to hide from conflict rather than to face it directly. This evasion only postpones and intensifies the ensuing difficulties.

Finally, it was observed that some conflict, such as that between management and labor, is institutionalized, so that its role requirements and procedures are relatively standardized. Role occupants enact scenarios that are familiar to both sides of the conflict and to interested outsiders; in so doing, they contain and organize the conflict situation and help fit it into the managerial ideologies.

The resolution of conflict is a vital process. It is brought about through administrative means, such as coordination, control, planning, or reorganization. Parties or units in conflict may accommodate to conflict resolution levels through gamesmanship and strategy and through experience that engenders trust. Participative management and leadership theory contain many ideas useful in conflict resolution.

_____ **INCIDENT CASE**

In a large insurance firm providing all types of coverage nationwide, the vice president for administration recommended a number of organizational changes to the president. Included in these was a plan to transfer the sales training functions out of the marketing department and into the training department, which came under the vice president for personnel relations. The personnel vice president had been trying to get the sales training function for over two years, and had finally persuaded the vice president for administration to make the change. When the plan was distributed to those affected, the vice president of marketing was outraged. Refusing to talk to the personnel vice president, he went directly to the vice president for administration and threatened to talk to the president himself "before this idiotic change goes too far." Forced to carry out this threat, he asked the president not to approve the change. When the president said he favored the change, the vice president of marketing threatened to resign.

Questions:

1. What should the president do, and why?
2. What is your opinion of the suggested change?

QUESTIONS FOR STUDY

1. What are the various forms of conflict that can occur within an organization?

2. What are some of the functional benefits and drawbacks of organizational conflict?

3. What is meant by *institutionalized conflict?* What is its purpose?

4. What behaviors of managers are important to creating conflict situations? What behaviors are necessary to minimize or contain undue conflict?

5. Could an organization be designed so as to have no conflict? Why or why not?

6. What does the analysis in this chapter have to say about the resolution of line-staff conflicts?

7. What is the definition of role conflict? What is a role? How does role conflict affect an organization?

8. Explain how leadership concepts are related to problems of conflict and conflict resolution.

SELECTED REFERENCES

Administrative Science Quarterly 14 (December 1969). Entire issue devoted to conflict within and between organizations.

BASS, BERNARD, and SAMUEL D. DEEP, eds. *Current Perspectives for Managing Organizations.* Englewood Cliffs, N.J.: Prentice-Hall, Inc., 1970. Pp. 445–488.

BLAKE, ROBERT F., HERBERT A. SHEPARD, and JANE S. MOUTON. *Managing Intergroup Conflict in Industry.* Austin, Tex.: Gulf Publishing Company, 1964.

DAVIS, MORTON D. *Game Theory: A Nontechnical Introduction.* New York: Basic Books, Inc., Publishers, 1970.

DEUTSCH, MORTON. *The Resolution of Conflict: Constructive and Destructive Processes.* New Haven: Yale University Press, 1973.

EMSHOFF, JAMES R. *Analysis of Behavioral Systems.* New York: Macmillan Publishing Co., Inc., 1971.

FILLEY, ALAN, ROBERT J. HOUSE, and STEVEN KERR. *Managerial Process and Organizational Behavior.* 2nd ed. Glenview, Ill.: Scott, Foresman and Company, 1976. Chapter 9.

HALL, RICHARD T. *Organizations: Structure and Process.* Englewood Cliffs, N.J.: Prentice-Hall, Inc., 1972.

KAHN, ROBERT L., and ELISE BOULDING, eds. *Power and Conflict in Organizations.* New York: Basic Books, Inc., Publishers, 1964.

LIKERT, RENSIS, and JANE GIBSON LIKERT. *New Ways of Managing Conflict.* New York: McGraw-Hill Book Company, 1976.

MARCH, JAMES G., and HERBERT A. SIMON. *Organizations.* New York: John Wiley & Sons, Inc., 1958. Chapter 5.

ROBBINS, STEPHEN P. *Managing Organizational Conflict: A Nontraditional Approach.* Englewood Cliffs, N.J.: Prentice-Hall, Inc., 1974.

SCOTT, WILLIAM G. *The Management of Conflict.* Homewood, Ill.: Richard D. Irwin, Inc., 1965.

THOMPSON, VICTOR A. *Modern Organization.* New York: Alfred A. Knopf, Inc., 1961. Chapter 5.

WIELAND, GEORGE F., and ROBERT A. ULLRICH. *Organizations: Behavior, Design, and Change.* Homewood, Ill.: Richard D. Irwin, Inc., 1976.

Chapter 18

Organizational Effectiveness

Many great social problems press in on us. We need the effective application of new knowledge through a diversity of skills drawn from many disciplines.   —James E. Webb

A good executive is judged by the company he keeps—solvent.
— Anonymous

Richard H. Hall states in *Organizations* (Prentice-Hall, 1972, p. 97) that "interest in effectiveness has not led to a definitive set of studies or conceptual approaches to the issue. A good part of the difficulty in assessing effectiveness lies in the problems surrounding goals." In his view, effectiveness, or efficiency, has not been defined because the concept denotes efficiency at achieving some good and that there are problems in identifying and measuring organizational goals and hence in organizational efficiency.

Questions to keep in mind as you read this chapter:

1. What characteristics of goals cause problems for research, concepts, and practices relating to effectiveness and its measurement?
2. Are the terms *effectiveness* and *efficiency* conceptually the same? Why or why not?
3. Can you explain why managers in organizations are not always very concerned about either effectiveness or efficiency?

How organizations are systematically to be judged is a difficult problem. Both those inside and those outside make continuous, critical evaluations, but it is hard to bring them together into a framework for action. Organizations face multiple expectations from employees, stockholders, customers, and the public. They work toward a number of goals simultaneously. Both the expectations and the goals may overlap or be in conflict. They may be idealistic, ambiguous, or unmeasurable.

Organizations seek, in general, to be effective in meeting expectations and achieving goals. The degree of effectiveness, then, becomes one major test by which an organization may be evaluated by those having a stake in its success. But the various stakeholders have differing amounts and kinds of power by which they pursue their interests. Managers often feel hard pressed to meet their conflicting demands. For example, environmentalists want antipollution devices in automobiles, whereas purchasers want low prices, and manufacturers want facility of production.

The effective organization, ultimately, is one in which the managers have harmonized conflicting demands, minimizing harmful conflict while pursuing the organization's goals and objectives. Fortunately there are grounds for believing that such resolutions are possible through common interests. Mott, for example, suggests that in any organization, the personal needs that workers most want fulfilled are the very needs whose fulfillment facilitates organizational effectiveness.[1]

Effectiveness is a matter of degree. No organization is as effective as it could be; perfect performance is without definition or measurement, and constituent interest groups will always be disappointed if their demands are inadequately heeded. In the absence of universal standards, we must judge organizations by relative comparisons and such other criteria as apply to particular situations. This chapter will explore the following aspects of organizational effectiveness: (1) the concept of effectiveness in organizations, (2) criteria and their measurement, (3) organizational correlates of effectiveness, and (4) problems in achieving effectiveness in organizations.

THE CONCEPT OF EFFECTIVENESS

Effectiveness is not a one-dimensional concept that can be precisely measured by a single, clear-cut criterion. Rather, effectiveness is a label that describes in a relative way the extent to which an organization has performed according to its capacities, potentials, and general goals.

[1]Paul E. Mott, *The Characteristics of Effective Organizations* (New York: Harper, 1972), p. 185.

Effectiveness centers more on the human side of organizational activity than on the technological side. Technology can be designed to provide a given level of effectiveness in an engineering or scientific sense, but it is always subject to the vagaries of the human beings who operate the technology. Thus effectiveness is the result of complex forces that combine technology with problems of human skills, values, and needs. That technology is not a sufficient base for analyzing effectiveness is illustrated by the changes that the Arab oil embargo of 1973 required in petroleum industry. According to Theodore Levitt, it took only one week of intensive around-the-clock work by managers to rearrange completely the entire sourcing, shipping, pipelining, and delivery of the world's petroleum products to get products rolling again to consumers. Managers made all the difference in rearranging the technology to fit urgent goals.[2]

Definitions

Both managers and researchers have used a variety of definitions of organizational effectiveness. The definitions differ according to the criteria by which effectiveness is measured.

Early writers defined effectiveness straightforwardly as the degree to which purposes are achieved. Barnard, for example, defines effectiveness as the condition of an organization in which specific, desired ends are attained. He makes an important distinction between effectiveness and efficiency: when unsought consequences are trivial, effective action is efficient; when unsought consequences are not trivial, effective action is inefficient.[3]

Georgopolous and Tannenbaum give this definition: *organizational effectiveness is the extent to which an organization, given certain resources and means, achieves its objectives without placing undue strain on its members.* This definition amplifies the concept by including as general criteria (1) productivity, (2) flexibility in the form of adjustment to internal change and successful adaptation to external change, and (3) the absence of excessive internal strain, tension, and conflict among subgroups.[4] Similarly, Mott defines organizational effectiveness as *the ability of an organization to mobilize its centers of power for action—production and adaptation.* This view adds to productivity the concept of adapting to environmental and internal problems.[5]

[2]Theodore Levitt, "Management: Engine of Progress," *MBA*, November, 1976, pp. 30–31.

[3]Chester I. Barnard, *Functions of the Executive* (Cambridge, Mass.: Harvard U. P., 1938), pp. 19–20, 55ff.

[4]Basil Georgopoulos and Arnold S. Tannenbaum, "A Study of Organization Effectiveness," *American Sociological Review* **22** (1957), 535–536.

[5]Mott, *Characteristics,* p. 17.

In addition to success in goal achievment and productivity, concepts of effectiveness have been based on such factors as indices of employee turnover or absenteeism, net profit, success in maintaining or expanding the organization, and the morale and job satisfaction of organization members. These approaches have the advantage of quantifiability and comparability over periods of time. However, the use of any single criterion as a measure of effectiveness is open to question. Further analysis of the various criteria will now be presented.

CRITERIA FOR EFFECTIVENESS

The definitions of effectiveness just presented indicate the presence of a criterion problem. That is, objective comparisons are difficult in the absence of criteria acceptable for consistent and valid measurement. Also, researchers need and use criteria that are different from those that are satisfactory to managers. Investigations have shown, for example, that managers in a complex organization may cite as many as two hundred criteria they believe are important. The reason is that organizations have multiple purposes, which are in a state of change. It is necessary, therefore, to use multiple criteria, and to use different kinds of measures for different purposes. Measures of total effectiveness against a single criterion are difficult, and they usually do not reflect the factors that influence the degree of effectiveness measured in this way.

Definitions of effectiveness based on goal achievement or on productivity are the most widely used. Other criteria such as those described above are also useful, but to a large extent they are oversimplified, or too narrow. For example, they do not take into account the problem of the organization's environment and the ability of the organization to cope with it. Moreover, they deal with ends, saying nothing of means to those ends. Morale, turnover, absenteeism, and other index types of criteria have frequently been inconsistent, insignificant, or hard to evaluate and interpret. Another difficulty is their differential sensitivity to additional factors such as the nature and volume of work, organizational level, and time of occurrence. Net profit is also a cloudy criterion because it is affected by unanticipated fluctuations external to the system, such as markets, sales and prices.[6]

Benge has suggested making performance comparisons by the use of indexes, covering industry comparisions, financial conditions, sales, manufacturing, purchasing, and profit. Each factor is weighted as to its importance by executive judgment. An average is calculated for each

[6]Mott, *Characteristics*, p. 17.

factor from historical performance data, and the deviations from the average at any point are expressed statistically in terms of standard deviations. The index of management effectiveness is the algebraic average of the weighted standard deviation of such factors.[7] Such systematic measurements may be useful in that they use multiple criteria, but they are subject to many limitations. The element of statistics implies more objectivity than is usually the case.

The use of goal attainment as a criterion of effectiveness is complicated by the tendency of goals to change, to be stated vaguely, and to exist in sets and at different levels. Also, because there are multiple goals, some will be in conflict. Moreover, the goals themselves must be evaluated if they are to be used as criteria for effectiveness. Although effectiveness can be measured only against a goal or standard, it is misleading to talk about effectiveness in attaining inadequate or wrong goals.

Even productivity or output as a measure of effectiveness is limited in scope and applicability. Such measures are historical. They reflect past effectiveness in adapting to problems and coping with emergencies, but they tell nothing about viability now or in the future. By the time productivity data are in hand, current conditions have changed. Also, productivity measures say nothing about such considerations as quality and efficiency.

Despite the drawbacks mentioned, productivity as a measure of effectiveness rates high among supervisory personnel as well as higher managers. Mahoney and colleagues found that the "man-in-the middle" supervisor holds priorities more similar to those of higher managers than to those of his own subordinates. Both supervisors and higher managers rate productivity very high. But supervisors assign less priority to human relations variables than do their superiors; they perceive such variables as instrumental in achieving productivity, not as ends in themselves; it is productivity that is often an important measure of effectiveness to those inside the organization at the middle and lower levels.[8]

Typologies

Multiple-criteria models of effectiveness are used to classify the relevant variables to be measured. Mott, Seashore, and Steers have each provided useful approaches to the selection and classification of effectiveness variables.

[7]Eugene J. Benge, "A Management Effectiveness Index," *Advanced Management* **17** (August 1952), 12–15.
[8]Thomas A. Mahoney, William Weitzel, and Norman F. Crandall, "A Supervisory View of Unit Effectiveness," *California Management Review* **13** (Summer 1971), 37–42.

Mott has developed the following criteria, based on his definition cited above:

A. Organizing centers of power for routine production (productivity)
   1. Quantity of the product
   2. Quality of the product
   3. Efficiency with which the product is produced
B. Organizing centers of power to change routines (adaptability)
   1. Symbolic adaptation
      a. Anticipating problems in advance and developing satisfactory and timely solutions
      b. Staying abreast of new technologies and methods applicable to the activities of the organization
   2. Behavioral adaptation
      a. Prompt acceptance of solutions
      b. Prevalent acceptance of solutions
C. Organizing centers of power to cope with temporarily unpredictable overloads of work (flexibility)[9]

Seashore has advanced a useful typology for different kinds of criteria of effectiveness. First, both ends and means are important. Some criteria are close to formal objectives in that they represent ends or goals that are valued in themselves; others are instrumental in achieving main goals. Second, the time frame must be considered. Some criteria refer to the past; others to the present and the future. Third, long-run and short-run perspectives are needed. Performance may be stable or highly erratic in the short run, but show a different pattern in the long run. Fourth, some criteria are "hard," others are "soft." Hard criteria consist of objective, measurable factors, whereas others, such as the level of morale, are qualitative. Hard data are not necessarily better than soft data, but both may be needed. Fifth, some variables are linear in value, that is, more is better than less; whereas others have a variable scale where some optimum is desired and more or less are both undesirable. Seashore also indicates the need to differentiate various criteria according to organizational level.[10]

Steers studied 17 multivariate effectiveness models developed by other researchers, in terms of their primary evaluation criteria, their normative or descriptive nature, their generalizability, and their derivation. He found little consistency in the criteria used in the models; he also noted problems that reduce their utility. He concluded that effec-

[9]Mott, *Characteristics*, pp. 17–20.
[10]Stanley E. Seashore, "Criteria of Organizational Effectiveness," *Michigan Business Review*, July 1965, 26–30. For additional studies, see Thomas A. Mahoney and William Weitzel, "Managerial Models of Organizational Effectiveness," *Administrative Science Quarterly* **14** (September 1969), 357–365.

tiveness measures should focus on operative rather than broad, strategic goals, and on goal optimization. That is, the specification of criteria should be flexible enough to account for diversity in goal preferences. Operative goals reflect the actual behavioral intentions of the organization, and hence it is possible to measure the extent to which those intentions are being achieved. Table 18-1 lists the 17 studies and indicates the type of model and the extent of its generalizability.[11]

Social Effectiveness

Among the "soft" criteria are those tests of effectiveness that relate to the organization's presence in the community. As corporate citizens, companies need to be aware of their social responsibilities. Bass, as early as 1952, suggested that the criteria of organizational worth need to be expanded. Instead of evaluating the success of programs solely by productivity, efficiency, and profits, he proposed that programs also be evaluated on their contributions to the organization's worth to its members and to society.[12]

Blum has also suggested a social responsibility measure, an "audit of progress in human relations." Both organizational and individual scores are used to reveal the status of the social audit and to serve as a basis for improving performance in that sector. Blum proposes that each company set aside a certain percentage of its profits for research and action in regard to factors influencing the satisfaction of human needs for unity and integrity, in order to improve human relations.[13]

Social responsibility audits have not been widely accepted, but there is a wellspring of social consciousness in the philosophies of managers and in the behavior of organizations. Social responsibilities, in the form of expectations of interest groups that comprise the public, are becoming increasingly important as criteria of effectiveness to be used alongside the more familiar ones.[14] We will return to this theme in Chapter 24.

[11]Richard M. Steers, "Problems in the Measurement of Organizational Effectiveness," *Administrative Science Quarterly* **20** (December 1975), 546–558. See also Paul M. Hirsch, "Organizational Effectiveness and the Institutional Environment," *Administrative Science Quarterly* **20** (September 1975), 327–344.

[12]Bernard M. Bass, "Ultimate Criteria of Organizational Worth," *Personnel Psychology* **5**, no. 3 (1952), 157–173.

[13]Fred H. Blum, "Social Audit of the Enterprise," *Harvard Business Review* **36** (March-April 1958), 77–86. See also S. Benjamin Prasad, "Organizational Effectiveness: A Theoretical and a Statistical Exploration," Midwest Division, *Proceedings of the 15th Annual Meeting* (Madison, Wis.: Academy of Management, 1972).

[14]See, for example, William A. McEachern, "The Managerial Revolution and Corporate Performance," *Challenge* **19**, no. 2 (May/June 1976), 36–40. See also Ronald J. Webb, "Organizational Effectiveness and the Voluntary Organization," *Academy of Management Journal* **17** (December 1974), 663–677.

TABLE 18-1. Evaluation Criteria in Multivariate Models of Organizational Effectiveness.

Study and Primary Evaluation Criteria	Type of Measure*	Generalizability of Criteria†	Derivation of Criteria‡
Georgopoulos and Tannenbaum (1957) Productivity, Flexibility, Absence of organization strain	N	A	Ded.; followed by questionnaire study
Bennis (1962) Adaptability, Sense of identity, Capacity to test Reality	N	A	Ded.; no study
Blake and Mouton (1964) Simultaneous achievement of high production-centered and high people-centered enterprise	N	B	Ded.; no study
Caplow (1964) Stability, Integration, Voluntarism, Achievement	N	A	Ded.; no study
Katz and Kahn (1966) Growth, Storage, Survival, Control over environment	N	A	Ind.; based on review of empirical studies
Lawrence and Lorsch (1967) Optimal balance of integration and differentiation	D	B	Ind.; based on study of 6 firms
Yuchtman and Seashore (1957) Successful acquisition of scarce and valued resources, Control over environment	N	A	Ind.; based on study of insurance agencies
Friedlander and Pickle (1968) Profitability, Employee satisfaction, Societal value	N	B	Ded.; followed by study of small businesses
Price (1968) Productivity, Conformity, Morale, Adaptiveness, Institutionalization	D	A	Ind.; based on review of 50 published studies
Mahoney and Weitzel (1969) General business model Productivity-support-utilization, Planning, Reliability, Initiative R and D Model Reliability, Cooperation, Development	D	B,R	Ind.; based on study of 13 organizations

432

Author (year) / Effectiveness criteria	*	†	Method
Schein (1970) Open communication, Flexibility, Creativity, Psychological commitment	N	A	Ded.; no study
Mott (1972) Productivity, Flexibility, Adaptability	N	A	Ded.; followed by questionnaire study of several organizations
Duncan (1973) Goal attainment, Integration, Adaptation	N	A	Ded.; followed by study of 22 decision units

Gibson et al. (1973)
Short-run
  Production, Efficiency, Satisfaction
Intermediate
  Adaptiveness, Development
Long-run
  Survival
	N	A	Ind.; based on review of earlier models

Negandhi and Reimann (1973)
Behavioral index
  Manpower acquisition, Employee satisfaction, Manpower retention, Interpersonal relations, Interdepartmental relations, Manpower utilization
Economic index
  Growth in sales, Net profit
	N	B	Ded.; followed by study of Indian organizations

Child (1974, 1975) Profitability, Growth	N	B	Ded.; followed by study of 82 British firms
Webb (1974) Cohesion, Efficiency, Adaptability, Support	D	C	Ind.; based on study of religious organizations

* N = Normative models, D = Descriptive models
† A = All organizations; B = Business organizations; C = Religious organizations; R = Research and development laboratories
‡ Ded. = Deductive, Ind. = Inductive
Source: Richard M. Steers, "Problems in the Measurement of Organizational Effectiveness," Administrative Science Quarterly 20 (December 1975), p. 548. Used by permission.

_____ **ORGANIZATION CORRELATES OF EFFECTIVENESS**

A different approach to problems of organizational effectiveness is to see whether structural characteristics are related to effectiveness. If so, structural criteria may be used to measure the degree of effectiveness of particular organizations.

Several studies have shown a relationship between organization or task structure and one or more measures of achievement, performance, or effectiveness. Leavitt and others, in communication net experiments, found that groups working on relatively simple and certain tasks tended to perform better when the groups had more structure, whereas groups working on uncertain, more complex tasks performed better with less structured communication nets.[15] Burns and Stalker found that organizations that were profitably coping with uncertain, changing environments had a low degree of formalized structure (similar to the adaptive model described earlier), instead of the higher degree of structure associated with success in more certain environments.[16]

In designing adaptive organization models, less reliance is placed the logic of similar or other related functions. Effectiveness is continuously judged by performers and peers, as well as by superiors in the system. Organization structure is looser, more flexible, and less important for its own sake. Mott's investigation of organizational effectiveness included a model of organization that embraces both the bureaucratic (closed) model and the adaptive (open) model. He treats organizations as ranging on a continuum of openness and closure. As roles and relationships become increasingly structured, the organization becomes more and more impervious to its environment. Mott believes that the degree of organizational closure is an important variable mediating many of the relationships between other organizational properties and organizational effectiveness.[17]

Likert has done extensive research on organizational performance. Like Bass, he suggests that traditional measures such as sales and profits deal only with end results and tell nothing about the state of the organization. Likert's research findings, which were based on comparisons of effective organizations with less effective ones, indicate that supportive employee-centered management using group methods of supervision coupled with high performance expectations obtains higher productivity, lower costs, and greater employee satisfaction than other forms of management. Because short-run gains can be obtained at

[15]Harold Leavitt, "Some Effects of Certain Communication Patterns on Group Performance," in E. Macoby et al. (eds.), *Readings in Social Psychology* (New York: Holt, 1958), pp. 546–563.

[16]Thomas Burns and G. M. Stalker, *The Management of Innovation* (London: Tavistock Institute, 1961).

[17]Mott, *Characteristics*, pp. 15–16.

the expense of the human characteristics of the organization, it is important to measure the state of the organization.[18]

Technology, Structure, and Performance

In major studies in Britain, Woodward found a relationship between the nature of the task and the structure of the organization, and noted that more profitable organizations tended to adopt structures consistent with the requirements of the technological environment.[19] However, more recent studies have failed to confirm Woodward's views. Blau, for example, rejects Woodward's notion of a "broad technological imperative" for internal structure.[20] Donaldson, reviewing four major studies, also concludes that the bivariate relationship between technology and structure has not been confirmed, and in fact has been disconfirmed.[21] The relationships between technology and structure are still controversial. They will require further studies before it is possible to relate these variables to performance. Moreover, all the major studies to date have focused on manufacturing firms.

Systems Analysis and Effectiveness

The systems view of organizations throws much light on problems of effectiveness. An important consideration is the way in which systems are analyzed, both internally and in relation to their environments.

Lawrence and Lorsch, who made a comparative study of six organizations in the same industrial environment, found a relationship between the extent to which the state of differentiation and integration in each organization met the requirements of the environment and the relative economic performance of the organization. The term *differentiation* describes the state of segmentation of the organizational system into subsystems, each of which develops attributes that relate it to the external environment. Thus differentiation includes not only formal divisions of labor, but also behavioral attributes of members of the organization. *Integration* is defined as the process of achieving unity of

[18]Rensis Likert, "Measuring Organizational Performance," *Harvard Business Review* **16** (March-April 1958), 41–50; also *New Patterns of Management* (New York: McGraw-Hill, 1961) and *The Human Organization* (New York: McGraw-Hill, 1967).

[19]Joan Woodward, *Management and Technology* (London: Her Majesty's Printing Office, 1958), pp. 16–24; see also Joan Woodward, *Industrial Organization: Theory and Practice* (New York: Oxford U. P., 1965).

[20]Peter M. Blau et al., "Technology and Organization in Manufacturing," *Administrative Science Quarterly* **21** (March 1976), 20–40.

[21]Lex Donaldson, "Woodward Technology, Organizational Structure and Performance: A Critique of the Universal Generalization," *The Journal of Management Studies* **13** (October 1976), 255–273. See also Thomas A. Mahoney and Peter J. Frost, "The Role of Technology in Models of Organizational Effectiveness," *Organizational Behavior and Human Performance* **11** (February 1974), 122–138.

effort among the various subsystems in accomplishing the organization's tasks. Differentiation and integration are seen as intrinsically opposing states—that is, one can be obtained only at the expense of the other. All six organizations studied had similar integrative devices (integrating teams and departments), but in the high-performing organizations, the integrative devices led to greater effectiveness by being more sensitive to the determinants of effectiveness and by having the ability to respond to changes in them. Such factors as patterns of influence in the organization and the modes of conflict resolution were significant.[22]

Negandhi and Reimann found in a sample of firms in India that decentralized organizations were more effective on economic measures than centralized enterprises. They suggest that firms having greater concern for task environmental forces (that is, firms viewing their task agents in long-term perspectives) are likely to have fewer hierarchical levels. They tend to use consultative approaches to decision making for major policies. The findings of the study in India differ from Lawrence and Lorsch's finding that to be effective, organizations must establish a fit between their internal structure and their external environments. Lawrence and Lorsch suggest that centralized structures in stable environments and decentralized structures in dynamic environments are associated with a high degree of effectiveness, whereas decentralized operations in stable environments and centralized operations in dynamic environments may be dysfunctional. Negandhi and Reimann found instead a positive relationship between decentralization and organizational effectiveness, despite India's relatively stable environment.[23]

Reimann found that the dimensions of organization structure differ substantially between relatively effective and ineffective firms. He also found, in studying 19 firms, that the organizational pattern of the high-performing firms contained three varying independent dimensions: decentralization, specialization, and formalization. The three dimensions can be visualized as a "structural space," as shown in Figure 18-1. An effective organization could be relatively decentralized, specialized, and formalized, as shown at Position A in the diagram. It could also be decentralized but not specialized or formalized, as shown at Position B. This finding confirmed earlier studies of the Aston group in England that organizations may be bureaucratic in a number of ways,

[22]Paul R. Lawrence and Jay W. Lorsch, *Organization and Environment* (Boston: Division of Research, Graduate School of Business Administration, Harvard University, 1967).

[23]Anant R. Negandhi and Bernard C. Reimann, "Task Environment, Decentralization, and Organizational Effectiveness," *Human Relations* **26** (January/February 1973), 203–214.

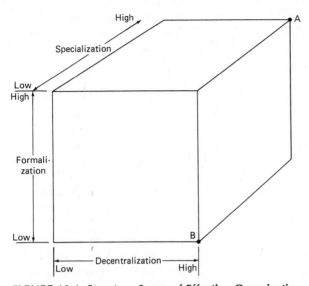

FIGURE 18-1. Structure Space of Effective Organization.

Source: Bernard C. Reimann, "Dimensions of Structure in Effective Organizations," *Academy of Management Journal* 17 (December 1974), p. 706. Used by permission.

and indicates that the multidimensional nature of bureaucratic organization structure may be unique to effective organizations.[24]

ACHIEVING ORGANIZATIONAL EFFECTIVENESS

Even though research throws considerable light on more effective organization designs, structural decisions are not always made according to the need for effectiveness. In bureaucratic models of organization, most decisions on organization structure are made according to similarities of activities and functions that are considered to be "logical" groupings. New functions and activities are contested for by managers in existing jurisdictions. Empire builders are aggressive in acquiring or inventing new activities. Decisions in this mode are likely to be temporary, for the criteria tend to be verbal, inaccurate, and subject to difficulties of prediction and change. To win at such a game, the manager has to carry out continuous moves of consolidation and defense.

Problems of effectiveness apply to the entire organization, but also to its subsystems—divisions, departments, sections, or other units. The

[24]Bernard C. Reimann, "Dimensions of Structure in Effective Organizations," *Academy of Management Journal* 17 (December 1974), 693–708.

subunits may vary extensively in their level of effectiveness. The total organization has to weigh the differential effectiveness of the subunits against other factors in its quest for improvement.

Knowing or appraising an organization's degree of effectiveness is a major step forward, but efforts to increase effectiveness need to be based on an adequate diagnosis of the source and nature of the causes of low effectiveness. Brown has noted seven defects that produce ineffective organizational results: failure of administrators to act when they need to, delay in taking action, taking the wrong action, lack of sufficient effort, wasted effort, excessive effort in relation to the need, and excessive quality of effort in relation to the problem. After proper diagnosis, it remains to determine which of four causes pertain to a given situation: people, organization, methods of administration, or external influences. The first three are controllable.[25]

Tannenbaum and his colleagues have constructed a set of diagnostic indices of organizational effectiveness. These elements pertain primarily to the human and organizational dimensions of organizational effectiveness:

1. *Understanding*—the extent to which prescribed relations are correctly perceived.
2. *Normative conformity*—the extent to which actual behavior conforms to prescribed behavior or to perceptions of the prescribed behavior.
3. Affective conformity—the extent to which actual behavior conforms to desires and reflections.
4. *Satisfaction and dissatisfaction*—the extent to which prescribed, perceived, or actual relations are also desired or rejected.
5. *Affective atmosphere*—the state of balance that exists in an organizational unit between affectively positive and affectively negative choices.
6. *Centralization*—the extent to which choices (prescribed, actual, desired, perceived, or rejected) are concentrated in a particular person or group.[26]

Organizational Health

Argyris, Bennis, and others have related the problem of total organization effectiveness to the concept of organizational health, which holds that because a system has multiple functions and its environment provides unpredictable inputs, effectiveness can be defined as the

[25]Alvin Brown, "Judging the Effectiveness of Organization," *Advanced Management* **20** (January 1955), 13–15.

[26]Robert Tannenbaum, Irving R. Weschler, and Fred Massarik, *Leadership and Organization* (New York: McGraw-Hill, 1961).

system's capacity to survive, adapt, maintain itself, and grow, regardless of the particular functions it performs. Bennis says that instead of static measures of output, effectiveness should be inferred from the processes by which the organization approaches problems. He argues that a single measure of output or slice of time will not provide an indication of organizational health. Instead, he suggests three kinds of criteria: adaptability, a sense of identity, and the capacity to test reality.[27]

Another criterion that is widespread in the literature of organizational health is that of the integration of individual and organizational goals. Argyris has researched the conditions that permit such an integration. He believes that restriction of output, destructive competition, and employee apathy—or any behavior that puts personal needs ahead of organizational goals—are symptoms of poor organizational health.[28] McGregor[29] argues that changing our assumptions about man and about the way organizations are run will produce integration and hence improve effectiveness. This assertion is supported by Katz.[30] Blake and Mouton present a case for better integration between concern for people and concern for production.[31]

Total organizational effectiveness is hard to measure and hard to achieve. What generally happens in organizations is that leaders are able to identify the less effective subgroups or individuals, and can work to improve matters at practicable levels. For example, the president of a university knows that it is not feasible to develop a university that is truly great in all fields of learning. The university may be great in certain areas, such as the humanities, medicine, or law, and less than good in education, engineering, or social science. The president therefore must be selective in his building efforts, for resources are scarce and it takes from five to ten years to change a department from "good" to "great." Efforts need to be concentrated on areas where it is feasible to improve and where the character of the university is shaped in relation to given communities of interest.

--- **SUMMARY**

A central problem in the concept of organizational effectiveness is the definition of standards or criteria by which an organization may be

[27]Warren G. Bennis, "Toward a Truly Scientific Management: The Concept of Organizational Health," *General Systems Yearbook* 7 (1962), 269–282.

[28]Chris Argyris, *Integrating the Individual and Organization* (New York: Wiley, 1964).

[29]Douglas McGregor, *The Human Side of Enterprise* (New York: McGraw-Hill, 1960).

[30]Robert L. Katz, "Toward a More Effective Enterprise," *Harvard Business Review* 39 (September-October 1969), 80–102.

[31]Robert R. Blake and Jane S. Mouton, *The Managerial Grid* (Houston, Tex.: Gulf Publishing Company, 1964).

judged. Although tangible measurements of productivity, profitability, or efficiency are useful, they are not sufficient measures of effectiveness. Both means and ends must be considered in determining the degree of effectiveness of the organization. The concept of effectiveness that is most useful in judging organizations is that of adaptability, change, and the capacity to mobilize the centers of organizational power for both productive and adaptive action.

Several organizational correlates of organization effectiveness were described. Lawrence and Lorsch found a relationship between the extent to which the state of differentiation and integration in each organization met the requirements of the environment and the relative economic performance of the organizations. Several studies have shown a relationship between organization or task structure and one or more measures of achievement, performance, or effectiveness.

In addition, the concept of organizational health has found considerable research support. According to this concept, a system has multiple functions, and its environment provides unpredictable inputs. Therefore organizational health and effectiveness is represented by the system's capacity to survive, adapt, maintain itself, and grow.

INCIDENT CASE

Two managers were arguing one day over lunch. One said, "The effectiveness of an organization depends entirely on hiring effective people. We look carefully at the track record of anyone we hire. With effective people, it doesn't really matter how you are organized." The other manager said, "You're wrong. In my company we make sure that the organizational system is sound. Nobody's perfect, so we don't expect to find people who are automatically successful. We develop them after they are hired, but we make sure that the organization structure and practices are sound."

Question:

1. Which manager is correct, and why?

QUESTIONS FOR DISCUSSION

1. Name some typical criteria by which organizations are judged. Which are concrete measures, and which subjective?

2. What criticisms can be made of achievement measures, or the managerial orientation toward results?

3. Discuss the means-ends dichotomy in relation to the evaluation of organizational effectiveness.

4. What is meant by the concept of organizational health? How is it measured? What research backs up the concept?

5. If achievement is a measure of only limited value, what else is necessary for adequate evaluation of organizational effectiveness?

6. What is meant by a social responsibility audit? How is it conducted, and to what uses can it be put?

7. Trace as many as you can of the elements of organizational or structural factors having an impact on organizational effectiveness.

8. Under what conditions would the concepts of efficiency and effectiveness merge?

9. Why is profit maximization not a useful ultimate goal for measuring organizational effectiveness?

SELECTED REFERENCES

BATY, GORDON B. *Entrepreneurship: Playing to Win.* Reston, Va.: Reston Publishing Company, 1974.

BLAKE, ROBERT F., and JANE S. MOUTON. *Corporate Excellence Diagnosis.* Austin, Tex.: Scientific Methods, Inc., 1968.

CAMPBELL, JOHN P., D. A. BOWNAS, M. G. PETERSON, and MARVIN DUNNETTE. *The Measurement of Organizational Effectiveness: Review of Relevant Research and Opinion.* San Diego: Leavy Research and Personnel Research and Development Center, 1974.

CAPLOW, THEODORE. *How to Run Any Organization.* New York: Holt, Rinehart and Winston, 1976.

CHAPPLE, ELIOT B., and LEONARD R. SAYLES. *The Measure of Management.* New York: Macmillan Publishing Co., Inc., 1961.

FINCH, FREDERICK E., HALSEY R. JONES, and JOSEPH A. LITTERER. *Managing for Organizational Effectiveness: An Experiential Approach.* New York: McGraw-Hill Book Company, 1976.

GRAY, JERRY L., ed. *The Glacier Project: Concepts and Critiques.* New York: Crane, Russok & Company, 1975.

HACON, RICHARD, ed. *Personal and Organizational Effectiveness.* New York: McGraw-Hill Book Company, 1972.

KATZ, DANIEL, and ROBERT L. KAHN. *The Social Psychology of Organizations.* New York: John Wiley & Sons, Inc., 1966. Chapters 6 and 12.

KENDRICK, JOHN W., and DANIEL CREAMER. *Measuring Company Productivity.* New York: The Conference Board, 1965.

KILMANN, RALPH H., and RICHARD P. HERDEN. "Towards a Systematic Methodology for Evaluating the Impact of Interventions on Organizational Effectiveness." *The Academy of Management Review* 1, no. 3 (July 1976), 87–98.

KOONTZ, HAROLD. *The Board of Directors and Effective Management.* New York: McGraw-Hill Book Company, 1967.

LAWLER, EDWARD E. *Pay and Organizational Effectiveness: A Psychological View.* New York: McGraw-Hill Book Company, 1971.

LEVINSON, HARRY. *Organizational Diagnosis.* Boston: Harvard University Press, 1972.

LIKERT, RENSIS. *The Human Organization.* New York: McGraw-Hill Book Company, 1967.

MOTT, PAUL E. *The Characteristics of Effective Organizations.* New York: Harper & Row, Publishers, 1972.

PRICE, JAMES L. *Handbook of Organizational Measurement.* Lexington, Mass.: D. C. Heath Company, 1972.

PRICE, JAMES L. *Organizational Effectiveness: An Inventory of Propositions.* Homewood, Ill.: Richard D. Irwin, Inc., 1968.

SCHEIN, EDGAR H. *Organizational Psychology.* Englewood Cliffs, N.J.: Prentice-Hall, Inc., 1965. Chapter 7.

SEASHORE, STANLEY. *Assessing Organization Performance With Behavioral Measurements.* Ann Arbor, Mich.: Foundation for Research in Human Behavior, 1964.

SPRAY, LEE, ed. *Organizational Effectiveness: Theory, Research, and Application.* Kent, Ohio: Comparative Administration Research Institute, 1976.

STINCHCOMBE, ARTHUR L. *Creating Efficient Industrial Administration.* New York: Academic Press, Inc., 1974.

THOMPSON, JAMES D. *Organizations in Action.* New York: McGraw-Hill Book Company, 1967. Chapter 7.

WIELAND, GEORGE F., and ROBERT A. ULLRICH. *Organizations: Behavior, Design, and Change.* Homewood, Ill.: Richard D. Irwin, Inc., 1976.

YUCHTMAN, EMPHRAIM, and STANLEY E. SEASHORE. "A Systems Resource Approach to Organizational Effectiveness." *American Sociological Review* **32** (December 1967), 891–903.

Cases for Part III

In one of the regional state mental hospitals in a highly populated, industrial state, the medical superintendent who ran the hospital had what many believed to be an impressive record of accomplishment. During his tenure of 16 years, the hospital was approved by the American Psychiatric Association for the complete three-year residency program for medical doctors seeking to become certified psychiatrists. Over one hundred physicians had taken this training by 1975.

Lawrence Novella, the medical superintendent, had greatly improved the hospital's facilities and services. He secured the full approval of the Joint Commission on Accreditation of Hospitals, making his the first such institution in his state to receive such approval.

When Novella, aged 56, first came to the hospital, there were over 3,000 patients. By 1976, there were fewer than 1,300. During this same period, the number of employees increased from 600 to 1,040, including an increase from seven doctors to thirty-four.

In early 1976, however, conflicts between Novella and some of the staff members occurred over changes Novella was recommending. Some of the changes were in the hospital's training and research section, but other changes were contemplated as well. During the following year, the complaints continued and their intensity increased. More and more frequently, the conflicts came out in the public press, further exacerbating the situation.

The director of public information for the state Department of Mental Health told press reporters that his department had received a number of letters both for and against Novella over the past two years. He said that he regarded the situation as one where people like to have someone to tell their gripes to, someone they think can do

443

something about their unhappiness. "There are always people who are unhappy," he said.

The disputes were called to the attention of the governor. An aide in the governor's office said that the office investigated the problems at the State Hospital, and that the governor decided to take a hands-off position in the matter.

A former psychiatric resident (M.D.) who had resigned after being drafted into the Army related the details of the complaints by staff members. "Many staff members," he said, "became discouraged when their proposals to the superintendent didn't bring any significant results."

According to the ex-resident, the protesting group took their dissatisfactions to the director of the State Department of Mental Health early in 1976. The director made an on-site visit to the hospital, talking with Novella and several staff members, but the situation was not satisfactorily resolved.

"During the past year, quite a few physicians left the hospital. Some may have left to return to private practice, but I think many left because of the continuing frictions with Novella," said the resident. He also said that although he himself was sympathetic with Novella's position, he felt that there was insufficient heart-to-heart communication. He reported that poor communication was revealed by the fact that staff members found out things about the hospital only through local newspapers.

In 1977 a local newspaper ran a series of articles exploring the circumstances of a death in the State Hospital. Low morale developed from the hospital's internal problems, the lack of communication, and the criticism generated by the mysterious death. "Our staff people are very proud of their work, and to receive such devastating criticism was a real blow to the hospital staff's morale," said the resident. The situation was reportedly further aggravated by the effort of Novella and certain other staff members to combat the unfavorable news accounts by threatening the paper's advertisers with a boycott if they continued to advertise. Stories about the boycott threats were carried in most of the State's newspapers, and *Time Magazine* gave the story national publicity.

The State Attorney General's office conducted a study of the attacks on the newspaper, concluding that hospital personnel had "set out to crush the newspaper because they did not like what was being printed," and stated that "such actions cannot be tolerated."

On the basis of the Attorney General's report, the State Director of Mental Health suspended Novella's pay for two weeks, and threatened his immediate dismissal if the State reported further misconduct.

At the end of 1977, Novella announced his resignation from the hospital's top administrative post, to work as a psychiatrist on the staff. Novella said that he had "thought it over over a long period of time."

The public relations director of the State Department of Mental Health stated, upon learning of the resignation, that the resignation was not forced. "The resignation was entirely voluntary, having nothing to do with the problems at the State Hospital. Neither the State nor the Mental Health Department asked for his resignation. There was no pressure applied," he said.

QUESTIONS

1. How does management in this case compare to management in a private company?

2. Does the fact that this case occurred in the context of a hospital have anything to do with what happened?

3. As a candidate for the superintendent's vacancy, what would your reactions be?

<hr>

B. THE TOUGH MANAGER

"I suppose I have inherited a reputation for being rough, tough, and independent," said Ellison Mudge, the new sixty-year-old president of the Gleamo Soap Company. The Gleamo Soap Company is a wholly owned British subsidiary of Varnex, Incorporated, a large, diversified conglomerate with headquarters in New York. Like other conglomerates, Varnex has in recent years been involved in extensive mergers that have greatly disrupted its industry.

Mudge's reputation for independence came from his career-long habit of bouncing in and out of different companies, often quitting and rejoining firms he had served before. Mudge is not regarded by colleagues as money-oriented; he has resigned from companies several times on matters of principle. He spent six years in his first company as a production manager. Finding it too bureaucratic, he went into the rubber industry for seven years. Then he disagreed with his boss on what he considered to be an important principle and resigned. The next two years he spent with his first company, but he resigned to return to the rubber company, working for his previous boss. The company was taken over by another firm, and talk of retrenchment led Mudge to quit.

Mudge next joined an adventurous conglomerate run by a notorious takeover king. He had major disagreements with top management, but ended up as president of an operating division. Two years later he returned to the rubber company, but had a difference of opinion with the chairman of the board and left. He returned for the third time to his first company, which by then was under new management. However, the new bureaucracy was no more satisfactory than the old one, so in 1965 Mudge resigned to return to Gleamo.

Mudge had worked for the Varnex enterprise on two brief previous occasions. In 1972 his position in the Gleamo Soap Company was that of executive director (equivalent to the position of general manager in U.S. firms). In 1974, he was promoted over the heads of the functional managers to the post of managing director (equivalent to the position of president in U.S. firms). Mudge's advancement over the heads of the functional managers who form the top management of Gleamo was unusual and created much talk in the industry as well as within Gleamo. This bypassing, said Mudge, "was completely out of character of both Gleamo and Varnex." Mudge had taken the assignment after a week's brainstorming session with top management in the New York office, where he and the president of the parent company, Varnex, became well acquainted.

Mudge felt that being rough, tough, and independent were qualities needed for the problems Gleamo then faced, which were primarily in the area of production. Orders were coming in at a rapid rate, but the company had difficulty operating profitably. To Mudge this pointed to the need for a major reorganization of the Gleamo unit. "No one coming in new would let things stay as they are," Mudge remarked, "so why should I?" He also remarked that "no two people run a business the same way, so I expect to make many changes." He proposed to reorganize Gleamo to strengthen each of its two main divisions—a consumer products division for cosmetics and toiletries, and an industrial chemicals and cleaning compounds division.

The reorganization plan that Mudge developed called for quick action, a reflection of Mudge's belief that an atmosphere of uncertainty is not a good one in which to manage a company. He proposed to accomplish the reorganization in logical stages. He told his subordinates that his philosophy was simple: "I believe men need three things: money, a feeling of security, and a sense of belonging. The latter is particularly important for those doing repetitive work. If one looks at these three things, they make sense because they are all interrelated, and it brings one back to the profit motive. The name of the game is money."

On taking over his new post, Mudge did not predict clashes between Gleamo and the parent Varnex company management, because Varnex has always had a philosophy that the top management of a foreign subsidiary must consist of nationals, and the degree of interference from New York is directly related to the confidence the central headquarters has in local management. After a new president took over at Varnex, according to Mudge, Gleamo experienced dramatic differences between being a British company with complete autonomy and being a part of an international company with complete autonomy. Mudge indicated, for example, that he worked out the basic principles for reorganization with the New York office. "Once we got the green light on principles, it was up to us to get on with it," said Mudge. However, he admitted privately that whether actions follow the principles laid down is often a question of interpretation. "But you have to be a good salesman, not the least in the matter of selling yourself to your bosses."

QUESTIONS

1. Appraise and discuss the philosophy of Mr. Mudge.
2. Analyze the problems of mobility and career patterns indicated in this case.
3. What forecast would you make, and why, concerning Mr. Mudge's probable effects, activities, and results in his new appointment as president of Gleamo?

C. AXTELLE COMPANY, INC.

Sam Snider was employed three years ago to head a group set up to design and install a highly computerized management information system in the Axtelle Company. Axtelle is a large, profitable manufacturing enterprise with over 22,000 employees, eight plant locations, and a unique product marketed nationally.

Despite the lack of top management support, Sam and his task force were able to proceed with the system design. There was no time pressure on Sam to produce. He set his own goals and managed his resources, generally, as best he saw fit. He was hired for his technical knowledge in computer systems, and for his ability to work with his peers in a consultative, goal-oriented relationship.

When the design was complete, it was presented to top management; after much agitation, promotion, and politicking by Sam's superiors, the design was approved.

Then the bottom fell out of company finances. A highly abbreviated version of the original plan was therefore developed which could be expanded to the full version as resources permitted. Sam fully participated in developing the briefer version, and he favored it. The new version was approved, but with a time schedule that was felt to be unrealistic by everyone familiar with the project. Many thought that the shortened time schedule was adopted to get the project approved.

Bill Mann, the operations manager, had been working with Sam on an ad hoc basis throughout this period, lending advice and cutting red tape as desired. Sam reported to him functionally but not on a line basis. With the renewed interest and tough time schedule, the time came to get down to the brass tacks. Here is how the project was structured:

(1) *Preliminary system design*—in which the user presents his needs in detail to the computer people.
(2) *System programming*—in which the system is programmed by the computer people according to user specifications.
(3) *System installation*—testing and installing alongside existing systems.

As the group moved into Step 1, the preliminary system design, the problem was to establish a realistic but tight schedule, and to publish the schedule to all concerned. However, Bill perceived that Sam was resisting this schedule. Being a high n-Achievement person, Bill thought, Sam was reluctant to set any schedule he was not reasonably sure to meet. The results of this problem were that:

(1) A schedule showing completion 30 May was published on 1 April.
(2) A schedule showing completion two weeks later was published in mid-May.
(3) A week later Sam proposed a third schedule, with yet another two weeks' slippage.

When Bill questioned Sam about this latest schedule, Sam said that the slippage was caused by additional detail required by users on parts of the computer system. When asked whether the remaining items had been rescheduled to reflect the added detail, he replied that the working team had set that schedule just as they had set the previous schedule. In further discussion, Bill said he had to have a schedule that he could defend, and that he couldn'd defend this one for the reasons mentioned. Sam became angry at that point, and said that to come up with such a schedule would take his time away from seeing that all the pieces of the project fit together, and in addition would further delay the project. Several times during the meeting Sam described how he had to "beat people over the head" to get something done. Finally, Sam asked to be relieved of his leadership of the project, threw his pen down, and sat back from the table after his angry outburst. Sam said, "I can't see why things have gone so well for two years, then all of a sudden there's this rush-rush-rush and everybody looking over my shoulder."

Bill analyzed Sam's problem as one of having deeply rooted problems with authority, as well as being a very high n-Achievement person. He is like a little boy who says "if you don't do things my way, I'm taking my toys home."

Bill analyzed the problem further, deciding that the central problem was getting on a realistic time schedule. He drew up the following plan of action:

(1) Explain again (for the 95th time) the effects of the changed atmosphere we are working under.

(2) Accept any delays (although a good schedule will serve as a rallying point and speed the project).

(3) Ask Sam to come up with a schedule that he regards as defensible (this will be tough because he is evasive as blazes, with a million reasons why it can't be done).

(4) Explain to Sam that he must realize that his hostility to the schedule will permeate the work group and that he has to find a way to come up with a schedule that he can support in a positive way.

(5) Agree that no schedule can be inflexible. However, it must be changed only as a last resort after all other alternatives are exhausted.

(6) After explaining all this, I will ask him how he feels about his angry behavior at the meeting. However, I don't know how to do this in a nonthreatening way. Perhaps the best thing to do is tell him he needs to think about how his effectiveness within the organization is a function of many factors, one of which is his choice of words—"beat so-and-so over the head," for example, but I'm not very confident of the outcome of this approach.

(7) Finally, if Sam is still recalcitrant, playing the hard-headed little boy, I'll ask him if he wants me to "beat him over the head." I doubt if I'd really do that, although I think he wants me to.

QUESTIONS

1. Will Bill's plan help to solve the problem? Why or why not?
2. Make an analysis that points toward an effective long-run solution.

D. DESIGNING AN ORGANIZATION STRUCTURE

1. Draw an organization chart for a single-plant, large manufacturing company, showing policy, staff, and operating levels. Assume that you are designing a bureaucratic structure. Use the following position titles and functions:

President
Manager of Research and Development
Vice President of Industrial Relations
Executive Vice President
Director of Purchasing
Vice President of Manufacturing
Plant Superintendent
Vice President of Finance
Vice President of Engineering
Production Manager
Chairman of the Board
Vice President of Public Relations
Manager of Labor Relations
Director of Corporate Planning
Manager of Industrial Engineering
Assistant to the President
Manager of Personnel

2. For the same organization, design an adaptive structure. You will use the same functions in your design, but you are free to eliminate or change any of the titles and functions, provided you explain your reasoning.

E. HUMAN RELATIONS IN THE OFFICE

In the personnel office of the Smith Manufacturing Company, two girls, Mary and Edna, disliked each other. This fact was known to the personnel manager, who had observed that the girls quarreled upon occasion. Although this lack of harmony in the office disturbed the personnel manager, he did not consider the situation serious enough to warrant anything more than a word of caution to the girls now and then. However, as time went on the situation became worse. Quarrels became more and more frequent. Each girl tried to hinder the other in her work. They openly refused to cooperate with each other and began to lose a great deal of time by going out of their way to interfere with each other's work. One day, while the personnel manager was sitting quietly at work, Mary rushed into his office, burst into tears, and exclaimed that she could no longer continue to work unless Edna was transferred or discharged.

QUESTIONS

1. If you were the personnel manager what would you do, and why?
2. What do you think could have been done to prevent this situation from happening?

F. THE TARFIELD COMPANY

Having completed a top management reorganization involving the appointment of three new corporate vice presidents, Arthur Benson, chairman of the board of the Tarfield Company, asked Howard Williams, the vice president of public relations, to release the news story to the press.

Williams asked Fred Foley, the head of the press relations section of his department, to prepare the story in detail. Foley wrote the release, and in accordance with Benson's express wishes, included photographs of the three promoted vice presidents. Two days later, the city's evening newspaper ran a brief story about the organizational changes, but did not use the photographs of the promoted executives.

On reading the newspaper account and noting that the pictures were missing, Benson lost his temper. He raged at Williams, who was unable to calm him down. When Benson discovered that Foley and not Williams had handled the matter, he ordered Foley to come to his office, where he called him unprintable names, stomping around his office in a fury. Foley, like Williams, tried to soothe Benson's feelings, with little success. After endeavoring to give Benson a rational explanation of the nuances of relations with the press, Foley hurriedly left the chairman's office, outwardly calm but inwardly shaken.

In desperation Foley had suggested to Benson that he talk to the financial news editor of the paper. The next day, still irate, Benson did so. The editor explained his guidelines for running pictures, saying that the heavy press of news on the day of the announcement prevented running the three photographs. He told Benson that the photographs were of the required quality, that they had arrived in time before the press deadline, and that it was not Foley's fault that the pictures were not used. Benson argued with the editor, but saw that he could not alter the decision.

One week later, Foley placed a letter on Williams's desk, saying "This is my letter of resignation. It has become clear to me that I am *persona non grata* in this firm; Benson considers me a failure for not getting those pictures in print. Therefore, I can no longer continue working here."

QUESTIONS

1. What should Williams do? What should he say, and why?
2. How can problems like these be prevented?

G. NORTON CANDY COMPANY

The Norton Candy Company is a national firm with a large line of candy products distributed under several well-known trade names. In recent years the firm has diversified into a number of related food lines, such as jams and jellies, diet foods, and imported cheese products. It is known among its competitors for aggressive selling. Inside the firm, however, the vice president of marketing was worried about the caliber of salesmen in contact with major outlets. The following memorandum is an example of the concern expressed by the vice president:

MEMORANDUM

To: Albert V. Nostrom, President
From: Lawson R. Nickels

I spent today with Jack Nellar, a new salesman on our payroll six weeks. He works for Mac Traynor in the southwest region, and what I found most disappointing about the whole day was the fact that Traynor is highly regarded as a top-drawer manager, and this, if anything, highlights the training problems we face. The following should make the point:

1. Nellar had one interview with Traynor, and was then hired by telephone.
2. Traynor worked with him for two weeks full time, teaching him, obviously as well as he knew how. He failed to teach him the following:
    (a) Nellar has absolutely no understanding of benefit selling.
    (b) Nellar doesn't realize the importance of securing retailers' names so as to establish a continually improving rapport.
    (c) Nellar didn't know that there is any importance in establishing the volume level at each retail account so that he could eventually identify high-volume from non–high-volume accounts.
    (d) Nellar has no concept that he was ever supposed to zone a territory.
    (e) Nellar did not once make a consumer effort during the entire day.
    (f) Nellar has no goals or objectives in his mind because none have been put there.

(g) Nellar does not call on supermarkets and thinks that there is apparently some unwritten law that states that for the first ninety days, a new man doesn't call on supermarkets.

(h) Nellar used the pronoun "I" constantly, as opposed to "you."

(i) Nellar did not walk into a store with a candy display under his arm and one of our free gift deals in his hands, because he had been told by his peers that "this really doesn't work." After the first five calls, we tried the gift plan together on the next five calls, and naturally it worked beautifully.

(j) What's in it for the retailer? Nellar's promotion isn't specific, and we don't help much. The retailer gets a deal of two free packages of candy worth in New York 84 cents, plus a gift item worth $1.98 retail. His 84 cents' worth of free candy gives him an extraordinary increase in his profit when added to the profit on selling the three boxes of candy it goes with. Obviously, there is a great benefit in this deal, much of which is unexplained in the blue pocket folder, but this folder apparently didn't get much attention from Nellar, which I attribute to lack of attention from Traynor.

(k) I think it is important that a salesman be creative. However, if it is the company policy to promote Norton Mixed Chocolates in a counter display, and if the display, coupons, header, etc., all talk about Norton Mixed Chocolates, its effectiveness is reduced if the salesman talks mainly about mint creams, or packaged nuts. Nellar did this on one of our calls.

The purpose of this memorandum is not to be critical of Traynor. He probably does as good a job as the next man. The purpose is to pinpoint, as specifically as I can, the crying need to get a training program at the Division Manager level going as soon as possible, and to have all the hard, basic fundamentals in that program.

I would particularly request that you do not discuss this matter with Traynor. The obligation of training an organization rests with higher levels than that of the regional manager.

LRN:CS

QUESTIONS

1. Cite what you feel are the purposes of this memo, and the probable results.

2. What training problems are in evidence here? Are there suggested remedies?

3. What organizational problems are indicated, if any?

4. What kind of training program do you think could be designed at the divisional level?

───── H. THE INDUSTRIAL NATIONAL BANK AND TRUST COMPANY

The Industrial National Bank and Trust Company was formed in 1928. By 1978 it had grown to be a large, full service institution with a number of branches in the major metropolitan centers of its state.

Over a long period of time, there came to be a proliferation of positions carrying high-status titles, plus other rewards and perquisites. People were rewarded not only for performance, but for achievements such as acquiring an advanced degree or obtaining a professional certificate or designation. As a result, minor promotions carried high prestige and inflated titles, and expectations were general among employees that these honorific appointments were made almost automatically.

These problems were intensified because they resulted in a large number of individuals being designated as "corporate officers." As officers the individuals received special perquisites such as travel expenses—along with their spouses—to meetings, and special fringe benefits originally intended for a small number of top managers designated as officers. Nearly 150 individuals had come to hold titles that also made them officers. Many in this group were professionals rather than managers with supervisors' duties.

Concerned with this proliferation and its cost burdens, the president asked the personnel vice president, Laurence N. Michaels, to develop a plan of corrective action. Michaels stated that he felt the situation was not easily reversible, but that he would retain a consultant to see what could be done.

QUESTIONS

1. As the consultant, what questions would you ask Michaels, and why?
2. Recommend the steps that could be taken to correct this problem and at the same time minimize negative effects on morale and motivation.

I. THE CORPORATION AND ITS ENVIRONMENT

In a speech to fellow industrialists, Henry Ford II pointed out that instead of getting on with the formidable job of rewriting the rules, public discussion wastes time and energy on irrelevant questions, such as how much of business profit should be diverted to environmental betterment. He asserted that the problems have become so huge that we would not necessarily make a dent in them with *all* the profits of American business.

Ford noted, "Hardly anyone disputes the proposition that service to society requires at least a short-run sacrifice of business profit." He then disputed that proposition. "This point of view," he said, "may have been tenable in the past. As long as public expectations with respect to the social responsibilities of business were relatively narrow and modest, business could pass muster by sacrificing only a little of its short-run earnings. Now that public expectations are exploding in all directions we can no longer regard profit and service to society as separate and competing goals, even in the short run. The company that sacrifices more and more short-run profit to keep up with constantly rising public expectations will soon find itself with no long run to worry about. Also, the company that seeks to conserve its profits by minimizing its response to changing expectations will soon find itself in conflict with all the publics on which its profits depend."

Ford went on to recommend not a middle course but an entirely different approach. Instead of regarding profits as competing with public expectations, such as environmental demands, he argued that business should look upon the rising public standards as opportunities for profit. "We have to ask ourselves, what do people want they didn't want before, and how can we get a competitive edge by giving them more of what they really want?"

Ford indicated that he was fully aware that in many cases governmental action will be required to translate the public's heightened desire for a better environment into effective market demand, as in the case of legal requirements for devices to reduce noxious emissions from cars.

QUESTIONS

1. What main reactions do you have to the above comments?
2. How would these reactions differ if you were a major stockholder? A high-level Ford Motor Company executive?
3. List some ways in which the selection of major objectives would be affected in the company if the above approaches were to be implemented.

J. COMPANIES A, B, AND C

Classical management theory emphasizes unity of command—with every manager reporting on a line basis to a single superior. The president or chief executive officer alone occupies the top command position. Revisionist theory, built around behavioral concepts of group decision, holds that all key decisions are in reality the product of a group effort. Therefore, it suggests the concept, quite widely adopted, of the president's office, a team of collaborating managers sharing the authority and responsibilities of top command in large, complex organizations.

Compare the following cases and appraise the probable effects, based on the information given or on assumptions you feel should be made:

Company A

This firm is a large conglomerate, which manufactures and sells liquor, shoes, clothing, tubular steel, chemicals, fluorescent equipment, and automobile batteries. It is very profitable, with pretax earnings rising in the previous five-year period from $50 million to $100 million. In 1976 its net income rose from $40 million to $51 million, on sales of $665 million.

The company's president, a former attorney, strongly believes in one-man rule, and in anti–free-form methods of management. He expects things to be done his way. Once, when asked by a stockholder to provide a financial forecast, he refused. The stockholder asked if a vice president could supply it. He responded, not entirely in jest, "In this company, if the president doesn't have an opinion, no one else does either." He also stated, "I am the antithesis of free-form management. People do much better when they know what is expected of them and to whom they report. They get nervous and anxious when these things aren't clear."

The president's philosophy is built around strong decentralization of day-to-day operations, and very strong central controls over planning, goals, and capital budgeting. He believes that any company belonging to a conglomerate is entitled to be managed in its own interest. The true test of a chief executive, he feels, is his ability to find, hire, and reward top-flight subordinates, with compensation tied to performance. He believes in the autonomy of the subordinate firms, to the extent that all central staff members can give suggestions only, not orders, to the constituent units.

The president works hard—seven days and nights a week—"to keep completely current." He is contemplating the establishment in his central office of four group vice presidents to be responsible for various operating companies.

Company B

This firm is a large, family-run garment company with important market shares in casual clothing, work clothing, and sports equipment. In 1977 it "went public," offering a large amount of stock for public sale.

Having hired nearly a hundred MBAs from leading business schools, the chief executive officer wanted to update the organization structure to take advantage of the abilities of the younger group, whose work was becoming highly effective throughout the company. To accommodate the "young Turks," he set up a troika at the vice-presidential level, and gave it more power than anyone not related to the founder had ever had.

With a limited range of products, the firm had maintained an ordinary, functional type of organization structure long beyond the point where most firms would have decentralized. Finding that growth and success led to the decline of the traditional pattern's effectiveness, the chief executive officer named a 13-person committee to study the problems and make recommendations. The troika resulted from their ideas, along with divisionalization and a new corporate staff group to monitor and coordinate the new divisions.

The troika of vice presidents paralleled the troika at the top level, which consisted of the chief executive officer and his two brothers, all grandsons of the company's founder.

Company C

This company is a giant firm in the insurance and financial industries. Its retiring board chairman, recognizing that lethargy and lack of competitiveness had grown within the firm, reorganized the company six months prior to his retirement. He set up a four-person "corporate office" to run the company, and selected the individuals assigned to these positions.

His successor accepted the new organization, apparently indifferent to its origin. The company turned into a more dynamic, tougher, and more successful firm, with higher profits and many changes.

The "corporate office" consisted of the new chief executive, the president and chief operating officer, and two executive vice presidents. The purpose was to bring more managers into the decision process, and to focus the attention of these officers on major problems and opportunities. The group is not regarded as a decision-making body, nor is it a committee. It is a device to bring together the special skills, abilities, and experiences of its members.

At their first meeting the four members decided to rule out all day-to-da, operating decisions from corporate office consideration. Each member would direct a major operating area. There was to be an emphasis on planning, delegation, control, and evaluation. The group meets twice weekly to focus on critical problems. It estimated it might take a year or possibly two for the influence of the new system to be felt. Meanwhile, the company's fortunes moved upward. Management by committee was avoided. One of the members even went ahead with a project that the other three opposed. "We act as peers, but anyone can speak his mind," one member said, "but the chairman is more equal than the others."

Postscript—Company C

Three years after the establishment of its corporate office the system broke down; one of the four key officers in the corporate office group, the company president, suddenly resigned to take a position elsewhere. The company quietly scrapped its group management system, leaving the chairman and chief executive officer as the sole boss.

The official explanation was that the abandoned structure tended to result in delays and on occasion to impede the decision process. The corporate office had come to be viewed as a decision-making body, with everyone feeling it necessary to pass decision problems through it for approval. This was contrary to the original intentions. Some of the delays were costly to the firm.

Two other giant firms in the same industry as that of Company C had also traded monolithic management for group management. One of these deemed the change successful, and there is a rumor—which the company denies—that the other is abandoning it. At the time that Company C abandoned its corporate office structure, seven other giant firms in various industries announced plans modeled after the corporate office system used in the General Electric Company for many years.

Question:

1. How do you account for the situations described in this case?

PART IV

Organizational Development and Managerial Behavior

Chapter 19

Organizational Development

We tried hard—but it seemed that every time we were beginning to form up into effective teams, we would be reorganized. I was to learn later in life we tend to meet any new situation by reorganizing, and a wonderful method it can be for creating the illusion of progress while producing confusion, inefficiency, and demoralization.

—Attributed to Gaius Petronious, d. ca. A.D. 66

In order to penetrate even further into their subject, the host of specialists narrow their field and dig deeper and deeper till they can't see each other from hole to hole. But the treasures their toil brings to light they place on the ground above. A different kind of specialist should be sitting there, the only one still missing. He would not go down any hole, but would stay on top and piece all the different facts together.   *—Thor Heyerdahl*

CHAPTER GUIDE

Systems are easier to change than people, and the effort expended has greater potential payoff. Daniel M. Duncan argues that, amidst a sea of regulation, one avenue of managerial discretion remains relatively untouched: the articulated design and administration of the systemic aspects of the organization ("A Systems View of OD," *Organizational Dynamics,* winter 1974, p. 29).

Questions to keep in mind as you read this chapter:

1. What are the implications of these statements for traditional views of management, organization, and training?

459

2. How does OD go about changing people, if at all?
3. In what ways might OD approaches have advantages over training approaches?

The term *organization development* (OD) is defined as *planned organization change to improve the effectiveness of people, structures, and processes*. OD applies an array of behavioral science concepts and methods to organizations. As a comprehensive term, it includes not only changes in organization design but also in organizational philosophy and in the skills of individuals and groups.

Organization development utilizes systems thinking, together with advanced techniques for understanding and improving the work behavior of organization members. It recognizes that organization structure and managerial performance are mutually interdependent. It treats the organization as an interrelated whole. From a systems viewpoint, organization development, called OD for short, is a set of concepts and techniques by which organization members learn to initiate, accept, and cope with change, to develop trust in each other, and to function effectively as members of groups and teams.

Many of the concepts and techniques of OD have been inherited from its predecessor, the human relations movement. Others are more recently developed, and consequently, are less well tested and accepted. The number of methods and approaches is large, and varies as to difficulty and feasibility. As a result, no two OD programs are alike, as organizations draw upon the growing knowledge in the field. The term *OD* is thus broadly used to describe a variety of change programs, even traditional training. Some organizations confine it to structural change; others to standard training programs; still others use it for the most sophisticated efforts for total, comprehensive change and development. This chapter treats OD in its broadest scope.

Some key assumptions underlying OD are these:

1. Piecemeal approaches to structural change and the development of people are less effective than OD methods.
2. Training and managerial development programs are only one part of the concept, and by themselves are inadequate for the complex needs of today's organizations.
3. The findings and techniques of behavioral science are more complex and more uncertain than older methods. Sociology, social psychology, and applied anthropology are now allied with psychology in their contributions to understanding organization behavior.

4. OD includes the effort to guide and direct change as well as to cope with or adapt to imposed change. It recognizes that goals change and the methods of attaining them are continuously changing.
5. The central focus of OD is on fostering the ongoing processes of renewal and regeneration so as to preserve organizational health.

This chapter is divided into two main sections. The first describes the fundamentals of organizational development. The second details selected OD techniques and procedures for the training and development of managers in organizations.

_____ THE FUNDAMENTALS OF ORGANIZATION DEVELOPMENT

Organization development is generally undertaken as an organization-wide program, although it has been applied in some cases only to parts of an organization, such as a research and development group. Conceptually its strengths lie in its capability for building unity and teamwork throughout an organization.

OD programs may be conducted by a special task force, an organization development department (if one exists), a team of behavioral science consultants, or appropriate members of the personnel department. Typically a combination of these is involved. An outside behavioral science consultant is very important. Ultimately all key managers, even including first-line supervisors, participate in OD processes. Managers themselves must change, not merely try to change others.[1]

Purposes of Organization Development

The basic rationale of OD programs is the recognition that traditional structures and processes, considered separately, cannot achieve the orientation to development that is possible by viewing the organization as a total system. Furthermore, the OD approach generates a much greater commitment and involvement on the part of organization members. It also provides for the effective utilization of outside consultants.

Organization development programs are largely based on open, adaptive systems concepts of the type described in Chapter 13; thus such programs are a primary means for modifying bureaucratic systems, for they point to new goals guided by planned change. Although some OD programs may not signify major departures from bureaucratic structure, most imply significant change for managerial leadership styles and the eventual loosening of bureaucratic tight-ship philosophies.

[1]Chris Argyris, *Management and Organizational Development* (New York: McGraw-Hill, 1971), chap. 5.

Another important purpose of OD programs is to foster participative management, and to develop attitudes of trust and confidence on the part of organization members. OD programs help people to work in groups and to develop self-insights that reduce tension, stress, and interpersonal conflict. They provide opportunities to gain experience in the use of personal and interpersonal skills.

OD Models

An OD program consists of a feedback cycle, the basic stages of which are diagnosis, action planning, action implementation, and evaluation. Evaluation findings relate back to continuous diagnosis, renewing the cycle with appropriate feedback. Figure 19-1 illustrates this process.

Within the over-all OD cycle, other cycles of varying duration appear at successive levels. Top management may follow a five-year cycle, middle management yearly or quarterly cycles, and lower management a monthly cycle. This scheme corresponds to typical planning horizons at these levels in other matters.[2] Figure 19-2 is illustrative.

The OD model presented in Figure 19-1 must now be expanded. Figure 19-3, a more detailed model, introduces three additional elements: the presence of change agents, the concept of intervention strategies, and the process and methods of developmental change. We will now analyze each of the main components of OD as shown in these basic models: (1) change agents, (2) diagnosis, (3) intervention strategies, (4) change processes, and (5) evaluation.

Change Agents

Change agents may be one or more members of the organization, or behavioral science consultants. Both are generally used in major OD programs. Groups may also serve as change agents.[3]

Outside consultants are needed for greater objectivity and for up-to-date technical knowledge. Their experience can help the organization

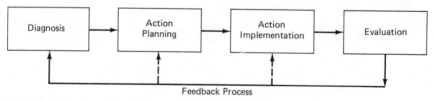

Feedback Process

FIGURE 19-1. An OD Program Cycle, with Feedback Mechanism.

[2]Jay W. Lorsch and Paul R. Lawrence, *Developing Organizations: Diagnosis and Action* (Reading, Mass.: Addison-Wesley, 1969), pp. 89–90.

[3]Alfred Jacobs (ed.), *The Group as Agent of Change* (New York: Behavioral Publications, 1974).

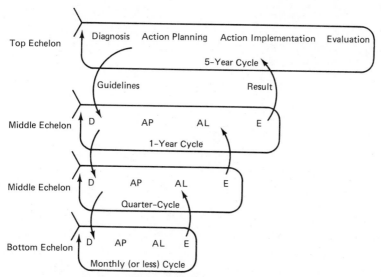

FIGURE 19-2. OD Cycles at Varying Levels.

Source: Jay W. Lorsch and Paul R. Lawrence, *Developing Organizations: Diagnosis and Action* (Reading, Mass.: Addison-Wesley Publishing Company, 1969), p. 90. Used by permission.

avoid the many pitfalls of OD. Change agents should enter the process at an early planning stage, preferably prior to, but certainly including, the diagnostic phase. The professional OD consultant guides the unfolding programs, serving in such helping roles as adviser, facilitator, catalyst, and problem solver.

The one role consultants avoid is that of decision maker, a function that is the responsibility of the organization's managers. The effective consultant guides organization members toward the goal of self-sufficiency, remaining aware of the need eventually to withdraw from involvement.[4]

Internal change agents may work far short of an OD program. When they are part of an OD effort, however, they function in much the same way as do external consultants. Both must be objective and careful analysts, and assist in diagnosis and evaluation. Both intervene in situations where people are unaware of the need for change or tend to resist it. Both need to be skillful in group leadership, communication, and interpersonal relations. Both must know a wide range of techniques and procedures, and how and when to get the most out of them.[5]

[4]Fritz Steele, *Consulting For Organization Change* (Amherst: University of Massachusetts Press, 1975).

[5]For additional information on change agents, see Richard Beckhard, *Organization Development: Strategies and Models* (Reading, Mass.: Addison-Wesley, 1969), chap. 10; Wendell French and Cecil H. Bell, Jr., *Organization Development* 2nd ed. (Englewood Cliffs, N.J.: Prentice-Hall, 1978), chap. 17; Lee Grossman, *The Change Agent* (New York: AMACOM, 1974); and chap. 15 of this book.

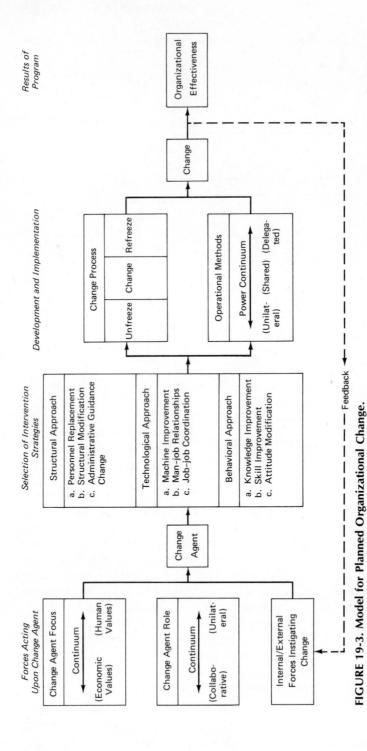

FIGURE 19-3. Model for Planned Organizational Change.

Source: Larry E. Short, "Planned Organizational Change," p. 56, *MSU Business Topics*, Autumn 1973. Reprinted by permission of the publisher, Division of Research, Graduate School of Business Administration, Michigan State University. Used by permission.

The change agent helps to raise the level of awareness and sensitivity to the complexities of planned change. The change agent helps also to avoid single-cause solutions, and can bring up alternatives that would otherwise be overlooked. Change agents help others raise relevant questions, seek critical data, expose false assumptions, and achieve a deeper understanding of their needs, values, goals, and expectations.[6]

Diagnosis

Diagnosis requires considerable skills of analysis and observation. In the diagnostic stage, over-all goals are stated in forms useful for guiding plans and actions. Consultants increase the likelihood of objectivity in sizing up problems that have led to the interest in OD. Moreover, because problems are often expressed by organization members in general and vague terms, they need to undergo substantial transformation before decisions are made.

The organization's leaders may have decided on an OD program because it is fashionable, or out of desperation, or from the desire to imitate others. They may also have launched the move without recognizing all its pitfalls, dangers, and costs, or with a shallow commitment to it. They may tend to take an overly simple view of change, and to be in a hurry for results.

It is usually not a single problem that is to be diagnosed. Rather it is a set of problems and the context in which they appear. Motives, attitudes, assumptions, and the availability of adequate resources must be considered in the diagnostic phase.

Change agents do not make the diagnosis. Instead, they help others to refine and sharpen their own diagnoses, face their feelings, clarify their assumptions, and state their true goals. The aim of diagnosis is to identify all the main components that cause difficulty in the existing situation. The initial diagnostic focus is on organizational variables rather than on the psychology of a group or of individuals, which becomes important at later stages.

Diagnosis begins with the total system, its structure and functioning. Work flows and communication processes are examined. Subsystems are observed in their relationships to each other. Diagnosis leads to locating the sources of specific problems, which activities break down or need improvement, and where casual methods can be systematized. Diagnosis helps the planners see what changes are needed in the system, the structure, or in people. Because it is easier to change

---

[6]For further descriptions of the change agent's functions, see Robert B. Duncan, "Dimensions to Consider in the Change Agent's Role," *Proceedings of the 34th Annual Meeting*, Academy of Management, Seattle, Washington, 1974; Len Sperry, Douglas J. Mickelson, and Phillip L. Hunsaker, *You Can Make it Happen: A Guide to Self-Actualization and Organization Change* (Reading, Mass.: Addison-Wesley, 1977).

systems than people, much of the value of OD is obtained thus. Changes in people, if necessary, can then be undertaken with the knowledge that system variables have been dealt with.[7]

Diagnosis depends heavily on the collection and analysis of relevant information. The necessary data are obtained by questionnaire and interview methods, as well as by the observations of trained change agents or outside consultants. Records and other information on past experience are often useful. Although factual information is helpful, it is also important to know the attitudes, feelings, and opinions of those involved in the change program.

Intervention

The concept of intervention is vital to the success of OD programs. Intervention, the action phase of OD, follows from diagnosis; it is a form of interference, but if it is regarded as only that its purposes are defeated. If intervention follows from the clearly perceived needs and goals of top management it becomes more than interference. It is a program of planned change.

Intervention is defined as *a set of planned, programmatic activities and techniques by which organizations and their clients collaborate in an OD program.* Interventions consist of the long-range, evolving applications of OD techniques targeted for changing individuals, groups, or the total organization.[8] Figure 19-3, shown earlier, shows five levels at which intervention may be needed, together with a listing of some of the major types of intervention associated with each level.[9]

The number and range of available interventions are extensive, as shown in Figure 19-4. Each form of intervention varies from others in the depth or intensity with which it penetrates the inner workings of the organization, and in the extent and nature of the changes it is designed to promote. An OD program does not use all the possible forms of intervention. Instead, it selects from the available alternatives those that best fit the aims resulting from the diagnosis. Within each form of intervention are appropriate techniques and procedures.[10]

A look at the various forms of intervention will show how they vary according to depth of penetration. Some are akin to more traditional

---

[7]Daniel M. Duncan, "A Systems View of OD," *Organization Dynamics* **2** (Winter 1974), 14–29. See also Noel M. Tichy, "How Different Types of Change Agents Diagnose Organizations," *Human Relations* **23** (December 1975), 771–799.

[8]French and Bell, *Organizational Development*, chaps. 9–14.

[9]See also Andrew M. Pettigrew, "Towards a Political Theory of Organizational Intervention," *Human Relations* **28** (April 1975), 191–208.

[10]Richard J. Selfridge and Stanley L. Sokolik, "A Comprehensive View of Organization Development," *MSU Business Topics*, Winter 1975, 45–61; Chris Argyris, *Intervention Theory and Method: A Behavioral Science View* (Reading, Mass.: Addison-Wesley, 1970).

Target Group	Types of Interventions
Interventions designed to improve the effectiveness of INDIVIDUALS	Life- and career-planning activities Role analysis technique Coaching and counseling T-group (sensitivity training) Education and training to increase skills, knowledge in the areas of technical task needs, relationship skills, process skills, decision making, problem solving, planning, goal setting skills Grid OD phase 1
Interventions designed to improve the effectiveness of DYADS/TRIADS	Process consultation Third-party peacemaking Grid OD phases 1, 2
Interventions designed to improve the effectiveness of TEAMS & GROUPS	Team building — Task directed — Process directed Family T-group Survey feedback Process consultation Role analysis technique "Start-up" team-building activities Education in decision making, problem solving, planning, goal setting in group settings
Interventions designed to improve the effectiveness of INTERGROUP RELATIONS	Intergroup activities — Process directed — Task directed Organizational mirroring (three or more groups) Technostructural interventions Process consultation Third-party peacemaking at group level Grid OD phase 3 Survey feedback
Interventions designed to improve the effectiveness of the TOTAL ORGANIZATION	Technostructural activities Confrontation meetings Strategic planning activities Grid OD phases 4, 5, 6 Survey feedback

FIGURE 19-4. Types of OD Interventions Based on Target Groups.

Source: Wendell L. French and Cecil H. Bell, Jr., *Organization Development: Behavioral Science Interventions for Organization Improvement,* ©1973, p. 107. Reprinted by permission of Prentice-Hall, Inc., Englewood Cliffs, N.J.

forms of organization change, such as altering the organization design or setting up management training programs. We may call this the manifest level of OD. It includes visible forms of change activity such as skill training, leadership development, coaching and counseling, task and role analysis, and career planning. Another category, more complex, may be termed the *latent* level of OD. Latent interventions are less visible, more normative, and more concerned with changing values and beliefs. Lorsch and Lawrence use a similar scaling of change methods from "modest change" to "fundamental change." Modest change entails essentially cognitive aspects, which correspond to manifest changes. The more fundamental the level of change sought, the more deeply it penetrates the emotional sector, which corresponds to the latent level of OD. The Lorsch and Lawrence typology is shown in Figure 19-5.

The scope and extent of the interventions to be used depends on what changes are desired and on the willingness of organization members to join with the change agent–consultant in grappling with problems not susceptible to routine, mechanical resolution. OD programs require substantial amounts of time, money, and energy, and the ability to accept uncertainty, ambiguity, and fundamental changes in attitudes and beliefs.The array of interventions is rich enough to permit adjusting the change and development techniques to accommodate each of the main OD stages: diagnosis, planning, implementation, and evaluation. Specific interventions and other techniques for training and development will be analyzed in the next main section of this chapter.

Change Processes and Strategies

A comprehensive OD program must deal with a blend of structural, personal, and interpersonal components. An important question is

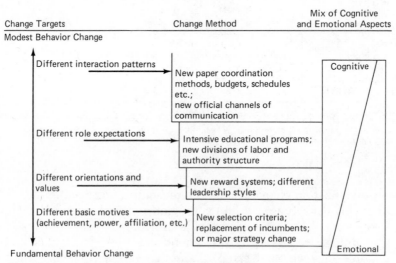

FIGURE 19-5. Range of Change Targets, Methods, and Emotional-Cognitive Aspects in OD.

Source: Jay W. Lorsch and Paul R. Lawrence, *Developing Organizations: Diagnosis and Action* (Reading, Mass.: Addison-Wesley Publishing Company, 1969), p. 87. Used by permission.

where to begin. Some feel that structural change should come first, whereas others believe that personal or interpersonal, group or intergroup relationships should be dealt with first. Argyris suggests that both approaches are valid under given conditions. He argues that one of the major tasks of the interventionist is to help organization members become aware of their roles in causing the problems they are attempting to overcome. Therefore the element of personal causation and responsibility is the critical factor in the effectiveness of OD interventions. If personal causation and responsibility are low, externally induced structural change will be effective, and one may begin the procedures with structural change. This approach would be effective at lower levels of the organization, for example. Where the organization seeks a more open or adaptive system, and where personal causation and responsibility are high, as in higher levels of the organization, one should begin with changing personal or interpersonal aspects.[11]

Because the major purposes of most OD programs are to institute enduring behavioral and attitudinal change, to increase the levels of trust and commitment in organizations, to produce internal change and self-renewal, and to foster the ability to cope with the changing external environment, OD techniques and procedures for change emphasize advanced concepts of behavioral science. Therefore a major task of the change agent–consultant is to help organization members learn new skills required for making changes effectively.

Evaluation and Feedback

Evaluation and feedback are not actually separate stages in the OD mechanism. They occur at every stage. As one stage ends and another looms, an evaluation will help assess the validity of what has been done, and show whether further work is needed before going on.

Evaluation proceeds by gathering and analyzing information. The consultant or other change agent may have impressions of informal information to start with, but the use of questionnaires, interviews, or group discussions is needed for systematic review of the results being assessed. Consequences of decisions are observed as the change processes move along.

Feedback is the process of relaying evaluations to appropriate individuals or groups, by means of special reports or in conference sessions.

[11]Argyris, *Intervention Theory*, pp. 156–173. See also French and Bell, *Organization Development*, chap. 14; Dale Zand and Richard Sorenson, "Theory of Change and the Effective Use of Management Science," *Administrative Science Quarterly* **20** (December 1975), 532–545; Gerald Zaltman and Robert Duncan, *Strategies for Planned Change* (New York: 1977).

Feedback must be carefully handled, because it leads to confrontations with the reality of change. Emotional factors may enter in; mistakes are recognized, with accompanying possibilities for resentment. Nadler has suggested that feedback suffers from relying too much on self-reports from organization members. Feedback should be based on a broad array of data, and include the assessment of the change model itself.[12]

A model showing the relationships of intervention, feedback, and evaluation is shown in Figure 19-6. It demonstrates that evaluation begins with a conceptual model for evaluating the intervention. Goals, change processes, and the needs of the recipients of the evaluation enter in. The receivers of the evaluations include the members of the organization, the consultants, and possibly the community or other

---

[12]David A. Nadler, "The Use of Feedback for Organizational Change: Promises and Pitfalls," *Group and Organization Studies* 1 (June 1976), 177–186. See also Herbert Kaufman, with Michael Couzens, *Administrative Feedback: Monitoring Subordinates' Behavior* (Washington, D.C.: The Brookings Institute, 1973).

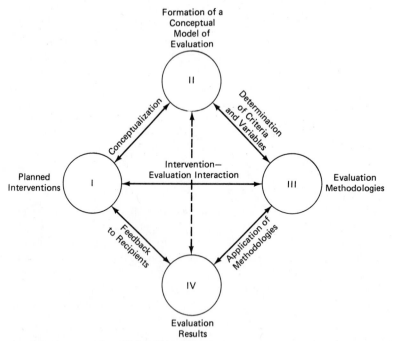

FIGURE 19-6. A Model of the Evaluation Process in Organization Development.
Source: Ralph H. Kilman and Richard P. Herden, "Towards a Systematic Methodology for Evaluating the Impact of Interventions on Organizational Effectiveness," *Academy of Management Review* 1 (July 1976), p. 89. Used by permission.

environmental sectors. It should be recognized that the personalities and perceptions of the evaluators and the recipients have an influence on the evaluations.[13]

ORGANIZATION DEVELOPMENT TECHNIQUES

The number of OD interventions is large. They vary in the range and depth of their penetration into the behavioral system of the organization and in the nature of the purposes they serve. Some have long been in use in traditional management and human relations training programs. As efforts shifted from improving individual skills to improvement at group, teams, or total organizational levels, new techniques emerged.

OD methods also vary as to the stage or stages of an intervention cycle where they are most appropriate; most encompass all the stages in one way or another. OD methods lead to action and change guided by learning theory, advanced educational and training approaches, and the development of skills and insights about groups, individuals, and interpersonal relations through actual practice. Diagnosis through information gathering and analysis, and appropriate feedback, continue throughout the use of the OD methods selected.

There is no single OD method capable of serving all the likely objectives. Typically several related methods are used together. For example, a traditional training method, such as a conference, becomes an OD method when it is linked to specific OD objectives, and when it is conducted according to behavioral insights designed to change the attitudes or performance of individuals or groups.

Classifications of OD Methods

OD methods are difficult to classify because of their overlapping and interrelated nature. Many interventions and methods are associated with widely known consultants who attach preferred labels to them. As these labels come into wider usage their meaning becomes more general and less precise. Classifications according to purpose or main use

[13]Ralph H. Kilmann and Richard P. Herden, "Towards a Systematic Methodology for Evaluating the Impact of Interventions on Organization Effectiveness, " *Academy of Management Review* 1 (July 1976), 87–98; David G. Bowers, "Organization Development: Promises, Performances, Possibilities," *Organization Dynamics* 4 (Spring 1976), 50–62; Robert L. Kahn, "Organization Development: Some Problems and Proposals," *Journal of Applied Behavioral Science* 10 (October 1974), 485–502; John R. Kimberly and Warren R. Nielsen, "Organization Development and Change in Organization Performance," *Administrative Science Quarterly* 20 (June 1975), 191–206.

are important for visualizing the scope of OD. The terms *OD, intervention theory, planned change, action research,* and *process consulting* have thus come to describe roughly the same methodological and conceptual approaches, with only slight variations among particular consultants.

The simplest classification employs three general groupings: technical, administrative, and social. Technical interventions include changes in work flow, organization structure, information flow, equipment, and the like. Administrative interventions focus on policies, procedures, programs, reward systems, or relations with the external environment. Social interventions include those directed toward team building, group and intergroup relations, conflict resolution, and improved communication.[14]

Bennis classifies interventions into nine categories according to theme or purpose. These focus on (1) discrepancies, (2) theory, (3) procedures, (4) relationships, (5) experimentation, (6) dilemmas, (7) perspectives, (8) structures, and (9) cultural problems.[15] Bennis's typology, though complex and overlapping, indicates the variety of problems that confront the OD specialist.

Different methods may be needed at the different stages of the OD cycle and for different purposes in a program. French and Bell, for example, designate twelve "families" of interventions: (1) diagnostic, (2) team building, (3) intergroup activities, (4) survey-feedback methods, (5) education and training programs, (6) technostructural activities, (7) process consultations, (8) the Management Grid, (9) mediation and negotiation activities, (10) coaching and counseling, (11) career planning, and (12) planning and goal-setting activities.[16] These categories also reveal the many strategic choices available to change agents and consultants.

Space does not permit a detailed elaboration of all OD methods. However, the sections that follow will describe the most widely used methods and approaches, including action research, survey feedback techniques, sensitivity training, process consulting, confrontation meetings, team building, behavior modification, and the Management Grid.®

Action Research

Action research emphasizes information collection and analysis, coupled with a feedback process. It declares that the organization intends

---

[14]Harold F. M. Rush, *Organization Development: A Reconnaissance* (New York: The Conference Board, 1975).

[15]Warren Bennis, *Organization Development: Its Nature, Origins, and Prospects* (Reading, Mass.: Addison-Wesley, 1969), pp. 37–39.

[16]French and Bell, *Organization Development,* pp. 102–105.

to act upon the findings, and implies that action will be based on pertinent data that describe the current situation. The concept of action research originated in the work of Kurt Lewin, from whose work the field of group dynamics emerged. Lewin believed that the direction and intensity of a change program should be based on analysis resulting from research on the scene of change.

Action research proceeds in ways similar to that of the OD cycle described earlier. It proceeds in the same way as any research: hypothesis formulation, data collection, analysis, testing of hypotheses, and evaluation. Action and feedback are the additional steps. It is a device for coupling the learning process with action planning. Action research generally focuses on actual problems, and findings are applied while the research is in progress, so that the applications provide a testing of the research as it progresses. It has the advantage of involving all those who take action or who are affected by change. It rationalizes and legitimates the action by providing accurate knowledge of the context in which it occurs. It accustoms the members of a group to working together objectively, paving the way for emotional and philosophical adjustments to change.

Some researchers regard action research as inappropriate. From a purely scientific point of view, coupling actions (change) with ongoing research might color the research. It is certainly an influence on the researcher's own thoughts and actions. Despite these drawbacks, however, action research will doubtless become increasingly important in organization development work.

The techniques of questionnaires, surveys, structured and unstructured interviews, and systematic observation are used to carry out action research.[17] Action research is particularly valuable as a planning and diagnostic intervention, but it is also useful at other stages, such as evaluation and feedback. Feedback is generally by means of group discussions in which those who will carry out changes are the main participants, with the consultant acting as a guide or resource person.

Survey Feedback Methods

Survey feedback methods bear a resemblance to action research in that they include the use of data collection and feedback. They are especially helpful in planning, diagnosis, and evaluation. Whereas action research is generally oriented toward system goals and overall planning, survey feedback methods focus on drawing out the attitudes of individuals toward problems of change and improvement, with team

[17]Newton Margulies and John Wallace, *Organizational Change: Techniques and Applications* (Glenview, Ill.: Scott, Foresman, 1973), pp. 22–43; French and Bell, *Organization Development*, pp. 84–96; Edgar F. Huse, *Organization Development and Change* (St. Paul, Minn.: West, 1975), pp. 103–110.

members working on their own data to produce change. The surveys deal mainly with superior-subordinate relations in job contexts, and analyze such problems as teamwork leadership style, organization climate, cooperation, and job satisfaction.[18]

The survey feedback approach was pioneered in 1947 by the Survey Research Center of the University of Michigan. A standardized survey instrument was developed to measure organizational data to be used by teams within the organization in bringing about change. Survey feedback methods have the advantage of high motivation through involving the organization members in studying matters that are immediately at hand and of practical interest, thus reducing the amount of resistance to change. They may be adapted to many types of groups and can be used to cut across the vertical and horizontal dimensions of the organization.

Following the survey, workshops or discussion groups are set up for feedback on the findings. Action alternatives are discussed, and the amount of support and agreement can be assessed for the actions proposed. The OD consultant is usually present at the feedback sessions. The consultant will have aided in the development of the survey instruments, for there are many technical pitfalls to be avoided. Poor survey methods can cause failure in the OD program and lead to difficulties that may endure long afterward.

Sensitivity Training

Sensitivity training has been used apart from OD programs, but in isolation it has not been effective in bringing about organizational change. It is especially valuable for many types of OD objectives when combined with other types of interventions. Its focus is on the individual—the discovery of self-insight, the learning of group and interpersonal skills, and the ability to face feelings and emotional tensions in oneself and others.

Sensitivity training originated in the work of Kurt Lewin and others associated with the pioneering work in group dynamics. Although the development effort focuses on the individual, group methods are employed in the training, because most people do their work in collaboration with others. Sensitivity training has appeared in many variations and forms, and is still evolving as research continues to refine its concepts and techniques. Widely used in the helping professions, such as education and social work, it has been used in management training less frequently because of its complexity and a general reluctance to risk its psychoemotional difficulties.

The core of sensitivity training is the laboratory—indeed, it is fre-

---

[18]French and Bell, *Organization Development*, pp. 130–153; George F. Wieland and Robert A. Ullrich, *Organization Behavior, Design and Change* (Homewood, Ill.: Irwin, 1976), chap. 17.

quently called laboratory training or T-group training. The laboratory or T-group is a small group established for the purpose of learning from actual experience in groups. The T-group is an unstructured, agenda-less group, usually of one or two weeks' duration. It requires a specially trained leader who functions as catalyst and facilitator. The content is provided by the interactions of group members. Discussions proceed from the interactions, behavior, activities, and feelings of the partici-pants. The leader reflects behavioral observations back to the group when appropriate, but relies chiefly on unstructured, subtle devices to keep the group going on its own. The leader probes, raises questions, and uses strategems for bringing out the feelings and attitudes of group members, and helping them learn from this process; he refrains from authoritarian, normative actions, from lecturing, and from injecting his own attitudes and values into the discussions.[19]

Types of T-Groups

T-groups have been set up as stranger labs, cousin labs, and family labs. *Stranger labs,* consisting of participants each from a different organiza-tion, are useful in "seeding" their organizations with the values and norms for various other change and OD interventions. *Cousin labs,* which enroll participants from the same organization but not the same work group, help in starting the change process in a particular organiza-tion. *Family labs* are made up of participants from the same work group. Such groups are useful for unfreezing, changing, and refreezing group values and norms and for improving group effectiveness.

Sometimes T-groups are referred to as *encounter groups.* This term is usually applied to groups emphasizing heightened personal aware-ness, more direct interpersonal communication, and greater self-insight for individuals. Encounter groups generally have a deeper level of penetration than T-groups. Allied to encounter groups are a wide range of "consciousness-raising" programs that attempt to go deeply into personality problems, psychic phenomena, transactional analysis and mystical ideas like transcendental meditation. This sector of develop-ment work is not closely related to organizational problems as such, and so will not be analyzed here.[20]

[19]Huse, *Organization Development and Change,* pp. 247–265; Margulies and Wal-lace, *Organizational Change,* pp. 65–82; Edgar H. Schein and Warren G. Bennis, *Per-sonal and Organizational Change Through Group Methods: The Laboratory Approach* (New York: Wiley, 1965); Kurt Back, *Beyond Words: The Story of Sensitivity Training and the Encounter Movement* (New York: Russell Sage Foundation, 1972).

[20]Huse, *Organization Development and Change,* pp. 260–265; Robert D. Joyce, *Encounters in Organizational Behavior: Problem Situations* (New York: Pergamon, 1972); Martin Lakin, *Interpersonal Encounter: Theory and Practice in Sensitivity Train-ing* (New York: McGraw-Hill, 1972); Gerard Egan (ed.), *Encounter Groups: Basic Read-ings* (Belmont, Calif.: Brooks/Cole, 1971); Lawrence N. Solomon and Betty Berzon, *New Perspectives on Encounter Groups* (San Francisco: Jossey Bass, 1972).

T-group training depends heavily upon the skills of the T-group trainer (leader). Although the overt role of the leader appears minimal, in reality it is crucial in the outcomes for participants. Leaders must themselves be sensitive and experienced in group processes and individual behavior, and skilled in nondirective methods. The National Training Laboratory at Bethel, Maine, which was founded in 1947 following experimental workshops on the use of discussion groups to achieve changes in behavior, trains and certifies qualified sensitivity training leaders.[21]

The numerous potential pitfalls in sensitivity training are most likely to arise from using a poorly qualified or ill-chosen trainer, from failure to select participants carefully, and from neglecting to fit the program into the other developmental efforts as part of an overall plan. The chief danger is the possibility of severe effects on the emotions and personalities of those participants who are unable to endure the stress and tension induced by the psychosocial techniques of the training. Such training need not be dangerous for the individual, but it can be for some.[22]

One large organization had a management training program in which managers were called in from all over the United States for a five-week period. At first, each week was devoted to standard subjects, such as management theory, planning, decision making, communications, and leadership. The training director, after reviewing the results over a period of time, decided that sensitivity training should be given during the first week. This change was instituted, with session leaders obtained through the National Training Laboratory. The plan failed because the initial week's program so greatly unnerved and disturbed the participants that the trainer in charge of the following week found it impossible to continue with standard approaches. He had to help the participants readjust to the differences between the first and the successive weeks, restoring their confidence and stability. The problem was caused by the participants' lack of advance preparation for what was about to happen, and by the unusual behavior of the session leaders brought in for the initial week.

Perhaps the most serious indictment of sensitivity training is that participants return from the sessions with heightened sensitivity to

[21]Achilles A. Armenahis, Hubert A. Field, and Donald C. Mosley, "Evaluation Guidelines for the OD Practitioner," *Personnel Journal* 54 (February 1975), 99–103, 106; John D. Aram and James A. F. Stoner, "Development of an Organizational Change Role," *Journal of Applied Behavioral Science* 8 (July–August 1972), 483–449; Argyris, *Intervention Theory*.

[22]Cary L. Cooper, "How Psychologically Dangerous Are T-Groups and Encounter Groups?" *Human Relations* 28 (April 1975), 249–260; Robert T. Golembiewski and Stokes B. Carrigan, "Planned Change Through Laboratory Methods," *Training and Development Journal* 27 (March 1973), 18–27. For an extensive review of T-group problems and research, see the special issue of *The Journal of Applied Behavioral Science* 11 (April 1975).

themselves and to interpersonal relations only to find that the work setting itself has not changed. After a time their training loses its effect through disuse or frustration. This is why sensitivity training is best used as part of an overall OD program, and along with other interventions.

Process Consulting

Process consulting focuses primarily on groups as the basic building blocks of organization. The groups may be permanent, or they may be temporary ones such as teams, task forces, project groups, or committees. Process consulting may deal with tasks, work flows, the processes by which the group accomplishes its task, and conflicts which arise between group members. Schein[23] and Argyris[24] are the chief developers of the process consulting method.

The concept of process consulting is built around a cycle similar to that of a total OD approach. Its problem-solving and decision methods are also similar to those of action research: defining the consultant's role, selecting methods and approaches, gathering data, making a diagnosis, intervening to take action, and evaluating—ending with the eventual departure of the consultant. Process consulting analyzes the roles and functions of group members, group problem-solving methods, decision making, the development of group norms, and the use of leadership and authority. The approaches of this technique are compatible with other OD methods and are often used in conjunction with them.

Like other types of OD consultants, the process consultant does not take the role of "expert." Instead, the aim is to help group members achieve their own diagnosis, action patterns, and decisions by examining the processes at work among group members. The consultant may use questionnaires, role playing sessions, coaching and counseling methods, and various review, feedback, and evaluation devices.

Confrontation Methods

Although confrontation methods are by no means a complete approach, they are a valuable adjunct to the problem-solving situations that inevitably arise in OD programs. Confrontation approaches aim to resolve intergroup conflict, which, if unresolved, can smolder and flare up in ways that are injurious to organizational health. Confrontation brings such conflicts into the open and attempts to find ways of reducing or eliminating their negative effects.

[23]Edgar Schein, *Process Consultation: Its Role in Organization Development* (Reading, Mass.: Addison-Wesley, 1969).

[24]Chris Argyris, *Intervention Theory;* and *Organization and Innovation* (Homewood, Ill.: Irwin, 1965). See also Huse, *Organization Development and Change*, pp. 218–227.

There are several forms of confrontation based on procedural strategy. Groups or their representatives may agree to negotiate their differences. Negotiation, however, implies compromise. Another way is for leaders to stress higher goals upon which agreement can be found, thus putting the conflict in a different perspective. Leaders can challenge the groups to find common ground from which their rewards will derive. A third technique is to deflect attention to a common adversary, getting the groups to work together to win out. Finally, a number of techniques for improving communication and understanding among the members of conflicting groups may be used.

The important common element in all confrontational methods is a face-to-face meeting of the conflicting groups or their representatives. The OD consultant or change agent can often help the groups to resolve key issues. In any case the skills of group leadership and discussion are important. Where such meetings use an "outside" leader or consultant, the method is called third-party intervention. The third party can and should maintain a neutral stance similar to that of mediators in labor negotations, though exercising more of a leadership role. The leader should also be able to diagnose the ongoing situation as discussions proceed.

Confrontation requires those in conflict to acknowledge and face their conflict together, and to join in the search for the sources of conflict. Emotional as well as logical elements of conflict are considered.[25] Surveys can be used to measure and compare the perceptions of those in conflict, focusing efforts on specific causes of problems.

One need not wait until major conflicts surface to use the confrontation approach. It can be used at early stages of the OD cycle to face conflict before it deepens and to head off some types of conflict. This flexibility broadens the scope to include diagnosis of potential conflict, and the opportunity to make plans and take actions to correct or prevent conflict. Confrontation can thus help a total group examine its own processes and needs, build group cohesion, and prepare for change. Used in this way, it closely resembles process consultation.[26]

Team Building Approaches

Team building interventions are designed to improve the work effectiveness of various groups or teams in the organization. Team building occurs in two contexts: the permanent organizational unit such as a section or department, and temporary teams such as committees, task forces, and project groups.

[25]R. E. Walton, *Interpersonal Peacemaking: Confrontations and Third-Party Consultation* (Reading, Mass.: Addison-Wesley, 1969); John A. Seiler, "Diagnosing Interdepartmental Conflict," *Harvard Business Review* **41** (September–October 1963), 121–132.

[26]Richard Beckhard, "The Confrontation Meeting," *Harvard Business Review* **45** (March–April 1969), 149–155.

Team building, though focused on the group's internal processes and relationships, uses procedures similar to those in other OD situations. These techniques are directed at improved diagnoses, planning of tasks and action programs, interpersonal relations, and organizational processes.

A consultant usually acts in a third-party capacity, working with the group's leader and its members. Meetings of various types and for various purposes are used, for diagnosis, analysis, and consensus. The group generates the data it needs, but the consultant also provides inputs from his research and observation.[27]

Training the team as a unit has distinct advantages over confining training to individuals. It reduces the need for political power struggle, intrigue, or stress on prestige and status. Recognition of a common future among group members leads to cohesion and solidarity.

Role Techniques

Role methods are useful in conjunction with major OD interventions. They are adaptable to any context that utilizes a meeting or training session to improve behavioral insights and understandings.

One approach is to engage in role clarification, by having group members explain various aspects of the role behaviors they deem important, and express their expectations about the roles of others. Through group discussion techniques, an improved understanding of the various roles can be achieved. Ambiguity and conflict among roles can often be greatly reduced.[28]

A more common role method is known as role playing (or role taking). Role playing can be used in T-groups, confrontation meetings, case studies, and team-building sessions. In this method two or more individuals are given a brief set of facts relevant to a problem under discussion. Each acts out, before the group, the role as he or she believes it should be carried out. Other group members observe, and later criticize, the role behavior. The players may be asked to reverse their roles to experience the other side of the situation.

Role playing affords participants an opportunity to test, in an off-the-job setting, their ability to handle personal and interpersonal relations and to use techniques under discussion. Individuals can try out their ideas; others see the results. It enables participants to generalize more carefully and apply the experiences of training, without the possible penalties of a real situation.

[27]Dave Francis and Mike Woodcock, *People at Work: A Practical Guide to Organizational Change* (La Jolla, Calif.: University Associates, 1975); Glen Varney, *An Organization Development Approach to Management Development* (Reading, Mass.: Addison-Wesley, 1976); Alfred Jacobs (ed.), *The Group as the Agent of Change* (New York: Behavioral Publications, 1974); Beckhard, *Confrontation Meeting*, pp. 26–35.

[28]French and Bell, *Organization Development*, pp. 117–119.

Role playing has the further advantage of high intrinsic motivation. It is realistic and practical. However, it does require involvement of the participants: the greater their involvement and commitment, the more effective the result. It must be used under the careful guidance of a leader, one of the pitfalls being the reluctance of some participants to engage in performance before the group. Some may resent it as a childish game and hesitate to take part.

Role playing originated in the 1940s as a psychological therapy technique called psychodrama or sociodrama. It gradually became a development and training technique for management and other groups.[29]

Managerial Grid®

The Managerial Grid® is a total OD approach that includes six phases, beginning with the individual manager and progressing to include the entire organization. The six phases may take from three to five years to complete. The approach was developed as an attitudinal formulation of concern for people and concern for production. The reasoning is that attitudes lead to behavior, which in turn has consequences.

The unique feature of this approach is the Managerial Grid® developed by Blake and Mouton.[30] The Grid, shown in Figure 19-7, depicts a range of management styles. On the horizontal axis are degrees of concern for production, and on the vertical axis are degrees of concern for people, particularly subordinates. Thus there are 81 possible combinations for the two dimensions. Questionnaires are used to measure various aspects of each manager's style, making it possible to plot his or her style on the Grid.® Thus a manager may be described as having a 1,1 style—that is, poor on both dimensions. A 9,9 style is asserted to be the ideal or best style. A 5,5 score is middle-of-the-road management. A 9,1 style emphasizes task management, and a 1,9 style indicates exclusive concern for the feelings and comfort of employees. At this point the Grid® is a useful tool for individual analysis and development.

The six stages begin with a seminar, usually of one week's duration, using the Grid.® Time is devoted to diagnosing problems, making analyses, and holding discussions based on the questionnaire findings

---

[29]See, for example, Norman R. M. Maier, Allan R. Solem, and Ayesha A. Maier, *The Role-Play Technique: A Handbook for Managerial and Leadership Practice* (La Jolla, Calif.: University Associates, 1975); Margulies and Wallace, *Organizational Change,* chap. 6.

[30]Robert Blake and Jane S. Mouton, *The Managerial Grid®* (Houston: Gulf Publishing Company, 1964); *Corporate Excellence Through Grid Organization Development: A Systems Approach* (Houston: Gulf Publishing Company, 1968); *Building a Dynamic Corporation Through Grid Organization Development* (Reading, Mass.: Addison-Wesley, 1969). The evolution of the Grid in Robert R. Blake and Jane S. Mouton, *Diary of An OD Man* (Houston: Gulf Publishing Company, 1976).

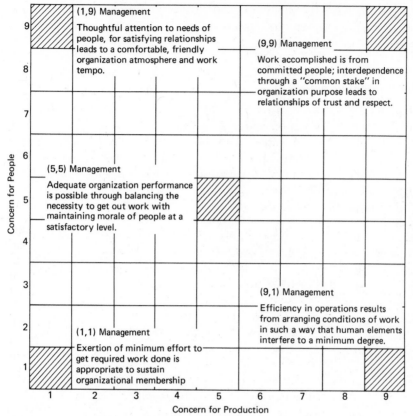

FIGURE 19-7. The Managerial Grid® Figure.

Source: Robert Blake and Jane Srygley Mouton, *The Managerial Grid*. Houston: Gulf Publishing Company, Copyright ©1964, p. 10. Reproduced by permission of the publishers and of Scientific Methods, Inc.

and other materials. Stage 2 consists of team development through applying the results of Stage 1. Stage 3 focuses on intergroup development among teams whose work requires coordination and integration. Stages 4, 5, and 6 attack problems of organization structure and design, aiming to develop the ideal organization and prepare for change. Actions are taken in Stage 5 to carry out the changes planned, and in Stage 6 to stabilize, evaluate, and reinforce the new organization and the managers' new skills. The complexities of these methods require a trained Grid consultant for maximum effectiveness.

Research on Grid® methods continues. The concept of the Grid® implies that there is one best management style. However, Grid® theory permits a versatile approach in which the best way is one designed to fit particular situations. Grid® methods are subject to limitations and difficulties similar to those of any other effort to change an organization to a more open, adaptive system. Likewise, the conditions favoring the success of Grid® methods are similar. The Grid® method has had mixed results, with some successes and some failures.[31]

Behavior Modification

Behavior modification, also called operant conditioning and positive reinforcement, is based on learning theory and directed toward changing individual behavior rather than that of the group or total organization. Strictly speaking, it is not an OD method, but it has been increasingly applied to a variety of organizations, including business firms.

Behavior modification applies Thorndike's Law of Effect, which asserts that behavior perceived to lead to a positive result will be repeated; behavior that has a neutral or negative result will tend not to be repeated.[32] Reinforcement of a person's behavior can be either positive or negative—positive if a desired behavior is rewarded, negative if an undesired behavior is punished. Most trainers and OD consultants prefer to avoid negative reinforcement and to rely on positive reinforcement.

Skinner, the foremost proponent of behavior modification,[33] has advocated the maximum use of positive reinforcement; he opposes negative reinforcement, because of its coercive implications. Reinforcement proceeds in three stages. First, the superior gives frequent positive reinforcement based on feedback from subordinates' performance, shaping their performance by constructive suggestions and the use of praise. In the second stage, reinforcement is infrequent and given at unpredictable times. Finally, supervisory reinforcement is reduced greatly, allowing task accomplishment to become the subordinates' primary source of reward. All this calls for training supervisors in reinforcement methods and getting them to accept the psychology involved. Stage three is an ideal that has proved difficult to reach in many cases.

Reinforcement methods have been extensively used in the Emery Air Freight Corporation. Its program begins with a performance audit to measure the individual's current results. Work standards are then adjusted or established by the superiors. Subordinates keep performance records, which are then scrutinized by their superior to recognize and praise good results and to criticize poor results. The program met with the difficulty that the progress reports remained necessary and

[31]Huse, *Organization Development and Change*, pp. 148–163; French and Bell, *Organization Development*, pp. 133–136; Filley, House, and Kerr, *Managerial Process*, pp. 503–506.

[32]F. Thorndike, *Animal Intelligence* (New York: Macmillan, 1911).

[33]See "Conversations with B. F. Skinner," *Organizational Dynamics* 1 (Winter 1973), 31–40; also B. F. Skinner, *Walden Two* (New York: Macmillan, 1970).

appeared to be a contrived reinforcement rather than the envisioned natural reinforcement. The company has nevertheless deemed the program successful.[34]

Behavior modification is controversial, chiefly because of its implications of manipulation and "control over people." It runs counter to beliefs in freedom and free will, and makes environment the basis of control. Skinner believes, however, that the *feeling* of freedom is the important thing, and that the individual feels free when he can act to avoid a negative reinforcement or to obtain a positive reinforcement.[35]

SUMMARY

Organization development has been explained in this chapter as a program of planned change for improving the effectiveness of people, organization structure, and management processes. OD recognizes the effects of the internal and external environment as well as the importance of improving the performance of individual managers. In this respect it is a more inclusive approach than traditional methods of training used in personnel management.

Several OD models were presented, based on systems thinking and feedback principles. OD programs generally cover a period of three to five years, and involve the participation philosophy of management. Consultants are used to guide and direct the evolving program, and to serve as resource persons.

The general OD approach is that of problem solving, in which the following main steps are followed: problem definition, diagnosis, planning of change goals, implementation of change, and evaluation. Rather than being a final stage, evaluation procedures are used at all stages as part of the feedback mechanism.

From the large number of available techniques and procedures, the following were analyzed: action research, survey feedback, sensitivity training, process consulting, confrontation meetings, team building, behavior modification, and the Managerial Grid®. All of these are forms of intervention; each has its corollary philosophies, instruments, procedures and frameworks, and each varies in the aim and reality of its results.

[34]"At Emery Air Freight," *Organizational Dynamics* **2** (July 1973), 41–50.
[35]See B. F. Skinner, *Beyond Freedom and Dignity* (New York: Alfred A. Knopf, Inc., 1971); Wieland and Ullrich, *Organization Behavior,* pp. 333–335; Huse, *Organization Development and Change,* pp. 278–283; Filley, House, and Kerr, *Managerial Process,* pp. 73–80; Don Hellriegel and John W. Slocum, Jr., *Organizational Behavior: Contingency Views* (St. Paul, Minn.: West, 1976), pp. 87–98; Fred Luthans and Robert Kreitner, *Organizational Behavior Modification* (Glenview, Ill.: Scott, Foresman, 1975); Clay Hamner and Ellen Hamner, "Behavior Modification on the Bottom Line," *Organizational Dynamics* **4** (Spring 1976), 2–21.

_____ **INCIDENT CASE**

The Parkinson Company is a large corporation in the electronics equipment industry. It has production divisions in eight states, and marketing centers in every state. The board of trustees has recently approved the president's plan for an organizationwide organization development program, which was launched on January 1. The consultant who helped develop the plan was retained for one year to help get the plan going, with the option of continuing if his services were needed after that. The consultant began by organizing a series of information meetings to acquaint everyone with the purpose of the plan and the procedures that would be followed. At the end of six months, the consultant was aware of severe opposition to the plan on the part of the corporate training director, who, although he appeared to have done nothing that would directly block the plan, gave only nominal cooperation to the consultant. He was late for many of the necessary meetings, and absent from some. The consultant also noticed that the opposition of certain other managers, who were friends of the training director, was on the increase.

Question:

1. What should the consultant do, and why?

_____ **QUESTIONS FOR DISCUSSION**

1. Work out a definition of organizational development and explain its principal elements.
2. Explain what OD programs attempt to accomplish, and why.
3. Is OD a cohesive body of ideas capable of becoming a discipline like psychology or economics? Why or why not?
4. How would you prepare an organization for the introduction of a comprehensive OD program?
5. Outline the principal pitfalls likely to be encountered in an OD program.
6. What are the advantages and disadvantages of sensitivity training as an OD intervention?
7. Explain how behavior modification techniques are used to improve the effectiveness of individuals.
8. Describe the various aspects of an OD consultant's role in the OD framework.
9. Evaluate the Managerial Grid® concept as an OD intervention.
10. How does OD methodology handle problems of resistance to change?
11. Select a desired organizational change, develop a sequence of organization development techniques to achieve this change, and explain how the techniques would interrelate.

_____ **SELECTED REFERENCES**

ARGYRIS, CHRIS. *Intervention Theory and Method: A Behavioral Science View.* Reading, Mass.: Addison-Wesley Publishing Co., Inc., 1970.

ARGYRIS, CHRIS. *Management and Organizational Development*. New York: McGraw-Hill Book Company, 1971.

BACK, KURT W. *Beyond Words: The Story of Sensitivity Training and the Encounter Movement*. New York: Russell Sage Foundation, 1972.

BECKHARD, RICHARD. *Organization Development: Strategies and Models*. Reading, Mass.: Addison-Wesley Publishing Co., Inc., 1969.

BENNIS, WARREN G. *Organization Development: Its Nature, Origins and Prospects*. Reading, Mass.: Addison-Wesley Publishing Co., Inc., 1969.

BLAKE, ROBERT R., and JANE S. MOUTON. *Building A Dynamic Corporation Through Grid Organization Development*. Reading, Mass.: Addison-Wesley Publishing Co., Inc., 1969.

BLAKE, ROBERT ROGERS. *Diary of an OD Man*. Houston: Gulf Publishing Company, 1976.

BOWERS, DAVID G. *Systems of Organization: Management of the Human Resource*. Ann Arbor: University of Michigan Press, 1977.

BROWN, PAUL L., and ROBERT J. PRESBIE. *Behavior Modification in Business, Industry, and Government*. New Paltz, New York: Behavior Improvement Associates, Inc., 1976.

FRANCIS, DAVE, and MIKE WOODCOCK. *People at Work: A Practical Guide to Organizational Change*. La Jolla, Calif.: University Associates, 1975.

FRENCH, WENDELL, and CECIL BELL, Jr. *Organization Development: Behavioral Science Interventions for Organization Improvement*, 2nd ed. Englewood Cliffs, N.J.: Prentice-Hall, Inc., 1978.

GOLEMBIEWSKI, ROBERT T. *Renewing Organizations*. Ithaca, Ill.: F. E. Peacock, Inc., 1972.

GROSSMAN, LEE. *The Change Agent*. New York: AMACOM, 1974.

HARVEY, DONALD, and DONALD R. BROWN. *An Experiential Approach to Organizational Development*. Englewood Cliffs, N.J.: Prentice-Hall, Inc., 1976.

HERBERT, THEODORE T. *Dimensions of Organizational Behavior*. New York: Macmillan Publishing Co., Inc., 1976.

HERMAN, STANLEY M., and MICHAEL KORENICH. *Authentic Management: A Gestalt Orientation to Organizations and Their Development*. Reading, Mass.: Addison-Wesley Publishing Co., Inc., 1977.

HUSE, EDGAR F. *Organization Development and Change*. St. Paul, Minn.: West Publishing Company, 1975.

JACOBS, ALFRED, ed. *The Group as Agent of Change*. New York: Behavioral Publications, 1974.

KURILOFF, ARTHUR H. *Organizational Development for Survival*. New York: AMACOM, 1972.

MAGNUSEN, KARL O., ed. *Organization Design, Development, and Behavior*. Glenview, Ill.: Scott, Foresman and Company, 1977.

McGILL, MICHAEL E. *Organization Development for Operating Managers*. New York: AMACOM, 1976.

MILES, RAYMOND E. *Theories of Management: Implications for Organizational Behavior and Development*. New York: McGraw-Hill Book Company, 1975.

MURRELL, KENNETH L., and PETER B. VAILL. *Organization Development*. Washington, D.C.: American Society for Training and Development, 1975.

SPERRY, LEN, DOUGLAS J. MICKELSON, and PHILLIP L. HUNSAKER. *You Can Make it Happen: A Guide to Self-Actualization and Organizational Change.* Reading, Mass.: Addison-Wesley Publishing Co., Inc., 1977.

STEELE, FRITZ. *Consulting for Organizational Change.* Amherst, Mass.: University of Massachusetts Press, 1975.

THOMPSON, DAVID W. *The Manager: Understanding and Influencing Behavioral Change.* Chicago: Bradford Press, 1974.

TOWERS, J. MAXWELL. *Role-Playing for Managers.* New York: Pergamon Press, 1974.

TRACEY, WILLIAM R. *Managing Training and Development Systems.* New York: AMACOM, 1974.

VARNEY, GLENN H. *An Organization Development Approach to Management Development.* Reading, Mass.: Addison-Wesley Publishing Co., Inc., 1976.

ZALTMAN, GERALD, and ROBERT DUNCAN. *Strategies for Planned Change.* New York: John Wiley & Sons, Inc. 1977.

Chapter 20

Organizational Climate and Morale

A company is known by the men it keeps.   —*Anonymous*

The country is where it is today on account of the real common sense of the big normal majority.   —*Will Rogers*

People can be divided into three groups: those who make things happen, those who watch things happen, and those who wonder what happened.
                                        —*John W. Newbern*

A story has been told about the president of a large bank in the South. He found a large world map in the center fold of a magazine. He cut it up into pieces and asked his ten-year-old son to put the world back together again. He thought it was an impossible job, but in a short time the son returned with the map of the world all put back together. "How on earth did you do this?" he asked. And the son replied, "On the other side of the page was a picture of a man, and I found that as I got the man together then the world was put together."

Questions to keep in mind as you read this chapter:

1. What are the main obligations of an organization toward the individuals within it?
2. What conditions should exist to make individuals feel that the organizational world makes sense?

Organizational climate and the morale of organization members greatly influence the behavior of people at work. In their leadership roles, managers must continuously monitor climate and morale, appraise the conditions affecting them, and take steps to maintain them at levels that keep the organization healthy and viable.

Climate and morale are examined in this chapter. Chapter 21 will discuss performance concepts, and Chapter 22 will analyze the element of motivation among employees of the organization.

ORGANIZATIONAL CLIMATE

Tagiuri defines *organizational climate* as *a relatively enduring quality of the internal environment that is experienced by its members, influences their behavior, and can be described in terms of the values of a particular set of characteristics of the organization.*[1] Climates vary from one organization to another, each reflecting a unique combination of circumstances. Climate is a commonly experienced phenomenon, and we have many expressions for it—such as *atmosphere, culture, environment,* and *milieu.* Yet climate remains an abstract concept dependent upon the perceptions of people.

Dissimilarities in the climates of different companies are quite apparent, but the characteristics of climate are relatively subtle. Often only insiders know the subtleties of the prevailing climate. But a given climate may change over time. New leadership, for example, may pay particular attention to the organizational climate at first. Moreover, climate may suffer as leaders age, become creatures of habit and tradition, and come to stand for old ways of doing things.

The importance of the quality defined as *climate* is its potential for influencing such important factors as efficiency, productivity, motivation, and job satisfaction. But the nature and effects of climate are hard to measure and evaluate.[2]

Measurement of Climate

Hellriegel and Slocum have proposed a contingency model for the measurement of organizational climate. They examined 31 studies, using three classes of contingencies for comparing them: type of technology, type of subsystems, and type of environment. They then examined the use of the organizational climate construct as an independent,

---

[1]Renato Tagiuri, "The Concept of Organizational Climate," in Renato Tagiuri and George H. Litwin (eds.), *Organizational Climate* (Boston: Division of Research, Graduate School of Business Administration, Harvard University, 1968), pp. 26–27.

[2]R. E. Johanneson, "Some Problems in the Measurement of Organizational Climate," *Organizational Behavior and Human Performance* **10** (August 1973), 118–144.

dependent, and intervening variable in the studies reviewed.[3] The following tentative conclusions are summarized:

1. *Independent variable, with job performance or job satisfaction as dependent variables.*
   (a) Job satisfaction often but not always varies according to the individual's perception of the organizational climate.
   (b) There is a significant relationship between job performance and organizational climate.
   (c) Individuals employ different work methods under different conditions of the climate.
2. *Dependent variable, with climate dependent on organization structure, and with change possible through human relations training.*
   (a) Perceptions of organizational climate vary among employees at different levels in the hierarchy.
   (b) The perceived degree of bureaucratization influences employees' perceptions of the climate.
   (c) Perceptions of climate vary with the employees' orientation to their environment.
   (d) There is a strong relationship between decision-making discretion and an employee's perception of climate.
   (e) Sensitivity training can be effective in changing employees' perception of climate.
3. *Intervening variable, with human relations, leadership, or managers' personality needs as independent variables, and performance and satisfaction as dependent variables.*
   (a) Results of human relations program were inconclusive, and the evaluation of training requires substantial time.
   (b) Leadership styles had a marked effect on creating different climates and hence on performance.
   (c) There is evidence that individual needs and climate can interact to influence performance and satisfaction.

It is possible that organizations may have more than one climate. If perceptions are measured, different groups may have different perceptions. Johnson found two climates in a study of professionals in one small consulting firm. In investigating the quality of relationships between the individual and the organization as a function of length of employment, he compared two samples, one consisting of those who had been present three or more years, the other of those employed less than three years. Each group perceived a different climate. The long-term employees deemed the climate flexible, supportive, nonauthori-

[3]Don Hellriegel and John A. Slocum, Jr., "Organizational Climate: Measures, Research, and Contingencies," *Academy of Management Journal* **17** (June 1974), 255–280.

tarian, concerned with integrating individual and organizational goals, and generally organic-adaptive in its environment. Newer employees saw the climate as rigid, procedural, strongly based on hierarchy and authority, more impersonal, and emphasizing organizational goals.[4] Climates have also been found to differ with respect to hierarchy[5] and to degree of environmental uncertainty.[6]

Although the rigor of research varies greatly among the different studies of climate, there is sufficient evidence to warrant practical interest in the application of the concept to organizations.[7] Lyon and Ivancevich found that different climate dimensions in a hospital influenced job satisfaction for nurses and administrators, and that the impact of climate on satisfaction varies with the climate dimension and the type of satisfaction.[8]

Meyer developed and used a questionnaire measuring several dimensions of organizational climate in two plants of the General Electric Company. The dimensions were nine in number: structure, responsibility, risk, standards, reward, support, conflict, warmth, and identity. The study was related to a larger overall study in the firm of problems of achievement motivation. Therefore as a first step Meyer used the questionnaire in two plants, one under a relatively permissive, participative manager, and the other managed by a more dominant, authoritarian person. No great claims were made for this short study of only two plants, but the differences on the studied dimensions were clear. The democratically managed plant was unusually successful in relation to its competitors, whereas the other, with only an average climate pattern, was less successful compared to its competitors.[9]

The internal environment contains two main types of elements: (1) the tangible, physical characteristics of the plant facilities, office arrangements, machinery and equipment, and other aspects of technology; and (2) the human environment—the relatively intangible cultural and social "atmosphere" evoked by leadership and human relations. These physical and social elements vary widely in strength and meaning, so that their influence on the members of an organization depends

[4]H. Russell Johnston, "A New Conceptualization of Source of Organizational Climate," *Administrative Science Quarterly* 21 (March 1976), 95–103.

[5]Roy Paine and Roger Mansfield, "Relationships of Perceptions of Organizational Climate to Organization Structure, Context, and Hierarchical Position," *Administrative Science Quarterly* 18 (December 1973), 515–526.

[6]Paul Lawrence and Jay W. Lorsch, *Organization and Environment* (Boston: Harvard Graduate School of Business, 1967).

[7]William R. La Follette, "How is the Climate in Your Organization?" *Personnel Journal* 53 (July 1975), 376–379.

[8]Herbert H. Lyon and John M. Ivancevich, "An Exploratory Investigation of Organization Climate and Job Satisfaction in a Hospital," *Academy of Management Journal,* 17 December 1974), 635–648.

[9]Herbert H. Meyer, "Achievement Motivation and Industrial Climates," in Tagiuri and Litwin, *Organizational Climate,* pp. 151–166.

heavily on the way individuals perceive them. Some elements influence the behavior of all or almost all organization members, whereas the influence of other elements is more selective. For example, an assembly line provides a concrete set of stimuli that is likely to affect all who work on it approximately the same way. But the workers on that assembly line may vary considerably in their perception of the group's morale or of the company as a place to work.

Organization climate affects the behavior of people in at least three important ways: (1) defining the stimuli that confront the individual, (2) placing constraints upon the individual's freedom of choice, and (3) providing sources of reward and punishment. Physical characteristics, task-related information, and the social interactions of individuals provide many of the stimuli presented to individuals. Their effects depend partly on the nature of the stimuli and partly on the perceptivity and personal attributes of the individuals. Constraints on individuals are necessary to achieve orderly and coordinated effort, to maintain the organization structure, and to direct activity in order to achieve desirable group goals. Defining jobs, roles, and responsibilities is a way of setting up some of these constraints. Rewards and punishments come not only from the formal systems of authority, but also from the informal system of colleagues and peers.

Organizational climate is important for its impact on the outlook, well-being, and attitudes of organization members, and thus on their performance. But research has not yet definitively established that the behavior of work groups has a significant effect on total organizational performance. Kaczka and Kirk, using methods of computer simulation, found that the performance of the firm is significantly affected by managerial climate, but that an employee-oriented managerial climate does not always lead to higher levels of performance.[10] Hinton found that a climate of frustration significantly reduced creative problem-solving performance measured against several assumptions about personality and ability characteristics of employees.[11]

Whether we consider the technological or the social environment, the executive's basic choice is to adapt to the environment or change it—an ancient dilemma, Simon notes, and one that we have traditionally solved by seeking and achieving a degree of simplification and stabilization of the environment.[12] The alternative is to reprogram

[10]Eugene Kaczka and Roy V. Kirk, "Managerial Climate, Work Groups, and Organizational Performance," *Administrative Science Quarterly* 12 (September 1967), 253–272; and "Managerial Climate and Organizational Performance," *Academy of Management Proceedings*, 1967 (Bowling Green, Ohio: 1968), 101–112.

[11]Bernard L. Hinton, "Environmental Frustration and Creative Problem-Solving," *Journal of Applied Psychology* 52 (June 1968), 211–217.

[12]Herbert A. Simon, "The Corporation: Will It Be Managed by Machines?" in Melvin Anshen and George Leland Bach (eds.), *Management and Corporations 1985* (New York: McGraw-Hill Book Company, 1960), pp. 33–37.

human beings so that they will possess the adaptive mechanisms that allow them to respond flexibly to the demands of the environment. The processes of automation and computerization, for example, are efforts to plan, control, and stabilize work environments, thereby reducing the need for adaptiveness and flexibility of the individual within the organization. Selection, training, and placement procedures also contribute to the stabilization of the managerial work force.

The idea of organizational climate raises many interesting questions, and appears to be significant in both practical and theoretical areas; but more research is needed. Meanwhile, organizational climate provides a useful focus for understanding such characteristics of organizations as communications, creativity and innovation, effectiveness, and stability.[13]

MORALE

The necessity for military organizations has familiarized many people with a general idea of morale. Belonging to many types of groups has also conveyed the importance of morale.

Definitions

Morale has many definitions, but there is no universally acceptable one. Definitions range from the purely operational (relevant mainly to a particular situation or type of situation) to the theorectical and often abstract concepts of researchers. Definitions also vary from one discipline to another.

Drucker,[14] McGregor,[15] and others refer extensively to "the spirit of an organization" and "the managerial climate." Such phrases denote the psychological and sociological characteristics of a particular environment. A typical work environment contains physical components— buildings, desks, files, tools—all of which have colors, odors, surfaces, and so on. But the most significant element of the individual's environment is the presence of other individuals and the formal and informal interactions that occur among individuals, within groups, and among groups. Morale is fundamentally a group phenomenon, consisting of the pattern of attitudes held by organization or by group members collectively.

[13]Stan Silverzweig and Robert F. Allen, "Changing the Corporate Culture," *Sloan Management Review* **17**, no. 3 (Spring 1976), 33–50.

[14]Peter F. Drucker, *The Practice of Management* (New York: Harper, 1954), chap. 13.

[15]Douglas McGregor, *The Human Side of Enterprise* (New York: McGraw-Hill, 1960), chap. 10.

Guion provides a "total situation" definition of *morale* that emphasizes the individual: "Morale is the extent to which an individual's needs are satisfied and the extent to which the individual person perceives that satisfaction is stemming from his total job situation." Morale is a complex mixture of several elements and is not a single dimension of organizational behavior; it is constituted by the attitudes of individuals. It recognizes the impact of the job situation upon the individual's attitudes, and includes the role of human needs as motivational forces.[16]

Blum[17] and Gilmer[18] state that the terms *job attitude, job satisfaction,* and *industrial morale* are by no means synonymous, although they are often used interchangeably. According to Gilmer, *job attitude* is the feeling of employees about their job and their readiness to react in certain ways to their job situation. *Job satisfaction* is the degree of favorableness of a person's various attitudes toward job, boss, work and other people, and even toward life in general. *Morale,* a group concept (differing from Guion), is the common expression of the attitudes of the various individuals in an organization. Individuals derive their personal morale out of their feelings of acceptance by the group and a sense of participation in a common enterprise.[19]

Levels of Morale

Morale is frequently described as being high or low, with the implication that morale exists in varying degrees and that it may change from time to time. There may be discerned an organizationwide state of morale, or morale may differ from one subunit to the next. But some degree of morale is always present. High morale exists when employee attitudes are favorable toward their job, their company, and their fellow workers—favorable to the total situation of the group and to the attainment of its objectives. Low morale exists when attitudes inhibit the willingness or ability of organization members to attain objectives or to obtain satisfaction from their jobs.

Morale is best regarded as a long-run condition. Those who point to businesses having low morale and good results may be taking a short-run view of the total situation. Morale is a state of balance and health within an organization, in which the participants view the total situa-

[16]Robert M. Guion, "Industrial Morale—The Problem of Terminology," *Personnel Psychology* (1958), chap. 11, pp. 59–61. As reprinted in Harry W. Karn and B. von Haller Gilmer, *Readings in Industrial Business Psychology,* 2nd ed. (New York: McGraw-Hill, 1962), p. 48.

[17]M. L. Blum, *Industrial Psychology and Its Social Foundations* (New York: Harper, 1956).

[18]B. von Haller Gilmer, *Industrial Psychology* (New York: McGraw-Hill, p. 198.

[19]Ibid.

tion with favorable attitudes. The significance of morale is in the level at which it exists in the group at given time. Managers need to recognize their influence on the patterns of morale prevailing in the groups with which they are working.

The concept of morale is often confused with that of teamwork, but the two are not the same. Teamwork is a condition in which individuals work together effectively in groups. Morale is the state of attitudes of members of the group. Teamwork may be high, yet morale may be low—although high morale is usually helpful in developing teamwork. Teamwork may also be absent when morale is high, as in cases where workers prefer individual effort and find satisfaction in their own performance.

Reasons for Maintaining High Morale

It has been widely assumed that high morale leads to high productivity. Research indicates that the relationship between morale and productivity is not so clear, direct, and simple as has been supposed. Research indicates the need for caution in attributing causal effects to high morale. For example, studies by the University of Michigan of insurance and railroad organizations revealed no great differences between high- and low-production groups with respect to morale. The extent to which workers reported that they liked their jobs, their bosses, and their work did not correspond to output levels.[20] Research has not proved, however, that a relationship does *not* exist, or that it can safely be ignored. Although one may occasionally encounter low morale and high productivity, or high morale and low productivity, research findings have *not* led to the conclusion that high morale is not important.

High morale is desirable for reasons other than productivity. For one thing, it is pleasant to work for an organization where a spirit of loyalty and good will prevails. Managers may feel proud of their ability to develop teamwork and an *esprit de corps* that is evident to others. Morale leads to a sense of unity and coordination that is apparent to outsiders—the community, customers, suppliers, and stockholders. Most important, too, is the attraction of such an organization for the better employees available in the labor marked.

During good times, when an organization is finding its product or service easy to make and sell, it may be able to endure, for a time,

[20]See, for example, Rensis Likert and Stanley E. Seashore, "Employee Attitudes and Output," *Monthly Labor Review* 77 (June 1954), 641–649; Daniel Katz, Nathan Maccoby, and Nancy C. Morse, *Productivity, Supervision, and Morale in an Office Situation* (Ann Arbor: Survey Research Center, University of Michigan, December 1950); Nancy C. Morse, *Satisfaction in the White-collar Job* (Ann Arbor, Mich.: Survey Research Center, University of Michigan, 1953); or Daniel Katz, Nathan Maccoby, Gerald Gurin, and Lucretia G. Flood, *Productivity, Supervision, and Morale Among Railroad Workers* (Ann Arbor: Survey Research Center, University of Michigan, 1951).

conditions of falling or low morale. High morale, however, prepares an organization for harder times, when it may have to tap all its resources in order to survive. With high morale, an organization is better prepared for the adverse circumstances that come to all sooner or later.

The problem of morale will now be analyzed in terms of two main aspects: (1) attitudes and job satisfaction, and (2) methods of building and maintaining morale.

ATTITUDES AND JOB SATISFACTION

Attitudes are a central component of morale. The nature of employee attitudes and the degree of their favorableness or unfavorableness reflect the morale of the organization or its subunits.

The attitudes of employees, at all levels, have both an objective and an emotional component. The objective component is a mental set, a view or opinion based on facts and on day-to-day experience. The emotional component centers around evaluations of these experiences—how people feel concerning them. In actual situations, it is not easy to separate the mental and emotional characteristics of an attitude. They go together. Unless managers are aware of both components, however, they are unlikely to deal with attitudes successfully.

The fact that mental and emotional attitudes are contagious has an important bearing on the way organizations function. Unrest among people can spread quickly once it starts. Favorable attitudes can also spread quickly as understanding and insights occur in a group, but such a movement tends to be slower than that typical of unrest. Little things that cause negative attitudes and low morale to develop can multiply rapidly, and the situation worsens. Once started, the spread of unrest is hard to stop. To head off growing unrest, managers should act preventively.

Too often, unrest provokes harsh sanctions rather than problem solving on the part of managers. Managers are tempted to act on their own negative evaluations of persons holding undesired attitudes. Value judgments of this kind interfere with objectivity.

The attitudes of members of an organization are often ephemeral and transitory, changing and dynamic. What counts for the manager and for the long-run stability of the enterprise is that a solid base of generally favorable attitudes continues to underly these day-to-day fluctuations.

The factors in an organization that most strongly influence morale are those that most closely touch people in their daily work and those that are frequently experienced in people's relations with immediate supervisors and fellow employees. Because managers have many, but of course not all, such factors under their influence, leadership is often stressed as necessary for high morale.

Extent of Job Dissatisfaction

Extensive studies indicate that job dissatisfaction is widespread. In general, studies in different industries show that many employees express dissatisfaction with their jobs; and members of organizations undoubtedly feel substantial unrecorded, generalized dissatisfaction that is never measured, chiefly because it is never expressed. Moreover, managers sometimes ignore the evidence of poor morale that does surface.

Job satisfaction tends to be higher in younger workers than in older ones, declining during the first few years of employment, then moving upward until middle-aged reactions set in. Job dissatisfaction tends to be associated with generalized maladjustments; those who express dissatisfaction are less friendly and more emotionally unbalanced than their satisfied co-workers; more boredom, daydreaming, and discontent prevail. The dissatisfied worker finds it hard to adjust to rules, employee standards, and the rigid requirements of bureaucracy. Also, the higher the level of occupation, the higher the level of job satisfaction found. Professional people, salaried workers, and shop workers fall in descending rank according to degree of job satisfaction. Dissatisfaction also appears to be closely related to income: those of higher incomes express greater job satisfaction.[21]

Size has also been found to have a negative relationship to job satisfaction and a positive relationship to such variables as absenteeism, turnover, accidents, and labor disputes. However, studies indicating this relationship have been mainly on rank and file rather than managerial employees. In this research size is generally measured in terms of four subunits: the employees, primary work group, the departmental unit, and the factory or office. Increasing the size of a total organization, therefore, would not necessarily lower employee morale if intraorganizational work units were kept small.[22]

Structure and technology also influence morale in complex ways. Research has not yet confirmed that any structural shape is superior to another in eliciting positive employee attitudes. Claims that flat structures result in higher morale have been largely unsupported. Furthermore, structural characteristics are related to size, so that differences in morale may be caused by size as well as structure.[23]

Low job satisfaction often occurs among workers in lower social strata; attitudes toward jobs are not simply a matter of individual

[21]Gilmer, *Industrial Psychology*, pp. 198–200.

[22]Lyman W. Porter, "Job Attitudes in Management: IV. Perceived Deficiencies in Need Fulfillment as a Function of Size of Company," *Journal of Applied Psychology* **47** (1963), 386–397.

[23]Lyman W. Porter and Edward E. Lawler, "Properties of Organization Structure in Relation to Job Attitudes and Job Behavior," *Psychological Bulletin* **64** (1965), 23–51.

opinions, but are conditioned by the value systems of the employee's social class. This means that managers can influence only a portion of the employee's attitudes, or affect the total patterns only in part. Some sources of attitude formation are beyond their ability to direct, control, or change. Attitudes arising directly from the organizational environment, however, offer ample scope and challenge for the decision maker.

The report of a special task force to the Secretary of Health, Education and Welfare, made in 1976, reported substantial discontent among managers, particularly in the middle echelons. This finding is surprising in view of earlier studies that viewed these relatively privileged and well-paid managers as highly satisfied. Whereas they were traditionally a loyal group, more than one out of three middle managers expressed some willingness to join a union. And an increasing number are considering career changes to gain greater independence or less responsibility, even at lower financial return. Some appear to reach a midcareer crisis of personality and obsolescence, where the game no longer seems worth the candle. This crisis was intensified in the sixties and early seventies, when they were vulnerable to value changes espoused by the counterculture.[24] Terkel's best seller, *Working*, also describes many cases of occupational discontent.[25]

Comparative studies in a single organization over time yield useful perspectives. One such study, using a sample of over 98,000 blue and white collar employees in a merchandise distributing firm, found a downward trend in job satisfaction between 1963 and 1972. Measures of satisfaction, including attitudes toward supervision, kind and amount of work, physical surroundings, and financial rewards, showed a consistent decline regardless of job tenure, job function, or geographical area.[26]

Measuring Attitudes and Morale

The questionnaire survey is the most widely used tool for the measurement of attitudes. Some firms have used extensive interviewing procedures, but these are more costly in time and expense, and are somewhat more complicated to analyze. A third means of measurement, index techniques, have been the least successful.

[24]*Work in America*, Report of the Special Task Force to the Secretary of Health, Education, and Welfare. Prepared under the auspices of the W. E. Upjohn Institute for Employment Research (Cambridge, Mass.: M.I.T. Press, undated), pp. 40–42.
[25]Studs Terkel, *Working* (New York: Pantheon, 1974).
[26]Frank Smith, Karlene H. Roberts, and Charles F. Hulin, "Ten-Year Job Satisfaction Trends in a Stable Organization," *Academy of Management Journal* 19 (September 1976), 462–468.

Standard questionnaire forms are available from such sources as consulting specialists and trade associations. But universally valid forms do not exist, and it is often necessary to devise a special questionnaire so that it fits the situation in which it is used.

The basic idea of a survey (by either questionnaires or interviews) is to obtain attitudinal responses from each individual, or a representative sample of individuals. Then by compiling and analyzing the data, a picture of the level of morale in a group can be developed. Knowing the nature of the responses and the state of over-all morale should indicate ways in which leaders and managers can improve morale by correcting the causes of poor attitudes.

This raises the question of whether attitudes relate to the quality of work performance of individuals and groups. Many surveys assume that they do; surveys used by organization development consultants and change agents are based on this idea. Lawler, however, indicates that the nature and quality of a survey's methods and contents have much to do with the survey's usefulness in building better performance; for to be effective, the content must take account of up-to-date motivation theory in planning and constructing the survey instruments.[27]

Most attitude surveys have focused on only two kinds of attitudes: those reflecting general job satisfaction, and those concerning the individual's feelings about supervision, pay, and other job rewards. Yet according to Lawler, these attitudes do not predict the extent to which individuals are motivated to perform better, although they may explain things like excessive absenteeism and turnover. Lawler believes that data are needed on how employees feel that important rewards are obtained in their organization. By coupling reward expectancy data with job attitude data, managers may assess the motivational state of their organization.[28]

Index methods are based on analyses of records or employee behavior that compare trends and changes over time. For example, records of grievances filed, turnover and absenteeism rates, accident rates, productivity, and the like may be systematically examined. Sudden changes may reflect a change in morale. By establishing base-line data for a given period and applying indexing techniques, the analyst can make ready comparisons against the base-line period. The index figures combine the results of a variety of measures. Efforts to establish index-number techniques combining such indicators have, in general, been relatively unsuccessful. The principal drawback of records is that they are historical—they point to low morale that has already occurred. They preclude a more preventive approach.

[27]Edward E. Lawler III, "Attitude Surveys and Job Performance," *Personnel Administration* **30** (September-October 1967), 485–487.
[28]Ibid.

Problems in the Use of Surveys

The use of attitude surveys has steadily increased, but the number of organizations using them is still relatively low. The decision to use this device regularly involves an assessment of the objectives that the organization is pursuing with respect to its employees. If surveys are part of a total program aimed at improving relations with employees and developing a better organization, the chances of success will be high. If, on the other hand, the decision is based on superficial reasons such as trying it because others do it, the chances of failure are great. Any tool or device can be misused and mishandled. Unfortunately, serious mistakes in dealing with employee attitudes may not be overcome for several years. In the realm of attitudes, personnel practitioners and line executives require special competencies. If these competencies are lacking, the organization is better off omitting survey work on employee attitudes.

Three conditions inhibit the successful application of systematic measurement of employee attitudes. First, not all managers themselves have attitudes that are conducive to the use of the survey technique. Some do not accept the importance of employee feelings, objectives, or opinions; and many who do acknowledge their importance are not convinced that employees can express their ideas and feelings in useful form in surveys or other methods of upward communication. Still others feel that it is wiser to "let sleeping dogs lie" and not take steps that might "stir up a lot of trouble." Such thinking is superficial, and is a rationalization. Clearly, ignoring unfavorable attitudinal situations among employees will not eliminate or improve a negative organizational climate.

A second obstacle to the acceptance of attitude surveys arises from the fact that such a survey is essentially an evaluation of the manager's leadership and supervision capabilities. A survey produces in tangible form a check on the quality of management and the success of personnel policies. Therefore, managers who are insecure or who have feelings of fear or inadequacy tend to resist their use. In the minds of executives who reject attitude surveys lies a curious ambivalence—a burning curiosity as to what employees really think about them and the organization, coupled with a gnawing fear that they won't like what they find out. Dread of uncovering unfavorable responses leads to rejection of the reliability of the medium through which the information is obtained.[29]

The third inhibiting factor in the use of surveys is caused by their

---

[29]Management and personnel literature contains many helpful methods and ideas for effectively conducting surveys, even in small organizations. See, for example, Gene Milbourn, Jr., "The Job Satisfaction Audit: How to Measure, Interpret and Use Employee Satisfaction Data," *American Journal of Small Business* 1 (July 1976), 35–43.

complexity and difficulty. Except in fairly large organizations there are few people qualified to conduct and analyze surveys, and inertia prevents managers from obtaining outside assistance. There are, however, genuine concerns for the reliability and effectiveness of surveys. Some measurement specialists and psychological researchers doubt the value of attitude surveys, partly because many organizations have had unsatisfactory experiences with them. That these bad experiences may be caused by improper use of the surveys does not diminish the problem for those opposed to them.

Likert has raised another objection to attitude surveys: they are usually designed to collect after-the-fact information, too late to guide decisions or prevent problems. Surveys tend to measure end results, rather than causal or intervening variables. Therefore they do not provide the right information for diagnosing organizational and motivational problems. Likert also suggests that it is difficult to obtain accurate reports from subjects who fill out surveys, because the motivation to fake the expected answers is often high. Likert does, however, advocate measurement—measurement of the causal and intervening variables through techniques of social psychology, psychometrics, sociometrics, and statistics. Clearly professionals are needed in using such survey methods. Likert's critique is well grounded, but there is ample room for a managerial tool that, when capably managed, provides information about the changing level of morale over time, and from one unit to another.[30]

Guidelines for Attitude Surveys

An attitude survey is an instrument of statistical measurement. Survey results do not, therefore, indicate a mathematically precise score for general attitudes. However, the statistical measurements provided by attitude surveys are based on probabilities, and they offer better guidance than haphazard guesses or intuitive feelings.

Periodic surveys provide a picture of trends and changes. Changes in morale do not necessarily appear suddenly but may emerge gradually. It is useful to draw comparisons about morale over significant periods of time. Surveys are occasionally made semiannually, but more commonly once a year.

Figure 20-1 shows sample items from an attitude survey. Surveys of this type collect only the perceptions or attitudes that people possess. Therefore it is important that the samples obtained be representative of the body of information being sought, and that the sample be adequate in size to permit the use of statistical analysis. Otherwise reliability and validity are lost. The writing and arrangement of questions in such a

[30]Rensis Likert, *The Human Organization: Its Management and Value* (New York: McGraw-Hill, 1967), chap. 8.

		Employee Questionnaire			
Yes	No		Yes	No	
☐	☐	My manager is fair and honest.	☐	☐	I have the necessary supplies and equipment I need to do my job.
☐	☐	I get paid for all the hours I work.			
☐	☐	Benefits provided by the company have been explained to me.	☐	☐	Employees are treated fairly.
			☐	☐	We are informed in advance of changes affecting us.
☐	☐	I have been properly trained to do my job.	☐	☐	My supervisor usually gets back to me with answers to my questions.
☐	☐	My supervisor handles employee complaints fairly.			
☐	☐	Employee terminations are for just causes.	☐	☐	I can usually count on management for a satisfactory answer about my benefits.
☐	☐	Rules and regulations are enforced fairly and consistently.	☐	☐	Pay raises are received on time.
☐	☐	I feel sure of my job as long as I do it well.	☐	☐	Our work load is reasonable.
☐	☐	We receive the Marriott "Crest" regularly.	☐	☐	I am satisfied with employee meals.
☐	☐	I am reasonably paid.	☐	☐	My supervisor thanks me for a job well done.
☐	☐	My supervisor will listen when I have a problem.	☐	☐	Employee meetings are held at least monthly.
☐	☐	I believe my job is important.	☐	☐	I believe this survey will bring some positive changes.

FIGURE 20-1. Sample Items from an Employee Morale Survey.

Source: G. M. Hostage, "Quality Control in a Service Business," *Harvard Business Review,* July–August 1975. Copyright © 1975 by the President and Fellows of Harvard College; all rights reserved. Used by permission.

survey are of crucial importance and should be undertaken only by trained persons.

To carry out a successful attitude survey program, executives should recognize and follow these policies:

1. Top management and lower echelons should be in accord as to the desirability of the program. The support of top management is essential.

2. The survey program is not a "gimmick" and, therefore, should be viewed as a long-range upward-communication program.
3. The program's objectives must include the intention to correct, wherever possible, all unsatifactory conditions under the organization's influence.
4. The cycle of communication must be carried to completion by matching the upward communication of the survey with the downward communication of results to those who participated in it.
5. Particularly at the start of a new program, the purposes, objectives, and policies should be carefully explained to those whose attitudes are being surveyed. Efforts are required to allay suspicion and fear and to win cooperation.
6. The direction of and responsibility for the program should be placed in the hands of a thoroughly qualified individual, so that the survey itself will be correctly prepared and the results properly analyzed and interpreted.

BUILDING AND MAINTAINING MORALE

Many organizations attempt to build high morale by fancy devices and gimmicks. Suggestion systems and open-door policies are adopted, not for their merit, but because others have them. Good morale cannot be developed on an unsound base of dissatisfaction with fundamental aspects of organization climate or with inept management. No technique of morale building can take the place of sound policies concerning pay, hours, and working conditions that dignify individuals and release their energies constructively.

The philosophies and methods of organization development that were described in Chapter 19 and the approaches to motivation that will be described in Chapter 22 will result in management styles and organizational conditions that work for high morale. At this point, four important concepts will be explained: (1) participation, (2) cohesiveness, (3) identification, and (4) loyalty.

Participation

Participation is a widely misunderstood concept. It has merited skepticism by managers and others who have "tried it" or who have seen it "tried." This notion of trial reflects the use of participation as a gimmick, a magic cure for the organization's ills. Moreover, organizations allegedly should adopt it because it is a humane, socially responsible idea. It fits respected value systems of goodness and democracy and therefore should be unquestionably accepted. Yet participation has led to disillusionment where it is used as a device for manipulating people or for deluding them into believing they have a voice in decisions when in fact they do not.

The Case for Participation

Participation is not only a group process reflecting democratic values; it is also a reflection of the extent and manner of delegating tasks and responsibilities to subordinates. Participation therefore is inherent in the superior-subordinate relationship; the skills of leadership and management include the ability to elicit effective participation in common enterprises.[31]

In the discussion of authority in Chapter 15, participation was shown on a continuum ranging from little or none under a highly authoritarian leader to almost completely democratic participation with a minimum of imposed authority. Managers can thus vary the nature and extent of participation so that it fits practical conditions experienced in their group's work life. The variables involved are the manager's own skills, experiences, and preferences, the content of the problem or situation, and the skills, abilities, and attitudes of the subordinates.

Organization members seek *meaningful* involvement. Participation, in the most meaningful sense, requires confidence in people's capacities and ideas and sincerity in extending significant opportunities for genuine participation of group members. An oversimplified notion of participation, such as that of voting on decisions with majority rule, or the intent to manipulate others or to abdicate managerial responsibilities, is futile.

It should be noted that participation may be managed differently under different circumstances. It may be applied to problems of change, to all decisions affecting a group, or to planning. It ranges from merely voluntary involvement to a programmatic system. It may be merely consultative or advisory; it may involve decisions of a minority or a majority, or it may require unanimity or consensus.[32]

Research on Participation

The desirability of developing the participation of subordinates is more than a mere value judgment. It is based on research findings that indicate its advantages in better performance of groups and higher satisfaction of individuals.

[31]James G. March and Herbert A. Simon, *Organizations* (New York: Wiley, 1958), chap. 4.
[32]H. Joseph Reiff, *Behavior in Organizations* (Homewood, Ill.: Irwin, 1977), pp. 389–393.

A classic study supporting the value of the participative approach first reported in 1948 by Coch and French, demonstrated the advantages of participation in overcoming the resistance of people to change. It tested the hypothesis that resistance to change is a combination of an individual's reactions to frustration with strong, group-induced forces. The researchers created three experimental groups, the first experiencing no participation in planning or deciding changes affecting the group. The second group experienced participation through representation, and the third experienced total participation by all members of the group. The no-participation group improved little beyond early efficiency ratings. The representation group showed an unusually good improvement, and the third group, through total participation, showed better efficiency ratings than either of the others. The conclusion was that total participation has about the same effect, in kind, as representative participation, but the former has a stronger influence.[33]

The Coch and French study was the forerunner of many in the Harwood Manufacturing Company, which has for years been operated by the participative approach. In 1962, the Harwood firm acquired the Weldon Manufacturing Company, and applied a participative approach to the rejuvenation of that firm with considerable success.[34]

Tannenbaum and Massarik, in an early study, found in a large chemical company's cost reduction program that participation led to concern and involvement by the total organization in the problems of cost. The result was higher output rates; improved product quality; lower turnover, absenteeism, and tardiness; and greater harmony in labor-management relations. Moreover, the company attributed to this participative cost-reduction approach a substantial profit increase as well as success in the cost-cutting goal.[35]

Participative approaches are consonant with the research literature that explores leadership, organizational change, communications, and human relations. McGregor's Theory X and Theory Y, Likert's System 4, and the literature on group decision are representative of the wide range of management approaches that point to the practical values of participation.[36]

[33]Lester Coch and John R. P. French, Jr., "Overcoming Resistance to Change," *Human Relations* 1 (December 1948), 515–532.

[34]Alfred J. Marrow, *Making Management Human* (New York: McGraw-Hill, 1957); Alfred J. Marrow, David G. Bowers, and Stanley E. Seashore, *Management by Participation* (New York: Harper, 1967).

[35]Robert Tannenbaum and Fred Massarik, "Participation by Subordinates in the Managerial Decision-making Process," Institute of Industrial Relations, Reprint No. 14 (Los Angeles: University of California), pp. 409–411.

[36]Raymond Miles, "Human Relations or Human Resources?" *Harvard Business Review*, July-August 1965, pp. 148–153; Raymond Miles and J. B. Ritchie, "Participative Management: Quality vs. Quantity," *California Management Review* 13 (Summer 1971), 48–56.

Likert's System 4

Most OD approaches rely extensively on the involvement and participation of organization members, individually and in groups. An
approach that puts participation and other concepts of the adaptive
organization at the center is Likert's System 4. Figure 20-2 shows a
Likert scaling instrument in abbreviated form. When the system is used
as a survey device, the descriptions of the operating characteristics on
the left, and the corresponding descriptive statements under the columns for Systems 1 through 4, are more detailed.[37] As can be seen from
Figure 20-2, System 4 characteristics are much the same as were
considered in the adaptive organization (Chapter 13).

Likert's concept is to utilize a variety of methods and techniques to
move an organization from the profile revealed by survey data obtained
with the form, and get it closer on each scale to the System 4 Column.
Surveys given in sequence yield new profiles indicating progress. To
Likert, System 4 is the ideal to be sought. On the basis of use over many
years, Likert believes that organization members prefer working for a
System 4 employer, and that System 4 is found in high-producing,
successful organizations, whereas low-producing, less successful organizations are using a System 1 or System 2 approach.

The validity of the System 4 approach is still being tested and
evaluated. It is subject to much the same criticisms and difficulties as
OD concepts, and has similar advantages. Evaluations to date have not
been sufficiently rigorous.[38]

The Advantages of Participation

In addition to the advantages revealed in the research just described,
many other advantages of participation can be demonstrated. With the
participation of subordinates, it is often possible to use fewer managers.
The need for close supervision, checking, control, and disciplinary
action is reduced. Subordinates derive a greater sense of responsibility
from the ability to influence events affecting them. Frequently, subordinates know things that deciding managers might overlook by proceeding alone. Subordinates often withhold vital insights and points of
view if they are afraid or coerced. Participation thus frees upward
communication. Not only is participation a pleasant experience for
people in an organization, but it also results in feelings of belonging
and of being wanted. Employees like to feel that they are an integral
and important part of the group.

[37]For a complete version of the questionnaire and a full rationale of its use and results,
see Rensis Likert, *The Human Organization.*
[38]Filley, House, and Kerr, *Managerial Process,* pp. 506–509; Wieland and Ullrich,
Organization Behavior, pp. 59–68.

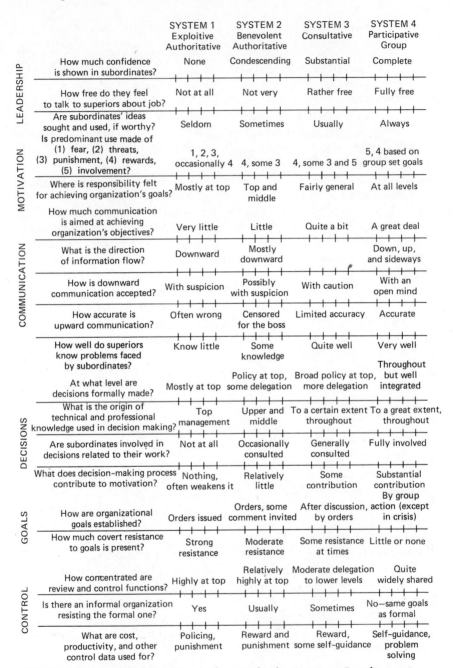

		SYSTEM 1 Exploitive Authoritative	SYSTEM 2 Benevolent Authoritative	SYSTEM 3 Consultative	SYSTEM 4 Participative Group
LEADERSHIP	How much confidence is shown in subordinates?	None	Condescending	Substantial	Complete
	How free do they feel to talk to superiors about job?	Not at all	Not very	Rather free	Fully free
	Are subordinates' ideas sought and used, if worthy?	Seldom	Sometimes	Usually	Always
MOTIVATION	Is predominant use made of (1) fear, (2) threats, (3) punishment, (4) rewards, (5) involvement?	1, 2, 3, occasionally 4	4, some 3	4, some 3 and 5	5, 4 based on group set goals
	Where is responsibility felt for achieving organization's goals?	Mostly at top	Top and middle	Fairly general	At all levels
COMMUNICATION	How much communication is aimed at achieving organization's objectives?	Very little	Little	Quite a bit	A great deal
	What is the direction of information flow?	Downward	Mostly downward		Down, up, and sideways
	How is downward communication accepted?	With suspicion	Possibly with suspicion	With caution	With an open mind
	How accurate is upward communication?	Often wrong	Censored for the boss	Limited accuracy	Accurate
	How well do superiors know problems faced by subordinates?	Know little	Some knowledge	Quite well	Very well
DECISIONS	At what level are decisions formally made?	Mostly at top	Policy at top, some delegation	Broad policy at top, more delegation	Throughout but well integrated
	What is the origin of technical and professional knowledge used in decision making?	Top management	Upper and middle	To a certain extent throughout	To a great extent, throughout
	Are subordinates involved in decisions related to their work?	Not at all	Occasionally consulted	Generally consulted	Fully involved
	What does decision-making process contribute to motivation?	Nothing, often weakens it	Relatively little	Some contribution	Substantial contribution
GOALS	How are organizational goals established?	Orders issued	Orders, some comment invited	After discussion, by orders	By group action (except in crisis)
	How much covert resistance to goals is present?	Strong resistance	Moderate resistance	Some resistance at times	Little or none
CONTROL	How concentrated are review and control functions?	Highly at top	Relatively highly at top	Moderate delegation to lower levels	Quite widely shared
	Is there an informal organization resisting the formal one?	Yes	Usually	Sometimes	No—same goals as formal
	What are cost, productivity, and other control data used for?	Policing, punishment	Reward and punishment	Reward, some self-guidance	Self-guidance, problem solving

FIGURE 20-2. Simplified Version of Likert Scales for System 4 Development.

Source: Rensis Likert, *New Patterns of Management* (New York: McGraw-Hill Book Company, 1961), pp. 223–233.

The advantages for participative management are, however, merely possible advantages. They do not follow automatically from ritualistic, insincere invitations to participate, but depend on confidence in people and on the manner and conditions under which the participation occurs.

Cautions About Participation

Criticisms of participative management together with its failures and difficulties reflect considerable skepticism. Some companies have reverted to a "get-tough" philosophy, which they regard as a rejection of the participation concept. Perhaps too much has been claimed for it. Even if some form of participation in decisions raises morale, improves job satisfaction, dignifies individuals, and so on, the decisions are not necessarily better. And they may be slower.

The skepticism of managers is matched by the hesitancy of many workers to participate in democratic groups. They often feel that it asks them to usurp managerial prerogatives; it seems an abdication of managerial responsibility.

Managers often prefer a pragmatic view; they want to solve problems and to get decisions made. Putting this responsibility on group members is an easy way for a manager to avoid involvement. Managers often adopt a superficial view of participation, settling for lip service or a vague kind of employee morale, or else they use it simply to gain popularity. They feel that to extend such opportunities to workers opens the door to full employee control. Therefore, they contend, the principle of democratic action should not be "carried too far."[39]

Additional difficulties in managerial acceptance of participative approaches are that (1) subordinates may reject decisions favored higher up, (2) subordinates may make a low-quality decision, (3) participation now leads to expectations for participation later, and (4) supervisors lose respect as leaders.[40] It is important that managers avoid undue rationalization in rejecting participative approaches, carefully weighing the advantages against the disadvantages.[41]

Cohesiveness

Cohesiveness and *identification* are sociopsychological concepts expressing certain relationships among individuals in a group and between individuals and the organization. *Cohesiveness* is defined as

---

[39]For example, see "Stonewalling Plant Democracy," *Business Week*, March 28, 1977.

[40]George Strauss, "Participative Management: A Critique," *ILR Research* 12 (1966) 306.

[41]Robert C. Albrook, "Participative Management: Time for a Second Look," *Fortune* 75 (May 1967), 166–170, 197–200; Edgar H. Schein, "In Defense of Theory Y," *Organizational Dynamics* 4 (Summer 1975), 17–30.

the degree of member attraction to the group or the degrees of power that the group has over the behavior of its members.[42] Cohesiveness has been studied largely as a small-group phenomenon.[43] Three major factors studied thus far are the group's attraction to members, the prestige of its membership, and the characteristics of the tasks in which the group is engaged.

Golembiewski, in comparing high cohesiveness (HiCo) and low cohesiveness (LoCo) groups, cites four aspects of cohesiveness that make it a strategic group property, capable of exerting control over the behavior of the members of an organization:

1. *Amount and hierarchy of communications.* Studies have generally shown that participation is more equal and more intense in HiCo than LoCo groups, consistent with the prediction that participation in HiCo groups is more valued by members;

2. *Rejection of deviants.* HiCo groups tend to reject those who deviate from group opinion more than LoCo groups do; and communications directed toward deviants tend to be initially more frequent as well as finally less frequent in HiCo groups than in LoCo, which reflects more marked attempts in HiCo groups to preserve the psychological group first by conversion of deviants and then by rejecting them convincingly when conversion does not result;

3. *Willingness to accept influence.* HiCo members are more susceptible to group influence than LoCo members, a relation more interestingly reflected in experimental demonstrations that HiCo groups are more successful in maintaining high *or* low production levels than LoCo groups; and

4. *Reactions toward external threat or deprivation.* HiCo groups are more capable of producing and sustaining a hostile reaction against "external" threat than LoCo groups.[44]

The existence of cohesiveness is at least in part an indication of the general level of morale, but extremely high cohesiveness is not entirely good for an organization, for it may introduce undue rigidity, fostering resistance to change and to outsiders with new ideas.

[42]Robert T. Golembiewski, *Behavior and Organization* (Skokie, Ill.: Rand McNally, 1962), p. 106. See also Stanley E. Seashore, *Group Cohesiveness in the Industrial Work Group* (Ann Arbor, Michigan: Survey Research Center, University of Michigan, 1954).

[43]Golembiewski, *Behavior.*

[44]Robert T. Golembiewski, "Management Science and Group Behavior: Work Unit Cohesiveness," *Journal of the Academy of Management* 4 (August 1961), 87–99. See also Bruce Buchanan II, "Building Organizational Commitment: The Socialization of Managers in Work Organizations," *Administrative Science Quarterly* 19 (December 1974), 535–546; Robert O. Hanson and Fred E. Fiedler, "Perceived Similarity, Personality, and Attraction to Large Organizations," *Journal of Applied Psychology* 3 (July–September 1973), 258–265.

Identification

Identification is a psychological concept describing an individual's reactions to the characteristics and achievements of an individual or group as though they were his own. Individuals in an organization tend to identify with their fellows—workers with fellow workers (especially those close to them or those on similar jobs) and managers with managers. This ability to identify with another person, group, or organization is a learning experience and a device by which a person derives security and confidence from the environment. Thus individual morale is strengthened by realizing that there are others who have the same problems, and even that they may have found at least some of the answers.

An interesting aspect of identification is the habit of dividing others into groups of friends and enemies—or, perhaps, less friendly and more friendly persons. Individuals tend to identify with those they can become close to on a friendship basis, and from such identification they derive feelings often characterized as a part of the concept of morale— having a good job, a good place to work, a good company to be part of.

Managers seeking to build morale into the environment can and do utilize the idea of identification. By strengthening the individual's identification, it is possible to intensify "we-they" feelings, marking out for the employer a clearer awareness of colleagues and the organization. To strengthen identification, managers employ symbolic devices, such as badges, emblems, long-service awards, departmental or company insignia, and newsletters and other communications media. But these outward manifestations are merely an aid, a reflection of the desire to create an environment making possible a degree of identification that increases the individual's feelings of importance and belongingness.

Many forces compete for the identification of a worker or a manager, in addition to colleagues and other internal groups. Indeed, all the "publics" to which the organization members belong pose such demands. Customers, suppliers, professional associations, community agents, labor unions, and trade associations are but a few of the many institutions that at various times will lay claim to, and pose conflicts for, the individual's propensity to identify with other individuals or groups. One's work, career, or occupation may also be a focus for the individual and the identification process.

Loyalty

Loyalty is often a garbled concept. Weak or insecure managers often demand a blind loyalty—a be-loyal-to-me-or-else attitude. Managers who verbalize excessively about loyalty are usually of such a type. True loyalty is a derived or an earned loyalty generated out of clarity of common purposes and respect for the goals, ideals, and activities of the organization, as well as for the people in it.[45]

One of the best descriptions of the ideological basis for loyalty, identification, and the integration of component interests in an organization is that of Philip Selznick in his classic study, *TVA and the Grass Roots.* He states:

> There is a vague and ill-defined quality which, unacknowledged and often poorly understood, represents a fundamental prize in organizational controversy. This is the evolving character of the organization as a whole. What are we? What shall we become? With whom shall we be identified? Where are our roots? These questions, and others like them, are the special responsibility of statesmen, of those who look beyond the immediate context of current issues to their larger implications for the future role and meaning of the group. To pose these questions is to seek more than the technical articulation of resources, methods, and objectives as these are defined in a formal program or statute. To reflect upon such long-run implications is to seek the indirect consequences of day-to-day behavior for those fundamental ideals and commitments which serve as the foundation for loyalty and effort.
>
> These considerations from the social psychology of the individual provide us with tools for organizational analysis. Organizations, like individuals, strive for a unified pattern of response. This integration will define in advance the general attitudes of personnel to specific problems as they arise. This means that there will be pressure within the organization, from below as well as from above, for unity in outlook. As unity is approximated, the character of the organization becomes defined. In this way, the conditions under which individuals may "live together" in the organization are established, and a selective process is generated which forces out those who cannot identify themselves with the evolving generalized character of the organization. The evolving character, or generalized system of responses, will be derived in large measure from the consequences of day-to-day decision and behavior for general patterns of integration.[46]

Loyalty poses personal and organizational pitfalls for managers. Loyalties may be in conflict with one another; loyalty may be demanded by a department in a way that runs counter to loyalties demanded by one's division, company, colleagues, profession, or even customers or other outside groups. Loyalty may also be rationalized to the point where it becomes a value over other values, such as honesty and integrity.

[45]For an interesting analysis of loyalty in business organizations, see William R. Gall, "Not by Loyalty Alone," *Journal of the Academy of Management* 5 (August 1962), 117–123; Nathaniel Stewart, "A Realistic Look at Organizational Loyalty," *Management Review*, January 1961, 13–19.

[46]Philip Selznick, *TVA and the Grass Roots* (Berkeley: University of California Press, 1949), p. 181.

Officials found guilty of illegal price fixing or of conflict-of-interest violations no doubt feel they are acting "for the good of the company."

Yet educated, intelligent loyalty is a desirable objective if accompanied by a genuine integrity on the part of all concerned. Where morale is high, questions of loyalty are not resolved issues; but loyalty in and of itself cannot condone mismanagement or incompetence or shield the insecure.[47] Note too that "loyalty" is influenced by such realities as alternative job opportunities and the influences of pension plans that are designed to reward longevity.

SUMMARY

In this chapter we have elaborated workable concepts of organizational climate and morale, identifying as their major elements the complex matter of attitudes toward work, company, job, boss, and colleagues. We considered the existence of organization climates, and the proposition that they can be measured and compared along different dimensions. Although research results are not yet plentiful, they indicate that the internal environment makes a difference to the organization member, and that it relates to his performance and job satisfaction.

The thesis of this chapter has been that such concepts involve legitimate questions of decision and action and that managers can run an organization better by understanding and learning to use these key concepts. Some aspects of morale as a condition or climate within the organization are measurable. Attitude surveys and analysis may reveal changing conditions and specific loci of morale problems. They are also used to identify which aspects of a situation call for remedial action by the organization.

Morale has a contagious quality. It can deteriorate rapidly when seriously unfavorable events occur, but high levels of morale must be patiently built up over long periods of time, and be maintained by sound policies and decisions rather than by gimmicks or one-shot actions.

We also examined the concepts of participation, cohesiveness, identification, and loyalty. Although participation theories of management are subject to criticism, they are current and are supported by considerable research evidence. Cohesiveness, a dimension studied mainly in small groups, is a measure of the extent to which the group will remain attractive to its members. Loyalty and identification do not appear automatically, but are engendered by qualities of leadership within the organization.

[47]John W. Lewis III, "Management Team Development: Will It Work for You?" *Personnel* **52**: 4 (July/August 1975), 11–25.

_____ **INCIDENT CASE**

Richard Helms, the personnel director of the Martin-Brown Company, became concerned over the indications of low morale he detected among the company's 1300 first-line supervisors. He believed that an attitude survey would show where the weaknesses were with respect to morale and organizational climate. The company's vice president of operations recommended against using a consultant, claiming that "our personnel department should have someone who can do it well enough." Helms assigned the task to Charles Dorwin, his manager of wage administration. Dorwin agreed with some reluctance, saying he really didn't know the right techniques. He drew up a list of questions, and using other surveys as a guide, prepared and issued a questionnaire. The resulting data were processed by six members of his clerical staff. Dorwin analyzed the data and issued a report to Helms. Helms reproduced 1500 copies of the 78-page report, which was ready to be mailed to the supervisors when the word came to him from the vice president of operations not to distribute the report, and to destroy all copies.

Questions:

1. What caused this situation to occur?
2. What would you do if you were in Helms' position?

_____ **QUESTIONS FOR STUDY**

1. How do you account for the fact that managers have so recently discovered the existence of human relations in the places where people work?

2. To what extent do you think morale is given inadequate attention by management? Is the subject given too much emphasis? If so, in what way?

3. How can the methods of science be applied to the problems of human beings at work?

4. What is meant by the concept of organizational climate? How can an organizational climate be improved?

5. To what extent can organizational climate be measured? What are the limiting factors?

6. Develop and administer an attitude survey for the members of your class. What problems did you encounter, and how did you solve them?

7. Is it true that complaints are inevitable in an organization and that little can be done except try to keep troublemakers out? Why or why not?

8. For what reasons should a manager pay attention to the state of morale within his department?

9. Can an individual have morale, or must it exist throughout the whole group?

10. What is the apparent relationship between morale and wages?

11. "Management can have good morale and high productivity without paying much attention to the wage structure." Is this statement true or false? Why?

12. How can the general level of morale be measured? Is it necessary to measure it, or will an estimate suffice?

13. What requirements would you impose to assure that an attitude survey to be made in your organization would be successful?

14. Explain as thoroughly as you can why executives are often reluctant to take concrete steps to measure morale.

SELECTED REFERENCES

BERNSTEIN, PAUL. *Workplace Democratization: Its Internal Dynamics.* Kent, Ohio: Kent State University Press, 1976.

BOWERS, DAVID G. *Systems of Organization: Management of the Human Resource.* Ann Arbor: University of Michigan Press, 1976.

BOWERS, DAVID G. *System 4: The Ideas of Rensis Likert.* Ann Arbor, Michigan: University of Michigan Press, 1975.

FROMKIN, HOWARD L., and JOHN J. SHERWOOD. *Integrating the Organization: A Social Psychological Analysis.* New York: The Free Press, 1974.

GELLERMAN, SAUL W. *Managers and Subordinates.* New York: Dryden Press, 1976.

HARRIS, O. JEFF, JR. *Managing People at Work: Concepts and Cases in Interpersonal Behavior.* New York: John Wiley & Sons, Inc., 1976.

HERSLER, WILLIAM J. and JOHN W. HOUCK, eds. *A Matter of Dignity: Inquiries into the Humanization of Work.* Notre Dame, Ind.: University of Notre Dame Press, 1977.

HUNT, JOHN W. *The Restless Organization.* New York: John Wiley & Sons, Inc., 1972.

HUNT, RAYMOND G. *Interpersonal Strategies for System Management: Applications of Counseling and Participative Principles.* Monterey, Calif.: Brooks/Cole Publishing Company, 1974.

KOEHLER, JERRY. *The Corporation Game: How to Win the War with the Organization and Make Them Love it.* New York: Macmillan Publishing Co., Inc., 1975.

LITWIN, GEORGE H., and ROBERT A. STRINGER. *Motivation and Organizational Climate.* Boston: Division of Research, Graduate School of Business Administration, Harvard University, 1968.

MALCOLM, ANDREW. *The Tyranny of the Group.* Totowa, N. J.: Littlefield, Adams and Company, 1975.

MARROW, ALFRED J., DAVID G. BOWERS, and STANLEY E. SEASHORE. *Management by Participation.* New York: Harper & Row, Publishers, 1967.

McGREGOR, DOUGLAS. *The Professional Manager.* New York: McGraw-Hill Book Company, 1967. Part 5.

PORTER, LYMAN W., and EDWARD E. LAWLER III. *Managerial Attitudes and Performance.* Homewood, Ill.: Richard D. Irwin, Inc., 1968.

SASHKIN, MARSHALL. "Changing Towards Participative Management Approaches: A Model and Methods." *The Academy of Management Review,* July 1976, pp. 75–86.

STEELE, FRITZ, and STEPHEN JENKS. *The Feel of the Work Place*. Reading, Mass.: Addison-Wesley Publishing Company, 1977.

SUSMAN, GERALD I. *Autonomy at Work: A Sociotechnical Analysis of Participative Management*. New York: Prager Publishers, Inc., 1976.

TAGIURI, RENATO, and GEORGE H. LITWIN, eds. *Organizational Climate*. Boston: Division of Research, Graduate School of Business, Harvard University, 1968.

TEDESHI, JAMES T., and SVENN LINBSKOLD. *Social Psychology: Interdependence, Interaction, and Influence*. New York: John Wiley & Sons, Inc., 1976.

WILLIAMS, ERVIN, ed. *Participative Management: Concepts, Theory and Implementation*. Atlanta: School of Business, Georgia State University, 1976.

Chapter 21

Managerial Performance: Appraisal and Improvement

The successful executive is critical of his own performance: the unsuccessful, of the performance of others.   —*Harry Levinson*

It isn't the incompetent who destroy an organization. The incompetent never get in a position to destroy it. It is those who have achieved something and want to rest upon their achievements who are forever clogging things up.
                                                  —*F. M. Young*

One of the troubles of our age is that habits of thought cannot change as quickly as techniques, with the result that as skill increases, wisdom fades.
                                                  —*Bertrand Russell*

CHAPTER GUIDE

Life can be very insecure for middle managers, who typically are not highly visible in their organizations. Reductions in force often lead to the firing of highly competent middle managers. One manager, a twenty-year employee in a medium-sized manufacturing firm, was fired as national sales manager in a reduction in force decision that ousted over five hundred managers. This discharge occurred only two months after a merit raise and praise for doing an "outstanding job." According to the president, "We had businesses that were inefficient. We had to restructure management to make it leaner, and we had to trim off people." Ten per cent of the salaried employees were discharged as a result of company panic over falling profits.

Questions to keep in mind as you read this chapter:

1. How might you, as a manager, protect yourself against a situation like this?
2. Was it a mistake for this company to fire competent, successful managers?
3. What steps should the discharged manager take next, and why?

The quality of managerial performance in organizations cannot be taken for granted. Managers are always subject to the judgments of others. Because individuals and organizational contexts constantly change, performance also can change and be changed. This chapter will describe how organizations provide for the development of managers and the improvement of their performance.

The organization development programs discussed in Chapter 19 are designed to improve the over-all performance of the organization, or units thereof. However, the individual's performance is only in part a function of the organizational context. Whether or not OD programs are used, the improvement of performance requires changes in managers' behavior. Many OD techniques are helpful, but managers also need planned training and development opportunities that enable them to develop their personal skills and abilities.

The problem of managerial performance will be analyzed in the following dimensions: (1) the nature of managerial effectiveness, (2) performance appraisal systems, and (3) methods and programs for training and development.

MANAGERIAL EFFECTIVENESS

Managers have at their command many resources that affect the quality of their work. Their personal experiences and capabilities are primary assets, but these are continuously influenced by the organization's climate and by the resources it devotes to training and development.

Ongoing organizations have a history and traditions that provide background. Role expectations provide continuity and cues as to how managerial work is to be done. To some extent, an organization runs almost automatically as long as the key roles are reasonably well performed. Effectiveness, however, is a matter of degree. Without continuous efforts to improve the effectiveness of managers, organizations would be accepting the status quo as satisfactory.

There are considerable differences in current definitions of *managerial effectiveness*. Campbell defines it as *any set of managerial actions that are optimal for identifying, assimilating, and utilizing internal and external resources with the aim of sustaining the functioning of the unit for which the manager is responsible.*[1] Reddin defines the concept as the extent to which a manager achieves the output requirements of his position—what he achieves rather than what he does.[2] Drucker defines it as a habit, a complex of practices that lead to getting the right things done.[3] All these definitions contain key elements: results, organizational objectives, and managerial action. The basic dichotomy lies in what the manager does and in what the manager produces. Both concepts are needed, for they refer to means and ends.

Efforts to measure the degree of effectiveness depend on clear and operational definitions. Not everyone agrees that effectiveness can be objectively measured, but subjective evaluations are made all the time. Whether we are measuring results or the determinants of the results, it seems clear that effectiveness does not lie entirely within the control of the manager himself, nor is it confined to a specific array of managerial traits. The environment, the organization structure, and the reward system are only a few of the factors that combine with the manager's personal characteristics in determining ultimate outcomes.[4]

It is easier to recognize ineffectiveness in managers than to measure effectiveness objectively. Ineffectiveness ususally creates problems that must be acted upon. An average degree of effectiveness may be tolerated until specific events demand more. The best defense against the ambiguities of measuring effectiveness is found in setting performance standards as objectively as possible, and using systematic procedures for appraising the performance of managers against those standards.

MANAGER APPRAISAL

Appraisal is often poorly done. The task is so complicated that managers often hesitate to devote the effort required by modern appraisal techniques. Many managers distrust formal methods and prefer to avoid direct confrontation with appraisals. They play hunches, guess, or decide the fate of subordinates by whim because they fear the criticism that systematic evaluations evoke.

Objectives of Appraisal

Appraisal is a continuous process. People working together cannot avoid forming and acting on judgments about their associates and what

[1]John P. Campbell et al., *Managerial Behavior, Performance, and Effectiveness* (New York: McGraw-Hill, 1970), p. 105.

[2]W. J. Reddin, *Managerial Effectiveness* (New York: McGraw-Hill, 1970), p. 3.

[3]Peter F. Drucker, *The Effective Executive* (New York: Harper, Publishers, 1967), p. 1.

[4]M. Sami Kassem and M. A. Moursi, "Managerial Effectiveness: A Book Review Essay," *Academy of Management Journal* 14 (September 1971), 381–388.

they do. Systematic appraisal methods help managers appraise subordinates fairly and as objectively as possible.

Appraisal is not the same as measurement. It is more subjective. Where performance results are measurable, measurement should be used; but in managerial work highly subjective factors are also important, so that appraisals are also needed.

The purpose of any systematic method of manager appraisal is to increase the objectivity and fairness in judgments of subordinates. It reduces subjectivity by the use of regular procedures for periodic appraisals, which thus provide up-to-date information for making decisions about people. Systematic procedures increase the consistency and equity of treatment, and help to assure that no one's talents, abilities, or potential are overlooked.

Uses of Appraisal Results

Appraisals result in systematically organized information about the performance of individual managers. This information can be used for making many kinds of decisions. The main uses are (1) to facilitate decisions about salaries and other rewards, (2) to identify promotable managers, (3) to determine the training needs of managers, and (4) to guide the growth and self-development of individuals.

Appraisals are often made at the time of considering periodic salary increases; individuals with favorable appraisals receive merit increases and other rewards. This provides tangible recognition, and may help to motivate individuals. However, many feel that appraisals and salary or promotion decisions should be made at different times to avoid having people strive for higher *ratings* rather than higher *performance*. If appraisals are tied to salary decisions, salary increases are automatically expected at appraisal time. Moreover, salary decisions are made on a number of complex factors, including social or emotional ones, and not on performance alone.[5]

Identifying promotable and trainable executives is important, for training resources are wasted if training occurs indiscriminately. Choices must be made as to who gets what, and these choices can be more readily justified under systematic procedures known to all. One large company with over fifty thousand executives eligible for training adopted a rule that its middle-management program would be restricted to those who had been on the job not more than two years. This rule then became the key to training objectives and course content; "being new on a job involving higher management responsibility" was a common factor among those attending. But the need remained for

[5]David W. Belcher, *Compensation Administration* (Englewood Cliffs, N.J.: Prentice-Hall, 1974); Herbert H. Meyer, "The Pay for Performance Dilemma," *Organization Dynamics*, Winter 1975, 39–50.

making choices among those who were eligible, and the individual appraisals were still necessary.[6]

Self-development is a keynote of the newer systems of appraisal that are supplanting traditional approaches.[7] The self-development concept has its roots in psychology and learning theory; it emphasizes the need for motivation, high aspiration levels, and the varying achievement drives of individuals. It also emphasizes the importance of a supportive organizational climate. The relevance of appraisal information for these purposes depends upon how the system is designed and applied.

A Systems View of Appraisal

The nature and role of the appraisal process can best be seen by taking a systems view such as that shown in Figure 21-1. There are three main subsystems: work planning and review, formal appraisal, and use or application of appraisal results. Work planning specifies the tasks, activities, and needs to be met, together with standards for their measurement or appraisal. In the second phase, appraisals are made, and adjustments may be made in the work as it progresses. Performance is the result of skills influenced by motivation. Appraisals are used in planning job changes or reassignments, training and development, and compensation.

We will now examine (1) the problem of performance standards, and (2) procedures for conducting the appraisal process.

Performance Standards for Managers

The overall performance of an organization depends on the performance of individual managers. Managerial performance is appraised by each manager's immediate supervisor. It is important that systematic procedures be used to measure or appraise results against clear standards.

The setting of performance standards has been widely neglected in organizations. In part, this neglect can be attributed to the complexity and rapid change in managerial tasks, and to the ambiguity or breadth that surrounds management tasks, especially at higher levels. But this reasoning begs the question: in the absence of standards of some kind, decisions about managerial performance are at the mercy of subjectivity and whim.

The determination of performance standards is difficult because

---

[6]James Rawls, Donna Rawls, and Raymond Radosevich, "Identifying Strategic Managers," *Business Horizons* 18 (December 1975), 74–78.

[7]Robert F. Pearse and B. Purdy Pelzer, *Self-Directed Change for the Mid-Career Manager* (New York: AMACOM, 1975); Hawdon Hague, *Executive Self-Development: Real Learning in Real Situations* (New York: Wiley, 1974).

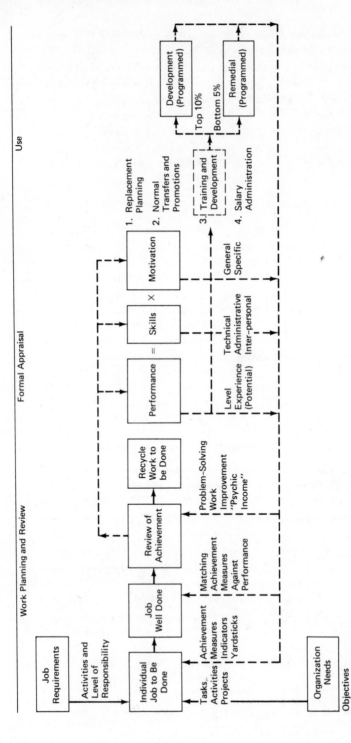

FIGURE 21-1. A Systems View of Appraisal and Management Development Planning.

Source: Nathan S. Winstanley, "Performance Appraisals and Management Development: A Systems Approach," *The Record* 13 (March 1976), p. 57. Used by permission.

human capabilities are difficult to define and understand.[8] A valuable approach is for managers to involve their subordinates in the process of choosing and defining the standards. In management by objectives (MBO) procedures used in many companies, the attainment of mutually agreed-upon objectives becomes the standard. In any case performance standards should be a matter of clear understanding between bosses and subordinates. Putting them in writing, as is the case in MBO programs, is helpful.

Appraisal Methods

Two main methodological approaches are used for systematic appraisals: (1) rating scales, sometimes called merit rating, and (2) results-oriented planning.

Early programs of appraisal centered on rating scales based largely on personality traits. This was a step in the right direction: it introduced system and regularity to the procedure. Although such scales are often used, their inherent weaknesses include the ambiguity of standards, the difficulty of defining the traits so that the raters apply them consistently, and doubt about whether there is a valid connection between the traits and the quality of performance. Rating scales are difficult to use without error and bias. There are also procedural problems of training supervisors to use the scales correctly and of interpreting appraisals with respect to subordinates. Newer systems of appraisal substitute a planning and coaching relationship between superior and subordinate for rating scales and use of traits. Where rating scales are used, they are adjuncts to a more comprehensive procedure designed as part of the total relationship of bosses and subordinates.[9]

The earliest systems of appraisal emphasized the role of the superior over the subordinate. The superior rated or appraised subordinates as part of the system of threats or coercion that was exercised over them. Trait scales provided labels with which to depict the weaknesses and strengths of subordinates in ways that placed all the blame on the subordinate. Subordinates had little choice but to please their bosses and to avoid antagonizing them. There is usually little recourse against unfair, erroneous, or biased ratings.

This one-way appraisal process has come to be widely modified in modern organizations, because assumptions about people at work have changed. Appraisal is now widely viewed as a two-way process, and as

[8]William W. Ronan and Erich P. Prien (eds.), *Perspectives on the Measurement of Human Performance* (New York: Appleton, 1971); Herman S. Jacobs and Katherine Jillison, *Executive Productivity* (New York: AMACOM, 1974).

[9]Marion S. Kellogg, *What to Do About Performance Appraisal* (New York: AMACOM, 1975).

part of the set of power and influence relationships inherent in every organization. The core of the new approach is the shift from personality-oriented, judgmental criticism (or reward) to a focus on results together with joint planning and contributions from both superior and subordinate. The concept of *performance control* has changed to an emphasis on appraisal as a tool of *performance planning and analysis.*[10]

This new approach to performance standards and manager appraisal is utilized in MBO programs; performance standards are set in mutual planning sessions by subordinates and their bosses. Because the ultimate aim of MBO is to use the mutually selected targets as standards for evaluating the subordinate's results, both superior and subordinate gain better understanding and more accurate appraisals through careful planning. They can better analyze how each contributes to the final results in a collaborative team effort.

The subordinate starts the planning and review cycle by choosing the performance targets he or she feels are most desirable. These are reviewed in a planning session by both superior and subordinate. The superior may accept or modify the targets, enlarging the horizon of a modest or apathetic subordinate, or restraining the overeager one who tries to tackle too much. The important result is mutual agreement, and recognition that both have a stake in what is done.

A central element in MBO or results-oriented approaches is that the focus is on performance and results rather than on the superior's opinions about the subordinate's personality or general behavior. Superiors are not forced to judge people or personality traits; instead they can evaluate what they are most qualified to recognize: the results achieved. Moreover, the mutual interests of the superior and subordinate are clear. Their relationship can be stripped of threats and coercion, which are at best negative motivators. Moreover, much of the burden for the selection of goals and the analysis of results is placed where it properly belongs—on the subordinate.[11] The results approach to performance appraisal is rooted in sound psychological principles applying to superior-subordinate relations. It gives greater dignity and worth to the roles of both, and transposes the evaluative process from subjectivity and emotion to a more objective basis.

Several difficulties must be considered in MBO or other results approaches. First, they represent a complex set of psychosocial behaviors for the supervisor, and an unfamiliar role for most subordinates. A higher set of skills is required of the appraising manager, who needs well-developed interviewing and observational capacities, substantial self-awareness, and sensitivity to the needs and feelings of others.

[10]Campbell et al., *Managerial Behavior.*
[11]George S. Odiorne, *Management by Objectives* (New York: Pitman, 1965); see also Stephen J. Carroll and Henry L. Tosi, *Management by Objectives: Applications and Research* (New York: Macmillan, 1973).

Participants also need commitment to the system, and superiors themselves should have experienced skillful treatment in the application of the system that is being applied to subordinates.

A second difficulty is that such procedures represent a way of life for the organization. They are a total system, not a piecemeal, casual affair that can be "tried out" by one group or another. Results approaches have to encompass all levels, including the very top; they need full support in the policies and actions of the entire management team.

A third problem is the potential criticism that results approaches emphasize ends and say little about means. Unless careful attention is given to the way the process works, subordinates may get the idea that results are wanted at any cost, and that the means do not matter. How work is done may also be important.[12]

A fourth problem follows from the other three. The training and development of managers in the philosophies, methods, and practices of MBO or other results appraisal systems is difficult. Success depends on winning the support of the participating managers, who need to feel confident in their ability to handle the complex social and psychological subtleties of the system. This confidence comes only through practice and training. Communicating the appraisal results to subordinates is the most critical step in the process.

Communicating the Results of Appraisal

Making appraisals without communicating them to the individual is not only unfair, but denies the supervising manager the use of a valuable tool in directing the efforts of subordinates. This is true even where rating scales are used.

Results are reported to subordinates in a feedback interview, a planned meeting between a boss and each subordinate, with four objectives: (1) giving the results, both favorable and unfavorable, to the subordinate, (2) analyzing the causes of performance problems, (3) planning constructive changes and actions to improve performance, and (4) reaching a mutual agreement on objectives for the next period. The feedback interview should occur as soon after the completion of the actual appraisal as possible, for delay may cause the subordinate undue anxiety.

The feedback interview is an example of the confrontation meeting described in Chapter 19. It does not necessarily center on conflict, however. The focus is on constructive approaches to the improvement of performance. Mutual interests are at stake; the parties to the meeting recognize their responsibilities for and influences over the results

[12]Harry Levinson, "Appraisal of *What* Performance," *Harvard Business Review* **54** (July-August 1976), 30–48.

being discussed. Nevertheless, it is also true that there will always be tension and emotion in such confrontations.

The way the feedback concept is used is important. In engineering applications of the feedback cycle, such systems are passive with respect to the information processed. They perceive no emotional content. By contrast, human feedback systems must take into account the emotions of the people involved—in this case, supervisor and subordinate. The manager who uses feedback opportunities in a threatening, coercive way will engender antagonism, resistance, and noncompliance. However, the manager who views the feedback process as a mutual learning and teaching experience, avoids a punitive approach, and fits the process into ongoing relationships with each subordinate will achieve greater self-control and more compliance, with less resistance and hostility.

Many managers are reluctant to discuss adverse aspects of the appraisal, but it is unfair to leave a subordinate in doubt. The superior can learn through practice how best to communicate unfavorable information. The aim is to help the subordinate improve and progress. Therefore the appraiser should discuss favorable factors and focus on results rather than simply criticizing personal characteristics, abilities, or traits. The inadequate performance of work may of course stem from problems of character and personality, a fact that the supervisor may have to face along with the subordinate. However, the organization's basic interest is in results, not in reforming or changing personalities or molding people in acceptable images. This approach is positive in that it reduces the impact of the subordinate's feelings of fear and anxiety.[13]

The subordinate's deficiencies are frequently traceable to defects in the superior's performance—failures to support the subordinate or to provide promised resources. This confrontation may increase the reluctance of superiors to report results to subordinates, for in so doing they expose their own actions to question or criticism. Yet the superior is protected by positional authority—by the fact that a boss is still a boss. The subordinate, too, has protections against unfair or biased treatment, for a well-developed appraisal system includes regular procedures for review and appeal apart from the boss's appraisal.

Appraisals and feedback interviews should be completed regularly on a periodic schedule. Some organizations schedule them every six months, but an annual basis is more often the case. However, periodic reviews do not take the place of continuous day-to-day coaching and development. In the employer-employee relationship, there is need for a review of wider scope than the daily work routines provide. It is the total result over significant periods of time that counts. But appraisals,

[13]John M. Ivancevich, "Changes in Performance in a Management by Objectives Program," *Administrative Science Quarterly* **19** (December 1974), 536–574.

even well-handled ones, are not magic remedies for deep-seated manager-subordinate problems. Some managers doubt that all subordinates really want to know where they stand. Subordinates who are confident and secure may wish to know more often than the anxious and insecure ones. The need for feedback, however, does not depend merely on what subordinates want.

Studies in learning theory show that performance improves when reliable information is processed to the performer from an authentic source in an unthreatening manner. However, the receptivity of the performer to the information is important. Human responses to information about results are likely to vary with the performer's degree of commitment to goals. The performer's needs, attitudes, and feelings affect the perceptions and interpretations of information received. Thus the manager should aim for a generally high level of commitment to improvement from subordinates rather than attack the compliance problem solely with disciplinary measures.[14]

Additional Approaches to Appraisal

Numerous variations in basic approaches to appraisal have been devised but are less widely used. Among these are peer ratings—ratings of one manager by other managers at the same level or working in the same kinds of activity.[15] Another is the use of self-appraisals, in which individuals appraise their own work prior to consultation with their superiors.[16] Systems calling for appraisals of superiors by their subordinates have also been tried, without impressive results. All these methods can be used as supplements to other systems such as the MBO approach, which itself often incorporates self-appraisals.

Dealing with Poor Performance

An effective appraisal system in which managers have confidence reveals those subordinates whose performance is below expectations. A decision must be made in each case whether improvement is possible, and what changes should be made.

---

[14]Alan L. Patz, "Performance Appraisal: Useful but Still Resisted," *Harvard Business Review* **53** (May-June 1975), pp. 74–80; E. Allen Slusher, "A Systems Look at Performance Appraisal," *Personnel Journal* **54** (February 1975), 114–117 Sanford M. Dornbusch and W. Richard Scott, *Evaluation and the Exercise of Authority* (San Francisco: Jossey-Bass Publishers, 1975).

[15]H. E. Roadman, "An Industrial Use of Peer Ratings," *Journal of Applied Psychology* **48** (August 1964), 211–214.

[16]George C. Thornton, "The Relationship Between Supervisory and Self-Appraisals of Executive Performance," *Personnel Psychology* **21** (Winter 1968), 441–455; Glenn A. Bassett and Herbert H. Meyer, "Performance Appraisal Based on Self-Review," *Personnel Psychology* **21** (Winter 1968), 421–430.

The improvement plan is based on analysis of the causes of poor performance. If a result-oriented appraisal method has been followed through the feedback stage, the manager and subordinate may have agreed on the causes, or at least have clarified their differences. If substandard performance is very low or has long continued, the manager has further decisions to make: Are the causes correctable? Who will do what? And is further effort worth the cost?

Some failures are caused by organizational problems that transcend the individual. A critical factor is the quality of selection and placement of newly hired employees. Miner estimates that about 70 per cent of all performance failures have some kind of placement error as a contributory cause, and that an investment in better selection and placement methods will greatly reduce performance failures.[17]

Even with the best of selection and placement procedures, managers must deal continuously with problems of individual performance. The alternatives are discharge, direct improvement efforts through retraining or disciplinary methods, or reassignment of the individual. To tolerate continued substandard performance would appear undesirable, but in practice this too is a chosen alternative. Some of the possible alternatives are shown in Figure 21-2. To deal with a poor performer, the manager needs to consider the subordinate's potential for improvement compared to the costs of the alternatives available. An impatient superior may decide not to salvage a slow or ineffective subordinate, preferring to take the hazard of selecting a replacement at some risk of another mistake.

The manager has help at his disposal. Perhaps he needs additional information, which may come from personnel records or from interviews with the subordinate and those with whom he works. Professional counselors, specialists, and psychological testing are available, usually from the personnel department. Clinical testing, as contrasted to selection testing, may throw additional light on the causes of performance problems, providing a better understanding of the individual. This information will also be useful in reassignment, which is often preferable to discharge. An individual not effective in one part of the organization is often successful in some other part, if a placement error was made and can be corrected.

The nature of the performance problem will determine the strategies needed for its solution. The types of problems are numerous.[18] One set of these, based on problems of motivation, will be considered in Chapter 22. Here we shall discuss three of the most common performance problems: (1) obsolescence, (2) shelf-sitting, and (3) human relations problems.

[17]John B. Miner, *The Challenge of Managing* (Philadelphia: Saunders, 1975), p. 324.
[18]Miner, *Challenge,* provides a comprehensive treatment of performance problems and methods of dealing with them.

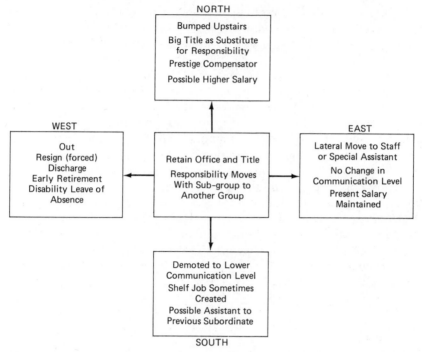

NORTH

Bumped Upstairs

Big Title as Substitute
for Responsibility

Prestige Compensator

Possible Higher Salary

WEST

Out
Resign (forced)
Discharge
Early Retirement
Disability Leave of
Absence

Retain Office and Title

Responsibility Moves
With Sub-group to
Another Group

EAST

Lateral Move to Staff
or Special Assistant

No Change in
Communication Level

Present Salary
Maintained

Demoted to Lower
Communication Level

Shelf Job Sometimes
Created

Possible Assistant to
Previous Subordinate

SOUTH

FIGURE 21-2. Organization Compass for Displacing Executives.

Source: Frank L. Bird, "The Displaced Executive or the Man on the Shelf," *MSU Business Topics,* Summer 1966, p. 34. Reprinted by permission of the publisher, Division of Research, Graduate School of Business Administration, Michigan State University.

Obsolescence

That a machine may become obsolete in its intended use is readily accepted, and a new machine is accepted with a sense of excitement. That a person can become obsolete is difficult to accept, and a replacement decision often generates fear and anxiety among those remaining. Yet the obsolescence of managers may be more significant to the organization. The cost of technological obsolescence is tangible and subject to engineering and accounting analysis; the costs of manager obsolescence are even greater, but they are also more intangible, harder to detect, and more difficult to deal with.

An obsolescent individual is one whose trained capacities and accumulated experiences have been outdistanced by changing technologies, new approaches, and demands hitherto not experienced.

Obsolete employees may be separated from the organization through layoff, early retirement, or some other means. Thus they join the ranks of the unemployed, where retraining is needed if they are to find useful employment again. Public programs of education and training at the adult level are required for a general attack on this part of the problem.

The alternative to discharging the obsolete employee is retraining or reassignment within the organization. This common practice accounts for a large share of the training and education effort of organizations. Sheer knowledge is becoming an increasingly important ingredient of all work, and because growth and change are rapid and abundant, obsolescence occurs in many forms. Everyone now needs to learn at an increasingly accelerated pace, and the required knowledge grows in complexity. Organizations need to develop educational and learning processes, even to the extent of making learning a formal part of the work requirement for nearly everyone.[19]

In addition to typical training and development programs, more imaginative plans are needed to combat obsolescence. Among these is the procedure, now adopted by a few companies, for executive sabbaticals. Under such plans, managers are assigned for six months or more, at full salary, to planned self-development activities. The manager whose obsolescence problem can be clearly identified may achieve new capabilities from a well-planned sabbatical. However, sabbaticals are more widely used for community service or as a change of pace for nonobsolescent managers.

Shelf-Sitters

Failures in work careers among managers may be caused by lack of skill or ability, a tapering off of aspiration and energy drives, or a lack of well-developed, practical career strategy. For any of these reasons, an individual may become a shelf-sitter—a person who has topped off at his present level of activities. The shelf-sitter has gone as far as he wants to go, or can go, barring an unusual motivating force.

Many shelf-sitters are capable of advancing or improving their performance, but have lost interest. Topping off at a relatively early age, they coast along to retirement unless unexpected events force them to change. They develop unusual attachments to what they are doing in the present, from which they derive security and contentment.

Obsolescent managers usually become shelf-sitters. Their careers are arrested. Technological developments have passed them by; their skills are no longer adequate. Shelf-sitting also occurs because managers, in the opinion of superiors, have reached the top of their capabilities and potentials.

Forcing a shelf-sitter to change runs the risk of generating anxiety, frustration, or hostility. Through proper motivation and direction, how-

[19]Harry Levinson, *The Exceptional Executive* (Cambridge, Mass.: Harvard U. P., 1968), pp. 110–111; Richard L. Shearer and Joseph A. Steger, "Manpower Obsolescence: A New Definition and Empirical Investigation of Personal Variables," *Academy of Management Journal* 18 (June 1975), 263–275; Allan Warrington, "Obsolescence as an Organization Phenomenon," *Journal of Management Studies* 11 (May 1974), 96–114.

ever, many will meet the challenge with unexpected interest and vitality. Therefore managers making decisions that affect the careers of subordinates bear a great deal of responsibility, for they affect their livelihood and welfare. This leads to procrastination in taking action with shelf-sitters and other obsolete managers. On the chance that the organization itself may be at fault in some way, the decision is delayed. Often it is hoped that the situation will work itself out or that the shelf-sitter will take action. This seldom happens. Tolerating the shelf-sitter entails great costs for the organization and for the individual.[20]

Human Relations and Performance

An individual's performance is only in part a function of knowledge, skill, or technical competence. Equally important is the ability to relate to others and to ongoing change situations. Political and social skills have a bearing on how an individual remains effective.[21]

If the manager is to hold a position, advance in an organization, or progress in his career, his abilities, task performance, and personality traits are important. Yet performance is always in an organizational context or climate that defines the rules of the game for the individual. The organization has its needs, demands, limitations, and problems, to which people must relate their experiences and abilities. To be effective and to progress in a career, managers must develop successful strategies by which to relate to the organization and to other individuals. These strategies consist of social and political skills that enhance the individual's relationships with others. In most organizations where change and growth are occurring, a certain competitiveness arises that calls for the selection of strategies that affect the manager's interactions with others.

A manager may follow given strategies for a number of reasons, not all of which are obvious. Managers are often unaware of the strategy implications of their own behavior: or they may be extremely shrewd and calculating in the pursuit of a particular strategy. Illustrations of personal strategies are abundant in organizations. For example, a manager may be power-oriented, and therefore eager to acquire power in all forms. His strategy might be to acquire control of resources such as office space and slush funds, or to enlarge the size of his staff. He wines and dines important people, especially those in a position to advance his interests. He is careful not to step on the wrong toes, and harsh with those who get in his way.

[20]Eugene E. Jennings, *Executive Success* (New York: Appleton, 1967).

[21]Abraham Pizam, "Social Differentiation: A New Psychological Barrier to Performance Appraisal," *Public Personnel Management* **4** (July/August 1975), 244–247; McLean Preston and Katherine Jillison, *The Manager and Self-Respect* (New York: AMACOM, 1975).

The personal strategies of managers are not entirely selfish. Many are good for the organization. If the preferred strategies are in the best interests of the organization they will be better accepted, and colleagues and rivals will be less likely to introduce countervailing strategies. The test of what is good for an organization, however, is uncertain, so that those who seek to endorse private strategies with the cloak of company welfare may meet skepticism from others; they may be deluding themselves into believing the nonexistent unselfish motives they declare. On the other hand, many personal strategies are congruent with the needs of the organization, which after all are numerous and complex.

A manager is both a rational being and an emotional one—a thinker, but an imperfect one. Managers act according to both what they know and how they feel. They have inner drives, needs, ambitions, and fears. They thrive on environments that make them feel secure and wanted; hostile or uncertain environments may either make them fearful and unable to act or evoke their best abilities in meeting challenging or threatening circumstances. Inner drives. aspirations, and motivations keep them going, at least until an outwardly respectable or inwardly satisfying level of accomplishment is attained.

Many of the manager's most important needs are either satisfied or relatively unsatisfied by the working environment. Therefore the manager's strategies are designed to (1) alter the environment so that it provides more net satisfaction; (2) defend against hostile, demanding, or threatening elements; and (3) extract from the environment certain levels of material, social, psychological and spiritual well-being.

TRAINING AND DEVELOPMENT OF MANAGERS

Leaving manager development to chance, to random events, or to the manager alone is simply not done in well-run organizations. However, *all* experience fundamentally involves learning (or unlearning), and the organization's problem is to encourage the sort of learning it finds important. Managers also make choices as to how and what they learn. Their motivation is important, for unless experiences are internalized as part of their personality, habits, and attitudes, the effects of training and development will fade.

Formal training programs therefore concentrate on those learning experiences that lead to the improvement of performance and are amenable to managerial direction. Much of the necessary motivation to learn is supplied by the leadership, example, direction, and control of managers who are willing to assist in their subordinates' plans for development. Motivation also comes from opportunities for greater responsibility and higher status, as well as through the intrinsic motivation of a task's demand for change and innovation, and through peer-group associations.

Training activities and programs are administered by a central training department whose director reports to the personnel or industrial relations manager. Programs and courses cover an enormous variety of subjects and purposes, ranging from specific skill development, such as appraisal feedback methods, to broad programs for higher managers. A major survey found that the nation's 7,500 largest firms spent an estimated $2 billion on employee education and training in 1975. This amount included only direct costs, exclusive of wages and salaries paid to employees while learning. Of the total, $1.6 billion went for company-operated programs, $220 million was spent on tuition-aid programs, and $180 million on courses provided by external sources. Of 32 million employees, 3.7 million took in-house courses during working hours; 700,000 were enrolled in company-run after-hours courses; and 1.3 million participated in tuition-aid programs.[22]

The scope of manager development programs is highly sensitive to budget and costs. Informal development is probably the least costly, but harder to plan, control, and achieve quality. Formal program maintenance can be expensive. For this reason an organization's allocations to development programs tend to fluctuate with economic and financial conditions as well as with the aims and philosphies of top management. When budget cuts come, informal training continues, but formal programs are curtailed, and outside training resources are less utilized. An organization may suffer if it depends too strongly on either a formal or an informal approach. A balanced effort uses the strengths of each, integrated by vigorous, supportive philosophies and policies from top management. In most cases, an organization cannot be self-sustaining in the area of manager development, but neither can it rely entirely on outside resources.[23]

Internal Resources for Manager Development

Formal programs of internal development include courses, seminars, and conferences conducted and administered by members of the training staff. Instructors may be recruited from outside sources, but most organizations prefer inside instructors, who are either borrowed for the purpose or maintained on a full-time basis in the training department.

Training specialists and line managers jointly assess training needs and design programs to meet them. Together with participants, they

[22]The Conference Board, *Education in Industry*, Report No. 719 (New York: The Conference Board, 1977).

[23]Bernard Taylor and Gordon L. Lippitt, *Management Development and Training Handbook* (New York: McGraw-Hill, 1975); William R. Tracey, *Managing Training and Development Systems* (New York: AMACOM, 1974).

carry out follow-up and evaluation procedures. Programs range over many subjects; some are close to immediate tasks and problems, and others are more broadly educational. The particular subjects offered depend on assessments of training needs, and the availability of qualified instructors and other resources. Usually the courses are offered on organization time, although less job-related activities may be scheduled on the individual's own time.

Selection of participants is a major problem in training and development. It is desirable to avoid the "fair-haired boy" complex by systematically choosing participants on the basis of need and ability to benefit, rather than on that of the boss's favoritism. It is also desirable to avoid undue promises of automatic promotion or salary increases. If programs are given on company time, participants are freed from their normal duties, with consequent adjustments needed by boss and colleagues.

In-house programs have the advantage of flexibility. Program units can be tailored as to length, subject, and approach. They can be utilized to bring managers up to date on changing ideas, to improve their skills and understanding, and to add to their knowledge.

Less formal approaches have special difficulties that can be met by devising appropriate aims, policies, rewards, and sufficient structure to lend visibility and importance to them. Two of these types of programs, both emphasizing learning on the job, will be discussed as illustrations: (1) coaching and (2) job rotation.

Coaching

Coaching is defined as *the developmental aim of a manager's ongoing relationship with subordinates.* It is a systematic, planned way of adjusting the working climate to bring out the best in both manager and subordinate. The extent to which people learn managerial skills through on-the-job experience depends heavily on the skills and attitudes of their immediate supervisors.

Fundamentally, coaching is a relationship of give and take between subordinate and superior. One requirement for effective coaching is the willingness of both to participate and to communicate. Because subordinates usually want to prove themselves, they have a strong incentive to cooperate in any relationship that will help them grow in their jobs. They are fortunate to have the opportunity to work with a boss whose knowledge and skills are worth emulating. Although there are persons who feel no need to learn and are therefore unresponsive to the coaching process, most subordinates appreciate the opportunity to enlarge their experience.

Coaching is difficult for many managers, who may be unwilling or unable to delegate authority to others—for coaching and delegating are closely associated. Another difficulty is that to develop a subordinate is to develop one's own replacement, and many managers fear being crowded out. Most important of all, the manager may not have the skills and attitudes essential to good coaching. These drawbacks can be overcome by including in every manager's development the expectation that he will be a good coach, and by making the ability to delegate and to coach part of all appraisals.

The advantages of the coaching relationship are numerous. First, the superior is in a strategic position to help the subordinate. The boss's experience and ability are usually greater than the subordinate's. As they work together day-to-day, the superior can reveal insights that would otherwise not become apparent to the subordinate for many years, if at all. The success of the coaching process depends upon the superior's capability for self-analysis, introspection, self-criticism, and perceptions, on his skills of communication, and the security of his relationships to his job and subordinates. It is somewhat unnatural to expect a person to discuss mistakes with others openly, but in the ideal coaching relationship, the superior would explain not only successes but also failures.

A second advantage of coaching is the improved performance of both the coaching executive and the subordinate. Working closely together, they have the opportunity to check each other and to pool their judgments. Analytical thought habits are developed and sharpened. A third advantage is the practical objective of developing necessary qualified replacements.

Coaching has a weakness that is not widely recognized: such a process may perpetuate outmoded ideas, policies, or work habits. The coach is likely to transmit both personal and organizational weaknesses. Coaching also demands patience and takes time, for it aims to develop the latent, untried, or undiscovered abilities of subordinates through planned work experience.

Three further aspects of the coaching relationship are important. The first is the analysis of the past: together superior and subordinate can see and evaluate what has been done. The second aspect is planning ahead: the superior and subordinate can join together their planning and thinking. Although the superior must take ultimate responsibility for decisions, a well-selected and alert subordinate can share it. The third aspect is the principle of learning by doing: subordinates need to test their abilities by trying them out. Some managers are reluctant to let subordinates make their own mistakes, but many realize that the cost of these mistakes is part of the price of developing talent; it is necessary to let subordinates make a mistake once in a while, to let them test their own judgment. Usually mistakes are not all black and white. There are different degrees of error, which can be discussed with the subordinate together with how the mistakes could have been minimized or prevented. The facts of each situation provide a central focus for objective discussion.

A basic hypothesis of the coaching process is that responsibility is one of the greatest developers of people. To effect in the subordinate the developmental benefits of responsibility, the supervising executive must delegate, giving subordinates just enough responsibility to expand their views and push them beyond what they were sure they could do. By delegation, a manager can stretch the abilities of subordinates without going so far as to destroy their self-confidence, for most people are modest about the things they can do and cautious in setting limits to their work.

Here a fundamental dilemma arises. An important step in coaching is to select wisely the person to whom particular tasks can best be assigned. A balance of judgment is required as to how much weight will be given to getting the job done and how much to developing a particular manager. Strictly speaking, if getting the job done is the most important value, the manager would often do the job himself. But to develop subordinates, the manager may assign tasks to subordinates that are beyond their obvious ability, risking that the tasks may not be done at all or done wrong.

Still another dilemma in coaching is how the manager can maintain a helping relationship throughout the subordinate's learning process, without oversupervision. Too close supervision is one of the frequent complaints of employees. It is important for the coaching manager to be available to give help and advice and to be receptive to questions from the subordinate. On the other hand, the superior should avoid undue interference.[24]

Rotation Plans

Many companies use job rotation plans to assure managers a broad experience in various parts of the organization. Rotation is less widely used in nonbusiness organizations, where opportunities for rotation are fewer.

The advantages and disadvantages of rotation plans are similar to those of coaching. The individual gains a variety of experiences and a broad knowledge of the organization and its work. However, there may be too great a sense of detachment and a lack of close involvement in vital matters. Much depends on the nature of the tasks and responsibilities. It is best if the work assigned is not simply busy work, but genuine, thus permitting involvement of the trainee and providing responsibilities to fulfill. It is a more realistic approach.

[24]Campbell et al., *Managerial Behavior*, pp. 447–451.

The success of rotation plans depends also on the ability of temporary superiors to communicate with and to teach the trainee. The trainer must be committed to the goals of the rotation system, and willing to undertake a teaching role. Through delegation, the superior should seek the best way of stretching the trainee's capabilities so that learning occurs.

A formal rotation plan is not necessary to achieve some of the advantages. A well-planned promotion system in effect does similar things. It cannot be counted on to do the whole job, but it is useful in conjunction with the rest of the training and development program.

External Resources for Executive Development

Most organizations utilize outside resources to supplement and complement their internal programs and activities. Outside resources become necessary when highly specialized subjects or methods are needed, or when special capabilities for instruction or for organizing materials are beyond the scope of organizational resources.

Organizations frequently use university-based development courses, conferences, and faculty services, as well as outside consultants. These resources assure a wider base from which to draw ideas and talent; they enrich and extend organizational programs, and support internal programs such as coaching.

One of the major functions of a university is to transmit the results of research to the channels of action in society. Recognizing this responsibility, universities provide a variety of extension services. A large share of the adult education activities of universities is devoted to management and human relations subjects, and to technical training. In addition to courses and conferences, many university programs undertake tailor-made programs for particular organizations or groups.

University and other outside programs have the advantages of flexibility and of the ability to discover and bring new subject matter to the attention of organization members. They are frequently costly, because the organization must not only pay fees but also release the individual for a period of time, pay participants' salaries while they are not working, and pay living and educational expenses for the duration of the program. However, it is an advantage for the participant to be away from the job, avoiding interruptions and concentrating on the learning experience. Moreover, a university program, unless it is tailor-made for a single organization, puts the participant in association with other managers having similar problems. They gain insight and help from each other, and this interchange is a valuable experience. Moreover, under expert guidance, they gain experience in team projects and group discussions.

Outside consultants may be retained to assist in developing internal programs. The principal value of a consultant is not to do the teaching, but to aid in the development of policies, programs, and plans, and to measure results. Smaller companies not having elaborate personnel or training departments can benefit from consultants, for the cost is less than that of operating a training department. However, some sacrifice of scope in the over-all program may result.

Unfortunately, many of the external agencies providing training programs are deficient in quality. A few are frauds and quacks, fad-followers out to make money from the popularity of training. The company's best protection against wasting its money is to follow all the guidelines for choosing any consultant.

Critique of Training and Development Programs

Practitioners and researchers alike have been dissatisfied with much of what passes for management training and development. All training is costly, and poor training may cost as much as the best. Misguided or ineffectual training is a needless waste of resources. According to one critic, the popular training activities dubbed management develop- ment' have been a disorganized assortment of, at best, educated guesses and, at worst, naive and overenthusiastic devotion to education for managers.

There are few, if any, reliable measures by which to judge the effectiveness of training or to predict the benefits. Yet guideposts for proper administration, design, and planning of management develop- ment programs are available. For example:

1. *Frills such as country-club or resort locations have no direct bearing on the quality of training,* although side benefits of increasing morale, vacation time, and so on, may be derived.
2. *Selection of participants should be carefully made.* There should be a reasonable chance for the managers selected to experience learning, growth, or change, and a reasonable chance for the organization to benefit through better performance from the par- ticipants. One company, for example, sent 25 men to an advanced training group, but two were near retirement, five had had recent coronary attacks, and another three had been on their current job nine or more years. These were selections of doubtful value.
3. *Selection for a given program should not mark the participant as a "comer" in the organization* or carry such high prestige that the individual loses status by remaining on the old job afterward. The business of training managers is not to create prima donnas, but rather to improve the skills, abilities, and understanding neces- sary for more effective management.
4. *The organization should systematically and rigorously evaluate its training and development activities.* Supervisors should

appraise the training results they see in their subordinates; participants should report on the quality of the programs and the
guidance that they have received.

5. *The organization should do only what cannot elsewhere be done
better or cheaper.* It should relate its activities to available community resources; it should determine a balance between internally and externally based programs.

6. *Development programs are not cure-alls for complex problems.*
Serious problems have deep causes that ordinary training cannot
touch. Training may help, but only if it is properly established
and conducted, with problem-solving objectives in mind. Training that categorically promises to solve problems should be considered with skepticism and caution.

The Evaluation of Training and Development

Compared to the amount of training and development activity in the
world of organizations, or compared to the amounts of money spent on
that aspect of management, little effort goes into systematic and reliable
evaluation. For the most part, development activity is sold on faith. Top
managers are expected to be believers, as are the participants.

Valid evaluations are hard to make, and experimental evidence is
even harder to produce. Evaluation is one of the greatest unsolved
problems in organizations. Yet useful tools and tested procedures are
available. Because any training or development activity leads to
change, there can be before-and-after measurements, to see if the
changes occurred. What is needed is a *criterion,* or set of criteria, by
which the changes can be measured. In addition, it is necessary to set
up a rigorous evaluation research design, following known research
principles, to show whether the measured changes resulted from the
development effort and not from an unrelated source.

The over-all design of the evaluation effort is important; simply
measuring a dimension of change is not sufficient. For example, program directors often administer a questionnaire after a course or conference program. Participants are free to give their opinions; most will say
they liked it and expect to benefit from it, and some will give minor
criticisms. It is often a popularity contest for the instructor. Clearly
there is no measure of the program's actual contribution to any changes
noted. A more objective model, and one that permits comparison of
before-and-after situations, is to measure an experimental and a control
group. It is necessary to have the two groups relatively homogeneous,
and either randomly selected or hand-picked. Any changes occurring in
the experimental group but not in the control group can be attributed
with some assurance to the program effort.

Evaluation procedures should be built into the planning when the development activity is originally undertaken. Provision should be made for the evaluation methods desired, preferably including the use of experimental and control groups. Building the evaluation scheme into the plans effort requires the definition of objectives, the specification of variables and training outcomes expected, and the selection of methods of training. A serious evaluation effort, therefore, enhances the need for thorough planning throughout the undertaking.[25]

SUMMARY

Appraisal is a central process in the working relationships of managers at all levels of the organization. Learning how to appraise subordinates systematically and objectively is an important skill of managers. Appraisal is the basis for coaching and other forms of development, as well as for promotion and salary decisions and other personnel actions.

Considerable promise for fair and objective performance appraisal is found in Management by Objectives programs, in which superior and subordinate mutually agree on targets, and following which the results of performance reviews are presented to the subordinate in a planning and analysis (feedback) session. The focus is on results rather than on personal character or personality defects, with the individual himself facing his deficiencies within the framework of their influence on results.

Training and development programs, whether external or internal, should provide rigorous evaluation procedures. The over-all program, and individual parts of it, should be subjected to evaluation against previously planned outcome criteria. Attention to group learning as well as to individual learning is vital.

INCIDENT CASE

Ed Thompson had a low opinion of the rating scale system the company required him to use in appraising the performance of subordinates. Consequently he hurried through the routines, without giving much thought to specific items. He thought of it as busy work, mere paper shuffling. He disliked having to report the results to each individual, so that in the interviews with subordinates he would not allow much discussion or opposition to his ratings. Thompson's boss, Don Rowan, was required to review the results of Thompson's appraisal of the subordinates. One day Rowan

[25]William R. Tracey, *Evaluating Training and Development Systems* (New York: AMACOM, 1975); Donald C. Swedmark, *Developing the Company Training Program: A Guide to Their Organization, Administration, and Evaluation* (Los Angeles: Davline Publications, 1975); Irwin L. Goldstein, *Training: Program Development and Evaluation* (Monterey, Calif.: Brooks/Cole, 1974).

called Thompson in to report *his* appraisal results. He said, "You are a good supervisor in most respects, but I've been getting complaints from subordinates that your ratings of them are extremely unfair." Thompson replied, "It doesn't make that much difference. They are protected by the union, so they don't really care what the ratings are. They know where they stand with me, and no rating form can tell anyone anything anyhow. I just don't let any of them argue over their ratings."

Questions:

1. What should Rowan do or say next?
2. What are the major defects of the system described here?

QUESTIONS FOR STUDY

1. State three policies that you would recommend as desirable in a well-managed program of managerial performance appraisal.

2. What are the main uses for the results of performance appraisal?

3. Examine some performance rating scales, and draw up a report on their advantages and disadvantages, weaknesses and strengths.

4. What is meant by a program of management by objectives? How does this relate to performance appraisal?

5. What is a feedback interview? How is it conducted? What are its major purposes?

6. How would you train supervisors in conducting high-quality feedback interviews?

7. What are the main training elements of an executive's career strategy? Why are they important?

8. What is meant by manager obsolescence? Why does it occur and what should an organization do about it?

9. What would you recommend doing about an individual in an organization who is clearly not performing up to the level of his ability?

10. Explain the philosophy and assumptions that pertain to the coaching process.

11. What are the chief problems that influence the quality of coaching?

12. Can organizations become obsolete? Under what circumstances?

SELECTED REFERENCES

BEHLING, ORLANDO, and CHESTER SCHRIESHEIM. *Organization Behavior: Theory, Research and Application.* Boston: Allyn and Bacon, Inc., 1976. Chapter 4.

BELCHER, DAVID W. *Compensation Administration.* Englewood Cliffs, N.J.: Prentice-Hall, 1974.

CAMPBELL, JOHN P., MARVIN D. DUNNETTE, EDWARD E. LAWLER III, and KARL E. WEICK, JR. *Managerial Behavior, Performance, and Effectiveness.* New York: McGraw-Hill Book Company, 1970.

COOPER, CARY L., ed. *Developing Social Skills in Managers: Advances in Group Training.* New York: John Wiley & Sons, Inc., 1976.

CUMMINGS, L. L., and DONALD P. SCHWAB. *Performance in Organizations: Determinants and Appraisal.* Glenview, Ill.: Scott, Foresman and Company, 1973.

DE MARE, GEORGE, with JOANNE SUMMERFIELD. *Corporate Lives: A Journey into the Corporate World.* New York: Van Nostrand Reinhold Company, 1976.

DRUCKER, PETER F. *The Effective Executive.* New York: Harper & Row, Publishers, 1967.

FARNSWORTH, TERRY. *Developing Executive Talent: A Practical Guide.* New York: McGraw-Hill Book Company, 1975.

FINKLE, ROBERT B., and WILLIAM S. JONES. *Assessing Corporate Talent.* New York: John Wiley & Sons, Inc., 1970.

HAGUE, HAWDON. *Executive Self-Development: Real Learning in Real Situations.* New York: John Wiley & Sons, Inc., 1974.

HANSON, AGNES O. *Executive and Management Development for Business and Government.* Detroit: Gale Research Company, 1976.

INGALLS, JOHN D. *Human Energy: The Critical Factor in Individuals and Organizations.* Reading, Mass.: Addison-Wesley Publishing Company, 1976.

KELLOGG, MARION S. *What to Do About Performance Appraisal.* New York: AMACOM, 1975.

KOONTZ, HAROLD. *Appraising Managers As Managers.* New York: McGraw-Hill Book Company, 1971.

MAIER, NORMAN R. F. *The Appraisal Interview: Objectives, Methods and Skills.* New York: John Wiley & Sons, Inc., 1958.

MCGREGOR, DOUGLAS. *The Professional Manager.* New York: McGraw-Hill Book Company, 1967.

PEARSE, ROBERT F., and B. PURDY PELZER. *Self-Directed Change for the Mid-Career Manager.* New York: AMACOM, 1975.

PORTER, LYMAN W., and EDWARD D. LAWLER, III. *Managerial Attitudes and Performance.* Homewood, Ill.: Richard D. Irwin, Inc., 1968.

ROSS, JOEL E. *Managing Productivity.* Englewood Cliffs, N.J.: Prentice-Hall, Inc., 1977.

ROWLAND, VIRGIL. *Evaluating and Improving Management Performance.* New York: McGraw-Hill Book Company, 1971.

SILBER, MARK B., and V. CLAYTON SHERMAN. *Managerial Performance and Promotability: The Making of an Executive.* New York: AMACOM, 1974.

YODER, DALE, and HERBERT G. HENEMAN. *Training and Development.* ASPA Handbook of Personnel and Industrial Relations, vol. V. Washington, D.C.: BNA Books, Inc., 1977.

Chapter 22

Motivation

A wonderful fact to reflect upon, that every human creature is constituted to be that profound secret and mystery to every other.   —*A Tale of Two Cities*

I was then and ever since filled with the fact that there were so many millions always living and each one is his own self inside him.
—Gertrude Stein

I always invent to obtain money to go on inventing.   *—Thomas Alva Edison*

CHAPTER GUIDE

The McDonald's fast-food chain has created a position in the corporate headquarters entitled "Vice President of Individuality." The purpose of the idea is to "maintain the growth and identity" of the individuals responsible for the company's success. Among the duties of the vice president are to listen to employee complaints, to offer advice, and to assist in career planning. The vice president is directed in his work to consider each employee's personality and abilities.

This firm also has an annual "store day," when top managers, from the board chairman down, work in restaurants cooking hamburgers and cleaning up, to keep in touch with workers. The new vice president is also making a study of the impact of the company on employee families by writing to spouses and children for suggestions.

Questions to keep in mind as you read this chapter:

1. As an employee in a McDonald's restaurant, how would you be likely to react to these ideas?
2. Do such techniques enhance employee motivation?

3. Look up the word *ombudsman*. Is it similar to the title of "Vice President of Individuality"?
4. Appraise the merits and demerits of this idea.

Motivation, like morale, covers many complex kinds of human behavior. People spend a large and important part of their lives in the organizations for which they work. They build their life styles, value systems, and central life interests to a large extent around their work. Those unfortunate enough to be out of a job are thereby deprived not only of money but also of a meaningful relationship to society and to their fellows.

This chapter discusses (1) a definition of motivation and its main characteristics, (2) theories of motivation, and (3) problems and methods of motivation.

THE NATURE OF MOTIVATION

Motivation refers to *the way in which urges, drives, desires, aspirations, strivings, or needs influence the choice of alternatives in the behavior of human beings.* Motives are forms of tension occurring within individuals; their resulting behavior is aimed at reducing, eliminating, or diverting that tension. Understanding the wide variety of needs and drives and their resulting tensions helps to explain and predict human behavior.

Merely knowing a motive or motives, however, is not sufficient for understanding the individual, for the actions that one takes to satisfy motives are also affected by the context or situation. The organization itself, its climate, and the managerial leadership styles that prevail must also be observed to understand the behavior of organization members. Furthermore, motives cannot be seen or precisely described. They must be inferred from overt behavior. Therefore managers must be cautious in their conclusions about what motivates particular individuals; they should not jump to unwarranted or erroneous conclusions.

The concept of motivation itself is mainly psychological. It relates to those forces operating within individuals that impel them to act or not to act in certain ways. Because such things as needs, drives, and wants are multiple and infinite in number, individuals are able, if not required, to assign priorities to the needs they try to satisfy. Questions of where and how as well as when, are also important. Employees with similar patterns of motives may thus behave differently depending on their beliefs, values, and environments, as well as their individual needs.

Motivation and Morale Contrasted

Important distinctions should be made between the terms *morale* and *motivation*. As indicated, these concepts can relate to both individuals and groups. *Morale,* however, describes a state of individual or group attitudes, judgments, and feelings about work, job, company, or supervisor, and so on, whereas *motivation* describes a propensity for particular behavior patterns to reduce or satisfy certain needs inducing tension. According to Stogdill, motivation is a function of drive and confirmed estimates of the desirability of various alternative satisfactions, whereas morale is freedom of restraint in action toward a goal. Thus an individual or a group may be highly motivated, but unable to act. With freedom to act, the degree of morale may be highly related to the strength of motivation. Morale may thus be regarded as motivation demonstrated in overt action toward a goal. Motivation, then, provides potential for morale. Morale is the condition of a group reflecting the member's willingness to cooperate and expressing the degree of integration existing among conflicting interests; motivation is an active force, directing behavior by causing individuals to seek one of several available goals, and to seek certain goals not present at the moment.[1]

From an operational rather than a conceptual point of view, however, the problem of motivating subordinates does have characteristics similar to that of maintaining and developing morale. It involves some of the same patterns of reluctance on the part of supervisors to tamper with personal characteristics or to interfere in the inner lives of subordinates. Changing worker motivation comes close, some believe, to manipulating individual behavior for ends that are not necessarily those of the employee. Motivation is also similar to the concept of morale in that the manager must appraise the degree of motivation of each subordinate. This appraisal cannot be made by surveys; it must come from observing and interpreting the subordinate's or group's behavior. A final similarity is that both morale and motivation require follow-up actions and continuous attention.

The Need Hierarchy

Most behavior is motivated, in that humans try to satisfy physical, emotional, socially conditioned, or psychic needs. Not many people

[1]Ralph M. Stogdill, *Individual Behavior and Group Achievement* (New York: Oxford U. P. 1959), p. 213.

limit their behavior to the satisfaction of physical needs; those with jobs find them relatively well satisfied. It is the psychological and sociocultural needs that pose difficult problems for organizations. Many forces act upon individuals simultaneously, causing them to pursue many kinds of needs.

The motivational process may be described as circular, in that it begins with a tension or drive; the individual is acutely conscious of unfilled needs. Next, there follows a restlessness and a search for the means of fulfilling the need. Finally, the need is to some extent fulfilled, or goals are redefined, and need satisfaction is attained. The process is completed when the individual evaluates the extent of satisfaction obtained and makes decisions about the behavior that is to follow. This process is diagrammed in Figure 22-1.

Need theory, as summarized here, underlies nearly all widely followed theories and practical approaches to motivation in work organizations. Because needs are infinite in number, some general classifications are required.

Needs are most frequently described in terms of a hierarchy or a continuum. One way is to classify them as primary or secondary. Primary needs are the basic physiological ones required for maintenance of the body and the individual's security. They are primary

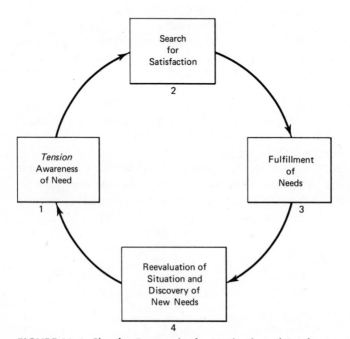

FIGURE 22-1. Circular Process in the Motivation of Employees.

because we attend to them first; other needs are satisfied after the basic ones are met. Secondary needs are psychological and sociological in nature and are strongly conditioned by culture, society, and our personality and temperament.

The most widely used need classification is that set forth by A. H. Maslow, as follows:

1. Basic physiological needs.
2. Safety from external danger.
3. Love, affection, and social activity.
4. Esteem and self-respect.
5. Self-realization and accomplishment.[2]

The value of Maslow's hierarchy lies in its greater differentiation of the sociopsychological needs. The five categories represent priority levels; individuals tend to satisfy the first before satisfying the second, and so on. Few individuals reach advanced stages of self-realization, which expresses the fullest accomplishment and achievement of the individual. Those who come close to attaining their ideal self-image have achieved self-realization or fulfillment.

That individuals tend to satisfy their needs in the order of priority described by Maslow's hierarchy is only an approximation because the categories are not absolute. Needs in the first two categories are basic and universal. Thus they are primary needs. Needs in the remaining three categories are highly situational and greatly influenced by society, culture, and the individual's own characteristics. The need for self-realization and accomplishment is the most difficult to satisfy. Few people actually attain adequate satisfaction of this need, but it provides a strong motivational force as individuals try to do so. Also, conditions may lead to a reversal of direction in the need hierarchy. Self-realization, if attained, may be lost.

Maslow's need hierarchy has been criticized for its lack of a rigorous research base. Maslow formulated his views from many sources, largely informal interviews and observations over many years, and many of his subjects were neurotic individuals. Nevertheless, the fact that so many theorists use his model as the foundation of their approaches is significant. It is important to remember that each need category is a general classification and not a name for specific behavior patterns.[3]

---

[2]A. H. Maslow, "A Theory of Human Motivation," *Psychological Review* **50** (July 1943), 370–396; *Motivation and Personality* (New York: Harper, 1954).

[3]For further information on need psychology see Clayton P. Alderfer, *Existence Relatedness and Growth: Human Needs in Organizational Settings* (New York: Free Press, 1972); David D. Van Fleet, "The Need Hierarchy and Theories of Authority," *Human Relations* **26** (September 1973), pp. 567–580; Benjamin Schneider and Clayton P. Alderfer, "Three Studies of Measures of Need Satisfaction in Organizations," *Administrative Science Quarterly* **18** (December 1973), 489–505; John W. Newstrom, "Self-Actualization: An Emerging Employee Need," *Personnel Administrator* **20** (April 1975), 31–32.

_____ **MOTIVATIONAL THEORIES**

Theories of motivation are important because they are the result of intensive research in organizations to find the best ways of motivating people. They are also widely translated into action programs by consultants and others who help organizations improve their effectiveness. Purely psychological treatments of motivation will not be analyzed here; we shall examine only the most notable organizational approaches, which include (1) participation theories, (2) interaction theories, (3) constraint theory, and (4) hygiene theory. There are substantial similarities and differences in these theories; they are not mutually exclusive approaches.

Participation Theories

In the previous chapter and at many points in this book, the concept of participative management has been discussed. Here it is necessary to note only that participation demands changes in typical assumptions about the nature of people and their probable responses to a participatory climate.

One of the best examples of the participatory approach to motivation is that of Douglas McGregor, the advocate of Theory Y. Theory Y posits the following assumptions which, if accepted, pave the way for better motivation through the involvement of people in work planning and decisions:

1. The expenditure of physical and mental effort in work is as natural as play and rest.
2. External control and the threat of punishment are not the only means for bringing about the effort toward organizational objectives. Man will exercise self-direction and self-control in the service of objectives to which he is committed.
3. Commitment ot objectives is a function of the rewards associated with their achievement.
4. The average human being learns, under proper conditions, not only to accept responsibility but to seek it.
5. The capacity to exercise a relatively high degree of imagination, ingenuity, and creativity in the solution of organizational problems, is widely, not narrowly, distributed in the population.
6. Under the conditions of modern industrial life, the intellectual potentialities of the average human being are only partially utilized.[4]

[4]Douglas McGregor, *The Human Side of Enterprise* (New York: McGraw-Hill, 1960), pp. 47–48.

Likert's work, cited in earlier chapters, also leads to participatory management through the concepts of System 4 management. The research Likert cites is of enormous value in its revelations about the nature of motivational forces. He states, in fact, that findings in study after study show that "those supervisors and managers whose pattern of leadership yields consistently favorable attitudes more often think of employees as 'human beings rather than just persons to get the work done.' Consistently, the data show that treating people as 'human beings' rather than 'cogs in a machine' is a variable related to the *attitudes and motivation* of the subordinate at every level in the organization."[5]

Interaction Theories

The interactionists consider an organization as a social system, existing in a more or less stable state in an environment. Inside the system are three classes of variables—activities, interaction, and sentiments. Activities can be observed and described; interaction (contacts or communications among individuals) can be measured and their purposes or results noted; the sentiments, feelings, attitudes, norms, and values of individuals are hard to specify and describe, but are part of the reality of the social system. The system, then, consists of activities, interaction, and sentiments and their mutual interrelationships. The concept of sentiments includes matters of motivation. Homans states that sentiments are "part of what is called individual self-interest" and that if we examine these motives, we shall find that for the most part they are "neither individual nor selfish but that they are the product of group life and serve the ends of the whole group, not just an individual."[6] Whyte relates interaction, activities, and sentiments to the motivation of individuals and group, if the participation and cooperation of employees are desired.[7]

Motivational Constraints

In their challenge to traditional (classical) management theory, March and Simon elaborate a theory of motivational constraints that affect (1) organizational decisions, and (2) the motivation for an individual to

[5]Rensis Likert, *New Patterns of Management* (New York: McGraw Hill, 1961); *The Human Organization: Its Management and Value* (New York: McGraw-Hill, 1967).

[6]George C. Homans, *The Human Group* (New York: Harcourt, 1950), p. 95.

[7]William Foote Whyte, *Money and Motivation* (New York: Harper, 1955), pp. 17–20. For further information on interaction approaches see Robert S. Sedwick, *Interaction: Interpersonal Relationships in Organizations* (Englewood Cliffs, N.J.: Prentice-Hall, 1974), and Dorothy Jongeward, *Everybody Wins: Transactional Analysis Applied to Organizations* (Reading, Mass.: Addison-Wesley, 1974).

remain in an organization. They hold that the "machine model" ignores the wide range of roles that individuals perform simultaneously without considering conflict and coordination among the roles. Supervision based on the machine model will therefore motivate behavior that the organization dislikes, even though the bureaucratic theorists have "devoted considerable attention to the problems of managing organisms whose motivations and learning behavior are much more complicated than those of the machine model."[8]

According to March and Simon, equilibrium reflects the organization's success in arranging payments to its members adequate to motivate their continued participation. Decisions by employees to remain in an organization differ from their decisions to produce. Because each employee can withdraw or remain, or can decide to enter some other organization, managers should think about the problems of motivating subordinates to remain. Measures or estimates of company inducements and employee contributions are required, and an inducement-contribution balance exists for each participant in the organization. This balance is a function of (1) the perceived desirability of leaving the organization, and (2) the perceived ease of movement from the organization, or the utility of alternatives a person foregoes in order to remain. The desire to leave is a function of the individuals's job satisfaction and his perception of alternatives within the organization. The perceived ease of leaving an organization is a function of the number of extraorganizational alternatives the employee has. The employee whose relationship or role in the organization is subject to change is free to negotiate, bargain, or argue over the nature of his participation; otherwise he must either accept or reject that role as is.[9]

The theory of motivation to remain in the organization reinforces the importance of meeting at least minimal job satisfactions for people and leads to a concern for their attitudes toward the organization, their job, their work, and their colleagues. Among the costs of operating an organization is that of maintaining high inducements to participate for those who are able to produce adequately. Frequently, organizations fail to adjust their inducement costs to match these utilities. The philosophy that "no person is indispensable" will sometimes force a good employee to withdraw because he has been underrewarded. Conversely, organizations may assign individuals inducement values that exceed their contributions. It is not simple to get a close fit between inducements and contributions, but organizations can use systematic job structure, wage and salary plans, and formal appraisal systems to narrow or eliminate the gap.

[8]James G. March and Herbert A. Simon, *Organizations* (New York: Wiley, 1958), pp. 33–34, 82–83.
[9]Ibid., pp. 83–111.

Achievement Theories

Achievement approaches to motivation focuses on human needs, particularly the need to achieve in competitive situations. Murray, for example, postulates that the strength of basic needs forms the core of an individual's personality.[10] Murray also developed the Thematic Apperception Test (TAT), which is widely used to measure basic needs, such as the need to achieve success, recognition, or security. McClelland and his associates developed a way of scoring the TAT to measure the need for achievement.[11] This is a generalized need to achieve success in any situation that involves comparison to a standard of excellence. It is not the common conception of achievement motivation defined in terms of drive, willingness to work, or ambition, but rather the need to achieve in a competitive situation, whether the competition be in relation to other persons or to some standard of excellence.

McClelland has shown that individuals who were given a thorough understanding of the concepts related to achievement motivation, and provided with insight into the meaning of their own scores on a fantasy measure of need for achievement, subsequently performed more effectively in competitive achievement situations.[12] Atkinson has shown that as expectation of failure increases in a competitive achievement situation, high-anxiety subjects show a decrement in performance, whereas low-anxiety subjects show an increment. Research on the development of measures of achievement motivation has also demonstrated that a positive, achievement-oriented frame of mind can be aroused in persons.[13]

Expectancy Theories

One of the most significant approaches to understanding motivation in organizations is based on the study of the way people behave in accordance with what they expect. Expectancy theory is reflected in the work of Mead, Elton, Roethlisberger and Dickson, and Barnard, as well as in the learning theory of Tolman, Hull, Skinner, Hilgard, and others.

Stogdill postulates three input variables as behavior patterns of group members: interactions, performances, and expectations. These inputs become translated into group structure and operations, ultimately producing the complex and interrelated achievements of the

---

[10]H. A. Murray, *Explorations in Personality* (New York: Oxford U. P., 1938).

[11]D. C. McClelland, J. W. Atkinson, R. A. Clark, and E. L. Lowell, *The Achievement Motive* (New York: Appleton, 1953).

[12]D. C. McClelland, *The Achieving Society* (New York: Van Nostrand, Reinhold, 1961).

[13]J. W. Atkinson, *Motives in Fantasy, Action and Society* (New York: Van Nostrand Reinhold, 1958).

group. The concept of expectation is the most unusual aspect of Stogdill's theory.[14] Expectation theory is related to motivation in that drive (level of tension) is assumed to operate in expectation. Expectation is defined as readiness for reinforcement and is a function of drive, the estimated probability of occurrence of an outcome, and the estimated desirability of the outcome. Estimates of probability and estimates of desirability interact to determine the level of expectation.[15]

Stogdill's theory relates primarily to group achievement. It is important in a theory of group achievement to account for individual drive and group motive power, but drive is hard to define. Drive can be inferred from persistent or vigorous activity or from the tension of heightened sensitivity directed toward certain goals. Drive can be partly a function of physiological conditions in the body—glands, state of nourishment, and so on. It may also be generated by fear, sense of danger, or by the presence of a highly valued object or stimulus. Motivation may be regarded as a function or drive of confirmed desirability estimates. Expectation and motivation are thus overlapping concepts, for drive and desirability estimates contribute to both motivations and expectations.[16]

The expectancy approach that has been most widely applied is that of Vroom. Vroom's conceptual model asserts that the probability of a person's performing an act is a direct function of the algebraic sum of the products of the valence of outcomes and expectancies that will occur given the performance of the act. This theory has the merit of viewing behavior as subjectively rational. It embraces the relationship of motivation to both the job satisfaction of the individual and the effectiveness of work performance.

Whereas Maslow's need theory holds motivation to be a function of habit and the drive for need fulfillment, Vroom's model takes motivation to be a function of the individual's expectation that an outcome can be attained multiplied by that person's utility for that particular outcome. The model assumes a mathematical expression which in its simplest form is F (E x V), where E is the individual's subjective probability or estimate of the expectation being attained, and V is the valence, or utility of the outcomes to the individual. It is, in effect, a decision model explaining the individual's perception of his environment and the probability of working successfully within it.

Vroom and other expectancy theorists seek to understand why behavioral forces lead a person in one direction but not in others.

[14]Stogdill, *Individual Behavior*, chaps. 2, 5. Note the similarity of the three input variables to the Homans-Whyte concepts of activity, interaction, and sentiments. Stogdill's concept of expectations appears to be more inclusive than and quite different from the Homans-Whyte concept of sentiments.

[15]Ibid., pp. 62–63. This concept exhibits numerous similarities to the March-Simon motivational constraint theory of organization.

[16]Ibid., pp. 59–68.

Individuals evaluate alternative actions by negative or positive valences of outcomes. If they are indifferent, the valence is zero. An action produces two types of outcomes, primary and secondary. The primary outcome is of value for its consequences, and the secondary outcome for its own sake.[17] Thus a person may expect his behavior to result in more productivity (primary level), which is also expected to lead to higher pay or better recognition (secondary level). The extent to which a primary outcome is seen as leading to a secondary outcome is dependent on the individual's perception of the situation. The individual's expectation that reward will follow the attainment of the desired primary outcome is the key factor.

Expectancy theory is still being tested and must await further validation. It is especially useful in explaining wage incentive systems, and has been the focus of research on a variety of performance-reward relationships.[18]

Hygiene Theory

Hygiene theory is essentially based on the work of Herzberg and his colleagues. Its focus is on job attitudes as the basis of motivation to work. Hygiene theory differs from expectancy and other theories in that the former is a two-factor theory, whereas other theories treat motivation as a single factor scalable on one continuum. The two sets of factors in Herzberg's concept are (1) intrinsic, related to the meaning of the work itself; and (2) extrinsic, involving elements of the work setting or context.

Extrinsic factors are hygienic—that is, they are more significant as sources of dissatisfaction when perceived as poor than sources of positive motivation when perceived as good. The route to positive motivation is through the intrinsic factors. Herzberg found that when people said they were satisfied with their jobs, they most frequently described factors related to their tasks, and to events that indicated successful performance of work and professional or occupational growth. By contrast, their dissatisfactions were related not to the work but to conditions that surrounded the work. These context (extrinsic) factors are quality of supervision, physical working conditions, interpersonal relations, salary, company policies and administrative practices, employee

[17]Victor H. Vroom, *Work and Motivation* (New York: Wiley, 1964); Victor H. Vroom and Edward L. Deci (eds.), *Management and Motivation* (New York: Penguin, 1974).

[18]Bernard Weiner, *Theories of Motivation: From Mechanism to Cognition* (Chicago: Markham Press, 1972); Edward E. Lawler III, *Motivation in Work Organizations* (Monterey, California: Brooks/Cole Publishing Company, 1973); Edward E. Lawler III, "Expectancy Theory and Job Behavior," *Organizational Behavior and Human Performance* **13** (June 1973), 482–503; Orlando Behling, Chester Schriesheim, and James Tolliver, "Alternatives to Expectancy Theories of Work Motivation," *Decision Sciences* **6** (July 1975), 449–461.

benefits, and job security. Herzberg calls them hygienic factors or dissatisfiers. He believes that the hygienic factors are more potent as dissatisfiers than as motivators. Hygienic factors may create job dissatisfaction when they deteriorate to an unacceptable level, but they are not the key factors in positive motivation.[19]

Vroom and others have criticized the Herzberg theory. Vroom disagrees with the two-factor nature of Herzberg's formulation, and attacks the research methods on which it is based.[20] Nevertheless, a number of replication studies have been made, extending the work to a number of occupations beyond those studied by Herzberg; and companies have widely applied the theory in management development and in organizational planning.[21]

------------------ **PROBLEMS AND METHODS OF MOTIVATION**

The theories of motivation described in the foregoing section vary in their applicability to practical situations. They show similarities in that they relate back to need concepts and to current understanding of personality theory. All involve the necessity of training managers in such understanding so that they may more adequately govern the situations of which motivation is a part. Applications require adopting the theoretical ideas to particular organizations, often with the help of a consultant. Of all the theories described, Herzberg's has had the widest application because it provides highly visible and specific procedures that can be embodied in training programs and total organization approaches to leadership and managerial styles, such as those of organization development.

Motivation remains a continuous problem to leaders and managers because for most people it is not fully achieved. The general level of motivation in most organizations is such as to obtain less than half the reasonable potentials of organization members for productive effort. There is always a goal farther out to be approached but never reached.

Managers should expect only a limited degree of success in motivating most workers highly. Skilled workers can be more readily motivated than unskilled ones because for them the intrinsic factors are greater. The chances of motivating managers to their peak performance

[19]Frederick Herzberg, Bernard Mausner, and Barbara Block Snyderman, *The Motivation to Work* (New York: Wiley, 1959); Frederick Herzberg, *Work and the Nature of Man* (New York: World, 1966).

[20]Vroom, *Work and Motivation*, pp. 126–129.

[21]Frederick Herzberg, "New Perspectives on the Will to Work," *Personnel Administrator* 19 (July/August 1974), 21–25; Robert J. House and Lawrence A. Wigdor, "Herzberg's Dual-Factor Theory of Job Satisfaction and Motivation: A Review of the Evidence and Criticism," *Personnel Psychology* 20 (Winter 1967), 369–389; William D. Reif, "Intrinsic versus Extrinsic Rewards: Resolving the Controversy," *Human Resource Management* 14 (Summer 1975), 2–10; G. R. Salancik, "Intrinsic Motivation," *Organizational Behavior and Human Performance* 13 (June 1975), 339–351.

are similarly greater than for rank-and-file workers, because the former have different definitions and goals for occupational success and tend to have higher levels of aspiration. Even among managers, however, the number who work hard to progress in their jobs and occupations is relatively small. Most persons tend to balance their efforts on an assessment of relative costs (time and energy) and benefits.

All employees face many demands upon their time, loyalties, and energies. The organization is not the only agency making these demands; the employee faces multiple interests—ideals, family, friends, community, and religious groups and other organizations all have expectations. Employees, for the most part, are capable of resolving the difficulties imposed on them by these multiple forces. However, it is possible that managers may, by excessive pressure, throw the employee's priorities out of balance. It is possible to demand too much. In one company, for example, the president caused an executive vice president to put the company's interest ahead of his personal interests. He worked seven days a week, never took a vacation, and was constantly driven by the president. He aged prematurely, developed neurotic symptoms and a cardiac condition, unduly neglected his family, and became an alcoholic. He endured this strain for nearly 15 years before he collapsed.

Some excessively work-motivated persons are driven by inner compulsions and a high need for achievement to sacrifice everything for the sake of their work. They are called "workaholics". They need help in restoring their sense of priorities.

The problem of motivating others can be seen in its full complexity by reflecting on the fact that motivation is an inner drive. The manager wishing to motivate others cannot decree that they will be motivated. Individuals must willingly motivate themselves. The manage can only try to arrange favorable conditions under which inner motivations will turn in a positive direction.

To motivate others, the managers themselves must be well motivated, so that the desire for accomplishment is pervasive. The skills of leadership and human relations provide useful ways of motivating others. By setting an example, managers demonstrate the value of motivation. A manager who understands his subordinates, their needs, and their sources of job satisfaction can provide the conditions of effective motivation.

Reward and Punishment Systems

Every organization selects policies and procedures for motivating and controlling the behavior of its members. In addition to applying the insights of motivational theory, organization behavior, and human relations, several other tools, techniques, and procedures are available to managers. Favorable behavior can be rewarded with higher pay, informal rewards, fringe benefits, and the like. Undesirable behavior can be restrained by various forms of punishment, such as reduced pay, reprimands, layoffs, discharge, and other disciplinary actions. Striving to attain rewards and to avoid punishment may take many forms, ranging from honest toil to devious manipulations of people and circumstances.

There can be no certainty that systems of reward and punishment are managed fairly. Most organizations try to achieve fairness in reward and punishment decisions, but even so, the fact that managerial work is not easily measured makes fairness an elusive goal. There are always elements of judgment and opinion, and facts present in the environment are subject to various interpretations. An intangible quality characterizes even concrete situations. The factors of evaluation and analysis that underlie the reward and punishment process are exceedingly complex.

To better understand the operation of reward and punishment systems in the motivation process we will now consider: (1) informal rewards and punishment, (2) the hierarchy and its reward potentials, (3) discipline, and (4) monetary rewards.

Informal Rewards

Some sources of reward and punishment are not within the direct control or influence of managers at all, partly because the definition of a reward or a punishment lies within the mind of the person being rewarded or punished. The informal organization, for example, may confer high status upon the rebellious employee. Workers' norms controlling production usually set too low a work standard. Rewards and punishments may also be provided by subsidiary groups and organizations external to the company itself. Thus trade associations, professional societies, and other associations may give or withhold recognition and reward, providing a forum within which persons in an organization may derive status and recognition beyond that possible from within.

A by-product of the formally specified systems of reward in complex bureaucracies is the evolution of unofficial rewards. These are not merely informal; they are outside the intended application of organizational resources. Even though organizations attempt to maintain the ability to recognize and reward outstanding performances beyond the call of duty, there are limits to the flexibility that can be built into job classifications, wage and salary ranges, and promotion plans. This forces unofficial use of company materials and services as supplementary rewards for those who go beyond the limits of the formal requirements. Taking these rewards is often theft, because the formal system forbids it. The implications of theft may be covered by ambiguous obeisance to fair play, wage plans, performance evaluation, and so on, but there is a gray area between theft and legitimate rewards. Esteemed personalities and power figures who perform unusual services can move closer to theft than others without censure. In addition to using company resources for maintaining social as well as productive factors in their situation, managers also manipulate situations to give employment to friends and relatives, to establish plush offices deriving from their rivalries and power struggles, and to build "slush funds" to help them play the game.

What is a reward for one is not a reward for another; what managers want at one time they do not want at another; the same inducements cannot be given to all on the same level because of differences in ability and expectations; offices and titles, such as "assistant to," are used as reward devices; and financial rewards are not usually enough.

Although informal rewards ideally are devised for genuinely unusual efforts, they are often granted for other reasons, some of which are taboo. For example, they may be given in lieu of a promotion or salary increase that could not be granted; as a bonus for doing unpleasant or low-prestige things; as an opiate to offset political, policy, or status defects; as a conciliation to irate colleagues or subordinates; as a way of getting around formal wage maximums; or as a reward for collusion in the operation of the unofficial reward system. These examples help us to understand that organizations exhibit enormous complexity in reward and punishment systems and that the formal mechanisms are supported by a vast array of satisfying and motivating inducements to produce and to participate. These elements should be calculated into the costs of obtaining a work force of well-motivated, highly satisfied employees.

The Hierarchy and Rewards

The bureaucratic model of organization builds reward and punishment systems into the hierarchical structure. Udy has reported a cross-cultural study of the evolution of organizational complexity. Studying 25 production organizations in 19 nonindustrial societies, he found a consistent pattern of relations among four characteristics: (1) dependence upon superiors for rewards—the allocation by higher authority of rewards to the lower levels; (2) specialization; (3) rewards for performance—the amount of the reward proportional to the work of effort contributed; and (4) contractual agreements permitting participation in the organization. All bureaucratic organizations that had three of the above characteristics had the first three; all with two had the first two; and if any had only one, it was the first.[22] Blau and Scott hypothesize

[22]Stanley H. Udy, Jr., "Bureaucratic Elements in Organizations," *American Sociological Review* **23** (February 1958), 415–418.

from this that unless there is a system of allocating rewards that ensures that the lower levels will be dependent on the higher ones, specialization is not likely to develop and that specialization in turn seems to be required before tendencies emerge in organizations to make rewards proportional to contributions. Also, contractual relations defining the conditions of participation (in the March and Simon sense) typically replace traditional reasons for participation when organizational complexity has developed.[23]

The structural hierarchy of an organization may be regarded as a system of prestige grading: the higher the position, the higher the status or prestige conferred upon the position holder. Motivation to climb upward in the hierarchy is elicited by the greater prestige and status obtained there, as well as by higher pay or greater spoils from the unofficial appropriation or use of resources.

Discipline

Industrial discipline today is a highly complex subject about which very little is really known. In unionized companies, disciplinary action by managers is subject to protest through the grievance procedures. A great many disputes that go to arbitration concern disciplinary cases.

Discipline, in its true sense, refers to conditions of orderliness in which the members of the organization conduct themselves with respect for the needs of the organization, subordinating to some extent their own needs and desires. Discipline must exist to a high degree in every organization. It is not the same as morale. Morale consists of attitudes that employees display toward the situation calling for discipline. If morale is high, however, discipline tends to prevail. Discipline could, however, exist to a large degree with low morale. In such a situation, the discipline would perhaps be controlled by force or fear.

All organizations impose restrictions on the behavior of individual members. We always find "rules of conduct" that prescribe orderly and safe behavior to protect the welfare and safety of group members and make it possible for the organization to do its work. We saw in earlier chapters that the existence of rules is one of the key characteristics of the bureaucratic model of organization. Rules, in effect, set up predetermined answers to questions that arise repeatedly as to what one should or should not do in given situations.

In every organization, no matter what its policies and no matter how good its techniques, there are individuals who do not subscribe to the rules and who become obstinate and oblivious to their responsibilities to the organization and its members. At this point, managers take

---

[23]Peter M. Blau and W. Richard Scott, *Formal Organizations* (San Francisco: Chandler, 1962), pp. 205–206.

disciplinary action—that is, action of a punitive nature to curb the undisciplined behavior. Among the usual punishments are fines, lay-offs, reprimands, and discharge. Penalties differ in their severity and in their significance to employees.

Disciplinary action needs to be undertaken with a wisdom and with sensitivity to the importance of just and fair treatment of employees. In many organizations, disciplinary action is taken in an effort to combat unionism. It often becomes a tool in a struggle between management and labor. Such a use of disciplinary action often breeds retaliatory measures among employees.

The constructive use of disciplinary action takes real talent, far more than its destructive use. Rules should be simple, clear, and sensible. They should be explained to all employees and fairly enforced. Rules carry an implied threat of punishment. If the threat is effective, punishment is avoided. It is often tempting for managers to rely on threat and the use of punishment. Instead, they should stress more positive approaches, with punishment as a last-resort method.

For disciplinary actions to have a motivating influence, they must be in line with the seriousness of the problem produced by the infractions dealt with. There must be an intent to handle situations fairly, and members of the group must be able to see and understand the rationale of what has been done. Even so, the presence of sanctions, pressures, or disciplinary actions is only one aspect of the problem of achieving conformity to group or organizational expectations.

Monetary Rewards

Paying the members of an organization is a highly complex process with an extensive technical apparatus. In addition to economic problems such as costs and labor market rates, pay entails a host of human relations and psychological problems. The organization must maintain an over-all pay and reward structure that is equitable to employees and to the organization as a whole. It must also incorporate pay into its superior-subordinate relations, and often into its relationships with labor unions, the government, and the public.

Pay is often misconstrued to be the primary motivating force, particularly for rank-and-file workers. The assumption that money is the sole or even primary motivator was shown to be in error by researchers of the human relations movement.[24] Herzberg saw this in placing pay among the hygiene factors rather than the motivating factors. In surveys, workers seldom place pay higher than fourth or fifth in the list of things that are important to their morale.

[24]Whyte, *Money and Motivation*; G. R. Salancik, "Interaction Effects of Performance and Money of Self-Perception of Intrinsic Motivation," *Organizational Behavior and Human Performance*, vol. 13, no. 3 (June 1975), 339–351.

558 *Organizational Development and Managerial Behavior*

Nevertheless, pay and how it is administered are important elements of the management system. Decisions about pay levels and individual pay are vital to the organization's welfare. Hence it is necessary to establish systematic procedures and concepts to maintain the monetary reward system in an equitable manner.

Efforts to use monetary inducements to generate more output by employees have not demonstrably produced the desired results. Bonus plans, profit-sharing, stock ownership, and other fringe benefits have been fairly successful for managers; profit-sharing and stock ownership have been helpful for rank-and-file employee motivation as well. Incentive systems based on piece rates or production formulas, generally applicable only to repetitive production work, are no longer as widely used as they once were.[25]

A wage incentive is a form of monetary payment that is calculated to induce a worker to produce work of the required quality beyond the amount reasonably expected of an average worker. An incentive system is a systematic and standardized way of calculating incentive payments for an individual or a group. Piece rates—payment of a stated amount per unit produced—are the most common form of incentive payments.

Numerous incentive systems have been devised by industrial engineers. Each has its own mathematical formula that results in a certain incentive value. The simplest system to understand is the concept of straight piecework, which means that the worker receives a stated amount per piece, no matter what quantity he produces. His reward is directly proportional to his putput. Other systems increase the incentive value by making the increase more than proportional to the additional units of production; still other systems make the increases at a less than proportional rate.

Monetary incentives of this type have certain drawbacks. Among them are the illusion of accuracy and infallibility; a complexity that baffles the worker and leads to numerous grievances and disputes; unions' dislike of them; and the difficulty of setting standards for the measurement of performance. Some incentive formulas have been regarded as so strong as to result in harm or injury to employee health.[26]

Profit-sharing and stock ownership are designed to give employees at all levels a stake in the total results of the organization's effort. They have only a general connection with group and individual effort, and are not directly motivating as are wage incentives.

Bonus plans have been successful in many companies. One of the most widely used in manufacturing firms is the Scanlon plan, devised in the 1930s by a steelworker named Joe Scanlon. It embodies a companywide effort to increase productivity, and to share the benefits

[25]H. G. Hunt and L. N. Turner, "The Abandonment of Wage Incentive Schemes," *Personnel Management* 49 (March 1967), 40–48.
[26]P. Shwinger, *Wage Incentive Systems* (New York: Wiley, 1975).

of the increases with all employees. A formula for this sharing is negotiated by management and the union. The plan embodies the participation of employees in goal setting, and makes heavy use of formal suggestion-box systems. All employees are strongly motivated to increase the company's productivity. The pressure on managers is often heavy, for their subordinates work hard at finding improvements that managers are ordinarily expected to find. At one Midland-Ross plant, the "normal" payroll was defined as 27 per cent of production costs. In one month the actual payroll was only 22 per cent of production, so the remaining five per cent was transferred to the bonus pool. The company receives 25 per cent of the monthly bonus pool; 25 per cent goes into a reserve fund to smooth fluctuation; and the balance is distributed as a bonus to all managers and rank-and-file workers. The bonus for hourly employees averaged about $1,500 in 1976 at Midland-Ross.[27]

Managerial compensation has its special problems. There has been a trend in recent years to emphasize pay for performance, both at middle and top management levels. Younger managers want their rewards immediately rather than after climbing to the top. For this they expect to perform outstandingly. Another trend is an increase in the number of perquisites—extra forms of compensation such as stock options or a company car. Still another trend is for managers to avoid situations where bonus pay and other rewards are held for the future and are lost upon resignation. More and more, it is necessary for an organization to negotiate a rather complex "compensation package" tailor-made to the requirements of each individual manager.[28]

Work Restructuring and Job Design

A major approach to more effective motivation has appeared in various forms of attention to job design and work restructuring. Herzberg's motivation concepts greatly spurred this movement by emphasizing the importance of the intrinsic motivations of work itself. He called it *job enrichment,* but much of the management literature now calls it *job enlargement.*

The basic idea of job enrichment is to restore to jobs the elements of interest that were taken away under intensive specialization. The emphasis is on the jobs of hourly workers rather than those of managers. For example, under the principle of specialization a machine operator simply runs the machine. Repairs are made by a specialist, and so are the different production set-ups. Tools and supplies are managed by

[27]*Wall Street Journal,* December 9, 1976, p. 1.
[28]See "Managers Want an Earlier Payoff," *Business Week,* May 4, 1974, pp. 10–12; "New Rewards in Executive Pay," *Business Week,* September 29, 1973, pp. 97–102; Alfred Marrow, *The Failure of Success* (New York: AMACOM, 1972); Herbert H. Meyer, "The Pay for Performance Dilemma," *Organizational Dynamics,* Winter 1975, 39–50.

others. Under job enrichment, the operator is given full responsibility for all aspects of the work, including machine set-ups, repairs, and procuring and caring for tools and supplies, thereby increasing the judgment and skills required. This is called horizontal job loading because it incorporates processes that are essentially at the same level.

In some plans for job enlargement, a vertical loading occurs—building up a job by adding factors from higher or lower levels. For example, a machinist may be given the responsibility of supervising a trainee or an assistant. Workers may be involved in departmental decisions, or run the department while the supervisor is on vacation. Vertical loading consists mainly of participative approaches to work systems. Both vertical and horizontal loading may be used together.

Several firms have designed integrated assembly units to replace standard assembly lines. This is a form of job enrichment. Among the more successful efforts are those of Volvo, Inc., in Sweden, the Olivetti Company in Italy, and American Telephone and Telegraph Company in the U.S.[29]

Volvo uses a system of computer-controlled trolleys that move about the plant carrying automobiles. This system replaces the standard assembly line, providing a flexible production system using the team approach. Observers have noted considerable unused space in the plant, which produces only thirty thousand cars per year (in contrast to the typical U.S. plant making two-hundred thousand per year). The plant cost 10 per cent more to build than other assembly plants, but the company claims that cost rose by only $7.74 per car. They have found fewer flaws per car to be corrected, and fewer supervisors are required. Because team members can change jobs among themselves, or change to different teams, or vary the pace of their work, the workers enjoy considerable flexibility and discretion. However, there remain the pressure of methods and time measurement, and the discipline of the expected pace of output comparable to the speed of the assembly line. Many worker comforts and benefits are incorporated into the construction and management of the plant. Dramatic changes in turnover and absenteeism were not experienced, although morale has appeared to be high. The company expects more of the potential and advantages of appear over time.[30]

Job enrichment squares not only with concepts of intrinsic motivation but also with theories of participation, involvement, and commitment. Nevertheless it has been widely criticized. It is not readily

[29]See Charles H. Gibson, "Volvo Increases Productivity Through Job Enrichment," *California Management Review* **15** (Summer 1975), 46–66; Peter Spooner, "Olivetti's Own Job Enrichment," *Business Administration*, April 1975, 25–29; "Making a Job More than a Job," *Business Week*, April 19, 1969, 88–89; Noel M. Tichy, "When Does Job Restructuring Work? Organizational Innovations at Volvo and GM," *Organizational Dynamics* **5** (Summer 1976), 63–80.
[30]*Wall Street Journal*, March 1, 1977, p. 1.

applicable to all situations. It presumes the capability or trainability of the individual in a wider range of work skills, and therefore has implications for selection and placement. It assumes that individuals want the greater challenges involved. Nevertheless, job enrichment has reflected the results of an increasing interest in practical methods of motivation.[31]

SUMMARY

This chapter has examined a wide range of motivation concepts and applications. Motivation is primarily a psychological construct explaining why individuals behave as they do. People try in their unique ways to fulfill their needs through their work. The need hierarchy describes varying levels of need categories through which individuals progress, from the most elementary to those that are founded upon social and cultural influences.

Managers cannot readily motivate others directly, but they can influence many factors that affect the motivations of subordinates and colleagues. The particular organizational climate may support or inhibit effective motivation.

Motivation theory has focused chiefly upon expectancies and rewards for performance. Motivation efforts have included the administration of wage and salary structures; job enrichment and job design; and methods of participation, commitment, and involvement. Underlying all serious efforts for effective motivation is the awareness that money is only instrumental—that is, it is desired not for its own sake but for what it can make possible. Money is not a primary or direct motivator and hence is not a managerial tool for forcing compliance. Intrinsic factors, such as the meaning of work, the challenges of work, and the opportunities it affords, are the basic elements of sound motivation.

INCIDENT CASE

Roger Burney, a brilliant industrial engineer in the Billings Company, was completely satisfied with his job. He put in his time conscientiously, and did his work thoroughly and skillfully. He was reliable, but rather easygoing. He did not like working overtime because he needed his evenings and weekends to pursue his

---

[31]Karl Simpson, "Job Enrichment: Just Another Half-Truth?" *The Personnel Administrator* **20** (November 1975), 42–45; Richard Hackman, "Is Job Enrichment Just a Fad?" *Harvard Business Review* **53** (September/October 1975), 129–138; E. Lauck Park and Curt Tausky, "The Mythology of Job Enrichment: Self-Actualization Revisited," *Personnel* **52** (September–October 1975), 12–21; *Atlanta Economics Review* **24** (May–June 1974), entire issue.

outside interests. Burney's boss, Jim Edwards, thought highly of him, but thought he was falling far short of his potential for advancement. Edwards knew that an opportunity to move into a line manager's job would be coming up, and felt that Burney would be an excellent person to promote into the vacancy when it occurred. When he broached the idea to Burney, Burney said, "That's nice of you to consider me, but I like what I am doing. I know my job and it is easy for me to do it without losing sleep at night. Staff work is my cup of tea, and that job in production would really cramp my style. And I don't need the extra money, so thanks but no thanks."

Questions:

1. What factors of motivation are at work in this case?
2. What should Edwards do next, and why?

_____ **QUESTIONS FOR STUDY**

1. What are the main categories of human needs? Why are these needs important?

2. Can managers actually motivate anyone else? Why or why not?

3. What disadvantages might follow as a result of consistently punitive actions on the part of a manager?

4. Define what you consider to be an adequate concept of motivation. Is there any difference between motivation and "manipulation"?

5. What is meant by a "need hierarchy"? How can executives make use of this concept?

6. What is an incentive *payment*? What is an incentive *system*?

7. What are the principle drawbacks and difficulties of an incentive system?

8. Why do automobile manufacturers not use wage incentive systems?

9. What is meant by the idea of "fair" wages? Outline the steps a company can take to achieve fair wages?

10. Explain what is meant by a piece rate. What objections do workers have concerning piece rates? Are these views justified?

11. Explain the interrelationships between the concepts of motivation and morale.

12. Evaluate the strengths and weaknesses of the bureaucratic model of organization structure in relation to problems of morale and motivation.

13. Can such techniques as recruiting, selection, and training have any demonstrable effect on morale and motivation? If so, explain how.

14. Explain the Herzberg concept of motivation. What are satisfiers and dissatisfiers? Hygienic factors?

15. In what ways are executives different from rank-and-file employees with respect to their expectations about remuneration?

16. What is meant by alienation? Does this concept apply to rank-and-file workers as well as executives? How does organization structure influence alienation?

17. Explain what is meant by extrinsic factors of motivation, and compare them with intrinsic factors.

SELECTED REFERENCES

ATKINSON, JOHN W., and JOEL O. RAYNOR. *Motivation and Achievement.* New York: Halsted Press, 1974.

BAER, EARL E. *The Sensitive I: People in Business.* New York: John Wiley & Sons, Inc., 1975.

COFER, D. N., and M. H. APPLEY. *Motivation: Theory and Research.* New York: John Wiley & Sons, Inc., 1964.

DOWLING, WILLIAM F., JR., and LEONARD R. SAYLES. *How Managers Motivate: The Imperatives of Supervision.* New York: McGraw-Hill Book Company, 1971.

EXTON, WILLIAM. *Motivational Leverage: A New Approach to Managing People.* West Nyack, N.Y.: Parker Publishing Company, 1975.

FEINBERT, MORTIMER R., ROBERT RANOFSKY, and JOHN J. TARRANT. *The New Psychology for Managing People.* Englewood Cliffs, N.J.: Prentice-Hall, Inc., 1975.

FORD, ROBERT N. *Motivation Through the Work Itself.* New York: AMACOM, 1969.

HENDERSON, RICHARD. *Compensation Management: Rewarding Performance in Modern Organizations.* Reston, Va.: Reston Publishing Company, Inc., 1976.

HUSBAND, TOM M. *Work Analysis and Pay Structure.* New York: McGraw-Hill, 1976.

KORMAN, ABRAHAM K. *The Psychology of Motivation.* Englewood Cliffs, N.J.: Prentice-Hall, Inc., 1974.

KOSSEN, STAN. *The Human Side of Organizations.* San Francisco: Canfield Press, 1975.

LITWIN, GEORGE, and ROBERT A. STRINGER. *Motivation and Organizational Climate.* Boston: Division of Research, Harvard Graduate School of Business Administration, Harvard University, 1968.

MCGREGOR, DOUGLAS. *Leadership and Motivation.* Cambridge, Mass.: The MIT Press, 1966.

MINER, JOHN B. *The Human Constraint: The Coming Shortage of Managerial Talent.* Rockville, Md.: BNA Books, 1974.

RUST, HAROLD M. F. *Job Design for Motivation.* New York: The Conference Board, 1971.

STEERS, RICHARD M., and LYMAN W. PORTER. *Motivation and Work Behavior.* New York: McGraw-Hill Book Company, 1975.

STAW, BARRY M. "Motivation in Organizations: Toward Synthesis and New Directions." In Barry M. Staw and Gerald R. Salancik, *New Directions in Organization Behavior.* Chicago: St. Clair Press, 1977.

SUOJANEN, WAINO W., SMACKY MCDONALD, GARY L. SWALLOW, and W. WILLIAM SUOJANEN, eds. *Perspectives on Job Enrichment and Productivity.* Atlanta: School of Business, Georgia State University, 1975.

TOSI, HENRY L., ROBERT J. HOUSE, and MARVIN D. DUNNETTE, eds. *Managerial Motivation and Compensation: A Selection of Readings.* East Lansing: Michigan State University Press, 1972.

VROOM, VICTOR H., and EDWARD L. DECI, eds. *Management and Motivation.* New York: Penguin Books, Ltd., 1974.

WALTERS, ROY W. *Job Enrichment for Results: Strategies for Successful Implementation.* Reading, Mass.: Addison-Wesley Publishing Co., Inc., 1975.

WEINER, BERNARD, (ed.). *Achievement Motivation and Attribution Theory.* Morristown, N.J.: General Learning Press, 1974.

YODER, DALE, and HERBERT G. HENEMAN, eds. *Motivation and Commitment.* ASPA Handbook of Personnel and Industrial Relations, vol. II. Washington, D.C.: BNA Books, Inc., 1975.

YORKS, LYLE. *A Radical Approach to Job Enrichment.* New York: AMACOM, 1976.

ZANGWILL, WILLARD I. *Success with People: The Theory Z Approach to Mutual Achievement.* Homewood, Ill.: Dow-Jones–Irwin, Inc., 1976.

- The more $ peo. receive the less they need $ as a motivator.

- 8% raise to clerical wrkr rec'd well ~ but to executive is an insult

- ceases to motivate peo. when they reach "comfort level" tho infla, ads make comfort level an unlikely prospect.

How impt is $?

Valence Approach: "Rank things you   (Vroom) want & prob of them happening

How to Analyze Mot'al Problems:

if have
① discrep. betw E & achieved results
② necessity of mgr. mkg dec. on basis of seniority.

EXAM: Chapt. 10 –22
                     10-18
              19   21 & 22
     skip 20

Chapter 23

Communication

The greatest problem of communication is the illusion that it has been accomplished.   —*George Bernard Shaw*

I *hear* and I *forget*
I *see* and I *remember*
I *do* and I *understand*   —*Confucius*

The most difficult and precarious enterprise in the world is effective communication. It is the ultimate art. In that respect, we all have a lot to learn.
—*Norman Cousins*

The quality of writing in most management communications is dull, obscure, and wordy. According to one authority, managers judge writing by intuition and personal habits rather than by any real skill or knowledge derived from training. Those who do have the skills of editing and writing seldom have the final say on copy; those without such skills can therefore ruin the message before it appears. They focus on content instead of the form and quality of the writing.

One suggestion is that managers who write need to become aware of the different ways in which language can be used to express meaning. One way to increase such an awareness is for managers to read more widely in the works of good writers such as Thoreau, Steinbeck, E. B. White, and others. Yet a few years ago *Fortune* reported a survey showing that after college, very few managers ever read a book of any kind.

Questions to keep in mind as you read this chapter:

1. How can reading help a manager improve his writing style? Why do managers seldom read books?

2. Under what conditions are written communications best? When are oral communications most effective?
3. What criteria should be used to evaluate an organization's communications?

Communication is a fundamental aspect of all human interaction. Through language, humanity has recorded its history and transmitted its cultures from one generation to the next. The ability to communicate has enabled humans to build societies, organizations, and other social groupings that make for survival and better living. At the same time, many of our problems—individual, organizational, and social—arise from the inability to communicate clearly.

In organizations, communication ties people and structure together. The influence of each manager upon others is in large part a function of communication. Managers typically spend at least 60 per cent of their time communicating, either orally or in writing and reading. In some cases the estimates reach 80 per cent. The working day of every manager is crammed with communications of many kinds—orders, directions, conversations, requests, reports, rumors, and so on. The mix includes not only oral and written forms of communication, but gestures, postures, dress, and other visual signals.

Our task in this chapter is to show how communication affects the work of managers and how they may improve organizational and personal communications. Three main topics will be analyzed: (1) the general nature of the communication process, (2) management information systems, and (3) the development of effective communication.

THE COMMUNICATIONS PROCESS

Communication may be broadly defined as *the process of meaningful interaction among human beings.*[1] More specifically, it is the process by which meanings are exchanged so as to produce understanding among human beings. This definition includes not only written and spoken words, but all the ways in which meaning is conveyed. Even silence may convey meaning and therefore must be considered a form of communication. In addition, gestures, facial expressions, and body

---

[1]The term *communication* is frequently used to refer to the integrative and signaling behavior of insects and animals. This kind of "communication," however, is much more limited than human communication, which involves language, speech, and complex visual cues.

postures communicate meaning to others. According to Jaques, communication is "the sum total of directly and indirectly, consciously and unconsciously transmitted feelings, attitudes, and wishes. . . ."[2]

This definition of the communication process must now be extended to include computers and related management information systems. It is important to distinguish between the systems and processes on the one hand, and interpersonal communications on the other. Computers and systems approaches are valuable as aids to greater accuracy and rapid processing of information, but it is ultimately managers who control and utilize communications.

Signs and Symbols

Signs and symbols are basic elements in communication. Signs are cues, or signals, to which we learn to respond because they stand for other stimuli. Signs become meaningful through "conditioned" responses—that is, responses learned through repeated association with a given stimulus, even though that particular response would not normally be evoked by that stimulus. For example, the sound of a dinner bell arouses salivation even without food, if we have learned that the ringing of the bell is associated with food. The bell cue stands in place of the food cue and hence is called a sign.

Symbols are special, complex kinds of signs. The meaning of a symbol is arbitrary and is less closely associated with its cues. The American flag, for example, brings forth complex feelings and images in the mind of the observer, who has learned that this symbol should evoke patriotic attitudes. The flag is an example of a nonverbal symbol, but words or mathematical notations are examples of other symbols in common use.

Language

Words are symbols whose meaning we learn as we grow up in a particular society. Their meaning is determined by the context of our particular society and culture. Thus a person using the English language refers to an object as a *pencil*, whereas a German-speaking person calls it a *Bleistift*. Language, however, is more complex than this, because words are used in sequences, and they commonly have more than one referent, with the meaning dependent on context. Cultural differences are also illustrated by the fact that "English" is the language of both the United States and Great Britain, but many words have greatly different meanings as used in the two countries.

[2]Elliott Jaques, *The Changing Culture of a Factory* (London: Tavistock, 1951), p. 301.

Semantics

Language is highly symbolic in that words refer to objects or ideas outside themselves. The meanings to which words refer are chosen arbitrarily, but communication is possible if senders and receivers of messages have some degree of agreement about the word and its referents.

Semantics is the science of meaning in language. We have all experienced the difficulty of understanding others when they use words that have several meanings. Because words are symbols, they stand for things or ideas that we learn to associate with those things. For instance, when we hear the word *dog,* each of us has an idea of its referent, if we have experienced dogs in the past. Yet this simple word conveys different meanings to people, depending on their experiences with dogs. Semantics teaches that communicating is difficult because a person does not always understand a word the same way as anyone else. Each interprets words through experience, and no two people have the same experiences. The meaning of words lies within the individual.

Another problem of semantics is that words represent different levels of abstraction. Abstraction is the degree to which a word is removed from an objective, tangible referent. The word *apple,* for example, can refer to a particular apple or to a generalized concept of apple. The word *democracy,* however, is on such a high level of abstraction that there is no specific referent for it. It is highly symbolic.

We cannot of course avoid abstract words like *democracy* or *management,* but whoever uses them should recognize their pitfalls. In talking with others, it is a good idea to distinguish among facts, inferences, and value judgments. For example, if we say that John Smith came to work late three days in a row, that would be a measurable fact. If we say that John Smith will lose his job because he has been coming to work late, we are drawing an inference. And if we say that John Smith is lazy and irresponsible, we have expressed a value judgment.

The best way to deal with abstractions in communications is to substitute specifics for abstractions wherever possible. One can ask for examples and clarification, and attempt to define carefully the abstractions used. It is wrong to assume that an abstract, conceptual word such as *freedom* has one specific meaning, or the same meaning, to other people. This is where organizational communications often break down.[3]

Semantic difficulties are compounded by our need to talk and write about ideals and values. Values express what people prize most highly.

[3]Arthur G. Bedeian, "A Historical Review of Efforts in the Area of Management Semantics," *Academy of Management Journal* **17** (March 1974), 101–114.

Organizations use values to motivate the desired behavior of employees. Loyalty, for example, is such a value. Values can motivate if they are effectively communicated and then internalized as part of the belief system of organization members. To be effectively communicated, they must correspond to the needs and perceptions of those members and must not do violence to other values they hold. If under these conditions an organizational value, such as "customer service is paramount," can be specified in terms of the behavior required by the value, the value becomes authentic and useful in concrete situations. Thus customer-service ideals become translated to mean service "at specified prices, times, and places if the official has an opportunity to render it without undue cost to himself or the company."

Two examples of confusion arising from semantic difficulties will be helpful in showing that it is not only words but actions, implications, and the entire situational context that produces misunderstandings.

> *Example 1.* A manager addressed the members of his organization after receiving a promotion. "In beginning my speech I said I was going to talk to them from the level of a store manager—which was the group I was addressing. What I meant was that all I know was what I learned as a store manager and I would talk at that level. Days later I started getting reports that said it was nice for me to drop back to their level again just to talk to them."
>
> *Example 2.* A superior told a worker to "take that carboy of acid and put it in that tub," whereupon he did just that—carboy, acid, and all.

MANAGEMENT INFORMATION SYSTEMS

The term *management information system* (MIS) has been defined in so many ways that the concept remains ambiguous. It is defined here as *a planned system of collecting, storing, and distributing data in the form of information needed to carry out the functions of management.* This definition implies that (1) formal communications of great significance for effective planning, decision, and control are related in a unified system; (2) that system is a subsystem of the organization and its technology; (3) order, arrangement, and purpose guide the establishment and use of the system; and (4) data are transformed into useful information.

Similar terms, such as *information* or *data processing* (or *handling*) and *information theory,* are sometimes used. Their common denominator is the idea that formal communications are subject to a regulated system that provides managers with information that they need, in a timely and relevant manner. Their systemic qualities are made possible largely by vast developments in computer technology.

Information Technology

Computers have virtually revolutionized information processing by providing the technology that greatly increases storage, retrieval, and the speed and volume of calculations.

The first application of computers in a business firm was made in 1954. There are currently more than 125,000 computers in the United States alone. They emerged from work in cybernetics and information theory, a rigorous effort to apply mathematics to communications engineering. This work began with the pioneering work of Shannon and his associates working in telephone communications[4] and is related to the field of cybernetics pioneered by Wiener.[5] Because information theory deals with the flow of information and communication networks, it has important implications for organization design and for man-machine relationships.[6] Information theory provides a means of measuring the information content of both symbolic and verbal languages and relating the characteristics of an efficient communication system to the information content of messages transmitted. This body of theory has been of use primarily in the design of large, complex communication systems and computers, but its application has been limited to communications directly involving people.

Computer technology is now in the fourth generation. The first generation has been dated from 1953 to 1958. In this period, applications were confined to simple, well-defined, formal systems such as payrolls, billing, and accounting. In the second generation, from 1958 to 1966, technology remained related to well-understood tasks and procedures, and the control of batch processing such as steel or paint manufacturing. Computers had the capacity to process large quantities of data in routine ways. On-line inquiry systems, as used by airlines and stockbrokers, evolved.

The third generation, from 1966 to 1974, saw the development of remote terminals to connect geographically separated units with central computers. Time sharing was developed to provide many users with the ad hoc services of a single large computer.

The fourth generation, beginning about 1974, is experiencing the evolution of application-independent data bases. The organization will then have a single, computerized, data-based system accessible to a variety of users for a wide range of purposes. One-line systems are also becoming easier to use.[7]

---

[4]Claude E. Shannon and W. Weaver, "The Mathematical Theory of Communication (Urbana: University of Illinois Press, 1949).

[5]Norbert Wiener, *Cybernetics* (New York: Wiley, 1948). Cybernetics deals with problems of communications and control in animals and machines.

[6]Everett M. Rogers and Rekha Agarwalla-Rogers, *Communication in Organizations* (New York: Free Press, 1976), chap. 5.

[7]John T. Small and William B. Lee, "In Search of an MIS," *MSU Business Topics,* Autumn 1975, 47–55.

The earliest computer systems were administered by accountants or controllers, because most of the use was in their departments. Now, however, with a variety of users, new organizational patterns have emerged that give the information system a place in the central organization or establish it as an autonomous unit. The result is that users are tending to lose direct control over their computer applications.[8]

Many firms have developed linkages among data processing, information flow, and computers. To form an integrated information system they have created data-processing departments. An example of a computer-based planning system utilizing computers, data processing, and management science is shown in Figure 23-1. The structure shown is not necessarily the most typical or the most desirable; there are alternative possibilities. Data -processing and related activities are essentially a staff function. Data-processing activities and associated operations are becoming more and more centralized, to gain increased efficiency for the organization as a whole.

Computers are constantly being improved and their capabilities increased. Smaller, less expensive models are being developed for use in smaller organizations. The tasks to which they are applied range from the pedestrian to complex scientific research procedures. They are used in fields hitherto limited by human ability to perform mathematical calculations. The economies made possible by the higher speed of the computers are suggested by the example of the company that used a computer to prepare a financial report in two hours that formerly took 320 man-hours. It prepares 1,200 manufacturing cost reports in 12 machine-hours, in contrast to the 1,800 man-hours formerly required. High-speed computers can handle data electronically at more than a thousand times the speed of conventional punched-card equipment.

Computers go far beyond conventional tabulating or punched-card office equipment—sorters, printers, verifiers, reproducers, and so on. The computer is a system that involves the work of all these, and more. As shown in Figure 23–2, the basic components are input, output, and an internal processing unit that provides control, computation, and storage. Input can be on standard punched cards, a random-access file, or magnetic tape. In the processing unit, the activity of the input is coordinated, and logical decisions or computations can be made at the rate of thousands per second. At the output stage, the computer translates its internal processing functions onto punched cards or a machine printout of tabulations. For many applications, the bottleneck is in the output part of the equipment, which generates mountains of paper but not usually at the same rate as the computations are performed.

Computer equipment is divided into *hardware,* which is the computer itself and its battery of associated equipment, and *software,* the collection of programs associated with the use of computers. A com-

[8]Ibid., p. 48.

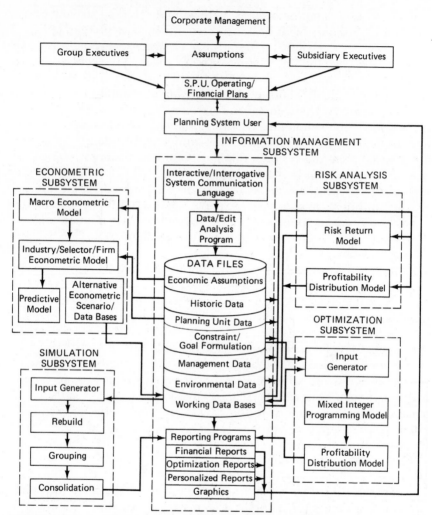

FIGURE 23-1. A Computer-Based Corporate Planning System.

Source: William F. Hamilton and Michael A. Moss, "A Computer-Based Corporate Planning System," *Management Science,* October 1974, p. 49. Used by permission.

puter program is a planned procedure for solving a problem or task through computerization. It consists of a series of instructions for calculations to be performed on the data. These instructions are in two parts, a statement that specifies an operation to be performed (such as "multiply") and a statement that identifies the location of data to be used. Each computer has a set of operational functions engineered into its logical design. Although the individual operations are often relatively simple, when used in combination by the person programming the

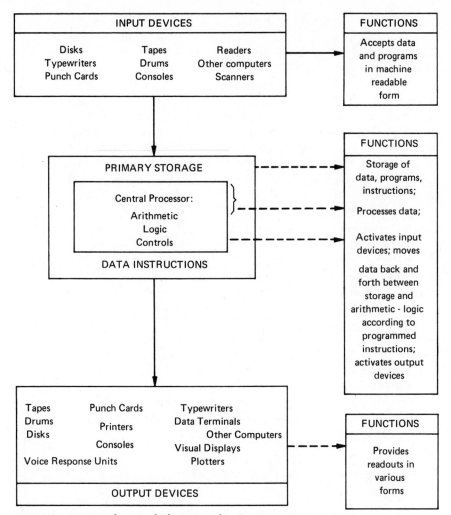

FIGURE 23-2. Fundamental Elements of a Computer System.

Source: George T. Hunter and Graham M. Clark, "Electronic Data Processing Machines," *Instruments and Automation* **28** (May 1955), p. 792.

computer the operational codes yield a powerful set of instructions to process enormous quantities of data and solve complex problems at heretofore impossible speeds.

Each computer has its own built-in machine language, into which it converts the language used by the programmer. This simplifies the programming because the programmer need not fully understand the machine language. Although special programs are written to accomplish unique tasks, most computers are supplied with various programs of wide application, and sometimes packaged programs are available. Considerable complexity exists in the fact that a number of languages for programming, are designated by acronyms such as FORTRAN, COBOL, and ALGOL, have been developed.

As applications of the computer increase, they will have a substantial impact on the design of systems and subsystems. Thus the organization design of business firms, government agencies, schools, and other types of organizations must be adapted to these changes in information technology. This means that information technology is focused on the relation of data to the need for making decisions. Inventory data, although computerized, is not necessarily an information system. An information system provides information in forms useful to the decision maker, not mere data. It transforms data into meaningful forms and delivers information to the right places at the right time. Hence such a system is more than a speed-up of processing clerical data. Increasing the quantity of information and the speed with which it is obtained, however, does not necessarily benefit the organization, for the improved techniques of generating and processing data can multiply the defects of a given system so that they become more harmful. Data for data's sake, moreover, are not needed. Therefore, electronic data processing must be applied only after an analysis of the uses for data and of the related information, communication, and work-flow systems. For example, some firms are using outmoded account classifications, and converting old accounting methods to electronic data processing compounds the defects and fails to provide useful information at reasonable cost. Reorganization of the system must therefore precede computerization.[9]

Organization Structure and Communication

Our earlier discussions of organization design indicated that one major purpose of structure is to provide a system of communication. It was also shown that different structures result in varying degrees of effectiveness in communication and hence in performance. Written and oral communications tie together the structural units, with great influence on the interactions of individuals and groups.

Adaptive organizations are less likely to maintain rigid lines of communication. The information system encourages open communication among people on a need-to-know basis. Individuals are responsible for knowing what they need to know and how to get it. Reporting relationships are not the main guidelines for legitimate communication.

[9]For a view of the manager's role in using the computer, see Simon Ramo, "The Computer in Management," *The Record*, February 1973, 14–16.

In bureaucratic, hierarchical organizations, the structure imposes formal relationships that tend to be regarded as important in regulating communications. Thus it is necessary to understand the upward, downward, and lateral dimensions of communication.[10]

Upward and Downward Communication

In bureaucratic organizations, the locus of authority at the top leads to an emphasis on downward communication. The process of delegation itself is a form of downward communication. Downward communication helps tie the levels together and is the means by which managers put their delegated authority to work. The role of the superior is to decide what subordinates need to know and to provide this information regularly, in sufficient quantities, in useful forms, and quickly enough for them to act in a timely manner.

Communications going downward in bureaucracies are highly directive—that is, they initiate actions by subordinates. Communications going upward are primarily nondirective—that is, they report results or give information, but generally do not initiate important activity by superiors. Upward communication occurs primarily to the degree that the superior encourages or permits it. The necessary minimum is that which enables managers to verify downward communications, to know that they are being received and carried out, and to know how and when to modify or discontinue them.

Encouraging adequate upward communication is difficult in bureaucracies. Subordinates must decide how, when, and what to communicate upward. Whereas downward communication fits traditional concepts of organizational behavior, upward communication tends to run counter to them. Consequently it is often poorly handled. Because of the need for a flow of information on which to base decisions and policies, managers must learn to tap the resources of subordinates by opening up the channels of upward communication to creative thought and the expression of ideas, without hasty value judgments from above.

The general orientation of upward and downward communication in an organization is depicted in Figure 23-3, which shows by means of arrows the frequency and intensity of the two dimensions of communication. The upward arrow is thin and the downward arrow is thick to symbolize the dominance of the supervisor over the subordinate in matters of communication. The objective of a skilled leader would be to adjust conditions so that the arrows are more nearly equal.

[10]Rogers and Agarwalla-Rogers, *Communication in Organizations*, chap. 4.

Communication
from **Supervisor**
to **Employee**

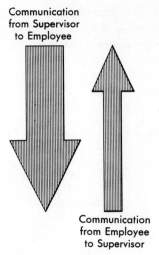

Communication
from **Employee**
to **Supervisor**

FIGURE 23-3. Frequency and Intensity of Communications Between Employee and Supervisor.

The Lateral Dimension

Lateral (horizontal) communication poses almost as much difficulty as vertical communication, but it has fewer implications of authority and status. Problems of interunit conflict arise from functional specialization and departmentalization. Management theory holds that such problems are resolved by coordination at the next higher level. This view emphasizes vertical communication flows, and lateral communication has not been extensively studied.

Landsberger has analyzed lateral relationships in a study of three British engineering plants producing similar products. In his view, the function of horizontal relationships is to facilitate the solution of problems arising from the division of labor. The nature of horizontal relationships is determined by individual managers, whose organizational subgoals are different but whose interdependent activities need to be blended. In these horizontal relationships, conflict and disagreement may be frequent and inevitable, but they are also often useful to the organization. Landsberger concluded that important things happen in the horizontal pattern of communications before the vertical processes are called upon to mediate a conflict or bring about a decision. The problems and dilemmas of an organization determine to a large extent the frequency and content of horizontal interactions and exert pressure to solve these dilemmas. Such problems determine the stands taken by the departmental units and the strength by which they are defended.[11]

[11]Henry A. Landsberger, "The Horizontal Dimension in Bureaucracy," *Administrative Science Quarterly* **6** (December 1961), 299–332.

Simpson, in an empirical study of superior-subordinate relationships, views horizontal communications as determined primarily by the state of technology, thus deemphasizing the frequency or content of horizontal interactions. He believes that vertical communication has been overemphasized, and in his case studies he found that communications among supervisors were mainly horizontal because of the mechanized nature of the work.[12]

Intergroup Communications

An important aspect of lateral communications is that between groups. For example, the relations among work flows, such as production or paper processing, can be computerized. A series of minicomputers at the various stages of a production process can be programmed to automate the entire process by controlling each step and communicating with the following step, and a central computer designed to keep top managers informed.[13]

Another example of intergroup communication of substantial complexity—and one in which computers are not useful—is labor-management relations. In unionized firms, workers form and join trade unions whose representatives bargain with management over wages, working conditions, and other terms of employment. Collective bargaining relationships are governed by highly institutionalized practices (procedures, roles, and habits of long standing that are confirmed by tradition, history, and legal requirements). Communications between labor and management representatives are fraught with problems of fact-gathering, analysis, and interpretation that are also laden with emotional content.

In a sense, it is difficult to imagine how such collective groups communicate. Is it reasonable to suppose that all communications must be from and among particular individuals? Not necessarily, because despite the fact that one individual is speaking to another, each is looked upon as representing the group from which he comes. The process of collective bargaining, for example, establishes authorized spokesmen for unionized workmen, and the company appoints managers to represent it.

Official management points of view in labor relations usually emanate only from the top echelons in a company, so that the top officers

---

[12]Richard L. Simpson, "Vertical and Horizontal Communication in Organizations," *Administrative Science Quarterly* 4 (December 1959), 188–196. See also George Strauss, "Tactics of Lateral Relationships: The Purchasing Agent," *Administrative Science Quarterly* 7 (September 1962), 188–196; Jerald Hage, Michael Aiken, and Cora B. Marrett, "Organization Structure and Communications," *American Sociological Review* 36 (October 1971), 860–871.

[13]"Minicomputers That Own the Factory," *Business Week*, December 8, 1973, pp. 68–78.

and managers are the chief spokesmen. By delegation, vice presidents or directors of industrial relations have key roles in communicating with employees, either directly or through collective bargaining. It is this top group of managers that determines the character of communications addressed both to the public and to working groups within the company.

As a whole, organizations have not been skillful at communicating with their employees. Despite large staffs of experts in communication, and the willingness to invest large sums of money, mass communications programs have for the most part failed. For example, the efforts of corporations to educate employees about the free enterprise system was based not only on genuine concern for economic illiteracy in our society, but also on alarm at the rising political influence of workers. Yet the programs had little impact because companies did not understand the nature of communication or the psychology of workers. The objective of reforming the workers, and converting them into individuals more like the employers wanted them to be, aroused their antagonism. Management proceeded on the erroneous notion that the way to cure misinformation and negative attitudes was to supply additional, correct information. The whole campaign underestimated the intelligence of workers, causing them to feel manipulated, and ignored the fact that information is inextricably interwoven with emotions and sentiments.

To equate communication with indoctrination or to view it merely as a tool for rendering workers more docile and subservient is to go wide of the mark in understanding communication as a basic element of interaction among people in organizations.

_____ **DEVELOPING EFFECTIVE COMMUNICATIONS**

Effectiveness in communications is generated by a multifaceted approach. Organizational designs must be analyzed for their effects on communication. This basic approach, discussed in preceding sections, can be implemented through: (1) research on the communication process in organizations, (2) communications audits, and (3) cost controls.

Research on the Communications Process

The problem of effectiveness begins with the need to measure communications variables. The next step is to relate the measured variables to desired outcomes, such as changed attitudes or better performance of work. Moreover, the measures used must be reliable, valid, and relatively inexpensive in the time and money required for their use. The possible variables in communication are numerous and difficult to define; it is often *perceptions* that are measured rather than directly observable phenomena.

Using standard research techniques, such as questionnaires, scaling methods, and statistical analyses, researchers can compare communications techniques in various organizations or groups. Among the principal variables measured are comparisons of modes of communication (written versus oral; face-to-face versus telephone); communication overloads; time required; directionality (vertical or lateral); accuracy; filtering and distortion; and many others. Not only must such variables be measured, but their impact on performance must be examined if we are to advance from folk wisdom to scientific knowledge.

An example of such research is that of O'Reilly and Roberts, who developed a 35-item measuring instrument and applied it to various organizations. In one project they studied upward communication as a function of three variables: (1) the subordinate's trust in his superior, (2) the subordinate's perception of the superior's influence over his future, and (3) the subordinate's mobility aspirations. They found that trust was the most important facilitator of open communication. The remaining two variables were also important, but to a lesser extent.[14]

In another study, O'Reilly and Roberts examined fifteen aspects of communications, collecting data from 327 subjects in ten branch organizations (five in the U.S. and five in Great Britain) of similar size, staffing, function, and physical facilities. They found it possible to differentiate these apparently homogeneous aspects on the basis of perceptions of communication, and that these differences in communication are related to both organizational climate and organization performance.[15]

Another aspect of organizational communication is to focus on process in relation to content or purpose. Gribbins, for example, has analyzed how communications processes work in relation to innovation. Innovation arises from forces in a company's environment, and the innovating organization is linked to aspects of the environment through the need to acquire relevant information, transmit the information, and to utilize the information in the assessment of the risks to individuals and to the organization.[16]

The concept of the communication network has proved to be a fruitful way of examining organizationwide communications. Farace and Pacanowsky devised a method of analyzing networks in large

[14]Karlene H. Roberts and Charles A. O'Reilly III, "Failures in Upward Communications: Three Possible Culprits," *Academy of Management Journal* 17 (June 1974), 205–215; see also Roberts and O'Reilly, "Measuring Organizational Communication," *Journal of Applied Psychology* 59 (1974), 321–326; Thad B. Green and Paul H. Pietri, "Using Nominal Grouping to Improve Upward Communications," *MSU Business Topics*, Autumn 1974, 37–43.

[15]Charles A. O'Reilly and Karlene H. Roberts, "Communication: A Way of Viewing Organizations," paper presented at the 34th Annual Meeting, Academy of Management, Seattle, Washington, August 1974.

[16]Ronald E. Gribbins, "Communication of Innovations: Predictions and Implications Utilizing a Sociological and Psychological Perspective," paper presented at the 34th Annual Meeting, Academy of Management, Seattle, Washington, August 1974.

organizations and applied it to a study of 961 organization members in a large bank, examining the relationships among the network role, the hierarchical level, and the individual's relative status. They found that as network roles become more centralized or involved in the network, the strength of the communication links of the individuals also increases, and that although hierarchical level is not related to role, relative status is so related. As involvement increases, the individual's relative status increases. Thus we need to view the importance of an individual's communication skills as related to fulfillment of a key role in the organizational network.[17]

Audits

Systematic audits are increasingly used for the diagnosis, evaluation, and control of organizationwide communications. Audit methods are generally based on the concept of the communication network. They have the advantage of comprehensiveness, integrating the study of such problems as information flow, message sending, or perception and attitudes.

A recently developed measurement system is called the ICA Audit. It establishes a normed data bank to provide comparisons between organizations and their communication systems, and establishes, through comparative studies, an external validation of organizational communication theories and propositions.[18]

Greenbaum has also developed an audit plan that analyzes four organizational networks of communication: regulative, innovative, integrative, and informative-instructive. Each network corresponds to an organizational goal—conformity, adaptiveness, morale, and institutionalization, respectively; each is also related to particular governing policies. The evaluation proceeds through fact-finding, analytical, and reporting stages.[19]

Cost Controls

Communication processes and activities require substantial organizational resources. Computer technology is expensive, although it has a

---

[17]Richard V. Farace and Michael Pacanowsky, "Organizational Communication Role, Hierarchical Level, and Relative Status," paper presented at the 34th Annual Meeting, Academy of Management, Seattle, Washington, August 1974; Richard V. Farace, and Donald MacDonald, "New Directions in the Study of Organizational Communication," *Personnel Psychology* 27 (Spring 1974), 1–19.

[18]Gerald M. Goldhaber, "The ICA Communication Audit: Rationale and Development," paper presented at the 36th Annual Meeting of the Academy of Management, Kansas City, Missouri, August, 1976. ICA audits have been used to evaluate communications in hospitals, schools, firms, universities, and governmental units.

[19]Howard H. Greenbaum, "The Audit of Organizational Communications," *Academy of Management Journal* 17 (December 1974), 739–754.

high potential for reducing costs. The time of managers who prepare, send, and receive communications is another area of costs, as are record keeping, filing, storage, and printing and mailing.

Many of these costs are hidden and indirect, and hence not readily measured. The costs of computerized management information systems are generally reviewed in feasibility studies prior to establishing them. Their operations too are subject to cost analysis and control.

Gallagher has devised a method for determining the value of an existing MIS report, based on user perceptions of monetary value, and the measurement of nonmonetary values by a semantic differential technique. In a test of the method he found that the value of information (1) was enhanced by the participation of managers in the report design, and (2) was related to the manager's organizational position.[20]

Costs are often analyzed in relation to their relationship with benefits. Strassman suggests that mangement information systems require a broadening framework for analysis, and that system development logically requires accounting for all labor costs at both the input and the output ends of the system.[21]

Improving Interpersonal Communications

In addition to the improvement of organizationwide communications, it is vital to focus organizational effort on the improvement of the communication skills of people. Day-to-day organizational activities are conducted through the continuous interaction of people who are communicating with one another. These communications are both formal (official) and informal. The distinction between formal and informal communications is not always clear, however, because a formal communication may be transmitted in an oblique, informal way. For example, when the boss says, "Would you like to take my place at the committee meeting next Tuesday?" he is actually giving an order.

To improve communications among people it is necessary to explore (1) the major barriers that interfere with the process, and (2) ways of improving human skills of communication.

Communication Barriers

Figure 23-4 shows a model of the communication process between a message sender and receiver. By means of a feedback process the receiver becomes a sender, reflecting an understanding, acceptance, interpretation, or rejection of the message, or the returning of a new

---

[20]Charles A. Gallagher, "Perceptions of the Value of a Management Information System," *Academy of Management Journal* 17 (March 1974), 46–55.

[21]Paul A. Strassman, "Managing the Costs of Information," *Harvard Business Review* 54 (September/October 1976), 133–142.

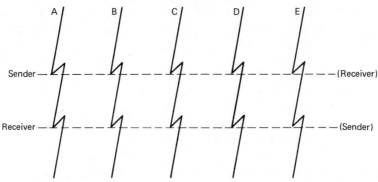

A—Personality: Human Needs

B—Status and Prestige

C—Language: Semantics, Jargon

D—Prejudices, Biases

E—Habits, Values, Traditions

FIGURE 23-4. Some Barriers to Effective Communication.

message. This diagram also depicts some of the main barriers that may distort the message, prevent it from going through, or slow it down.

The chief aim of communication is to influence others by conveying meanings that will be understood and accepted. We try to gauge the degree of acceptance and understanding by the responses, both verbal and behavioral, of receivers. This estimate can mislead, however, if the receiver is only pretending. There are possible ulterior aims in communication, such as the deliberate intent to confuse or to propagandize. Much warping and blockage of the communication process can occur, intentionally or not. Communication seldom results in perfect understanding. There are degrees of success.

The barriers between senders and receivers are both functional and dysfunctional. Functional barriers serve useful purposes, such as eliminating unnecessary communication or slowing it down for greater care and understanding. Dysfunctional barriers impede the amount, clarity, and usefulness of necessary information transmission.

Not all communications are worth disseminating. A completely free system of communication in an organization would be chaotic. Some of the barriers that inhibit the free flow of communications are therefore intentional. In studying a British factory, Jaques judged the effectiveness of communication on the quality of selectivity in the transmission of information, rather than on the free flow of all communications.[22] There is no rule for determining the degree of "freeness" that should prevail in communication within organizations, but in order to hold an

[22]Jaques, *Changing Culture*, p. 302.

organization together as a unit, the communication process must be subject to the direction of managers in the same way as other important aspects of organization behavior.

As computerization of information and data systems takes place, and as organizations are increasingly designed with work-flow and systems concepts predominating, unplanned or random communication patterns are less likely to occur in the formal system. It will be more likely that people in organizations will have the information they need to do their job, but also that they will not have access to information they might like to have but do not need. Thus political and power factions in organizations will be affected.

We have noted that organizational hierarchy itself affects communications by imposing the notion of "channels" through which communications must officially travel. Some organizations put undue emphasis on sticking to channels, causing difficulties for those who are prevented from contacting anyone but their immediate superior or subordinates. The resulting frustration leads people to circumvent the restrictions and to operate more within the informal organization. Such restrictions overlook the interrelated nature of activities going on within the segments of an organization. Thus the over-all management information system must facilitate needed communications and restrain or eliminate unneeded or unused information.

Objectives may constitute dysfunctional barriers to effective communication. Unworthy or undesirable purposes need communication as much as desirable ones do. Therefore those who seek selfish ends may try to distort or block communication, bending it to their own strategies. Embezzlers and other criminals may, for example, injure the organization by illegitimate uses of the computer. Propagandist objectives, such as antiunion information or attempts to change employee attitudes toward the economic system, are hard to achieve because the message receivers are prone to resist.

The relative status and power of senders and receivers may prove to be a barrier to effective communication. Status reflects the attitudes of regard, approval, deference, and so on, that people display toward others. In part status is attached to the position, and in part it is derived from the personality of the individual. Status reflects the degree of importance others ascribe to a position or to the individual occupying it.

Status is implied in job titles, salary distinctions, and privileges that go with rank. Objects that go with status are called status symbols. For example, managers with carpets in their offices have higher status than those with tile floors. Some may be entitled to a company-furnished desk set, which becomes a status symbol to the extent that others notice it and regard it as a privilege of that position. Status is also conferred upon individuals by reason of the group or category to which they belong. This source of status is not necessarily related to position or hierarchy. For example, there are status differences between men and women, night shift and day shift, main plant and branch plant, or shop workers and office workers.

Status impedes upward communication because subordinates are conscious of it in their relationships with superiors. To begin with, the subordinate's future is in the boss's hands. What the boss thinks and does is so important that the subordinate is cautious about speaking to him. Most workers like to have a happy and pleasant boss, so they hesitate to report their own shortcomings and mistakes or to relay upsetting information. Status is also a communications barrier because it reinforces the belief that it is impossible to talk the same language as the superior. Status hinders because it discourages subordinates from bringing vital information to their bosses. Subordinates may prefer a happy but ignorant boss to an informed but upset one. They filter the information going through to him. Some of it drops out; some is greatly changed to achieve a carefully calculated effect.

Although status usually prevents or distorts communications, it also facilitates them, provided that the superior's status is earned or maintained along with the confidence and trust of subordinates and has not been accompanied by abuses or misuses of authority. Status helps individuals to know at least approximately how others see them. People tend to evaluate communications partly by the initiator's status. When subordinates need to authenticate and validate the information they receive, they may look to their superiors.

Emotions also block communication among managers. People vary in their emotional sensitivity; although subordinates may appear generally rational and logical in their behavior, careful listening and observing often show that feelings take precedence. Efforts to be impersonal or strictly factual and logical will fall flat. It is far better to give emotions a chance to find expression, for unexpressed emotions cause personality problems. If the boss is highly emotional, for example, subordinates are reluctant to communicate.

In the communication of feelings, we find much confusion because of semantic difficulties. Therefore, when a manager wishes to understand the feelings of others, he cannot always rely on what they say but must be a keen observer of how they behave. People do not always express themselves well in words, but they can usually find an action that will be eloquent indeed, especially when they are trying to influence the boss.

We often notice that what people do does not correspond at all to what they say. If the two disagree, behavior is a more reliable guide than words. People will say again and again that they are happy and safisfied, and that nothing is wrong—then suddenly they will quit. Subordinates expect the boss to know some things without their having to communicate in so many words. If the boss is a good listener and looks for feelings as well as for the explicit meaning of words, a better understanding will result. For example, one boss noticed that a secretary who does not want to do something will not refuse; but it will take several days longer than it should, if it gets done at all.

Context, or the situational element, may block or facilitate communications. Words, sentences, facts, figures, and other components of communications must be understood with reference to the situation in which they occur. The key to understanding the context is to see the latent meanings in facts or events as well as the surface—or manifest—meaning. Workers' wage grievances, for example, are only symptoms of deeper employee doubts, problems, and conflicts, and on careful analysis the root of the trouble often does not concern wages at all. To illustrate, a manager assigned sorting work, previously performed by men on overtime pay, to a group of women. When the output of the men fell, they asserted that the loss of overtime pay was the cause of their discontent. By observing carefully, however, the manager learned that the real source of the lowered output and morale was the violation of a strong group norm that sorting was a man's work.

Another communications barrier is the tendency to make value judgments an actual or implicit part of communication. When communications directly or indirectly include such elements as judgments, evaluations, and opinions, emotions and resistance are likely to be aroused, leaving room for only two opposing ideas, feelings, or judgments. Overcoming this barrier requires listening to the other person with understanding and with an effort to see the other person's point of view.

A final major barrier to effective communications is the lack of authenticity and legitimacy. Acceptance depends on the credibility of the source of information.[23] If authentic formal communications are absent, poorly timed, or too long delayed, information needs will be filled by the informal system. Such problems often occur because managers try to avoid being connected with unfavorable information. For example, a manager might withhold an announcement of a promotion, an outsider to be hired, or an imminent layoff of workers, to put off criticism as long as possible. Such cases invite the rumor mill to supply information based on whatever cues and signals are visible.

Rumors pervade all organizations. Information containing elements of surprise may pass through an organization rapidly, encountering distortion along the way. Distortion is normal in verbal communication chains; it takes the form of exaggeration, incompleteness, and error. Rumors are interesting, exciting, entertaining, and even therapeutic; they are also informative in a general way even though details may be

[23]Bernard Bass and Rudi Klauss, "Communications Styles, Credibility, and Their Consequences," *The Personnel Administrator* **20** (October 1975), 32–36.

wrong. The grapevine serves as a warning device in advance of impending change. Rumors are generally accurate in announcing that change is about to occur, although the exact nature of the change may lack detail. Distortions occur because rumor transmitters fill in the missing details. The longer a rumor persists the greater the distortion, but rumors tend to be more accurate than most managers believe.

Rumors of unpopular or controversial change are prone to wild exaggeration and tend to create unfounded speculation. Davis suggests that rumors have causes that can be controlled: lack of information, insecurity of employees, and emotional conflicts. Handling serious rumor problems by preventive action is best, but once such a rumor starts, managers should constrain or subdue its force. The best tactic is to release the truth or relevant facts without repeating the rumor itself. Facts speak louder than efforts to argue against the rumor, especially if they come from a reliable and authoritative source.[24]

Improving Human Skills of Communication

In the final analysis, the effectiveness of communication depends on the intelligence, judgment, and discretion of individuals, and on their skills in writing and speaking. Skill in oral and written communication is subject to improvement through learning and practice.

Oral Communication

The directness of oral communication is unsurpassed. It is usually face to face between individuals, the principal exceptions occurring in the use of telephones, public address systems, and other media.

Face-to-face communication has many advantages. Communicators have a chance to appraise the degree of understanding achieved, to ask questions, check responses, and clarify meanings. More of the personality of each person is brought to bear in the communication process, adding zest and interest to the message. Through oral communication, an employee relates himself to others in the work situation. Visual signs, such as gestures or body posture, may facilitate or inhibit the communication.

Oral communications have the disadvantage that perception of the spoken word is likely to be less accurate or enduring than perception of the written word. The scope of oral communications is limited to those situations where time and the nature of the message permit direct contact. Lengthy communications and those that require permanence of form, such as creeds, policies, or rules, are beyond the scope of oral

---

[24]Keith Davis, "Cut Those Rumors Down to Size," *Supervisory Management,* June 1975, 2–6; "Understanding the Organizational Grapevine," *Business and Public Affairs* **2** (Spring 1976), 5–10.

forms. Oral communications can be misunderstood, and it is difficult to check them later when contradictory claims arise.

Talking a lot has been shown in one experimental study to be a simple way of convincing others that one is a leader, and it makes little difference what the content is. The researchers explained the preference for quantity over content by noting that the quality of verbal interaction is a reflection of a person's ability, whereas quantity is an indicator of a person's motivation.[25] In another study, researchers found that fast talkers make people think they are competent, but not very nice. Slow talkers appear to be bumblers.[26]

Written Communications

Written communications play an extensive part in managerial effort. As has been indicated, some messages must be relatively permanent so that they can later be referred to for checking and instruction. Such communications as reports, research information, policies, rules, and agreements are nearly always in writing.

Written material has the advantage of being (usually) more carefully thought through than spontaneous conversations or other oral communications. Individuals often understand what they read better than what they hear. They are accustomed to written messages in many situations. Through printing and duplication procedures, written material can be widely disseminated. Written messages can be checked for accuracy.

There are also disadvantages, such as the difficulty of keeping written material up to date and the impossibility of clearing up obscure meanings for the reader. A further problem is that written documents can become the instruments of excessive legalism and formality, and hence the source of disputes. Finally, one must find ways of making sure that the written messages are read by those for whom they are intended. Many people are reluctant to read or find it difficult; and they are always highly selective in what they read. Moreover, the writer has the burden of using clear, plain English.

Relationships in written communications can be direct, although not actually face to face. For example, when a supervisor sends a note to a worker to assign a task, it is not face-to-face communication, but the effect is nearly the same in the sense that the worker will usually carry out the directive as if the supervisor were present.

Written communications can become burdensome, giving the means more emphasis than the ends deserve. Most managers who have experi-

---

[25]Richard M. Sorrentino and Robert G. Boutillier, "The Effect of Quantity and Quality of Verbal Interaction on Ratings of Leadership," *Journal of Experimental Social Psychology* **11** (September 1975), 403–411.

[26]Bruce Smith, Bruce Brown, William Strong, and Alvin Bencher, "Effects of Speech Rate on Personality Perception," *Language and Speech* **18** (April–June 1975), 145–152.

enced the floods of paper that cross their desks daily seek ways to reduce the task of reading. In some cases, managers have been found writing memoranda to other managers at desks nearby. Often a telephone call or a personal visit will serve the purpose better. For internal communications, written items can be confined primarily to the issuance of instructions and the assignment of duties. Such written communications should be supplemented by oral communication, either at the time they are submitted or shortly thereafter.

Developing Communications Skills

The entire communications program must be built upon sound foundations that include (1) demonstrated willingness of all executives to communicate in a timely way all information that affects the organization, its work, and its employees; and (2) policies and objectives that support and augment top management's sincere desire for a vital communications program.

Maintenance of the communications program depends on (1) training managers in the understanding necessary for improving their skills of communicating, (2) checking activities to appraise the effectiveness of communications, and (3) altering the communications program as circumstances require.

Much so-called human relations training is actually communications training. Specifically, managers may study and practice oral communication, effective speaking, report writing, and methods of giving orders and reprimands—skills that enhance leadership and develop better managers.

Yet communications training is inadequate if it overemphasizes one-way communication. The art of listening and understanding must also be cultivated. The ability to listen with genuine understanding is rare among executives and supervisors, but it can be acquired through practice. However, the training process is difficult because it leads to an incisive examination of the relationships of people to each other. Listening develops different relationships from those of habitual nonlistening behavior.

Technical or professional jargon often inhibits clear communication. For example:

Message from the Army Corps of Engineers:
If it snows heavily, federal officials should use a "four-sided matrix" to "monitor the condition of ingress and egress routes," and a decision group working with data from four information providers will "execute their determination."

Translation:
Any of four administrators will call to see if snow has made the roads hazardous. If so, they will ask radio stations to tell federal employees to stay home.

In addition to avoiding the use of jargon, here are some additional ways to make written or oral communications more effective:

1. Listen attentively; find areas of common interest; listen for main ideas.
2. Withhold value judgments about context or delivery, until strategically appropriate.
3. Plan ahead; be prepared; avoid impromptu situations if possible.
4. Keep messages brief.
5. Attend to behavioral cues as well as language or diction.
6. Avoid stereotyping and the assignment of individuals or ideas to rigid categories.
7. "Small talk" has a function, but be aware of misusing it by taking it literally.
8. Distinguish between the desire to know and the need to know.
9. Distinguish among facts, references, and conclusions.
10. Say what you mean or feel, but use judgment in how you do so.
11. Avoid attributing motives to others.
12. Say enough, but leave some things unsaid.
13. Don't shun all conflict, but avoid unnecessary conflict.

SUMMARY

Managers and administrators work in an environment filled with demands posed by the need to receive and disseminate communications in various forms, both written and oral. Immersed in a sea of semantics and symbolic behavior, the manager sorts out what is important to communicate, and what is needed for decision making.

Skill in careful, effective communication can be learned through attentive practice. Deciding what and when to communicate is important to the manager. The desire to communicate is not always present, but when present it goes far toward preventing problems that otherwise clog organizational channels.

Every action of the executive should be accompanied by planning the communication needs and problems associated with it. Appropriate communications thus become a key part of every plan. It is important to determine who will be affected and how, and to smooth the transition or change by well-timed information to those affected and involved. Communications involve emotional overtones as well as factual content. Therefore the manager needs to be aware of all the implications of communication or the failure to communicate.

The bureaucratic model is designed for upward and downward communication, with emphasis on the downward flow. On the other hand, open-system, adaptive models are less formal about communication protocols, the test being what a communication contributes to the end results sought by an individual or a group.

Organizationwide communications are referred to as *management information systems.* Such systems today are built around computers, which far exceed the limited capabilities of humans to find, sort, store, receive, and analyze data. Work flows are regulated and directed by computers, which are widely used also in operations research methods of problem solving.

INCIDENT CASE

A consultant was making some studies in the Ottawa Products Company. Because he was a person who could be trusted, various managers told him different things about a new line of products recently introduced to the market. The plant manager said, "We are in good shape—of course, sales of the new line are lower than we expected. It takes time to work the bugs out and get a new line established."

The assistant plant manager said, "We've got reports from dealers who don't like the new product line. I've tried to leak this idea quietly to my boss, but he doesn't want to hear about it. The new designs were his, and he thinks he's an expert on product design. The sales manager wants me to tell him in no uncertain terms, but that would only make him more determined. If we wait, he'll catch on."

The sales manager said, "The new line is really a dud. If we don't do something, we'll lose dealers, and that would be hard to recover from. It's not my job, though, to tell our top man because he'd blame me for not selling it properly. The assistant plant manager could do it, but he wants to protect the brass from hard knocks."

Questions:

1. What communications problems are evident here?
2. Can the consultant do anything?

QUESTIONS FOR STUDY

1. What is the science of semantics? How did the field of study develop?
2. Give a comprehensive definition of the concept of communication.
3. Explain why managers may actually desire *not* to communicate with others.
4. Draw up a set of criteria that you feel can be used to help decide what to communicate and when.
5. What implications for organization design do you see in the research on communication?
6. In what ways can human relations, morale, and motivation, be affected by communications patterns?
7. Why do communication bottlenecks occur? How can they be avoided or broken up?
8. Why were economics education campaigns considered a failure? Is

knowledge of economics important? If so, how should the company communicate it, if at all?

9. Find some company documents, bulletins, announcements, and other literature, and analyze them as to their probable effectiveness as communicating media.

10. What factors do you feel are conducive to acceptance of particular communications as legitimate and authentic?

11. How can there be too much communication? Why will completely free communication not necessarily produce efficiency of task performance?

12. Describe the main features of a computer. What planning activities precede the installation of a computer?

13. Evaluate the assertion that computers are useful only for routine activities of large volume in large companies.

14. Explain the ways in which it is possible that computerization may affect an organization. Make an analysis of the validity of the arguments you raise.

15. What are the main components of an organizationwide management information system?

16. What major applications exist for computer-processed information?

SELECTED REFERENCES

APPLEBAUM, RONALD L., et al. *The Process of Group Communication.* Chicago: Science Research Associates, 1974.

BASS, BERNARD M., and SAMUEL D. DEEP, eds. *Current Perspectives for Managing Organizations.* Englewood Cliffs, N.J.: Prentice-Hall, Inc., 1970. Chapters 22–24.

BEER, STAFFORD. *Management Science.* Garden City, N.J.: Doubleday & Company, Inc., 1967. Chapters. 6, 7.

BENTLEY, T. *Information, Communication, and the Paperwork Explosion.* New York: McGraw-Hill Book Company, 1976.

BERLO, DAVID K. *The Process of Communication.* New York: Holt, Rinehart and Winston, Inc., 1960.

BIRKLE, JOHN R., and RONALD YEARSLEY. *Computer Applications in Management.* New York: John Wiley & Sons, Inc., 1976.

BRENNAN, JOHN. *The Conscious Communicator: Making Communication Work in the Work Place.* Reading, Mass.: Addison-Wesley Publishing Co., Inc., 1974.

BUENING, CHARLES R. *Communicating on the Job: A Practical Guide for Supervisors.* Reading, Mass.: Addison-Wesley Publishing Co., Inc., 1974.

BURCH, J. G., and F. R. STRATER. *Information Systems: Theory and Practice.* New York: John Wiley & Sons, Inc. 1974.

DAVIS, GORDON B., and GORDON C. EVEREST, eds. *Readings in Management Information Systems.* New York: McGraw-Hill Book Company, 1976.

EMERY, F. E., ed. *Systems Thinking.* London: Penguin Books Ltd., 1969.

FABUN, DON. *Communications: The Transfer of Meaning.* Beverly Hills, Calif.: Glencoe Press, A Division of Benziger Bruce & Glencoe, Inc., 1972.

GOLDHABER, GERALD M. *Organizational Communication.* Dubuque, Iowa: W. C. Brown, 1974.

HAMPTON, DAVID L., ed. *Modern Management: Issues and Ideas.* Belmont, Calif.: Dickenson Publishing Company, 1968. Pp. 189–219.

HUSEMAN, RICHARD C., CAL M. LOGUE, and DWIGHT L. FRESHLEY, eds. *Readings in Interpersonal and Organizational Communication,* 3rd ed. Boston: Holbrook Press, 1977.

KEEFE, WILLIAM F. *Open Minds: The Forgotten Side of Communication.* New York: AMACOM, 1975.

KOEHLER, JERRY W., KARL W. ANATOL, and RONALD L. APPLEBAUM. *Organizational Communication: Behavioral Perspectives.* New York: Holt, Rinehart and Winston, 1976.

LEWIS, PHILLIP V. *Organizational Communication: The Essence of Effective Management.* Columbus, Ohio: Grid, Inc., 1975.

LAWLER, EDWARD E., III, and JOHN G. RHODE. *Information and Control in Organizations.* Pacific Palisades, Calif.: Goodyear Publishing Company, 1976.

MINTZBERG, HENRY. *The Nature of Managerial Work.* New York: Harper and Row, Publishers, 1973. Chapter 6.

OWEN, JAMES L., PAUL A. PAGE, and GORDON I. ZIMMERMAN. *Communication in Organizations.* St. Paul: West Publishing Company, 1976.

NIXON, S. R. *Handbook of Data Processing Administration Operations and Procedures.* New York: AMACOM, 1976.

RADLEY, G. W. *Management Information Systems.* New York: Intext Educational Publishers, 1974.

ROSENBURG, JERRY M. *The Computer Prophets.* New York: Macmillan Publishing Co., Inc., 1969.

ROGERS, EVERETT M. *Communication in Organizations.* New York: The Free Press, 1976.

ROSS, JOEL E. *Modern Management and Information Systems.* Reston, Va.: Reston Publishing Company, Inc., 1976.

SCHNEIDER, ARNOLD E., WILLIAM C. DONAGHY, and PAMELA J. NEWMAN. *Organizational Communication.* New York: McGraw-Hill Book Company, 1975.

SELIGMAN, BEN B. *Most Notorious Victory.* New York: The Free Press, 1967.

SIMON, HERBERT A. *The Shape of Automation for Men and Management.* New York: Harper and Row, Publishers, 1965.

STAW, BARRY M., and GERALD R. SALANCIK. *New Directions in Organization Behavior.* Chicago: St. Clair Press, 1977. Chapter 6.

THAYER, LEE. *Communication and Communication Systems.* Homewood, Ill.: Richard D. Irwin, Inc., 1968.

VARDAMAN, GEORGE, and PATRICIA VARDAMAN. *Communication in Modern Organizations.* New York: John Wiley & Sons, Inc., 1973.

VOICH, DAN, HOMER J. MOTTICE, and WILLIAM A. SHRODE. *Information Systems for Operations and Management.* Cincinnati: South-Western Publishing Company, 1976.

WEAVER, BARBARA N., and WILEY L. BISHOP. *The Corporate Memory.* New York: Wiley-Interscience, 1974.

WOFFORD, JERRY, EDWARD A. GERLOFF, and ROBERT C. CUMMINS. *Organizational Communications.* New York: McGraw-Hill Book Company, 1977.

Chapter 24

Managerial Ethics and Social Responsibility

Without work all life goes rotten. But when work is soulless, life stifles and dies.
—*Albert Camus*

Blessed be he who has found his work; let him ask no other blessedness.
—*Thomas Carlyle*

This place isn't organized enough to be Machiavellian.　　—*Anonymous*

CHAPTER GUIDE

"I never dreamed this could happen to us," says Daniel C. Searle, chairman of drug-maker G. D. Searle & Co., his voice trailing off sadly. The traditionally low-profile Skokie (Ill.) company was shaken to its roots in July when its integrity was challenged at televised hearings of the Senate subcommittee on health, headed by Edward M. Kennedy (D-Mass.). The hearings involved Food & Drug Administration charges that Searle midhandled research data on two of its top-selling drugs, Aldactone and Flagyl.

The controversy continues to plague the company since the findings of the Kennedy committee have been turned over to the Justice Department for possible criminal action and the FDA is reinvestigating all Searle research data filed since 1968.

Although some Searle executives refer to the Senate hearings as a "circus," the experience was traumatic enough to force the company to make basic changes in its research practices and its relations with regulatory agencies and the public. It has:

(1) Established a corporate committee of social scientists to study economic and political trends and determine how these are likely to affect Searle.
(2) Started to educate employees on major issues, ranging from drug pricing to

the workings of free enterprise, and is urging employees to take more active roles in local civic affairs.

(3) Begun to update its corporate research standards and to install an audit system to insure compliance.

(4) Set up a council of Searle managers to review community relations and public attitudes toward business and to recommend ways to deal with these problems.

(5) Shifted the regulatory compliance function from the division to corporate level to clarify communications and improve cooperation with the FDA and other government agencies.

(6) Hired Timmons & Co., the Washington lobbyists, to gain more insight into what is happening in Congress and to push Searle's views more effectively.*

Questions to keep in mind as you read this chapter:

1. How do you assess the value of the company's remedial actions?
2. What are the principal elements involved in the socially responsible behavior of a corporation?

Within an organization are reflected many of the characteristics of society as a whole. The organization is a subculture of the larger society; thus sentiments and attitudes prevailing outside are exhibited by the people inside. Yet the organization also influences their feelings, beliefs, attitudes, and values. Organizations prefer values that strengthen it in relation to its environment of competitive and economic forces. They reinforce cohesion by reinforcing guidelines that suggest appropriate and acceptable behavior; they help establish organizational unity and identity and sharpen the distinctions between "we" and "they."

Although people's attitudes, beliefs, and feelings are deep seated, having been inculcated by school and home over years of maturation, organizations may at least shape certain situational applications or interpretations of these sentiments, especially where there are no obvious conflicts with society's views. Thus a company's advocacy of "free enterprise" poses no direct dilemma, because such a view is congruent with opinions outside and because such a sentiment can be verbalized without specifying any precise behavior for individuals. If on the other hand a company desires its employees to view labor unions as an evil, employees may find such a concept unconvincing, for both outside and inside experiences have, for many, been quite the reverse.

*As reported in *Business Week*, September 8, 1975, pp. 62–64.

Remarkable changes have occurred in society at large. There has been substantial and covert resistance to the postures of the establishment. The level of education in all sectors of society has risen, and the past two decades have seen the increasing importance of consumerism, government regulation, human rights, egalitarianism, assertiveness, and autonomy of the individual. All this has led to changes in the way organizations function in relation to people and to society.

This chapter explores two of the most critical types of problems posed by these changes: (1) issues of social responsibility, and (2) the ethics of managerial decision and action.

SOCIAL RESPONSIBILITY

Much of today's questioning of the social responsibility of business has centered on the large corporation as a type of social institution. One should not, however, lose sight of the importance of social responsibility for small business, professionals, and government, and other public or quasi-public agencies.

Social responsibility in business has been an issue for over a century. However, there has been a change of emphasis. Earlier discussions centered on three areas: (1) distinctions between public and private ethics, that is, how managers resolved ethical questions as individuals when they differed for the apparent good of the organizations, (2) the responsibility of employers toward employees by reason of their greater power and wealth; and (3) the need for the organization to be a good citizen of the community by supporting the arts and giving money to philanthropic causes. Although these areas continue to pose problems, they focus upon expected ethical behavior of individual managers. Now, however, the emphasis goes beyond this level to demand that organizations themselves tackle and solve the problems of society.[1]

The pressures on organizations for greater social responsibility come from two main sources. Through its regulatory and goal-setting powers, the federal government is the most important source. The second source is action groups, such as those formed by environmentalists or consumers, which not only bring pressures of their own, but also exert a strong influence on what state or federal governments do.

Awareness of Social Responsibility

There is little doubt that today's managers are concerned with their roles as members of society. They control great wealth and power. Yet they own relatively little of that wealth and power, fulfilling a function

---

[1]Peter F. Drucker, *People and Performance: The Best of Peter Drucker* (New York: Harper's College Press, 1977), pp. 237–238.

of trusteeship for the owners of capital and, indirectly, for society. In addition, many managers are increasingly concerned with what the role of the large corporation should be in a highly complex industrial society. Thus there are two kinds of social responsibility—that of the corporation itself as an instrument designed to serve the ends of society, and that of managers as employees and as trustees empowered by owners to run the organization in the quest for profit and other goals.

There are three reasons for the growing social concerns of managers: (1) they have been *forced* to be more concerned because of informed public opinion, governmental regulation, threats of public ownership, the better education of individuals, the rise of labor unions, and increasingly effective communication among people; (2) they have been *persuaded* to become more concerned by the fact of being sharers and participants in the developing attitudes and values of people in society and by the growth of knowledge, managerial skills, and the need to grapple with problems of change in society; and (3) the separation of ownership and control has set up conditions favorable to growing concern, such as the values associated with the professional point of view.[2] The statements of managers themselves attest to the growth of socially responsible values, both their own and those of their companies. These views are expressed in books by company presidents, government officials, and others, which address such matters as trusteeship, views on the right use of power and wealth, the meaning of professional status and associated constraints upon businessmen, and the belief that profits, business growth, security of assets, and service to consumers are the best way to maximize social contributions. Many assert that a systematic management philosophy should be made more explicit.[3]

Social Responsibility: Pro and Con

At superficial levels, social responsibility is a self-evident good. Like motherhood, everyone can be for it. But when we probe the meaning of the phrase more deeply, as managers who espouse it must, we encounter basic dilemmas and conflicts about how managers achieve social responsibility.

A problem for decision makers is that there are no clear guidelines for the socially responsible action. There can be no certainty that one given decision will benefit society more than another, and the various

[2]Howard R. Bowen, *Social Responsibilities of the Businessman* New York: Harper, 1953); Marquis W. Childs and Douglas Cater, *Ethics in a Business Society* (New York: Harper, 1954).

[3]See, for example, Thomas G. Spates, *Human Values Where People Work* (New York: Harper, 1960); Abram T. Collier, *Management, Man, and Values* (New York: Harper, 1960); Thomas J. Watson, Jr., *A Business and Its Beliefs* (New York: McGraw-Hill, 1963); *Journal of Contemporary Business* 4 (Summer 1975), entire issue.

pressure groups have different and often conflicting concepts of social responsibility. The problems of society have existed for a long time; they are seemingly intractable, highly complex, and baffling. Often the remedies attempted seem to worsen a problem or generate new ones. A nuclear plant may increase available power, but pose enormous problems of waste disposal.

The dilemma is that not everything good for the organization is good for society, and what is good for society may not be good for the organization. There are many who believe that current pressures give too much weight to social objectives, causing managers to let up on traditional standards of organizational performance to achieve those social objectives. Clearly such a dilemma must be resolved by judgments and trade-offs negotiated on a case-to-case basis.

Another dilemma is whether managers can justify, legally or otherwise, any use of organizational resources other than for the direct interests of owners. That is, do managers have the right to use organizational assets for social purposes? If corporations fail to accept some measure of social responsibility, the environment conducive to their survival and growth may be endangered. But if the corporation goes too far in assuming a burden of social responsibility, it can weaken itself through spending its energies and resources on matters not related to the profit motive. Thus the manager must be conscious of the dangers inherent in philosophies that stress commitments to extreme positions for or against social responsibility.[4]

The case against social responsibility is based chiefly on hard-boiled management that puts the needs, interests, rights, and values of the organization ahead of all others. Such an emphasis discounts the role of the corporation as "balancing" the many interests and claims of non-owner groups; its philosophy becomes legalistic, independent, and self-centered. Profit-centered behavior is the only permissible behavior; making money is the only acceptable goal.[5]

The case for social responsibility for most managers is to be found in pursuing that responsibility in such a way as to enhance the attainment of profit, production, or service objectives. That is, the conflict between social purpose and economic performance is more apparent than real, and there are grounds for believing that the two realms of effort are compatible. A growing sense of social responsibility is reflected in greater awareness of organizational purpose and social ends; in the development of professional attitudes of managers in improving organizational climate through more attention to such goals as human rela-

[4]Richard Eells and Clarence Walton, *Conceptual Foundations of Business* (Homewood, Ill.: Irwin, 1961), pp. 456–457.

[5]Ibid., pp. 458–474. See also Milton Friedman, "The Social Responsibility of Business Is to Increase Its Profits," *New York Times Magazine*, September 13, 1970; Gilbert Burck, "The Hazards of Corporate Responsibility," *Fortune*, June 1973.

tions, job satisfaction, individual development, and democratic rights; in recognition of the potentialities of power and wealth for both good and evil; in closer involvement of business firms with social agencies and other institutions; and in increases in corporate donations to education, foundations, community welfare, and service agencies.[6]

Critique of Business as a Social Institution

All social institutions have come under severe criticism about their failures to measure up to the enormous range of serious problems in society. Such problems as crime, corruption, drug addiction, resource depletion, air and water pollution, war, and disease continue or worsen despite the resources devoted to their solution. The resulting frustration has led to disillusionment about the effectiveness of the political, social, and economic means of improving the human lot on earth. Managers and their organizations are now facing the brunt of this criticism. It is not entirely a matter of finding scapegoats; there are deep undercurrents that press for extensive change in every aspect of our lives. Nowhere is this more clear than in the business world, where business—more accurately "big business"—is the target of attacks that range from cynicism to radical upheaval.

Critics of corporate social responsibility are often cynical about the motives of businessmen. They cannot believe that businessmen's motives in social responsibility arise from anything less than pure selfishness, aggrandizement, or exploitation of the gullible public. "No one is less realistic than the cynic," says Drucker.[7] Yet cynicism often hides behind a mask of realism. The "practical-man" orthodoxy acclaims the realist and the cynic without discriminating between them, hence advancing both and creating a fallacy. Managers who can recognize cynicism in themselves and others can help keep the distinctions clear. Cynicism, however, must not be equated with skepticism. A healthy skepticism prevents deals and naïveté from obstructing the company's efforts. But cynicism destroys the bases for effective managerial action because it is essentially negative and defeatist in its orientation.

Radical criticism of business enterprise holds that only a radical restructuring of the entire fabric of society will suffice to solve society's problems. The radical attack has been long on criticism but short on specific and valid proposals for action. Radical arguments are strident

---

[6]George A. Steiner, "Institutionalizing Corporate Social Institutions," *Business Horizons* 18 (December 1975); Archie B. Carroll (ed.), *Managing Corporate Social Responsibilities* (Boston: Little, Brown, 1977); Stahrl W. Edmunds, "Unifying Concepts in Social Responsibility," *Academy of Management Review* 2 (January 1977), 37–45.

[7]Peter F. Drucker, *The Practice of Management* (New York: Harper, 1954), p. 157. See also Benjamin M. Selekman, *A Moral Philosophy for Management* (New York: McGraw-Hill, 1959), part III.

and emotional, and some include violent overthrow as a means to the sought-for ends. During the turbulence of the sixties, such views got a hearing, with substantial support from younger age groups. But in the seventies, although serious criticisms remain, the activism has faded, replaced by the steady pressure of interest groups for gradual change.[8]

The extent of the gradual but persistent changes occurring throughout society are as yet largely unappreciated by businessmen.[9] Lodge argues that a new ideology is supplanting the old. He sees the traditional Lockean ideology—individualism, property rights, competition, limited government, and scientific specialization—that supported our social institutions in the nineteenth and twentieth centuries as dangerously eroded, so that it no longer makes traditional authority legitimate. A new ideology is emerging, based on managers deriving authority from the managed; corporations will serve community needs rather than community desires, and managers will need to learn how to think in terms of interdependencies in all things.[10] Similar views have been expressed by Anshen,[11] Levitt,[12] and Bell.[13]

The responses of managers to criticism, whether radical or otherwise, have been generally inept. Defending the status quo has always been difficult, and managers have appeared weak in confronting specific issues, particularly those advanced by radical advocates. Yet defenses there are, and some are made eloquently. Jacoby, for example, has argued that the corporation has served us well, and although it can be improved, it need not be destroyed as a valuable economic institution.[14] Lundborg argues that the future need not shock us,[15] and Beichman decries the societal distortions that are used to support radical change.[16] Maddox puts the doom-sayers in society in a different perspective.[17] But among the refuters of extreme views managers are few indeed. It is difficult for them to transcend the thinking of the Lockean ideology.

---

[8]For a review of the criticism of business, see Dalton E. McFarland, "Management and its Critics: A Look at Social Pluralism," *Journal of Business Research* 2 (October 1974), 395–408. For radical perspectives on business and other types of organizations, see Charles Perrow, *The Radical Attack on Business* (New York: Harcourt, 1972).

[9]For example, see C. Spencer Clark, "Management's Perceptions of Corporate Social Responsibilities," *Journal of Contemporary Business* 4 (Summer 1975), 15–30.

[10]George C. Lodge, *The New American Ideology* (New York: Knopf, 1975).

[11]Melvin Anshen (ed.), *Managing the Socially Responsible Corporation* (New York: Macmillan, 1974).

[12]Theodore Levitt, *The Third Sector: New Tactics for a Responsive Society* (New York: AMACOM, 1973).

[13]Daniel Bell, *The Coming of the Post-Industrial Society* (New York: Basic, 1973).

[14]Neil H. Jacoby, *Corporate Power and Social Responsibility* (New York: Macmillan, 1973).

[15]Lewis B. Lundborg, *Future Without Shock* (New York: Norton, 1974).

[16]Arnold Beichman, *Nine Lies About America* (New York: The Library Press, 1972). See also Ben J. Wattenberg, *The Real America* (New York: Doubleday Bros., Inc., 1974).

[17]John Maddox, *The Doomsday Syndrome* (New York: McGraw-Hill, 1972).

Social Audits

Although the extent of an organization's social responsibility is a subjective concept that is not susceptible to effective measurement, efforts in that direction are increasing. One recommendation is that companies be required to prepare *social* as well as financial balance sheets. Granting the difficulties of quantification, Elbing and Elbing argue that measurements that go beyond the purely economic should be made to depict the extent of the organization's social contributions and liabilities. For example, we could perhaps measure the enhancement of natural resources, compared to their depletion; the socialization processes of citizens, the effects of the corporation on its community, or the gains from the development of human resources.[18]

Social audits are similar to financial audits: they generally employ independent experts; they set up a continuous monitoring system by which to measure the effects of organizational activities on society; and although subjective factors are always present, social audits generally cover areas that can be quantified. For example, scientists and engineers are developing ways of measuring the extent of pollution, environmental danger, or waste-disposal problems. Such matters as the effects of personnel policies on ethnic minorities are hard to measure, but are nevertheless important.

Although measurement problems are difficult, some believe that it is organizational politics rather than technical difficulties that inhibit the use of social audits. This view highlights the fact that measurement or review carries emotional and other overtones that in turn affect the behavior that is being measured.[19]

The concept of the social audit for monitoring, measuring, or appraising social performance is at least 35 years old. The use of this concept has evolved through the three stages shown in Figure 24-1. The first stage envisioned a governmental evaluation by an outsider, and defined social performance largely in economic terms. The second stage was the concept of the management evaluating itself and the organization's social performance. In the third and current stage, audits cover a wider range of activities and serve multiple purposes, such as satisfying the

[18]Alvar O. Elbing, Jr., and Carol J. Elbing, *The Value Issues of Business* (New York: McGraw-Hill, 1967). See also Lee J. Seidler and Lynn L. Siedler (eds.), *Social Accounting* (New York: Wiley, 1975); Meinoff Dierkes and Raymond A. Bauer (eds.), *Corporate Social Accounting* (New York: Praeger, 1973); Ralph W. Estes, *Corporate Social Accounting* (New York: Wiley, 1976).

[19]William C. Frederick and Mildred S. Meyers, "The Hidden Politics of Social Auditing," *Business and Society Review* 11 (Autumn 1974). See also John Humble, *The Social Responsibility Audit: A Management Tool for Survival* (London: Foundation for Business Responsibility, 1973), and John J. Corson and George A. Steiner, *Measuring Business Social Performance: The Corporate Social Audit* (New York: Committee for Economic Development, 1974).

corporate conscience, improving social programs, enhancing public relations, and increasing the credibility of the firm.[20]

An approach similar to social audits, but more closely relating social costs to economic costs, is social cost-benefit analysis, which develops an assessment profile that can be used as a guide to improvement programs.[21]

An example of the use of social audits to check on specific problems is provided by the Monsanto Company, which used a *special purpose audit* to investigate whether it had engaged in bribery or illegal political contributions overseas, as a number of firms had done. In assuring stockholders that nothing illegal had occurred, the chairman of the board said that the company "does and will act with integrity," and that Monsanto personnel "are expected to comply fully with company policies and the laws of each of the nations in which we do business." The audit team was headed by an outside director and consisted of a subcommittee of the firm's standing audit committee. The committee also included a partner of the accounting firm retained for financial audits.[22]

Structural Development

Another way to improve the social responsibility of management is to set up a top-level unit with special concerns in that area. In a sense every manager should be a "keeper of the corporate conscience," but many organizations have found it helpful to combine a number of specific functions into a special type of unit with staff authority. An example is shown in Figure 24-2.

Social Responsibility in Focus

Issues of social responsibility will doubtless continue to be vigorously debated, and with mixed feelings. In 1975 the *Wall Street Journal* asserted that morbidity had overtaken the concept of social responsibility. The evidence cited included the cancellation of a national seminar on the subject for lack of participants, and the discontinuation of the *Business and Society Newsletter*. The editorial expressed doubts that the idea of corporate social responsibility has had impact on the business community.[23] A wave of protests followed. Arguing the opposite

[20]Archie B. Carroll and George W. Beiler, "Landmarks in the Evolution of the Social Audit," *Academy of Management Journal* 18 (September 1975), 589–599.

[21]Thomas A. Klein, *Social Costs and Benefits of Business* (Englewood Cliffs, N.J.: Prentice-Hall, 1977).

[22]*St. Louis Post-Dispatch,* April 23, 1976.

[23]*Wall Street Journal,* January 16, 1975; January 17, 1975; February 23, 1975.

Subject	Kreps's 1940 Audit	Bowen's 1953 Audit	Today's Audit
Definition	Acid test of business performance	Evaluation of the performance of business from a social point of view	Measurement of companies' progress toward social goals
Purpose	Government evaluation of business's social performance	The firm's evaluation of its social performance	The firm's evaluation of its social performance
Apparent motives	Establish criteria for future evaluatons Establish the technique for society to influence business performance	Bring social point of view to management	1. Satisfying the corporate conscience 2. Improving financial wisdom of social programs 3. Public relations 4. To enhance credibility of the business firm
Nature of issues audited	Quantifiable areas: 1. Employment 2. Production 3. Consumer effort commanded 4. Consumer funds absorbed	Company policy toward: 1. Prices 2. Wages 3. Research and development 4. Advertising	Company performance in: 1. Minority employment 2. Pollution/environment 3. Working conditions 4. Community relations

	5. Payrolls 6. Dividends and interest	5. Public relations 6. Human relations 7. Community relations 8. Economic stabilization	5. Philanthropic contributions 6. Consumerism issues
Use	By society to assess business performance	By management to assess its performance	Divided between two schools of thought. One group feels it should be only for management's use. Another group feels it should be a public document.
Methodology	Evaluation of public information employing economic indices	Judgmental appraisal of company policy	Monitor, measure, and appraise all aspects of social performance using various techniques—cost vs. benefit, accounting, etc.
By whom conducted	A government bureau	Internal personnel or an industry agency	Internal personnel or a consultant

FIGURE 24-1. Evolution of Social Audit Concepts.

Source: Archie B. Carroll and George W. Beiler, "Landmarks in the Evolution of the Social Audit," Academy of Management Journal 18 (September 1975), 598. Used by permission.

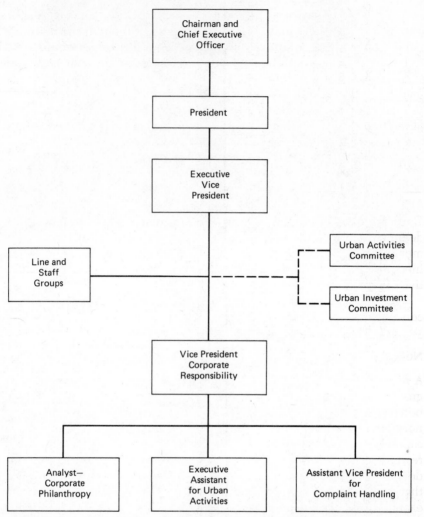

FIGURE 24-2. Organization of the Social Responsibility Functions in a Large Insurance Company.

case, rebuttals stressed the need to judge corporations by their actions, not by the quantity of media references or attendance at meetings. A consulting firm offering a "Corporate Responsibility Planning Service" proclaimed that on the basis of philanthropic actions:

> Corporate responsibility is very much alive. In 1975, three out of every four companies are maintaining or increasing both departmental and contributions budgets from the 1974 levels. The average department budget increase is 12.5%; the average contributions budget increase is slightly more than 19%.

The illegal behavior of many corporations and their managers has outraged citizens and managers alike, and has brought the closer regulation that many also deplore but accept. Behaving legally would seem to be a minimum requirement of socially responsibile managers and corporations, to say nothing of devising safeguards against violations of law and policy, and developing planned contributions to society's problem solving. Socially irresponsible decisions have their roots in the fabric of society as a whole, but this does not absolve corporations from the need for social concern and more acceptable behavior.

MANAGERIAL NORMS, ETHICS, AND VALUES

Corporate acts, being the manifestation of great wealth and power, are dealt with through the due process of law and the machinery of governmental regulation. Individual acts and decisions must also be examined, for the behavior of the organization is compounded out of cumulative effects of the work of human beings.

We will now examine the behavior of managers in terms of three concepts: norms, values, and ethics.

Norms

A norm represents a common acknowledgment by most members of a group (though not necessarily by all of them) that the members ought to behave in certain ways under certain circumstances.[24] Conformity to norms brings an individual certain rewards that are within the group's capability to bestow. Variation from a norm carries a risk that those rewards will be withheld or sanctions will be employed against the deviant. Group members feel rewarded when their own behavior and that of others conforms to the ideal prescribed in the norm.[25] An example of a norm established by a group is the level of output that a work team deems satisfactory. The group often sets a norm that differs from the standard expected by the supervisor. The norm is compelling to the group members, for the reward for conforming to it is bestowed by peers. Another type of norm found in some organizations is that of dress codes. A person appearing in a sports coat and slacks might be looked down on by peers—and, in this case, also by those above him, to whom he looks for recognition and approbation. Thus a norm is a kind of standard, developed by a group, against which behavior can be measured. It includes ways of reinforcing desirable or conforming behavior and of ruling out undesired behavior.

[24]George C. Homans, *The Human Group* (New York: Harcourt, 1950), p. 123.
[25]George C. Homans, *Social Behavior: Its Elementary Forms* (New York: Harcourt, 1961), p. 46.

Norms fulfill a special social function—that of harmonizing the relations of people by authenticating what is and is not appropriate. They exist both for the total organization and for its subgroups.

Values

Organizations possess values of their own, as well as being the instruments through which broader social values are applied from the culture at large. Many organizational values are parallel to the broader ones; others are related to the nature of the organization or to its classification as to product or industry; still others are unique and particular to a single organization.

The organization institutionalizes norms, values, and ethical standards by incorporating them into management practice. Service awards, for example, show the extent to which a company values longevity of employment and the loyalty of its employees; a bank clerk handling other people's money learns that the bank values honesty and accuracy; the factory employee learns that the company and the boss value productivity and efficiency; the union lets its members know that it values solidarity and brotherhood. Such values reflect the expectations and their relative weights that various claimants exert on an individual's time and attention.

Whereas norms are codes or standards of conduct a group espouses, values describe what individuals consider important. Values may be expressed verbally, or implied in the way people behave. They represent preferences for particular things, conditions, or situations, as compared with others. A person's values describe things or ideas that count the most to him, and that he will strive for or make sacrifices to maintain or achieve.

The extent to which a person will work or sacrifice, or otherwise behave so as to reinforce and maintain the value, is a measure of its strength for him. Thus a person who insists on going fishing instead of working overtime appears to value leisure and recreation more than pay.

Values must be distinguished from beliefs. Beliefs are ideas about what is real. People's beliefs are what they "know"—what can be tested and found to be true, false, incomplete, and so on. Values, which consist of the degree to which persons define what is right, fair, just, or desirable, are not subject to scientific or objective validation. Most human discourse consists of a mixture of both beliefs and values; people do not always distinguish between what they think they know and what they like or dislike. In our society, however, most people think they are rational and objective. Therefore, they have "reasons" for the values they hold, and they usually express only those values for which they have reasons. Moreover, behavior that departs from traditional, established, or announced values is generally rationalized, the aim being to gain acceptance for the behavior.[26]

Because values take the form of opinions, concepts, or ideas that people hold to be important, they appear to possess an inherent or self-evident rightness that removes them from dispute. Most managers hold firm values—as to how people should be treated, or how the business should be conducted, or how the economic, political, and social system should operate—that they regard as uncontestable.

Values may be stated explicitly or may be implicit in the actions of managers. Often the explicit values are those that are most widely accepted in a public sense or that are most closely tied to the wider society. Actual behavior may reflect values somewhat different than those offered for public consumption. There is often a situational willingness to ignore or modify the explicit values. For example, values surrounding the idea of "free enterprise" in our economic system do not deter the marketing executive whose job is to destroy the competitive strength of other firms in his industry. Or a supervisor may affirm democratic values while cracking down on the creative impulses of group members. The fact that implicit values may differ from ideal or expected values does not invalidate the values of either type. Managers may derive guidance and satisfaction from the values they are expected to hold, even though they cannot or do not always live up to them. For example, a manager may agree that people should be treated kindly, yet at times will deal harshly with subordinates.

Values exist in a scale or hierarchy of their relative importance. Patterns of values are called value systems; there may be an organization's value system or a society's value system, as well as an individual's value system. The integrity of an individual is based on consistency of behavior with respect to personal value systems. Managers do not merely follow a system of values varying as to strength and importance—they also, from time to time, shift the ordering of these values or vary the intensity with which certain values are held compared to others. Under certain conditions, therefore, a manager may rearrange values that are potentially in conflict—putting the high-order value (treating people kindly) temporarily below a lesser value (climbing the hierarchy). This does not necessarily mean, however, a change in the value system; if need be, the manager finds rationalizations "explaining" the actions actually taken.

These complexities in the hierarchy of values make the task of describing and analyzing them difficult. Managerial values have not been described in detail, or completely cataloged. But an awareness of value systems and how they affect behavior in organizations is of

[26]Gunnar Myrdal, *Value in Social Theory* (London: Trench, Trubner & Co., 1958), pp. 71, 119–164.

utmost importance. Values are broad guides to action, rather than correct, simple, straightforward rules that govern absolutely every detail of the manager's work. Values do not necessarily control behavior or assure reliable predictions of behavior, but they are influential and are therefore vital to understanding organizational behavior. The element of judgment is important, giving considerable scope in the interpretation and application of values.[27]

Peers and Colleagues

We have seen that, in the case of norms and such matters as status and prestige, what one's fellows think is important to how one behaves. This is also the case with values. However, individuals may verbalize and even act upon values that are important throughout a group without permanent or genuine changes in their personal value structures. Yet there tends to be congruence between the values of an individual and those of colleagues and peers, as we see in the professions, where enforcement of appropriate value systems is largely in the hands of one's colleagues. Teachers, lawyers, doctors, and dentists all develop and apply similar beliefs, attitudes, and values derived from the groups of peers and colleagues with whom they are professionally associated.

An individual in a work group tends to conform to the group's norms as long as he values the friendship and approval of his associates or fears the possibility that they will cut him off from rights, privileges, and benefits they can offer. In the case of values, the individual feels an intimate involvement with others: a nation, a society, or even a business firm or work team. Values strengthen, protect, and solidify a group, and although departure from values may not result in immediate penatly, a sense of guilt or estrangement may follow. Vague, disturbing doubts notify the individual that he has violated the long-range wisdom of the group.

Ethics

Ethics is a branch of systematic philosophical inquiry. Joad defines it as a theoretical treatment of moral phenomena that fall into three classifications: moral judgments, moral emotion, and moral volition. Ethics concerns "right" or "wrong" conduct by individuals. Ethical behavior is that which "ought" to prevail. The central ethical phenomenon of concern to philosophers is moral judgment, which subsumes moral emotion and moral volition. Moral judgment is the opinion that something is "right" or "wrong." Moral emotion is the feeling of remorse and self-disapproval, or satisfaction and approval, that accompanies judgments of what is right or wrong. Moral volition includes choices and

---

[27]See Elbing and Elbing, *Value Issues.*

decisions between alternatives that are based on ideas of right or wrong. In ethical studies philosophers seek truths about ideas of right and wrong, good and evil.[28]

Many social institutions are concerned with the moral aspects of human behavior. The emotional and volitional elements are in large part the province of psychology and physiology; organized religions concern themselves with moral judgments. Schools, families, and churches teach moral behavior. Thus managers concerned with the morality of decisions have a basis for testing beliefs and values against those of society. But the phenomena of ethics remain the special province of philosophers rather than scientists, and the achievement of a "scientific morality," with universal rightness or wrongness, is generally regarded as impossible.[29]

Ethical judgments, like norms and values, are usually accompanied by strong emotions. When they are challenged or attacked, feelings of defensiveness are provoked; feelings of hostility, anger, and aggressiveness may be directed at the attacker. When individuals act in violation of norms, values, or moral standards, such emotions as disapproval, fear, and guilt are likely to occur unless rationalization or other psychological phenomena are used to offset them.

In ethical conduct, there is an implicit awareness of the need to transcend selfishness, greed, and striving exclusively for material wealth. The desire for profit is seldom the sole motive in managerial decisions. As managers become more professionally oriented, and as corporate social consciousness expands, the ethical foundations of managerial actions will increase in importance.[30]

Studies of Ethics in Business

All organizations pose ethical problems for managers. All decisions have ethical aspects. Research on ethical problems, however, has been largely confined to business organizations, no doubt because they are numerous, powerful, close to money and its potential evils, and strongly tied to other institutions in society.

Serious studies of the ethics and ethical attitudes of businessmen reveal much uncertainty about what constitutes ethical behavior, and even about whether ethics are important. Clearly we can see that ethical behavior does not consist of clear-cut choices between right and wrong. Managers incorporate ethical implications into decisions along with other criteria only if they so choose, and many do not.

Research on ethics is typically in the form of questionnaire surveys.

[28]C. E. M. Joad, *Philosophy* (New York: Fawcett World Library, 1962), chap. 6; see also P. H. Nowell-Smith, *Ethics* (London: Penguin, 1954), chaps. 1, 2.

[29]Nowell-Smith, *Ethics.*

[30]Leonard Silk and David Vogel, *Ethics and Profits: The Crisis of Confidence in American Business* (New York: Simon & Schuster, 1976).

Three studies, which reveal the general nature of such surveys, give rise to disquieting feelings about the ethical beliefs of managers.

One of the earliest studies is that of Father Raymond Baumhart, who surveyed 1,700 subscribers to the *Harvard Business Review*. Most respondants acknowledged that some practices were unethical, but many were uncertain as to exactly what determined their ethical behavior. Twenty-five per cent cited unfair pricing as an ethical problem; 25 per cent also cited bribes, gifts, and call girls as unethical practices. Forty-three per cent said they would use inside information to better themselves financially; 20 per cent would pad their expense accounts; 50 per cent would hire a competitor's employee to learn trade secrets. The study also found that older managers professed higher ethical standards than younger ones, but that there was no connection between formal education or religious affiliation and the ethical sensitivity of the managers.[31]

A study by Father John F. Clark found results similar to Baumhart's. He found in a sample of 100 training program participants a general sense of ethics, but weak positions on specific issues.[32]

More recently, Carroll surveyed 238 managers, asking them to indicate agreement or disagreement with selected ethical propositions. Sixty-five per cent agreed with the statement that "managers today feel under pressure to compromise personal standards to achieve company goals." Seventy-eight per cent agreed with the statement "I can conceive of a situation where you have sound ethics from top to bottom, but because of pressures from the top to achieve results, the person down the line compromises. Three fourths of the managers agreed that the social responsibility of business is a question of ethics. On whether illegal campaign contributions are realistic examples of business ethics today, 54 per cent said yes and 40 per cent said no. It was chiefly the top managers who disagreed, whereas middle and lower managers agreed.[33]

Remedies for Questionable Ethics

There are no easy solutions to the problems of corporate crime or corruption. Many feel that punishments for organizations and individuals found quilty are too light. This problem pervades the society at large, and can be dealt with only by the complicated processes by

[31]Raymond Baumhart, S.J., *Ethics in Business* (New York: Holt, 1968).

[32]John W. Clark, S.J., *Religion and Moral Standards of American Businessmen* (Cincinnati: South-Western Publishing Company, 1966).

[33]Archie B. Carroll, "Mangerial Ethics: A Post-Watergate View," *Business Horizons* 17 (April 1975), 75–80. See also James A. Wilson, "Morality and the Contemporary Business System," and George C. S. Benson, "Business Ethics in American Society," in Journal of *Contemporary Business* 4 (Summer 1975), 31–55, 59–74; and "The Pressure to Compromise Personal Ethics," *Business Week*, January 31, 1977, p. 107.

which society acts. Legislative and judicial processes themselves have problems which prevent them from making more headway on substantive and procedural issues.

The matter of managerial ethics and values is even more complex than that of obedience to law. The studies already cited reflect roughly an even split between the number who believe ethics are important and those who do not, and between those who feel current ethics are bad and those who feel behavior is for the most part satisfactory. On the dilemma of illegal payoffs, for example, one survey showed about 75 per cent of the respondents believe bribes and payoffs are not problems in their industries. Fifty two per cent said U.S. companies should adhere to U.S. standards in conducting overseas business, whereas 48 per cent said the commercial modes and standards of the foreign countries should be followed.[34]

Despite the complexities, organizations—particularly large and powerful corporations—are increasing their efforts to include combinations of the following: (1) establishing policies and guidelines for ethical behavior, (2) incorporating ethics and values into processes of education, (3) developing codes of conduct, and (4) using advisors on ethical and moral problems.

Policies and Guidelines on Ethics

Organizations can develop improved ethics by clearly stating their policies toward behavior that is considered unethical. Clear guidelines, with specific ways of handling situations, are needed. To assume that everyone will do the right thing in the absence of such guidelines is to invite laxity in the ethics of decision making.

Much unethical behavior results from uncertainties about what is right for the organization compared to what seems right to individuals. Overambitious managers intent on corporate goals are often willing to use questionable means, and to avoid criticizing, or even knowing, what their subordinates are doing. There is an element of self-protection that leads an individual to questionable ethics in the light of pressures for profit or productivity. Drug company employees, for example, have falsified research data to get a product on the market. In such cases, it is always difficult to find out who is actually liable. Damages are hard to assess even though it is widely believed that corporations should pay for their mistakes. Thus prevention is the better strategy, and this means, at the least, firm policies.[35]

In disseminating policies designed to improve the ethical tone of an

---

[34]"Unusual Foreign Payments: A Survey of the Policies and Products of U.S. Companies Abroad," Report No. 682 (New York: The Conference Board, 1976).

[35]Christopher D. Stone, *Where the Law Ends: The Social Control of Corporate Behavior.* (New York: Harper, 1975).

organization, it is necessary to transcend mere public relations pronouncements. When policies are coupled with strong internal controls, they are translated into more ethical actions.

The waves of scandal, bribery, kickbacks, illegal campaign contributions, fraud, and corruption emerging in the 1970s has engendered a deep distrust of business enterprise. The level of moral anxiety in the public mind is high, and has no doubt led to efforts directed at improvement. Reliance on the economics of the marketplace and on government regulation by law no longer seem adequate to the burgeoning ethical chaos prevalent in society.[36] Ethical demands are today far more complex than ever before. Therefore it is important for organizations to find a way of adhering to standards that blend self-interest and altruism into an acceptable whole.[37]

Educational Influences

Some companies have conducted seminars and conferences on ethics for their managers. This procedure no doubt helps, for it calls attention to the ethical aspect of other problems, provides a sharing of experience, and furnishes an opportunity to explain and reinforce corporate standards and policies.

A more serious problem of education exists in the schools and colleges that train a large proportion of our managers. Today's business schools are talking more about ethics, and are doing more research in the area. There is a dilemma, however. Because ethics boils down to the individual's personal values and standards, but action occurs in the goal-oriented context of the organization, what to do about ethics in the classroom remains a puzzle. One method is to infuse all courses with ethical considerations, something that has been done extensively at places using the case method, as for example in the Harvard Business School. Another tactic is to set up special courses designed to address issues in ethics and social responsibility. The number of courses and programs in this area has been increasing rapidly.[38]

Many have reservations about the extent to which formal courses actually increase ethical sensitivity. Some doubt that ethics can be taught at all. Nevertheless it seems useful for professional schools, such

---

[36]This does not minimize the importance of the need for efforts on the part of government to elevate its own ethical standards, as well as those of corporations and managers. See "Stiffer Rules for Business Ethics," *Business Week,* March 30, 1974, pp. 87–90.

[37]Max Ways, "Business Faces Growing Pressure to Behave Better," *Fortune,* May 1974, 193–195 and 310–320; Andrew Mann, "The Ethics Puzzle," *MBA,* September 1974, 23–25; John A. Newstrom and William A. Ruch, "The Ethics of Management and the Management of Ethics," *MSU Business Topics* 23 (Winter 1975), 29–37.

[38]Mann, *Ethics Puzzle.*

as those in business, law, medicine, engineering, and education, to face the ethical dilemmas that exist in the profession they serve. Practice in ethical decision making can be given through cases so that the student need not discover ethics for the first time after taking a job. Courses can help students clarify and discern their own values, incorporating them into the analysis of all decision problems. But more than courses is needed. The ethical postures of the faculty can also have a substantial influence.[39]

Codes of Conduct

Many organizations have confronted problems of ethical and social responsibility by establishing formal creeds and codes of conduct. In this they are emulating the professions, which have long used codes of ethical conduct to guide the behavior of members. More recently state and federal governmental units have adopted codes as the result of public pressure for better conduct by legislators and other public officials. Trade associations, like the professions, attempt to maintain ethical guidelines for members. Figure 24-3 shows an example of a code of ethics developed by a group of professional management consultants.

The use of codes of ethics by business firms and government agencies is more controversial than in the case of professions and trade associations. Codes are criticized on the grounds that they are unworkable, and are only a public relations gesture. Still others say they are impractical, not worth the effort. On the other hand, a firm that takes no positive ethical stand may be thought to have something to hide.

What the well-managed firm needs to refute the skeptics is a clear, simple, written creed of beliefs as a code of conduct expressing the ideals it strives for. Such a creed becomes a benchmark for judging conduct and recognizing ethical problems. Preparing the code or creed leads to valuable thought and analysis on the part of managers. It is important, however, to get as much general agreement as possible without delaying, stalling, or avoiding entirely the preparation of a code.

There have been occasional movements to establish codes for all managers or for business firms generally. These general approaches have not been successful, and it is not likely that they will be. Codes work better when individual firms or other organizations design their own and keep them current.

[39]Derek Bok, "Can Ethics be Taught?" *Change*, October 1976, 26–30; Edgar H. Schein, "The Problem of Moral Education for the Business Manager," Carl R. Anderson and Martin J. Gannon, (eds.), *Readings in Management: An Organizational Perspective* (Boston: Little, Brown, 1977).

ETHICAL STANDARDS OF PRACTICE

Membership in the Society of Professional Management Consultants is a symbol of experience, competency, and trustworthiness in the profession. These qualities are amplified by the following statements of ethical standards in the consulting profession to which members of the Society subscribe:

1. A MEMBER conducts his business and private affairs with integrity and high moral purpose.
2. A MEMBER will serve his clients with professional fidelity, and act only for the client's best interest and benefit. A member will relinquish a client's account rather than compromise his personal standard of integrity.
3. A MEMBER will be certain about his qualifications to perform any assignment which he accepts from a client; and it will be his sincere intention and wholehearted purpose that the client derive substantial benefits as a result of his services.
4. A MEMBER will respect all information relating to the business affairs of his client as confidential.
5. A MEMBER can be depended on to be truthful and forthright with the client in his observations and recommendations.
6. A MEMBER's promotional announcements will be accurate, and made in a professionally dignified and proper manner.
7. A MEMBER strives at all times to uphold the honor and to maintain the dignity of the consulting profession. He finds the highest honor in a deserved reputation for fidelity to private trust and to public duty. The member endeavors to hold the esteem of others in his profession who subscribe to these standards; and he will condemn unethical or illegal conduct by other consultants which may come to his attention, and expose it for proper investigation and action.

FIGURE 24-3. A Typical Code of Ethics.

Enforcement is one of the chief difficulties of codes of ethics. Associations have some capabilities for enforcement in dealing with occasional or minor deviations, although it would be impossible to contain a widespread member rebellion against the code. Firms too can take disciplinary action. But codes are not laws, and the sanctions are limited and usually reluctantly applied. At best the codes set standards that a majority of the group prefers and voluntarily agrees to abide by, and they exert influences in directions that favor the organization in the sphere of ethics.

Most association codes are consonant with customs, mores, beliefs, social values, public laws, and generally desirable behavior. However, ethical codes are voluntary on the part of group members. Ethical codes persist because of common agreement within the group that such behavior is the "right" behavior for the individuals in the group. To keep the confidence, respect, and cooperation of his fellow association members, a manager must act within the limits of the code. The ultimate sanction would be a withdrawal of the offender's rights of affiliation. By its very nature, an ethical code exerts a strong emotional and mental hold upon individuals who participate in ethic-forming groups.[40]

The existence of ethical codes serves a number of important functions. They usually specify behavior that is required for the protection and continuity of the group as a whole. They reflect a group's unity and cohesiveness, and are evidence of its solidarity. Such codes also provide a measure of protection for the general public against fraudulent, misleading, or unfair treatment. They offer definitions of undesirable practices and denote methods of recourse available in cases of deviation from the code. The codes, moreover, reflect the movement of trade associations into the sphere of greater professionalization, for they emphasize service and performance within standard standards and deemphasize monetary rewards for their own sake. It is the professional associations, rather than the trade or industry associations, that have been the most concerned about codes of ethical conduct and that have gone farthest in the adoption of formal codes.

Some critics feel that adopting ethical codes is a form of "spurious ethics"—that is, they provide a false sanction for behavior that tends to be more in the interests of a narrow group than in the interests of the public good. Moreover, such concepts as "fair trade practices," however arguable on economic grounds, are clothed with a spurious respectability in the name of ethics. It seems clear that what passes for "ethics" needs to be carefully examined so that subtle biases thought desirable by a few are not merely clothed by a mantle of ethics to win the respect of many. Motivation, however, is difficult to assess. Although selfish motives at one time or another influence the use of ethical principles, one must be wary of generalizations that claim that the ethical conduct of businessmen always arises from sinister motives.

Ethical Advisors

Ethical problems are so highly situational that only those involved can know enough to make effective decisions. Still, some organizations find consultants helpful. Chaplains, long used in prisons and in the military services, are now widely used in hospitals and business firms. Occasionally, clergymen are appointed to boards of directors or retained as consultants to help wherever needed. Although the organization's relationships with ethical advisors may be rather casual, one cannot fault those who admit that they need help. Nevertheless, advisory roles are limited and provide no easy or permanent solution to ethical questions.[41]

---

[40]See *Wall Street Journal*, March 16, 1976, p. 1., and "How Companies React to the Ethics Crisis," *Business Week*, February 9, 1976, pp. 78–79.

[41]John F. Steiner, "The Prospect of Ethical Advisors for Business Corporations," *Business and Society* **16** (Spring 1976), 5–10.

_____ **THE ETHICS OF WORK AND SUCCESS**

The meaning of work to individuals has important influences on their behavior in organizations. They derive their basic values and beliefs about work from society at large, the family, their educational experiences, and many other sources.

The Puritans, who were Calvinists by religious faith, brought what is known as the work ethic to the United States. The work ethic, sometimes called the Protestant Ethic because of its origins in religion, holds that labor is good in itself and good for the person's soul; the person helps both himself and others by the act of working. This ethic thrived during the country's industrial growth and the expansion of its frontiers. It flourished under successive waves of immigrants in search of security and the good life. The Great Depression reinforced the work ethic through the scarcity of available work; wars made work a patriotic duty.

Today work has lost much of its religious significance, and labor is seldom regarded as good in itself. Yet the work ethic remains, in a different form. Drudgery and menial work are widely rejected, as are monotonous, routine, and meaningless tasks. Whereas work was formerly the avenue to financial success and higher social status, it is more and more valued today for its intrinsic worth to a problem-burdened society, and for the extent to which it corresponds to newer ideals that transcend material affluence as the measure of success. Work to attain wealth is no longer the motivation it was when the Puritan work ethic was more dominant. Young people today question their parent's pursuit of money through work. Leisure, and even hedonism, are important values, even though these are made possible mainly by wealth produced by our business system.

Some say that the work ethic no longer exists. This is a distortion based on the cynical views of those frustrated by the newer attitudes toward work. Instead of disappearing, the work ethic is undergoing drastic change. People will work hard and long, but not merely for money. They want meaningful work, recognition, personhood, and fulfillment—needs that collide with traditional views of work, people, and jobs widely held by managers, who now must reach new understanding about people and work. It will not be easy for organizations to realign their technology, management styles, and work patterns to meet the new demands. The work ethic remains, although success is being redefined.[42]

_____

[42]Dale Tarnowieski, *The Changing Success Ethic* (New York: AMACOM, 1973); Sar A. Levitan and William B. Johnston, *Work is Here to Stay, Alas* (Salt Lake City: Olympics Publishing Company, 1973; Harold L. Sheppard and Neal P. Herrick, *Where Have All the Robots Gone? Worker Dissatisfaction in the Seventies* (New York: Free Press, 1972).

THE FUTURE OF MANAGEMENT

The future of management will be filled with challenges and opportunities. Today's management must not only cope with current problems and activities, but also prepare to meet new and unknown needs in the future.

Change in the ever-present reality. Social change underlies organizational behavior and change, and hence affects the philosophy and leadership style of managers. People are better and better educated; values are changing as society progresses in the solution of its problems. Communications have greatly improved, providing information that is widely distributed not only to those who decide and act but to all whose lives are affected by change.

Society has declared its intentions to reduce poverty, improve medical care, cut back crime, and establish peace. We have moved to a more egalitarian posture for the fair treatment of minorities; ethnic, social, religious, and sex discrimination is being curbed. Such movements as consumerism have arisen to seek the protection of various sectors of the public against careless, capricious, or indifferent treatment. In all these matters, the intrusion of government into the management of organizations has reached a newer, higher, and, to many, a more undesirable level.

Managers and their organizations have a role and a responsibility in public affairs, along with commitments to their employees, to their communities, and to other stakeholders. The skills and insights of managers will have much to do with the success of society's efforts to bring abundance and security to all peoples.

SUMMARY

In this chapter we have examined the ethical and philosophical dimension of management, as that dimension appears in the processes of managerial decision and action. It also appears in the web of corporate life, in which the corporation seeks to relate to the economic, social, and political life around it.

Values, norms, beliefs, attitudes, philosophies, creeds, and feelings are all inextricably involved in the decision process. They constitute a legitimate area of management study, for they are reflected in the daily realities of corporate behavior.

Organizations today place a strong emphasis on social responsibility. Businesses particularly corporations, are heavily criticized for indifference to society's problems, but they are taking steps to meet the increasing demands that they join with others in solving such problems as crime, pollution, urban decay, and poverty. Crimes like bribery, corruption, embezzlement, and theft are dealt with by laws, but the processes of legal action are slow and often uncertain. More difficult are problems in which the corporation itself must be regulated, controlled, or punished. Standards of proper conduct of business firms are hard to set, but these too are being rapidly codified into regulatory and other laws.

Management today is an exciting and challenging opportunity for the creative energies of human beings. The executive devoid of philosophical and ethical insight is not prepared adequately for these great challenges. Although there are no quick or easy answers to the problems and dilemmas of management, intelligent minds are required to maintain and improve the progress already under way.

QUESTIONS FOR STUDY

1. Show how ethical considerations play a part in management thinking. Cite some examples.

2. Compare the relative merits of liberal arts and professional business curricula in preparing prospective executives for their careers.

3. How can ethical behavior on the part of businessmen be enforced?

4. How can you reconcile the profit motive with the idea of professional management? With the idea of ethical management?

5. Find a copy of the ethical practices code adopted by the AFL-CIO. Of what value are these statements?

6. What are the differences among such concepts as ethics, values, beliefs, attitudes, and norms?

7. Can the company actually determine for people what their attitudes and beliefs should be? To what extent do companies control or influence employee values? Employee beliefs?

8. The government orders you to install air-cleansing equipment or close your plant—equipment that you, as company president, don't think is needed. How do you sort out your conflicting obligations to the stockholders, the workers, and the community?

9. The district court has upheld the school discrimination suit that Lawyer Thomas brought on behalf of ten black students, and now asks him for his proposed remedy. Does he consider only the needs of the black students, or those of the white students and the entire neighborhood too?

10. What can corporations do to become more socially responsible?

INCIDENT CASE

In the early days of its training program to prepare disadvantaged community residents for entry-level positions, the Lexton Company encountered many difficulties. After two to four months of orientation training and job exposure, trainees were placed on beginning jobs if their attendance and performance were judged satisfactory. Between 1970 and 1974 only about half of the trainees were placed on jobs. The training staff attributed this result to poor selection, with trainees having poor backgrounds. Researchers later found that there were layoffs and cutbacks in employment at the company, and that the program's trainees would not participate adequately without the existence of clear job opportunities.

Questions:

1. What are the relevant probable causes of these difficulties?
2. What can be done to improve this situation?

SELECTED REFERENCES

ACKERMAN, ROBERT W. *The Social Challenge to Business.* Cambridge, Mass.: Harvard University Press, 1975.

ANSHEN, MELVIN, ed. *Managing the Socially Responsible Corporation.* New York: Macmillan Publishing Co., Inc., 1974.

ASHFORD, N. A. *Crisis in the Workplace.* Cambridge, Mass.: The M.I.T. Press, 1975.

BARLETT, LAILE E. *New Work, New Life: Help Yourself to Tomorrow: A Report from People Already There.* New York: Harper & Row, Publishers, 1976.

BAUMHART, RAYMOND, S.J. *Ethics in Business.* New York: Holt, Rinehart and Winston, 1968.

BELL, DANIEL. *The Coming of the Post-Industrial Society.* New York: Basic Books, Inc. 1973.

BRAUDE, LEE. *Work and Workers: A Sociological Analysis.* New York: Praeger Publishers, Inc., 1975.

BYARS, LLOYD L., and MICHAEL H. MESCON, eds. *The Other Side of Profit.* Philadelphia: W. B. Saunders Company, 1975.

CARROLL, ARCHIE B. ed. *Managing Corporate Social Responsibilities.* Boston: Little, Brown and Company, 1977.

CASS, EUGENE LOUIS, and FREDERICK G. ZIMMER. *Man and Work in Society.* New York: Van Nostrand Reinhold Company, 1975.

CHAMBERLAIN, NEIL W. *The Limits of Corporate Responsibility.* New York: Basic Books, Inc., 1973.

DEUTSCH, JAN G. *Selling the People's Cadillac: The Edsel in Corporate Responsibility.* New Haven: Yale University Press, 1976.

DUNCAN, W. JACK. *Decision Making and Social Issues.* New York: The Dryden Press, 1973.

EASTON, ALLAN. *Managing for Negative Growth: A Handbook for Practitioners.* Reston, Va.: Reston Publishing Company, 1976.

ESTES, RALPH W. *Social Accounting.* New York: John Wiley & Sons, Inc., 1976.

HACKMAN, J. RICHARD, and J. LLOYD SUTTLE. *Improving Life at Work: Behavioral Science Approaches to Organizational Changes.* Santa Monica, Calif.: Goodyear Publishing Company, 1977.

HILL, IVAN, ed. *The Ethical Basis of Economic Freedom.* Chapel Hill, N.C.: American Viewpoint, Inc., 1976.

JACOBY, NEIL H. *Corporate Power and Social Responsibility.* New York: Macmillan Publishing Co., Inc. 1973.

KLEIN, THOMAS. *Social Costs and Benefits of Business.* Englewood Cliffs, N.J.: Prentice-Hall, Inc., 1977.

LEVITT, THEODORE. *The Third Sector: New Tactics for a Responsive Society.* New York: AMACOM, 1973.

LITSCHERT, ROBERT J., and EDWARD A. NICHOLSON. *The Corporate Role and Ethical Behavior: Concepts and Cases.* New York: Petrocelli/Charter, 1977.

LODGE, GEORGE C. *The New American Ideology.* New York: Alfred A. Knopf, Inc., 1975.

O'TOOLE, JAMES. *Work, Learning, and the American Future.* San Francisco: Jossey-Bass, Inc., 1977.

SCHMIDT, WARREN H., ed. *Organizational Frontiers and Human Values.* Belmont, Calif.: Wadsworth Publishing Company, 1970.

SETHI, S. PRAKASH, ed. *The Unstable Ground: Corporate Social Policy in a Dynamic Society.* Los Angeles: Melville Publishing Company, 1974.

VIOLA, RICHARD H. *Organizations in a Changing Society: Administration and Human Values.* Philadelphia: W. B. Saunders Company, 1977.

WALTON, CLARENCE C. *Ethics and the Executive.* Englewood Cliffs, N.J.: Prentice-Hall, Inc., 1969.

Cases for Part IV

A. LAWRENCE PHARMACEUTICALS, INC.

A. LAWRENCE PHARMACEUTICALS, INC.

In 1959, chemists at Lawrence Pharmaceuticals, Inc., discovered a new chemical that proved useful as a muscle relaxant. It was patented and sold in liquid form as Brytol, after receiving FDA clearance. Ten years later, the volume of sales was such that the company decided to explore the feasibility of building a new plant for the manufacture of Brytol rather than continuing to purchase the chemical ingredients from chemical workers. Up to this point the firm had made only finished pharmaceuticals and had no units producing raw chemicals.

The president reasoned that the chemicals used in Brytol were derivatives of other chemicals used in its other products, so that a new plant could be designed to produce the ingredients of several of its products. Moreover, inflation and petroleum shortages, in his opinion, made the firm "too much a slave of the market." However, in 1971 the FDA suddenly gave the main chemical in Brytol a "questionable" rating, and it was four years before the substance was again cleared.

In 1975 the president set up a secret, high-level task force to "make recommendations for compounds to be considered, acquisition possibilities, site selections, and financial justifications" for entering upon the manufacture of selected chemicals. The task force divided into two groups, one exploring the "build" possibilities, and the other studying the opportunities to acquire an existing facility.

The "build" unit retained an engineering consulting firm, which developed design criteria, the manufacturing process, an equipment list, an environmental impact statement, project schedules, and preliminary cost estimates that showed that the investment would pay for itself in three years.

Consultants for the "buy" team found one hundred available plants of interest, of which twenty were contacted. One was already a big supplier to Lawrence and

621

would have required little modification. However, it was rejected because it was located in an area where expansion would not be feasible. Also, it was unionized, and according to a senior official, "We've always tried to steer clear of unions." The "buy" group finally selected a plant in another state.

An intense rivalry developed between the two teams, with the members of each feeling that their personal reputations were at stake. Their egos were involved in the outcome. The "buy" team members wanted a big, visible win over the rival team. The "build" team members wanted their cause to triumph. The president regarded the rivalry as the creative tension he had hoped for in creating the teams. Meanwhile, the company's banker recommended against building because of the cyclical nature of the chemical business. The president rejected the bank's argument, pointing to the danger of possible future oil embargoes that might cause an interruption of supplies.

After ten months of study, the task force presented the details of its "build" and "buy" options. The arguments were equally persuasive and the costs were about equal for both options. The president and the chairman of the board jointly made the decision in favor of the "build" team.

QUESTIONS

1. Appraise the problems and advantages of project teams as reflected in this case.

2. Evaluate the decision processes involved.

3. If you were a stockholder, what reactions might you have to the actions and problems in this case?

B. THE PEMBROKE COMPANY

The Pembroke Company is a long-established firm operating fifteen branch plants located in the eastern part of the United States. The branch plants are engaged in manufacturing and processing chemicals, packaging materials, and wood and fiber items on a job-shop basis; in the processing of various farm products; and in the manufacturing and sale of food and paper items purchased by housewives for use in their homes and on a large scale by institutions.

The president, William Hagers, had built up in Chicago a head office organization that coordinated the branch plants and provided them with the special services they needed. Selling and advertising were planned primarily at the head office, with variations possible and permitted at the local level if not in conflict with over-all company policy. In 1974 Hagers decided that a marketing specialist should be added to the promotions department, as Loomis, the sales and advertising manager, had proposed. With Hagers's approval, Loomis interviewed various candidates; after considerable deliberation, and with the assistance of the personnel department, he hired Harvey Robbins. Robbins was a tall, powerful, energetic man forty years old. His first impression on others was always favorable. Robbins had a varied experience in light manufacturing industry and had at one time worked for a chemical firm. Robbins had a college degree in business administration with special emphasis on marketing and statistics, and this, in addition to his experience, seemed to make him qualified as far as the technical features of his job were concerned. During the preemployment interview, Loomis noticed Robbins's persistence in asking pointed questions about the company and its policies. Robbins was very aggressive. He would begin with a fairly innocuous question and then ask a whole series of them which kept getting Loomis further and further out on a limb. However, as soon as Robbins saw that Loomis was getting uncomfortable, he would switch to another question to avoid upsetting Loomis. During the interview, Robbins also made some extreme assertions, which he stated dogmatically without allowing Loomis to question their validity. However, only one former employer had mentioned this trait, and that employer had stated he would rehire him if possible. Loomis concluded that the man's technical qualifications made him the best bet for the job and thought that if personality problems existed, they could be satisfactorily handled.

On the day Robbins reported for work, Loomis took him to lunch, and while going through the company cafeteria, an office boy thoughtlessly elbowed his way ahead of Robbins. Robbins put down his tray, grabbed the boy, and in very strong language reprimanded him in front of everybody. The office boy argued back, and it was all Loomis could do to prevent a fight. Because there was some provocation, Loomis was not inclined to make too much of the incident at the time. However, during the next few months, a pattern developed in which Robbins showed a tendency to divide people's thoughts into two categories—those he agreed with and those with which he disagreed. Robbins seemed anxious to make sure where everybody else stood on all controversial issues and constantly questioned people in an effort to back them into a corner and prove that they were wrong and he was right. Robbins's associates were both amused and puzzled, but few took any offense at it.

During the year, other instances similar to the one in the company cafeteria occurred. On one such occasion Robbins noticed that one of his colleagues was engaging in a project of which he did not approve. He went directly to the colleague and told him to stop the project. The colleague responded angrily and pushed Robbins out of his office. The word got around that Robbins had been poking into the affairs of several other people. He made several specific suggestions to both Loomis and Hagers about where his colleagues were failing to do their jobs and where they could improve. He openly criticized Loomis himself in several departmental meetings. His comments and suggestions often had some merit to them, but he was not always practical or logical in his thinking. Loomis tolerated this behavior: "It'll blow over after he's been here a while. Besides, his work is tops. He's helped us get our marketing strategy back where it belongs. And I think our people dislike the way he criticizes me openly in our meetings."

At this point, Loomis was transferred, and a man named Nelson replaced him. Nelson had a different background, ability, and temperament from Loomis. Whereas Loomis was easygoing, mild-mannered, and inclined to let the Robbins's problem take its natural course in the hope that he would improve, Nelson was a man of action, with very high standards, and capable of strong leadership. He soon realized that one of his major concerns was Robbins. Robbins had so offended the other people in the group that they would no longer work with him. At first, Nelson thought that the problem was one of immaturity and that after a while Robbins would "grow up." He did not wish to discharge Robbins because of his excellent technical record on the job. However, he asked Hagers to have a talk with Robbins, which Hagers did. Robbins told Hagers he realized he was at times a bit upsetting, but everything he did was for the good of the organization. After this talk, Hagers told

Nelson to be patient and try to work with Robbins. Hagers told Nelson, "Robbins is just a reformer, that's all." Later, Nelson called in Robbins for a talk, in which the conversation went as follows:

Nelson: Harvey, I don't like these fights you get into every so often.

Robbins: I know it's not good, but they always blow over. The fellows soon get over it. I don't know anyone who's holding a grudge against me, unless it's that Bill Vincent. Has he been needling you about me?

Nelson: No, no, not that at all. I just can't believe you know what you're doing to our group. You've got everyone upset. They say they won't work with you any more.

Robbins: I can't help it if they feel guilty about what they're doing and go crying to you. Incidentally, what did you report me to Hagers for?

Nelson: We were discussing your future here, Harvey. Naturally, I had to tell him, and he's very concerned.

Robbins: Oh, yeah? Well, I've got him on my side now. What do you think of that? He saw some truth in what I told him about some of the guys around here. He wants to run a first-class organization here, and I think he'll listen to me.

Nelson: I don't think you can afford to be too cocky about it. We've been in business a long time, Harvey. I've seen men come and go. We need your talent. We realize you've done an excellent job. But we've got to have some assurance you know your faults and want to correct them, especially the matter of rubbing everybody the wrong way. There's more to your job than just the technical side, you know.

Robbins: I don't enjoy fighting. You certainly know that. You've got too many fellows here who do enjoy it, though. Well, I'm glad you like my work at least. I'm not trying to go out of my way to upset people, especially you or Hagers. I don't go out of my way to pamper them, either. Anyhow, I think you ought to be out looking for some better men to replace the duds we got around here.

Nelson: Well, where do we go from here? What about yourself?

Robbins: Don't expect miracles, Nelson. I know I should get along better, and you know that usually I do, too. It's just these incidents. I'll try to cut down on them. Maybe that'll make you and Hagers appreciate me more. After all, you know, I'm expecting a healthy raise in three more months. I'm way ahead of Bill Vincent in the way I do my work—that's for sure. I should get a raise before he does.

Nelson: You'd better concentrate on how to get along with your fellow workers, Harvey. That's the main thing now.

Nelson told Hagers about this conversation. Hagers said he doubted if he'd approve any promotions or raises for Robbins for a long time yet—not until Robbins improved a lot. He told Nelson to keep trying to work with him. Nelson told Hagers that he was going to call a meeting of the entire department and order everyone (including Robbins) to mind his own business and not worry about the other fellow. Hagers told Nelson to tell the group that the order was from him as well as from Nelson.

From some weeks, Robbins worked quietly and no incident occurred. Then late one afternoon, Bill Vincent came to Nelson and said, "Robbins told me I didn't have enough competence to do my job. He told me he was going to tell Hagers that, too. He said anyone else could do my work better, and I lost my temper. If you don't get rid of him, you're going to have a hard time keeping me. Who does he think he is, anyway?"

QUESTIONS

1. What should Nelson say to Vincent?
2. What should Nelson say to Robbins?
3. Has Hagers helped the situation or made it worse? How?
4. What, if anything, can Robbins's associates do about him?
5. How do you evaluate Nelson's way of handling Robbins?

C. THE LTD CORPORATION

The LTD Corporation, a large, nationwide service organization with subsidiaries in every state, is widely known for its applications of advanced concepts of organization development, and for encouraging the use of sophisticated behavioral science knowledge in its training and development programs.

In one of the western states, the subsidiary had launched a management development program for engineering, scientific, and technical personnel. This program consisted of half-day sessions once a week for periods of twenty weeks. However, because facilities in the main office building were not adequate for all the groups of twenty, some of the training groups went in company cars to outlying motels or other suitable quarters where space could be leased. About half the groups were accommodated in the main building, where most of the participants had their offices.

One morning Henry Haldane, the supervisor of technical information, was approached by John Dunn, one of his ablest men:

Dunn: Can I have a few minutes of your time, Henry? There's something I've been asked to take up with you.

Haldane: Sure. Come into the office and tell me what's on your mind. Make it short, though, because I've got another man coming in here in a few minutes.

Dunn: I'll come right to the point. You know that a lot of the guys in our management training program get to go to those other locations. Some of them are in nice spots, and they get to have lunch and a few drinks before their meetings.

Haldane: So what?

Dunn: So some of the fellows and I were talking and we decided that to be fair, you should give us the same total time off. They get four hours off for two hours of training time, and those of us who have our meetings right here in the building have to stay on duty except for the training period itself. We'd like to have the same amount of time before and after sessions that the rest of the guys get.

Haldane: That's pretty small potatoes, and I must say I don't think any of you guys have any kind of case at all. You go back and tell them I said that. Tell them the training course is here for their benefit, and that I expect them to work like hell on it, and to do their jobs on top of that.

Dunn: Wouldn't it be possible for us to go home right after the training session like the guys who go outside do? They are free to go home at four o'clock.

Haldane: It's out of the question.

Dunn: Then how about two hours' extra pay to make up the difference?

Haldane: No soap.

Dunn: O.K. The fellows asked me to inquire. I'll tell them what you said.

QUESTIONS

1. What are some of the hidden ramifications of this case?

2. If this problem was brought to you as training director, what would be your response?

D. QWIK-KLEEN LINEN SUPPLY COMPANY

John Warren was the president and general manager of the Qwik-Kleen Linen Supply Company, which specialized in supplying linen to its business and professional customers. Under the guidance of Warren, the business had grown to the point where it covered the entire state and was grossing over $20 million a year. Warren had built up a competent staff of people, including Henry Worth, the chief accountant, Sam Trent, plant superintendent, and Bill O'Grady, in charge of purchasing and fleet maintenance. In addition, Warren had an assistant manager, who reported directly to him. Exhibit 1 shows the relationships of these top men, as pictured by Warren. Warren followed the practice of concentrating on major decisions and on planning and coordinating the work of the others. For handling day-to-day problems, Warren relied on his assistant manager, Ben Nelson.

Late in the fall of 1978, Bill O'Grady, the purchasing agent and fleet maintenance man, informed Warren that he was giving two weeks' notice and resigning. When Warren inquired what the trouble was, O'Grady said that he had come to the conclusion that he had gotten about as far as he could go in this particular concern and that he had better look for another job. He told Warren that he did not yet have anything definite in mind but that he expected to find a new position after a short vacation. Warren invited O'Grady to come into his office and talk the matter over. O'Grady reluctantly agreed. The following conversation ensued:

Warren: Bill, this comes as a surprise to me. I really don't know what to say. I can't understand what is bothering you.

O'Grady: Well, you know how it is; after you've been in a job about so long you get to thinking more about it and wondering where the future lies. I just have a general feeling that it would be a good idea for me to move.

Warren: A general feeling? Aren't there any specific things which have gone into this feeling of yours?

O'Grady: Well, of course, it isn't entirely without a basis in fact, but it's hard to talk about things like this. The last thing I want to do is to get someone else in trouble.

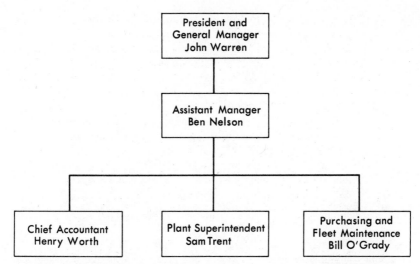

EXHIBIT 1. Organization Chart of the Qwik-Kleen Linen Supply Company.

Warren: Do you think if you tell me what's wrong you'll get somebody else in trouble?

O'Grady: Well, it isn't that I lack confidence in your judgment, but if I were to get down to brass tacks I would have to mention someone else in an unfavorable light and I hate to do that.

Warren: I'd like to assure you that anything you or I might say here will go no farther. You know from past experience that I haven't violated confidences, don't you?

O'Grady: Yes, I know that, Well, the problem is that, as you know, I've been working pretty hard in my job here. I came with you five years ago and at that time you were just ready to give our competitors a stiff fight. We did pretty well in this struggle, and I like to feel that in some part at least it was due to the new purchasing policies and procedures that I worked out and to the new procedures we developed for scheduling the trucks. Now, I don't like to go around blowing my own horn, but for the kind of job I've been doing I ought to be getting more money. I don't think it would be too hard for me to get a couple thousand dollars a year more in some other company, and I wouldn't even have to move out of town. I've hesitated so far because I like you and I have enjoyed working with the company. I've kept hoping that something would develop to change the picture for me, but lately I've been feeling that the only way to do it is to make a change.

Warren: Bill, I realize you may not have known my feelings on this, but I have had a lot of confidence in your ability, and I'd be the first one to give you credit for your part in our success. What does Nelson have to say about all this?

O'Grady: That's the point I was getting at. For the last six months, I've been talking with Nelson at every chance I got, to get him to talk with you about giving me a raise. I hated to go around him this way, but since you asked me I might as well tell you. Whenever I talk with Nelson, he is friendly about it, and he agrees that there's no question about the value of my contribution. But he keeps putting me off with some vague answers about having to take it up with you when the time is most strategic, and he never says anything to me about it unless I go to him first.

Warren: I can recall no discussion whatsoever between Nelson and myself on this. I don't know why he would hold a matter like this up, but this is something we can fix right away. Would you stay on with us doing the same fine job you're doing? We'll give you a raise of fifteen hundred dollars for the first year, starting the first of next month, and unless we get a bad setback in business volume, we'll give you another raise of $1,000 the year following. How does this sound to you?

O'Grady: Well, I'd really wanted to leave, and I've put out a few feelers around town. How about giving me a week to think it over?

Warren: Fine, Bill. I think that's entirely a fair request. You let me know within a week.

Warren was very much disturbed about this matter and determined to talk with Nelson about the situation on the following Monday. He was two hours late in getting to his social affair, but congratulated himself with the thought it was fairly certain that O'Grady would stay on with the firm.

QUESTIONS

1. What connection do you see between the communications problem in this case and the organization structure of the firm?

2. Write the dialogue that will take place when Warren holds his discussion with Nelson the following week.

3. What do you think of Warren's interviewing skills? What are his weak and strong points as an interviewer? As a boss?

4. What do you think are likely to be the relationships between Nelson and O'Grady if O'Grady decides to stay, and why?

5. What other management problems does this case indicate?

E. THE U.S. POSTAL SERVICE

A group of postal employees decided to make a few extra dollars on the side. They had a good arrangement: report to work on time, punch in on the time clock, then scurry around and get all their work completed by noon. As soon as they had finished their work for the day, three of the group would leave the office and paint houses the rest of the day. At quitting time the fourth man in the group punched the others out on the clock. Each member took turns working and covering up for the other three.

In the postal service, inspectors are supposed to catch such operations at the local level. The normal procedure is for the manager in charge of the unit to request an investigation when he finds something wrong. In this particular case, however, investigators in the district office found out about the group first, and unknown to the local manager or local investigator bugged the post office and took pictures of the group painting during working hours. After the district investigators got the evidence they nabbed the group and took them to the local manager for dismissal.

Instead of dismissing the employees, the manager became furious because the chain of command had been violated. He had not known an investigation was going on. He insisted that rules and the chain of command are very important in an organization. Three weeks later, none of the employees had been dismissed and the manager was still arguing with district headquarters about the violation of the chain of command.

QUESTIONS

1. Analyze the management problems implied by this case.
2. How could the situation have been dealt with more effectively?

F. BILL FREMONT

In 1977 Ralph Swenson, head of the traffic department in the Blake Products Corporation, announced plans for expanding his department in order to keep pace with the company's rapid growth. Swenson, after deliberating with the people in his department, had decided to establish three section heads who would report to him, and to organize the departmental activities under these three section heads. Swenson appointed Tom Logan as head of the incoming traffic section. Logan had been with the company approximately five years and had been in the traffic department for three years. Like Swenson, Logan was a college graduate in business administration. He had made steady progress in the company, and his semiannual performance reviews showed a pattern of considerable ability to get results. Logan displayed a willingness to assume responsibility, had the habit of working hard, and had a thorough knowledge of the technical problems of the business. His weaker points included a tendency to get results at the expense of his associates' feelings. In making this appointment, Swenson felt that Logan's good points merited his advancement to section head, and that his weak points could be strengthened as he learned to handle his new job.

About four months after Logan became head of the incoming traffic section, he decided that he needed a statistical and operations research specialist to do planning work and conduct cost analyses for other parts of the company. Swenson authorized Logan to hire a college graduate in business administration. After interviewing twelve candidates suggested to him by the personnel department, Logan decided that Bill Fremont was his man.

Fremont had concentrated his studies on marketing and statistics and had also taken courses in traffic and transportation. However, Fremont was reluctant to take the job because he felt that he might start for a higher salary in some other company. Logan discovered in talking with him that they were about $50 apart in their salary bargaining. Logan met this problem by emphasizing the tremendous expansion plans of the company and the consequent opportunities for advancement. He told Fremont, "If you'll just come with us and let us teach you how to do the job we want, you'll be a valuable man to us and we'll see to it that you are rewarded accordingly." Fremont accepted the position.

During the following year, Fremont showed every evidence of fulfilling Logan's expectation. Fremont was eager to learn, and proved to be bright and intelligent.

Moreover, his education had given him a grasp of many of the technical details and problems of traffic management, and he appeared to be good at finding ways of applying this knowledge. However, Logan began to notice after this first year signs of discontent on Fremont's part. On one occasion, Logan had suggested that for Fremont's development in his job he attend a special school being sponsored by the company at one of the colleges in the community. Fremont had replied, "I spent four years going to school and I got tired of it. Now I want to keep my mind strictly on learning this business. My family responsibilities are such that I would hate to take even one night a week off right now to attend these classes." On that occasion, Logan replied that he understood and said that perhaps some later opportunity would arise. On another occasion, Logan had found himself under pressure to get out certain traffic reports and had asked Fremont to give him a hand by coming down on Saturday morning, when everything else in the office would be quiet, to finish the work. Fremont replied that he hated not to be cooperative but that the work he was doing was not connected with those reports, and he didn't want to get his mind on some other problem at that time. Besides, he had made some important plans for that Saturday and didn't feel he could change them in order to work. Again, Logan said he understood how Fremont felt, but privately he felt that Fremont was not giving him the cooperation he expected.

During the next few weeks, Logan noticed still other changes in Fremont. Fremont began to put off various projects he was working on without finishing them. Moreover, Logan observed him starting new projects before the others were satisfactorily finished. When he mentioned this to Fremont, Fremont replied that he was still learning the ropes and that he had to tackle a variety of jobs to get to know the business. Fremont also promised to clean up the unfinished work, but Logan noticed that in the weeks following, very little was actually completed. Logan also noticed that Fremont often came back late from lunch. When asked about this, Fremont replied that he had joined a couple of community service clubs, both of which met for lunch at noon each week, and he felt that he was fulfilling his public relations responsibilities by representing the company at their luncheons. On another occasion, Logan discovered that Fremont had taken on a project for one of the other section heads. When asked about this, Fremont said that he had become a very close friend of the other section head and was doing him a favor by helping him out in an emergency.

Ralph Swenson, the head of the traffic department, had also noticed many of these situations and decided to talk with Tom Logan about it without delay. The same morning that Logan had decided he would have to take some positive action with regard to Fremont, he received a telephone call from Swenson, who told him that at ten o'clock he would like to meet with him concerning his new employee, Fremont.

_____ **QUESTIONS**

1. How should Swenson handle this situation in his talk with Logan?
2. What can Logan say to Swenson?
3. What can Logan say and do with respect to Fremont?
4. Was Fremont a wise choice for Logan to hire into this section?
5. From the facts given us, does Logan seem to have been a wise choice as section head?

G. THE PROGRAM CLERKS

A government office is staffed with a manager and three program clerks (women of approximately the same age). The work load is divided quite evenly among the three program clerks. However, each is expected to help the other program clerks during the periods of peak work. Programs are generally well administered, but frequently there is some overload of work on clerk B because clerk C, even though she has some available time, does not readily help without being directed to do so. Clerk A helps the other two without direction and accepts the responsibilities as part of her job. There are indications that clerks B and C have a personality conflict from years ago before being employed by the office. Reassignment of duties cannot be used to change the working arrangement.

QUESTIONS

1. What should the manager do to improve the office work, and why?
2. Analyze the causes and prevention of problems of this type.

H. WELLINGTON ELECTRONICS, INC.

Wellington is a firm of 450 employees engaged in the manufacture and sale of electronic equipment. It is basically a one-product company, with that product based on patents held by the owner and founder, Thomas T. Lawless.

In 1976, Lawless decided to undertake an unusual morale-building plan. In addition to regular pay scales, this nonunion firm had a cash bonus system based on production goals mutually set by supervisors and workers. The quarterly bonus often results in the equivalent of six weeks' pay per year for the better performers.

The new plan consisted of closing the plant down for a week to send all 450 employees who wished to go either to London or to Disney World at company expense. The president viewed the trip as a reward for doubling the company's profits of the previous year. He viewed it also as a memorable reward to generate a continued team effort. The cost of the plan was estimated at $150,000.

The employees received the plan enthusiastically, although the workers were aware that they would be liable for federal income taxes on the value of the trip. At first the plan included only a trip to London, but after the employees requested alternatives such as Rome or Paris, Disney World was added. By the end of the first month, over half of the employees had signed up. Those who stayed home were given a week off with pay, since the plant would be closed. Workers with less than one week of service would have to pay 35 per cent the trip costs.

"If this plan is a success, we'll consider doing another one in return for achieving some other objective," said the president.

QUESTIONS

1. Evaluate the plan as a device for building morale and improving motivation.

2. What is the incentive value of such a plan?

3. Would this plan work in companies in other industries? In large firms? Why or why not?

_____ **I. OLIVER WHITE**

Oliver White, age 59, had been with the Williams Division of the Noller Corporation for most of his working career. Starting in the bookkeeping department as a clerk, he had gradually developed an interest in purchasing. When the Williams Corporation became a division of Noller, he was assistant director of purchasing. One year later he was made director. He was unaware of any particular problems until an interview that took place on June 2. Here is a summary of this meeting and two more that followed it, from notes Oliver White made afterwards:

(1) Meeting on June 2, 1978:

Mantoni advised me today that I was not going to represent the company at the New York meeting of the Purchasing and Materials Managers Association, because the company reorganization does not include me among the managers of the purchasing department. Mantoni read me his appraisal of me from the new form that he had just filled out and was about to turn in to the Personnel Department. He praised me highly as a "doer," someone who gets things done. In that, he said, he had no better employee. He criticized my planning, saying that I had not made a plan of action, but that he had made my plan (which was being achieved). He said he had other responsibilities and could no longer do this for me. Therefore, he had to put someone in my job as manager. He criticized my administrative ability. He said I allow my personnel to do the administrating, and he can't let this go on, so, therefore, he must replace me as manager.

He then proceeded to compare my current appraisal with those of previous years. Everyone, he said, praised me and gave me favorable reports. In fact, he called them "rave reports," with nothing wrong with my performance or operation. He said that the fact that (1) the department was on schedule as to our basic plan; (2) the budget was in fine shape—being achieved; (3) shortages were at an all-time low; and (4) the variance was the most favorable it had ever been, made it hard to tell me I was not qualifed for what they wanted in a department manager. He also said he did not want me to feel it was personal because it was not. In fact, that was what was making it so hard for him to tell me. He wished I had not done so well as a performer because this made the decision so hard for him. He also said my knowledge of materials and the job were so great he did not want to lose them. He said his plans were to move me to a job as one of his administrative assistants. I would advise and assist on purchasing matters.

I advised him I might or might not stay on in that capacity. He said that would naturally be my choice, but he hoped that I would. He told me that he had felt I would be upset and due to previous health problems might want to retire early. I asked him if I had company permission to retire early (this is necessary on early retirement) and he answered in the affirmative. I further stated I had five and a half years at Ford Company and that if I could add to it up to ten years, that would net me another pension. I told him I intended to explore this. He then offered me time off—not as vacation, but just time off with his permission—to seek out anything I wanted to along these lines.

He profusely apologized for his procrastination in telling me and getting this review done. I accepted his apology and told him I was of the opinion he was only doing as he had been told to do, and I held nothing against him. He asked me to sign the appraisal he had read to me. I signed it—without reading it—and promptly left the office.

(2) Meeting on June 4, 1978:

I asked Mantoni to furnish me a copy of my June 2 appraisal form. I stated I wanted it for self-improvement, and he assured me he would give me a copy. I further asked for early retirement figures, which he gave me.

I asked him if he planned to cut my salary if I accepted the new position he had offered. He replied that he did not; he would have to come up with a very strong Hay Plan writeup to justify my present wage, but he felt he could justify it.

Mantoni then expounded on what he intended I do as administrative assistant:

1. Review all new products on the "C to C" procedure:
   (a) Obtain new quotations on all new purchased material use.
   (b) Attend group meetings to give authentic purchasing advice.
   (c) Review all materials to see if they are the best obtainable.
   (d) Provide second sources for "C to C" items before they hit production.
2. Provide second sources for items now single-sourced.
3. Be available to keep him advised of market and material situations.

(3) Meeting on June 16, 1978:

I was called up to Vice President Freeman's office for meeting with him and Messrs. Mantoni and Leighton. Freeman stated that rumors were circulating around town to the effect that I had been fired. One rumor said I was given thirty days' notice; another said ninety days' notice. Bailey had heard this rumor at the Country Club, and Bart Carl had heard it from a person outside the company. Therefore, they wanted to know what I had told people because these untrue rumors damaged the company's image.

I stated I had no idea how these rumors started because I had written notes on my meeting with Mr. Mantoni, June 2, and they did not indicate anything about being fired, or of my having been given notice. I offered to get a copy of this for them to read, but the offer was declined. I was given assurance I was not fired; in fact, I was advised I could stay until I was 65 years old if I wanted to.

It was further brought out that when a company moves from $200 million in sales to $360 million in sales, new and different people are required in many functions. Purchasing was indicated as one of these areas. Freeman asked if I had read the new appraisal given to me by Mantoni on June 2. I stated that I had not read it, but Mantoni read it to me, and I signed it. I further requested that a copy of the appraisal be furnished to me. All three agreed to this. Mr. Kennedy then asked if I agreed with the appraisal, to which I answered no. I stated that my signature only meant that I had heard it, and not that I agreed to it.

I further stated I thought everyone was entitled to his opinion, and I did not hold any animosity toward Mantoni because of the appraisal. I was given further assurance that I could stay until I was 65, but not in my present assignment.

Freeman pointed out how some companies would not have given me the fair treatment I was receiving here due to the rumors that were being spread. He asked me to do some serious soul searching and see if I hadn't said something that could have caused these rumors. I agreed to do this and to endeavor to spike these ugly rumors. I left reassured that I could stay until 65 if my plans for early retirement to Florida did not mature.

The following excerpts are taken from the new appraisal form completed on Oliver White by Frank Mantoni:

1. *Employee's Major Responsibilities:* To coordinate and supervise all functions assigned to the purchasing department.
2. *Performance Appraisal:* His purchasing experience is extensive. As a result, he has a solid knowledge of materials and material sources. His attitude toward the job is positive and he has been extremely cooperative with his supervisor. He is successfully executing the 1978 Operating Plan, and his department is performing below budget.
3. *Methods:* Managing is accomplished in three phases—planning, administration, and execution. Oliver prefers to execute. He tends to leave the planning to superiors and delegates administrative functions to his subordinates. This is a serious weakness. He appears to have the loyalty of subordinates, and they respond favorably to his direction. There is room, however, for improvement when he is working with and through people outside of his department. More diplomacy would help.
4. *Management Qualifications* (general): Oliver is aggressive and with constant direction he gets the job done. He is a self-starter once a course of action has been planned but prefers to leave the planning to others.
5. *Strongest Qualifications:* Knowledge of materials and material sources.
6. *Strongest Secondary Qualifications:* Expediting the materials required for production.
7. *Requirements for Improved Performance:* More attention must be devoted to the planning and the administrative phases of management. He must approach people outside of his organization with more diplomacy.
8. *Employee's Own Idea of His Future:* Mantoni left this section blank.
9. *Action Agreed Upon Between Employee and His Supervisor for Employee's Improved Performance in His Present Position or Other Management Developmental Steps Looking Toward Employee's Advancement, Including Promotional Potential:* Mantoni left this section blank.

In addition to the above, a check mark was placed by Mantoni opposite the choice: "Leave in present position until . . . ," but no information was filled in. Mantoni also checked another part of the list that said "Services Satisfactory."

--- **QUESTIONS**

1. Evaluate the appraisal system being used in the Williams Division.
2. Appraise the behavior of White and Mantoni as revealed by this case.

Analyzing Management Cases*

A case study presents a body of information describing a particular problem situation. In an organizational context, it is an account of thoughts, behaviors, and interpersonal relations among managers, employees, and clients, as well as an accounting of general environmental condtions and priorities that characterize a specific decision/action field.

Such cases are to be analyzed rather than solved. Analyses may develop or evolve through classroom discussions or be offered in a written report. In either form, each analysis starts with a focus on a central issue or question representing an accurate reflection of the total problem or situation. Within this definition, optional courses of action may be hypothesized. An argumentative thesis explaining further detail of important action elements of the case can, then, be developed. This argument should be supported by factual and interpretive evidence from the case itself, not from vague generalizations and opinions. A final step in the analysis may be a set of recommendations suggesting actions or decisions logically following such argumentations.

PURPOSES OF CASE ANALYSIS

Analyzing a case in such a manner will serve one or a combination of the following purposes:

1. *Increase awareness of environmental conditions.* Assessment of the field giving rise to the problem will often cast attention to

*Written in collaboration with Fremont A. Shull, of the University of Georgia.

imperatives of variables in the external environment. In this modern world of rapid change, organizational problems seemingly of an integral nature are often directly related to external dynamics. Thus, environmental relationships may become significant concerns in case analyses.

2. *Add knowledge of organizational behavior.* It is likely that factual materials in a case will give insight into the conditions, problems, and decisions facing management in various organizational situations. Moreover, because past decisions and actions leading to the issue under study may or may not have been appropriate and effective, causalities are exposed and can be examined within the structure of the case. Therefore, such studies offer a realistic flavor to academic training.

3. *Strengthen abilities in identifying situational problems.* Because tradition and emulation often dominate exploration and study in problem solving, the latter skills of management are often neglected. A decreasing cost curve does not necessarily mean that the organization is operating in the most efficient and effective manner, nor does it necessarily manifest long-run potential. Thus a major fucntion of management is to locate and define accurately the problems facing the organization if it is to remain relevant to its environment.

4. *Enhance skills in framing appropriate questions.* Calling upon intuition, experience, and logic, the analyst is required to use his creativity in discerning intelligent and comprehensive alternatives and substantiating logical solutions. Without this phase of analysis, various influencing forces or pertinent hypotheses may be overlooked. In many cases, an executive must deal with insufficient facts, matters of compromise, and human vagaries. Thus it is of major importance that the analyst ask himself how a particular decision will affect other areas of the enterprise and to what extent combined abilities and willingness are present to pursue a particular course of action.

5. *Offer realistic training in problem-solving skills.* This function contains elements of both heuristic thinking and resolution or closure. Analyses may point to (a) decisions in which additional facts or more pertinent evidence is needed and for which appropriate machinery must be created to provide such information, or (b) a culling, evaluation, and integration of available evidence, so that a definitive course of action can be proposed. Information reported in a case can conceivably lead to a number of different conclusions, depending on the ways in which the information is treated. The existence of several options or outcomes, however, does not mean that all possible courses of action have equal merit. Generally, the analyst must order his recommendations in the light of logical predictions of desirable outcomes.

Depending upon the learning experience desired from case analyses, a variety of processing models may be used. These would include the following:

1. *A problem-solving format.* The traditional approach to a case analysis is the format described above. However, the learning experience may relate more fully to social interactions where, for example, a group of participants is assigned the case. Moreover, a particular phase of the problem-solving approach, such as generating alternatives or problem-definition, may be emphasized.

2. *Level of analysis.* A case study will usually present a generic focus—a generalized area of concern, for example. It may concentrate on: (a) institutional/political interfacing with the external environment, where strategic issues of long-run survival are paramount; (b) internal managerial-judgment issues, where questions of policies on coordination and effectiveness dominate; or (c) technical-tactical concerns with efficiency, where questions on procedures and methods require solution.

3. *Solution strategy and decision rules.* Various solution strategies are available for analyzing cases. They include straightforward computational methods, working backwards (from conclusion to premise), and heuristic branching. None of these is equally applicable to all cases, but each might be tentatively explored for any particular analysis. Furthermore, various decision rules may be more appropriate or less to the case under study. These rules include optimistic gambling, regret minimization, and computed mathematical expectations. Each will direct a different solution and any one of them should be applied knowingly.

4. *Analytic technique.* A number of data collection/analysis techniques can be applied to a case study. Most cases involve analyzing precedent conditions and future expectations. On the one hand, if knowledge about relations or causality exists, statistical and financial analyses may be made. If simple extrapolations are sufficient, techniques like a PERT diagram may be helpful. On the other hand, if the state of the future is under inquiry, simulation and the Delphi method may be most useful. The temporal dimensions of the issue in the case will dictate the appropriate analytic technique(s).

_____ **PREPARATION OF ANALYSES**

There is no one best way to analyze a case, nor is there a standard form in which to present the data. The manner of presentation depends upon

(1) the nature of the case, (2) the need for detail and supporting evidence, and (3) the purpose for which the analysis is being made. Unless instructed to the contrary, the governing principle is brevity and consiseness. It is well to remember that difficulties of reporting multiply at a rate greater than an increase in the detail contained in the analysis.

Conciseness should not be obtained by eliminating significant areas of discussion, but rather by economy of writing and clarity of style. Both depth and breadth are essential elements of analyses; a comprehensive analysis will not be superficial, nor will it omit consideration of important data bearing upon the thesis or exposition.

The follwing suggestions will help the preparation of a case analysis, whether oral or written:

1. Read the case thoroughly and completely; absorb all of the information in the case. Then put the case aside for a period of time and, if possible, carefully reread the case once or twice, trying to get an accurate picture of the dynamics of that particular situation. Let unusual solutions surface.

2. If the case description is long, review notes or summaries of pertinent information before proceeding with the analysis. Lawyers call this phase *briefing a case*. A principal difficulty at this stage is to sort out important pieces of information from "red herrings" and data of little significance.

3. Formulate in writing a precise statement of the problem. Superficial questions in the case may not penetrate real dimensions of the problem. Distinguish between the symptom (such as high labor turnover) and the cause (such as low pay) of the problem. Even though the symptom (such as a physical alteration) may need treatment, preventive remedies must be directed toward the cause of the problem.

4. Elaborate on the problem statement in such a way as to show (a) which incumbent(s) must take some kind of action, and (b) why some kind of action must be taken at this particular time.

5. Describe alternative decisions or courses of action that can be taken. These become hypotheses that require testing by marshaling evidence available in the case material.

6. Raise questions concerning the various hypotheses providing the reasoning that moves toward evaluation. These crucial questions constitute the heart of an analysis in terms of goal and priority assessments.

7. A useful evaluation model includes two types of assessments: (1) cost-benefits of a particular action, versus (2) testing such evaluations against accepting/rejecting that decision.

8. Organize the evidence so as to substantiate a specific recommendation, while stating conclusions clearly. Point out further actions

which, if made, would improve the situation or prevent a recurrence. Noncrisis management is related to the question: What might we have done to reduce the probabilility of this problem's having happened?

9. Completion of the recommendations may require the specifications of method of follow-through and monitoring for control during the changeover. Specifications can include processing standards, signaling mechanisms, and possible corrective actions.

--------------- **ALTERNATIVE ORAL TECHNIQUES OF PRESENTATION**

The common method of presenting a case orally is take a particular stand and logically support that position. If the presentation is made by a panel, members may rotate in articulating the different phases of the presentation. Questions from the audience are often restricted to those of a factual nature; overall evaluation of the recommendations is held to the conclusion of the analysis.

However, audience participation may be desirable. If so, the following techniques may be used:

1. *Propositional defense.* This technique, used by external consultants, involves responding to specific questions from the audience during each phase of the presentation. Defending the recommendations may be required in terms of facts and inferences, exhaustiveness of alternatives generated and their evaluations, and the logic and feasibility of the conclusions.

2. *Socratic method.* Audience involvement and heuristic learning may suggest a fairly nondirective consultant-audience dialogue; in such a case major deviations from any preconceived trains of logic may be necessary, and the analyst may be required largely to raise pertinent questions to the audience. The Socratic method is especially useful where the audience is as much, if not more, informed of the case situation as the person or persons who present it.

3. *Jury system.* Where the consultant wishes to employ the experience and wisdom of the audience, he may use the jury system. Here, after briefing the audience on the nature of the problem and its implications, he acts only as a resource person. At the conclusion of the dialogue, with equal vote, the audience can move toward majority or consensus resolution.

4. *Decision negotiation.* If the audience has developed its own preconception of a solution different from that of the analyst's, he may feel the need to bargain or negotiate toward resolution. The process may involve attitudinal changes, different descriptions of resource bases, and/or redefinitions of the problem. This tech-

nique can result in creative or integrative solutions Negotiation can place the analyst in a compromise position, however; thus detailed knoweldge of the situation and its implications is demanded.

_____ **SUGGESTIONS FOR WRITTEN REPORTS**

Organize your logic so that the reader can identify a well-stated problem, an organized solution, and a summary of actions recommended. But putting a case analysis into writing suggests the following considerations:

1. Because implementation requires operational concerns, clarity and simplicity of written statements are essential. Thus: (1) use short sentences; (2) be sparing in the use of descriptive adjectives; and (3) avoid using the passive voice.
2. Because accountability and control must be localized, tell who is doing what, and specify whose responsibility it is to take action and what areas are weak.
3. Because an analyst deals only with selected data, as much as possible avoid argumentative matters unless the facts cannot be contested in the context of the information provided. The analysis must be supported primarily by facts and situations supplied in the case itself, and not generalizations that have been obtained elsewhere.
4. An almost universal weakness in analyses of consultants is that the writer fails to evaluate outcomes or possible effects of alternative suggestions made.
5. And finally, spelling, punctuation, and sentence structure are vital in every piece of writing. Judges heavily weigh writing skills, so the sooner they are mastered, the better.

Name Index

A

Abarbanel, Jerome, 294
Abell, Peter, 294
Ackerman, Robert W., 619
Ackoff, Russell L., 123, 143, 281
Adams, John E., 397
Adorno, T. W., 216
Agee, Marvin H., 120
Aguilar, Francis J., 294
Aiken, Michael, 403, 577
Aitken, Hugh G. J., 39
Albert, W. W., 389
Albrook, Robert C., 507
Albrow, Martin, 325
Alderfer, Clayton P., 545
Aldrich, Howard, 282
Alexander, Harold L., 253
Allen, Robert F., 492
Alpin, John C., Jr., 164
Alutto, Joseph A., 413
Alvares, Kenneth, 224
Amundsen, Kristen, 253
Anatol, Karl W., 592
Anderson, Carl R., 613
Anshen, Melvin, 294, 491, 599, 619
Ansoff, H. I., 143, 166
Anthony, Robert N., 143, 189, 211
Applebaum, Ronald L., 591, 592
Applewhite, Philip B., 215
Appley, M. H., 563
Aquarius, Qass, 65

Aquilano, Nicholas J., 208
Aram, John D., 65, 81, 476
Argenti, J., 143
Argyris, Chris, 20, 37, 216, 228, 230, 236,
    332, 387, 439, 461, 466, 469, 477, 484–85
Armenakis, Achilles A., 476
Ashford, N. A., 619
Athos, Anthony G., 416
Atkinson, J. W., 549, 563
Avots, Ivar, 344

B

Babbage, Charles R., 23
Bach, George Leland, 294, 491
Back, Kurt, 475, 485
Bacon, Jeremy, 45
Baer, Earl E., 563
Baiardi, Peter, 125
Baill, Peter B., 7, 51
Bales, Robert F., 36
Barlett, Laile E., 619
Barnard, Chester I., 32, 80, 93, 162, 317,
    359–60, 381, 427
Barnes, Louis B., 381
Basil, Douglas, 402
Bass, Bernard M., 406, 423, 431, 585, 591
Bass, Lawrence W., 352
Bassett, Glenn A., 525
Bates, F. L., 294, 352
Baty, Gordon, 286, 441

Bauer, Raymond A., 183, 600
Baughman, James, 39
Baumgartner, John Stanley, 343
Baumhart, Raymond, S. J., 610, 619
Bavelas, A., 333
Beaudine, Frank F., 246
Becker, Selwyn, 277
Becker, Theodore M., 18
Beckett, John A., 337, 352
Beckhard, Richard, 463, 478, 485
Bedeian, Arthur G., 568
Beer, Stafford, 14, 97, 101, 120, 211, 337, 402, 591
Behling, Orlando, 9, 225, 338, 539, 551
Beichman, Arnold, 599
Beiler, George W., 601–3
Belasco, James A., 20, 413
Belcher, David W., 518, 539
Bell, Cecil H., Jr., 463, 466–67, 469, 472–79, 482, 485
Bell, Daniel, 599, 619
Bencher, Alvin, 587
Benge, Eugene J., 429
Benne, Kenneth D., 216
Bennis, Warren G., 10, 37, 216, 230, 283, 330, 333, 352, 387, 403, 432, 439, 473, 475, 485
Benson, George C. S., 610
Bentley, T., 591
Berle, Adolph A., Jr., 173
Berlo, David K., 591
Bernstein, Paul, 236, 513
Berzon, Betty, 475
Billmeyer, Fred W., 61
Bird, Frank L., 527
Birkle, John R., 591
Bisconti, Ann Stoufer, 62
Bishop, Wiley L., 592
Bishoprick, Dean W., 326
Blake, Robert R., 20, 230, 236, 419, 423, 432, 439, 441, 480–81, 485
Blanchard, Kenneth H., 403
Blau, Peter M., 325, 435, 556
Blum, Fred H., 431
Boddewyn, J., 29
Boehm, George A. W., 100
Bohr, Niels, 98
Bok, Derek, 613
Bonge, John, 183
Bownas, D. A., 441
Boulden, James, 144
Boulding, Elise, 424
Boulding, Kenneth E., 157
Boutillier, Robert G., 587
Bowen, Howard R., 596
Bowers, David G., 471, 485, 504, 513
Bowers, Raymond V., 282
Bowman, James S., 11
Brandenburg, Richard G., 139
Braude, Lee, 619

Bray, Douglas W., 253
Brech, E. G. L., 24, 29, 40
Brennan, John, 591
Brown, Alvin, 438
Brown, Bruce, 587
Brown, Courtney, 45, 325
Brown, Donald R., 485
Brown, Paul L., 485
Brown, Ray, 180, 183
Brown, Warren B., 389, 394
Brumbaugh, Robert B., 12
Bucalo, John P., Jr., 253
Buchanan, Bruce II, 508
Buchele, Robert B., 20
Buck, John A., 253
Burack, Elmer H., 255
Burch, J. G., 591
Burck, Gilbert, 597
Burns, Thomas, 230, 330, 352, 434
Burtt, H. E., 222
Buskirk, Richard H., 166
Butler, Wm. F., 144
Byars, Lloyd L., 619

C

Cafferty, Thomas P., 412
Campbell, John P., 66, 441, 517, 522, 534, 539
Cannon, Warren M., 144
Canter, Rosabeth Moss, 358
Caplow, Theodore, 432, 441
Carlisle, Howard M., 16
Carrigom, Stokes B., 476
Carroll, Archie B., 601–3, 610, 619
Carroll, Stephen J., 166, 522
Cartwright, Dorwin, 36, 218
Carzo, Rocco, Jr., 281, 352
Cass, Eugene Louis, 619
Cater, Douglas, 596
Chambers, John C., 144
Chamberlain, Neil W., 294, 619
Chandler, Alfred D., Jr., 158, 166, 358
Chapman, Richard L., 352
Chapple, Eliot D., 283, 441
Chase, Richard B., 208
Chemers, Martin M., 236
Child, John, 48, 433
Childs, Marquis W., 596
Chin, Robert, 216, 283
Churchman, C. West, 13, 120, 294
Clark, C. Spencer, 599
Clark, Graham, M., 573
Clark, John W., S. J., 610
Cleland, David I., 144, 184, 294, 344, 352
Cleland, Sherrill, 157
Coch, Lester, 504
Coelho, George V., 397
Cofer, D. N., 563

Coffey, Robert E., 416
Coggin, William C., 339
Coleman, Bruce R., 183
Coleman, Charles, 311
Coleman, John R., 414
Collier, Abram T., 596
Collins, Orvis, 43
Collins, Roger D., 39
Cook, Curtis W., 402
Coon, Carleton S., 283
Cooney, Thomas E., 403
Coons, A. E., 222
Cooper, Cary L., 476, 540
Copeman, George, 166
Corson, John J., 600
Cotton, Donald B., 144
Couzens, Michael, 470
Cox, Allan J., 242, 255
Crandall, Norman M., 234, 429
Creamer, Daniel, 441
Chessey, Donald R., 416
Crozier, Michel, 325
Culbert, Samuel A., 410
Cummings, L. L., 540
Cummins, Robert C., 592

D

Dahl, Robert A., 381
Dale, Ernest, 24, 231, 255, 325
Dalton, Gene W., 325, 381, 403
Dalton, Melville, 34, 211
Dauten, Paul M., 24
David, Stanley M., 353
Davis, Gordon B., 591
Davis, Keith, 586
Davis, Morton D., 423
Davis, Ralph C., 211
Deci, Edward L., 551, 563
Declerck, R. P., 143
De Cotis, Thomas A., 221
Deep, Samuel D., 406, 423, 591
De Greene, Kenyon B., 336
Delbecq, Andrew L., 83
Del Mar, Donald, 39
De Mare, George, 61, 540
Deming, Robert H., 189, 209
Dessler, Gary, 16, 226
Deutsch, Jan G., 619
Deutsch, Morton, 423
Dickson, William J., 35
Dierkes, Meinoff, 600
Dill, William R., 53, 287–89, 295
Dimock, Marshall, 59, 214
Donaldson, Lex, 435
Donnelly, James W., Jr., 325
Donoghy, William C., 592
Dornbusch, Sanford M., 525
Douglas, Thomas W., 11, 12

Douglass, M., 286
Dowling, William F., Jr., 563
Dreyfack, Raymond, 20
Drucker, Peter F., 4, 17, 20, 25, 30, 66, 97,
    127, 150, 166, 200, 205, 377, 492, 517,
    540, 595, 598
Dubin, Robert, 417
Duncan, Daniel M., 466
Duncan, Robert B., 465, 469, 486.
Duncan, W. Jack, 12, 97, 619
Dunnette, Marvin D., 245, 420, 441, 539,
    563
Dutton, John M., 12, 335, 412
Dyer, Lee, 66, 353

E

Easton, Allan, 97, 619
Ebert, Ronald J., 97
Edmunds, Stahrl W., 598
Eells, Richard, 285, 597
Egan, Gerard, 475
Elbing, Alvar O., Jr., 600, 608
Elbing, Carol J., 600, 608
Ellis, Tony, 43
Emerson, Harrington, 32
Emery, David A., 50
Emery, Douglas R., 91
Emery, Fred E., 281, 291, 294, 591
Emory, C. William, 109, 116, 120
Emshoff, James R., 353, 407, 423
England, George W., 160
Estes, Ralph W., 600, 619
Evan, William, 286, 294
Everest, Gordon C., 591
Ewing, David W., 137, 403
Exton, William, 563
Eyring, Henry B., 295

F

Fabun, Don, 295, 591
Famularo, Joseph J., 325
Farace, Richard V., 580
Farmer, Richard N., 6, 21
Farnsworth, Terry, 540
Faux, Victor, 66
Fayol, Henri, 21, 25, 356
Feinbert, Mortimer R., 563
Fiedler, Fred E., 224–25, 236, 508
Field, Hubert A., 476
Filipetti, George, 31, 39
Filley, Alan C., 313, 381, 424, 482–83, 505
Finch, Frederick E., 441
Finkle, Robert B., 540
Fleishman, E. A., 222, 236
Flippo, Edwin B., 9
Flood, Lucretia G., 494

Follett, Mary Parker, 32, 357
Ford, Robert N., 563
Form, William, 35
Forrester, Jay W., 10, 346
Francis, Dave, 479, 485
Frankenhuis, Jean Pierre, 18
Frederick, William C., 9, 600
French, John R. P., Jr., 218, 504
French, Wendell, 230, 463, 466–69, 472–79, 482, 485
Freshley, Dwight L., 592
Friedlander, Fred, 432
Friedman, Milton, 597
Fromkin, Howard L., 513
Frost, Peter J., 435
Fuchs, Jerome H., 21

G

Gaines, George S., 108
Galbraith, Jay R., 339, 353
Galbraith, John Kenneth, 43, 152
Gall, William R., 510
Gallagher, Charles A., 581
Gamson, W. A., 381
Gannon, Martin J., 21, 613
Gantt, Henry L., 95
Gardner, Burleigh, 35
Gardner, Neely, 335
Gellerman, Saul W., 513
George, Claude S., 236
Georgopoulos, Basil, 427, 432
Gergen, Kenneth J., 183
Gerth, H. H., 299
Gibb, Cecil A., 223
Gibson, Charles H., 560
Gibson, James L., 235
Giesbrecht, Martin Gerhard, 43
Gil, Peter P., 10
Gillespie, D. F., 286
Gilmer, B. von Haller, 493, 496
Gilmore, Frank F., 139
Glans, Thomas B., 337
Glasser, Gerald F., 115
Glueck, William F., 255, 400
Goetz, Billy E., 112, 114
Gold, Bela, 295
Goldman, Max, 225
Goldstein, Irwin L., 538
Golembiewski, Robert T., 476, 485, 508
Goodman, Richard A., 292, 351, 377
Gordon, Robert Aaron, 43
Gordon, Thomas, 215
Gouldner, Alvin W., 217
Graen, George, 224
Graham, Gerald H., 66
Gray, Jerry L., 441
Green, Paul E., 116
Green, Thad B., 579
Greenbaum, Howard H., 580

Greene, Charles N., 221
Greenlaw, Paul S., 112, 114, 120
Greenwood, Ronald G., 379
Greiner, Larry E., 385, 403
Gribbins, Ronald E., 579
Grinold, Richard C., 255
Gross, Bertram M., 147, 166
Grossman, Lee, 394, 403, 463, 485
Gruber, W., 325
Gruenfeld, Elaine F., 255
Gue, Ronald L., 112, 114
Guest, Robert H., 403
Guetzkow, Harold, 282, 333–34
Guion, Robert M., 493
Gulick, Luther, 10, 238
Gurin, Gerald, 494
Gustafson, David H., 83

H

Haber, Samuel, 39
Haberstroh, Chadwick J., 203, 334
Hackman, J. Richard, 561, 619
Hacon, Richard, 441
Hage, Gerald, 403, 577
Hague, Hawdon, 519, 540
Haire, Mason, 37, 387
Hall, Douglas T., 61, 255
Hall, Francine S., 61
Hall, Richard H., 424
Hall, William K., 128
Hamburg, David A., 397
Hamilton, William F., 572
Hamner, Ellen, 483
Hamner, W. Clay, 16, 483
Hammond, Robert A., 103
Hampton, David R., 20, 592
Haner, F. T., 183
Hanson, Agnes O., 540
Hanson, Robert O., 508
Harris, O. Jeff, Jr., 513
Harrison, E. Frank, 97
Harris, E. F., 222
Hartley, E. L., 219
Harvey, C. C., 352
Harvey, Donald, 485
Havens, A. Eugene, 161
Hayes, R. L., 143
Hedburg, L. T., 335
Hegarty, Edward J., 66
Hein, Leonard W., 112, 114
Heirs, Don, 137, 144
Hellriegel, Don, 16, 483, 488–89
Helmich, Donald L., 394
Hemphill, J. K., 223
Henderson, A. M., 299
Henderson, Richard, 563
Heneman, Herbert G., Jr., 256, 540, 564
Herbert, Theodore T., 485
Herden, Richard P., 441, 470–71

Herman, Stanley M., 485
Herold, David M., 221
Herrick, Neal P., 616
Hersey, Paul, 403
Hersler, William J., 513
Herzberg, Frederick, 230, 552
Hickson, David J., 325
Hill, Ivan, 620
Hinton, Bernard L., 491
Hirsch, Paul M., 431
Hoagland, John H., 24, 29
Hodgetts, Richard M., 377
Hodgson, Richard C., 66
Hofer, Charles W., 125
Hofshi, Rami, 358
Hollander, Stanley C., 18
Homans, George C., 34, 223, 547, 550, 605
Hostage, G. M., 501
Houck, John W., 513
House, Robert J., 226, 316, 351, 381, 414,
    424, 482–83, 505, 552, 563
Howard, Ann, 253
Huber, George, 282
Huck,James R., 253
Hulin, Charles F., 497
Humble, John, 600
Hummel, Ralph, 325
Hunsaker, Phillip L., 465, 486
Hunt, H. G., 558
Hunt, John W., 513
Hunt, J. G., 222, 226, 236, 286
Hunt, Raymond G., 513
Hunter, George T., 573
Husband, Tom M., 563
Huse, Edgar F., 403, 475, 477, 482, 485
Huseman, Richard C., 592
Hussey, David, 144

I

Ingalls, John D., 540
Ishikawa, Akira, 144
Ivancevich, John M., 325, 490, 524

J

Jablen, Fredric, 245
Jacobs, Alfred, 462, 479, 485
Jacobs, Herman S., 521
Jacoby, Neil, 282, 599, 620
James, Lawrence R., 300
Jaques, Elliott, 325, 567, 582
Jay, Antony, 381
Jenks, Stephen, 514
Jennings, Eugene E., 216, 231, 529
Jeuck, John E., 285
Jillison, Katherine, 521, 529
Joad, C. E. M., 609
Johanneson, R. E., 488

Johnson, Richard A., 211
Johnson, Rodney D., 109, 120
Johnston, H. Russell, 490
Johnston, William B., 616
Jones, Allan P., 300
Jones, Garth N., 403
Jones, Halsey R., 441
Jones, Harry, 144
Jones, William S., 540
Jongeward, Dorothy, 547
Joyce, Robert D., 475
Juran, J. M., 45

K

Kaczka, Eugene, 491
Kahn, Herman, 122
Kahn, Melvin, 21
Kahn, Robert L., 83, 223, 236, 337, 403,
    424, 432, 441, 471
Kakar, Sudhir, 39
Karn, Harry W., 493
Kassem, M. Sami, 517
Kast, Fremond E., 211
Kastens, Merritt L., 144
Katz, Daniel, 83, 223, 236, 337, 403, 432,
    441, 494
Katz, Elihu, 217
Katz, Robert L., 184, 439
Katzell, Raymond A., 51
Kaufman, Herbert, 151, 403, 470
Kavesh, Robert A., 144
Keefe, William F., 592
Keen, Peter G. W., 53
Kefalos, Asterios G., 295
Kelley, Harold H., 216
Kelley, Joe, 408
Kelley, Richard N., 61
Kellogg, Marion S., 21, 521, 540
Kendrick, John W., 441
Kerr, Clark, 417
Kerr, Steven, 164, 381, 424, 482–83, 505
Kilman, Ralph H., 325, 441, 470–71
Kimberly, John R., 471
Kindall, Alva F., 164
King, William R., 144, 184, 294, 344, 352
Kirk, Roy V., 491
Klauss, Rudi, 585
Klein, Lisl, 353
Klein, Thomas A., 601, 620
Klein, Walter H., 184
Knight, Kenneth, 339
Knowles, Henry P., 236
Knowles, M. C., 279
Kochan, Thomas A., 221, 286
Koehler, Jerry, 513, 592
Koontz, Harold, 9, 45, 184, 441, 540
Korda, Michael, 358
Korenich, Michael, 485
Korman, Abraham K., 563

Korsch, James F., 358
Kossen, Stan, 563
Kotter, John P., 66
Kraut, Allen I., 253
Kreitner, Robert, 483
Kubr, M., 21
Kuriloff, Arthur H., 485

L

La Follette, William R., 490
Lakin, Martin, 475
Lamone, Rudolph P., 111
Lamar, Charles, 108
Landau, Martin, 335
Landsberger, H. A., 411, 576
Larson, L. L., 226, 236
Laszlo, Erwin, 13
Latham, Gary P., 160
Lawler, Edward E., III, 211, 255, 441, 496,
    498, 513, 539–40, 551, 592
Lawrence, Paul R., 289, 295, 325, 352, 393,
    403, 419, 432, 436, 440, 462–63, 467–68,
    490
Lazarsfeld, Paul F., 217
Leavitt, Harold J., 219, 295, 297, 333, 434
Lee, James A., 394
Lee, William B., 570
Leifer, Richard P., 282
Lerner, Allan W., 97
Lertzman, Sidney I., 351, 414
Levinson, Daniel J., 66
Levinson, Harry, 66, 441, 515, 523, 528
Levin, Richard I., 111
Levitt, Theodore, 427, 599, 620
Levy, Ferdinand K., 209, 212
Lewin, Arie Y., 184
Lewin, Kurt, 36
Lewis, John W., 511
Lewis, Phillip V., 592
Likert, Jane Gibson, 424
Likert, Rensis, 37, 211, 230, 424, 435, 441,
    494, 500, 505–6, 547
Lilienthal, David E., 21
Linbskold, Svenn, 514
Lippitt, Gordon L., 403, 531
Lippitt, R., 219
Litchfield, Edward H., 10
Litschert, Robert J., 620
Litterer, Joseph A., 406, 410, 441
Litwin, George H., 488, 490, 513–14, 563
Lodge, George C., 173, 599, 620
Logue, Cal M., 592
Lombard, M., 236
Lopez, Felix E., 51, 52, 245, 255
Lorange, Peter, 125, 144
Lorsch, Jay W., 289, 295, 325, 393, 419, 432,
    436, 440, 462–63, 467–68, 490
Louden, J. Keith, 45

Luke, Robert A., Jr., 247
Lundborg, Lewis B., 49, 599
Luthans, Fred, 16, 483
Lyon, Herbert H., 490
Lyon, John, 120

Mc

McCall, M., 236
McCarthy, Robert J., 253
McClelland, D. C., 381, 549
McDonald, Alanzo, 415
McDonald, Donald, 580
McDonald, John, 114
McDonald, Smacky, 563
McEachern, William A., 431
McFarland, Dalton E., 11, 31, 61, 413, 599
McFeely, Wilbur F., 403
McGill, Michael E., 485
McGregor, Douglas, 48, 66, 211, 217, 223,
    230, 381, 439, 492, 513, 540, 546, 563
McKenney, James L., 53, 141
McMurray, Robert, 36
McNair, Malcolm, 36
McNichols, Thomas J., 184

M

Maccoby, Michael, 63, 236
Maccoby, Nathan, 494
Maddox, John, 599
Magee, John F., 116–17
Magnusen, Karl O., 485
Mahar, Linda, 236
Mahler, Walter R., 245, 381
Mahoney, Thomas A., 234, 429–30, 432,
    435
Maier, Ayesha A., 480
Maier, Norman R. F., 540
Maier, R. M., 480
Malcolm, Andrew, 513
Mann, Andrew, 612
Mansfield, M. J., Jr., 125, 141
Mansfield, Roger, 490
March, James G., 10, 32, 37, 297–98, 325,
    333, 348, 406, 419, 424, 503, 548, 550
Margerison, Charles J., 144
Margulies, Newton, 403, 473, 475
Marrow, Alfred J., 504, 513, 559
Marrett, Cora B., 577
Marshall, Kneal T., 255
Maslow, A. H., 230, 545
Martella, Joseph A., 224
Martin, Charles C., 344, 353
Massarik, Fred, 217, 439, 504
Mathes, Sorrel M., 403
Mathies, Leslie H., 295
Maurer, John G., 295, 353

Mausner, Bernard, 552
Means, Gardiner C., 173
Mee, John F., 39, 339
Melcher, Arlyn, 353
Merrill, Harwood F., 31, 40
Merton, Robert K., 160, 286
Mescon, Michael H., 619
Metcalf, Henry C., 21, 32, 47, 236, 357, 381
Meyer, Herbert H., 490, 519, 525, 559
Meyer, Marshall, 325
Meyers, Clark E., 40
Meyers, Mildred S., 600
Mickelson, Douglas J., 465, 486
Middleton, C. J., 343
Migliore, R. Henry, 166
Milbourn, Gene, Jr., 499
Miles, Raymond E., 9, 12, 21, 255, 485, 504
Miles, Robert H., 229, 414
Mileti, D. S., 286
Miller, David W., 79, 99, 108, 115, 120
Miller, Delbert C., 35, 421
Miller, Ernest C., 147
Miller, Kenneth M., 255
Mills, C. Wright, 299
Mindlin, Sergio F., 282
Miner, John B., 9, 21, 316, 526, 563
Mintzberg, Henry, 21, 54, 66, 88, 592
Mitchell, James O., 253
Mitchell, Terence R., 97, 403
Mockler, Robert J., 211
Modler, Joseph J., 211
Mollick, Atinderez K., 144
Moment, David, 215, 218, 231
Monczka, Robert M., 16
Mooney, James D., 24
Moore, David G., 43, 157
Moore, Wilbert E., 21
Morgenstern, Oskar, 114
Morse, Dean, 403
Morse, Nancy C., 494
Mosley, Donald C., 476
Moss, Michael A., 572
Mott, Paul E., 426–30, 432, 434, 442
Mottice, Homer J., 120, 592
Moursi, M. A., 517
Mouton, Jane S., 20, 230, 236, 419, 423,
    432, 439, 441, 480–81, 485
Munsterberg, Hugo, 33
Murdock, Robert G., 102, 120
Murphy, David C., 184
Murray, H. A., 549
Murrell, Kenneth L., 485
Myrdal, Gunnar, 607

N

Nadler, David A., 470
Nadworny, Milton J., 40
Naumes, William, 184

Naylor, T. H., 125, 141
Negandhi, Anant R., 337, 353, 433, 436
Neuhauser, Duncan, 277
Newcomb, T. M., 219
Newman, Pamela J., 592
Newman, William H., 21, 144, 211
Newport, M. Gene, 233, 236
Newstrom, John A., 612
Newstrom, John M., 16, 545
Newell, Allen, 118
Nicholson, Edward A., 620
Nielander, Edward E., 255
Nielson, Warren R., 471
Niland, Powell, 109, 116, 120
Niles, J., 325
Niles, Mary Cushing, 45
Nisbet, Robert, 381
Nixon, S. R., 592
Norlen, Urban, 120
Nowell-Smith, P. H., 609
Nystrom, Paul, 325, 335

O

O'Connor, Rochelle, 144
Odiorne, George S., 166, 522
O'Hanlon, Thomas, 346
Oldham, Greg R., 162
Optner, Stanford L., 100–101, 339
O'Reilly, Charles A., 579
Orris, James B., 224
Osborne, Richard N., 286
O'Shaughnessy, John, 325
O'Toole, James, 620
Owen, James L., 592

P

Pacanowsky, Michael, 580
Page, Paul A., 592
Page, Wm. J., Jr., 164
Paine, Frank T., 184
Paine, Roy, 490
Park, E. Lauck, 561
Parsons, Talcott, 299
Pascucci, John J., 346
Patten, Thomas H., Jr., 233, 239
Patz, Alan L., 525
Pearse, Robert F., 519, 540
Pehrson, Gordon, 137, 144
Pelzer, B. Purdy, 519, 540
Perrow, Charles, 329, 353, 385, 392, 599
Person, H. S., 40
Peterson, M. G., 441
Petrofesa, John, 255
Pettigrew, Andrew M., 466
Pettit, Thomas A., 211
Petty, M. M., 229

Pfeffer, Jeffrey, 227
Phillips, Cecil R., 211
Pietri, Paul H., 579
Pigors, Paul, 223
Pizam, Abraham, 529
Platt, Robert B., 144
Pollard, Harold R., 40
Pondy, Louis R., 325, 410, 420
Porter, Lyman W., 217, 255, 496, 513, 540, 563
Prasad, S., Benjamin, 11, 431
Presbie, Robert J., 485
Presthus, Robert, 53, 58
Preston, McLean, 529
Price, James L., 432, 442
Price, Karl F., 20
Prien, Erich P., 521
Pugh, Derek S., 325

Q

Quick, Thomas L., 403

R

Radley, G. W., 592
Radosevich, Raymond, 519
Raia, Anthony P., 166
Raiffa, Howard, 120
Ramalingam, P., 120
Ramo, Simon, 574
Randolph, Robert M., 144
Ranofsky, Robert, 563
Raven, B., 218
Rawls, Donna, 519
Rawls, James, 519
Raynor, Joel O., 563
Ready, R. K., 66
Reddin, W. J., 66, 517
Reichley, James A., 214
Reif, William D., 16, 552
Reiff, H. Joseph, 503
Reiley, Alan C., 24
Reimann, Bernard C., 433, 436–37
Renwick, Patricia A., 410
Rhodes, John Grant, 211, 592
Rice, George H., Jr., 326
Rich, Joseph, 300
Richards, Max D., 112, 114, 120, 255
Rietman, Walter R., 53
Ritchie, J. B., 504
Rizzo, John R., 351, 414
Roadman, H. E., 525
Robbins, Stephen P., 21, 424
Roberts, Karlene H., 497, 579
Roeber, Richard J. C., 295
Roethlisberger, F. J., 35, 233
Rogers, David C., 184

Rogers, Everett M., 570, 575, 592
Rogers, Rekha Agarwalla, 570, 575
Ronan, William W., 521
Rosenberg, Jerry M., 592
Rosenzweig, James E., 211
Ross, Joel E., 102, 120, 540, 592
Rothermel, T., 286
Rotondi, Thomas, Jr., 278
Rowland, Virgil, 540
Rubenstein, Albert H., 334
Rubin, Irwin M., 225
Ruch, William A., 612
Russell, Bertrand, 98, 515
Rust, Harold M. F., 472, 563
Ryan, William G., 342–43, 353

S

Salancik, G. R., 552, 557, 592
Sanford, Fillmore, 216
Sashkin, Marshall, 513
Saxberg, Borje O., 236
Sayles, Leonard, 9, 54, 212, 441, 563
Scheer, Wilbert E., 144
Schein, Edgar H., 16, 216, 397, 432, 441, 475, 477, 507, 613
Schein, Virginia E., 358
Schelling, T. C., 406
Schermerhorn, John R., Jr., 282
Schmidt, Stuart M., 221, 286
Schmidt, Warren H., 620
Schneider, Arnold E., 592
Schneider, Benjamin, 255, 545
Schoderbek, Charles G., 295
Schoderbek, Peter P., 164, 209, 295
Schriesheim, Chester, 225, 338, 539, 551
Schrode, William A., 120
Schuster, Fred E., 164
Schwab, Donald P., 540
Scott, W. Richard, 403, 525, 556
Scott, William G., 424
Seashore, Stanley E., 403, 430, 432, 441–42, 494, 504, 508, 513
Sedwick, Robert S., 547
Segall, J. E., 389
Seidler, Lee J., 600
Seidler, Lynn L., 600
Seiler, John A., 281, 421, 478
Selekman, Benjamin M., 598
Selfridge, Richard J., 466
Seligman, Ben B., 592
Selznick, Philip, 160, 236, 510
Senger, John, 350
Sethi, S. Prakash, 620
Sexton, William P., 236, 353
Shaeffer, Ruth G., 256
Shannon, Claude E., 570
Shaw, Philip, 18
Shearer, Richard L., 528

Sheldon, Oliver, 21
Shepard, Herbert A., 419, 423
Sheppard, Harold L., 616
Sherman, V. Clayton, 540
Sherwood, Frank P., 164
Sherwood, John J., 513
Shirley, Robert C., 396
Short, Larry E., 464
Shrode, William A., 592
Shubik, Martin, 115, 120
Shull, Fremont A., 340, 421
Shwinger, P., 558
Sikula, Andrew F., 378
Silber, Mark B., 540
Silk, Leonard, 609
Silverman, Melbin, 344
Silverzweig, Stan, 492
Simmons, Roberta G., 233
Simon, Herbert A., 10, 32, 37, 77, 79, 81–
    82, 91, 99, 102–3, 118, 120, 187, 325,
    333–34, 348, 359, 406, 419, 424, 491, 503,
    548, 550, 592
Simon, Leonard S., 108
Simpson, Karl, 561
Simpson, R. L., 411, 577
Sisken, Bernard R., 109, 120
Skinner, B. F., 482–83
Slevin, Dennis P., 325
Slocum, John W., Jr., 16, 483, 488–89
Slusher, E. Allen, 525
Small, John T., 570
Smith, Bruce, 587
Smith, Clagett G., 406, 410
Smith, Donald D., 144
Smith, Frank, 497
Smith, Theodore, 166
Snyderman, Barbara Block, 552
Sofer, Cyril, 45
Sokolik, Stanley L., 466
Solem, Allan R., 480
Solomon, Lawrence N., 475
Solomon, Lewis C., 62
Sontoff, Herbert, 50, 332
Sorenson, Richard, 469
Sorrentino, Richard M., 587
Spates, Thomas G., 596
Sperry, Len, 465, 486
Spivey, W. Allen, 157
Spooner, Peter, 560
Spray, Lee, 442
Spriegel, William R., 40, 382
Stagg, Jerry, 348
Stalker, G. M., 230, 330, 352, 434
Starbuck, William H., 12, 325, 335
Starr, Martin K., 79, 99, 108, 115, 120
Staw, Barry M., 563, 592
Steager, Joseph A., 528
Steele, Fritz, 463, 486, 514
Steers, Richard M., 431–33, 563
Stein, Robert N., 18

Steiner, Gary A., 286
Steiner, George A., 139, 144, 342–43, 353,
    598, 600
Steiner, John F., 615
Stephens, James C., 66
Stewart, Nathaniel, 510
Stewart, Rosemary, 51
Stinchcombe, Arthur L., 442
Stogdill, R. M., 222–23, 236, 334, 543,
    550
Stone, Christopher D., 611
Stoner, James A. F., 476
Strater, F. R., 591
Strauss, George, 507, 577
Straussman, Paul A., 581
Stringer, Robert A., 513, 563
Strong, William, 587
Sullivan, John F., 18
Summerfield, Joanne, 540
Suojanen, Waino W., 563
Suojanen, W. William, 563
Susman, Gerald I., 514
Suttle, J. Lloyd, 619
Swallow, Gary L., 563
Swanson, Huntington S., 120
Swedmark, Donald C., 538
Swingle, Paul G., 382
Swinth, Robert, 326, 353

T

Tannenbaum, Arnold S., 212, 406, 427
Tannenbaum, Robert, 217, 432, 438, 504
Tarnowieski, Dale, 616
Tarrant, John J., 563
Tausky, Curt, 561
Taylor, Bernard, 531
Taylor, Frederick W., 24–31, 38, 40
Tead, Ordway, 354
Tedeshi, James T., 514
Terkel, Studs, 497
Terreberry, Shirley, 289
Thayer, Lee, 592
Thibaut, John W., 216
Thomas, Kenneth W., 420
Thomas, Michael E., 112, 114
Thompson, David W., 486
Thompson, James D., 158, 289, 326, 389,
    411, 442
Thompson, Victor A., 212, 326, 332, 347,
    382, 403, 413, 421, 424
Thorelli, Hans B., 288
Thorndike, F., 482
Thornton, George C., 525
Tichy, Noel M., 466, 560
Todd, H. Ralph, 236
Tolliver, James, 551
Toren, Nina, 326, 332
Torgerson, Paul E., 120

Tosi, Henry L., 16, 166, 522, 563
Tournier, Paul, 407
Towers, J. Maxwell, 486
Toynbee, Arnold, 285
Tracey, William R., 486, 531, 538
Tracy, Lane, 239
Trist, Eric L., 136, 291
Tuden, Arthur, 158
Tuggle, Francis D., 91
Tushman, Michael, 403

U

Udy, Stanley H., Jr., 555
Ullrich, Robert A., 353, 403, 424, 442, 474,
    483, 505
Unwalla, Darab B., 43
Urwick, Lyndall F., 24, 29, 31–32, 40, 47,
    236, 238, 357, 410

V

Vaill, Peter B., 485
Valenzi, Enzo R., 226
Vance, Stanley, 45
Vancil, Richard F., 125, 144
VandeVen, Andrew H., 83, 84
Van Fleet, David D., 545
Vardaman, George, 592
Vardaman, Patricia, 592
Varney, Glen H., 479, 486
Vickers, Geoffrey, 184
Viola, Richard H., 620
Vogel, David, 609
Voich, Dan, Jr., 120, 592
von Bertalanffy, Ludwig, 14
Von Maanen, John, 21, 66
von Neumann, John, 114
Vroom, Victor H., 551–52, 563

W

Wager, L. W., 233
Wagner, Harvey M., 120
Wallace, John, 403, 473, 475
Walters, Roy W., 564
Walton, Clarence C., 597, 620
Walton, Richard E., 412, 478
Warr, Peter, 166
Warner, Aaron W., 403
Warner, W. Keith, 161
Warner, W. Lloyd, 157
Warren, E. Kirby, 21, 144
Warrington, Allan, 528
Watson, Thomas J., Jr., 596
Wattenberg, Ben J., 599

Ways, Max, 612
Weaver, Barbara N., 592
Weaver, W., 570
Webb, James E., 425
Webb, Ronald J., 431–33
Weber, Max, 32, 239, 277, 298–99, 359
Weick, Karl E., Jr., 539
Weinberg, Gerald, 120
Weiner, Bernard, 551, 564
Weist, Jerome D., 118
Weitzell, William, 234, 429–30, 432
Weschler, Irving R., 217, 438
Wheelwright, Steven C., 144
Whistler, T. L., 389
White, D. J., 120
White, Harrison C., 256
White, R. K., 219
Whyte, Lancelot Law, 185
Whyte, William Foote, 34, 63, 217, 547,
    550, 557
Wieland, George F., 353, 403, 424, 442,
    474, 483, 505
Wiener, Anthony J., 122
Wiener, Norbert, 284, 570
Wiest, Jerome D., 209, 212
Wigdor, Lawrence, 552
Wilbur, Ray Lyman, 75
Wilensky, Harold, 287
Williams, Ervin, 514
Williams, Raymond, 5
Williamson, Oliver E., 212
Wilson, James A., 610
Winstanley, Nathan S., 520
Wofford, Jerry, 592
Woodcock, Mike, 479, 485
Woodward, Joan, 392, 435
Woolf, Douglas Austin, 9, 40
Woolsey, Robert E. D., 120
Wortman, Lillian A., 21
Wren, Daniel A., 40

XYZ

Yanouzos, John N., 281, 352
Yearsley, Ronald, 591
Yoder, Dale, 12, 256, 540, 564
Yorks, Lyle, 564
Young, F. M., 515
Yuchtman, Ephraim, 432, 442
Yukl, Gary A., 160
Zaleznek, Abraham, 66, 215, 218, 231, 381–
    82
Zaltman, Gerald, 469, 486
Zand, Dale, 469
Zander, Alvin, 36, 218
Zangwill, Willard I., 564
Zimmer, Frederick G., 619
Zimmerman, Gordon I., 592

Subject Index

A

Action research, 472–73
Adaptive—coping cycle, 397
Administration, *See* Management
Administrators, *See* Managers
Applied anthropology, 34
Appraisal, performance, 517–25
Aspiration, level of, 58
Assessment centers, 252–53
Attitudes, employee, 373, 594
    See also Morale
Audits
    control and, 201
    of communications, 580
    social, 600–1
Authority, 354–80
    acceptance of, 359–61
    accountability and, 367, 370–72
    in adaptive organizations, 376–77
    clarity of, 364, 374–76
    conflicts in, 363–65
    decentralization, 377–79
    defined, 355–56
    delegation of, 193–94, 366–72
        basic steps in, 366–70
        nature of, 366–70
        problems of, 370–77
        responsibility and, 193–94, 370–72
        scope of, 360–61, 368–70
    exceptions concept and, 374
    power and, 355–59

types of
    functional, 365–66
    knowledge, 356
    line, 361–62
    positional, 355
    situational, 356
    staff, 362–63
    unity of command, 346–50
    zones of indifference, 360–61
Automation, 205–7, 570–74

B

Behavior modification, 482–83
Budgets, 199–200
Bureaucracy, 296–323
    conditions giving rise to, 298–300
    defined, 298–300
    dysfunctional consequences of, 330–33
    evolution of, 32, 298–300
    mobility and, 58–59, 249–52
    size and, 32
    See also Organization structure
Businessman, defined, 42

C

Careers, managerial, 8
    defined, 57
    strategies for, 60–64
    See also Promotions

Change
    in basic roles, 48–50
    See also Organization change
Clark Equipment Company, 153
Committees, 84–85
    structural, 313–15
Communications
    audits, 580
    barriers to, 568–69, 581–86
    decision making and, 93–94
    defined, 566–67
    effectiveness of, 578–89
    information technology and, 569–74
    interpersonal, 581–87
    between management and labor, 577–78
    oral, 586–87
    organization structure and, 277, 574–78
        horizontal, 576–77
        intergroup, 577–78
        upward and downward, 575–76
    process of, 566–74
    research on, 578–80
    semantics and, 568–69
    symbols and, 567
    training in, 588–89
    written, 587–88
Communication nets, 333–35
Comparative management theory, 13–14
Computers
    control and, 205–7
    information technology and, 392, 570–74
    nature of, 570–74
    simulation and, 108–10
Conflict organizational
    functions and dysfunctions of, 407–9
    institutionalized, 417–18
    interdepartmental, 191–92
    intergroup, 477–78
    leadership and, 409
    line and staff, 363–65, 412–13
    nature of, 404–7
    of policies, 179–81
    power struggles and, 414–16
    resolution of, 418–22
    roles and, 413–16
    strategy of, 406–7
    types of, 409–13
        horizontal, 411–12
        structurally based, 409–13
        vertical, 410–11
Conglomerate firms, 345–46, 388–89
Consultants, management, 17–19, 477
Control
    auditing for, 201–2
    automation and, 205–7
    cycle, 196–97
    decisions and, 202–3
    defined, 187–88
    functional differentiation and, 191–92

    human factors in, 190–91, 195–96
    mechanical element and, 204–7
    methods of
        budgets and, 199–200
        disciplinary action, 203
        example setting, 198
        information and observation, 200–202
        standards, 197–9
        standing limitations, 198–99
        standing orders and, 199
    planning and, 188–90
    of scheduling, 207–9
    social, 204
    specialization and, 192–93
    statistical, 204–5
    systems, computers and, 205–7
Coordination
    achievement of, 130–33, 193–95, 313
    committees and, 194–95
    decisions and, 194
    defined, 186–87
    organizational mechanisms for, 194–95
    problems of, 190–93
    self, 187
    specialization and, 192–93
    staff meetings and, 195
Critical Path Method, *See* PERT
Cybernetics
    See Feedback cycle

D

Decentralization
    of authority, 377–79
Decision making
    administrative problems in, 85–87
    commitment in, 78–79
    committees and, 84–85
    communication and, 93–94
    control and, 202–3
    coordination and, 194
    decision trees, 115–18
    defined, 77–78
    delegation and, 366–70
    effectiveness of, 88–89
    environment and, 92–93, 290–93
    evaluation of, 89–91
    group, 82–84
    heuristic programming, 116–18
    information systems, 100–102, 570–74
    nature of, 77–78, 99–102
    operations research methods, 99–119
        game models, 114–15
        inventory management, 112–13
        linear programming, 110–12
        resource allocation and, 110–12
        simulation, 108–110
        waiting-line problems, 113–14
    participation in, 94–96

problem solving and, 85–87
as process, 77–78
psychological elements in, 93
quality of, 92–96
    satisficing and, 91–92
quantitative methods of
    classes of, 106–8
    models in, 76–77, 106–8
    nature of, 99–108
    systems framework for, 100–102
rationality in, 79–80
roles in, 88–89
simulation models in, 108–110
timing of, 93–94
types of, 80–85, 104–5
    basic and routine, 81
    committee, 84–85
    group decision, 82–84
    organizational and personal, 80–81
    programmed and nonprogrammed,
        81–82
Delegation
    See Authority
Discharge, 253–54
Discipline, 203, 253–54, 553–59

E

Ecology of management
    See Environment
Effectiveness
    of executives, 516–17
    organizational, 425–40
Efficiency, organization structure and,
        276–77, 299
Emery Air Freight Corporation, 482–83
Employment contracts, 245–46
Entrepreneurs, 42–43, 51–52, 88
Environment
    impact of, 285–86, 390–91
    interpretation of, 288–89
    models of, 288–89
    of organizations, 284–93
    task, 287–88
    types of, 291–93
Ethics of executives, 605–17
    codes of, 613–15
    concepts of, 608–9
    education and, 612–13
    norms and, 605–6
    policies and, 611–12
    professions and, 16–18
    studies of, 609–10
    values and, 606–8
Executive development, 530–38
    critique of, 536–37
    evaluation of, 537–38
    external resources for, 535–36
    internal resources for, 531–35
        coaching, 532–34

courses and conferences, 535
    rotation plans, 534–35
personnel department and, 531
programs for, 530–38
team building, 478–79
training departments and, 531
    See also Organization development;
        Performance, managerial
Executives
    appraisal of, 517–25
    capabilities of, 60
    career mobility and, 57–64, 247–49
    effectiveness of, 516–17
    levels of, 43–46, 53
    obsolescence of, 527–29
    responsibilities of, 26–27, 54–57, 193–
        94
    stereotypes, 46–48
    See also Executive development;
        Performance, managerial

F

Federal Trade Commission, 292
Feedback cycle, 5–6, 107, 283–84
    control and, 196–97
Forecasting, *See* Planning

G

Gamesman, the, 63–64
Goals, 153–55, 159–62, 428–29
    changes in, 162–63
    conflict in, 160–61
    congruence of, 161–62
    displacement of, 161
    multiple, 160–61
    See also Objectives
Group decision, 82–84
Group dynamics, 36
    growth and decay of organizations, 387–
        88, 438–39

H

Hawthorne Studies, 35
Hierarchy of needs, 543–46
Hierarchy, organizational, 43–46, 277,
        300–301, 332, 410–11
    rewards and, 555–56
    See also Organization
History, managerial, 22–39
Human relations, 32–36, 477–78, 488–92,
        581–87
    communications and, 581–87
    as a movement, 32–36
    performance and, 529–30
    See also Morale; Organization climate

I

Incentives, wage, 28–29
Individualism, 599
Industrial democracy, 219–21
Industrial psychology, 33
Industrial sociology, 34
Influence, 217–18, 219–21
   See also Authority; Power; Leadership
Information processing, 134–35, 200, 570–74, 581
   See also Decision making
Institutions, social, 4, 598–99
Interpersonal relations
   See Human Relations

J

Job enrichment, 559–61
Job satisfaction, organizations and, 277–78, 496–97
   See also Attitudes; Morale

L

Labor-management relations
   communication and, 577–78
Leadership
   abilities and, 214
   conflict and, 409
   definitions of, 217–21
   effectiveness of, 227–29
   influence and, 217
   nature of, 215–26
   organizational factors in, 231
   power and, 218
   problems of, 227–29
   shortage of, 214
   styles of, 229–35
      authoritarian and democratic, 219–21
      charismatic, 229–31
      organizational and personal, 231
   supervisory, 232–34
   theories of, 214–26
      contingency, 223–26
      early, 215–16
      multidimensional, 221–26
      Ohio State Studies, 221–23
      path-goal, 226
      situational, 223–26
      traits, 216–17
Line-staff relations, 363–65

M

Management
   administration and, 6–7
   consulting, 17–19
   defined, 4–8
      as an applied science, 11–12
      as a career, 8–9, 16–17, 57–58
      as a collective noun, 8
      as a formal discipline, 7–8, 37–38
      as a process, 5–6
      as a profession, 16–17
   ecology, 284–93
   history of, 9–11, 22–38
      early influences, 23–25
      human relations movement, 9–10, 32–36
      incentives, 28–29
      management science, 9–10, 37–38
      research techniques, 27–28
      revisionist movement, 9–10, 36–38
      scientific management movement, 25–32
      Taylorism, evaluation of, 9–10, 29–31
      work methods, 27–28
   by objectives (MBO), 163–64
   theory, 8–16
      comparative, 13–14
      contingency approach, 15–16
      development of, 9–11, 22–38
      functional vs. revisionist, 36–38
      and practice, 12–13
      state of, 9–11
      systems approach and, 14–15, 51, 100–102
Management science, 26–31, 37–38
   See also Operations Research
Managers
   characteristics of, 46–48
   defined, 42–46
   responsibilities, 26–27, 54–57, 193–94
   roles of, 50–52, 413–16, 479–80
   stereotypes, 46–48
Managerial grid, 480–82
Managerial tasks, 48–54
   See also Performance, managerial
Manpower planning, 239–40
Middle management, 45, 175–76
Missions, *See* Objectives
Mobility of managers, 57–64, 247–49
   career strategies and, 61–64
   occupational, 58
Models, 106–8
   See also Decision making, quantitative methods of
Morale, 492–511
   attitudes and, 373, 495–97
   building and maintaining, 502–11
   cohesiveness and, 507–8
   definitions of, 492–93, 543
   factors influencing, 488–92
   identification and, 509
   job satisfaction and, 277–78, 495–502
   levels of, 493–94
   loyalty and, 509–11

measurement of, 488–92, 497–502
   attitude surveys, 499–502
   participation and, 502–7
   reason for maintaining, 494–95
   See also Organizational climate
Motivation
   human needs and, 543–45
   job design and, 559–61
   morale and, 543
   nature of, 542–43
   organizational hierarchy and, 555–56
   problems of, 552–61
   rewards and, 553–59
      discipline and, 553–54, 556–57
      informal, 554–55
      monetary, 557–59
   of subordinates, 552–61
   theories of, 546–52
      achievement theory, 549
      constraints theory, 547–48
      expectancy theories, 549–51
      hygiene theory, 551–52
      interaction theory, 547
      participation theories, 546–47

N

Negotiations, 88

O

Objectives
   acceptance of, 162
   advantages of, 147–49
   changes in, 162–63
   defined, 146–47
   effectiveness of, 156–62
   evaluation of, 159–60
   general, 149–55
   growth and, 151–53, 387–88
   hierarchy of, 148
   management by (MBO), 163–64
   nonbusiness organizatons and, 151–52
   planning and, 146, 148
   profit and, 154–55
   social obligations and, 153–54
   specific, 155–56
   strategies and, 156–58
   survival, 150–51
   See also Goals
Officers, corporate, 43–44
Operations research
   See Decision making
Organization
   boundaries of, 281–82, 290–91
   defined, 274–75
   environment and, 273–93, 290–93
      external, 290–93, 390–91
      internal, 390–91

job satisfaction and, 277–78
   politics and, 58–60
   as process, 275–76
   systems and, 279–84, 336–39
   theory of, 328–30
   See also Organization structure
Organization change, 275–76, 278, 384–401
   agents of, 394–95
   conditions of, 385–86
   domino effect in, 395
   environment and, 390–93
   equilibrium theory of, 283
   growth and decay, 387–88, 438–39
   mergers and acquisitions, 388–89
   nature of, 384–85
   planning for, 399–401
      organization planning departments, 399–401
   reorganization and, 389–90
   resistance to, 397–99
   sources of, 387–90, 393–94
   strategies of, 395–401
   technology and, 391–93
Organization charts, 318–20
Organization design
   adaptive structures and, 328–51
      conglomerate firms and, 346, 388–89
      definition of, 275, 328–30
      free-form organization, 345–46
      matrix and project designs, 339–45
      systems designs, 336–39
      task forces, teams and, 344–45, 478–79
   bureaucracy and, 279, 298–323, 329–33
   communications nets and, 333–35
   decentralization, 377–79
   definitions and concepts of, 297–98, 328–30
   departmentalization, 301–7
      functional, 302–3
      geographical, 305–7
      process, 303–4
      product, 304
   general models of, 297–98, 335–46
   hierarchy and, 43, 46, 277, 300–301
   matrix designs, 339–44
   multiple leadership, 346–50
   position titles, 307, 321–23, 355–56
   project designs, 339–44
   span of control and, 316–18
   tall vs. flat, 316–18
   unity of command, 346–50
Organization development, 459–83
   change agents and, 462–65
   definition of, 460–61
   diagnosis stage, 465–66
   evaluation and feedback in, 469–71
   fundamentals of, 461–71
   intervention and, 466–68
   models for, 462–64

Organization development (*cont'd*)
    purposes of, 461–62
    strategies of, 468–69
    techniques of, 471–83
    See also Executive development
Organization manuals, 320–21
Organization structure
    adaptive, 327–51
        defined, 275, 328–30
    basic types, 307–15
        committee structure, 313–15
        functional structure, 311–13
        line organization, 308
        matrix, 339–44
        project, 339–44
        staff structure, 308–11
        strategies and, 158
    bureaucratic, 279, 296–323, 329–33
    characteristics of, 279, 293–323, 324–33,
        335–46
    communication nets and, 333–35
    functions of, 276–79
    levels of, 43–46, 277, 300–301
    span of control, 316–18
    See also Organizational design
Organizational climate, 487–513
    measurement of, 488–92
    effectiveness, 425–39
        achievement of, 437–39
        correlates of, 434–37
        criteria of, 428–29, 431
        definitions of, 426–28
        models and, 432–33
        nature of, 427–43
        organizational correlates of, 434–35
        social responsibility and, 431
        systems and, 435–37
        technology and, 427, 435
        typologies of, 429–31
    growth, 151–53, 387–88
    health, 438–39
    identity, 278
    survival, 150–51
    See also Morale; Motivation

P

Participation
    decision making and, 94–96
    employee morale and, 502–7
    motivation and, 546–47
    planning and, 140–142
Performance, managerial, 516–39
    appraisal of, 517–25
        communicating results of, 523–25
        methods of, 521–25
        modified approaches to, 525
        objectives of, 517–18
        standards for, 519–21
        uses of, 518–19

    obsolescence and, 527–29
    poor performance, dealing with, 525–30
    See also Leadership, training and
        development
Personnel management, 238–40
PERT networks, 207–9
Planning, 123–42
    basic elements of, 123–33
    change and, 122–23
    control and, 188–90
    coordination of, 130–33
    data collection and, 129–30
    defined, 123
    effectiveness of, 137–40
    evaluation of, 137–38
    forecasting and, 126–29
    levels of, 132–33
    long range, 124–26, 131
    obstacles to, 133–37
        administrative problems, 133–34
        costs of, 135
        human element and, 136–37
        information flows, 134–35
    organization for, 138–40, 399–401
    participation and, 141–42
    problems and, 123–24
    simulation and, 140–41
    specialists and, 140
    staff groups and, 139–40
    time as a factor in, 124–26
Policy, managerial
    administration of, 175–82
    application of, 168–69
    changes in, 181–82
    conflicts in, 181
    criteria for, 178–80
    defined, 168–70
    dissemination of, 176–78
    examples of, 168–69
    formation of, 172–75
    general, 168–69
    hierarchy of, 172–75
    implied vs. stated, 176–78
    makers of, 172–75
    middle managers and, 175
    rules and, 169–70
    specific, 168
    structure of, 170–71
    supervisors, first line, and, 175
    top management and, 173–75
Politics, organizational, 59–60
Position titles, 307, 321–23, 355–56
Power, 218, 355–59
Problem solving, 85–87, 123–24, 465–68
Process consulting, 477
Professionalization in management, 16–17
Profit making, 154–55
Project management, 339–44
Promotions, 243, 249–52, 518–19
    from within, 249–52
    staffing and, 243, 249

R

Resources, allocation of, 88
Responsibilities, managerial, 26–27, 54–57, 193–94
  conflicts in, 56–57
  delegation of, 366–72
Revisionist movement, 36–38
Reward systems, 553–59
Roles, managerial, 48–54, 413–16, 479–80
  changes in, 48–50
  conflict in, 413–14
  definition of, 48
  groups and, 474–77
  leadership and, 219–21, 229–31
  organizational development and, 394–95, 462–65, 479–80

S

Satisficing, 91–92, 160–61
Scientific management, 25–32
Sensitivity training, 474–77
Shelf-sitters, 528–29
Simulation, 108–10
  planning and, 140–41
Social psychology, 34
Social responsibilities, 153–55, 204, 595–605
  arguments for and against, 596–98
  audits of, 600–601
  awareness of, 595–96
  business and, 598–99, 601–5
  See also Ethics of executives
Span of control, 316–18
Specialists, 138–40, 192–93
Specialization, 192–93
Staff planning units, 138–39
Staffing
  definition of, 238
  discharge and, 253–54
  employment contracts and, 245–46
  manpower planning and, 239–40
  matching people and jobs, 247
  mobility of managers and, 247–49
  personnel departments and, 238–39
  problems in, 246–54
  procedures for, 240–45
    applicants, 244
    external, 241–43
    internal sources, 243
    interviewing, 244–45
    recruiting, 240–43
  promotions and, 249–53
  selection processes, 243–46, 252–53

Strategies
  conflict and, 406–7
  decisions and, 104–6
  of forecasting, 126–27
  objectives and, 156–58
  in organizational change, 395–401
  organization structure and, 158, 399–401
  types of, 157–58, 358–59
Supervisors, first-line, 45–46, 232–34
Surveys, methods of, 473–47, 499–502
Synergy, 389
Systems
  boundaries, 281–82, 290
  classifications of, 279–84
  decision making and, 100–102, 290
  development of, 336–39
  elements of, 14–15, 51, 101–2, 328–30
  equilibrium and, 283
  feedback and, 283–84
  open and closed, 290, 335–36, 338
  organization and, 279–84, 435–37
  subsystems and, 282–83
  theory of, 14–15, 336–39

T

Task environment, 287–88
Technology, 391–93, 427, 435
Top management, 43–45, 393–94
Training, managerial, 530–38
  in communication, 588–89
  See also Executive development

U

Unions, trade
  See Labor-management relations
Unity of command, 346–50

V

Values, corporate and managerial, 606–8

W

Wage administration
  incentives and, 28–29, 557–59
Western Electric Company, 35
Work planning and measurement, 27–28
Work, meaning of, 616